Management

Leadership in Action

Management

Leadership in Action

Fifth Edition

DONALD C. MOSLEY
University of South Alabama

PAUL H. PIETRI
University of South Alabama

LEON C. MEGGINSON
University of Mobile

HarperCollins*CollegePublishers*

Executive Editor: *Michael Roche*
Developmental Editor: *Rebecca Strehlow*
Supplements Editor: *Julie Zasloff*
Project Coordination and Text Design: *Thompson Steele Production Services/Interactive Composition Corporation*
Cover Design: *Linda Wade*
Cover Photograph: *Tony Stone Worldwide*
Photo Researcher: *Carol Parden*
Electronic Production Manager: *Eric Jorgensen*
Manufacturing Manager: *Hilda Koparanian*
Electronic Page Makeup: *Interactive Composition Corporation*
Printer and Binder: *RR Donnelley & Sons Company*
Cover Printer: *New England Book Components*

For permission to use copyrighted material, grateful acknowledgment is made to the copyright holders on p. C–1, which is hereby made part of this copyright page.

Management: Leadership in Action, Fifth Edition.

Library of Congress Cataloging-in-Publication Data

Mosley, Donald C.
Management, leadership in action / Donald C. Mosley, Paul H. Pietri, Leon C. Megginson. — 5th ed.
p.   cm.
Rev. ed. of: Management, concepts and applications / Leon C. Megginson, Donald C. Mosley, Paul H. Pietri, Jr. 4th ed. c1992.
Includes index.
ISBN 0-673-99264-0
1. Management.   I. Pietri, Paul H.   II. Megginson, Leon C.   III. Megginson, Leon C. Management, concepts and applications.   IV. Title.
HD31.M394   1995
658—dc20   95-8641
                                                                              CIP

96 97 98   9 8 7 6 5 4 3 2

*B*rief *C*ontents

Contents

Chapter 2

Chapter 3

Chapter 4

Chapter 5

ART 2 **Managing Strategies and Processes   172**

Chapter 8

Organization Design, Authority, and Power

Chapter 9

Managing Human Resources and Diversity

PART 3 Leading and Developing People in Organizations

324

Chapter 10

Chapter 11

Chapter 14

PART 4 Control and Information, Small-Business Management, and Your Future in Management   488

Chapter 15

Chapter 16

Chapter 17

vision of showing students how the theoretical concepts of management relate and apply to actual practice at all management levels and in a broad range of managerial settings, be they service, manufacturing, not-for-profit, domestic, global, large, or entrepreneurial organizations.

As one of the first texts to emphasize real-world managerial practices, this edition continues to provide an abundance of current examples and references. Also, for the first time, a special complementary book, *Experiential Approach to Modern Management*, by Drs. Terry Armstrong and Esther Long of the University of West Florida, has been especially prepared to complement this text. Terry has been a valued colleague for years as a member of the management consulting division of the Academy of Management and served as program chair in 1995. The book provides a wealth of live, real-world experiences that reinforce the key concepts in each chapter and breathe life into theory.

Content and Organization

Because basic management textbooks have grown in length and number of chapters covered, addressing all material in a quarter or a semester often results in a superficial treatment of many topics. Thus, many reviewers suggested a shorter, more compact, concise text. This fifth edition consists of 17 chapters, 3 fewer than the previous edition. That reduction was achieved in several ways: First, the material was rearranged to create a tighter organization "fit." For example, the concept of organizational culture now appears much earlier in the book—in Chapter 3, "The External and Internal Environment." "The Global Environment" has been moved forward to Chapter 4, to closely follow the "External Environment." Several chapters have been combined to form single chapters. These include Chapter 7, "Strategic and Operational Planning;" Chapter 8, "Organizational Design and Authority;" and Chapter 15, "Managing Information and Control." These chapters are now slightly longer, but the combination is more unified and concise than the separate chapters were. Also, since many important "quality"-oriented issues have been incorporated into other chapters, the fourth-edition chapter "Managing Production and Operations" has been omitted. Chapter 16, "Entrepreneurship and Small-Business Management," is new to this edition. Since the small-business sector plays such an increasingly important role in our economy and will serve as employer for many students, we felt it important to include a new chapter devoted to this sector's unique managerial challenge.

The book is subdivided into four major parts. Part One, "Managing the Dynamics of a Changing World," introduces the student to the study of management and the major changes influencing theory and practice today. It features chapters examining what management is and what managers do, traces the evolution of management thought from antiquity to contemporary times, identifies the changing external and internal environments within which managers and organizations must function, examines in detail the global environmental issues facing managers, and highlights the most pressing ethical and social considerations managers and organizations must address.

Part Two, "Managing Strategies and Processes," features chapters on managerial decision making, strategic and operational planning, organizational design and authority, and the managing of human resources. Part Three, "Leading and

Developing People in Organizations," is the book's longest. Communicating with people is covered in Chapter 10; motivating, in Chapter 11; leadership processes and styles, in Chapter 12; managing change and conflict, in Chapter 13; and team development—in essentially new coverage—in Chapter 14.

Three final chapters form Part Four, "Management Control and Information, Entrepreneurship, and Careers." Chapter 15 examines the control function and the role of information, Chapter 16 examines the role of management in small-business settings, and Chapter 17 examines managerial career implications, as well as what organizations are doing to facilitate career growth.

Special Features

As always, we continue to focus on making *Management: Leadership in Action* as student oriented as possible. Accordingly, we have included numerous features to capture students' interest, facilitate the learning process, and make the book enticing to read and study. Many of these features are designed to show students how the material they are learning is put into practice in the actual world of management, while others are geared to making the text an effective learning aid. In keeping with the increased emphasis on issues related to the cultural diversity, global, quality, and ethics and social responsibility aspects of management, every chapter contains applications that highlight these areas.

Part Overviews. Each of the text's four parts begins with a brief, introductory overview of the chapters that make up that part.

Chapter Objectives. Each chapter begins with a clear statement of learning objectives. These help orient the reader to the chapter content, provide direction for learning, and may be used by students to review material and check whether they understand important points.

Chapter Opening Cases. Each chapter opens with a real-world case example that sets the stage for the material subsequently discussed in the chapter. Unlike many other texts, this one includes references to each Opening Case *throughout* the chapter to reinforce key ideas. In some chapters, the Opening Case serves as the basis for an end-of-chapter Learning Exercise. Eight of the 17 chapter Opening Cases are new to this edition—cases such as Harley Davidson (Chapter 1), as Chick-Fil-A (Chapter 5), as Ritz-Carlton (Chapter 13), as Cianbro (Chapter 14), and as Nike (Chapter 16).

Management Application and Practice (MAP). The popular boxed items called Management Application and Practice (MAP) appear in each chapter to highlight a concept discussed in the text and to show how the concept has been applied in actual practice. Collected from current sources such as the *Wall Street Journal, Business Week, Fortune, USA Today*, and other professional publications, over 30 such MAPs strongly reinforce cultural diversity, global, ethical, quality, and leadership issues. Examples include "Cultural Clash Leads to Troubles" (MAP 3.3), "Two Quality Cup Winners of 1994" (MAP 6.2), "Unethical Applications of Motivation Theory" (MAP 11.2), and "What to Expect If You Work for a Japanese Firm" (MAP 17.4).

CHAPTER-OPENING CASES

Chapter-opening cases use real-world companies with profile managers and their management approaches to set the stage for the material discussed in the chapter.

GE's Fight with Bureaucracy

In 1981, at the age of 45, Jack Welch took over the reins of General Electric (GE) from the popular and well-thought-of chairman and CEO Reginald H. Jones. Under Jones's leadership, earnings per share, adjusted for inflation, had risen an average of 4.9 percent a year as compared to 1.9 percent a year under his predecessor, Fred Borch. A major reason for the high regard for Jones was that GE had moved from a state of chronic cash shortage to one of tremendous financial strength. On the other hand, Jones's thirst for information and control led to the building of a bureaucracy, causing decisions to be reviewed at many levels.

Almost immediately after taking office, Jack Welch went to war with the bureaucracy that had developed during Jones's tenure. In the process, the world's tenth largest industrial corporation has been remade and—perhaps—revitalized. During this time, Welch has gained a reputation as a tough and ruthless manager. Noel Tichy, a consultant who often works for GE, says Welch stoked the fire beneath the corporate cauldron to avoid the boiled-frog syndrome. Tichy explained, "If you put a frog in a pan of water and turn up the heat gradually, the frog will just stay put 'til it dies. But try to put a frog into boiling water and it will jump right out—and survive."

A key question is, Has it been worth it? If you were to ask one of the over 100,000 workers whose jobs were eliminated through layoffs, attrition, or sales of businesses, you would get one answer. If you were to ask stockholders who have [...] rise from 4.9 percent [...] under Welch, you

Jack Welch went to war with General Electric's bureaucracy.

would get another answer. What kind of man is it who has streamlined the company from 100 business units down to 14?

Welch was an only child whose father was a hardworking railroad conductor. Like many prominent leaders, he considers his mother the dominant influence in his life and his earliest role model. It was she, he says, who influenced his core values: "She always felt I could do anything. It was my mother who trained me. She wanted me to be independent. Control your own destiny—she always had that idea. Saw reality. No mincing words. Whenever I got out of line, she would whack me one. But always positive. Always constructive. Always uplifting." These core values have been translated into a GE strategy of ranking either first or second globally in the markets it serves. The strategy has succeeded, as 12 of GE's units are considered market leaders.

Today Jack Welch is considered one of the stars of American industry. His newsletter in GE's annual report is a much anticipated event by business leaders, stockholders, and scholars, who read it searching for creative ideas. In the 1993 annual report he states:

We are betting everything on our people—empowering them, giving them the resources and getting out of their way—and the numbers tell us that this focus has not only pointed us in the right direction, but it is providing us with a momentum that is accelerating.

With the objective of involving everyone, we use three operating principles to define the atmosphere and behavior at GE:

Boundaryless . . . in all our behavior;

Speed . . . in everything we do;

What Is Communication?

The term *communication* is relatively new to organizations. *Communication* itself was not an important part of management's vocabulary until the late 1940s and early 1950s. But as organizations became more "people conscious" with the beginning of the behavioral approach to management (see Chapter 2), communication became one of management's chief concerns, as shown in an interview of Jack Welch, CEO of General Electric, for the *Harvard Business Review*. When asked, "What makes a good manager?" Welch responded largely in terms of managers' communication practices: "They go up, down, and around their organization to reach people . . . countless hours of eyeball to eyeball, back and forth. . . . It's not pronouncements on a videotape; it's not announcements in a newspaper. It is human beings coming to see and accept things through a constant interactive process."[2]

Communication is the process of transferring meaning from one person to another in the form of ideas or information. It uses the chain of understanding that links the members of various units of an organization at different levels and in different areas. An effective interchange involves more than just the transmission of data. It requires that the sender and receiver use certain skills—speaking, writing, listening, reading—to make the exchange of meaning successful. In spoken conversation, a true interchange of meaning encompasses shades of emphasis, facial expressions, vocal inflections, and all the unintended and involuntary gestures that suggest real meaning.

A large part of the typical manager's time is spent in some form of communication—reading, listening, writing, or speaking. It has been estimated that around 80 percent of a manager's time is spent in verbal communication.[3] Despite its importance, there is much evidence that communication is not handled effectively in organizations.

> Of the 30,000 managers, professionals, and clerical personnel surveyed by Opinion Research Corporation over a four-year period, 60 percent felt that their organizations were not doing a good job of keeping them informed about company matters. Moreover, fewer than 30 percent felt that their companies were willing to listen to their problems.[4]

communication The process of transferring meaning from one person to another in the form of ideas or information.

Formal Communication Channels in an Organization

You can better understand organizational communication if you examine the basic directions in which it moves. **Formal communication channels** are the prescribed means by which messages flow inside an organization. The three basic channels are downward, upward, and lateral or horizontal.

formal communication channels The prescribed means by which messages flow inside an organization.

Downward Communication

Communication that follows the organization's formal chain of command from top to bottom is called **Downward communication**. It tends to follow and reflect the authority-responsibility relationships shown in the organization chart. Some examples of downward communication are

downward communication Communication that follows the organization's normal chain of command from top to bottom.

PRACTICING MANAGER BOXES

"Practicing Manager" boxes spotlight an actual manager's background, career movement, values, and managerial philosophies. These features illustrate how real people are involved in building their careers in management and demonstrate what students can expect in their future management careers. "Practicing Manager" boxes feature managers at different organizational levels, and provide examples of both traditional career path managers and entrepreneurs.

PRACTICING MANAGER

Michael Dell, CEO, Dell Computer Corporation

Not many managers are 29, CEO, and founder of a ten-year-old, $3 billion company with over 3,000 employees. But Michael Dell, founder of Dell Computer Corporation (DCC), is no ordinary manager.

When he was younger, Michael Dell would drive to school on the I-610 loop that circles Houston, Texas, and imagine that one day he would run a business in one of the many ultramodern skyscrapers along the route. During his morning drive, Dell would further imagine that the building from which he ran his business would come complete with flagpoles in front bearing company flags with a private elevator to take him up to his CEO chambers.

Now, Michael Dell looks back and says, "I've never imagined myself not doing something significant." What Dell has done by the ripe old age of 29 is nothing short of spectacular. As CEO of DCC, this college dropout, who started selling computer parts by mail from his college dorm room when he was a freshman at the University of Texas at Austin, is now worth $1.2 billion.

Dell, who has been interested in business since he was 12, began tinkering with computers when he was 16. He remembers his first Apple II: "I bought the Apple as soon as it came out, took it apart, and put it back together." Describing himself as a teenage hacker, Dell spent a great deal of time exploring [how] computers use software and trying to find ways to speed up the process. He even taught himself the raw programming code called assembly language.

When he was 19, Dell began selling parts by mail from his dorm room. By the end of the year, he was shipping $80,000 worth of equipment a month. "The opportunity looked so attractive, I couldn't stay in school," Dell says of his initial success.

Dropping out of school, Dell created PC's Limited, rented a small office across town from the University of Texas campus, and placed an ad in a computer magazine. The results were phenomenal: The first month, sales were $181,000; the first year, $6 million; the second year, $33 million; the third year, $69 million; and so on. Ten years out, 1994 sales reached over $3 billion.

Because of his incredible early success, Dell was able to hire a team of veteran executives to help manage the company's rapid growth. He added telemarketing to his direct response advertising and later hired a sales force to go after large corporate contracts.

Although Dell computers are highly regarded in the computer industry, the secret of Dell's success is not *what* he sells but *how* he sells it. Technically trained salespeople take phone orders from customers who choose from a wide variety of options to create a PC suited to their specific needs. Once the order is placed, it is sent to DCC's state-of-the-art factory, where the just-ordered computer is custom-built and ready for shipment within four days. The finished computer

MICHAEL DELL, FOUNDER OF DELL COMPUTER CORPORATION.

Organizational Noise

Organizations, by their very nature, tend to inhibit effective communication. A communication consultant can examine the organization chart of a firm and immediately see that communication barriers exist. Four organizational barriers are (1) organizational levels, (2) managerial authority, (3) specialization, and (4) information overload.

Organizational Levels As pointed out earlier, when an organization grows, its structure expands, creating many communication problems. If a message must pass through added levels—among increased numbers of people or departments—it will take longer to reach its destination and will tend to become distorted along the way.

As a message goes through various organizational levels, it passes through several "filters." Each level in the communication chain can add to, take from, modify, or completely change the intent of a given message.

One explanation for this tendency is that messages are usually broader and more general at higher levels of management and must be made more specific as they filter down to lower levels. If the broad message is misinterpreted, then the specifics that are added may be incorrect.

What is your view?

When you miss a class, you probably check with a fellow student to get the class assignment. But have you ever completed the assignment only to arrive in class and find that it was not what the teacher wanted? Dependence on others' interpretations of firsthand communications, even though it risks loss of accuracy and interpretation, is an important part of organizational communication. Can you think of some real or hypothetical cases in which one *must* rely on an intermediary either to send or receive information in an organization?

Managerial Authority Authority is a necessary feature of any organization. Yet the fact that one person supervises others creates a barrier to free and open communication. Many bosses feel that they cannot fully admit problems, conditions, or results that may make them look weak. Many subordinates, on the other hand, avoid situations that require them to disclose information that might make them appear in an unfavorable light. As a result, there often is a lack of openness between managers and subordinates. Job problems, frustrations, below-standard work, disagreements with the superior's policies, and other types of unfavorable information

---

WHAT IS YOUR VIEW SECTIONS

"What Is Your View" features present thought-provoking questions and problems designed to stimulate students to apply key concepts presented in the text.

MANAGEMENT APPLICATION AND PRACTICE 12.1

The Godmother of Quebec's Businesswomen

Jeannine Guillevin Wood has been called the godmother of Quebec's businesswomen. Although she shrugs off the designation, the 65-year-old CEO of Montreal's Guillevin International Inc. has become a business legend in the province and beyond. In 25 years, she transformed a small family appliance wholesaler in the city's east end into a multimillion-dollar electrical products distribution empire spanning Canada and stretching into the United States.

"It is true that I was one of the first to show that women could do certain things around here, and for that I am glad," she says. But the battle is not yet completely won, for there are still a few people who will not accept [women in business]. Those kinds of people I find it best to ignore."

Few colleagues or competitors have managed to ignore Guillevin Wood. The company of which she is CEO and principle shareholder is Canada's third largest distributor of electrical products and a major vendor of automation, security, and safety equipment. It employs 1, 100 people in 105 offices, distributing 82,000 products to 33,000 customers. Annual sales in the company year ending January 31, 1990, exceeded $422 million (Canadian) and showed profits of $5.9 million.

Guillevin Wood also sits on the boards of several major Canadian concerns. In October 1990, in the face of a recession, her company expanded in the Maritimes—part of a commitment to Canada-wide growth and community service. That same year, she became the first woman appointed to the policy committee of the blue-ribbon Business Council on National Issues. "You might say that I have won some

recognition," she concedes.

Guillevin Wood's life might have taken a far different course. Until 1965, she led an obscure but comfortable existence as a Montreal housewife and mother, content to spend the summers golfing and the winters in Florida. But her first husband, François Guillevin, died suddenly, leaving her with a 15-year-old daughter to care for, as well as control of the family business. (She is now married to businessman Keith Wood.) At the time, F. X. Guillevin & Son Ltd. was an electrical wholesaler with 35 employees and annual sales of $1.5 million, mostly from the distribution of household appliances. Guillevin Wood decided to take the reins into her own hands rather than sell the business. "I had no other choice," she recalls. "It was a good old family firm with a lot of good employees who had given their lives to the company. How could I let them down?"

It was a brave decision, considering that she had no business experience of any kind. Over the next 20 year, however, she acquired 11 other companies and forged working partnerships with firms in France and the United States to fashion what is now Guillevin International. She also gained wider recognition so that by 1976 she had twice been named "Man of the Month" by Montreal business organizations. Other accolades followed.

"There really is no secret to my success," she says. "It was just the result of plain old discipline and a lot of hard work." It is advice that she offers by example to others, male and female—the kind of advice expected from a godmother.

Source: Adapted from "MacLean's Honor Roll: Advising by Example," MacLean's, December 31, 1990, pp. 22-23.

Jeannine Guillevin Wood.

In India, it is considered highly improper to discuss business in the home on social occasions. To invite someone to one's home to further a business relationship violates sacred hospitality rules.[50]

ethnocentrism The tendency to believe and act on the belief that one's own cultural value system is superior to others.

Ethnocentrism. One of the primary causes of cultural conflict is **ethnocentrism,** the tendency to believe and act on the belief that one's own cultural value system is superior to all others. If an overseas executive persists in such self-centered views in dealing with people in a new culture, his or her behavior will probably be resented by the host country and may lead to rejection or conflict. The cure for this problem may be to avoid sending that type of individual overseas, or to take additional time and training to acquaint the manager with local customs and practices before he or she is assigned overseas.

A Ford Foundation resident adviser on management development in Pakistan would sharpen half a dozen pencils to use at his desk. He noticed that his Pakistani counterparts used only one pencil and would ring for the "peon" to come and sharpen it. The adviser considered this quite inefficient until he learned that his failure to use the peon "broke the rice bowl" of seven people. That is, if the peon were fired, he and six family members would go hungry. The adviser learned to use the services of the peon.

A manager's inability to cope emotionally and psychologically with the problems posed by cultural differences may interrupt harmonious relationships between the manager and the local personnel. Thus, the manger may tend to rely on rigid rules and regulations to ensure control over local operations. The inability of the manager to cope with the conflicts may also result in an emotional or irrational response to the local personnel. This may be the beginning of a vicious circle of irrational responses.

Production suddenly started falling behind schedule at an American-controlled plant in Bangladesh. The newly arrived manager noticed that the workers were listless and apparently uninterested in their work. He tried speeding up the operations, which resulted in a strike. Then he found out that it was the religious holiday Ramadan, during which the Muslims fast from before dawn until after dark.

Recall the opening case in which Rudolph Carter avoided falling into this type of trap. Instead, his managerial philosophy of respecting the local personnel permitted him to adjust to the new environment that was similar to the one in which he had grown up.

Miscommunication. A major factor contributing to cultural conflict is miscommunication. Communication, as shown in Chapter 10, is the transfer of meaning from one individual to another, and many barriers filter the sender's meaning. Difference in language, customs, feelings, and cultures may cause miscommunication when managing people of a culture different from your own. The entire complex of human life, with its individual variations, offers opportunities for misunderstandings. Language, however, is the most serious source of miscommunication because it is the means of communication most often used. In addition to a lack of knowledge of the language itself, the manager's intonation, pronunciation, and facial expressions may also cause misunderstanding. Carter's knowledge of Spanish led to rapport with Gonzales, which ultimately led to the workers accepting Carter.

An American executive may find many English-speaking people in the culture in which he or she operates, but may also find that relying on them still leads to problems. First, nationals are often unfavorably impressed when a foreign manag-

REAL-WORLD
EXAMPLES

A hallmark of the text is its abundance of current, real-world examples and references which reflect diverse organizations and clearly illustrate the relevance of management and how the concepts being explained are applied in actual situations. This edition also includes more examples of entrepreneurs and small business managers.

The research currently being done in this area does not assume that leaders are born, not made, but looks at traits in a different light. For example, some researchers take the position that, if the characteristics of successful leaders can be identified, then these characteristics can be developed in others who aspire to leadership. In a study involving over 2600 top-level managers at Santa Clara University and several corporate locations, the superior leaders were found to be most often honest, competent, forward-looking, inspiring, and intelligent.

Robert Crandall, chairman of AMR Corporation, the parent company of American Airlines, is such a leader. In 1990, he was selected as "*USA Today*/FNN CEO of the Year." A competitive impulse and the use of technology have made him "a lethal adversary."

In a nation where short-term thinking is the norm, the tough-talking, fast-driving CEO stands out. In the face of a recession, an annual operating loss, and an industry slump, "Crandall is charging ahead . . . managing for the long term." He's been successful "because he developed a strategic vision and put his entire energy into achieving it," according to *USA Today* and FNN (Financial News Network)."

Robert Crandall, CEO of AMR Corporation, exhibits the traits of a superior leader.

Bloomin' Lollipops In September 1989, Michelle Statkewicz, Renee Sossaman, and their parents, Jiggs and Dot Martin, quit their jobs to start Bloomin' Lollipops. It opened in January 1990, after over six months of research and planning. The small business makes chocolate flowers, hard candy lollipops, and candy animals, which are placed in gift baskets for sale to gift shops, institutions, and the general public. Candy lollipop bouquets are available in a variety of colors and more than 50 different flavors, including lime, strawberry, grape, apple, lemon, watermelon, licorice, root beer, and piña colada. The owners have 150 or more career-, sports-, holiday-, and hobby-related molds with which to work. The Mobile, Alabama, business is booming, and the owners say several people from as far away as Texas are interested in obtaining franchises. Bloomin' Lollipops formulated the following statement of objectives:

> *We will make the best products, under environmentally sound conditions, deliver them to the customers as quickly as feasible, and charge a reasonable price—based upon our costs plus a satisfactory return on our investment of knowledge, time, and effort. We will set up satellite shops in Mobile and surrounding areas, and feed those shops from our kitchen. Afterward, we hope to franchise throughout the country.*

Even small businesses such as Bloomin' Lollipops need well-stated objectives.

STRONG COVERAGE OF DIVERSITY

In keeping with the increased emphasis on issues related to cultural diversity, every chapter contains applications that highlight diversity in management.

The Disabled The *Vocational Rehabilitation Act (VRA)*, passed in 1973, prohibits employers with federal contracts from discriminating against the disabled. Job opportunities—including special facilities, if needed—must be provided. A **disabled person** is defined as anyone who has a physical or mental disability that substantially restricts major normal activities such as physical movement or learning, seeing, speaking, or hearing.

disabled person
Anyone with a physical or mental disability that substantially restricts major normal activities such as physical movement, learning, walking, seeing, speaking, or hearing.

Deaf workers have traditionally been hired by the printing industry as compositors and printing press operators because they are not easily distracted, and the noise of high-speed presses and other machinery does not bother them.

The Americans with Disabilities Act (ADA), passed in 1990, expanded the scope and coverage of the VRA. In essence, the ADA prohibits discrimination on the basis of disability in hiring, promotion, and all other terms, conditions, and privileges of employment. The ADA applies to virtually all employers with 15 or more employees, not just government contractors. But unlike the VRA, it does not require employers to develop AAPs.

FIGURE 9.5
Topics to avoid when interviewing applicants.

Here is an up-to-date summary of ten of the most dangerous questions or topics you might raise during an interview.

1. *Children.* Do not ask applicants whether they have children, or plan to have children, or have child care.
2. *Age.* Do not ask an applicant's age.
3. *Disabilities.* Do not ask whether the candidate has a physical or mental disability that would interfere with doing the job.
4. *Physical characteristics.* Do not ask for such identifying characteristics as height or weight on an application.
5. *Name.* Do not ask a female candidate for her maiden name.
6. *Citizenship.* Do not ask applicants about their citizenship. However, the Immigration Reform and Control Act does require business operators to determine that their employees have a legal right to work in the United States.
7. *Lawsuits.* Do not ask a job candidate whether he or she has ever filed a suit or a claim against a former employer.
8. *Arrest records.* Do not ask applicants about their arrest records.
9. *Smoking.* Do not ask whether a candidate smokes. While smokers are not protected under the Americans with Disabilities Act (ADA), asking applicants whether they smoke might lead to legal difficulties if an applicant is turned down because of fear that smoking would drive up the employer's health care costs.
10. *AIDS and HIV.* Never ask job candidates whether they have AIDS or are HIV-positive, as these questions violate the ADA and could violate state and federal civil rights laws.

ords, copyright 1954, 1953 and renewed 1982, 1981 by Stuart Chase, reprinted by
novich, Inc.

SUMMARY

Since business organizations operate as open systems, they are especially vulnerable to factors within their environments that can favorably or adversely affect them. An organization's environment consist of those factors or elements that influence the way it functions. Three specific subenvironments constituting an organization's environment are the general, task, and internal environments.

Environmental complexity refers to the number of key factors in the macro and task environments and the extent of similarity of subfactors within a given factor. Environmental change refers to the frequency with which relevant environmental factors change—are the factors stable or dynamic? A four-cell environmental matrix illustrates four possible combinations: simple/stable, complex/stable, simple/dynamic, and complex/dynamic environments. The least difficult managerial challenge is posed by an organization with a simple/stable environment; the most difficult challenge involves a complex/dynamic environment.

General environment factors are broad variables that tend to affect all organizations, including legal/political, economic, social technological, and international factors. The organization's task environment includes factors that interact *directly* with the specific organization as it operates. Task environment factors include suppliers, regulatory agencies, competitors, customers, and special interest groups.

Organizations cannot afford to be passive about the environments in which they function. Therefore, environmental forecasting is helpful in anticipating the impact of factors affecting future operations. Influencing the environment is a more active approach that typically involves lobbying, public relation efforts, and forms of ownership ranging from joint ventures to mergers and acquisitions. The use of boundary-spanning roles—organizational positions that maintain contact with external environmental factors—is an important vehicle for anticipating potential effects of the external environment.

An important factor in an organization's internal environment is culture—the set of shared philosophies, values, beliefs, and behavior patterns that give the organization its identity. Rites and rituals are important components of an organization's culture. Founders and leaders influence organizational culture by what they pay attention to, how they conduct themselves, how they respond to crises, how they allocate rewards, and how they hire and fire.

KEY TERMS

organizational environment
general environment
task environment,
internal environmen
environmental complexity
environmental change
simple/stable environment
complex/stable environment
simple/dynamic environment

CHAPTER-ENDING PEDAGOGY

Each chapter concludes with a summary, a key terms list, discussion questions, and learning exercises and/or cases.

complex/dynamic environment,
legal/political factors
economic factors
social factors
demographic forces
social forces
technological factors
international factors
coproducer arrangement
environmental forecasting
partnering, or partnership alliances (PALs)
organizational culture
heroes
rites
rituals

DISCUSSION QUESTIONS

1. In which cell of the complexity/change environmental matrix would you
   place each of the following organizations? Why?
   a. Manufacturer of breakfast cereals
   b. Local chain of laundromats or dry cleaners
   c. University bookstore on campus

2. What are the most significant general environment factors for each of the following organizations? Why?
   a. Godfather's Pizza
   b. HarperCollins College Publishers (books)
   c. Walt Disney theme parks

3. Do you think that there is one *best* type of culture an organization can have? If
   so, what is it? How could you, as CEO, develop and shape the firm's culture so
   that it is the most appropriate for the organization's environments?

4. Give some examples of rites or rituals that you are familiar with and that are
   part of an organization's culture.

CHAPTER-ENDING PEDAGOGY (CONTINUED)

These pedagogical aids cover main points in the chapter, reinforce key concepts, facilitate reviewing for exams, and enable students to think beyond basic ideas.

PRACTICING MANAGEMENT

4.1

case

To Move or Not to Move?

John S. Chamberlin, chairman and chief executive officer of Lenox, Inc., of
Lawrenceville, New Jersey, was asked what was the hardest decision he ever made
as a manager. He answered that it was one he made as an executive with General
Electric. Although the decision had to be approved by GE's board, he had to
make a recommendation and defend it.

GE had been manufacturing clock radios and table radios in Utica, New York,
for several years. The workers and townspeople considered the GE operations a
permanent fixture. But the company had started to lose its market share because
its AM-FM clock radios were selling for $29.95 each, while a comparable Japanese
model sold for about $9.95.

Based on tough economic realities, Chamberlin had two alternatives: to remain
in Utica or to move operations to Singapore. There were about 2,000 workers
employed in Utica. Labor costs for the U.S. workers were about $5.00 an hour,
while the cost for workers in Singapore would be about 50 cents an hour. If the
operation left Utica, the workers would have to be laid off, since there was
nowhere in the company to transfer them.

Source: Based on "My Toughest Business Decision Was . . . ," *Wall Street Journal*, February 14, 1983, p.
16.

Questions

1. What do you think Chamberlin recommended?

2. Can you think of any alternatives besides the two mentioned? Discuss them.

END-OF-CHAPTER EXPERIMENTAL EXERCISES

Thirty-one chapter-ending "Practicing Management" cases and exercises provide structured activities and self-assessment exercises to help students apply the key concepts and theories in each chapter. All of the cases are based on actual managerial situations and events in real organizations.

PART

1

Managing the Dynamics of a Changing World

Welcome to the dynamic world of management! Part One of this book achieves two purposes: (1) to provide an introduction to your study of management and (2) to explore the external and internal environments within which managers of today's organizations function.

Chapter 1 explains what management is—making things happen in an organization—and what managers do—how they make things happen. The development of management from ancient times to the present is discussed in Chapter 2. Chapter 3 describes the changing environments—both external and internal—in which you will function as a manager. One increasingly dynamic environmental factor, the global environment, is covered in detail in Chapter 4. Chapter 5 discusses the major factors requiring that today's organizations place ethical and socially responsible behavior high on their list of managerial priorities.

> The difference between a company that is a leader in its industry and one that is a follower is management—superior human performance.
>
> –RICHARD S. REYNOLDS, JR.

What Management Is—*and* What Managers Do

After studying the material in this chapter, you should be able to:

- **State** why you should study management.

- **Identify** and **explain** five critical challenges facing organizations and managers.

- **Describe** the overall functions performed by managers.

- **Differentiate** between management and leadership.

- **Describe** how management is needed to reach organizational objectives, balance conflicting goals, and achieve efficiency and effectiveness.

- **Discuss** how different organizational levels and types of activities affect managers' performance.

- **Describe** the three skills used by managers.

The Hog Comeback

Harley-Davidson, written off in the 1980s as another casualty of Japanese superiority, is running full throttle once again. The demise and resurgence of the 90-year-old motorcycle company has become a story told again and again in boardrooms of corporate America and in business schools throughout the United States.

The Harley story begins in the 1970s, when AMF Corporation still owned the company. In response to the surging popularity of motorcycles late in the decade, Harley tripled production over a short four-year period, in the process deferring styling and engine performance upgrades. However, in the rush to get more motorcycles out the door, the company suffered a noticeable decline in quality. Engines came off the line leaking oil, lacking parts, and evidencing serious vibration problems. The once great American motorcycles were simply no competition to high-quality, fully equipped Japanese bikes. As a result, market share fell from 40 percent in 1979 to 23 percent in 1983.

Former CEO Vaughn Beals and a group of top Harley executives decided to kick-start the company one more time with a buyout of AMF in 1981. As Beals explains, "We were being wiped out by the Japanese because they were better managers. It wasn't robotics, or culture, or morning calisthenics and company songs." Under the direction of Beals and managers from every department, a strategic planning audit was conducted. Harley management used the audit results to determine company strengths, weaknesses, opportunities, and threats, and developed a long-range, ten-year plan—something the company had never done before. The audit revealed the importance of quality in every aspect of the firm.

Harley managers became quality obsessed. They implemented a new quality and inventory control system based almost entirely on employee participation—both in its planning and in its implementation. Employees were taught statistical techniques and were empow-ered to manage their own work. Plant managers were trained in team leadership techniques, replacing the old domineering style of bosses. In an effort to build new relationships with current and prospective customers, Harley executives began sponsoring and participating in weekend cross-country Harley rallies. During these outings, managers would listen to what other Harley riders had to say. Customer feedback provided managers with ideas that led to engine and styling improvements.

It wasn't long before Harley employees had formed the Harley Owners Group, more popu-larly known as the HOGs, the name riders affectionately call their Harleys. HOGs began sponsoring motorcycle events almost every week-end somewhere in the United States. Today, over 100,000 members participate in the nationally advertised events frequently held to support charity causes. As Harley began recouping market share and, more importantly, customer loyalty, the Japanese motorcycle manufacturer Honda was faltering. When Honda tried to start a rival club, it never got off the starting line and dropped out of the race.

By 1993, Harley had taken command of 60 percent of the big cycle market (1,200 cc and larger), and profits and stock prices doubled. The Harley motorcycle once again led the ranks as a symbol of American ingenuity and quality craftsmanship. Today, under the direction of CEO Richard Teerlink, Harley-Davidson is one of America's most admired corporations. Speaking to the Academy of Management, Teerlink emphasized that the company's continual chal-lenge was to keep open communication channels and use all the abilities and ideas of its employ-ees. Additionally, the company operates as a unified team with a "whole company" perspective among the individual departments—engineer-ing, manufacturing, marketing, and design. These objectives enable employees to focus on quality and keep the company running smoothly and efficiently at the same time.[1]

No question about it: Managers make the difference between success and failure for their companies. AMF Corporation managers had not been able to run Harley-Davidson profitably and efficiently. CEOs Beals and Teerlink, through strategic planning, effective problem diagnosis, and changes in the company's leadership style, were able to turn the company around and put it on the success track. When we think of managers, we may picture high-profile personalities such as General Electric's Jack Welch (whom many consider the outstanding CEO in America); former general Colin Powell, chairman of the Joint Chiefs of Staff in both the Bush and the Clinton administrations; or David Thomas, founder and well-known ad spokesperson for Wendy's, the fast-food chain. However, if you are currently employed, your boss is a manager, as were the principals of schools you attended, your head coach if you played organized sports, or the pastor of your church. Managers in organizations of all sizes, in all industries, and at all levels, from CEOs to supervisors of operating personnel, have an impact on performance.

In this chapter, we begin by discussing the importance of management to all organizations and how this relates to your study of business in general and management in particular. A clear definition of management is presented, followed by an examination of the functions performed by managers and how the functions relate to each other. The chapter closes with a look at the different levels and types of management in organizations today.

Harley-Davidson CEO Richard Teerlink on his Hog.

Management Is Needed in All Organizations

organization Two or more individuals interacting to achieve a common objective.

You may think of management primarily in connection with business. That idea is partially correct, but it is incomplete—management is also needed in all types of organized activities and in all types of organizations. In fact, every time two or more people interact to achieve a common objective, an **organization** exists. And management is needed in all organizations—families and clubs; small businesses and large ones; public and private organizations; profit-oriented and not-for-profit organizations; manufacturing firms, service organizations, and retail concerns; and American, foreign, and multinational firms.

Managers Are Found in Every Organization

In what kinds of organizations do you think most managers are employed? Perhaps you would think "manufacturing," which includes our largest industrial firms, such as GE, IBM, General Motors, or Boeing, which create products. Yet as you can see from Table 1.1, almost twice as many managers and administrators work in services as in other industries, including manufacturing. Also notice that one out of every four employees in finance, real estate, and insurance is classified as a manager. In other words, managers are found in every organization, from the largest employer in the United States (the federal government, with over 3 million civilian and 1 million military personnel) to the approximately 14 million small businesses with fewer than 100 employees. From 1983 to 1992, the number of executives, managers, and administrators increased from 10.7 million to 14.7 million. Analysts predict this growth will continue to reflect about 14 percent of projected employment growth through 2005, and will account for 11 percent of all employees in the United States.[2]

TABLE 1.1   NUMBERS AND PERCENTAGES OF MANAGERS, CLASSIFIED BY TYPE OF INDUSTRY

Type of Industry	Number of Managers and Administrators (in thousands)	Percentage of All Managers	Percentage of All Employees in Industry Who Are Managers
Services	4,891	34	12
Manufacturing	2,396	16	12
Wholesale and retail	2,191	15	9
Finance, real estate, and insurance	1,941	13	25
Public administration	1,180	8	21
Transportation and public utilities	907	6	11
Construction	911	6	13
Mining	100	1	15
Agriculture	35	>1	3

Source: Data compiled from U.S. Bureau of the Census, *Statistical Abstract of the United States* (Washington, D.C.: Government Printing Office, 1993).

Why Study Management?

Perhaps you aspire to a management position in the near future, perhaps not. Even if you do not aspire to be in management, studying management can do several things for you:

1. Everyone can find ways to apply management skills in everyday life.
2. Most people currently work for or in the future will work for some type of organization, and understanding management can help you draw conclusions about the effectiveness of your own manager, top management, or both. This may prove helpful in decisions regarding your career.
3. Even if you initially pursue a nonmanagerial position, such as a technician, nurse, salesperson, accountant, or computer programmer, if you perform well, you will probably be given an opportunity to become a manager.
4. Understanding management is valuable when interviewing with prospective employers, since it will help you ask questions that will (a) give you a better picture of where you would fit in the organization and (b) enable you to make a better impression on your interviewer.

Management is an exciting field, always changing, and critically important to many people on many levels. In 1992, 96,857 incorporated businesses failed; poor management is a major reason.[3] This chapter will establish the framework for your study of management. In it, we provide a basic discussion of what management is and what managers do—that is, the job of management.

Critical Challenges to Management

The world of organizations, whether domestic, foreign, or multinational, has changed dramatically in the past decade. This section of the chapter focuses on five critical challenges facing present and future managers: globalization of competition, increased emphasis on quality, diversity of the workforce, ethical and social responsibility issues, and empowerment of employees.

Globalization of Competition

Globalization refers to the opening of markets to competitors throughout the world. As an example, until the late 1970s, U.S. firms faced little foreign competition in domestic markets. However, during the 1980s, U.S. businesses lost domestic market shares to Asian and Western European firms in many industries, including electronics, computers, automobiles, and, as illustrated in the opening case, even motorcycles. U.S. firms had become complacent about quality and had failed to build positive relationships with customers and employees. Foreign companies, on the other hand, emphasized quality and customer and employee satisfaction, creating a competitive advantage. U.S. firms became easy targets for high-quality, customer-oriented foreign firms. Figure 1.1, for example, illustrates how the United States measured up in 1992 against major competitors in 13 key industries in Japan and Europe. The grades given on the report card reflected production data, company performance, and expert opinion.

globalization The opening of markets to competitors throughout the world.

A	Pharmaceuticals
A	Forest Products
B+	Aerospace
B	Chemicals
B	Food
B	Scientific & Photographic Equipment
B	Petroleum Refining
B-	Telecommunications Equipment
C+	Computers
C	Industrial & Farm Equipment
C	Motor Vehicles
C-	Metals
D	Electronics

Scoring: **A** = Dominant worldwide
B = Solid leadership, shared with others
C = Vulnerability; risk of continued decline
D = Basically on its back

Source: "How American Industry Stacks Up," by Andrew Kupfer, *Fortune*, March 2, 1992, p. 30. Reprinted by permission.

FIGURE 1.1
U.S. competitiveness relative to Japan and Europe, 1992.

Since then, U.S. companies have improved performance dramatically in a number of these industries, including motor vehicles, computers, and industrial and farm equipment, to name a few.

In much the same way that foreign firms have perceived the U.S. market as an opportunity, U.S.-based firms have viewed foreign competition not only as a threat on their own home front but also as a source of new global opportunities. For instance, many large U.S. corporations such as Exxon, IBM, and Dow Chemical generate well over 50 percent of their sales revenues in foreign countries. Free trade agreements such as the North American Free Trade Agreement (NAFTA) and the European Common Market, which eliminate or reduce tariffs among agreeing member nations, have helped to create open, nonrestricted markets for their member countries. In the future, globalization is expected to open even more markets for free trade. One of the critical challenges facing management will be gaining an advantage in an increasingly aggressive and competitive world.

The Increasing Emphasis on Quality

Organizations of the 1990s are more quality conscious than ever before, both in the United States and abroad. Customer demands and intense competition have created quality awareness in large and small organizations in both the private and the public sectors. The emphasis on quality improvements was popularized by the late W. Edwards Deming. Although his concepts and work were largely ignored in this country, they found fertile ground in post–World War II Japan. Deming's approach to quality enabled Japanese companies and their products to overcome their reputation for poor quality at a low price. As a result, Japan is now a major competitor in the world and a prime example of the benefits of quality management to organizations and to a country as a whole. Today, Japan is considered a world leader in producing quality products.[4]

Total quality management (TQM) refers to an organization's commitment to quality and continuing improvement in all areas of its operations, including processes as well as goods and services. In the opening case, Harley-Davidson's quality focus involved strengthening customer relationships, improving inventory and inspection systems, training employees, and creating a team approach to overall company effectiveness.

Quality is not just an issue in the United States. As trade barriers are removed among European nations, quality standards have become crucial. In response to this need, the International Standards Organization established the **ISO 9000** standards as a framework for product quality assurance among countries doing business within the community of European nations. Over 50 nations, including the United States, have endorsed the ISO 9000, yet this is viewed as only the beginning of a worldwide move toward global quality standards. ISO 9000 certification requires rigorous assessment of an organization's quality practices, including design, manufacturing, inspection and testing, training, and service. Seeking, finding, and maintaining quality standards pose special challenges to managers at all levels in the organization.

total quality management (TQM) An organization's commitment to quality and the continuing improvement in all areas of its operations, including processes as well as goods and services.

ISO 9000 A framework for product quality assurance among countries doing business within the community of European nations.

The Added Challenge of Diversity

Today's managers must have strong human relations skills, for the workforce includes people from a broad range of educational backgrounds, ethnic origins, age-groups, genders, and cultures. Traditionally, the U.S. workforce was dominated by white males, but times changed rapidly. In 1985, U.S.-born white males accounted for 47 percent of the U.S. workforce, but by 2000 they will account for only 15 percent of new workforce entrants. Women, Hispanics, and African Americans fill an increasingly larger portion of jobs in the United States today, and the number is growing. In addition, the U.S. workforce has grown older, from a median age of 30 in the early 1980s to an expected 39 by 2000.[5]

As shown in MAP 1.1, the growing workforce diversity challenges managers by affecting many human resource–related issues, including recruitment, training, compensation and advancement, flexible working hours, part-time employment, and greater interpersonal sensitivity to the values and needs of the workforce.

Ethics and Social Responsibility in Management

Organizations today and in the future will continue to be evaluated by their commitment to ethical behavior and social responsibility. But despite the fact that companies have become more sensitive to these legal and social expectations, virtually daily one reads about violators. Citicorp fires the president and senior executives of

MANAGEMENT APPLICATION AND PRACTICE 1.1

Managing the Firm While Meeting the Needs of a Diverse Workforce

Top managers in U.S. firms are more conscious than ever before of the need to provide employment opportunities to special groups within their organizations, including women, minorities, and the physically and mentally challenged. As the workforce becomes increasingly diverse, managers need strong human relations skills as well as managerial and technical skills.

Today, two out of every three jobs are filled by women, and women are now moving into top management positions. For example, several companies are now considered "woman friendly." The following companies are leaders in this effort:

▶ *Avon Products* (cosmetics). Of 47 officers, 27 percent are women.

▶ *CBS Inc.* (television, radio). Approximately 25 percent of the upper ranks are women.

▶ *Dayton Hudson Corporation* (retailing). Women account for almost 20 percent of company officers and 68 percent of management trainees.

▶ *Kelly Services* (temporary services). Women make up 90 percent of the workforce and 30 percent of the company's top managers.

▶ *U.S. West* (telecommunications). Of the firm's top executives, 21 percent are women.

▶ *Pitney Bowes* (office equipment). The company has a minimum requirement that 35 percent of its new hires and promotions go to women and 15 percent to minorities.

▶ *Gannett Company* (newspaper publishing). Bonus pay is tied to a manager's record of promoting women and minorities.

▶ *Tenneco* (diversified). Executive bonuses are linked to the successful mentoring of women.

For African Americans, the figures are more mixed. Nearly 14 percent of African Americans in the workforce (as compared to 17 percent of whites) are in professional and technical jobs. But only 6 percent are managers, and only 4 percent of all corporate officials and managers are African American. Although discrimination still exists, most firms are now equal opportunity employers. At Levi Strauss, for example, 43 percent of the workforce are Hispanic, 14 percent are African American, and 30 percent are women. Hispanics make up almost one-fourth of all managers and officials and 13 percent of professionals.

Black Enterprise magazine identified 50 other companies that were committed to improving black employment statistics. Among them are Adolph Coors Company, where 31 percent of managers are African American, and Federal Express, where managers are graded on minority hiring and 34 percent of the employees are African American. In the auto industry, Ford Motors boasts 246 African American–owned dealerships, General Motors has 114, and Chrysler has 64.

The Americans with Disabilities Act (ADA) was passed to protect and prevent discrimination against the physically and mentally challenged, which include anyone who is substantially restricted from performing normal activities. "Normal activities" include walking, seeing, hearing, speaking, working, or learning. The ADA also covers persons with certain types of diseases, such as AIDS.

Sources: "Diverse by Design," *Business Week*, "Reinventing America," 1992 issue; Walecia Conrad, "Welcome to the Woman-Friendly Company," *Business Week*, (August 5, 1990), pp. 48–55; and Rick Mendoza, "The Best Places to Work," *Hispanic Business*, (February 1994) pp. 26–36.

a credit card division for overstating revenues; American Express terminates several managers for passing off a number of bankrupt accounts as current; Sears auto centers in California and Florida inflate customers' auto repair costs; legal actions continue against executives involved in the fraud-ridden S&L failures of the 1980s, which cost taxpayers over $500 billion. While organizations have grown more vigilant recently, the end to unethical practices or breaches of socially responsible actions is nowhere in sight. Michael Josephson, a prominent ethics consultant for some of America's largest corporations, feels that the pressure on individuals to perform—for themselves and their company—is the major factor.

But violations can prove costly. Corning's stock declined some 15 percent after the breast implant scandal implicated Dow Corning breast implants, despite the fact that it had sufficient coverage to handle all claims. Mandatory fines can reach hundreds of millions of dollars for a broad range of criminal actions—antitrust violations, breaches of security and contract law, bribery, fraud, and EEO violations, to name some. But not everything that is legal is necessarily ethical. Even if businesses don't land in court, the media have given greater attention to business investigative reporting, an additional incentive to businesses to keep their acts clean in today's environment. Landing on page one of *USA Today* or being the subject of an exposé on *60 Minutes* is every CEO's nightmare.[6]

The Challenge of Empowerment

Today's internal organizational environment differs markedly from environments of just a decade ago. Organizations recognize that all employees, not just managers and executives, are key players in their success. Organizations are implementing total quality management (TQM) programs that help create open and participative corporate cultures. Empowering employees, and especially teams of employees, gives them more decision-making freedom regarding their own work, group projects, and the achievement of company objectives. Whether or not firms have formal TQM programs, employee empowerment has become a focus of most successful organizations today. Note in the opening case how employees at Harley-Davidson were empowered to make decisions to improve quality.

Examples of employee empowerment are reflected in such changes in management programs and policies as ensuring employee representation on committees normally reserved for upper managers, sharing plans and performance data with employees at all levels, and creating employee problem-solving groups. At Kodak's precision components manufacturing division, empowered operating personnel now assume more responsibility in arranging their own work hours, keeping track of their own productivity, maintaining and repairing their own equipment, training fellow workers, meeting with suppliers, helping manage inventory, and interviewing prospective job candidates. As a result of Kodak management's commitment to employee empowerment, production time for X-ray cassettes was reduced by 67 percent.[7] Effective empowerment has been documented at relatively small organizations as well as at major corporations.

Despite its overall success, management must address several issues surrounding empowerment, such as the following:

1. Developing empowerment skills of managers
2. Overcoming the traditional management viewpoint that empowering employees results in the loss of managerial power
3. Gaining employee acceptance of the increased responsibility that accompanies empowerment

Meeting the Five Challenges

Throughout this text, we will be emphasizing these five contemporary management challenges. In fact, individual chapters are devoted to the discussion of ethics and social responsibility (Chapter 3), the impact of globalization on management

Management–union disputes often reflect differences in how best to deal with issues of global competition, increased quality, and employee diversity.

(Chapter 5), and the importance of managing diversity and human resources (Chapter 9). Several discussions focus on new management techniques, with particular emphasis on empowerment and total quality management programs (Chapter 14). The *Managerial Application and Practices* feature provides examples of how these important issues are affecting management today and in the future.

Defining Management

The following scenario helps explain what management is to trainees who attend the authors' workshops and seminars.

> Jan Bolton operates a one-person shoe repair shop. Jan performs all the necessary activities, including serving customers, repairing shoes, buying equipment and supplies, maintaining equipment, keeping records, paying bills, and borrowing money when necessary. In effect, she does everything associated with the operation of her shoe repair shop.

After reading about Jan, trainees are asked, "Does Jan perform management?" How would you answer that question? Perhaps you are thinking that the answer is *yes*, since Jan makes decisions about the business and must manage her time. Perhaps you are thinking that the answer is *no*; Jan is not performing management, since she is "doing"—performing sales, purchasing, maintenance, and operating-level work. Consider your answer for a moment, and then read the second scenario.

Business is so good that Jan leases the adjacent office and removes the wall, creating five times more floor space in the shop. Jan hires four employees: three repairers and one counter clerk.

Now consider the question once again: "Does Jan perform management?" Although almost all trainees in the management workshops now answer *yes*, occasionally one or two trainees will argue that it depends on how one defines management. These few protagonists are absolutely correct—the answer does depend on one's definition of management.

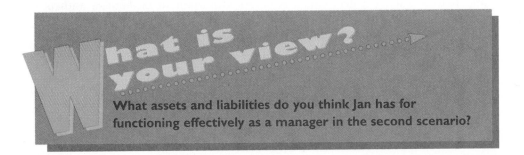

What assets and liabilities do you think Jan has for functioning effectively as a manager in the second scenario?

A body of management knowledge accumulated since the early part of the century serves as one basis for providing an appropriate definition of management. This definition, consistent with those found in management texts, workshops, and seminars, is illustrated in the second scenario, where Jan must achieve results through the efforts of others.

Throughout this text, then, **management** is defined as the process of planning, organizing, leading, and controlling the activities of employees in combination with other resources to achieve organizational objectives (see Figure 1.2). This definition reflects a broad number of situations consistent with Jan's situation in the second scenario—one shared by CEOs, middle managers, and supervisory personnel in organizations such as the U.S. Army, the Girl Scouts of America, the Charity Hospital of New Orleans, Exxon, Kmart, and Jan's Shoe Repair.

management The process of planning, organizing, leading, and controlling the activities of employees in combination with other resources to achieve organizational objectives.

FIGURE 1.2
What management is.

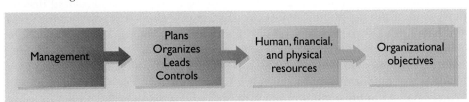

Functions Performed by Managers

Regardless of the type of industry, the organizational level, or the organizational function involved, at least four functions must be performed by anyone who is a manager—planning, organizing, leading, and controlling organizational activities. This section provides a general overview of these functions. They are discussed in detail in Parts Three, Four, and Five of the text.

Planning

planning The management function of choosing an organization's mission and objectives and then determining the courses of action needed to achieve them.

Management at every level of the organization is involved in some aspect of planning. Before making a decision, it is always important to be familiar with past events, but it is even more important to have a plan for the future. **Planning** is the process of choosing an organization's mission (or purpose) and objectives, and then determining the policies, projects, programs, procedures, methods, systems, budgets, standards, and strategies needed to achieve them.

Organizing

organizing The management function of determining resources and activities required to achieve the organization's objectives, combining these into a formal structure, assigning responsibility for them, and delegating authority to carry out assignments.

Organizing is the management function of determining how a task is to be accomplished. Management must consider the resources necessary to achieve the organization's objectives and then assign responsibility and authority to the appropriate people. The task is typically broken down into several steps or processes, and employee groups are formed with the purpose of achieving their part of the overall task.

An organization's hierarchy or structure reflects the organizing function. The chain of command, determination of departmental groupings, and establishment of communication flows should enable the organization to effectively achieve plans. For instance, lower-level managers perform organizing functions, note the requirements of a job, and assign people with the necessary skills to work on that job.

Leading

leading The management function of influencing employees to accomplish objectives, which involves the leader's qualities, styles, and power as well as the leadership activities of communication, motivation, and discipline.

Plans—and the organization and staff that result from them—are useless without the function of leading employees. The **leading** function, simply stated, is getting employees to do the things you want them to do. Therefore, it involves the leader's qualities, styles, and power as well as the leadership activities of communication, motivation, and discipline.

Leading involves a face-to-face manner of assigning tasks and issuing instructions, transmitting goals and objectives, requesting cooperation, asking for ideas, and handling other communications with employees. However, leading can also be achieved through indirect communications with employees, such as publishing standing orders, standard operating procedures (SOPs), and job descriptions. Leading communications can be personal or impersonal. Often, the higher managers move in the organization, the more impersonal their methods of communication, while lower managerial positions typically involve more personal methods.

At Wal-Mart, late founder Sam Walton stayed visible by walking around, a leadership style that became a key factor in the company's success. Walton enjoyed interacting with employees and for years made it a practice to visit each store at least once a year, meeting employees face to face. He insisted that top managers "get into the stores frequently." David Glass, his successor, spends several days each week visiting stores, as do other top managers. The cost of keeping the firm's fleet of 11 turboprop airplanes busy flying executives to stores across the country is considered necessary in maintaining strong relationships and leadership in the giant Wal-Mart discount store chain.[8]

Controlling

All the previous functions discussed in this section are ineffective without the last one, **controlling**—the process of devising ways and means of ensuring that planned performance is actually achieved. The concept of control in achieving planned performance can be seen in many of our daily activities. Keeping a running balance in a check register helps prevent overdrafts and the costs associated with them. Periodically inspecting a car's oil, water, belts, and hoses helps meet the objective of keeping the vehicle in good running condition and maintaining engine performance. Forms of control commonly used by managers in organizations include inspections, progress reports, and financial statements.

controlling The management function of devising ways and means of ensuring that planned performance is actually achieved.

In essence, control involves five basic steps:

1. Setting performance standards
2. Determining methods for measuring performance
3. Measuring actual performance
4. Comparing performance with established standards
5. Taking corrective action when necessary to bring actual performance into conformity with the standard

Therefore, for effective control, there must first be planning, organizing, and leading.

Relationships Among Managerial Functions

It is important to differentiate the four basic functions that managers perform, but it is just as important to understand how they are interrelated to each other. For example, a manager whose department faces a large project must plan the project. Part of the plan may involve whom to assign to what project tasks, which is organizing. Whom she assigns to which tasks (whether they are seasoned, proven performers) influences whether she will use a looser or tighter leadership style, which is leading. Her leadership style will influence the frequency and formality of employee progress reporting, which is controlling. While the functions can be performed in any order, they are typically performed in the following sequence: planning, organizing, leading, and controlling.

No single function is more important than another; all are needed. However, the four management functions must be coordinated to achieve the optimum level of performance.

The Contemporary Emphasis on Leadership

Managers of U.S. organizations have come under considerable fire recently for everything from being shortsighted, resistant to change, and satisfied with the status quo to lacking vision and failing to develop employee commitment to the organization's objectives. Critics, who have attacked every managerial level in business, government, and not-for-profit organizations, are calling for less emphasis on the traditional management functions of planning, organizing, and controlling, and more on leading or "leadership." Figure 1.3 illustrates how United Technologies Corporation views the difference between *managing* and *leading*.

The call for effective "leading" in organizations reflects a shift from the traditional view that management's primary job was to maintain the status quo. Prior to the 1980s, organizations functioned in relatively stable environments compared to today's rapidly changing technological, economic, legal, and sociocultural environments. Turbulent external and internal environments surround the challenges pointed out earlier—increased global competition, a new focus on continuous quality improvement, diversity in the workforce, ethics and social responsibilities, and employee empowerment. Additional turbulence has been created by **corporate downsizing**—a popular technique designed to eliminate layers of hierarchy and reduce the number of operating personnel in general and of managers in particular. Managers at all levels face the challenges of motivating employees and maintaining morale under these most difficult conditions.

Empowerment has created other problems in organizations, as managers' roles are being shifted from those of traditional bosses to team leaders. Team leaders are essentially colleagues and peers within the organization who must use influence

corporate downsizing A popular technique for eliminating layers of hierarchy and reducing the number of operating personnel in general and managers in particular.

FIGURE 1.3
Differentiating management from leadership.

Let's Get Rid of Management

People don't want to be managed.
They want to be led.
Whoever heard of a world manager?
World leader, yes.
Educational leader.
Political leader.
Religious leader.
Scout leader.
Community leader.
Labor leader.
Business leader.
They lead.
They don't manage.
The carrot always wins over the stick.
Ask your horse.
You can *lead* your horse to water, but you can't *manage* him to drink.
If you want to manage somebody, manage yourself.
Do that well and you'll be ready to stop managing.
And start leading.

Source: Cited in Warren Bennis and Burt Nannus, *Leaders: The Strategies for Taking Charge* (New York: Harper & Row, 1985), p. 22. Message published in the *Wall Street Journal* by United Technologies Corp., Hartford, CT 06101.

rather than authority to achieve tasks and objectives. Thus, in today's environment of dramatic, ongoing change, managers at all levels must perform the leading function effectively in order to achieve organizational objectives.

In the stable, status quo environments of the past, managers who weren't particularly adept at leading—but who were effective planners, organizers, and controllers—could still be reasonably effective at achieving goals. However, in today's organizational environments, the need for effective leadership skills makes this far less likely.

John Gardner, former secretary of the U.S. Department of Health, Education, and Welfare and noted author on leadership, addresses the leadership-management issue by stating that managers who are effective at leading (whom he refers to as leader/managers) distinguish themselves from narrower, traditional planning-organizing-controlling managers. He points out that leader/managers do the following:

1. Think longer-term, beyond the daily crises.
2. Grasp their unit's relationship to the bigger organizational picture—their overall organization, industry trends, and so forth.
3. Reach constituents beyond their own department's boundaries, such as suppliers and customers.
4. Emphasize intangibles of vision, values, and motivation to work with and understand people.
5. Have political skill in coping with conflicting requirements of multiple stakeholders, such as other departments, customers, suppliers, unions, and top management.
6. Think in terms of renewal. They don't let the status quo, bureaucracy, or company policy dictate their limits.[9]

Gardner's view makes sense in light of the changing environments affecting organizations today. All managers, by the nature of their jobs, must provide strong leadership in order to be effective.

The terms *manager* and *leader* are used interchangeably throughout the text when referring to managers. However, it is important to remember that the *processes* of managing and leading differ, as explained in this section, managing being the broader term.

Throughout this text, an emphasis has been placed on the discussion of leadership and its role in management. In Part Three, five chapters focus on human relations skills in successful organizations: "Communicating for Results" (Chapter 10), "Motivating Employees" (Chapter 11), "Leadership in Action" (Chapter 12), "Managing Change, Organization Development, Conflict, and Stress" (Chapter 13), and "Team Development and Empowerment Strategies" (Chapter 14). Other chapters, as appropriate, include discussions and examples of leadership.

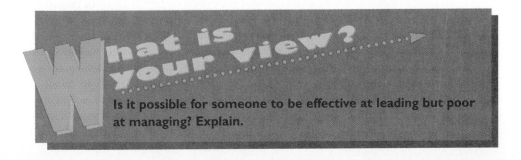

What is your view?

Is it possible for someone to be effective at leading but poor at managing? Explain.

Management as Both Art and Science

In general, effective managers use a scientific approach in making decisions. They systematically observe that a problem exists, gather data about the problem and potential solutions, generalize about the potential outcomes, then make the necessary decisions. However, in many aspects of management—especially decision making and human relations—managers also use an artistic approach, basing decisions on personal judgment, intuition, or "gut feeling." The question, therefore, is not whether effective management is a science, based on application of a systematic body of management knowledge, or an art, based on judgment and intuition. Rather, effective management is a combination of both, in varying proportions in different situations.[10]

Management is not really a hard science, like chemistry or physics. Rather, it has more in common with the social sciences, such as psychology and sociology. Take, for example, a law of physics: Newton's Third Law of Motion states that "to every action, there is always an equal and opposite reaction." This law describes a relationship that is invariably true, without exception. Management, however, has few laws that are always true in all situations. On the other hand, management has numerous *concepts*—generalizations that *tend* to be true but are not always. This is especially the case with many of the human aspects of management. Take the management concept that "people support decisions they have helped to make." This is generally true, but *not always*. Therefore, it is different from a law, which is invariably true under all circumstances.

The art of management, then, involves knowing when it is appropriate to apply management concepts and when it is not, depending on the situation. Moreover, it requires managers to use insight and judgment when past experience or training provides no firm principle on which to rely. Many managers, in fact, have never been formally trained in management but are extremely successful, relying on their "art" in practicing management.

Many discussions in this text are based on the assumption that there is a systematic body of knowledge—management theory—comprising a core of management concepts that tend to apply in most situations. *If you understand this body of knowledge and know how to apply it to given situations, it will greatly increase your likelihood of success in managerial situations.* However, understanding the body of knowledge and practicing the skills are two different things! For example, this book is designed so that each chapter helps you understand management principles, while end-of-chapter questions and exercises help you develop your managerial skills.

Management Is Universal

universality of management The concept that the functions of management must be performed by managers at all levels and in all organizations and cultures.

Understanding where and why management is needed depends on understanding the concept of **universality of management,** which states that the functions of management must be performed by managers in all types of organizations, in all cultures of the world. Management is universal in that it has a systematic body of knowledge comprising principles, guidelines, and other components of management theory. This body of knowledge tends to be broadly applicable to all situations, in a variety of organizations—business, government, educational, social, and religious, among others. It is generally applicable to all levels of management in an organization, from the lowest to the highest.

The functions of management must be performed; however, they may be applied differently by different managers and depend on variables such as the type of organization, employer, and employees and the organizational culture.[11] Lou Holtz, head football coach of Notre Dame's Fighting Irish, must set objectives, make plans to achieve them, and organize and coordinate his coaching staff. A continuing responsibility is leading his coaches and players by inspiring and communicating with them. At all times, but especially during games, he must assess team performance and modify plans according to his assessments. Every manager performs the same basic management functions, whether it be Holtz; CEO Karen Horn of Cleveland, Ohio's Bank One; Principal Larry LeDoux of Kodiak (Alaska) High School; or Maintenance Supervisor Buddy Teague of Bowater Carolina. What is important to note is that Holtz's methods or style of planning, organizing, leading, and control-ling college athletes may differ markedly from Principal LeDoux's management of five or six school department heads and Teague's style of managing his crew of ten union mechanics. All, however, must perform the four managerial functions.

All managers must achieve organizational goals through the coordinated efforts of other people. For that reason, managers often transfer from one depart-ment to another or even from one organization to another and still perform their management roles effectively. Consider the following examples:

▶ Elaine Chao went from a vice-president's job at BankAmerica to chairman of the Federal Maritime Commission, then became undersecretary of the U.S. Department of Transportation, director of the Peace Corps, and, in 1992, president and CEO of United Way of America.

▶ IBM CEO Louis Gerstner moved from the presidency of American Express, to CEO of RJR Nabisco (tobacco, food), to his current position with IBM in 1993. The credit card business (financial services industry) differed markedly from RJR Nabisco's tobacco and food processing industry, and both are different from the high-tech environment of IBM.

▶ Dr. Marshall Hahn left the academic world as president of Virginia Tech for Georgia-Pacific's (forest products, paper) chemical operations. He was not a chemist, yet he performed effectively as a manager of the chemical division and ultimately became CEO.

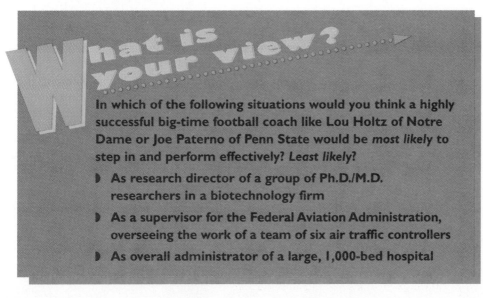

What is your view?

In which of the following situations would you think a highly successful big-time football coach like Lou Holtz of Notre Dame or Joe Paterno of Penn State would be *most likely* to step in and perform effectively? *Least likely?*

▶ As research director of a group of Ph.D./M.D. researchers in a biotechnology firm

▶ As a supervisor for the Federal Aviation Administration, overseeing the work of a team of six air traffic controllers

▶ As overall administrator of a large, 1,000-bed hospital

If managers perform their functions effectively in one situation, there is some probability that they will do the same in other situations. Do not interpret this to mean that an effective manager can manage anything. Because of the many variables involved, there is no assurance of success. Numerous factors may differ in various management positions, including organizational size, level of management, complexity of subordinates' tasks, subordinates' education and skill levels, number of subordinates, and other variables in the management environment.

Why Organizations Need Management

So far in this chapter, we have established that management is needed by all organizations and have described the functions performed by managers. This section explains the three primary reasons why organizations need management:

1. To establish objectives
2. To maintain balance among stakeholders
3. To achieve efficiency and effectiveness

Establishing Objectives

Objectives are the focus of organizational energy. Thus, a major management task is to establish objectives for the unit(s) being managed. Once objectives are established, the organization's human, financial, and physical resources attempt to accomplish them.

Top management typically establishes overall objectives for such areas as profitability, market share, growth, or new product development. At lower levels, objectives are set so as to achieve those of higher levels. Objectives for production output, quality, costs, and safety are typical. While objectives for lower-level managers may be established at higher levels, today it is becoming increasingly common for all employees to participate in determining the objectives they will work to meet.

Maintaining a Balance Among Stakeholders

stakeholders All those having a stake in the organization's success, including employees, owners, customers, government authorities, and creditors.

In working to achieve objectives, managers need to maintain balance among the conflicting objectives, goals, and activities of the **stakeholders** of an organization—those people who have a stake in the organization's success, including employees, owners, customers, government authorities, and creditors.

As shown in Figure 1.4, management holds in trust and must balance the interest of many different groups. It performs the function of stewardship on behalf of the *owners*, who are seeking a satisfactory return on their investment. The return may be profits (as in a business) or service (as in local, state, or federal governments). Management must also consider the interests of its *employees*, who seek good pay, safe and comfortable working conditions, fair and equitable treatment, the greatest possible job security, and more time off. The interests of the *public*, including consumer groups, environmentalists, and civil rights advocates, must be considered. Management must also please its *customers*, *clients*, and *consumers*, for without

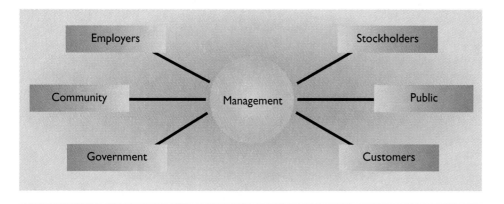

FIGURE 1.4
Effective management balances conflicting interests.

them the organization would have little purpose. Other stakeholders include *creditors*, *suppliers*, *union leaders*, and *trade associations*. Finally, management must satisfy the needs and demands of various *governments*. If management favors one stakeholder group at the expense of others, it will, in the long run, create an imbalance that will be detrimental to the organization.

Achieving Effectiveness and Efficiency

In management, the concept of **effectiveness** relates to a manager's ability to set and achieve objectives. For example, if a restaurant has, among other objectives, a 1996 profitability target of $1.75 million in sales and reaches or exceeds it, then

effectiveness The managerial ability to set and achieve proper objectives.

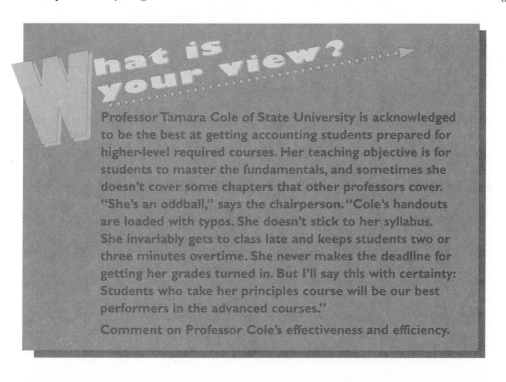

What is your view?

Professor Tamara Cole of State University is acknowledged to be the best at getting accounting students prepared for higher-level required courses. Her teaching objective is for students to master the fundamentals, and sometimes she doesn't cover some chapters that other professors cover. "She's an oddball," says the chairperson. "Cole's handouts are loaded with typos. She doesn't stick to her syllabus. She invariably gets to class late and keeps students two or three minutes overtime. She never makes the deadline for getting her grades turned in. But I'll say this with certainty: Students who take her principles course will be our best performers in the advanced courses."

Comment on Professor Cole's effectiveness and efficiency.

PRACTICING MANAGER

Not many managers are 29, CEO, and founder of a ten-year-old, $3 billion company with over 3,000 employees. But Michael Dell, founder of Dell Computer Corporation (DCC), is no ordinary manager.

When he was younger, Michael Dell would drive to school on the I-610 loop that circles Houston, Texas, and imagine that one day he would run a business in one of the many ultramodern skyscrapers along the route. During his morning drive, Dell would further imagine that the building from which he ran his business would come complete with flagpoles in front bearing company flags with a private elevator to take him up to his CEO chambers.

MICHAEL DELL, CEO, DELL COMPUTER CORPORATION

What Dell has done by the ripe old age of 29 is nothing short of spectacular. As CEO of DCC, this college dropout, who started selling computer parts by mail from his college dorm room when he was a freshman at the University of Texas at Austin, is now worth $1.2 billion.

Dell, who has been interested in business since he was 12, began tinkering with computers when he was 16. He remembers his first Apple II: "I bought the Apple as soon as it came out, took it apart, and put it back together." Describing himself as a teenage hacker, Dell spent a great deal of time exploring how computers use software and trying to find ways to speed up the process.

When he was 19, Dell began selling parts by mail from his dorm room. By the end of the year, he was shipping $80,000 worth of equipment a month. "The opportunity looked so attractive, I couldn't stay in school," Dell says of his initial success. Dropping out of school, Dell created PC's Limited, rented a small office across town from the University of Texas campus, and placed an ad in a computer magazine. The results were phenomenal: The first month, sales were $181,000; the first year, $6 million; the second year, $33 million; the third year, $69 million; and so on. Ten years out, 1994 sales reached over $3 billion.

Although Dell computers are highly regarded in the computer industry, the secret of Dell's success is not *what* he sells but *how* he sells it. Technically trained salespeople take phone orders from customers who choose from a wide variety of options to create a PC suited to their specific needs. Once the order is placed, it is sent to DCC's state-of-the-art factory, where the just-ordered computer is custom-built and ready for shipment within four days. The finished computer is sent to the customer within a week. By using the existing telephone network and highly developed U.S. transportation system as an extension of his company's factory and sales operation, Dell has eliminated regional warehouses and huge inventories.

From 19-year-old whiz kid to 29-year-old CEO, Dell catapulted DCC into one of the four largest PC producers in the United States. What began in such a small way in a university dorm room has evolved into a corporation headquartered in Austin, Texas—with subsidiaries in the United Kingdom, West Germany, France, and Canada, and sales to 94 countries.

The next few years, though, pose important managerial challenges as DCC tries to parlay its desktop PC success into similar successes with portables and advanced business computers. And despite the meteoric 100x sales growth since 1985, getting a handle on costs and operating margins has been a problem. In 1993, DCC lost $35 million due to bloated inventory, a canceled computer line, and costs associated with global expansion. "We've grown so fast, we're having growing pains," Dell acknowledges. In 1994, he undertook a program to build the "infrastructure to take us to $10 billion in sales." Dell brought in a number of new top executives and high-level managers, five from rivals Compaq and Apple and one new chief financial officer from Sun Microsystems. Motorola's executive vice-president, Morton Topper, was lured to become vice-chairman and share power with Chairman Dell in a two-member office of the chief executive. Industry analysts praised Dell for his maturity in recognizing the need to share power. "We have established a powerhouse reputation for desktop personal computers," Dell said in 1994. "Our goal for the coming year is to extend our reputation with the markets for advanced systems and portable computers."

Sources: Jeremy Main, "A Golden Age for Entrepreneurs," *Fortune*, February 12, 1990, p. 120; Tom Richman, "The Entrepreneur of the Year," *Inc.*, January 1990, pp. 42–43; Peter Burrow and Stephanie Forest, "Dell Computer Goes into the Shop," *Business Week*, July 12, 1993, pp. 138–140; Peter Burrows, "Beyond Rock Bottom," *Business Week*, March 14, 1994, pp. 80–82; and "Dell Computer Creates Two-Man Chief's Office," *New York Times*, May 10, 1994, p. D5.

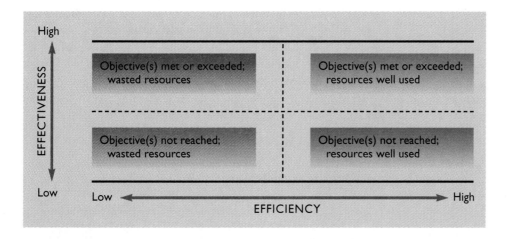

FIGURE 1.5
The effectiveness-efficiency matrix.

management would be considered *effective*. The other side of the management performance coin is **efficiency**—the ability to fully use resources while pursuing objectives. In the case of managing a restaurant, this would include such resources as employees, food, and time. The restaurant manager who achieves the same sales volume as another restaurant, while having only 15 percent of the payroll and food costs, would be considered more *efficient* in using resources.

The matrix in Figure 1.5 illustrates how meeting objectives directly relates to the effectiveness and efficiency of managers. A seafood restaurant manager, for example, might reduce the number of employees by efficiently using human resources and might reduce the cost of spoilage by controlling the expensive, perishable food inventories. However, if the restaurant does not meet its profitability objectives due to slower customer service and fewer sales, then the manager's effectiveness would remain low. Successful managers employ resources in a way that enables them to get the job done (effectiveness) with the least cost (efficiency).

Managers have multiple objectives to accomplish, many of which are complementary. For example, an "effective" restaurant manager would probably have objectives such as food quality and customer satisfaction, as well as sales objectives, all of which must be met through optimum use of resources.

efficiency A manager's ability to get things done, achieving higher outputs relative to inputs.

Levels of Management

There are many levels of management. In general, management activities vary at different organizational levels and with different organizational functions. The management levels are characterized by three features: the number of employees, the activities performed, and the managers' titles. The traditional way of depicting the different levels of management is with a pyramid, as shown in Figure 1.6.

Managers are given more authority and responsibility at higher levels. They perform different organizational functions and engage in different activities depending on their level. The time and skills required of managers also differ according to their level.

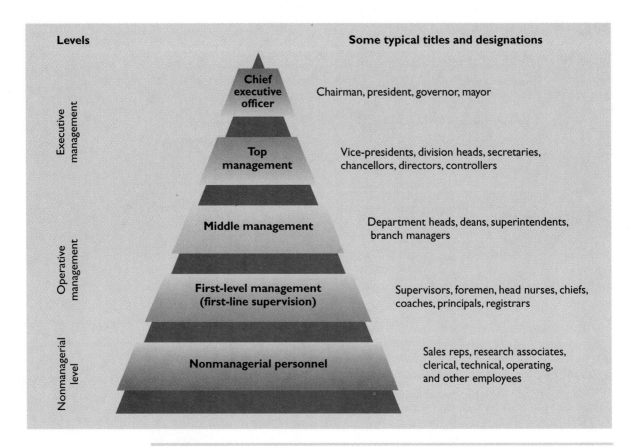

FIGURE 1.6
Management levels in an organization.

Number of Employees Differs at Different Levels

The majority of an organization's employees are nonmanagerial personnel who are at the base of the management pyramid. Among nonmanagerial workers, status and pay vary widely. This level includes not only low-skill-level positions, such as physical laborers and assembly line workers, but also high-skill-level positions, such as engineers, scientists, and technicians.

Within the managerial ranks, the number of managers at each level decreases as individuals move up from the operative to the executive level. Finally, at the apex of the organization, there is normally only one person.

Activities Differ at Different Levels

In general, people in the lower levels of management spend most of their time directly supervising and working with subordinates to meet the operating goals of higher management. People in higher levels spend more time setting goals and objectives, determining policies, establishing and controlling budgets, and making long-range forecasts.

Titles Differ at Different Levels

Another characteristic of the management hierarchy is that titles and designations differ at successively higher levels. Managers at lower levels typically have titles such as supervisor, head nurse, or chief. At the next higher level, managers may be called by titles such as superintendent, department head, or dean. In the third tier, managers have titles such as division head, director, and vice-president. The individual at the top of the management hierarchy may be called chief executive officer, president, chairman of the board, governor, or administrator.

Different Types of Organizational Functions

The way managers perform their jobs tends to vary according to the organizational functions they perform. The missions or purposes of organizations vary greatly. There are, however, many similar functions that all organizations must perform in carrying out their missions. Basically, these functions can be classified as either primary or support functions.

Primary Organizational Functions

Most organizations are built around three **primary functions** that are essential to their survival:

1. *Operations:* production, manufacturing, or the generation of service
2. *Marketing:* distribution, promotion, sales
3. *Finance:* acquisition and use of funds, budgeting

primary functions
The three functions essential to organizational survival: operations, marketing, and finance.

Support Functions

Several **support functions** are necessary to keep the organization's primary functions operating effectively. The major support functions include personnel, accounting, maintenance, research and development, legal, clerical, engineering, purchasing, and public, community, and legislative relations.

support functions
Functions necessary to keep the primary functions operating effectively.

Functional and General Managers

Managers and management positions are typically classified as one of two types. In general, **functional managers** are responsible for the activities of only one of the primary or support functions, such as production, marketing, finance, personnel, or accounting. **General managers** oversee a total operating unit or division, including all the functional activities of that unit. Figure 1.7 illustrates these relationships.

Examples of functional managers found within the production function, for instance, include vice-president of operations, production manager, production

functional managers
Managers responsible for activities of any one primary or support function.

general managers
Managers who oversee a total operating unit or division, including all the functional activities of the unit.

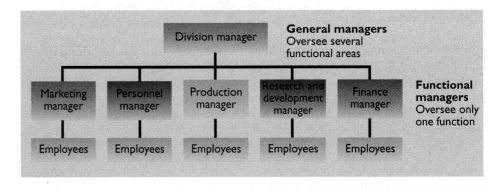

FIGURE 1.7
Relationship between functional and general managers.

superintendent, and general foreman. A general manager is typically a CEO, president, division manager, plant manager, or branch manager. Functional and general managers are found throughout all levels of the managerial pyramid.

Nature of Managerial Duties

As pointed out earlier in this chapter, managers must perform the four basic managerial functions of planning, organizing, leading, and controlling. However, this description of management functions doesn't indicate the true nature of managers' duties, such as how they spend their time, what specific jobs they typically perform, and which roles and skills they use.

Management researcher Henry Mintzberg identified ten different managerial roles. These roles, shown in Figure 1.8, are further divided into three broad categories: interpersonal, informational, and decisional. *Interpersonal roles* involve working directly with other people, such as subordinates, supervisors, peers, or people outside the organization. *Informational roles* require a manager to receive important information and disseminate it among the appropriate people. *Decisional roles* involve making decisions that affect other people.[12]

Taking a somewhat different viewpoint from Mintzberg's, Fred Luthans and his colleagues studied some 450 managers at various organizational levels.[13] They identified four major sets of activities:

▶ *Routine communication*: processing paperwork and exchanging information

▶ *Human resource management*: the "people" side of managing—coaching, training, influencing, and appraising

▶ *Traditional management*: planning, organizing, and decision making

▶ *Networking*: socializing, politicking, and interacting with people outside the organization

Figure 1.9 shows the percentage of time managers in the survey spent on each of the four activities, as well as the averages for managers who were considered effective. Note that effective managers spent much time on communication-related activities.

Interpersonal Roles	
Figurehead	Performs ceremonial activities, attends social functions, greets visitors. (Rides Hog at motorcycle rallies.)
Leader	Motivates, encourages, and builds enthusiasm among employees. (Visits dealers, employees.)
Liaison	Serves as connecting link with important others outside the unit or organization. (Calls on government officials to push for lower tariffs by Japan.)

Informational Roles	
Monitor	Seeks out and receives relevant information. (Requests information from vice-presidents regarding current sales, production levels.)
Disseminator	Circulates and transfers relevant information. (Shares information at weekly Monday meeting of key managers.)
Spokesperson	Makes official statements to outsiders. (Conducts meetings with stock analysts, sharing company forecasts for profits, growth.)

Decisional Roles	
Entrepreneur	Tackles special problems, seeks changes that will improve the unit or organization. (Visits foreign countries, selling licensing or manufacturing agreements.)
Disturbance handler	Responds to problems and pressures among employees or units, resolves conflicts. (Reconciles dispute among vice-presidents over styling changes for new model.)
Resource allocator	Decides why, when, how, for what, and to whom organizational resources are allocated. (Determines finalized departmental budgets for the fiscal year.)
Negotiator	Bargains with subordinates, other organizational units, or outsiders to reach agreements. (Calls key supplier to help negotiate contract for purchased parts.)

FIGURE 1.8
Ten managerial roles (hypothetical examples of each role per Harley CEO Richard Teerlink).

The study also revealed that managers who were considered successful in receiving promotions spent the largest percentage of their time (48 percent) engaged in networking, much more than the time spent by the entire group of managers studied as well as those managers considered effective. The point is that interacting with a broad constituency—bosses, peers, subordinates, and people outside the organization—is an important factor in obtaining managerial promotions.

In performing their roles, managers experience crowded and hectic workdays. Frequently, activities are interrupted by others; most of the tasks managers perform are brief, taking less than ten minutes. Consequently, management jobs are extremely fast paced. One study found that average first-line managers dealt with several hundred job-related problems each day. Even top-level managers can have 30

	Managers		
	All (450) Managers		Effective Managers
Traditional management	32%		19%
Human resource management	20%		26%
Communication	29%		44%
Networking	19%		11%

Source: Fred Luthans, Richard Hodgetts, and S. A. Rosenkrantz, *Real Managers* (Cambridge, Mass.: MIT Press, 1988).

FIGURE 1.9
How managers spend their time.

or more separate episodes in a typical day. The hurried pace means that managers have little opportunity to close a door in order to spend even one hour alone.

Additional research about managers confirms that they also work long hours. A workweek of 50 hours is typical, and the higher the level, generally the longer the hours. Studies of CEOs, for example, show they spend four out of five nights working: one at the office, one entertaining, and two at home. Workweeks of 55 to 65 hours or more, especially at higher managerial levels, are not uncommon.[14]

Owner Richard Branson performing the role of spokesperson for Virgin Airlines.

Types of Managerial Skills

The skills that effective managers generally use can be sorted into three major types:

1. Conceptual skills
2. Technical skills
3. Human relations skills

The relative importance of any one of these skills to a given manager at a given time depends on the type of organization, the managerial level, and the function being performed. Figure 1.10 reveals the relative importance of the various skills at different management levels. While each of these skills is required to some degree by all managers, top managers generally use conceptual skills more than middle and first-level managers, and first-level managers typically use technical skills more than the other two levels of managers. Human relations skills are used about the same by all managers.

Conceptual Skills

Effective managers are able to obtain meaning from inadequate—and often conflicting—data. They do this using **conceptual skills,** the mental ability needed to acquire, analyze, and interpret information received from various sources and to make complex decisions. Conceptual skills include diagnostic skills and involve the ability to understand cause-effect relationships and to see the whole of a situation as well as the parts.

For example, in the opening case, Harley CEO Vaughn Beals most likely used conceptual skills in assessing the severity of problems facing Harley-Davidson. He probably talked with various managers; listened to customer complaints; noted

conceptual skills
Mental ability needed to acquire, analyze, and interpret information received from various sources and to make complex decisions.

FIGURE 1.10
Relative importance of managerial skills at different levels in the organization.

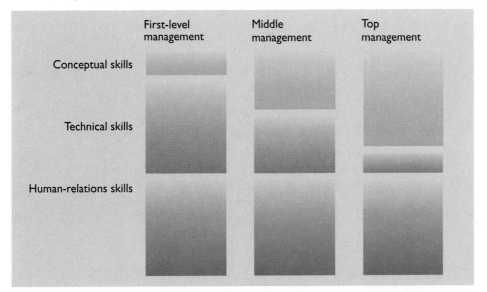

styling changes taking place in competitors' products; visited dealers; analyzed production, sales, and financial assessments; and concluded that drastic action was needed if Harley was to survive. His conceptual skills helped him to recognize, diagnose, and understand the problem and to develop various approaches to change Harley's strategies.

Managers who do not have strong conceptual skills tend to respond alike to all inputs without considering their relative importance. This can result in a loss of control and sense of direction.

Managers need to develop conceptual skills that will enable them to see what goes on in their work environments and help them take appropriate actions. In essence, this is the ability to "see the big picture," to plan ahead rather than react. Studies tend to confirm the conclusion that these conceptual skills are used more by people in top management than by those in any other level of management in an organization.[15]

Technical Skills

technical skills Ability to use the knowledge, tools, and techniques of a specific field, such as accounting, engineering, production, or sales.

Technical skills include the ability to use the knowledge, tools, and techniques of a specific discipline or field, such as accounting, engineering, production, medicine, or sales. Managers still need some knowledge of the technical functions they are supervising, although the amount of time they spend performing technical activities decreases as they move up the organizational ladder. Examples include the ability to program a computer, operate a machine (such as a lathe, printing press, or typewriter), or prepare financial statements.

Technical skills are relatively more important for first-line supervisors than for top managers. First-line supervisors are closer to the actual work being performed. As a result, they often must tell or show others how to do the job. They also must know when the work is being done properly. Every industry, every company and enterprise, and every job has special technical skill requirements.

Even though John Scully was a top manager at Pepsico, Apple Computer was interested in hiring him as CEO for his marketing strengths. Apple executives felt that their company management had exceptional technological strengths but

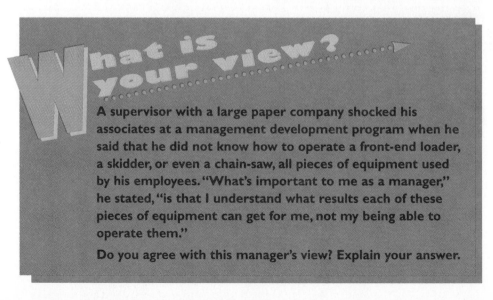

What is your view?

A supervisor with a large paper company shocked his associates at a management development program when he said that he did not know how to operate a front-end loader, a skidder, or even a chain-saw, all pieces of equipment used by his employees. "What's important to me as a manager," he stated, "is that I understand what results each of these pieces of equipment can get for me, not my being able to operate them."

Do you agree with this manager's view? Explain your answer.

needed someone at the top with leadership, administrative, and especially marketing expertise to maximize Apple technological know-how. In his early days at Apple, Scully was tutored in computer technology by two young programmers. As he admitted, leading Apple without knowing much about technology was "like trying to do brain surgery in the first year of medical school."[16]

Human Relations Skills

The many diverse abilities required to understand other people and to interact effectively with them are known as **human relations skills.** For example, these skills are needed in leading, motivating, and communicating with subordinates, peers, bosses, and even outsiders.

human relations skills
Ability required to understand other people and interact effectively with them.

A study conducted by the Center for Creative Leadership interviewed close associates of 21 managers who were at one time considered highly promising, but later in their careers had plateaued, been fired, or been forced to retire early. The reason most frequently mentioned by associates for these managers' derailment was their insensitivity to people—having an abrasive, intimidating, or bullying style.[17]

According to the American Management Association, the people side of managing is one advantage that global firms have over their U.S. counterparts. Global competitors in Japan, Germany, and other industrial countries enjoy greater skills at leading and building a climate in which personnel are committed to creating quality goods and services. In the United States, fingers are pointed at our financial and analytical approaches to managing. The "number-crunching" approach too frequently overlooks the importance of human relations skills.

SUMMARY

Management is alive, challenging, and complex. Moreover, if you possess management skills, a career in management can offer many opportunities.

People form organizations because they can accomplish more by cooperating than they can by working alone. An organization is a group of two or more people working together to achieve a common objective. Management is needed whenever people work together in an organization, and this is particularly true in the increasing numbers of small businesses and service industry companies. Five current challenges facing managers and organizations are (1) the global environment, (2) a continuous emphasis on quality improvements, (3) the diversity of today's workforce, (4) social responsibility and ethical concerns, and (5) employee empowerment.

Management is defined as working with human, financial, and physical resources to achieve organizational objectives by performing the planning, organizing, leading, and controlling functions. Because of the dramatic changes taking place in organizations today, the leadership function of management has received increasing attention in recent years. Management can also be portrayed as a combination of art and science.

The universality-of-management concept states that the functions performed by managers are the same at all organizational levels and in all organizations. Management serves three main purposes: (1) to establish objectives; (2) to maintain balance among the conflicting demands of stakeholders, including owners, employees, and customers; and (3) to achieve efficiency and effectiveness.

The three primary functions that must be performed in any organization in order to succeed are operations, marketing, and finance. Support functions, which include purchasing, research and development, and accounting, assist in accomplishing the three primary functions. A functional manager has narrow job responsibility for only one of the primary or support functions. A general manager, on the other hand, has much broader responsibilities, overseeing several primary and support functions.

Three broad roles are assumed by managers: interpersonal, informational, and decisional. In performing these and other roles, managers find that their jobs are hectic, characterized by many relatively brief episodes that vary widely in nature. Managers commonly work 50 or more hours weekly.

Managers need certain skills in order to do their jobs effectively. These include conceptual, technical, and human relations skills, which can be acquired through education and experience.

KEY TERMS

organization, 8
globalization, 9
total quality management (TQM), 11
ISO 9000, 11
management, 15
planning, 16
organizing, 16
leading, 16
controlling, 17
corporate downsizing, 18
universality of management, 20

stakeholders, 22
effectiveness, 23
efficiency, 25
primary functions, 27
support functions, 27
functional manager, 27
general manager, 27
conceptual skills, 31
technical skills, 32
human relations skills, 33

DISCUSSION QUESTIONS

1. Explain the importance of total quality management in organizations today. In your answer, consider issues internal as well as external to the organization. How is globalization affecting the quality movement?

2. Figure 1.9 reveals how effective managers spend their time performing various functions. Why do you think managers in upper-level positions spend most of their time on communications?

3. What managerial function is being performed when sales managers go over their salespersons' reports to see how they are doing?

4. Of the types of skills required by managers, which, if any, are more desirable for the president of a college fraternity, the head of a church, and a drill sergeant in the U.S. Army?

5. How do you explain the fact that managers are needed in all organizations, whether large or small, public or private, profit-seeking or not-for-profit?

PRACTICING MANAGEMENT

1.1

learning exercise

Understanding the Job of Managing

Managers perform a great variety of activities on their jobs. These activities can range from simple telephone calls to major investment decisions. They can also vary in relative importance and in the time they consume. This exercise is designed to help you gain some first-hand knowledge of managerial work.

The Procedure

1. Find a manager (plant manager, office supervisor, general manager, personnel manager, production manager, or the like) whose job primarily involves supervising the work of other people. Then arrange an interview to obtain information about that person's job.

2. Ask the manager to identify the activities he or she considers important and those that are time-consuming. You can use the Managerial Job Questionnaire as a guide.

3. Prepare a managerial job profile by compiling your findings and those of other students. You can use the average of importance scores and time-consumption scores as a basis of the profile. You can make rankings from these average scores.

4. On the basis of other students' data, compare answers of managers in different functional groups (marketing, production, and so forth) and in different hierarchical levels.

5. Discuss the implications of these findings for improving managerial performance and for educating future managers.

The Managerial Job Questionnaire

Instructions: The items in the Managerial Job Questionnaire concern the activities you perform as a manager. The purpose of this survey is to identify the relative importance you attach to various managerial activities and the amount of time per week you devote to each activity or role. Enter an appropriate number for each activity on the basis of a 5-point scale, with 1 representing the *least important* or *least time-consuming* and 5 representing the *most important* or *most time-consuming* activities.

Source: Kae H. Chung and Leon C. Megginson, *Organizational Behavior: Developing Managerial Skills* (New York: Harper & Row, 1981), pp. 23–25.

Managerial activities	Importance	Time consumed
Interpersonal roles		
Figurehead: Activities involving ceremonial, social, or legal duties (dinners, luncheons, signing contracts, civic affairs, etc.)		
Leader: Motivating, guiding, and developing subordinates (staffing, training, and rewarding employees)		
Liaison: Maintaining contacts with people outside your chain of command (staff meetings, lunches with peers, customers, and suppliers)		
Informational roles		
Monitor: Seeking and obtaining information through verbal and written communication media (meetings, memos, reports, and telephone calls)		
Disseminator: Transmitting information to subordinates (through meetings, memos, briefings, and telephone calls)		
Spokesperson: Transmitting information to people outside the work group (speaking to groups, reporting to outsiders, and briefing stockholders)		
Decision roles		
Entrepreneur: Searching for business opportunities and planning new activities for performance improvement (new venture, new product, and planning)		
Disturbance handler: Taking corrective actions on problems or pressures (labor strikes, material shortages, and personal conflict resolutions)		
Resource allocator: Deciding which organizational units get what resources and how much (budgeting, capital expenditure decisions, and personnel assignments)		
Negotiator: Negotiating with employees, customers, suppliers, and unions (sales negotiations, labor contract negotiations, and salary negotiations)		

1.2 The Personal Interest Inventory

learning exercise

Directions: Each of the following questions is worth a total of 3 points. For each question, assign more points to the response you prefer and fewer points, in order of preference, to the others. For example, if one response receives 3 points, the other two must receive 0; if one receives 2, then the others must receive 1 and 0; or each may receive 1 point. Enter your scores in the Score Matrix.

1. Which activity interests you most?
   - 0 | a. Working with your hands
   - 3 2 b. Working with people
   - 0 0 c. Reading books
2. Which skills would you invest time in learning?
   - 0 0 a. Research and writing
   - 3 3 b. Organizing and leading
   - 0 0 c. Crafts and art
3. Which job activities would you enjoy most?
   - 3 1 a. Counseling and coaching
   - 0 1 b. Building and doing
   - 0 2 c. Thinking and planning
4. Which trait is most characteristic of you?
   - 1 1 a. Helper
   - 2 2 b. Doer
   - 0 0 c. Scholar
5. Which would you most enjoy doing?
   - 3 3 a. Talking with people
   - 0 0 b. Writing a book
   - 0 0 c. Building a house
6. How do you prefer to use your spare time?
   - 0 2 a. Outdoor projects
   - 2 1 b. Social activities
   - 1 1 c. Thinking
7. Which of these traits is most important to you?
   - 0 0 a. Physical coordination
   - 1 1 b. Ability to deal with people
   - 2 2 c. Mental ability
8. Which jobs most reflect your interests?
   - 2 0 a. Teacher, social worker, counselor
   - 0 2 b. Engineer, surveyor, craftsman
   - 1 1 c. Researcher, historian, author
9. Which ability is your strongest?
   - 2 1 a. Communication skills
   - 1 1 b. Creative thinking
   - 0 1 c. Physical skills
10. Which tasks do you perform best?
    - 0 2 a. Operating and maintaining
    - 2 0 b. Communicating and motivating
    - 1 1 c. Developing and planning

11. Which occupation interests you most?
    - 0 1 a. Pilot
    - 2 2 b. Judge
    - 1 0 c. Politician
12. Which of the following is most interesting to you?
    - 2 1 a. Helping others
    - 1 2 b. Thinking things through
    - 0 0 c. Using your hands
13. Which skills could you learn with the least effort?
    - 1 2 a. Leading and negotiating
    - 0 0 b. Artwork and handicrafts
    - 2 1 c. Language and theoretical reasoning
14. What tasks appeal to you most?
    - 0 0 a. Developing new theories
    - 2 2 b. Helping people with problems
    - 1 1 c. Developing a skill
15. What assignment appeals to you most?
    - 1 1 a. Working with ideas
    - 2 2 b. Working with people
    - 0 0 c. Working with things
16. Which is your greatest attribute?
    - 0 0 a. Creativity
    - 1 2 b. Competence
    - 2 1 c. Sensitivity
17. For which occupation do you have a natural talent?
    - 3 0 a. Counselor
    - 0 3 b. Builder
    - 0 0 c. Scientist
18. Which subject interests you most?
    - 0 0 a. Practical arts
    - 0 0 b. Philosophy
    - 3 3 c. Human relations
19. To which group would you prefer to belong?
    - 0 0 a. Scientific society
    - 1 2 b. Outdoor group
    - 2 1 c. Social club
20. How do you like to work?
    - 2 1 a. In a group, discussion and recommending solutions
    - 1 2 b. Alone, using ideas and theories
    - 0 0 c. Alone, using tools and materials

Question	Things		People		Ideas	
1.	a.	1 0	b.	2 3	c.	0 0
2.	a.	0 0	b.	3 3	c.	0 0
3.	a.	1 3	b.	1 0	c.	1 0
4.	a.	1 1	b.	2 2	c.	0 0
5.	a.	3 3	b.	0 0	c.	0
6.	a.	1 0	b.	1 2	c.	1 1
7.	a.	0 0	b.	1 1	c.	2 2
8.	a.	0 2	b.	2 0	c.	1 1
9.	a.	1 2	b.	1 1	c.	1 0
10.	a.	2 0	b.	0 2	c.	1 1
11.	a.	1 0	b.	2 2	c.	0 1
12.	a.	1 2	b.	2 1	c.	0 0
13.	a.	2 1	b.	0 0	c.	1 2
14.	a.	0 0	b.	2 2	c.	1 1
15.	a.	1 1	b.	2 2	c.	0 0
16.	a.	0 0	b.	2 1	c.	1 2
17.	a.	0 3	b.	3 0	c.	0 0
18.	a.	0	b.	0	c.	3
19.	a.	0	b.	2	c.	1
20.	a.	1	b.	2	c.	0
		16		30		14
		TOTAL		TOTAL		TOTAL

Instructions: The Personal Interest Inventory should give you some insight into the strengths you would bring to a management position. Basically, if you enjoy an activity, it is likely to be something that you do well. The three areas shown in the Score Matrix—things, people, and ideas—correspond to the following skills, which managers must use in doing their job:

Things:	Technical skills
People:	Human skills
Ideas:	Conceptual skills

1. After scoring your inventory, break into groups of three to five and discuss your profiles. To what extent are they similar? Different? Are any of the areas dominant in the group? Underrepresented? Discuss.

2. Generalize about the kinds of supervisory jobs that might call for
   a. High technical skill
   b. High human skill
   c. High conceptual skill

3. Are your answers on this inventory consistent with the type of management job that you have in mind? If there are inconsistencies, what do they mean?

Source: Based on an exercise designed by Billie Stockton, Anita Bullock, and Anne Locke, Northern Kentucky University, 1981.

The Evolution *of* Management

LEARNING OBJECTIVES

After studying the material in this chapter, you should be able to:

- **Understand** that the development of management thought has been a slow, evolutionary process.

- **Describe** the early beginnings of management knowledge.

- **Explain** the basis and characteristics of the classical approaches, the reasons for using them, and the reasons for their decline in popularity.

- **Explain** the basis and characteristics of the behavioral approaches, the reasons for using them, and the reasons for their decline in popularity.

- **Discuss** the development and uses of the management science approach.

- **Discuss** the origin and applications of the systems approach.

- **Discuss** how Deming's emphasis on total quality management (TQM) has affected management thought.

- **Explain** why the contingency approach is useful to the study of management.

- **Describe** some of the changes occurring in the environment that affect management.

The Decline of the Roman Empire

Arnold Toynbee, the great British historian, believed that there are recognizable cycles in the rise and decline of human organizations. For example, during its ascendancy, the Roman Empire went through a period of expansion through arms, diplomacy, and building—especially of roads and aqueducts. The empire was successful for many years because of its intelligent rule of conquered peoples.

Most provincials found life improved under Roman rule. They were allowed to retain their language and were granted Roman citizenship. After a long period of growth characterized by innovation, development, and high energy, the empire began to stagnate and decline. As the wealthy elite moved into the so-called good life—without having to work hard for it—Roman citizens gained a reputation for hedonism, depravity, and corruption. Under the rule of the wealthy aristocracy, they became conservative and resisted change because they felt the old ways were best. Bribery of officials was rampant, and there was widespread scheming for power and control. Eventually, the rulers lost control and the decline accelerated.

Some experts see many parallels between the rise and fall of civilizations and the rise and fall of large bureaucratic organizations such as the former government of the USSR, Pan American airlines, and IBM. (See the case at end of this chapter for details of changes at IBM.) Certainly, many lessons can be learned from historical developments. In fact, some management experts, such as Lawrence Miller,

author of *American Spirit*, maintain that stagnancy and decline are not inevitable, and that organizations can go through processes of renewal and have the ability to offset stagnation and decline.[1]

To what extent do you think parallels exist between the growth, stability, and decline of the Roman Empire and those of organizations—including governments—today?

The temple at Leptis Magna was built during the period of expansion of the Roman Empire.

The opening case reinforces the conclusion of author and philosopher George Santayana: "Those who cannot remember the past are condemned to repeat it." Modern managers face many new, bewildering, and often contradictory ideas and situations. In order to handle them, managers need to understand not only *what* is happening around them but also *why* it is happening. And that *why* can best be understood when viewed from a historical perspective.

Therefore, reviewing the evolution of management from the earliest days to the present should help you understand what is happening in the managerial world you are about to enter. A study of the unfolding drama of managerial relationships of the past should contribute greatly to your understanding of how to practice the dynamic, evolving process called *management*.

The Evolution of Management Knowledge

People have always used management, management concepts, and management techniques, either consciously or unconsciously. For example, around 3800 B.C., people built the great pyramids of Egypt under a highly developed managerial and technological system that still awes us today.

Early Management Was Slow to Develop

Yet early management thought was slow to develop for several reasons. First, from the days of the Greek philosophers through the Middle Ages, and into the early modern period, business was not considered a respectable occupation. Second, early economists and political scientists did not concern themselves with managerial or entrepreneurial aspects of business. Third, businesspeople themselves did not aid the development of management, since they considered their profession an art rather than a science, explaining that principles cannot be applied to management as they can to sciences. Fourth, until the last third of the nineteenth century, businesses were operated principally on a small, personal basis, as sole proprietorships or partnerships. Thus, there was little real incentive to develop management theory into the dynamic field it is today.

Some Early Developments in Management Still in Use

Management has been around for a long time, and we can see its effects in a wide variety of ways. In fact, many of the early developments in the practice of management are still in use today. For this reason, it is important to understand why and how these early management principles evolved.

Early Civilizations The great civilizations, such as Babylon, Egypt, Assyria, and Persia, had expert managers. Their many achievements—the walled cities and canals of Sumer (whose builders relied on the use of merit wages); the hanging gardens, irrigation system, and astronomical and mathematical achievements of the Babylonians; the highway and library systems of Assyria; and the great cities and wealth of Persia—all required considerable organization and managerial genius.

The Code of Hammurabi included incentive and minimum wages as early as 1800 B.C. Moses used such management concepts as establishment of policies, division of labor, delegation of authority and placement of responsibility, organizational structuring, and the exception principle—whereby the leader lets subordinates handle routine activities while the leader handles only exceptional cases—during the exodus from Egypt around 1250 B.C.[2]

Citizens of ancient Greek cities worked under the piecework system on government contracts. Rome, which once controlled the known world from England to Asia, achieved its greatness by using a well-developed infrastructure of roads, records, and laws, and the application of highly developed and complex management knowledge.

China's Great Wall, massive armies, intercontinental road system, and silk trade required considerable management expertise, including utilizing the principles of specialization (division of labor) and the concept of labor turnover.

Machiavelli   Over 400 years ago, Niccolò Machiavelli, a diplomat and civil servant in the city-state of Florence, wrote *The Prince*, a book that focused on how to rule successfully. He stated that "whoever desires to found a state and give it laws, must start with the assumption that all men are bad and ever ready to display their vicious nature whenever they may find occasion for it."[3] Thus, according to Machiavelli, a leader is justified in using any leadership style or tactic to achieve the desired objective.

The Renaissance Period   Economic development and business activity almost disappeared during the *Middle Ages*, which began with the decline of the Roman Empire and lasted until the Renaissance. It was a period often referred to as the *Dark Ages* because of the lack of intellectualism, as well as extensive poverty and disease.[4]

The Great Wall of China required considerable management skills to build.

The Dark Ages were followed by the *Reformation*, which, in turn was followed by the *Renaissance* period. It was during the Renaissance that science, reason, exploration, and discovery were emphasized, and the systematic development of management theories, principles, and practices began to occur. By the late 1700s, these developments produced the many new ideas, practices, and inventions that resulted in what is known as the *Industrial Revolution*.

Forerunners of the Industrial Revolution

During the *Industrial Revolution*, machine and factory production replaced hand production. This revolution began in Europe shortly after 1700 and continued for over 150 years; however, its impetus was not felt in the United States until after 1865. The Industrial Revolution is considered one of the fastest and greatest periods of change and growth in world history.

Prior to the Industrial Revolution, the feudal system was primarily found in rural areas, while the guild system thrived in urban areas. These systems later merged into the cottage system of production, which in turn was supplanted by the factory system. At the heart of the Industrial Revolution was the factory system, which is still the most popular system of production today.

The Feudal System

The *feudal system* reached its peak of development in Europe during the Middle Ages. *Serfs*, the lowest order of workers, performed all the work on manors. They were neither slaves nor hired laborers. Economically, serfs were bound to the land and could not leave it, but they did have certain privileges that generally corresponded to their responsibilities. For example, they could not be sold, and they received part of their produce as compensation. The *lord* of the manor was responsible for protecting serfs from bandits, hostile lords, and other dangers. In doing this, the lord had to use such management duties as planning, organizing, and controlling.

The feudal system was best adapted to rural and agrarian production. Consequently, with the emergence of manufacturing and commercial industries as dominant economic forces, serfdom declined in importance and had largely disappeared from Europe before the end of the Middle Ages. It is interesting to note, however, that as late as 1861, there were still 20 million serfs in Russia.[5]

The Guild System

The development of manufacturing brought laborers to the cities and led to the use of the *guild system*. Within the guild itself were clear-cut differences among master craftsmen, journeymen, and apprentices. The *master craftsman* was typically the owner of the shop, who employed the traveling *journeyman* to work for him. The *apprentice* was a young learner who usually worked for his board, his lodging, and a small allowance. During the initial stages of the system, since all three levels worked closely together in the same industry, they were a tightly knit social group. The guild system involved selecting, training, and developing workers as well as wage and salary administration, and was the forerunner of modern human resource management. Vestiges of the guild system can be found in today's labor unions, especially construction trade unions.

The Cottage System

During the seventeenth century, the *cottage system* (also known as the *domestic system*, *home industry*, and *putting-out system*) was the most common form of production system. Work was performed in the homes of workers in rural or semirural areas. An independent merchant capitalist would pay the master craftsman for his products on a piecework basis, and he in turn would pay the workers who did the actual production in their simple thatched cottages. The merchant capitalist and the master craftsman had few management problems, since the place and conditions of work were not their concern. During Japan's rapid industrialization following World War II, the cottage system was widely used. And even after large factories were built, industry has continued to rely on thousands of suppliers that are really just expanded cottage industries.[6] With some modifications, this system is still used for producing handcrafted items like clothing and wooden products in places such as Hong Kong, Italy, and some parts of New England and Appalachia in the United States.

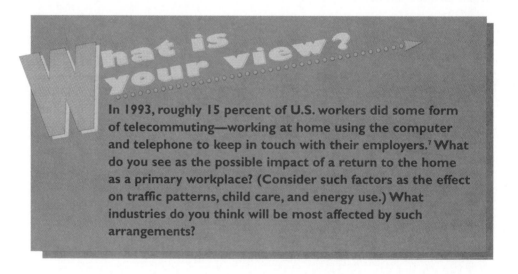

What is your view?

In 1993, roughly 15 percent of U.S. workers did some form of telecommuting—working at home using the computer and telephone to keep in touch with their employers.[7] What do you see as the possible impact of a return to the home as a primary workplace? (Consider such factors as the effect on traffic patterns, child care, and energy use.) What industries do you think will be most affected by such arrangements?

Industrial Revolution The period of change that began during the eighteenth century when machine and factory production replaced hand production.

How the Industrial Revolution Affected Management

The **Industrial Revolution** was a major impetus behind the evolution of management thought. During this period, emphasis was placed on quantity output, which resulted from a new production system, a new economic doctrine, and a new factory system.

A New Production System

The Industrial Revolution was precipitated by a new production system made possible by the invention and use of new tools, processes, and machines for manufacturing cotton and woolen products. A new energy source—the coal-driven steam engine— powered the machines. These developments resulted indirectly from the growth of knowledge during the period of vigorous intellectual activity following the Renaissance. Also, one of the first entrepreneurial efforts toward cleaning up the environment occurred when Robert Owen tried it at his mills in Scotland (see MAP 2.1).

A New Economic Doctrine

laissez-faire, laissez-passer Theory stating that if entrepreneurs were left alone to pursue their own self-interests, they would be guided by an "invisible hand" that would cause them to act in "the interest of the whole society."

The new production system was based on the French economic concept of **laissez-faire, laissez-passer,** that is, "Let manufacturers be free to make what they please, and let them be free to trade when they please." Adam Smith, a Scottish professor of moral philosophy—and the world's first economist—used the term in his book *The Wealth of Nations* to stress that the government should not interfere with economic affairs, either domestic or foreign. Smith felt that if entrepreneurs were left alone to pursue their own self-interests, they would be guided by an "invisible hand" that would cause them to act in "the interest of the whole society."[8] Natural laws, such as the law of supply and demand, would also regulate economic activities to the greater benefit of society. Finally, Smith believed that a mutual interest

The Eli Whitney gun factory used interchangeable parts to make muskets for the U.S. Army.

MANAGEMENT APPLICATION AND PRACTICE   2.1

Robert Owen: Father of Human Resource Management

One of the first practitioners of social responsibility in management was the successful industrial executive and management pioneer Robert Owen (1771–1858).

Reared in a poor family, Owen had little formal education but was an avid reader. He was an apprentice in the textile industry before the age of 10, and by age 23 had become a successful cotton manufacturer in Manchester, England. At 29, he moved to New Lanark, Scotland; bought the mills of David Dale; and married Dale's daughter.

On the basis of his reading, Owen believed that in order to improve the lot of his workers, it was necessary to eliminate the influences of a hostile environment. He felt that negative circumstances affected not only people's physical condition but also their mental and psychological development. This in turn determined their thoughts, emotions, and value systems. To improve the plight of workers—and thus achieve increased productivity—it was necessary to change their adverse physical, social, and economic environments by providing more satisfactory living and working conditions.

Owen implemented this philosophy by developing New Lanark into a model community. He provided good housing and sanitation and had employees plant trees, shrubs, and gardens around their homes. He improved working conditions in factories and installed such unheard of facilities as shower baths and toilets. Although real estate taxes at that time were based on the number of windows in a building, he put many windows in his factory to provide light and ventilation. This drastically increased his taxes and cost of production, but factory productivity and profits increased as well. Day schools were organized for employees' children, and night schools were provided for the workers themselves. The minimum working age for children was increased from 8 to 11 years, and their workday was shortened from 12 hours to 10; Owen later abolished child labor entirely.

Devoting himself to management as a profession, Owen tried to spread his ideas to all of Scotland and England by encouraging the cooperative and labor movements, unfortunately with little success. Yet his efforts have earned him recognition as the "father of human resource management."

Sources: Elbert Hubbard, *Little Journeys to the Homes of the Great*, anniversary ed. (New York: Wm. H. Wise, 1916), pp. 9–49; Lyndall Urwick, ed., *The Golden Book of Management* (London: Newman Neame, 1956), pp. 5–9; and Leon C. Megginson, Geralyn M. Franklin, and M. Jane Byrd, *Human Resource Management* (Houston, Tex.: Dame Publications, 1995), p. 33.

existed among workers, who worked harder for more money, and owners, who benefited from the profits derived from the increased production.

Smith's concepts became the central core of the American free enterprise economic system. They are also central to many modern management concepts, such as self-management work teams (see Chapter 14 for more details) and group decision-making techniques (see Chapter 6).

A New Factory System

factory system
Productive system based on the use of machines and equipment to achieve output.

The new economic doctrine and the invention of numerous machines that improved manufacturing led to the **factory system** of production and eventually resulted in mass production processes. For example, although Eli Whitney is best known for his cotton gin, his fortune resulted from selling muskets made with interchangeable parts to the U.S. Army. (See page 45.) His method of using interchangeable parts in production was a direct forerunner of the assembly line method of production.

While the factory system led to a higher standard of living, it also brought about extensive changes in management, shifting production from workers' homes to factories. Supporting the factories were new fuel- and water-powered machines that supplanted the effort and energy of human and animal power. Master craftsmen and merchants became employees of the emerging group of capitalists. Many of the jobs requiring human skills could now be performed by redesigned and newly invented tools and machines.

Along with the factory system, however, came many physiological and psychological problems, such as monotony, fatigue, noise, strain, and the ever present danger of accidents.

Development of Management in the United States

Within a short time, the new factory system made existing European production and distribution activities obsolete. Entrepreneurs and managers became aware of challenges they had not faced before, but they did not realize the relationship between the changing environments—such as truly international operations, mass production and distribution, trade unionism, and employee rights—and their managerial activities. Neither did these European managers understand the nature and results of the new challenges provided by the new environments.

Although the development of management in the United States has paralleled that in Europe, there are several differences. For example, as the supply of capable workers has been relatively scarce since colonial days—except for two or three periods—U.S. managers have had to be more adept at selecting, training, and motivating employees than their European counterparts. As a result, many innovative management practices have evolved since the late nineteenth century to cope with these shortages. Figure 2.1 shows some of the management approaches used by U.S. organizations of all types—public and private, profit and not-for-profit.

FIGURE 2.1
The development of management approaches.

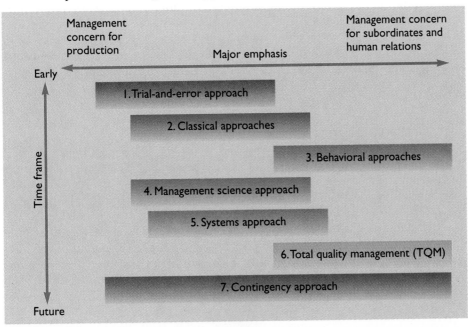

Early Management Practices

Because of the potato famine in Ireland and severe weather problems and political turmoil in Central and Western Europe, there was an influx of immigrants into the United States during the 1840s. This trend was followed by many Orientals arriving to work in the California goldfields. Then, a massive inflow from Southern Europe following the War Between the States (1861–65) led to an oversupply of workers relative to demand. This imbalance led to many labor problems for the emerging managerial class. Managers tended to exploit workers, assuming them to be a commodity that could be bought and sold. Consequently, workers were treated as simply another factor of production, and the gap between managers and workers widened as factories grew larger and more complex.

Performance of managerial activities was based on *trial and error*, whereby managers and workers kept trying different methods until they found one that worked. Unfortunately, successful methods were rarely communicated to other managers or workers. Managers, therefore, had to rely on their own judgment, intuition, and business records to remedy immediate and critical problems, and they had little or no idea how to plan for the long run. Under these conditions, management became increasingly ineffective and inefficient.

Later Management Practices

The failure of the trial-and-error approach led to two distinct schools of management thought. First, the *classical approaches* to management sought efficiency in organization and operations. They were followed by the *behavioral approaches*, which emphasized favorable treatment of employees rather than focusing solely on their performance or the organizational system.

The reaction to these two movements resulted in the development of several contemporary approaches, including the *management science (quantitative methods) approach*, the *systems approach, Deming's emphasis on total quality management (TQM)*, and the *contingency approach*. These were a rational synthesis of the two previous approaches, using the better elements of each. We believe that the approach most commonly used in the future will be a contingency approach, whereby management decisions and actions are determined by the prevailing situational elements.

The Classical Approaches

It was not difficult for early American entrepreneurs and managers to supervise small groups and obtain desired results under the trial-and-error management system. Each business could be directed personally, and what little planning and control was needed could be done by the individual worker or foreman. During the late 1800s, however, with the expansion of transportation (railroads) and communications (telegraph, telephone, and postal systems), the development of the western frontiers, and mechanized plants and factories in the East, organizations became larger and the need for more systematic management became evident. The people highlighted in Figure 2.2 were largely responsible for the development of

Frederick W. Taylor (1856–1915)	Henri Fayol (1841–1925)	Carl Barth (1860–1939)	Henry Gantt (1861–1919)
Motion and time studies Worker incentive programs Philosophy of gain sharing by increasing productivity	Developed universal functions of management Developed universal management principles	Developed slide rule	Developed production scheduling methods Used graphic methods and created the Gantt chart

Frank Gilbreth (1868–1924)	Lillian Gilbreth (1878–1972)	Henry Ford (1863–1947)	Max Weber (1864–1920)
Expanded principles of time and motion study	Pioneered in selection, placement, and training of personnel	Expanded mass production, assembly line	Emphasized role of bureaucracy

FIGURE 2.2
Contributors to the classical approaches.

the **classical approaches,** which sought efficient operations and regarded workers as just another factor of production, along with land and equipment.

A forerunner of the classical approach, Charles Babbage, a Cambridge professor and eminent mathematician, is credited with writing the first treatise on management in the industrial age. Entitled *On the Economy of Machinery and Manufacturers*, it was published in 1832.[9] One of his main contributions was the *principle of the transfer of skill*, which states that, to the extent that a machine becomes more automatic and is able to produce large quantities of goods accurately and more rapidly, the worker using it requires less skill and becomes a machine tender rather than a skilled craftsman. Babbage is also known for inventing the differential calculating machine, which foreshadowed the computer.

Frederick W. Taylor's Scientific Management

The concepts of the scientific approach to improving existing management methods were introduced into the United States by Frederick W. Taylor (1856–1915). Having joined the Midvale Steel Works in Philadelphia as a machine shop laborer in 1878, Taylor began to research ways to improve efficiency. Considered the father of efficiency engineering, Taylor developed what is known today as the **scientific management movement,** an approach that advocates increasing production while improving employees' working conditions and increasing earnings.[10] His main contribution was codifying certain principles previously developed and used in well-managed European factories and stating them coherently, thereby making them available to American factory managers.

The "Mental Revolution" of the New System The heart of Taylor's approach was to create a *"mental revolution,"* which assumed that managers would want to increase productivity and share those gains with the workers through easier work and

classical approaches Management approaches that sought efficient operations and regarded workers as just another factor of production, along with land and equipment.

Frederick Winslow Taylor (1856–1915).

scientific management movement Frederick W. Taylor's enlightened approach to management, which advocated increasing production while improving employees' working conditions and earnings.

improved material well-being. Unfortunately, some of the *systemizers*, or *efficiency experts*, during the early 1900s made use of the mechanics and techniques of scientific management without undergoing the mental revolution. Being concerned primarily with speeding up production and increasing output, they often neglected to pay proper attention to the human element involved. It was this type of thinking that led the labor movement and government officials to oppose Taylor's system.

What is your view?

Have you seen the classic silent movie *Modern Times*, starring Charlie Chaplin? The film is a satire on the scientific approach. In one scene, a manager has Chaplin, the worker, use his right hand to run a machine, then both hands, then both knees. Finally, the actor is using both hands, both knees, both elbows, and his head to run the machine. Do you think this is a valid use of the scientific approach? Explain.

Management Responsibilities Under the New System   On the basis of his philosophy and experiments with selected workers, Taylor developed the following duties of professional managers using his system. Each manager would do the following:

1. Develop a science for each element of a worker's job that would replace the old rule-of-thumb method
2. Select, train, teach, and develop workers scientifically (in the past, workers had chosen their own method of production and trained themselves as best they could)
3. Cooperate heartily with employees to ensure that all work was done in accordance with the best available methods of operation
4. Divide the work and responsibilities between management and workers
5. Use incentive wages to motivate workers to produce more

The following example illustrates how Taylor's methods were applied to improve the handling of pig iron:

Having determined the best way to do the work, Taylor sought "high-priced" workers to demonstrate the improvements. A man named Schmidt was selected and trained in the new method. He and others were told when—and how—to pick up a 60-pound slab of iron (called a pig), when and how to walk, and when and how to put it down, as well as when and how long to rest. The results were impressive. Schmidt increased his daily output from 12.5 tons to 47 tons, for which his daily pay increased from $1.15 to $1.85.[11]

Evaluation of Taylor's Contributions   Taylor designed better work methods to enable workers to produce more. His research, experiments, speeches, and writings were directed toward the lowest *operating level of the organization* rather than the *higher management levels*. The emphasis Taylor and his followers placed on small work groups at lower levels of the organization gave little attention to middle and top management and, therefore, resulted in little improvement in these management levels in U.S. organizations.

Taylor actually did much more than he is usually given credit for. He developed an entire production and management system that was far ahead of its time. In fact, Taylor's contributions were partially responsible for the great production systems during World Wars I and II.

Henri Fayol (1841–1925).

Henri Fayol's Administrative Management

While Taylor's scientific management movement was being studied, praised, criticized, and expanded in the United States, Henri Fayol (1841–1925) was revolutionizing management thinking in France through his management studies and writings, which developed principles that could be applied to all levels of management in all types of organizations.[12]

Administrative management, as developed by Fayol, is very close to our definition of management. It focuses on the process of management concerned with setting goals and planning, organizing, commanding, coordinating, and controlling activities in such a manner that organizational objectives are achieved.

Fayol is one of Europe's most distinguished contributors to the field of management theory and practice. Trained as a mining engineer, he worked his way up and eventually became the head of Comambault, a coal mining and iron foundry combine. He brought it from near bankruptcy to an extremely strong economic position. Whereas Taylor's focus was on activities at the bottom of the organization, Fayol zeroed in on management from the chief executive's point of view.

Fayol's Two Main Concepts Fayol's most important contribution to management involved two fundamental concepts. The first one concerned the *universality of basic management principles*, discussed in Chapter 1. These principles are applicable to all forms of organized human endeavor. His second major concept was that there is a body of knowledge related to the functions of management that can—and should—be taught. This concept led to the development of a management discipline that can validly be taught at the college level.

Basic Principles of Management. Fayol developed 14 general principles of management that applied to all types of organizations: (1) division of work, (2) authority and responsibility, (3) discipline, (4) unity of command, (5) unity of direction, (6) subordination of individual interest to general interest, (7) remuneration of employees, (8) centralization, (9) the scalar chain, (10) order, (11) equity, (12) stability of personnel, (13) initiative, and (14) esprit de corps. These principles were considered to be flexible and capable of meeting every managerial need if one had the intelligence, experience, decision-making ability, and sense of proportion to use them effectively. Many of these principles—including division of work, authority and responsibility, unity of command, and the scalar chain—have proved to be valid and, therefore, are discussed in more depth in later chapters.

administrative management The process of management concerned with setting goals and then planning, organizing, commanding, coordinating, and controlling activities to attain organizational objectives.

Basic Functions of Management. The functions or elements of management required to effectively apply Fayol's principles include planning, organizing, commanding and coordinating (now called leading), and controlling. Fayol explained each of these in detail, and although they were discussed briefly in Chapter 1, they will be developed more fully throughout the text.

Evaluation of Fayol's Contributions   Fayol's ideas and concepts continue to have great influence today. The concept of management as a process with universal functions that are carried out by managers in different environments is a central theme of many management texts and disciplines. The one area in which Fayol's contributions have been challenged is the rigid application of his principles without due consideration of the environment in which they are being applied. In some situations, his principles may not be applicable, but even then they can still be used as guidelines, for example, when using the contingency approach to management (which will be covered later in the chapter).

Other Contributors to the Classical Approaches

Several associates of Taylor also made contributions to the scientific approach in industry. Among these were Carl G. Barth, Henry L. Gantt, and Frank and Lillian Gilbreth. Henry Ford and Max Weber were also contemporaries who made significant contributions to management thought.

Carl Barth   Carl G. Barth (1860–1939), who worked closely with Taylor, had as much to do with developing, testing, and perfecting the mechanisms of scientific management as Taylor himself. Barth's greatest contribution was the development of the slide rule that bears his name. A predecessor of the computer, the slide rule was eventually replaced by hand-held calculators.

Henry Gantt   The greatest contribution of Henry L. Gantt (1861–1919) to the scientific approach was the Gantt chart, the extension of the use of graphic methods to record performance. (See Chapter 15 for further detail.) Gantt also began the production scheduling methods on which modern scheduling techniques are based.

Frank and Lillian Gilbreth   Taylor's ideas were expanded by the husband-and-wife team of Frank and Lillian Gilbreth. Frank B. Gilbreth (1868–1924) arrived at some of his management techniques independently of Taylor. Today he is considered a pioneer in the development of time and motion studies. He was interested in efficiency, especially in finding "the one best way to do the work." He was able to obtain—without undue fatigue—output that union bricklayers in England considered impossible nearly 50 years later.[13]

Lillian Gilbreth (1878–1972) was most interested in the human aspects of work, such as the selection, placement, and training of workers. She published the first book on management psychology.[14]

Henry Ford   No discussion of the evolution of management would be complete without mention of Henry Ford (1863–1947). In 1913 and 1914, he implemented modifications—based on Whitney's concept of interchangeable parts—to the

Lillian Gilbreth (1878–1972).

Frank Bunker Gilbreth (1868–1924).

assembly line method of production long used in the meatpacking industry. In addition to mass producing his Model T car (the "Tin Lizzie" or "flivver"), Ford introduced some of the most innovative personnel policies of the time. He increased the daily wage to $5.00 for an eight-hour day—almost double the previous rate for a nine-hour day. In addition, Ford gave attention to employee health and safety, employed the handicapped, and provided medical care.[15] However, he also removed all the stools out of the clerical spaces because clerks worked better/faster if they did not sit down on the job.

Max Weber Max Weber (1864–1920) developed the concept of **bureaucracy,** whereby an organization is characterized as having specialized jobs, rigorous rules of behavior, clear-cut authority and responsibility relationships, employment and promotions based upon merit and seniority, and lifelong employment.[16] We tend to criticize bureaucracies, especially governmental agencies and organizations that tend to become rigid, inflexible, and heavily reliant on official routines and procedures marked by excessive complexity. Yet some such organizations may be quite effective for they do provide order and guidance. Unfortunately, as otherwise prosperous organizations—such as IBM—become older and larger, they tend to become more bureaucratic.

bureaucracy An organization with strict rules and regulations, well-defined authority and responsibility, and lifelong employment based on merit and seniority.

The Classical Approaches in Perspective

Under the classical approaches, managers' main responsibilities were to plan, direct, and control the actions of their subordinates in order to obtain the highest output from them—on schedule. Subordinates were expected to carry out the plans, directions, and controls imposed on them without question; this type of supervision resulted from the accepted use of authority by the manager and obedience on the part of subordinates.

The classical approaches did have many benefits and may still apply to certain types of work. This type of approach can be useful (1) when time is a critical factor in accomplishing the task, (2) when the number of people involved is high relative to the space available to bring them together, and (3) under conditions of stress or when a question of survival is involved. For example, a classic study found that leaders who maintained an authoritative type of structure tended to be more effective under stress conditions than leaders who were more permissive.[17]

The approaches also had some limitations. A basic assumption underlying the approaches is that there is little need for social groupings, since it is desirable to prevent the interaction of subordinates from interfering with their work. The primary concern was to design the workplace to minimize worker effort and fatigue so that maximum output could be obtained. Rewards were based on the "*economic man*" *concept*, which assumed that motivation and rewards were achieved through providing employees with "a fair day's wage for a fair day's work."

In effect, what happened under these approaches to management was that managers told individuals what their needs were and also how they were to be satisfied. Consequently, the primary thing workers had to do was submit to management's dictates. In all deference to Taylor, Fayol, and their colleagues, although managers applying their principles often obtained increased production, they frequently failed to take sufficient account of the human factors present in the organization. The approaches worked well from their inception and through the Great Depression of the 1930s, a period of massive unemployment and poverty. However, they failed with the advent of World War II, which created an increase in the demand for workers but also caused the number of people in the workforce to decline.

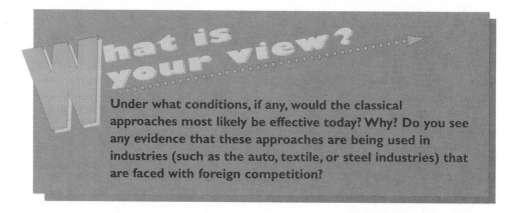

What is your view?

Under what conditions, if any, would the classical approaches most likely be effective today? Why? Do you see any evidence that these approaches are being used in industries (such as the auto, textile, or steel industries) that are faced with foreign competition?

The Behavioral Approaches

By the 1920s, the mechanization resulting from the Industrial Revolution, the assembly line technology introduced in the meatpacking and automobile industries, and the "mental revolution" of Taylor's scientific management combined to create what became known as a period of perpetual prosperity. Some of the leading entrepreneurs and managers had accepted the new classical approaches and were using them in their operations.

Criticisms, however, were already being directed toward the principles upon which the approaches were based, at least in the form in which they were being practiced. Many critics found contradictions among the various principles. Other thinkers felt that these principles were only a part of management thought, and some were already suspecting that many of the assumptions on which these principles were apparently based might not necessarily be true.

Forerunners of the Behavioral Approaches

The **behavioral approaches,** also called the *organic* or *humanistic* approaches, emphasized favorable treatment of employees instead of focusing solely on their output or performance. These approaches were foreshadowed by the work of three outstanding thinkers of the time.

Robert Owen, profiled earlier in the chapter, was not only the father of human resource management, but also a socialist, reformer, philanthropist, and early practitioner of the behavioral approach. Hugo Munsterberg (1853–1916), the father of industrial psychology, emphasized as early as 1913 the need for studying human behavior, in addition to scientific management.[18] Max Weber, also discussed earlier in the chapter, had theorized that bureaucracy was an ideal way to ease the transition from small-scale entrepreneurial management to professional management of large-scale enterprises.

Based on these beginnings, this group of pioneers, whose contributions are summarized in Figure 2.3, dramatically changed the direction of management theory and practice.

behavioral approaches Management approaches emphasizing favorable treatment of employees instead of focusing solely on their output or performance; also known as the *organic* or *humanistic* approaches.

Oliver Sheldon's Philosophy of Social Responsibility

In 1923, Oliver Sheldon (1894–1951) emphasized in his book *The Philosophy of Management* that a business has a "soul" and that management has social responsibilities "as a major partner in the community," alongside capital and labor.[19] Furthermore, he thought of management in a much broader sense than Taylor or

FIGURE 2.3
Contributors to the behavioral approaches.

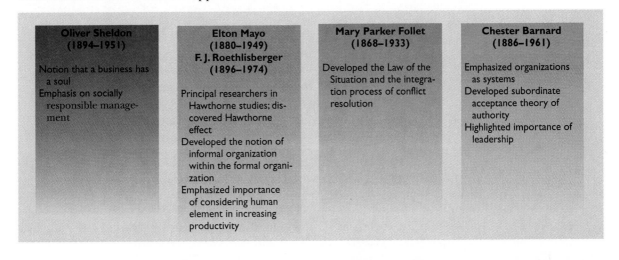

Oliver Sheldon (1894–1951)	Elton Mayo (1880–1949) F. J. Roethlisberger (1896–1974)	Mary Parker Follet (1868–1933)	Chester Barnard (1886–1961)
Notion that a business has a soul	Principal researchers in Hawthorne studies; discovered Hawthorne effect	Developed the Law of the Situation and the integration process of conflict resolution	Emphasized organizations as systems
Emphasis on socially responsible management	Developed the notion of informal organization within the formal organization		Developed subordinate acceptance theory of authority
	Emphasized importance of considering human element in increasing productivity		Highlighted importance of leadership

even Fayol did. Sheldon included the determination and execution of policy, the coordination of functions, and other organizational processes as valid and integral activities of management.

The Hawthorne Studies

Hawthorne effect The feeling of importance and value, which served as an incentive toward increased production, experienced by workers who were chosen as subjects for a scientific study.

The behavioral approach is generally considered to have started with a series of studies conducted at the Hawthorne plant of the Western Electric Company near Chicago from 1924 to 1932. The *Hawthorne studies,* as they are called, revealed that a powerful incentive toward increased production was due not solely to physical working conditions or financial rewards but also to the **Hawthorne effect,** whereby workers felt important and appreciated because they were chosen as subjects for a scientific study.

The Western Electric Company was a progressive organization that had applied many of the philosophies, theories, and principles of scientific management. Yet worker dissension and dissatisfaction were so prevalent at its Hawthorne plant that when unloading workers at the plant, the streetcar conductor would announce, "All out for the jail!" Researchers from the National Research Council of the National Academy of Sciences began a series of experiments at the Hawthorne plant in 1924 in an attempt to find a causal relationship between the physical environment and employee performance.

The original experiment focused on the relationship between lighting intensities and productivity. Two groups of workers were selected: one group on which experiments would be conducted and one to be used as a control group. Illumination was increased for the experimental group, and productivity increased. This was consistent with original expectations and hypotheses. What was not expected was the increase in productivity of the control group, whose lighting had not been changed! To test the findings further, the lighting of the test group was lowered, but to the amazement of the researchers, the productivity of the test group increased again. Completely baffled, the researchers withdrew from the experiments.

What is your view?

If the changed illumination level was not responsible for the increases in productivity in the experimental and control groups, what do you think was responsible?

In 1927, a group of industrial psychologists began another series of experiments at Hawthorne, led by George Elton Mayo (1880–1949), an associate professor at the Harvard School of Business. F. J. Roethlisberger (1898–1974), Harvard's on-site representative who wrote a definitive account of the activities, explained that

The six participants in the Relay Assembly Test Room experiment at Western Electric's Hawthorne plant in 1927. In the world-famous book about the Hawthorne studies, *Management and the Worker*, Theresa Layman Zajac, fourth from the left, was described as "Operator Number Three." She was 16 when the renowned Relay Assembly Test Room experiment began, and Theresa was still working at the time of the Fiftieth Anniversary Symposium of the studies, held at Oak Brook, Illinois, in November 1974.

the inquiry was concerned primarily with the relation between output and work conditions, such as shorter workdays and workweeks, rest periods, company-provided lunches, and varied starting and stopping times and the resulting fatigue and monotony.[20]

The experimental subjects, selected because they were experienced, willing, and cooperative, were six 15- and 16-year-old girls—five relay assemblers and one layout operator, who assigned work and obtained parts. The group, pictured in the photo above, worked in its own room, and each girl did the same job, one that could be completed in a short time. The group's performance was observed, measured, and recorded. Members' output, attendance, and morale increased steadily over a period of two and a half years.

Other experiments were performed with the relay-assembly group, a mica-splitting group, and a bank-wiring group. Both supervisors and subordinates were interviewed using listening techniques and general, nondirective questions designed not to influence the subjects' responses. As a result of the magnitude of the studies, the inquiry stretched on until 1932, when the experiment was suspended for external reasons—including the Great Depression.

The findings of these studies, which contradicted some of the traditional principles of industrial efficiency, became the basis for the **human relations movement**—the process of motivating individuals in a given situation to achieve a

human relations movement
Management approach emphasizing motivation of employees to achieve a balance of objectives that yield greater human satisfaction and attain organizational goals.

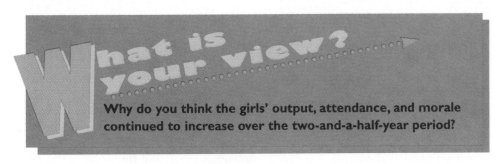

What is your view?

Why do you think the girls' output, attendance, and morale continued to increase over the two-and-a-half-year period?

social ethic A concept that has as its foundation the corporate well-being of society and the value of harmony in interpersonal and intergroup relationships.

balance of objectives that would yield greater human satisfaction and achieve organizational goals. Another result was a shift away from the individualistic ethic toward the **social ethic** and the value of harmony in interpersonal and intergroup relationships.

Mary Parker Follett's Integration Process

integration or **collaboration** A method of constructive conflict resolution whereby the people involved look for ways to resolve their differences so that everyone gets what he or she wants.

While Mary Parker Follett (1868–1933) served as a link between the scientific and humanistic periods, she leaned toward the latter. One of her contributions was her analysis of how to deal with conflict. She believed that any conflict could be resolved by (1) voluntary submission of one side, (2) struggle and victory of one side over the other, (3) compromise, or (4) integration—known today as *joint problem solving*. Her preferred solution was **integration** or **collaboration,** whereby everyone wins, as opposed to a win-lose situation, or a watered-down compromise by which neither side gets all it wants.[21]

Follett also believed that the essence of good human relations was creating the feeling of working with someone rather than over or under someone—the notion of *power with* rather than *power over*. For example, if an accounting manager discovered that a person working in the office was making a mistake, instead of giving a reprimand and specific instructions on how to correct it, he or she might say, "We seem to be short $5,000. Let's look at the statement and see what needs to be done to correct it." Thus, instead of giving a direct order, the manager works *with* the other person, and the order (correction) is derived from the situation.

Mary Parker Follett (1868–1933).

Chester Barnard's Acceptance Theory of Authority

Chester Barnard (1886–1961), president of the New Jersey Bell Telephone Company, wrote widely on a variety of management subjects, but his most influential book was *The Functions of the Executive,* published in 1938.[22] He saw organizations as systems of goal-directed activities. Management's primary functions, in Barnard's view, are formulating objectives and acquiring the resources required to meet the objectives.

acceptance theory of authority The theory that subordinates will accept orders only if they understand them and are willing and able to comply with them.

Barnard emphasized communication as an important means of achieving group goals. He also introduced a new **acceptance theory of authority.** According to his theory, subordinates will accept orders only if they understand them and are able and willing to comply with them. Barnard was a pioneer in advocating the *systems approach* to managing.

The Behavioral Approach in Perspective

Like the scientific management movement, the behavioral approaches were not immediately recognized and accepted for what they were—namely another revolution in management philosophy, theory, and practice. The environment of the early 1930s was characterized by a deepening worldwide depression, massive unemployment, new political experiments, an expanding labor movement, and an economy based on restricting output, increasing demand, and sharing the work. It did not encourage acceptance of the behavioral approach. As a result, the general implementation of the behavioral approach came during the period from World War II to the late 1950s. Although it is still quite prevalent and will continue to be for some time, the behavioral approach is gradually being augmented by new approaches discussed in the next section.

Basic Model Under the behavioral approach, managers tend to be more concerned with building morale and maintaining social interactions than with improving performance. The model for this approach was as follows:

high morale → job satisfaction → increased performance

Yet there are at least three possible relationships between satisfaction and performance, not just one:

1. Satisfaction can contribute to, or influence, performance: satisfaction → performance.
2. There may be an uncertain relationship between satisfaction and performance, whereby it could go in either direction: satisfaction ↔ performance.
3. Performance itself may contribute to satisfaction: performance → satisfaction.

The behavioral approach assumes that two insights are needed. First, managers must regard the organization as an operating system designed to produce and distribute a good or service efficiently and effectively. And second, the organization is to be viewed as a social system through which individuals try to find expression for their hopes and aspirations as well as satisfy their economic needs.

Some of the early practitioners of the behavioral approach, however, either were ignorant of or tended to ignore this dual relationship. Consequently, in many organizations, strong interpersonal and intergroup relationships were seen as more important than efficient production and other organizational objectives.

Limitations of the Behavioral Approach The behavioral approach has had its share of critics. Malcolm McNair, a vocal critic, and many others have frequently attacked human relations as representing "sloppy sentimentalism," "warm-feeling management," and even worse.[23] As with the classical approaches, however, most of the attacks seem to have come as a result of overzealous advocates using the form and techniques of the school of thought but disregarding its underlying philosophy. Regardless of the justice of criticism of the general theory, the fact remains that the humanistic approach has served to broaden the concepts of management theory and practice.

Contemporary Approaches

Several contemporary approaches have evolved since World War II from a blending or meshing of the classical and behavioral approaches. The starting point for the contemporary approaches was dissatisfaction with the principles proclaimed by the earlier writers. Today's scholars believe that neither of these early movements was sufficiently rigorous in its methods to provide valid principles and theories.

The theorists of these approaches were predominantly engineers, sociologists, or psychologists. The classical theorists studied the work areas for more efficient production; the behavioralists studied job satisfaction, morale, productivity, and conflict resolution.

Contemporary researchers come from varied disciplines—behavioral sciences (psychology and sociology), systems theory, operations research (quantitative experts), decision theory, statistics, computer science, and other areas of research methodology. With the strengthening of the basic disciplines underlying earlier approaches, and an increased understanding of the use and application of behavioral, statistical, and mathematical techniques, more valid theories have resulted from rigorous testing of propositions and more reliable knowledge of management processes and techniques.

The most popular contemporary approaches are as follows:

1. The management science (quantitative methods) approach
2. The systems approach
3. Total quality management (TQM)
4. The contingency approach

Management writer Peter Drucker has contributed to the development of these approaches through his insightful studies, writings, and consulting. Drucker's influence runs through all contemporary approaches, as you'll see in MAP 2.2.

The Management Science Approach

management science approach Management approach that uses decision-making techniques involving mathematical models and computer technology; also known as the *quantitative methods approach.*

Recall that Taylor's scientific management approach was a systematic way of making management decisions instead of using a "seat of the pants" approach. Scientific management was primarily applied to production and operations problems but was limited in its use of mathematics and statistics. On the other hand, the **management science approach** refers to decision-making techniques developed over the past 45 years that involve mathematical models and usually require the use of a computer. These techniques can be used to help solve problems in a broad range of situations, including decision making and operations management.

operations research (OR) Method of pooling the knowledge of research specialists to develop quantitative models that behave similarly to the real-world situations confronting decision makers.

Management science approaches originated during World War II in the form of **operations research (OR).** Basically, OR involved pulling together teams of scientists—such as mathematicians, physicists, and statisticians—rather than military experts to help the Allied forces make strategic operating decisions. OR was highly successful and was credited with many Allied successes. OR specialists successfully resolved problems such as the following:

1. What distribution of ground antiaircraft batteries and what firing patterns would maximize protection against enemy air raids?
2. What cluster of bombing patterns would inflict maximum damage on enemy targets?
3. What deployment of depth charges would result in the greatest number of enemy submarine "kills"?

After the war, many operations research specialists returned to their positions in U.S. universities, businesses, and government organizations and applied some of the OR techniques to a wide variety of business problems.

In management science and operations research, specialists pool their knowledge to develop mathematical models, which represent the behavior of the variables in each situation. Once the models are designed, they can be manipulated to reflect changes in the variables and to select solutions for optimum results.

MANAGEMENT APPLICATION AND PRACTICE 2.2

Peter F. Drucker: Management Popularizer

Peter F. Drucker can be called the father of modern management for his pioneering work in the 1940s and 1950s. Born in Vienna in 1909 and educated in Austria and England, Drucker came to the United States in 1937. After working as an economist for a group of British banks and insurance companies, he became a consultant for some of the largest U.S. companies. His lengthy study of General Motors in 1943 was the first detailed study of the inner workings of a major U.S. corporation. From this and later studies by Drucker, there emerged the concept that management is a job separate and distinct from other activities in an organization.

Drucker's greatest contribution to the evolution of management has been to codify and popularize some of today's basic management concepts and practices. For example, in the 1950s he formulated the concept of *management by objectives (MBO)*, a method of redesigning an organization to allow managers and subordinates to set their own goals. He also applied the military concept of strategy to organizations. And his idea that innovation can be fostered by management within an organization is a cornerstone of today's concept of *intrapreneurship*.

How does Drucker manage to have companies lining up to pay him two or three times as much as

other consultants charge? Why are people clamoring to get into his courses and management seminars at Claremont Graduate School? His success is based partly on his ability to see the world differently from the way others see it and to arrive at practical solutions to difficult problems.

But his scholarly and free-wheeling approach to problems is not without its critics. For example, some academicians find his analysis insufficiently rigorous, and some consultants find it impractical. Despite what admirers and critics say about him, however, he has greatly influenced the evolution of management thought. In fact, his latest publications, *Managing for the Future: The 1990s and Beyond* and *Post Capitalist Society*, have led Walter F. Wriston, former chairman of Citicorp, to say, "Peter Drucker's perceptions on the trends and forces at work shaping today and tomorrow not only fascinate but may be ignored at our peril."

Sources: Peter F. Drucker, *The Practice of Management* (New York: Harper & Row, 1954); Amanda Bennett, "Management Guru: Peter Drucker Wins Devotion of Top Firms with Eclectic Counsel," *Wall Street Journal*, July 28, 1987, pp. 1, 12; Kathy Rebello, "Peter Drucker: His 'Management by Objectives' Is a Commandment for Execs," *USA Today*, October 26, 1987, p. 4B; Peter F. Drucker, "A Turnaround Primer," *Wall Street Journal*, February 2, 1993, p. 15A; Peter F. Drucker, *Managing for the Future: The 1990s and Beyond* (New York: Dutton, 1992): and Peter F. Drucker, *Post Capitalist Society* (New York: HarperBusiness, 1993).

This approach is used in most high-tech, transportation, automobile manufacturing, and aerospace industries today. It is used for activities such as finding the optimum location and layout of facilities, improving sequencing of operations, and designing products.

The Systems Approach

Change is probably the most critical factor affecting the lives of individuals as well as the operations of organizations. Those who can adapt to it survive; those who cannot stagnate and may even die. The relative stability of the 1950s was shattered

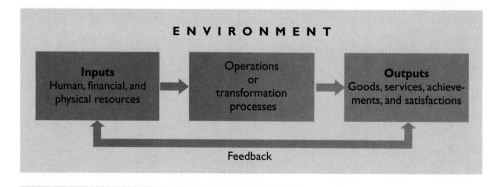

FIGURE 2.4
The systems approach involves processing inputs into outputs.

systems approach
Management approach that integrates universal management functions and strategic planning with the consideration of external factors.

system An assemblage or combination of things or parts forming a complex or unitary whole, made up of inputs, operations, and outputs.

closed system System that tends to move toward a static equilibrium.

open system System that tends to be in a dynamic relationship with its environment, receiving various inputs, transforming them in some way, and producing outputs.

by the political activism of the 1960s. Managers of organizations found the external social, political, and legal environments influencing almost every decision. As previous approaches to managing no longer worked, a new approach—the **systems approach**—was needed. It integrated universal management functions and strategic planning with consideration of external factors.

The leading pioneers in the development of the systems approach were Richard Johnson, Fremont Kast, and James Rosenzweig, who defined a **system** as "an organized or complex whole; an assemblage or combination of things; or parts forming a complex or unitary whole."[24] A system is composed of *inputs, operations* (or transformation processes), and *outputs*, as shown in Figure 2.4. A management system can be compared to the human body, in which each organ is related to, interacts with, and is dependent on the proper functioning of the other organs. If something happens to one part of the body, the other parts are affected.

Types of Systems   Systems can be either closed or open. A **closed system** is not interactive with the outside environment and thus is not influenced by what is happening there.

On the other hand, an **open system,** such as an organization, tends to be in a dynamic relationship with its environment, receiving inputs from both internal and external sources, transforming them in some way, and producing outputs for the internal and external environments. Receiving inputs in the form of material, energy, and information, along with feedback regarding outputs, allows the open system to offset the process of decline. Moreover, the open system adapts to its environment by changing the process of its internal components or structure as the need arises.

All of us are familiar with individuals who deserve the label "closed-minded." Closed-minded people have difficulty coping with the changes that occur in their environment. For example, during the 1970s, Japanese car companies were more open to their environments, from a systems standpoint, than their American competitors. Consequently, while American companies continued to produce the large gas-guzzlers that had been so popular during the 1950s and 1960s, Japanese firms were producing smaller cars with high gas mileage in response to what was happening in the environment: changing consumer needs and higher gasoline prices. Many management experts recognize that the exceptional leadership and salesmanship of Lee Iacocca, which resulted in a more open system at Chrysler, prevented the company from going bankrupt during the late 1970s.

An Organization as a System   The systems approach is essentially a way of thinking about the organization—its goals, objectives, and purposes—and the relationships among its parts. The systems approach to management has three goals:

1. To define relationships both internal and external to the organization
2. To see and understand the pattern of these relationships
3. To see the overall purpose of the relationships

The concept of the organization as a system is not new, since many successful businesspeople have used the approach, now called the *systems concept.* For example, many of the builders of great corporations, such as Theodore Vail of AT&T and Alfred Sloan of General Motors, had the ability to view the business as an integrated whole or system. They were able to identify strengths and weaknesses and to see how they were critical to success.

On the other hand, many of the 100 largest U.S. corporations in 1900 are not around today because their top managers ignored systems concepts. One such failure involved a manufacturing company that moved south to avoid labor unions. It was a family-owned concern that had been producing quality goods for several generations. Yet within two decades of moving, it was nearly bankrupt and was forced to sell out to a larger corporation. The company's decline was not caused by declines in product quality; rather, the decline resulted from an obsolete and inefficient marketing system and closed-minded top managers who would not accept suggestions for improvement from lower-level managers and professionals.

As we discussed in Chapter 1, conceptual skills—the ability to see the big picture and take a systems approach—are very important for top management. Today, more than ever before, systems thinking on the part of top management can protect a company from the same circumstances that caused buggy manufacturers to go bankrupt. A systems type of analysis can also help explain recent developments in Eastern Europe, especially in the newly formed Russian republics.

Total Quality Management (TQM)

From the mid-1940s to the mid-1970s, the United States led the world in developing, producing, and selling a broad range of quality products at home and abroad. Its inventiveness, willingness to improve and invest in new processes, emphasis upon high quality and productivity, and effective marketing created a worldwide business environment that caused us to be a world leader.

However, as will be shown in Chapter 5, during the last two decades the "Made in America" label has been disappearing as foreign producers have replaced us in industries such as computers, machine tools, and semiconductors.[25] Many factors have led to this decline. Adverse U.S. tax and fiscal policies, increased product liability and other litigation costs, increasing building costs, inefficient labor, and ineffective management have led to a decline in investment in plant and equipment. Private and public research and development expenditures have declined or increased slowly. Labor costs, made up of wages and employee benefits, have risen relative to those in other countries. As a result of these and other factors, our **productivity**—the amount of goods or services produced by a worker in a given period of time—has lagged behind that in many other countries.

One of the primary problems in the United States in recent years has been competition from Japanese producers. In the past, products made in Japan were considered to be of poor quality. Even during the post–World War II reconstruction

productivity The amount of goods or services produced by a worker in a given period of time.

W. Edwards Deming
(1900–1993).

statistical quality control (SQC)
Control of quality output by using statistical methods so that variations from the desired quality can be attributed to chance or random causes.

total quality management (TQM)
Approaching quality improvement from a total corporate, process-oriented, and customer-driven concept.

period, the Japanese were embarrassed by the shoddiness of their goods.[26] Having recognized the superior quality of American-made products, they bought them, disassembled them for study, improved them, and then produced and sold them at cheaper prices.

In an effort to change their position as well as their image, Japanese businesses turned to an American quality expert, W. Edwards Deming (1900–93). Deming was educated and trained in the value of quality, especially **statistical quality control (SQC),** whereby variations in the desired quality can be measured by using statistics. It was Deming's philosophy and approach to quality developed during the 1930s and 1940s that form the basis of the **total quality management (TQM)** approach.[27] TQM approaches quality improvement from a total corporate, process-oriented, and customer-driven concept.

Deming found an audience of top management in Japan and taught them how quality demanded a total commitment to it, starting at the top of the organization and proceeding down through the middle and lower levels. Deming explained that executive promotions and salary increases had to be directly tied to quality in order for the commitment to be a concern of everyone in the organization. Above all, quality had to be central to a company's purpose. According to Deming, when quality improves, costs decrease, productivity increases, more quality products are sold, and, as a consequence, more people are employed. When Deming's ideas were applied by Japanese firms, they found that improvements in quality transformed wasted employee hours and machine time into more and better products. Deming showed the Japanese that improved quality naturally and inevitably begets improved productivity. Once management adopted the concept, quality became everyone's aim.[28]

Japan's most prestigious award for quality, the *Deming Award*, is so named in recognition and appreciation of Deming's contributions to improved quality and productivity. During the 1980s, Deming became recognized and honored as an advocate of quality in his own country as well. Until his death in 1993, Deming remained a proponent of the inevitable need for continuous quality improvement in the world today.

The rediscovery of Deming's work in the United States, the success of Japan's industrial complex in the 1980s, and the emphasis upon employee empowerment and teamwork have combined to make TQM a major theme in many U.S. organizations. (See Chapter 14 for more details.)

The Contingency Approach

While all these approaches have some validity, they also have weaknesses and limitations. Experts agree that there is no one best method of management. Instead, managers of today and the future will use the **contingency approach,** the assumption that different conditions and situations require the application of different management techniques. The contingency approach, shown in Figure 2.5, combines the best aspects of the other approaches, customizing management methods to different circumstances at any given time.

Advocates of the contingency approach say there are few if any universal truths, concepts, or principles that can be applied under all conditions. Instead, every management situation must be approached with an "it all depends" attitude. Contingency theorists attempt to explain what styles or approaches would best apply under different circumstances.

Contingency theories have been developed in such areas as organization design, leadership, motivation, strategic planning, and group dynamics, all of which are discussed in this text. One such contingency theory is the **eclectic approach,** which draws on the best available information from all approaches and disciplines, including sociology, psychology, cultural anthropology, and industrial engineering. It is the eclectic approach that the authors have chosen in writing this text.

contingency approach Management approach advocating the combined use of various other approaches, based on the assumption that different conditions and situations require the application of different management techniques.

eclectic approach Management approach that draws on the best available information from all approaches and disciplines.

FIGURE 2.5
The contingency approach combines aspects of the other approaches.

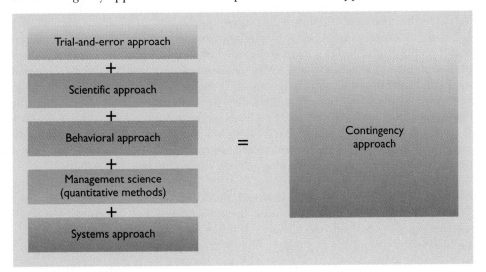

Some Contributions of Contemporary Approaches

Contemporary researchers and writers have contributed important insights into the practice of management, and the ideas of these professionals are followed closely throughout this book. The contemporary theorists use the most recent advances in research methods, mathematics, and computer technology for making many types of decisions. The mark of the new approach is its emphasis on sophisticated research methods, empirical investigation (based on observation and experience), and rigorous testing of hypotheses.

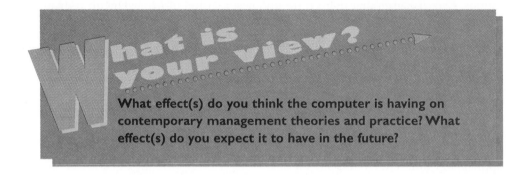

What is your view?

What effect(s) do you think the computer is having on contemporary management theories and practice? What effect(s) do you expect it to have in the future?

The Rapidly Changing Environment of Management

Although management philosophies, and the resulting improved practices, have been developing for centuries, the pace has quickened during the last few decades. During those decades, many major progressive organizations have tried to apply some of the newer management concepts to improve performance. There are, however, many differences, variations, and inconsistencies in the theories, concepts, and programs that organizations are presenting to their employees—as well as in the reactions of employees to these new ideas.

Since nearly all human behavior can be explained by the history of institutions and organizations, today's managers need to understand how management philosophies and practices have evolved. Knowing and understanding what has happened in the past should help one to recognize evolving patterns of human behavior. Recognizing these patterns can help managers avoid repeating the mistakes of the past.

A most interesting development is the movement away from communism toward socialism and the free enterprise system in Eastern Europe. There will be much need for management training and development to encourage this movement.

Finally, as this chapter has pointed out, if we are to learn our lessons well, we must understand not only what changes have occurred but why *they have occurred*. This will be done throughout the book, but especially in the next three chapters.

S U M M A R Y

The development of management has been a long and complicated evolutionary process, one that is still evolving and is revolutionizing management theory and practice throughout the world.

People have applied management techniques to achieve objectives since ancient times. But modern management did not begin until the late 1800s and early 1900s, with Taylor's *scientific management movement* in the United States and Fayol's *administrative management* concepts and practices in Europe.

Under these classical management approaches, managers' main responsibilities were to supervise subordinates' actions in order to obtain the most efficient output from them. The principal goal was to achieve maximum production in the shortest period of time and at the lowest cost. The system did produce a large volume of products—cheaply—but it did little to enhance the dignity and worth of employees.

The behavioral approaches that developed from the Hawthorne studies attempted to fill the gaps in the classical approaches fostered by the practitioners of scientific management. The discovery of new factors affecting employee productivity and morale opened up broad new fields to research and experimentation.

The main contributions of the behavioral scientists were the identification, isolation, and revelation of the importance of human and social factors in organizational relationships. It was also learned that managers, instead of dealing with discrete individuals, had to operate within cultural and social systems and subsystems.

With the increasingly professional role of management since the 1930s, a most significant development has been the tendency of professional managers to be concerned with human and social relations as well as with maximizing profits. Therefore, today's managers must be ready to face new problems and make quick decisions involving more systematic and longer-range planning and development.

Contemporary approaches to management have created a rational synthesis of the classical and behavioral approaches to be applied to varied and changing situations. We can view these situations in the light of a scientific and a systems approach that considers the effects of the environment on management decisions and uses quantitative techniques to study behavior.

Yet none of the classical approaches is completely acceptable in today's rapidly changing, and often hostile, environment. None of them fits all situations, so future managers must use a *contingency approach*; that is, every management situation must be approached with an "it all depends" attitude.

One definite factor that must be considered is the emphasis on quality and the ways to achieve it throughout the organization. The total quality management (TQM) movement is in the forefront of management advances, as are employee empowerment, partnering, and reengineering. These concepts are the next generation in the evolution of management, one that will be interrelated with the social, economic, political, and technological environments in organizations throughout the world.

Industrial Revolution, 44
laissez-faire, laissez-passer, 45
factory system, 46
classical approaches, 49
scientific management movement, 49
administrative management, 51
bureaucracy, 53
behavioral approaches, 55
Hawthorne effect, 56
human relations movement, 57
social ethic, 58
integration or collaboration, 58

acceptance theory of authority, 58
management science approach, 60
operations research (OR), 60
systems approach, 62
system, 62
closed system, 62
open system, 62
productivity, 63
statistical quality control (SQC), 64
total quality management (TQM), 64
contingency approach, 65
eclectic approach, 65

1. Management knowledge evolved slowly over centuries, but more recently has experienced rapid change. How do you explain this change?

2. How did the Industrial Revolution affect the long-term development of management?

3. In what ways was the scientific management approach successful? What were its limitations?

4. What were the responsibilities of management under Taylor's scientific management system?

5. What were Fayol's two primary contributions to the development of management?

6. How would you compare the contributions of Taylor and Fayol?

7. What did the behavioral approaches accomplish? What were the disadvantages in using these approaches?

8. How would you describe the current trends in Eastern Europe?

9. To what extent do you think Deming's TQM will affect management thinking in the future?

10. Do you think the contingency approach will be effective in the rapidly changing environment of management today? How will it differ from the eclectic approach? Explain.

11. Which of the three possible relationships between job satisfaction and performance do you think best explains what happens in actual work situations? Explain.

PRACTICING MANAGEMENT

2.1

case

IBM—A Changing Organization

When you think of IBM, you think of computers, right? Well, yes and no. Although computers are now IBM's most visible product, this was not always the case. Few people realize that for several years after the computer's introduction in the late 1940s, IBM resisted developing computers of its own, since it controlled 97 percent of the tabulating equipment then in common use, including the cards it used.

IBM actually began in 1884 when Herman Hollerith patented an automatic punch-card tabulating machine and won a contract to process the U.S. census in 1890 and again in 1900. Losing the 1910 census contract, he sold the company to Computer-Tabulating-Recording Company (CTR), a maker of time clocks, butcher scales, and tabulators.

Thomas J. Watson was hired to run CTR in 1914. He revitalized the company by transforming its sales force into dedicated supersalesmen wearing dark suits, white starched shirts, and conservative striped ties. Each day began with a pep rally at which Watson gave a motivational speech to the salesmen and led them in singing from the company's songbook, *Ever Onward*. After 1920, CTR concentrated on tabulators, and, having changed its name to International Business Machines Corporation in 1924, the firm totally dominated its field until the early 1950s. Then came the computer, and Watson was not interested in the newfangled "electrical brains," as he believed that businesses would not buy over "5 to 10" of them.

After Remington Rand had placed the first giant computer (the Univac) at the U.S. Census Bureau in 1951 and another at General Electric in January 1954, IBM changed its mission and sold its first commercial computer to Monsanto in 1955. Though a late starter, IBM soon took the lead in the computer field because of its marketing expertise, and, thanks to its organization principles, managed to hold that lead until 1977. Then, smaller, more dynamic and innovative firms such as Apple, Commodore (Pet), and Tandy (Radio Shack) began selling desktop computers. As in the 1950s, IBM had to change its mission and organizational principles in order to survive.

Thomas Watson, Jr., had become CEO in 1956 when IBM had developed into the world's largest and most respected computer maker. Its name was synonymous with excellence and American ingenuity. After Watson retired in 1974, IBM began to stagnate, with one notable exception.

In 1980, William C. Lowe, a typical IBM executive but also a risk-taking entrepreneur, led an independent, 12-person team to develop the IBM-PC in an obscure laboratory in Boca Raton, Florida—far away from IBM's other operations. An autonomous division—Entry Systems Division (ESD)—was set up to design, develop, manufacture, and sell the new device, which IBM hoped would become a centerpiece of its office automation system.

An IBM computer in a Japanese warehouse.

This switch in mission and strategy led to many fundamental changes. As an independent unit, ESD was spared many of the controls and formal reporting structures of other divisions. Thus, the original PC took only 13 months from preliminary planning to introduction in 1981, whereas most other IBM products took years to develop. The PC was built from off-the-shelf parts instead of parts designed and produced by IBM. ESD used software from an outsider, Microsoft, rather than developing its own. Instead of having only highly trained salespeople and commercial users, ESD sold computers to millions of customers through its own retail stores and other dealers, such as Computerland outlets and Sears, Roebuck's new nationwide chain of business machine stores. IBM also used massive advertising blitzes with a Charlie Chaplinesque character in order to sell its product to the public. But in the spring of 1985, IBM curbed ESD's autonomy by moving it from Florida to New Jersey and making it part of the IBM monolith.

Like all large organizations, IBM became bureaucratic over the years, even before Tom Watson, Jr., retired. For example, although IBM was "America's most admired" corporation for several years, by 1987, it had fallen to fourth (out of ten) in its industry in "innovativeness."

The company's biggest problem was its blind reliance on the product that made it so profitable, the giant mainframe computer. In 1992, these computers contributed 50 percent of IBM's revenues and perhaps 60 percent of its profit. Yet the end of the mainframe era was in sight by the mid-1980s, long after workstation and personal computers were coming into prominence.

IBM's entrenched management structure dominated a highly centralized organization with virtually no delegation of authority. For example, while PC marketers could get new models in six months, they were fettered by layers of bureaucracy spiraling out from company headquarters in New York. It often took from 60 to 90 days to get a price change OK'd, as each layer of management had to concur.

The company's inbred corporate culture also had a devastating effect on manufacturing operations. Until recently, it used the same approach to make PCs that it had long used to make mainframes. Yet producing a mainframe is like making a giant airplane, while producing a PC is like making a TV set.

In summary, IBM was losing out because its bureaucratic, centralized organization had been unable to compete with fast-moving competitors like Apple, Compaq, and Dell. In fact, the hallmark of IBM—customer service—had become an oxymoron in many quarters of the company.

In 1993, a new CEO, Louis Gerstner, was brought in to transform IBM—which had lost $5 million in 1992—into a new company. Gerstner, who had no computer experience, cannot effect the transformation by slashing staff and cutting costs; he must do it by changing the basic nature of the company.

Sources: Patricia Lamiell, "AT&T Turnaround a Lesson for IBM," *Mobile* (Alabama) *Register*, January 29, 1993, p. 8B; Kevin Maney, "A Great Leap for IBM," *USA Today*, March 29, 1993, pp. 1B–2B; Leslie Cauley and John Schneidawind, "Gerstner Expected to Get IBM Post Today," *USA Today*, March 26, 1993, pp. 1B–2B; James Cox and Bill Montague, "Inside IBM Search: Lots of Games," *USA Today*, March 29, 1993, pp. 1B, 4B; and Bill Laberis, "By the Numbers," *Computer World*, January 17, 1994, p. 34.

Questions

1. How do you explain the stagnation that occurred at IBM?

2. Do you think IBM will make a successful turnaround? Explain.

3. What suggestions would you make to Gerstner for improving IBM?

2.1 Studying an Organization's History

learning exercise

In 1989, Vartan Gregorian assumed the presidency of Brown University. One of the first things he did was to study the university's history in depth because, he explains, "How many corporate leaders have read the histories of their own firms? How many read the biographies of their founding fathers? I know what my constituents want, and I also know that today's problems are not new problems."

Gregorian goes on to say, "Each institution has its own customs and traditions, and you cannot presuppose outside formulas to it—you have to develop it from within. You can't bring textbook solutions to organizations."

Source: "Profiting from Nonprofits," *Business Week*, March 26, 1990, p. 68.

Questions

1. Specifically, what might you learn from studying the history of an organization?

2. Choose an organization on campus (fraternity, student government association, academic department, or other) and study its history. Examine correspondence, meeting minutes, profiles of past leaders, and past accomplishments and problems. After gathering this information, explain what you learned from this historical study. What recommendations would you make to the present organization leaders?

The Managerial Environments

After studying the material in this chapter, you should be able to:

- **Discuss** the systems view of organization.

- **Distinguish** the general, task, and internal environments of an organization.

- **Explain** the complexity/change environmental matrix.

- **Identify** the important factors in the organization's task environment.

- **Explain** some of the actions organizations can take to help manage their external environment.

- **Discuss** the concept of boundary-spanning roles within an organization.

- **Identify** the important elements of organizational culture.

Exxon Valdez

Not many organizations can weather a single incident that costs them over $2 billion—and still counting—as well as a great deal of adverse publicity. Shortly after midnight on March 24, 1989, the supertanker *Exxon Valdez*, after running aground, leaked 10 million gallons of crude oil into Alaska's environmentally chaste and beautiful Prince William Sound.

The resulting oil slick covered 3,000 square miles of ocean, ruining valuable spawning grounds and fish hatcheries. Newspapers, magazines, and television featured photos of thousands of dead seals, birds, and other wildlife, as well as the oily sludge that contaminated formerly pristine beaches. Television programs such as Ted Koppel's *Nightline* ran specials on the subject, featuring interviews with local Eskimos and small-business entrepreneurs whose livelihoods from the sea were threatened.

Needless to say, it was a crisis of the worst kind for Exxon—and the public perception added to the problem when it seemed that Exxon's management responded too slowly in initiating cleanup operations. Despite the magnitude of the crisis and the adverse publicity, Lawrence G. Rawl, Exxon's CEO, was forced to admit to a congressional investigative committee that he had not visited Prince William Sound personally until two weeks after the incident. His reason was that he felt he was more effective at his corporate desk in New York. Even if this was true, it did little to reverse the general opinion that he should have gone to Alaska to evaluate the disaster area himself.

Exxon's customers, however, were quick to respond. Thousands of them mailed their sliced credit cards back to the company to protest the way the crisis had

been handled. Furthermore, Exxon was indicted on five criminal counts, and more than 150 separate civil lawsuits were filed against the international giant. The company is still paying lawyers' fees, and adverse public opinion continues today.

But while things were bad for Exxon, they were also bad for Alaska. The state legislature had provided tax breaks to the oil industry for years amid ongoing attempts by environmentalists and others to reverse them. When the concessions previously given on the two huge North Slope oil fields were eliminated, the once calm political waters between the state and the oil companies became stormy. Alaska's new legislation created an estimated $2 billion expenditure for the oil industry over the next two decades. "There's no doubt," said Governor Steve Cowper, "the spill made the political atmosphere different from what it was before."[1]

The Alaskan oil spill.

We indicated in Chapter 1 that one of the functions of management is to balance conflicting objectives among and between organizational stakeholders, many of whom are outside the firm. The *Exxon Valdez* oil spill provides an excellent example of how several important groups were affected by this single disaster:

1. Organizations and entrepreneurs whose activities and livelihoods were damaged by the spill
2. Special interest groups such as environmentalists
3. The state of Alaska, which devoted energy and financial resources to the cleanup
4. The federal government, which had a large interest in maintaining domestic petroleum production to reduce dependence on foreign oil
5. Competitors—Mobil Oil, Atlantic Richfield, and others—with strong investments in Alaskan oil production
6. Exxon customers, whose loyalty to the company diminished
7. Exxon employees, who saw their organization under attack publicly and whose morale was adversely affected
8. The public, whose sympathy toward tighter environmental controls over oil production and transport increased

This chapter examines these and other factors that affect the environments of organizations today and the ways in which management seeks to function effectively within both external and internal environments. The material in this chapter serves as an excellent background for other parts of the book, including Chapter 4 ("Managing in the Global Environment"), Chapter 7 ("Strategic and Operational Planning"), and Chapter 9 ("Managing Human Resources and Diversity").

Organizations: The Systems View

In Chapter 2 you learned that the systems approach is an important contemporary approach in the evolution of management. We defined a *system* as "an organized or complex whole; an assemblage or combination of things or parts forming a complex or unitary whole." Notice that a system is a network of interrelating components that, when taken together, functions as a whole. Moreover, organizations were shown to be examples of *open* rather than *closed* systems.

As shown in Figure 3.1, to function effectively over time, an open system must respond appropriately to external forces. But while organizations are indeed open systems, the danger is that some managers, perhaps smug after years of success or being unaffected by external factors, begin to think of their organization as a closed system. That is, they may grow a bit complacent, feeling almost immune to potentially adverse forces. These managers then discover—to their shock—the reality that their system is indeed an open, dynamic one.

The degree of dynamism within an open system varies. Included among the variables that may affect the system dynamics are the type of industry or service offered, the nature of competition, and the sheer volatility and importance of external factors that influence the system. What has occurred in the banking industry is a good example of changes in a system's dynamics.

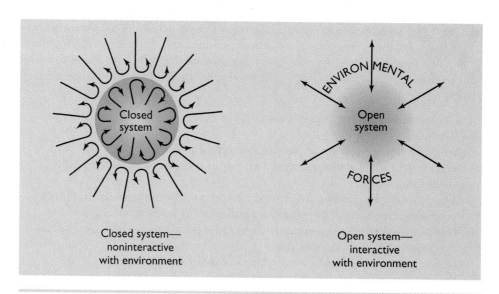

FIGURE 3.1
Open and closed systems.

Operating in a government-regulated environment, the banking business was for years a stable, conservative, profitable industry. Competition was limited by law to other banks, savings and loan institutions, and credit unions. Government regulations controlled the number of new entrants, limited the kinds of business services banks could perform, established maximum and minimum interest rates for loans and savings accounts, and severely restricted acquisitions and mergers.

With deregulation in the early 1980s, the system dramatically changed. Interest rate floors and ceilings have generally been removed. Nonbanks, such as Sears Roebuck, Merrill Lynch, and Prudential, have been allowed to offer "banking" services such as universal credit cards, interest on savings, and personal loans. Banks were allowed to branch out into nonbank services, such as insurance and brokerage services. Restrictions regarding mergers and acquisitions were liberalized, permitting giants like Citicorp, BankAmerica, and Chase Manhattan to compete on a national level, and regional superbanks to compete intensely in a several-state area. Perhaps those most severely affected were small, rural, independently owned banks, which saw down-the-street competitors acquired by lager bank holding companies and suddenly offering more services at lower prices.

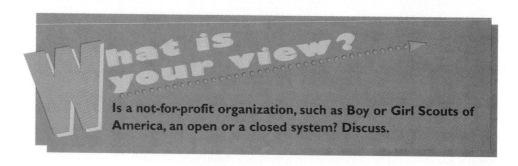

What is your view?

Is a not-for-profit organization, such as Boy or Girl Scouts of America, an open or a closed system? Discuss.

Thus, banking is a far more dynamic, open system today than it was before deregulation, as are the airline, trucking, telephone, cable television, and other industries that were deregulated in the 1980s.

Many of our most successful organizations, such as Sears Roebuck, IBM, and General Motors, to name a few, have experienced recent difficulties because of their inability to keep pace with changes that occurred in the system in which they operate. As many management experts note, the short-term solution of personnel layoffs and other cost-cutting measures seldom is, by itself, the answer. These organizations must modify their set of managerial assumptions—about customers, markets, competitors, technologies, and other factors—that have become outdated and were based on an operating system that was once valid but no longer is. In other words, they must keep in touch with their changing environment.

The Environments of an Organization

The **organizational environment** is composed of external and internal factors or elements that influence the way it functions. In this section, you will learn about the types of environments and how change and complexity influence an organization's environment.

organizational environment The combination of factors or elements that influence the way an organization functions.

Types of Environments

Basically, three specific subenvironments constitute an organization's total environment. As shown in Figure 3.2, these are (1) the general environment, (2) the task environment, and (3) the internal environment.

The **general environment** is composed of those external factors—legal/political, international, technological, economic, and social factors, for example—that generally affect all organizations. In the opening case, for example, the Alaska legislature's mood with regard to big oil companies shifted in the wake of the *Exxon Valdez* spill—a shift in the legal/political environment affecting others as well as Exxon.

The **task environment** refers to specific external factors that interact *directly* with the organization as it seeks to operate; factors such as customers, competitors, regulatory agencies, special interest groups, and suppliers fall into this category. To take the opening case again as an example, the governmental bodies with which Exxon was required to interface—the Environmental Protection Agency, the U.S. Coast Guard (which oversaw cleanup operations), and then other federal and state of Alaska agencies—are part of its direct task environment.

The third environment is the organization's **internal environment,** which includes factors over which the organization has a large degree of control, such as its organizational culture, structure, human resources, policies, and technology.

The primary focus of this chapter is on the first two external environments— the general environment and the task environment. An overview of the internal environment is covered in greater detail in other chapters throughout the text.

general environment The external environment composed of broad factors (legal/political, international, technological, economic, social, and so on) that affect all organizations.

task environment The external environment composed of factors (customers, competitors, suppliers, and so on) that interact directly with the organization as it seeks to operate.

internal environment The subenvironment composed of factors (its organization structure, personnel, policies, and so on) over which the organization has a large degree of control.

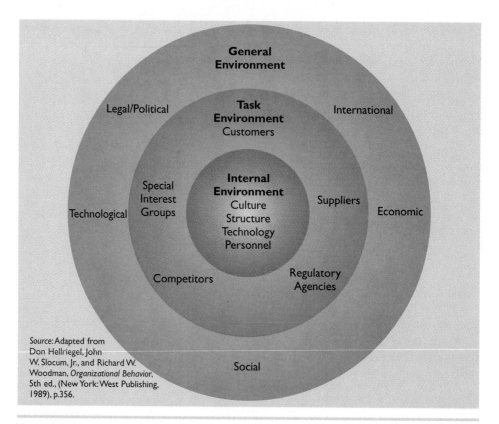

FIGURE 3.2

The environments of an organization.

Complexity and Change in the External Environment

Organizations' external environments differ dramatically. Some have numerous important factors in their external environment; some have few. Some must constantly adjust to changes in the factors, while others operate in environments in which factors change more slowly. Having a framework in which to view these differences permits a greater understanding of the organization-environment interface. The framework is based on two dimensions: (1) the complexity of the environment and (2) the degree to which the environment changes.

environmental complexity The number of key factors in an organization's environment and their similarity.

Environmental Complexity   The first dimension, **environmental complexity,** refers to two things: (1) the number of key factors operating in the organization's environment and (2) their similarity (homogeneity). For instance, an organization operating in a highly complex environment is affected by a number of key factors, such as numerous special interest groups, very different types of competitors, and broad customer groups, each with different needs or purchasing requirements. An organization operating in a simple, low-complexity environment may not be affected by special interest groups; have only a few clearly defined competitors, all of whom are similar; deal with customers whose needs and buying requirements are similar; and so on. Take, for instance, a chain of four movie theaters, as contrasted to an airline. The movie chain operates in a low-complexity, simple environment, in contrast to the airline, which is more likely to be affected by legal/political, global, and many other factors that are not critical for the movie chain. Moreover, within a given factor, say suppliers, the airline's important suppliers—maintenance service firms, manufacturers of sophisticated information technology equipment, food service vendors, and aircraft manufacturers—are quite dissimilar.

Environmental Change   The second dimension, **environmental change,** refers to the frequency and extent of changes in the organization's environment. Again, a movie theater's environment is relatively stable compared to an airline's environment: Competition does not change greatly; nor do customer tastes and needs. On the other hand, an airline faces great and rapid environmental changes. Competitors constantly change routes, schedules, prices, and travel incentives. New technological advances influence airline scheduling, maintenance, and interaction with passengers. Changes in the economy have a great impact on the number of passengers and miles flown, while changes in petroleum prices greatly affect financial performance. For example, Pan Am filed for Chapter 11 bankruptcy in 1991, partly because of escalating fuel prices, which increased from $600 million in 1989 to $740 million in 1990.[2] Regarding the degree of environmental change, we would, therefore, say that a movie theater chain operates in a relatively stable environment, an airline in a dynamic environment.

environmental change The frequency and extent of changes in an organization's environment.

The Complexity/Change Environmental Matrix   Every organization can thus be plotted somewhere on a four-cell matrix, as shown in Figure 3.3. The four cells are (1) simple/stable, (2) complex/stable, (3) simple/dynamic, and (4) complex/dynamic.

Simple/Stable Environment.   In a **simple/stable environment,** organizations are involved with relatively few key factors. Moreover, there is relatively little change within and among the factors. This is the easiest cell in which to manage, for there is relatively little uncertainty in the external environment.

simple/stable environment An organization environment composed of relatively few factors with little change within and among them.

Complex/Stable Environment.   Organizations operating in a **complex/stable environment** interact with many important and dissimilar factors. However, the factors do not tend to change frequently or dramatically.

complex/stable environment An organization environment composed of many important and dissimilar factors that do not frequently or drastically change.

Simple/Dynamic Environment.   In a **simple/dynamic environment,** the organization interacts with relatively few key factors, but those that do affect it are dynamic and constantly changing. Precious metals mining, for example, uses a relatively straightforward technology, competition is clearly defined, and government agency requirements are fairly well understood. However, changes tend to occur frequently in demand, prices, and regulatory requirements.

simple/dynamic environment An organization environment composed of few key factors that are, however, dynamic and constantly changing.

Complex/Dynamic Environment.   Managers operating in a **complex/dynamic environment** have the most difficult managerial challenge of all, for organizations operating in such an environment face a great many complex environmental factors, which change rapidly.

complex/dynamic environment An organization environment composed of numerous, complex, rapidly changing factors.

Genentech, the progressive biotechnology firm, operates within such a complex/dynamic environment. Some of the key factors influencing the complexity dimension are (1) competitors in the race for new research;

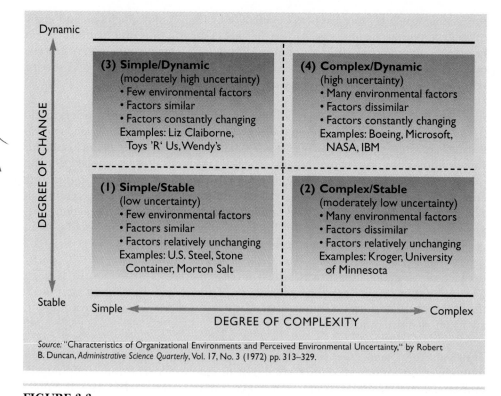

#3u

FIGURE 3.3
The complexity/change environmental matrix.

(2) numerous regulatory agencies, such as the Food and Drug Administration (FDA); (3) research and advisory groups, such as the National Cancer Institute; (4) newly approved drugs; and (5) technological advances in equipment and processes. Furthermore, the key external forces themselves are dynamic and constantly changing: New competitors enter the field, new drugs or processes are discovered, FDA regulations change, and so forth. To be successful, Genentech—like other biotechnology firms—must find efficient means of operating within this environment.

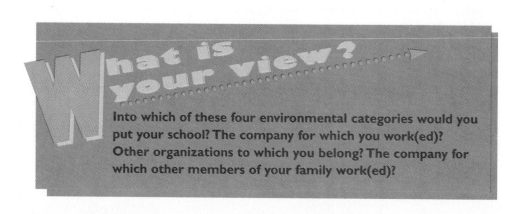

What is your view?

Into which of these four environmental categories would you put your school? The company for which you work(ed)? Other organizations to which you belong? The company for which other members of your family work(ed)?

General Environment Factors

The general environment consists of factors that broadly affect all organizations. Among these are the (1) legal/political, (2) economic, (3) social, (4) technological, and (5) international factors. We will consider each of these in turn.

Legal/Political Factors

The legal/political factors have far-reaching implications for organizations. **Legal/political factors** refer primarily to activities of federal, state, and local governments that may have a significant impact on organizations.

An example of a legal/political factor was the election of Bill Clinton as president in 1992. Since he ran on a platform of downsizing the military establishment and controlling spiraling health care costs, his election boded poorly for defense industry firms such as General Dynamics and Rockewell International, and for pharmaceutical firms such as Merck and Pfizer. After Clinton's election, a number of mergers in the health care industry occurred as firms sought to protect their flanks by finding the right combination of products and services to compete in the more tightly managed, cost-controlled environment Clinton envisioned.

legal/political factors Activities of federal, state, and local governments that have a significant impact on organizations.

How each influence Envi

Economic Factors

Economic factors are another major aspect of the general environment. For example, the stage of the business cycle—growth, stability, or decline—has a direct bearing on a nation's gross national product (GNP), level of business investment, and total sales. Moreover, inflation and interest rates strongly influence customer behavior, as well as management's investment decisions and ability to borrow money. Also, as many organizations' debts are tied directly to the fluctuating prime lending rate, when inflation drives up the prime rate, organizations are faced with larger debt service payments. A slow economy, on the other hand, means less disposable income and higher unemployment, which in turn will determine how much customers spend. In summary, economic factors affect all organizations.

economic factors Factors in the economy that affect organizations, including the gross national product, interest rates, inflation, and so on.

Social Factors

A broad range of **social factors** shape the general environment of organizations. Two categories of such factors are (1) demographic forces and (2) social forces.

Demographic Forces   The population's size, density, age, sex, and other associated characteristics are referred to as **demographic forces.** For instance, age is definitely a force shaping the general environment. Americans are living longer, with an average life expectancy approaching 75 years. This trend has strong implications for housing, health care, recreation and leisure, financial planning, and numerous other activities. Additionally, the *baby boom* of the 1940s and 1950s and the subsequent decline in birthrates (the *baby bust*) have resulted in an older workforce and, in fact, a working-age population that in many cases cannot match employment

social factors Factors, including demographic and social forces, that help shape the general environment of organizations.

demographic forces Characteristics of the population—size, density, age, sex, and other related features —that contribute to shaping the general environment.

demand. When the baby-boom generation entered the workforce in the 1970s, more women than men sought jobs; today, slightly over half the new hires are females. Dual wage-earner couples are also increasing, and mobility patterns and population shifts are becoming more significant.

social forces Society's values and lifestyles that affect the general environment.

Social Forces   Society's values and lifestyles are referred to as **social forces.** With a Gallup poll showing that over 75 percent of Americans consider themselves "environmentalists," and in the wake of major oil spills (such as that of the *Exxon Valdez*), acid rain, and other issues, the environment is perhaps the dominant social—and economic—issue to influence U.S. business commitment in the 1990s.[3] Shifting attitudes toward minority rights and the power of minorities subjected many firms doing business with South Africa to increased scrutiny. In the 1980s and 1990s, the same can be said for the consumerism and proenvironment movements. Attitudes toward such issues as alcohol and drugs, more open sexuality, and smoking have had—and will continue to have—a strong impact on organizations, some more directly and intensely than others. The same can be said for today's obsession with fitness and personal health and the resultant interest in jogging and other exercise, and proper diet and nutrition.

Technological Factors

technological factors The component of an organization's general environment by which inputs are transformed into outputs, including equipment, materials, personnel, and facilities.

Technological factors are another important component of the organization's general environment. These are the means by which organizations transform inputs into outputs, which can vary from simple, inexpensive equipment or materials to costly, complex facilities using computers, automation, robots, or other sophisticated mechanisms. The technology of service-oriented firms, such as education systems, nursing homes, restaurants, and hotels, is also important. New technology can quickly make products or services obsolete, or offer advantages in the way in which organizations function. Recent increases in the speed with which information can be transmitted between and among locations is revolutionizing

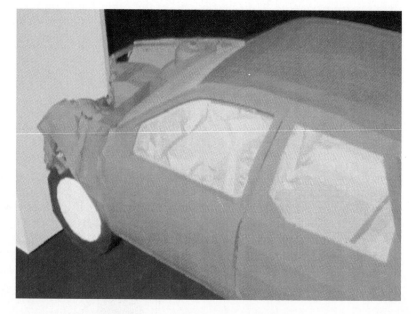

Information technology advances in the auto industry. In 1991, this car crashed on a computer, one of the world's first digital smashups. Such simulations, now widely used in the industry, cost as little as $5,000, versus $1 million for a crash on a test track.

information management. Whereas regular mail takes days, special services such as Federal Express and Express Mail promise it overnight, and facsimile (fax) transmissions are instantaneous. Cellular phones permit continuous contact, and electronic mail systems allow users to flash messages worldwide in a matter of seconds to however many persons need the information. It is expected that the use of electronic mail will double annually through the year 2000.

Companies that for decades have dominated manufacturing and distribution of music, movies, and books face the prospect of being replaced by the electronic alternative—a high-speed network that runs into every home and can deliver video, music, and text quickly and inexpensively. In 1993, IBM and Blockbuster announced a plan to transmit recorded music over optical fibers to Blockbuster's retail stores and manufacture CDs on the spot, on demand. Xerox is near completion of a technology that would enable a customer to walk into Kinko's, the copier chain, and receive a novel, such as *Gone with the Wind*, printed, glued, and bound in about eight minutes.[4]

Surprisingly, perhaps, many major technological breakthroughs affecting an industry do not originate within it. BIC, for instance, was not in the razor business when it developed technology for the disposable razor that strongly threatened industry leaders Gillette and Schick. Nor was Seiko or Timex in integrated circuit technology when Texas Instruments developed technology that led to the digital watch.[5] Personal computers originated outside the computer industry. Technology affects all organizations, and none can afford to overlook it.

International Factors

Other factors making up the general environment are the **international factors.** Occurrences on the international scene—be they economic, political, or social— have a strong impact on U.S. organizations. Just a few such recent events are (1) the

international factors
Economic, political, or social events throughout the world that have a strong impact on domestic organizations.

The explosion of western products in Moscow, advertised on buildings, buses, and sidewalks, has triggered a backlash among many Russians that has been partly responsible for a resurgence of nationalism.

move toward democracy and the free enterprise system in Eastern Europe; (2) the reunification of Germany; (3) the signing of important trade agreements with Japan, China, and Russia; (4) the failure of Third World countries to meet their debt payments to U.S., Canadian, and other lenders; and (5) the continued problems arising from tension among Middle Eastern countries—including Iraq's invasion of Kuwait and the war that followed, as well as the ensuing political upheaval within these and other countries.

A particularly important international event was "Europe '92"—when Western European countries became one united market of 320 million people. This has strongly affected U.S. companies' decisions to acquire or merge with European firms in order to gain a toehold.

Task Environment Factors

An organization's task environment, sometimes called the *operating environment*, refers to elements within the external environment that interact directly with the organization. In this section, the following task factors in the environment are discussed: (1) suppliers, (2) regulatory agencies, (3) competitors, (4) customers, and (5) special interest groups.

Suppliers

Suppliers are important elements in the organization's task environment, accounting for a whopping 60 percent of the total cost of operations in the manufacturing sector.[6] Accordingly, the role of suppliers in the supplier-vendor relationship has changed dramatically in recent years. Once considered adversarial, the relationship today is more likely to follow the Japanese model of a **coproducer arrangement:** fewer suppliers, longer customer-supplier relationships, high interaction, and close physical proximity, as shown in the following examples.

coproducer arrangement A relationship between organization and supplier that depends on high interaction and close proximity, and results in fewer suppliers and longer customer-supplier relationships.

> Motorola, a big supplier to Hewlett-Packard (HP), is linked into HP's electronic data system. Demand from HP's factories for supplies from Motorola can in turn trigger Motorola's purchases and production schedule. Needless to say, a very trusting relationship is needed.[7]
>
> Motorola extends its reputation for high quality to its suppliers by teaching them how to implement quality systems consistent with Motorola's needs. Motorola teams tour suppliers' plants every two years, conducting a quality audit and gathering feedback and suggestions for improvement. Moreover, the company has established a 15-member Council of Suppliers, which rates Motorola's purchaser-supplier practices from its suppliers' perspectives.
>
> Honda is also involved in improving supplier relationships. It recently selected one of its former suppliers, highly reputable Donnelly Corporation, to make outside mirrors for all of its U.S.-produced vehicles. The only problem was that at the time of the selection, Donnelly produced only inside mirrors—a new plant was required to consummate the deal. Donnelly was selected based on Honda management's knowledge of Donnelly's values and cultures, which matched their

MANAGEMENT APPLICATION AND PRACTICE 3.1

The Fed Cracks Down on Auto Safety

With automobile recalls in 1994 running at the highest levels in 17 years, the potential defects being probed by the government sound like consumer and manufacturer nightmares—fires, exploding air bags, seats that collapse, faulty steering, and seat belts that don't perform. In March 1994, federal officials dramatically warned all drivers of station wagons, hatchback models, sport utility vehicles, and even minivans—the industry's newest and most profitable model—that tailgates could open during a crash, ejecting the passengers. As Transportation Secretary Frederico Pena indicated in the formal warning statement: "We recognize the great popularity of minivans and will be working very aggressively to get to the bottom of this issue." But according to Auto Service Monitor, a private firm that tracks recalls, only about a third of the recalled vehicles are taken to the shop for the necessary repair.

But how can there be so many safety problems at a time when the public has been hearing and reading so much about auto quality? Certainly, there are problems, and they are not limited to the Big Three U.S.

automakers. Honda Accords and Civics and BMWs have also been victimized by technology. Part of the problem is the complexity of automobile manufacturing today. Increasing the number of wires, tubes, and fluid containers in an automobile also increases the risk of electrical shorts, leaks, crimps, and overflows. Another factor in the quality problem is that manufacturers rely on suppliers for quality parts. Chrysler recently repaired 15,000 Neons, its newest small car model, due to a faulty ignition part from one of its suppliers—not to poor design or shoddy assembly by Chrysler employees.

Still another reason for the increased attention to quality today is that the Clinton administration is more diligent than preceding administrations in addressing issues of public safety. Critics claim the consumer was victimized by the Reagan-Bush administration's lack of attention to issues affecting consumer safety, and thus there has been a rise in the number of automobile recalls in recent years.

Source: Adapted from "Quality Woes Are Spreading Like a Rash," *USA Today*, March 18, 1994, pp. B1, B2.

own. Building on the strength of its earlier relationship, a handshake—and an expected $60 million in Donnelly sales—was all it took for Donnelly to commit to the new partnership.[8]

Regulatory Agencies

As indicated earlier, the general trend of government, despite much criticism from business, has been to assume a more active role in the regulation of business, as shown in MAP 3.1. Basically, regulation can be divided into four categories of laws that protect the following:

1. The legal rights and safety of employees
2. Consumers
3. Competition and the marketplace
4. The ecological environment

Table 3.1 presents some of the major regulatory agencies of the federal government responsible for enforcing these and other federal laws. Individual states also have regulatory counterparts paralleling the federal agencies.

TABLE 3.1   Important Regulatory Agencies Affecting the Task Environments of Organizations

Agency	Year Created	Function	Type of Organization Affected
Occupational Safety and Health Administration	1970	Regulates safety and health conditions in the workplace	All firms with more than 10 employees
Consumer Product Safety Commission	1972	Attempts to reduce problem-related injuries to consumers through improved design, labeling, and instructions	Consumer products makers
Equal Employment Opportunity Commission	1964	Issues guidelines on employment discrimination, investigates charges, determines reporting and recordkeeping requirements of businesses, resolving cases through settlements or litigation	All private employers of 15 or more persons; educational institutions, labor unions
Federal Trade Commission	1914	Broad discretion to protect consumers from unfair trade practices such as deceptive advertising and sales practices; to maintain competition	Consumer products firms
Antitrust Division (Justice Department)	1890	Regulates all activity affecting interstate commerce from trade restraints to illegal agreements to mergers	Primarily large firms
Environmental Protection Agency	1970	Sets and enforces air, water, and noise pollution standards and standards for using and handling pesticides and toxic wastes	Manufacturers that produce emissions, chemical firms, firms generating toxic waste
Federal Reserve Board	1913	Regulates state-chartered banks that belong to the Federal Reserve System; has jurisdiction over bank holding companies; sets money and credit policy	Most large banking institutions directly; indirectly, all financial institutions
Food and Drug Administration (Health and Human Services Department)	1906	Responsible for safety and effectiveness of drugs and medical devices; safety and purity of food; requires labeling	Pharmaceutical, medical equipment, food processing firms
Federal Aviation Administration	1958	Regulates aircraft manufacturing through certification of airplane airworthiness, pilot certification, aircraft maintenance procedure	Aircraft and aircraft parts manufacturers, airlines, airline maintenance firms
National Highway Traffic Safety Administration (Transportation Department)	1966	Regulates manufacturers of motor vehicles and tires so as to reduce number and severity of vehicular accidents	Auto, truck, trailer, and tire manufacturers, auto safety products manufacturers

Competitors

Competitors represent a key group of players in an organization's task environment. An organization's relationship with its competitors, unlike that with most other task players, is indirect rather than direct, and involves adversarial—and often aggressive—behavior. One organization may modify its pricing or advertising behavior, differentiate its product or service, change its distribution strategy, or innovate in order to gain a competitive advantage over others.

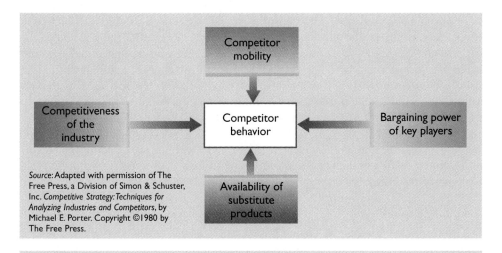

Source: Adapted with permission of The Free Press, a Division of Simon & Schuster, Inc. *Competitive Strategy: Techniques for Analyzing Industries and Competitors*, by Michael E. Porter. Copyright ©1980 by The Free Press.

FIGURE 3.4
Factors influencing competitive behavior in a firm's task environment.

Professor Michael Porter of Harvard developed a model, shown in Figure 3.4, that helps depict the nature of competitive behavior in a given industry.[9] Porter says there are four important variables affecting competitor behavior: (1) competitor mobility, (2) the relative bargaining power of key players, (3) the availability of substitute products, and (4) the competitiveness of the industry.

Competitor Mobility   *Competitor mobility* refers to the relative ease with which competitors can enter or leave a particular market, given the market's attractiveness. It is relatively simple, for example, for competitors to enter the videotape rental, restaurant, fitness center, convenience store, or computer software business. On the other hand, it is highly unlikely that a new automobile or airplane manufacturer could spring up overnight, as the need for capital and the cost of technology, know-how, and labor would be massive—not to mention the difficulty of developing products better than the intended competition's, at a competitive price.

Similarly, the difficulty or ease of market exit is also important. When the going gets rough in an industry, how easy is it for competitors to pick up and leave? A problem may develop for a company if its competitors do not abandon a stagnant, nongrowth, or low-growth market that is overcrowded. Then excessive supply will drive prices down and lead to price cutting to capture greater market share.

Sometimes aggressive competition, rather than stagnant markets, forces out competitors.

> In the 1980s, two firms, Procter & Gamble (Luvs and Pampers) and Kimberly-Clark (Kleenex and Huggies) dominated the disposable diaper market. First one, then the other, gained the dominant market share through aggressive pricing, promotion, and product differentiation. The new line of thinner diapers gave Procter & Gamble the lead in 1988; Kimberly-Clark imitated it and has since overtaken P&G. The hardball strategies these two firms have used to become market leader have chased away three highly respected competitors; Scott Paper Company, Union Carbide, and Johnson & Johnson suffered huge losses and left the industry.[10]

Sometimes a business will continue making an unprofitable product as a service to customers who buy its other products or services. IBM had difficulty exiting the copier market for this reason. There may even be an emotional commitment to a product, as when Singer hung on to its unprofitable sewing machine line simply because sewing machines were its original product and its "bread and butter" for so long. Such decisions to "hang on" keep the level of competition at higher than normal levels in a particular industry.

Relative Bargaining Power of Key Players   The relative bargaining power of key players also influences the degree of competition in an industry. Anheuser-Busch, with close to 45 percent of the beer market, generally sets the tone for prices in the industry. In early 1990, Heinz announced that its market leader, StarKist, under pressure from "Save the Dolphin" groups, would no longer buy tuna from suppliers whose nets also catch and kill dolphins; two other smaller tuna canners with small market shares made similar announcements within hours.

Suppliers are also capable of strongly affecting competition through their own demonstrations of power within the market. For example, the Organization of Petroleum Exporting Countries (OPEC) has a significant effect on the oil industry by setting the prices its members will charge and the amount of oil each member agrees to produce.

Nowhere is the bargaining power of key customers reflected more than in the pharmaceutical industry. In 1993, drug manufacturers such as Merck and Pfizer began bowing to demands for price discounts from large, consolidated consumers such as hospital chains, HMOs, and large drug mail-order houses. Drugstore chains such as Revco and Rite Aid have charged pharmaceutical companies with price discrimination and are demanding similar discounts.[11]

Availability of Substitute Products   Another important factor affecting competitive behavior is the extent to which products in one industry are closely related to those in other industries. For example, Coke competes not only with Pepsi and 7UP but also with a number of other beverage products, such as tea, milk, fruit juice, and even alcoholic products like wine and beer. Producers of fiberglass insulation compete with manufacturers of substitutes—cellulose, polystyrene foam, and rock wool; steel companies compete against wood, aluminum, and plastic manufacturers; and so on.

When substitutes exist, their competitive presence is felt in two important ways. First, and more importantly, they place a ceiling on the prices an industry can charge without risking buyers switching to less expensive—or, in some cases, higher-quality—substitutes. Second, unless sellers of a product upgrade quality, reduce costs (and prices), or in some way differentiate their product from substitute products in buyers' eyes, they invite more direct, intense competitive behavior from substitute producers. This is especially true in industries that have a high growth potential.

Competitiveness of the Industry   The competitiveness of the industry also strongly affects organizations' behavior in pricing, promotion, new product development, and other areas. Some industries, by their nature, lend themselves to very strong competition, others much less so. The intensity of competitor rivalry results from such factors as the number of firms, the industry's rate of growth, and the degree of product differentiation. While the automobile industry is highly competitive, the paper and forest products industry, until recently, has been characterized by stability—few new entrants, follow-the-leader pricing, and no major additions to overall industry capacity. More recently, however, foreign competition, mergers, and increased capacity of U.S. and Canadian producers have shaken the industry and depressed prices.

Customers

Customers are also a critical part of the task environment; without them, no organization could survive. Moreover, customers' values, tastes, and needs tend to change over time, and organizations—both profit-seeking and not-for-profit—must stay attuned to these if they want to survive. Many organizations now have well-defined, organized systems for keeping up with their customers through special programs. Volvo, for instance, has established a 100,000-mile club for Volvo owners, which entitles them to discounts on vehicle maintenance and repairs.

Other companies establish formal contacts, inviting customers to offer feedback about the quality of service or to participate in helping make product design changes. It is estimated that, in some industries, as many as 80 percent of all important innovations have originated with users.[12]

Special Interest Groups

More recent but powerful players in the task environment are *special interest groups.* These groups, such as Greenpeace, the American Association of Retired Persons (AARP), and Planned Parenthood, have arisen for various reasons, including (1) the feeling that government, business, labor unions, and other powerful organizations are unresponsive to people's needs and wishes; (2) the fact that media attention has been an ally of many such groups; and (3) the knowledge that favorable rulings in the courts have made many groups financially feasible. Thus, a wide variety of special interest groups, including consumer groups, social cause groups, and labor unions, may affect an organization's task environment.

Consumer Groups *Consumer groups* support consumer interests in their relationships with big business. Although consumerism is not new, its modern renaissance can be traced to Ralph Nader, who took on General Motors in the early 1960s. Nader's book *Unsafe at Any Speed* condemned GM's rear-engine Corvair as a death trap and indicted GM for lack of concern about safety. GM's attempts to discredit Nader—he sued them and was awarded over $400,000—and the furor over the Corvair catapulted Nader and the consumer movement into the public eye.[13]

Numerous regulatory agencies discussed earlier provide much consumer protection, but many private groups, such as trade associations, the Consumer Research Institute, and Better Business Bureaus, are also very active. Specific areas of consumer attention and challenges to organizations are advertising, packaging, safety, and pricing.

Social Cause Groups *Social cause groups* pursue a variety of social interests and causes. The National Association for the Advancement of Colored People

(NAACP), for example, has successfully influenced firms with investments in South Africa, and Mothers Against Drunk Driving (MADD) has affected the advertising practices of the beer and liquor industries considerably. Under continued pressure from antipornography groups, several major convenience store chains—including 7-Eleven, the largest at the time—stopped selling *Playboy* and similar magazines.

> Hundreds of Minnesotans destroyed their Dayton Hudson credit cards to protest the retail chain's decision to stop providing money to Planned Parenthood. Even though the money was used for birth control and education—not abortions—the company, like many others, decided to stop funding such controversial causes. Abortion rights groups pledged to launch a "Holidays Without Dayton's" campaign if Dayton did not reverse its decision.[14]

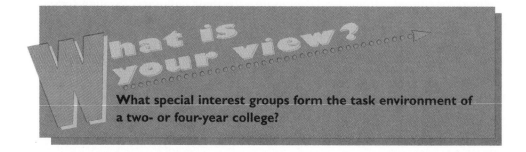

What is your view?

What special interest groups form the task environment of a two- or four-year college?

Labor Unions   The percentage of U.S. workers who are union members has declined considerably in recent years. According to the Bureau of National Affairs, union membership (as a percentage of the U.S. workforce) declined from 35 percent in 1945 to 17 percent in 1990.[15] While unions are losing membership in the private sector—now only 12 percent of private workers are members—union membership in governmental organizations is gaining and will soon hit 40 percent.[16] Yet unions still wield considerable power, especially political power. Knowledgeable managers know it could be dangerous to take them too lightly, as the following example illustrates.

> In the early 1990s, Mazda, one of the three unionized Japanese auto plants in the United States, began to experience labor difficulties, which embarrassed not only Mazda but also the United Auto Workers (UAW) union. Mazda agreed to union representation before opening its doors and worked out an arrangement— supported by the UAW—to screen out potential troublemakers from its workforce. However, the UAW's hand-picked representatives were voted out by its members and replaced by activists.
>
> In response to the local union's militance, Mazda retaliated by (1) replacing several important American managers at the plant with Japanese managers, (2) using its *Kaizen* (continuous improvement) productivity approach to increase pressure on employees to turn out more cars, and (3) hardening its attitude toward sick leave and absenteeism. The result was severely strained company-employee relations and an atmosphere far removed from the cooperative, "family"-style atmosphere of traditional Japanese-managed companies.[17]

Managing the External Environment

The number and variety of environmental factors—both general and task—that strongly affect an organization are mind-boggling. Add to this the fact that most organizations do not operate in the simple/stable cell of the environmental matrix but, rather, in a complex and/or dynamic cell, and you will better understand the need to understand and adapt to one's environment. Many organizations no longer simply assume that they are passive victims of their environment, but actively seek to enhance and influence their relationship with it.

> For example, Edgar Woolard, on becoming CEO of Du Pont shortly after the *Exxon Valdez* oil spill (Opening Case), started meeting once each month with leading environmentalists.[18]

Basically, organizations can pursue one of three avenues regarding their environment. They can (1) attempt to forecast potential impacts in order to react more effectively, (2) attempt to influence the environment through boundary spanning, or (3) take other forms of defensive action.

Environmental Forecasting

Environmental forecasting is monitoring the environment and attempting to forecast its future. An ever growing number of firms are now peering into crystal balls and examining predicted social, international, and technological changes.[19] The results have been mixed, as the following example illustrates.

environmental forecasting The examination of future social, international, and technological changes.

> In 1989, McDonnell Douglas, one of the largest U.S. aircraft manufacturers, completed a major research project on what its environment would look like in the year 2000. Despite studying world politics in great detail, forecasters failed to foresee the changes in Eastern Europe, the fall of the Berlin Wall, or the political upheaval in China. They did, however, identify several important future actions, including the possibility of joint ventures with Japanese and European aerospace companies and the potential development of space aircraft that would make possible intercontinental commuter travel in less than two hours.[20]

Boundary-Spanning Roles

The interrelationships that occur when an organization interacts with its environment are conducted by various personnel, including executives, formal representatives, and task forces. These people are called *boundary spanners*—individuals who span the environment between the organization and its external forces. The roles of some boundary spanners, such as CEOs, governmental relations representatives, and public relations officers are created expressly to achieve such a relationship with key external forces.

TABLE 3.2 BOUNDARY SPANNERS	
Position/Department	**Relevant Macro/Task Factors**
CEO	All
Marketing	Competitors, customers
Public relations	Society, community, special interest groups
Human resources	Potential employees
Engineering, production	Technological, suppliers
Purchasing	Suppliers
Industrial relations	Unions
Government relations	Legal/political, regulatory agencies, international
Forecasting	Economic, international
International	International
Strategic planning	Competitors, legal/political, economy, customers, suppliers
New product development	Customers, competitors
Research and development	Technological, competition, regulatory
Joint venture representatives	Competitors, suppliers

Mazda has over 100 employees whose job is to work inside suppliers' plants to make sure that Mazda's policies are followed.[21]

Sun Oil's vice-chairman of the board of directors is assigned responsibility for environmental assessment, overseeing Sun's chief economist, a specialist in technological assessment, and a public issues consultant.[22]

A number of boundary spanners include contact with external factors as only a part of their job. For example, a CEO who attends a professional meeting or trade show and interacts with suppliers and competitors may also learn about new technological developments. Even corporate travel planners may act as boundary spanners. Table 3.2 illustrates a number of boundary spanners found in more progressive organizations.

Other Managerial Actions

Other actions management can take to help influence the impact of external factors include (1) entering partnerships or join ventures and (2) diversifying ownership. (These will be discussed in greater detail in Chapter 14.)

Partnerships/Joint Ventures   Recently, a number of joint ventures by two or more partnering firms have occurred in a number of industries. This form of cooperation is called **partnering, or partnership alliances (PALs).** Computer hardware and software firms such as IBM and Microsoft, automobile manufacturers such as GM and Toyota, and pharmaceutical/health-related firms such as Johnson & Johnson and Merck have all gotten into the act as joint venture partners.

partnering, or partnership alliances (PALs)
The establishment of joint ventures by two or more firms or industries.

MANAGEMENT APPLICATION AND PRACTICE 3.2

Partnering, or Becoming PALs

Diamond/Star Motors is the result of an alliance/partnership between U.S.-based Chrysler and Japan's Mitsubishi Motors. On the one hand, the arrangement allows Chrysler to domestically produce a high-quality car using Mitsubishi's expertise; on the other, Mitsubishi avoids U.S. tariffs and restrictions.

Many well-known organizations today, including Anheuser-Busch, Avis, Coca-Cola, Hilton, KFC, McDonald's, and PepsiCo, have for many years been engaged in licensing arrangements with foreign distributors. This practice is a popular means of entering foreign markets. Trade agreements such as NAFTA and the European Common Market are reducing if not eliminating many of the barriers in establishing a truly global economy.

By linking national and international organizations much more closely, partnership alliances, or PALs, will be an effective organizational strategy toward future globalization. Suppliers and customers from around the world that formerly saw their roles as adversarial will gain greatly from the strengthened relationships. Management writer Rosabeth Moss Kanter offers advice and tips for successful partnership arrangements:

1. *Make the PAL important.* It should be sufficiently relevant that the players provide adequate resources, attention, and sponsorship. If there is not a lot at stake for one or both parties, the partnership is more likely to come unglued.

2. *The PAL members should be interdependent.* This results in a balance of power. For example, 50 Ford and IBM executives have worked carefully together to design IBM equipment that will be used in Ford's new office system. Moreover, the team will oversee the actual installation and initial implementation of the system.

3. *The PAL organizations should be integrated.* This maximizes appropriate points of contact. Some purchaser-supplier relationships today are linked together and share each other's information systems so as to determine product needs, dates shipped, and so forth. Suppliers are automatically involved in providing inputs about the design of purchasers' products. Polaroid, for instance, saved $27 million over a two-year period by helping its suppliers improve their own cost structures.

4. *The PAL partnership must be institutionalized.* It should be bolstered by an ongoing organization and have mechanisms for dealing with issues from legal to social ties and shared values.

A key to partnering is trust. The steps above, when taken by suppliers and their customers, establish and maintain a high level of trust.

Sources: John A. Pearce II and Richard B. Robinson, Jr., *Strategic Management*, 5th ed. (Burr Ridge, Ill.: Irwin, 1994), pp. 243–246, and Rosabeth Moss Kanter, *When Giants Learn to Dance* (New York: Simon & Schuster, 1989), pp. 141–173.

Experts point to GE's jet engine subsidiary and Snecma, its French counterpart, which together form CFM International on a 50-50 basis and make engines used to power Boeing, Douglas, and Airbus airplanes, as a model alliance. In its 17 years, the alliance has taken orders for $38 billion worth of engines.[23]

In many cases PALs involve customers and suppliers; in others, such as the companies that combined interests by investing in the Alaska pipeline, they involved competitors. As shown in the profile of Herman J. Russell, one reason for the popularity of joint ventures is the sharing of financial risks that would prove too large otherwise; in other cases, however, joint ventures are a direct attempt to gain some control over the external environment. Rueben Mark, CEO of Colgate-Palmolive, says partnerships "will be the thrust of the '90s and beyond."[24]

MAP 3.2 provides some insight into what makes for an effective partnering relationship.

PRACTICING MANAGER

When the pensive and intro-spective Herman J. Russell, chairman of Atlanta-based H. J. Russell & Co., recalls his entrepreneurial accomplish-ments, it is no surprise that he focuses on a strong founda-tion as the key to his success. Russell turned the bricks and mortar company founded in 1956 into a diversified con-struction and engineering powerhouse with 1993 sales of $150 million, placing it among the largest African American–owned organiza-tions in the United States.

HERMAN J. RUSSELL, H. J. RUSSELL & CO.

Russell, whose father owned a small plastering subcontracting business in Atlanta, learned from his father not only the tricks of the trade but also the value of saving. While still in junior high, he purchased a plot of land for $125 from the city of Atlanta, and during his senior year in high school, he began building a duplex on it. The duplex was finished a little over a year later, during the summer break of his freshman year at Alabama's Tuskegee Institute.

Upon graduation from Tuskegee in 1957, Russell founded Russell Plastering Company. The small company quickly gained an excellent reputa-tion throughout the Southeast as one of the best plastering subcontractors in the business. Russell soon moved into the residential market, where he became a builder of apartment complexes. From there, his company grew steadily and eventually became involved in large joint venture construc-tion projects. In 1962, Russell became the first African American member of the Atlanta Chamber of Commerce. In 1980, he was elected its president.

The span of those 18 years saw Russell involved in a number of major joint venture projects with other contractors, including the Georgia-Pacific headquarters building in Atlanta, numerous other office buildings and apartment complexes in the Southeast, the Martin Luther King Community Center in Atlanta, four under-ground stations for Atlanta's rapid rail system, the underground people mover at the Atlanta airport, and the new terminal at Atlanta's Hartsfield International Airport. The contractors with whom Russell participated in these and other projects have often been competitors, yet the beauty of joint ventures lies in the mutual sharing of the financial risks that could not possibly be under-taken by most individual firms.

Drawing from personal experience, Russell observed that "real joint ventures are going to have total participa-tion. It is one of the finest ways to learn new techniques." However, he is quick to add that "the worst thing in the world is for people to use their name in joint ventures and to not develop that resource."

Russell values well-managed growth as opposed to the meteoric, get-rich-quick philosophy of wheeler-dealers. "I think it is ridiculous for any young person to adopt a concept of getting rich overnight," he asserts. "I've always believed in a philoso-phy of controlled growth. There is no quick fix to success; it requires lots of hard work and sacrifice." In other words, Russell believes in taking the stairs—not the elevator—to the top.

Russell credits his extensive knowledge of the construction industry as a vital factor in his success. While he can tell from computer print-outs "where we are, I don't only read the print-out—I go into the field to see things for myself. Once I go out on a job, I will pick things up auto-matically. My eyes, my feet tell me things the computer can't because I've been trained."

Another characteristic that has become Russell's trademark over the years is his consis-tent dependability. He has a splendid reputation for completing high-pressure projects on time and within budget.

This reputation is a direct result of another element that has played a major role in his rise to the top—planning. "If you are a builder and do not put it together right," he says, "you are going to lose your shirt. You have to be precise in putting together the bid package and the real-estate deal. Then you have to monitor the situation to make sure you are managing the process. . . . We never do a job unless we have a system in place to check everything."

Source: Excerpted from Russell Shaw, "Herman J. Russell: Chairman, H. J. Russell & Co.," *Sky*, August 1990, pp. 41–47. This article has been reprinted through the courtesy of Halsey Publishing Co., publishers of Delta Air Lines's *Sky* magazine. See also Alfred Edmund, "Coming on Strong: With the Economy on the Upswing, the B.D. 100s Broke the $10 Billion Barrier and Got Back into the Business of Job Creation," *Black Enterprise*, June 1994, p. 75.

Diversified Ownership   Another way for an organization to affect its external environment directly is through diversified ownership. Such action allows an organization to spread its risks and avoid having "all its eggs in one basket," by agreeing to coproduce products, share distribution channels, or cooperate with another organization in some other manner beneficial to both, allowing them to do jointly what neither could achieve independently.

Chevron, for example, concerned about its future supply of oil reserves because of international uncertainly in the Middle East, acquired Gulf Oil—which was later acquired by BP. This move provided Chevron with a greater diversity of oil reserves in politically stable countries, particularly the United States and Canada. The large tobacco giants Phillip Morris and R. J. Reynolds have both diversified into other industries, including beer, soft drinks, other beverages, and food, which enabled them to be less dependent on cigarettes. It is not unusual for a firm to acquire a major financial interest in a key supplier, which not only diversifies its ownership but also gives it some control over a major resource dependency.

Internal Environment Factors

The third major environment of importance to organizations is the internal environment. Unlike the general and task environments, which are external, the internal environment is more directly controllable by an organization. Moreover, it reflects the organization's efforts to adapt effectively to its general and task environments. Important factors making up the internal environment are the organization's culture, personnel, structure, and processes. In this section, we emphasize culture, since it represents the broader, more fundamental factor of the internal environment. Other chapters throughout the text discuss the remaining three factors.

What Is Organizational Culture?

As individuals come into contact with organizations, they become familiar with the organization's formal rules and practices, the dress norms, the stories of co-workers, and the informal codes of behavior, rituals, tasks, pay systems, jargon, and jokes understood only by insiders. These elements are some of the manifestations of organizational culture.[25]

Organizational culture can be defined as the shared philosophies, values, beliefs, and behavior patterns that form the organization's core identity.[26] Marvin Bowen, former managing director of McKinsey and Company, defines it more succinctly as "the way we do things around here."[27]

organizational culture
The shared philosophies, values, beliefs, and behavior patterns that form the organization's core identity.

In their search for excellently managed organizations, Peters and Waterman, also former McKinsey and Company consultants, found that the best companies distinguished themselves from the also-rans by their "coherent" corporate culture. An organization with a strong culture has consensus on the values that drive the organization. These values are deeply held, widely shared, and highly resistant to change. At 3M, *innovation* is a key value; Honda is a *team*-oriented company where people achieve with others, not by themselves.

Culture also involves other internal matters, such as the organization's structure, employee characteristics, and the company's reward and promotion system.

It also influences how processes and decisions are determined. Over the years, IBM's culture has reflected a strongly conservative, deeply customer-service–oriented firm, with deep loyalty between the company and its employees. This strong sense of loyalty led former CEO John Akers to postpone IBM's downsizing until the late 1980s.

Elements of Organizational Culture

The area of organizational culture has a rich vocabulary. To help you understand the importance of culture and its impact on performance, we will focus on three of its components: *heroes, rites,* and *rituals.*

heroes Role models who make attaining success and accomplishment possible.

Heroes   Those who provide role models and make attaining success and accomplishment human and possible, or **heroes,** are essential to a strong organizational culture. They symbolize the values of the organization not only internally but also to the outside world. They preserve what makes the organization special, but they also set high standards and are masterful at creating a motivating environment.

> Richard A. Drew, a banjo-playing college dropout working in 3M's research lab during the 1920s, [helped] some colleagues solve a problem they had with masking tape. Soon thereafter, Du Pont came out with cellophane. Drew decided he could go Du Pont one better and coated the cellophane with a colorless adhesive to bind things together—and Scotch tape was born. In the 3M tradition, Drew carried the ball himself by managing the development and initial production of his invention. Moving up through the ranks, he went on to become technical director of the company and showed other employees just how they could succeed in similar fashion at 3M.[28]

In an organization with a long history of a strong culture, some of the most notable heroes may still have significant influence even when they are no longer with the organization, and perhaps the most influential heroes are the ones who create an environment in which many ordinary members can become heroes.

> The legendary Mary Kay Ash of Mary Kay Cosmetics is an example. She trains her salespeople not only to represent the firm but also to believe that they can do what she has done. To inspire them with her own confidence, Mary Kay awards diamond bumblebee pins to outstanding performers and explains that, according to aerodynamic engineers, the wings of the bumblebee are too weak to support its heavy body in flight. But bumblebees do not know this, and so they fly anyway. The message is clear: Anyone can be a hero given the confidence and persistence to try.[29]

rites Relatively elaborate, dramatic, planned activities that combine various forms of cultural expression.

Rites   At one time, Napoléon was criticized for awarding so many Legion of Honor medals. His reply was, "You lead men by baubles, not words." Napoléon understood that achievement deserves recognition and that recognition is a powerful motivator. Both rites and rituals call attention to and reinforce what is desired from organization members. **Rites** can be defined as relatively elaborate, dramatic, planned activities that combine various forms of cultural expression. An awards luncheon or

Mary Kay's awards seminar participants whoop it up at the annual rite held in 1993 in Dallas.

banquet at which a number of people are recognized (for years of service, outstanding performance, innovative suggestions, or the like) is a widely used rite, as is a college fraternity initiation ceremony.

> IBM has major conventions for its managers each year, the 100 Percent Club for those who make their sales quota, and the Quarter-Century Club for those with 25 years or more of service with the company.

Rituals Detailed methods and procedures faithfully or regularly followed are called **rituals.** In essence, these are company policies—or at least should be in harmony with policies. Among other things, a ritual can be the way an awards rite is carried out or the way a quality circle ideally functions. Rites and rituals can be designed for such activities as work, play, recognition, and management meetings. A ritual can be as simple as the way a manager greets her secretary when she comes in every morning, or the way she sorts her mail and arranges it on her desk, or the fact she always holds staff meetings Monday mornings at 10:00 A.M. The following example illustrates how Wendy's founder, R. David Thomas, performs such rituals.

rituals Detailed methods and procedures faithfully or regularly followed.

> R. David Thomas checks his watch and notices that he is making very good time on this Alabama highway. Thomas is on one of his famous cross-country tours to inspect each Wendy's along the way.
>
> Thomas spends about four days on the road each week, a company ritual that promotes solidarity and encourages industry. The ritual includes stopping at Wendy's restaurants, chatting with customers and employees, and eating his favorite—a cheeseburger with mustard, pickles, and onions. Does he spend much time behind the counter? "No," he says, "if I went back there it would be a

disaster. The crew would be petrified and everything would come to a stop." Yet to one and all, the multimillionaire owner of the third largest restaurant chain says, "I'm a short-order cook," and to his customers he proudly proclaims, "I'm Wendy's dad." [30]

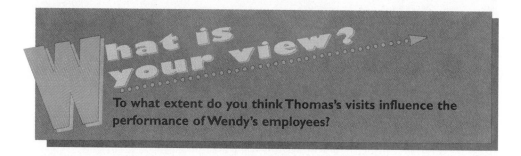

What is your view? ⋯⋯▷

To what extent do you think Thomas's visits influence the performance of Wendy's employees?

How Leaders Develop and Shape Culture

Organizational cultures develop and are shaped in various ways. Founders, for instance, have a strong mark on corporate culture. Ray Kroc, McDonald's late founder, strove for excellence in quality, service, cleanliness, and value. His objectives guided McDonald's as it grew to become the largest restaurant chain in the world. Sam Walton and Mary Kay Ash are other examples of founders whose values permeate their organizations.

Edgar Schein, a leading organizational writer, consultant, and academician from MIT, feels that leaders influence culture by the following:

1. What they pay attention to
2. How they conduct themselves
3. How they respond to crises
4. How they allocate rewards
5. How they hire and fire [31]

Leaders, by their actions, send signals about what they value. And regardless of what may be written in corporate value statements, it is the actions of leaders that send the clear message. For example, it is quite in vogue for an organization today to describe its culture as one that is "totally quality conscious" or "believing in the empowerment of personnel." However, when employees see a key leader contradict the written values, development of the culture is undermined.

A classic example was a microcomputer manufacturer that was featured in several magazines, including *Time*, as one of the rising stars of Silicon Valley. It hired a management consulting firm to meet behind closed doors with the president and vice-president to develop "Falcon Culture." These meetings were referred to as "culture meetings" and later as "values meetings." Eventually, a two-page culture document espousing—among other things—open communication, participative decision making, and ethical behavior toward customers was issued.

The basic problem was that the firm did not practice what it preached. One of the values was "attention to detail is our trademark: our goal is to do it right the first time." However, even though employees at lower levels reported that a ship-

MANAGEMENT APPLICATION AND PRACTICE 3.3

Cultural Clash Leads to Trouble Between French and American Magazines

To understand why global mergers often don't work, look no further than two Manhattan restaurants called Gallagher's and Le Bernardin. Gallagher's is a former speakeasy turned smoky, he-man steak house. Le Bernardin is an expensive French seafood restaurant where black bass stewed with zucchini, tomato, and basil is part of a $65 lunch.

American magazine magnate Peter Diamandis is a regular patron of Gallagher's, while executives of the French magazine empire Hachette dine at Le Bernardin. And when Hachette acquired Diamandis Communication, Inc., both parties got a large case of indigestion. Hachette, publisher of *Elle*, saw the deal as the most promising of media marriages, supported by a dowry of such popular American magazines as *Woman's Day*, *Road & Track*, and *Popular Photography*.

But the relationship presented unexpected problems. Diamandis, a self-made millionaire who grew up in a Greek family in Newark, New Jersey, stayed on as company CEO. However, after several months of private disagreement with French executives over the direction of their newly acquired U.S. company, Diamandis had a tense confrontation with Hachette's vice-chairman, Daniel Filpacchi. Diamandis and his top two aides abruptly left the firm, and Filpacchi took over as CEO the same day. Early the next morning, telephone operators were answering the phones, "Hachette Magazines."

The primary cause of the disagreement reflected major differences in French and American magazine operations. Diamandis, like his American contemporaries in the publishing industry, put a lot of faith in editorial meetings and in market research techniques such as focus groups, in which a group of readers is asked about the magazine. Hachette executives, on the other hand, preferred to make decisions based on their "gut feelings" rather than on meetings or marketing studies. Louis Oliver Gropp, an American editor of *Elle Decor*, a U.S. spin-off, explains, "There is an unmistakable French assurance. . . . Americans are more bureaucratic. Europeans do it in a shorthand, instinctive way."

This was not the first American joint venture for Hachette. The French media giant had previously entered a deal to publish a French version of Time Warner's *Fortune* magazine. Hachette partners wanted to make it spicier, with a stronger emphasis on lifestyles. *Fortune* editors were horrified, and the joint venture collapsed, taking with it plans for a Spanish-language *Fortune* as well.

Source: Patrick M. Meilly, "Mal de Marriage," *Wall Street Journal*, February 15, 1992, pp. A1, A6.

ment of computers was defective, two members of the executive group decided to ship it anyway.

As a result of this type of performance, sales began slipping, and other aspects of the values statement were violated—secret meetings, firings without just cause, and so on. Yet even as the firm declined into bankruptcy and the "culture statement" had become a joke to the employees, top management continued to hold "culture meetings." Today, the firm is no longer in existence.[32]

SUMMARY

Since business organizations operate as open systems, they are especially vulnerable to factors within their environments that can favorably or adversely affect them. An organization's environment consists of those factors or elements that influence the way it functions. Three specific subenvironments constituting an organization's environment are the general, task, and internal environments.

Environmental complexity refers to the number of key factors in the macro and task environments and the extent of similarity of subfactors within a given factor. Environmental change refers to the frequency with which relevant environmental factors change—are the factors stable or dynamic? A four-cell environmental matrix illustrates four possible combinations: simple/stable, complex/stable, simple/dynamic, and complex/dynamic environments. The least difficult managerial challenge is posed by an organization with a simple/stable environment; the most difficult challenge involves a complex/dynamic environment.

General environment factors are broad variables that tend to affect all organizations, including legal/political, economic, social, technological, and international factors. The organization's task environment includes factors that interact *directly* with the specific organization as it operates. Task environment factors include suppliers, regulatory agencies, competitors, customers, and special interest groups.

Organizations cannot afford to be passive about the environments in which they function. Therefore, environmental forecasting is helpful in anticipating the impact of factors affecting future operations. Influencing the environment is a more active approach that typically involves lobbying, public relations efforts, and forms of ownership ranging from joint ventures to mergers and acquisitions.

The use of boundary-spanning roles—organizational positions that maintain contact with external environmental factors—is an important vehicle for anticipating potential effects of the external environment.

An important factor in an organization's internal environment is culture—the set of shared philosophies, values, beliefs, and behavior patterns that give the organization its identity. Rites and rituals are important components of an organization's culture. Founders and leaders influence organizational culture by what they pay attention to, how they conduct themselves, how they respond to crises, how they allocate rewards, and how they hire and fire.

KEY TERMS

organizational environment, 77
general environment, 77
task environment, 77
internal environment, 77
environmental complexity, 78
environmental change, 79
simple/stable environment, 79
complex/stable environment, 79
simple/dynamic environment, 79
complex/dynamic environment, 79
legal/political factors, 81
economic factors, 81
social factors, 81

demographic forces, 81
social forces, 82
technological factors, 82
international factors, 83
coproducer arrangement, 84
environmental forecasting, 91
partnering, or partnership alliances
  (PALs), 92
organizational culture, 95
heroes, 96
rites, 96
rituals, 97

D I S C U S S I O N   Q U E S T I O N S

1. In which cell of the complexity/change environmental matrix would you place each of the following organizations? Why?
   a. Manufacturer of breakfast cereals
   b. Local chain of Laundromats or dry cleaners
   c. University bookstore on campus

2. What are the most significant general environment factors for each of the following organizations? Why?
   a. Godfather's Pizza
   b. HarperCollins College Publishing (books)
   c. Walt Disney theme parks

3. Do you think that there is one *best* type of culture an organization can have? If so, what is it? How could you, as CEO, develop and shape the firm's culture so that it is the most appropriate for the organization's environments?

4. Give some examples of rites or rituals that you are familiar with and that are part of an organization's culture.

PRACTICING MANAGEMENT

3.1

case

Anheuser-Busch Versus Miller

Recently, the Fortune 500 list of manufacturing firms ranked giant beer brewer Anheuser-Busch (AB) no. 49 overall, and in profitability it came in at no. 30 with $767 million. In the beverage companies subcategory, it came in second only to PepsiCo in annual sales. These impressive figures, however, are viewed as just another average year for the top-notch U.S. firm.

AB's best-selling Budweiser brand has been the leading beer in America for a number of years, maintaining the company's reputation as the best in the beer industry since the mid-1950s. The Budweiser product line captured 44.3 percent of industry sales in 1992, including imported beers. But competition from Miller Brewing Company has forced AB to hustle to keep its place in the market.

By examining past production rates of barrels of beer, industry analysts as well as company management can evaluate the trend over the last 50 years. Over this period of time, AB has remained a leader in the industry, gathering larger percentages of the booming beer market.

As you can see from the market share figures in Table 3.3, smaller national breweries have declined in importance, and there has been a shift in the positions of the beer giants. Schlitz, the nation's no. 1 brewer in 1950, never recovered from price discounting and lost its billing as a premium beer when it altered its recipe. Stroh ultimately bought Schlitz and Schaefer in the 1980s. Pabst also fell on hard times and was acquired by S&P. The new entry to the top is Bond, USA's Heilman brand, which has won its position by acquiring smaller regional breweries, including Carling, Lone Star, and Colt .45 malt liquor.

In 1991, the beer industry was faced with a new 8 percent federal excise tax, which increased taxes and prices by about 32 cents per six-pack of beer. The beer industry has also been the target of protest groups such as Mothers Against Drunk Driving (MADD) and antidrug groups campaigning against alcoholism. As a result, the beer market has seen little increase in production rates in recent years. Fewer new products have been marketed by beer companies, the last three being in the late 1970s with the introduction of light beers, in 1986 with bottled "draft" beers, and in 1993 with "ice" beers. Not coincidentally, the first two new beers were introduced by Miller; ice beers originated in Canada.

Philip Morris, the tobacco giant, bought Miller in 1970. Realizing that 30 percent of beer drinkers consume some 80 percent of the nation's beer, Miller embarked on a theme aimed at blue-collar

TABLE 3.3   BEER MARKET SHARE FIGURES

Year	Rank	Brewer	Barrels (%)
1950	1	Schlitz	6.8
	2	Anheuser-Busch	6.5
	3	Pabst	4.1
	4	Falstaff	3.7
	5	Miller	3.1
1960	1	Anheuser-Busch	9.6
	2	Schlitz	6.4
	3	Falstaff	5.5
	4	Pabst	5.0
	5	Schaefer	3.6
1970	1	Anheuser-Busch	18.2
	2	Schlitz	12.4
	3	Pabst	8.0
	4	Coors	5.8
	5	Schaefer	4.6
1980	1	Anheuser-Busch	28.1
	2	Miller	21.0
	3	Pabst	8.5
	4	Schlitz	8.4
	5	Coors	7.8
1992	1	Anheuser-Busch	47.3
	2	Miller	20.5
	3	Coors	10.8
	4	Stroh	7.9
	5	Bond, USA (Heilman)	5.3

workers. The "It's Miller Time" campaign featured ordinary working people knocking off after a hard day for a few beers at a local establishment. Within four years, Miller jumped back into fourth place. In 1976, Miller Lite was introduced with celebrity ad campaigns featuring Bubba Smith, Rodney Dangerfield, Mickey Spillane, and Joe Frazier. In 1992, while Bud had held on to its first-place position, Miller Lite had become America's second favorite beer.

Anheuser-Busch has continued to steadily improve its market share. One AB strength has been its ability to position its beers strongly in the various market segments, with its Natural Light and Busch on the lower end and Michelob and Lowenbrau on the premium end. Unlike most other breweries, AB operates at full capacity and earns almost $15 per barrel in operating profits, compared to under $5 per barrel for Miller and Coors.

The name of the game is, therefore, market share, and AB has no plans to sit by and allow other brewers to whittle away at its share. August Busch III, CEO and grandson of the founder, predicted that AB would hold 50 percent of the market by the mid-1990s. However, the opening of global markets, plus the pressures of government regulation, changing social values in the United States, and rising popularity of local microbreweries, has made this a difficult challenge to meet. As a result, global markets and alliances between foreign companies and countries are more important to an organization's growth strategies. Recognizing this importance, AB acquired a 5 percent stake in China's Tsing Tao brewery in 1993.

In addition to brewing, AB operates several related—and some not-so-related—businesses. Its Container Recovery Corporation collects and recycles aluminum cans; Busch Agricultural Resources processes barley and rice into brewer's malt and engages in commercial rice sales; Metal Container Corporation manufactures cans; Busch Industrial Products is the nation's largest producer of baker's yeast; St. Louis Refrigerator Car Company deals with commercial repair, scheduling, and maintenance of railroad cars, in addition to operating AB's fleet of specially insulated and cushioned railroad cars. AB also owns the St. Louis Cardinals baseball team and major theme parks in Florida, Virginia, and other states.

Sources: *Standard and Poor's Industry Surveys*, December 16, 1993, pp. F29–F31; Patricia Sellers, "Busch Fights to Have It All," *Fortune*, January 15, 1990, pp. 81–88; *Anheuser-Busch Fact Book*, 1989; and Milton Moscowitz, Michael Katz, and Robert Levering, *Everybody's Business* (New York: Harper & Row, 1980), pp. 783–786.

Questions

1. Where would you place a beer manufacturer such as Anheuser-Busch or Miller on the complexity/change matrix? Why?

2. Identify some of the most important general social factors that brewers must be aware of during the 1990s. In what way might these affect the industry?

3. Indicate some of the actions Miller and Anheuser-Busch have taken that reflect favorably on their interacting with their external environment. Discuss.

3.1

learning exercise

Analyzing Environmental Factors

1. Select a major company in the industry of your choice, such as Wal-Mart, Coca Cola, *National Geographic*, or Schwinn. The primary criterion is that it be a company familiar to your classmates.

2. Identify where you would position that company on the complexity/change environmental matrix (Figure 3.3) and be prepared to defend your choice.

3. Assume that you have been appointed by the CEO of the company to present to the board of directors an overview of your findings, including the three most important factors that will affect the firm in the next five years. Write your report.

Managing *in the* Global Environment

Time and space cannot be discarded, nor can we throw off the circumstances that we are citizens of the world.

–HEYWOOD BRAUN

LEARNING OBJECTIVES

After studying the material in this chapter, you should be able to:

▸ **Describe** the perspective of the world as one vast market.

▸ **Discuss** the importance of global operations, including their changing nature.

▸ **Explain** some of the opportunities and risks involved in global operations.

▸ **Describe** the levels at which global operations occur.

▸ **Discuss** how global managers differ in performing management functions, as compared to other managers.

▸ **Explain** some of the problems involved in staffing global operations, such as human resources and personnel training.

▸ **Describe** the major factors leading to managerial effectiveness in global operations.

▸ **Identify** criteria for selecting managers for global operations.

▸ **Explain** the motivational factors influencing a person's decision to accept or reject a foreign assignment.

Rudolph Carter: International Manager

Rudolph Carter, a young electrical engineer in a dead-end job with a small-town utility firm in Louisiana, received an attractive job offer from the SEMA Company, a major sugar company in the tropics. Although the job offered a very substantial increase in salary, good promotional promise, and numerous fringe benefits, it did have certain drawbacks. Carter was well aware of these, having been born, reared, and educated (through his school years) on a tropical plantation where his father had worked until his death five years earlier. He knew that one of the chief difficulties was getting to know the local people—working with them and winning their acceptance.

Carter accepted the job and within two months reported for his first assignment. The first few days on the job proved to be very difficult because of the human relations problems resulting from the chief electrical engineer's sudden return to the States for medical treatment. The electrical plant was being run by the senior electrical engineer, Jose Gonzales, a national who was a graduate of the technical college on the island. Gonzales, about 45 years old, had 16 years' service in the department. The chief engineer had left full written instructions with Gonzales (with a copy for Carter) outlining Carter's job assignments and responsibilities. The instructions left little doubt that Carter was to assume full responsibility and authority for operating the electrical plant.

The beginning of the crop-grinding season was only two weeks away, and Carter found himself in a crush of people rushing around trying to put all the facilities into operating condition. The plant's workforce consisted of about 40 locals, most of whom could understand some English but could not speak it well. This was true even of Gonzales.

Carter saw that Gonzales, a competent engineer, had, in fact, been effectively running the entire operation for many years. Gonzales's word was law as far as the workers were concerned, for they respected him highly. Moreover, Gonzales was keenly ambitious, possessing a strong desire and motivation to become the chief electrical engineer.

Gonzales quickly let Carter know that his presence was resented; he offered no cooperation, advice, or help. The only factor that kept Carter from being totally ineffective was his ability to speak Spanish.

Three days before the grinding season began, the plant manager requested a detailed report on the start-up status of all equipment. Carter requested a report from Gonzales, who replied that everything was "completely OK, and ready to go" and that he had never before prepared such a detailed status report, since the chief engineer had always been content with his word alone.

Carter located in the files the status report submitted by the chief engineer the previous year—with copies to no one. The report went

A major dimension of management today—managing global operations—is illustrated by the opening case. Increasingly, the emphasis in business is on global activities, and those interested in management need to appreciate some of the opportunities and problems associated with management practices throughout the world.

We have entered an age of global competition that is characterized by a one-world market. Although globalization is not new, what is different today is the speed and extent of growth in global markets. This growth has been made possible by advances in technology, communications, and transportation. Successful managers

into considerable detail, listing all electrical items and showing everything in a ready-to-go condition.

Carter wondered whether he should simply duplicate the previous report, showing everything as satisfactory—thus relying on Gonzales's verbal assurance—or take the list to Gonzales and insist on witnessing the testing and operation of all components. Carter did not want to antagonize Gonzales this early in the game, yet he did want to be certain that his first report to the plant manager would be correct and accurate.

He decided to show the report to Gonzales, who was surprised to see it and immediately became defensive. But after Carter emphasized his willingness to accept Gonzales's assurance that all items were ready to go and made it clear that he wanted merely to recheck the equipment listing, Gonzales cooperated graciously.

During the check, the two men found that numerous items had been physically removed from the field and from a few of the installations. Gonzales even pointed out that one major piece of equipment had not checked out to his satisfaction, since his people were having trouble hooking up instruments to test it. Gonzales seemed relieved when Carter suggested that they work together to see if they could find the difficulty.

Carter quickly spotted the difficulty, but instead of pointing it out directly, he guided Gonzales's analysis so that he was able to spot the problem. The workers were impressed that their man had located and corrected the difficulty. Carter could tell that Gonzales realized he had been allowed to save face with his workers.

This was the beginning of a very pleasant and cooperative relationship, with Gonzales slowly and surely recognizing and accepting Carter's position and authority over him.

In order to manage a sugar plantation in the tropics, a U.S. engineer has to get to know the local workers and win their acceptance.

are increasingly treating the world market as their domain. The importance of global markets is making the job of managers—today and in the future—more challenging. This chapter is designed to provide an understanding of some of the factors leading to managerial success in an international assignment.

As a result of the changing environments discussed in Chapter 3, more and more American organizations are engaging in global activities. And an increasing number of Americans will be involved in some aspect of international operations during their work lives. We estimate that up to one-half of all college graduates will work with international activities in one way or another.

The World as One Market

If you are to understand the global dimension of management, you should first understand the history and characteristics of international operations.

Colonialism

mercantilism An economic system based on exporting manufactured products in exchange for gold, silver, and raw materials.

During the period of European colonialism, international operations were merely an extension of domestic operations and were based primarily on the concept of **mercantilism,** under which international enterprises operated almost as agencies of the government, trying to improve the wealth of the home country by increasing its gold and silver. To that end, the cost of production in the home country was to be held low, raw materials were to be imported from the colonies and converted into finished products, and the finished goods were to be exported back to the colonies or to other countries at a substantial profit to the firm and government. In return, the importing countries were to send the industrial nation additional raw materials.

Under this arrangement, personnel sent to other countries were simply the sales agents of domestic producers or were agents sent to exploit the raw materials in the foreign countries. These managers tended to carry their own culture with them and to create a small extension of the mother country as they traveled in other areas of the world. They did not accept the local people as equals. England's experience in India is an excellent example. The East India Company and the British government built roads, railroads, schools, and hospitals and developed agriculture, industry, and commerce. Yet even in 1948, when India won its independence, there were many clubs that the Indians could not enter as either members or guests.

The Trend Toward Nationalism

nationalism A nation's attempt to maintain and protect its natural resources as well as its socioeconomic, cultural, and political systems.

Following World War II, colonialism began to be replaced by **nationalism,** whereby a nation tries to maintain and protect its natural resources as well as its socioeconomic, cultural, and political systems. Formerly colonial nations wanted not only the improved economic position resulting from producing their own finished products from their own raw materials but political and social equality as well. This movement is very evident today in the oil-rich countries of Saudi Arabia, Kuwait, Iraq, and Nigeria.

This trend can also be seen in Latin America, where countries such as Mexico and Venezuela are emerging as industrial competitors. Likewise, South Korea, Singapore, Malaysia, the Philippines, and other Asia-Pacific nations are competing with the United Kingdom, the United States, Canada, and other industrialized nations.

The Growth of Global Corporations

Due to the rise of nationalism and other trends, the form of the international business organization began to change significantly in the 1960s. Replacing the strong, dominant companies that merely extended their national operations into the international arena to exploit raw materials were **multinational corporations (MNCs),** which use investments from owners in several countries to secure resources to produce and sell goods or services in many different countries. They operate, produce, and distribute goods or services to the mutual benefit of the host and home countries.

Now **global corporations,** which operate worldwide, with little regard for national boundaries, are developing. The MNCs treated foreign operations as an extension of their national operations, producing and/or marketing abroad products that were designed and engineered "back home." The nationality of the corporation was clear, as was the chain of command. In the 1980s, however, a wave of mergers, acquisitions, and strategic alliances made the nationality of these global firms difficult to determine and resulted in truly worldwide management of the companies.

These global firms locate their activities (design, finance, production, marketing, and so forth) in the most advantageous place. Their products, wherever they are produced or assembled, are then sold globally—in a standardized form—wherever demand exists. This results in a much greater need for coordination by top management, which in turn results in less autonomy for individual operations.

Alvin Toffler, the noted futurist, summarized this trend by saying, "Many large companies are no longer American—they are nonnational, they are stateless, and this is just the beginning." He points out that as operations across national boundaries increase, we are going to see "truly post-national corporations; and national governments are going to have a harder time regulating these huge organizations."[1]

Obviously, there are many variations of MNCs and global corporations. Some of these giants are making tremendous technological breakthroughs (such as superconductivity and supertrains), selling stock on markets around the globe, and putting people from all nations on the fast track to the top.

Headquarters for ABR of Sweden are located in Switzerland, 85 percent of its sales are outside the home country, 50 percent of its stock is held in other countries, and its managers are Swedish, Swiss, and German.

ICS, a British company, has 78 percent of its sales, 50 percent of its assets, and 16 percent of its stock outside Britain—and 40 percent of its top management are not British but of four other nationalities.

The Coca-Cola Company, with 54 percent of sales and 45 percent of assets outside the United States, has a thoroughly international management group. For example, the CEO is Cuban and the chief financial officer is Egyptian.[2]

Few Americans know that the brand names and the manufacturing facilities for consumer products for sale with RCA and GE brand names are owned by a French company, Thompson SA. Magnavox and Sylvania are owned by Phillips of the Netherlands. Quasar is made by Japan's Matsushita Electric Industries.

Innovations, technology, capital, talent, and marketing flow in many different directions in these global companies. Peter Drucker explains this trend by showing that the primary resources are no longer land, labor, or capital, but knowledge. And "money and information flow around the world, oblivious to its borders."[3]

From its Geneva base, Morgan Stanley Capital International tracks the economic performance of over 2,000 international companies from 21 countries. According to one of its surveys, 7 of the top 14 firms in total sales were U.S. companies: General Motors, Exxon, Ford, IBM, Mobil, GE, and Sears, Roebuck. In addition, 9 of the top 13 most profitable companies—IBM, General Motors, GE, Ford, Exxon, Philip Morris, AT&T, Dow Chemical, and Du Pont—were also U.S. organizations.[4]

multinational corporations (MNCs)
Corporations that use investments from owners in several countries to secure resources and produce and sell goods or services in several countries.

global corporations
Corporations that operate worldwide, with little regard for national boundaries.

Miss Thailand gives out free samples of Palmolive soap.

The Changing Philosophy of Global Operations

It was once thought that successful managers of foreign operations were "shrewd Yankee traders," notorious for their slick salesmanship. Although salesmanship is still important in foreign operations, today's overseas personnel must possess other qualities as well. There are many complicating factors that should be judged carefully by an international company, the government of its "home country," and the host nation. As indicated earlier, one important factor to consider is that the character of international operations has changed from the earlier colonial imperialism to the present philosophy of mutual benefit to the participating countries.

A classic study found that global mangers operate within four systems: technical, political, cultural, and economic. As shown in Figure 4.1, these systems are interrelated, interacting, and—to a certain degree—conflicting.

FIGURE 4.1
Four interrelated systems in which global managers operate.

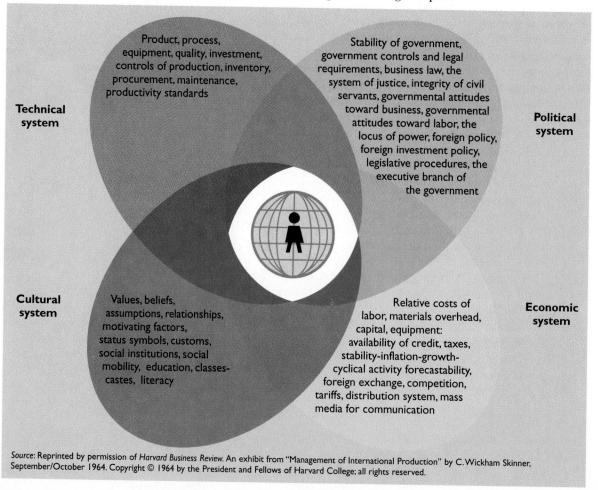

Technical system

Product, process, equipment, quality, investment, controls of production, inventory, procurement, maintenance, productivity standards

Political system

Stability of government, government controls and legal requirements, business law, the system of justice, integrity of civil servants, governmental attitudes toward business, governmental attitudes toward labor, the locus of power, foreign policy, foreign investment policy, legislative procedures, the executive branch of the government

Cultural system

Values, beliefs, assumptions, relationships, motivating factors, status symbols, customs, social institutions, social mobility, education, classes-castes, literacy

Economic system

Relative costs of labor, materials overhead, capital, equipment: availability of credit, taxes, stability-inflation-growth-cyclical activity forecastability, foreign exchange, competition, tariffs, distribution system, mass media for communication

Importance of Global Operations

As Heywood Broun puts it, "Time and space cannot be discarded, nor can we throw off the circumstances that we are citizens of the world." We must realize that when there is fighting in the Middle East, we pay higher prices for gasoline. When television manufacturers in one country developed high-definition TV (HDTV)—a wide-screen set with a display that is as vivid as a 35-millimeter photograph—it revolutionized the industry globally (an excellent example is the introduction of color television in the 1950s and its impact throughout the world). And when there is political unrest, such as there was in South Africa due to apartheid, foreign firms operating there are affected. Some U.S. firms even ceased operations in South Africa entirely.

Similarly, when Japanese managers in one industry outperform those in other countries, Japanese exports will far exceed the exports of those other countries. The resulting trade imbalance gives Japanese companies the ability to buy faltering competitors. In recent years, the Japanese have purchased some of the most prestigious and productive companies in the United States, including MCA Corporation, as well as prime real estate properties, such as San Francisco's Mark Hopkins Hotel.

In other words, as all of these examples have illustrated, what happens in one part of the world has a resounding impact on the rest of the world, directly or indirectly. An effective managerial perspective must consider domestic and global events as integral parts of the whole.

Television is now a global medium. CNN is available to more than 85 million households in 185 countries. It also airs reports from news organizations the world over. The Financial News Network produced segments of *America's Business Today* for Japan's NHK, which in turn produced segments of *Japan's Business Today* for FNN. USA Network's *Counterstrike* was produced jointly by USA's Grosso-Jacobson Productions, Canada's Alliance Entertainment, and France's Altantique Production.[5]

The Growing Global Economy

In 1989, the United States and Canada signed a free trade agreement that is breaking down economic barriers between the two countries. And the United States and Mexico finalized such an agreement in 1993. It is expected that this **North American Free Trade Agreement (NAFTA)** will surpass all other trading blocs and extend from the Arctic to the equator. NAFTA creates a market with 370 million people and a gross national product of $6.8 trillion.[6]

North American Free Trade Agreement (NAFTA) Trade agreement that eliminates or reduces barriers among Canada, Mexico, and the United States.

Meanwhile, drastic and extensive changes are occurring in other parts of the world that affect managers, businesses, and the overall economy of many nations. Eastern Europe—including Russia and the newly formed republics—is going through an economic reformation as a result of recent political restructuring.[7] The Berlin Wall has fallen, and the East and West German economies are being integrated. Western Europe's 12-member European Union (formerly the European Economic Community) is a powerful trading bloc as a result of free trade agreements and removal of trade barriers. This means that U.S. companies and their managers must be adept at competing more often with fierce competitors.

Even the "less developed" Asian nations are no longer that: Japan is an economic powerhouse, and countries such as China and Indonesia are now major players in the global economy. U.S. business managers today are eagerly seeking

Eugene Matthews, in 1992 the only U.S. business consultant in Hanoi.

business opportunities in Vietnam, since the Clinton administration lifted barriers there as well.

Asia's escalating role in global operations was put into perspective by George Baeder, head of the Pacific Rim Consulting Group in Hong Kong, when he said, "Asia is clearly emerging as the largest market in the world."[8] As evidence of this truth, trade among Asian nations is increasingly replacing trade with the slower U.S. economy. And Asian capital—especially from Japan and China—is becoming more important than investment from the West.

Southeast Asian governments are attempting to create a more cohesive market by endorsing a regional free trade area and a broader Asian economic bloc. Following are some examples of expansion in the Pacific Rim:

▶ Li Ka-shing, a Hong Kong multimillionaire, broadcasts television programs— with commercials—to the whole region via his own space satellite.

▶ Japan, South Korea, Hong Kong, and Taiwan are moving some of their older industries into lower-cost Asian lands.

▶ Singapore is spreading its labor-intensive factories into neighboring Indonesia and Malaysia.[9]

Most recently, China has emerged as "the economic powerhouse of the 21st century." Enticed by a 13 percent growth in China's economy, production rates up 23 percent, booming retail sales, and a customer base of 1.17 billion, many U.S. marketers are rapidly moving into China.[10] Procter & Gamble, for example, is already selling a vast array of shampoos and other products in Beijing, Canton, and Shanghai department stores. Johnson & Johnson currently makes Band-Aids in Shanghai and has another factory planned to produce baby shampoo. And Colgate-

Palmolive is building a new toothpaste plant in southern China.[11] U.S. firms are also moving to China's service market. American International Group, Inc., has 140 representatives knocking on Shanghai doors selling insurance. In just eight months, 12,000 policies were sold.[12]

Still, many management problems must be overcome if business efforts such as these are to succeed in China.[13] The primary obstacle is China's decaying infrastructure. Beijing plans to invest billions of dollars (much of it foreign) in major transportation, telecommunications, and power projects. Another problem is the shortage of trained professional and technical personnel, such as accountants. Many Chinese CEOs refuse to delegate authority, and many government regulations stifle foreign managers' efforts to modernize systems and procedures. As these events indicate, political democracy and market economies are emerging everywhere, and the United States must again become competitive in this global market.

The U.S. Role in Global Operations

While there is concern that foreign investors from Britain to Taiwan have brought prime U.S. real estate and large "American" companies such as Smith & Wesson guns, MCA, and Burger King, the United States is still very competitive. For the first time in over two decades, the United States has the most competitive economy in the world.[14] Productivity is at one of its highest levels, labor costs are relatively stable, and quality once again means "world class." The conclusion is that the United States offers a large, stable, and capitalistic market to attract further flows of capital and to continue to build markets abroad. For example, in 1993, AT&T went through a massive top-level reorganization in order "to accelerate AT&T's "globalizations" and move into multimedia products and communications services worldwide.[15]

Exports   According to Ben Wattenberg, a senior fellow at the American Enterprise Institute, it is no accident that the United States still holds the technological lead in aircraft, pharmaceuticals, biotechnology, plastics, synthetic fibers, telecommunications equipment, and petroleum explorations.[16] But the U.S. share of computers, semiconductors, machine tools, and apparel is declining. The last U.S. producer of television sets now assembles them in Mexico.

The large proportion of the United States' gross domestic product (GDP) that results from global activities is another indication of the importance of such activities. International sales by U.S. multinationals in 1991 were $1.2 trillion—20 percent of all corporate revenues. Also, export sales have had a 7.6 percent compound annual rate for the last decade. Foreign operations account for 51 percent of nonelectrical sales, as well as 59 percent of computers and office equipment revenues.[17]

U.S. exports of services are growing even faster than product exports. During the last year alone, service exports have grown at an average rate of 12.6 percent, almost double the 6.7 percent growth in merchandise exports.[18] Also, the U.S. services trade balance is consistently positive, while the merchandise balance is negative.

Another indication of the importance of exports is the large percentage of revenue selected companies receive from international operations. Colgate-Palmolive received 64 percent of its revenues from foreign sales; IBM, 62 percent; Avon Products, 58 percent; Dow Chemical, 52 percent; and Du Pont, 47 percent.[19]

Another success story is the Coca-Cola Company, which commands one-third of Japan's total soft drinks market and 60 percent of its carbonated drinks market.[20]

In 1992, the United States exported $440 billion worth of goods. Its top export markets were Canada, Japan, Mexico, the United Kingdom, Germany, France, Taiwan, South Korea, the Netherlands, and Singapore.[21]

The free enterprise system and the high level of entrepreneurship in the United States are tremendous assets. This spirit—or philosophy—is now being imported by many countries, most recently by former socialist and communist countries.

Britain started the trend by reducing the top tax rate from 90 percent of income to 60 percent and providing tax breaks for small businesses. The result? The number of self-employed people escalated from 1.8 million to 2.6 million in seven years.

Entrepreneurship is also popular in Japan, especially with young people who do not want to tie themselves to larger firms. Although the chances of failure are greater for small companies than for larger ones, many people are willing to take the risk in order to have greater freedom. According to one venture capitalist, some 70,000 to 80,000 new ventures are created in Japan each year.[22]

In addition to entrepreneurship, the United States is also exporting technology by educating students from other countries in U.S. undergraduate and graduate schools. The knowledge they acquire is helping their countries improve their standards of living and making them more competitive in the world's markets. Students from countries in Southeast Asia predominate—especially Taiwan, whose students form the largest international bloc on U.S. campuses.

The export of technology was also seen during the Persian Gulf War and Operation Desert Storm. In 1991, an Austin, Texas, company, Alpha Environmental, Inc., sent 5,000 pounds of microbes (bacteria that feed on hydrocarbons) and a crew of 36 to fight the 460-million-gallon oil slick.[23] And Red Adair and other U.S. firefighting contractors mobilized to try to put out at least 600 oil well fires in Kuwait. U.S. crews and equipment were used in the massive endeavor.[24]

Imports   The importance of global operations to this country is shown by the fact that foreign-owned firms account for 10 percent of total U.S. sales, 7 percent of its manufacturing employment, and 9 percent of its assets.[25] Increasing investment by foreign interests in the United States creates more jobs.

Foreign investment has also added to the diversity of many well-known firms here in the United States:

▶ Alcon Laboratories and Carnation Company are owned by Nestlé, a Swiss firm.

▶ The Great Atlantic & Pacific Tea Company (A&P) is owned by Tengelmann, a German company.

▶ The Exxon building in Rockefeller Center and the Tiffany building on Fifth Avenue have Japanese landlords.

▶ Brooks Brothers Clothiers is a British-owned company.

▶ Shell Oil is owned by Royal Dutch/Shell Group.

▶ Altos Computer Systems is owned by Taiwan-based Acer Group.

Foreign investment works both ways—many U.S. companies have recently acquired larger percentages of foreign companies to increase their global market share. This has been especially true in the automobile industry:

▶ General Motors owns 100 percent of Lotus, 50 percent of Saab, and 38 percent of Isuzu.

▶ Ford Motors owns 100 percent of Jaguar, 75 percent of Aston-Martin, and 25 percent of Mazda.

▶ Chrysler owns 100 percent of Lamborghini and 12 percent of Mitsubishi.[26]

An increasingly common question today is, Do you really know who makes the product you are buying? In 1992, a Mazda 626, built by members of the United Auto Workers in Flat Rock, Michigan, qualified as an American-made auto, but the Ford Crown Victoria did not.[27] Consumers must now decide between buying the Mazda, which qualifies as an American-made auto even though the company is primarily owned by the Japanese, and buying the Crown Victoria, which qualifies as non-American-made despite the fact that Ford is a U.S.-owned firm.

Until 1987, the primary foreign owners of U.S. businesses were Great Britain, Canada, Australia, France, and West Germany. According to the Bureau of Economic Analysis, however, Japan is now the primary owner of companies over which foreign control of operations is exercised. Figure 4.2 illustrates the top foreign investors in the United States.

What are the results of these changes? First, these investors have created millions of new jobs and pay many billions of dollars in wages and benefits. Second, by one measure of productivity, foreign-owned factories averaged sales of $131,430

FIGURE 4.2
Japan: Now the top foreign investor in the United States.

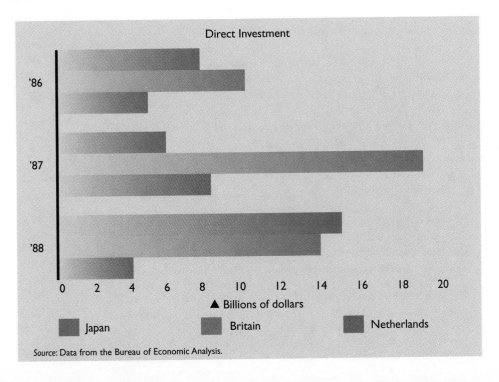

Source: Data from the Bureau of Economic Analysis.

per worker in a recent year, compared to $118,846 for plants owned by U.S. companies.[28] Finally, new management and production methods are being introduced. For example, Toyota Vehicle Processors, Inc., the Toyota subsidiary that supplies Toyota plants in Japan with U.S.-made components, has pioneered in using just-in-time inventory methods to save time and money in supplying these parts.[29]

Japanese companies are becoming a dominant factor in U.S. manufacturing, and in many cases the Japanese managers of these companies, using American workers, are more productive and have higher-quality results than their counterparts in Japan.

Opportunities and Risks in Global Operations

As global operations continue to develop in importance, it is necessary to look at some of the opportunities they offer as well as the risks they pose. Table 4.1 summarizes some of the primary opportunities and risks involved in global operations.

At present, the potential for growth for U.S. managers and entrepreneurs is especially great in Central and Eastern Europe. A recent Opinion Research Corporation study of the 1,500 largest U.S. companies found that 35 percent of them planned to do business in Eastern Europe during the coming year. Among the most popular countries were East Germany (48 percent), Poland (31 percent), and Hungary (27 percent).[30] In 1991, GUM—the largest department store in Russia, located in Moscow's Red Square—prepared to become a joint stock society. Stockholders would include GUM's present employees, the members of the

TABLE 4.1   OPPORTUNITIES AND RISKS IN GLOBAL OPERATIONS

Opportunities and challenges available
1. Expansion of markets
2. Lower wages and labor costs in most countries
3. Availability and lower costs of certain desired natural resources
4. Potential for higher rates of return on investment
5. Strong demand for U.S. goods in many countries
6. Benefit to the receiving country: Investment can provide needed capital, technology, and/or resources

Problems and risks involved
1. Higher possibility of loss of assets by nationalization, war, or other disturbances
2. High potential for loss of earnings, or difficulty or impossibility of retrieving the earnings from investment
3. Favored treatment usually given to local organizations by the host government
4. Rapid change in political systems, often by violent overthrow
5. Lower skill levels of workers in underdeveloped countries
6. Difficulties in maintaining communication and coordination with home office because of distance, time difference, and poor communication systems
7. Unfair competition, particularly from state-subsidized firms
8. Fluctuating foreign exchange rates, possibly resulting in lower profits (or a loss)
9. Cultural differences and misunderstandings

Moscow city council, and others. Many companies in the United States and other countries were interested in collaborating with the new society. [31]

Shoppers parading the malls in GUM's department store in front of the Kremlin in Moscow.

Some of the Opportunities

One of the primary reasons for engaging in global operations is the opportunity for a business to expand its markets. This opportunity is available not only to manufacturers but to service and trade businesses as well. Also, profitability from foreign operations is often significantly higher than in the United States.

Since almost half of Canada's 26.6 million people live within an hour's drive of the U.S. border, and because of high prices in Canadian stores, many U.S. retailers have expanded operations by appealing to customers from north of the border. Canadians make up nearly 40 percent of the customers at a new $55 million mall in Massena, New York. And they account for a quarter of the weekend shoppers in Duluth, Minnesota. A travel agent in Toronto promoted a "shop 'til you drop" bus trip to Erie, Pennsylvania, 200 miles away. Retail analysts estimate that Canadian shoppers spent almost $2 billion in the United States in 1990.[32]

U.S. firms expand their operations overseas because they can obtain a higher rate of return on their investment from foreign operation than from domestic activities. This is due in part to the fact that foreign wages and total labor costs—including employee benefits—are considerably lower than in the United States. Another reason is the availability and lower cost of many natural resources in other countries. As shown in Figure 4.3, high percentages of metals used in producing the F-15 and F-16 jet fighters are imported.

FIGURE 4.3
Imported metals in F-15 and F-16 jet fighters.

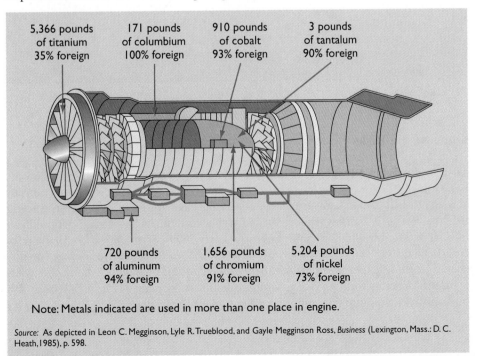

5,366 pounds of titanium 35% foreign

171 pounds of columbium 100% foreign

910 pounds of cobalt 93% foreign

3 pounds of tantalum 90% foreign

720 pounds of aluminum 94% foreign

1,656 pounds of chromium 91% foreign

5,204 pounds of nickel 73% foreign

Note: Metals indicated are used in more than one place in engine.

Source: As depicted in Leon C. Megginson, Lyle R. Trueblood, and Gayle Megginson Ross, *Business* (Lexington, Mass.: D. C. Heath, 1985), p. 598.

Another incentive for U.S. foreign investment is the strong demand for many American goods. The "Made in the U.S.A." label, particularly in the apparel industry, is an important factor in the recent popularity and strong demand in foreign countries for U.S.-made products.[33]

U.S. investments also benefit the host country by providing the needed capital and technology to produce economic development in those countries. In fact, foreign countries, once thought of as "capitalistic exploiters," are now being viewed as a means of assisting the economies of the receiving countries rather than taking from them. The investment firm Chinavest has had considerable success. In 1985, Chinavest started putting U.S. institutional money in China. Headed by Robert Theleen, a former U.S. Army intelligence officer in Vietnam, the group underwrote a $3.8 million entertainment center that opened in Guangzhou in 1994.[34]

Many Third World countries are now buying used equipment from U.S. factories that is obsolete here due to size, environmental problems, or high energy or labor costs. The seller gets rid of unwanted equipment, and the buyer gets a bargain. Often, a manager from the selling firm is thrown into the deal to install and operate the equipment. Consider, for example, the used equipment from an alkali plant that was shipped from Canada to India, where it was put into operation for only $4 million, compared to the $10 million cost of new equipment. Venezuela bought the equipment from a cement plant in Pennsylvania for $30 million, a saving of over $20 million.[35]

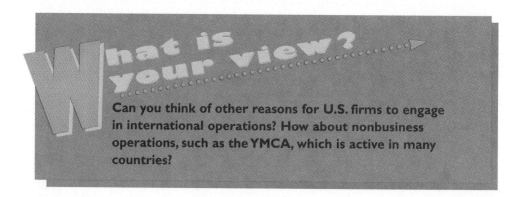

What is your view?

Can you think of other reasons for U.S. firms to engage in international operations? How about nonbusiness operations, such as the YMCA, which is active in many countries?

Some of the Risks

As shown in Table 4.1, several risks and problems are involved in global operations. For example, economic activities around the world may be reducing opportunities abroad. In fact, some American businesses that have gone global are now finding that the domestic market is more attractive because of the increasing competition in international trade. For example, in the early 1990s, Scott Paper Company refocused its resources on its highly rewarding U.S.-based core businesses: quality coated printing paper and personal care and cleansing products. Among the assets Scott sold were its food service business, a paper converting plant in Belgium, and bulk nonwoven manufacturing, including a plant in Germany.[36]

Danger of Expropriation One of the problems of doing business in a foreign environment is the risk of **expropriation,** the seizure of foreign-owned assets by a government. In a highly publicized case, Iran seized the assets of all U.S. banks and many other companies when it seized American embassy personnel in 1979. Similarly, in 1990 when Iraq declared Kuwait a province, it also seized all U.S. assets in Kuwait.

expropriation Seizure of foreign-owned assets by a government.

Differing Attitudes, Customs, and Tastes Often the attitudes and policies of the host government can be difficult to deal with. For example, having the host government as a "partner" is in many cases a condition of entry. Or the host government may require that the foreign firm enter into a joint venture partnership with a local firm. Sending profits back to the firm's home country is usually restricted, sometimes severely so.

Additionally, the host government's foreign policy can be a problem. Many U.S. firms have to contend with the tensions caused by strained Arab-Israeli relations and with the uncertain status of Vietnam.

Weak Infrastructure A nation's infrastructure includes variables such as transportation networks, power and energy supplies, communication services, the quality of educating, and water and sewer systems. A weak infrastructure directly hinders the distribution system for industrial and consumer goods. When Honda Motor Company began a major expansion of U.S. production capacity, it predicted that in five years, 50,000 Ohio-built cars would be exported to Japan. But in 1990—four years into the plan—only 12,000 U.S.-made Accord coupés were sold in Japan. Despite the Japanese craving for flashy imports—especially sports cars—the Accords wouldn't sell. Investigations found that Honda's small sales force—about one-fourth that of Toyota and one-third that of Nissan—was a serious handicap, since Japanese customers expect high-quality service, including regular home visits by auto salespeople.[37]

Staffing Problems Constraints are usually imposed on the staffing of the foreign firm. A frequent pattern for U.S. firms is to start with a cadre of U.S. managerial, professional, and technical people; gradually hire and train native operating personnel; and ultimately turn the entire operation over to local personnel or staff hired from other countries. A few Americans do take up permanent residence and assume monitoring roles. The reason for the host country's insistence on such a pattern is no mystery: It wants jobs for its people.

Local workers may be less productive or not motivated in the fashion U.S. managers expect, or they may present other kinds of management problems. In some cases, the American concepts of regular job attendance, punctuality, adherence to the work schedule, and so on, are simply not a part of the local norms. In other cases, local workforces have had little prior involvement with a money economy and with the idea of accumulating some wealth and consequently are not motivated by monetary compensation.

Furthermore, cultural differences in the environment may be great enough to lead to culture shock. For example, American executives working in Japan have complained that their Japanese counterparts stall endlessly before getting down to business. This obstacle reflects two different value systems with respect to the use of time.

Violence and Terrorism   Unfortunately, violence and terrorism are all to prevalent throughout the world, making international activities and managerial assignments less attractive and more risky. For example, because of kidnappings and killings, no American teachers are left at the once great American University in Beirut, Lebanon. And AT&T temporarily banned all employee travel in 1991 during the Persian Gulf War and continued to limit business travel abroad afterward.[38]

Stages in Global Operations

Global operations are an evolving process for most companies, and the usual evolution is through the five stages shown in Figure 4.4.

First Stage

In the *first stage*, a small company entering the global arena might start exporting on a limited scale. It may not even realize it is exporting, as the good or service may be sold to an intermediary who resells it to foreign buyers. Also, management may export only occasionally, when there are surplus or obsolete items in its inventory.

Second Stage

A company in the *second stage* of global operations actually makes a continuing commitment to seek export business. This step implies that management will make an ongoing effort to sell its products overseas.

Giordana Chiaruttini, deputy director of international trade for the U.S. Small Business Administration, is encouraging small firms to start exporting to Canada as a result of the Free Trade Act signed with Canada in 1989. Top prospects for export

FIGURE 4.4
Stages of involvement in global operations.

Degree of Product Control	Stage	Risk to Your Company
Great	Producing, as well as marketing, your product overseas	Great
	Beginning to actually market your product overseas by maintaining an office or subsidiary in a foreign country	
	Initiating foreign licensing, involving a formal agreement with a foreign country to produce, and/or distribute a product or service	
	Becoming actively involved by making a continuing effort to export	
Little	Doing some exporting on a casual or accidental basis, usually through an intermediary	Little

are medical equipment, building materials, computers and telecommunications equipment, auto parts, and furniture.[39]

Today's most likely exporters are not the manufacturing giants but companies with fewer than 500 employees. The results of a survey by Cognetics, Inc., are shown in Figure 4.5. An example of this stage is Vita-Mix, a small company in Ohio, which began operating at the second level in 1991 when it hired an international sales manager. Now, it sells its high-powered blenders to 20 countries, and faxed orders are pouring in from Norway to Venezuela. Twenty percent of its $15 million sales in 1992 were exports.[40]

Third Stage

The *third stage* of global involvement is reached when a company makes a formal agreement with a foreign firm to produce the product under a licensing arrangement.

Bruce Nevins, the marketer who brought Perrier to the United States, is seeking another fortune by taking licensed Coca-Cola sportswear and accessories to Asia and Latin America. As chairman of Hong Kong's Berleca, Ltd., he is trying to sell the image of a youthful, energetic American lifestyle to people in those areas. He believes that when people buy such products as Coke sweaters, shoes, and handbags, they are really buying "the good things of life"—the American style.[41]

Fourth Stage

In the *fourth stage*, the company sets and maintains a separate sales office or marketing subsidiary in a foreign country. Levi Strauss & Company, the only U.S. apparel maker that has a truly global strategy, is an example of a major corporation in the fourth stage of global operations. In order to maintain control over its brand identity and quality, its foreign operations are carried out by subsidiaries. Strauss has adopted strict ethical guidelines for its foreign contractors.[42]

FIGURE 4.5
Small firms are largest exporters.

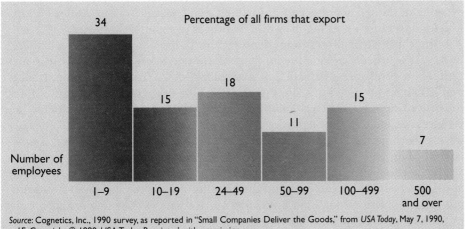

Percentage of all firms that export

Number of employees: 1–9: 34; 10–19: 15; 24–49: 18; 50–99: 11; 100–499: 15; 500 and over: 7

Source: Cognetics, Inc., 1990 survey, as reported in "Small Companies Deliver the Goods," from *USA Today*, May 7, 1990, p. 1E. Copyright © 1990, USA Today. Reprinted with permission.

Bruce Nevins is marketing licensed Coca-Cola sportswear and accessories in Asia and Latin America.

Fifth Stage

Finally, at the *fifth stage*, the company begins to actually produce and sell its products in another country. It can do this by (1) setting up its own production and marketing operates as a subsidiary in the other country, (2) buying an existing company, or (3) forming a joint venture.

An example of the first alternative is Basler Electric Company of Highland, Illinois, which operates two plants in Mexico that make small transformers used as power supplies in consumer electronics.[43]

Crawford & Company, an Atlanta-based independent claims adjuster, is an example of the second alternative. In 1990, it purchased Graham Miller Group, a London insurance adjusting firm with 56 offices in some 40 countries.[44]

joint venture A partnership formed for a specific undertaking, usually sharing the foreign costs of operation, risks, and management with a host government or firm.

The third alternative, a **joint venture,** is a partnership formed for a specific undertaking, usually sharing the foreign costs of operation, risks, and management with a host government or firm. For example, PepsiCo, Bausch & Lomb, Nabisco, and KFC have become household names in China during the last decade. In fact, the official *Beijing Review* has identified them as "among the most profitable joint ventures in China."[45] Although a joint venture is one of the quickest (and cheapest) ways to become involved in global operations, it is also one of the toughest and riskiest. Many joint ventures fail, and one partner can be swallowed up by the other.

Since problems can exist with international business partners—as they can in any partnership—how can one gain the benefits of such an alliance without suffering ill consequences? Figure 4.6 provides suggestions of consultants and business professors specializing in the field.

◆ Pick a compatible partner and take the time to get to know and trust him.

◆ Choose one with complementary products or markets, rather than one who competes head-on with you.

◆ Be patient. Do not rush into a deal, and do not expect immediate results.

◆ Learn all you can about your partner's technology and management, but try not to give away your core secrets. In other words, trust your partner, but ... !

Source: Jeremy Main, "Making Global Alliances Work," Fortune, December 17, 1990, p. 122.

FIGURE 4.6
How to choose a joint venture partner.

Management Functions Performed by Global Managers

The successful practice of global management is based on the universality of management concept discussed in Chapter 1; that is, management tends to be universal, since many of its activities, principles, and functions are the same anywhere, anytime, in any type of organization, and in any country. Thus, management is management whether it is performed in Minneapolis, Montreal, Madrid, or Moscow.

Differences do exist, however, in the way management functions are carried out and in the principles applied to given situations. The extent of these differences varies with the country, organization, and ability of the personnel involved. Managerial resources and skills, philosophies and values, operating environments, and differing cultural backgrounds may cause variations in the performance of these functions. Yet the functions managers perform, as well as the principles on which they are based, are universal.

Planning

International managers, like their domestic counterparts, engage in two types of planning, namely strategic, or long-term, and operational, or tactical. As discussed in Chapter 7, strategic planning significantly affects what an organization does and how it does it, whereas operational planning deals with management's day-to-day, ongoing operations.

Strategic Planning In global operations, strategic planning may involve one or more of the firm's basic strategies for achieving organizational objectives, such as its role in various environmental societies, its choice of nations in which to operate, the mix of goods or services to provide, its competitive positioning in each of its markets, the formulation of long-term objectives and how to achieve them, and the allocation of resources among units in the various countries.

South Korea's powerful business group once produced everything from sausages to ships. More recently, efforts are being made to reduce the technological gap between Korea and Japan. Samsung, for example, no longer emphasizes growth over quality. According to Lee Byung-Chull, a Samsung executive, the objective is to pare down the Samsung empire and concentrate on its core business of machinery, electronics, and chemicals. This change in strategy is necessary because, Lee explains, "If we don't move into more capital- and technology-intensive industries, our very survival will be at stake."[46]

Operational Planning   While strategic planning is aimed toward effectiveness, operational decisions are made to reach efficiency. *Effectiveness* is the ability to "do the right things," or to get important things accomplished; *efficiency* is the ability to "get things done correctly," or to improve the ratio of output to input. Operational planning is thus aimed at the efficient delivery of the company's goods and services to the marketplace. It involves planning for more routine activities, such as production and marketing of goods and services, personnel management, plant operations, organizational charts, management information systems, sales meetings, and advertising campaigns.

Operational planning, then, involves developing highly detailed plans, procedures, methods, and budgets for the global organization and its subsidiaries. In global operations, these plans are usually from one to two years—subject to very rapid modification as the situation dictates. They are used as a framework for day-to-day operations in the different countries. They are also used as a basis for monitoring, evaluating, and controlling operations.

An example of operational planning is that done by Tokyo retailer Ito-Yokado Company, which for over 20 years has operated 7-Eleven franchises in Japan. While the franchisor, Southland Corporation, and its U.S. 7-Eleven stores have filed for bankruptcy, Ito-Yokado, Japan's most profitable retailer, has exceeded all expectations. This has been possible due to its high standards of operation. In fact, president Masatoshi Ito, whose family owns part of Ito-Yokado, even checks for dust during store inspections. The Japanese parent has copious, detailed procedure manuals from which employees are taught everything from how to greet customers to how to persuade them to have their film developed at 7-Eleven. A key ingredient of the operating procedures is the computerized inventory control system used in the Japanese stores, which allows managers to track sales of goods and place orders almost instantaneously. According to Barclays de Zoete Wedd Securities Ltd. (Japan), the 7-Elevens in Hawaii do not have computerized systems and still generate about the same level of sales, but must carry four times the inventory of the Japanese stores.[47]

Organizing

Global business operations usually take one of three forms: exporting, contractual agreements with foreign entities, or direct investment. Only the last of these requires a major modification of the corporation's structure.

Organizing to Facilitate and Exporting Strategy   Firms implementing a strategy of direct exporting typically use one of three organizational forms: a part of existing departments, a separate export department, or an export sales subsidiary.

Having exporting activities provided by the same groups performing the domestic functions, such as advertising, finance, accounting, and shipping, is the simplest form because it uses existing resources and personnel.

As export sales and profits increase, the company will probably expand to a separate export department. Usually, all the functional areas and activities found in domestic sales divisions are found in these units. The divisions are usually organized on a product or geographic basis.

Finally, export sales subsidiaries may be set up instead of a sales division. With headquarters either in the United States or abroad, these subsidiaries are usually independently incorporated, wholly owned subsidiaries of the parent company. The subsidiary president is usually a corporate vice-president, with directors or vice-presidents for each of the geographic areas or product groups. The primary distinction between sales subsidiaries and the traditional international subsidiaries is that the former do not involve manufacturing. Instead, they buy products from the parent company or from others for export.

Organizing for Direct Foreign Operations   As indicated earlier in the chapter, when a company makes a direct foreign investment by establishing a branch or subsidiary abroad, its assets and future earnings are put at risk. To reduce that risk, there must be effective and efficient coordination and control of global activities.

One of the most important changes in global operations since World War II has been the growth of international operating divisions, which replaced export sales divisions. This change represented a fundamental philosophical and strategic shift, for foreign countries are now viewed as locations for expanding all business activities rather than merely as markets for U.S. exports. Now, activities such as research, product design, manufacturing, warehousing, and services are conducted abroad in order to enhance the firm's competitive position. If economically justifiable, this is the organizational structure now used by most progressive U.S. and foreign companies.

As the international division replaced the export division, the organizational structure of the home office usually took the form of an international headquarters company. This arrangement ended the pretense that global business was merely an offshoot of domestic operations. Instead, management said that global business was to be handled as an operationally independent and autonomous enterprise, with its own factories, warehouses, sales offices, and employees scattered among the different countries.

In 1991, Sony Corporation announced the formation of a new U.S.-based company, Sony Software Corporation, with responsibility for managing its movie and record units, thereby bringing its vast entertainment operations under one corporate umbrella. According to Sony's CEO, Norio Ohga, "Uniting our software companies in one structure will enhance our worldwide initiative." Sony Software includes Sony Music Entertainment (formerly CBS Records) and Sony Pictures Entertainment Inc. (formerly Columbia Pictures).

Sony Software was set up to boost sales of Sony's home electronics hardware. The new compact has developed and coordinated computer-related software businesses in an effort to create new products merging electronics and entertainment. In 1993, Sony Music introduced a series of remastered "classic compact discs." These "Legacy MasterSound" series, plated with 24-karat gold, were supposed to reproduce music with unprecedented accuracy and clarity. Sony and Sony Music have established another company to develop and market hardware and software for a new 32-bit video system for home use. Sony's U.S. investment seems to be paying off.[48]

Leading

The leading function is one of the most affected by global operations, as it depends on the manager's ability to adapt to often extreme cultural differences. Thus, companies trying to satisfy the growing needs of global consumers can gain an edge if they are willing to cross not only national boundaries, but also cultural ones.[49]

culture The knowledge, beliefs, art, morals, laws, customs, and other capacities and habits acquired by a person as a member of a society.

How Culture Affects Leading   **Culture** is defined as the knowledge, beliefs, art, morals, laws, customs, and other capacities and habits acquired by a person as a member of a society. People who are born—and learn—in a given cultural system will, therefore, have a behavioral pattern different from that of people who grow up in other societies. The Practicing Manager profile of Petra Dziamski illustrates this principle.

If a manager cannot learn to adjust to another culture, the cultural differences, or cultural conflict, may lead to ineffective management of international operations.

Causes and Effects of Cultural Conflicts   When managers enter a different cultural system, they frequently encounter human traits and behavior that are alien to their own. These differences have the potential to result in conflict. The different cultural environment typically causes frustration and insecurity until the manager becomes accustomed to it. For example, the Japanese perceive time very differently from the way Americans do. To them, months and years may be required to make important decisions. Americans interpret this as lack of interest, when in actuality it is not.

French managers are much more likely than their American counterparts to use space as a network of influence. Whereas American managers cherish their private corner office, French managers will normally be found in the center of their subordinates' work areas, where these managers feel they can exert control.

In the Middle East and Latin America, the American businessperson feels overcrowded. People get uncomfortably close, violate our sense of personal space, and are more physical with each other. Unless the businessperson reciprocates, he or she is perceived as cold and distant.

In India, it is considered highly improper to discuss business in the home on social occasions. To invite someone to one's home to further a business relationship violates sacred hospitality rules.[50]

ethnocentrism The tendency to believe and act on the belief that one's own cultural value system is superior to others.

Ethnocentrism.   One of the primary causes of cultural conflict is **ethnocentrism,** the tendency to believe and act on the belief that one's own cultural value system is superior to all others. If an overseas executive persists in such self-centered views in dealing with people in a new culture, his or her behavior will probably be resented by the host country and may lead to rejection or conflict. The cure for this problem may be to avoid sending that type of individual overseas, or to take additional time and training to acquaint the manager with local customs and practices before he or she is assigned overseas.

A Ford Foundation resident adviser on management development in Pakistan would sharpen half a dozen pencils to use at his desk. He noticed that his Pakistani counterparts used only one pencil and would ring for the "peon" to come and sharpen it. The adviser considered this quite inefficient until he learned that his failure to use the peon "broke the rice bowl" of seven people. That is, if the peon were fired, he and six family members would go hungry. The adviser learned to use the services of the peon.

When asked if management is universal, Petra Dziamski of Siemens Corporation says, "Management is in the process of becoming universal—it is, however, not there yet."

Dziamski (the D is silent) moved to the United States in 1990 to assume the position of manager of methods and training for the Corporate Purchasing, North America, Division of the German-based Siemens Corporation. Her responsibilities at the Iselin, New Jersey, office included corporate-level coordination of U.S. domestic purchasing methods, information systems, and training. Finally, Dziamski acted as a liaison between her American and German constituents in order to "enhance the effectiveness of Siemens's worldwide purchasing activities."

Dziamski rose rapidly in the corporate infrastructure at Siemens. From 1983 until 1985, she was in the management training program. For three years following, she served as an agent in the Methods and Training Department of Corporate Purchasing in Munich. During that period, she also studies electronics as Munich's Technical University. After completing that program, Dziamski was promoted to manager of the international reporting system. A year later, she was promoted again to manager of the "Compact Disc Read Only Memory" project of the Production and Logistics Division.

One of the tenets of Siemens's corporate philosophy is to have well-rounded, international managers. Consequently, being an international operation, Siemens encourages employees to transfer to different countries in order to realize this philosophy. When the opportunity arose for Dziamski to be transferred abroad, she jumped at the chance, for as she explains, "I've always wanted to live and work in another country. I thought that immersing in another lifestyle would be both a personal and professional learning experience. I also thought that showing an ability and a willingness to work abroad would speed up my career."

In early 1990, Siemens offered Dziamski two choices: Europe or the United States. She says she chose the United States for several reasons: "Working in a similar position within Europe would not have been as great a challenge, as it was so close to Germany. First, there would be no language problem because I've spoken English since I was 11 years old. Second, I had studied U.S. history and

PETRA DZIAMSKI OF SIEMENS CORPORATION

geography, and its culture fascinated me." More specifically, though, Dziamski states that "the United States is one of the few countries where women are more accepted in managerial positions."

The department Dziamski managed consisted of ten employees, four of whom she describes as working "for/with me." Siemens exercises what Dziamski calls "a philosophy of low hierarchy"—a horizontal rather than vertical chain of command. Therefore, the employees who worked with and for her reported directly to the director of Corporate Purchasing, Bernard Nagel—not to her.

The move to management in the United States, was nonetheless, an adjustment for Dziamski. She considered the practice of calling co-workers and even her boss by their first names a welcome change. However, she found it irritating that she reported only to her immediate supervisor and not to the vice-president of Corporate Logistics in Germany, as she had before the move. In addition, Dziamski asserts, "I was not able to be as outspoken as I was in Germany—the Americans whom I worked with were very polite and took great pains to describe in detail what they wanted and what they could offer."

Dziamski's responses to the question of what she liked and disliked about her position in the United States reflect her feelings about the universality of management. "I like traveling, but what I particularly enjoy," she says, "is encouraging our employees to fight for pragmatic 'purchasing.'" What she dislikes most is "having to deal with unmotivated employees within our company."

Dziamski believes that management transcends cultural and geographic boundaries: "In order for a manager to be successful, that person must be willing to be effective; that is, the manager must put forth a great deal of effort to achieve results." She explains that the atmosphere within the company must be supportive of management. Dziamski also emphasizes that in order to maintain good management "companies have to pay well." Some things truly are universal.

In early 1993, Dziamski returned to Germany, where she is now commercial sales manager with the Siemens Transportation Systems Division in Nuremberg.

Source: Conversations with and correspondence from Petra Dziamski.

A manager's inability to cope emotionally and psychologically with the problems posed by cultural differences may interrupt harmonious relationships between the manager and the local personnel. Thus, the manger may tend to rely on rigid rules and regulations to ensure control over local operations. The inability of the manager to cope with the conflicts may also result in an emotional or irrational response to the local personnel. This may be the beginning of a vicious circle of irrational responses.

Production suddenly started falling behind schedule at an American-controlled plant in Bangladesh. The newly arrived manager noticed that the workers were listless and apparently uninterested in their work. He tried speeding up the operations, which resulted in a strike. Then he found out that it was the religious holiday Ramadan, during which the Muslims fast from before dawn until after dark.

Recall the opening case in which Rudolph Carter avoided falling into this type of trap. Instead, his managerial philosophy of respecting the local personnel permitted him to adjust to the new environment that was similar to the one in which he had grown up.

Miscommunication.   A major factor contributing to cultural conflict is miscommunication. Communication, as shown in Chapter 10, is the transfer of meaning from one individual to another, and many barriers filter the sender's meaning. Difference in language, customs, feelings, and cultures may cause miscommunication when managing people of a culture different from your own. The entire complex of human life, with its individual variations, offers opportunities for misunderstandings. Language, however, is the most serious source of miscommunication because it is the means of communication most often used. In addition to a lack of knowledge of the language itself, the manager's intonation, pronunciation, and facial expressions may also cause misunderstanding. Carter's knowledge of Spanish led to rapport with Gonzales, which ultimately led to the workers accepting Carter.

An American executive may find many English-speaking people in the culture in which he or she operates, but may also find that relying on them still leads to problems. First, nationals are often unfavorably impressed when a foreign manager makes no attempt to learn their language. Hence, citizens of the host country are less receptive to the manager's ideas. Second, the chances of miscommunication may be greater if the executive does not learn the new language, because the capacity of the nationals to understand English may be limited. Dealing with translators may also create problems, as shown in MAP 4.1.

Evaluating and Controlling

As mentioned throughout this text, planning and controlling are inseparably intertwined. Thus, when planning for operations, managers should build into the process procedures for evaluating and controlling those plans, as global strategic management processes are interrelated.

Ordinarily, controlling is an important function for global managers. Their companies will use some form of contingency planning; that is, strategists consider several scenarios in the foreign environment, together with the anticipated strengths and weaknesses of each scenario and their effect on the domestic company and its international operations. The managers then formulate several

MANAGEMENT APPLICATION AND PRACTICE 4.1

"How's That Again?"

Following are some examples of miscommunications in business situations that illustrate the difficulty in achieving an effective translation:

▶ Macy's, of New York, ran the following headline in an advertisement for cosmetics: "Macy's Introduces the Fabulous Fall Faces by PUPA." The problem was that the Polish translation of *pupa* means "buttocks" or "behind."

▶ An American manufacturer of a touch-toe industrial drill included an instruction manual containing a sentence that, when translated into Italian, reads, "The dentist takes off his shoe and sock and presses the drill with his toe."

▶ Another American manufacturer encountered the same problem when it discovered that in Arabic its hydraulic ram was translated as a "water goat."

▶ A PepsiCo campaign carried the slogan "Come alive with Pepsi." In Chinese, however, this meant, "Pepsi brings your ancestors back from the grave."

---

strategies and implementation guidelines for each of the strategies, and exercise control to see that they are implemented. In the future, the strategy that most nearly fits the actual environmental conditions, as developed in the earlier strategy, will be put into effect. The other contingency plans will be retained for later use if necessary.

Finally, some organizational procedures should be set up for periodically evaluating the global operations and bringing them under control if results are unsatisfactory. Evaluation and control are accomplished through feedback to determine whether or not the strategy is working.

Staffing Global Operations

The three primary sources of human resources for global operations include current employees who have been educated and trained and who have gained experience in the firm's domestic operations; individuals who have received their education, training, and experience in the host country; and citizens of a country other than the home country or the country of operation.

As illustrated in Figure 4.7, it can be generalized that top management comes from the parent firm, middle and lower management comes from nationals of the host country and of third countries, and other employees are nationals of the host country. It is important to note, however, that no specific figures are available for the proportionate degree of use of these three types of employees.

Staffing with Employees from the Firm's Home Country

The first alternative—staffing with people from the home country—is desirable because it protects the parent company's interests. Yet it has limitations. The number and quality of capable managers that can be trained in this way are limited,

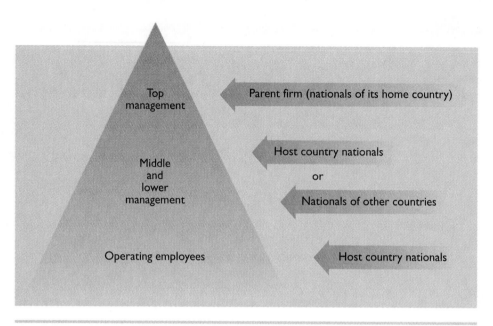

FIGURE 4.7
Sources of human resources for global operations.

because the training is costly and because many countries have legislation requiring employment of nationals.

Selecting employees for global operations is more difficult than selecting them for domestic operations. Those selected must have not only professional skills but also traits that will help them understand the complex world in which they must operate. Ideally, they should be able to move from one culture to another without much difficulty.

Employees going on international assignments need predeparture training that exposes them to the customs, language, and living conditions of the country in which their operations will be situated. This training can be done by the company itself, in one of the home country's government training centers for overseas diplomatic personnel, or by an educational institution.

Many colleges and universities have instituted curricula in global business. These usually include courses in the individual's specialized functional area, other business courses, at least two foreign languages, cultural anthropology, sociology, international economics, geography, and others—with special emphasis on the "cultural" courses.

But the responsibility for training managers for overseas assignments rests with the company itself. Apparently, the more progressive companies are now accepting the responsibility of preparing capable and experienced executives ready to tackle overseas assignments.

For example, Colgate-Palmolive started a program in 1987 to attempt to groom recent college graduates for globe-hopping careers. Each year it trains about 15 recent college graduates—call *globalites*—for 15 to 24 months prior to multiple overseas job stints. The program has become such a powerful recruiting tool that "more than 15,000 people vie for the 15 slots each year."[51]

Staffing with Host Country Nationals

Willingly or otherwise, most firms today employ nationals of the host country to fill vacancies. This source is limited, especially in relatively undeveloped countries, where the supply of capable personnel is small.

Referring again to the opening case, notice that top personnel had to come from outside the country because the skills required were not available locally. Yet Gonzales aspired to the chief engineer's position and thought he was in line for it.

When local nationals are used, it is because (1) it is less costly; (2) it is good politics, helping the local employment situation; (3) it may facilitate cultural understanding between the company's home country and local personnel; and (4) their employment creates purchasing power. Also, local law often requires that nationals be employed to fill the majority of the managerial positions and all the supervisory positions. Mexico, for example, has a law requiring that 90 percent of the employees of foreign firms' operations in Mexico be Mexican citizens.

This source of supply also has some drawbacks. As mentioned earlier, a shortage of qualified personnel may exist in some countries. National pride may deter qualified local managerial and technical personnel from working for a foreign company if the top positions are reserved for employees from the home country. In some countries, a strong paternalistic urge limits layoffs and dismissals of employees. Brazil had a law requiring that all employees with ten years' seniority be granted lifetime employment. Both foreign and domestic firms got around this by firing employees in their tenth year and then rehiring them later.

Once local nationals are hired, they must be prepared to work for the foreign firm. One persistent problem is the amount to pay these employees. In general, it is necessary to determine a wage that is consistent with what the foreigners are making and yet not too far out of line with local earnings. A significant personnel problem in underdeveloped countries is the major social and psychological adjustments required when a foreign firm draws local people from a rural setting and introduces them to the Western economic system.

Staffing with Nationals from Other Countries

The practice of employing nationals of countries other than the home or host country has been used extensively since World War II. The breakup of large colonial empires such as those of Great Britain, France, Belgium, Germany, and the Netherlands has resulted in freeing many qualified nationals of those countries who have been engaged in international operations. Their extensive experience makes them very attractive to both the host nations and foreign firms. Other reasons for hiring nationals of other countries are their fluency in languages and their ability to move from one culture to another with a minimum of disruption.

Factors Leading to Managerial Success in Global Operations

Managers operating in global assignments must be able to adjust to the different culture and customs of the country in which they are working. Therefore, it is highly desirable to be able to predict whether a manager is likely to succeed in such assignments.

Criteria for Selecting Global Managers

When considering hiring a manager, certain background information can be used to forecast his or her effectiveness in operating in another culture.

First, managers must have demonstrated *professional competence* in their chosen field to be successful in global business activities. The engineer must be a good engineer, the chemist a good chemist, and the manager must understand and know how to use the body of knowledge that constitutes the science of management.

Second, managers must possess an *adventurous attitude*, an *optimistic outlook*, a *broad liberal education*, a mind that is more attuned to cultural similarities than differences, and a personal philosophy that accepts value differences in other people. Therefore, they should conceive of people, places, cultures, and so forth, as being similar rather than different. Dealing with similarities leads to cooperation among people, whereas an overemphasis on differences leads to competition and ultimately to conflict. A recent Dunhill Personnel Systems study found that the most important factor "in becoming a good global manager is understanding a foreign culture."[52]

Third, people are needed who have a history of *success in various activities* other than their professional activities. In other words, a person who has been successful in sports, or in extracurricular, church, or social activities, has a greater chance for success in international operations than one who has not.

Fourth, people with *greater self-reliance* have a greater chance of success than those who depend on others; managers in another culture are on their own more than those engaged in domestic activities.

Fifth, *experience in overseas assignments*, such as military, diplomatic corps, Peace Corps, or similar activities, is considered advantageous. As many companies' global ambitions grow, many fast-track executives now see foreign assignments as necessary for career advancement.[53]

One of the basic problems encountered in the intercultural movement is learning to trust others, but probably more important is the *ability to have others trust you*. This is best accomplished through your actions. An overgeneralization is that one's perception of and sensitivity to the values found in another's culture are important to success as an international manager.

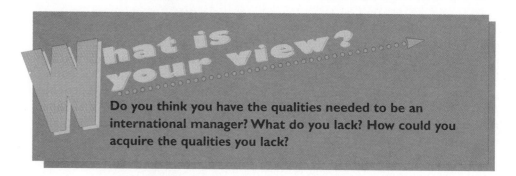

What is your view?

Do you think you have the qualities needed to be an international manager? What do you lack? How could you acquire the qualities you lack?

Different Perceptions of Foreign Assignments

Employees engaged in global operations may be viewed as either heroes or martyrs. In the eyes of their colleagues at home, they are heroes living romantic lives in faraway places. To themselves, they may also be heroes who help to better people's standard of living. But at the same time, they may see themselves as martyrs, since they may be ill equipped to deal with cross-cultural operations. An individual accustomed to living in a given cultural setting (consisting of customs, norms, value judgments, language, and other factors) may find it difficult to become comfortable with a new pattern of life. Figure 4.8 presents some reasons for accepting and rejecting foreign assignments.

Motives for Accepting Foreign Assignments   An individual may feel some frustration and insecurity and may make some personal sacrifices, but there is much opportunity to enjoy "the good life" while experiencing another culture in depth. Research has shown that the usual motives for choosing foreign assignments are greater administrative responsibility, experience for more rapid promotion, personal satisfaction from living abroad (U.S. executives overseas attained considerably more job satisfaction than their domestic counterparts), higher net income, desire for adventure, less competition from other personnel, and a chance to widen one's horizons.

Motives for Rejecting Foreign Assignments   The Conference Board found in a recent survey of 112 U.S. and 18 foreign multinational companies that only about one out of four U.S. managers is eager for foreign duty.[54] The usual reasons for refusing foreign assignments are children of school age whom you would like to have educated in their own country, a spouse's reluctance to live abroad, and fear of severing connections for career opportunities at home. Change of habit and routine is also a negative factor.

An increasingly important factor in refusing a foreign assignment is the social and political unrest in many foreign countries. For instance, it is more difficult for

FIGURE 4.8
Reasons for accepting or rejecting foreign assignments.

Reasons for accepting

Chance for greater authority and responsibility

Less competition from others in the organization

Source of greater sense of achievement and personal satisfaction

High after-tax income

Chance for travel and adventure

Chance for broadening experience

Reasons for rejecting

Fear that children will not receive a good education

Spouse's reluctance to live abroad

Fear of losing career opportunities in own country

Reluctance to change customs

Fear of or inability to learn another language

Reluctance to leave familiar surroundings, entertainment, and recreational opportunities

energy companies to get employees to go to Iran or Saudi Arabia today than it was just a few years ago.

Returning to the organization's home base after the overseas tour is completed creates another problem. Loyalties and positions have been realigned while the employee was away. Unfortunately, "out of sight, out of mind" is truer for those overseas than "absence makes the heart grow fonder."

On balance, though, the benefits of accepting an overseas assignment tend to outweigh the disadvantages. And, in general, U.S. managers do not mind jobs abroad if "the assignment is for three to five years and there is an end in sight."[55]

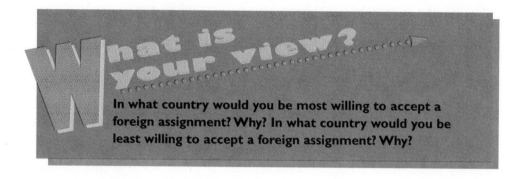

What is your view?

In what country would you be most willing to accept a foreign assignment? Why? In what country would you be least willing to accept a foreign assignment? Why?

SUMMARY

The interest in global business is mushrooming, and those interested in management must understand some other opportunities and problems involved in today's global economy.

The nature of global operations is changing. New economic opportunities being created in Eastern Europe, the maturing of the European Union, the passage of NAFTA, and exploding economic developments in Pacific Rim countries are creating new trading opportunities. The multinational corporations are becoming truly global firms, with products, capital, and personnel moving in many directions.

Global operations are very important to the United States as a whole, to individual firms, and to you as a future manager. Some of the reasons U.S. firms seek overseas opportunities are (1) expansion of markets, (2) the possibility of higher return on investment, (3) lower wages and labor costs, (4) availability and lower cost of some natural resources, (5) the enthusiastic demand for American goods abroad, and (6) the realization that U.S. investments can provide needed capital and technology to produce development and growth in host countries.

Foreign direct investment in the United States is surpassing U.S. investment abroad, so that many American firms now have a foreign accent. The United States is making a distinct contribution to international operations by exporting entrepreneurship and technology—even to socialist countries.

But there are problems and risks involved. Recent economic conditions and political activities—such as worldwide recession and new trade restrictions—may be reducing opportunities. Also to be considered are (1) the danger of expropriation; (2) differing attitudes, customs, and policies; (3) staffing problems; and (4) violence and terrorism.

The stages of global operations are (1) engaging in casual exporting, (2) becoming actively involved in exporting, (3) granting foreign licenses, (4) maintaining an office or subsidiary in another country, and (5) producing and marketing in another country.

Global operations are based on the concept that management principles are universal and can be applied effectively in any country; however, the global manager must in some cases perform the managerial functions differently.

Ethnocentrism, inadequate consideration of local customs, different perceptions, miscommunication, and cultural attitudes can lead to cultural conflicts.

Global operations may be staffed with (1) nationals of the home country, although there is a limited number of such capable people, and it is very costly to maintain them overseas; (2) nationals of the host country, although again, the supply of capable people is limited, and it is often difficult to discipline or terminate them; and (3) nationals of third countries who have become available following the breakup of the English, French, Dutch, German, and Belgian colonial empires.

Some criteria to look for when selecting managers to operate in another culture are (1) professional competence, (2) an optimistic outlook, (3) success in various activities in addition to professional tasks, (4) self-reliance, (5) the ability to trust others and gain their trust, and (6) previous overseas experience in some capacity, such as serving in the Peace Corps, diplomatic corps, or military.

KEY TERMS

mercantilism, 108
nationalism, 108
multinational corporations (MNCs), 109
global corporations, 109
North American Free Trade Agreement
(NAFTA), 111

expropriation, 119
joint venture, 122
culture, 126
ethnocentrism, 126

DISCUSSION QUESTIONS

1. Do you agree with the authors' projections of the future trend of global business and its management? Explain.

2. Do you think the universality of management principle is valid in global operations? If so, how do you explain the divergence of management practices in different cultures?

3. Why is the study of cultural variables important for cross-cultural business operations?

4. What are some problems global firms face when trying to staff overseas operations with their own nationals?

5. What are some of the problems associated with staffing with local and foreign nationals in a global firm?

6. Do you think the global economy is really here? Explain.

PRACTICING MANAGEMENT

4.1 case

To Move or Not to Move?

John S. Chamberlin, chairman and chief executive officer of Lenox, Inc., of Lawrenceville, New Jersey, was asked what was the hardest decision he ever made as a manager. He answered that it was one he made as an executive with General Electric. Although the decision had to be approved by GE's board, he had to make a recommendation and defend it.

GE had been manufacturing clock radios and table radios in Utica, New York, for several years. The workers and townspeople considered the GE operations a permanent fixture. But the company had started to lose its market share because its AM-FM clock radios were selling for $29.95 each, while a comparable Japanese model sold for about $9.95.

Based on tough economic realities, Chamberlin had two alternatives: to remain in Utica or to move operations to Singapore. There were about 2,000 workers employed in Utica. Labor costs for the U.S. workers were about $5.00 an hour, while the cost for workers in Singapore would be about 50 cents an hour. If the operation left Utica, the workers would have to be laid off, since there was nowhere in the company to transfer them.

Source: Based on "My Toughest Business Decision Was . . . ," *Wall Street Journal*, February 14, 1983, p. 16.

Questions

1. What do you think Chamberlin recommended?

2. Can you think of any alternatives besides the two mentioned? Discuss them.

4.2 case

Move to Tokyo?

Top management at Global Aerospace Products & Systems, Inc. (GAPS) decided on a join venture in Japan to manufacture their commercial jet aircraft, developed by Sonic Aircraft Company (SAC), a subsidiary of GAPS. Factors affecting this corporate decision included the following:

1. A joint venture with a Japanese partner would be a practical method of entering the tightly controlled Japanese market.

2. A joint venture would give GAPS the benefit of comparatively low Japanese manufacturing costs while maintaining the high quality level needed to ensure flight safety of the SAC aircraft.

3. A joint venture would give GAPS more control than a licensing agreement would.

GAPS shares the concern of other U.S. aerospace companies regarding Japanese efforts to enter the aerospace business. The Japanese are "getting ready to learn how to develop commercial aircraft," says William Purple, head of Allied's big Bendix aerospace unit. If the next major Japanese industrial thrust is in aerospace, it would "trigger aerospace companies like us to want to joint venture with them," he adds. A Boeing company spokesman stated that, if the Japanese go into the aircraft business, it will be "worth our while to be working with them." He notes that the Japanese might go elsewhere for technology or develop it on their own. Another aerospace official adds, "It's better to find a way to join forces with the Japanese than exhaust your energies trying to beat them."

Tokyo, the capital of Japan, is one of the largest cities in the world, with a population of more than 12 million people. Over 70 percent of the 900 or so corporations listed on the Tokyo stock exchange have their headquarters there. In addition, countless industrial associations, research institutions, and prefectural agencies are set up in Tokyo to be near the centers of business and government. The cost of living in Tokyo is twice as high as that in New York City, according to the *Business International Index*. In downtown Tokyo, the sidewalks are crammed full of people, most in Western dress—men in suits and ties, women in skirts and blouses—and all in a big hurry. Lights at each street crossing control the movement of pedestrians and the dense traffic—a mass of cars, taxis, buses, trucks, motorcycles, and bicycles. The noise level is high, as is the level of air pollution.

As a young manager employed by GAPS, you have mixed feelings about the offer from the personnel department to move to Tokyo and fill a management position in the project office for this joint venture. The assignment is for a period of two to three years. On the one hand, you know it is an important job. GAPS basically has a "promote from within" policy, although occasionally GAPS will recruit selected management professors from leading universities to meet specific higher-management needs. Furthermore, GAPS personnel policy regarding promotions to vice-president requires the completion of a successful overseas appointment. You also know that your selection has been reviewed and approved by top management because of the promotion potential of the position. Compensation includes a 25 percent salary increase (in part to compensate for the high cost of living), a housing allowance, and reimbursement for travel expenses, including shipment of furniture and one automobile to Tokyo. No federal income taxes would be paid until after meeting the IRS requirements for exclusion of the first $70,000 of income earned abroad. GAPS would pay any Japanese taxes on income and/or property.

On the other hand, you are concerned about having to move halfway around the world to live in Tokyo, with terrible noise and air pollution levels. You do not want to pay the sky-high rent on a small, five-room unfurnished apartment with doorways so narrow that your U.S.-made refrigerator cannot fit through. Even a McDonald's Big Mac is expensive—about twice as much as at home. Finally, you are quite concerned about the loss of your legal rights as a U.S. citizen while living abroad. A foreigner, by entering Japan, implicitly consents to be treated as a national (which means no discrimination or special treatment as a foreigner); that is the essence of the Calvo Doctrine (named after the outstanding Argentine jurist).

You have one week to accept or reject this job assignment in Tokyo. GAPS personnel policy leaves the decision entirely up to the individual manager, who must decide on a strictly voluntary basis.

Sources: Prepared by Professor John E. Setnicky, Xavier University, New Orleans, Louisiana, from "More U.S. and Japanese Companies Decide to Operate Joint Ventures," *Wall Street Journal*, May 10, 1983, p. 33, and "Tokyo's High-Priced Office Real Estate," *Focus Japan*, April 1981, p. 3.

Questions

1. Would you accept or reject the job in Tokyo? Why?

2. If the project office were located in London or Paris, would your response be different? Why or why not?

3. If you reject his job offer, what do you think would happen to your career progression at GAPS?

chapter

5

Ethics and Social Responsibility

LEARNING OBJECTIVES

After studying the material in this chapter, you should be able to:

◗ **Explain** the need for social responsibility.

◗ **Explain** the need to balance social responsibility and profits.

◗ **Discuss** how the concept of social responsibility has evolved.

◗ **Describe** what types of action plans are needed to fulfill management's social responsibility.

◗ **Describe** what ethics are and discuss some aspects of management in which they are involved.

◗ **Discuss** how ethical standards can be developed and maintained.

Chick-Fil-A: Lending a Helping Hand

Truett Cathy, founder and CEO of Chick-Fil-A Inc., has converted a 24-hour short-order business into a $325 million chain of chicken restaurants. With some 500 company-owned units, Chick-Fil-A is the country's third largest chain of chicken restaurants.

Cathy, the sole stockholder of the Atlanta-based business, refuses to sell stock in the company—or even to sell franchises. Instead, he handpicks operators to sublet his restaurants. After each operator remits 15 percent of gross sales to the company, the unit's net proceeds are evenly split between the operator and Cathy. Another unique operating standard is Cathy's refusal to open for business on Sundays. He insists his "never-on-Sunday" policy gives Chick-Fil-A an edge in attracting and retaining a high-quality staff.

Since it is a private company, Cathy can run Chick-Fil-A the way he thinks is best. For Cathy, "best" includes a strong commitment of time and money to charitable activities. He says that "serving customers great-tasting food and serving America's young people through enrichment programs" are the company's mission as well as his own. "It is much easier to build boys and girls than men and women, especially if they are given the proper guidance, direction, and example— an example that demonstrates a caring and loving spirit." He accomplishes the company's mission through its charitable activities, which include employee scholarships, the WinShape Center Foundation, Inc., Camp WinShape, and the WinShape Foster Care Program.

A Chick-Fil-A employee who has worked in a restaurant a minimum of 20 hours per week for two consecutive years can be nominated by the manager to receive one of the company's $1,000 college scholarships.

The WinShape Center Foundation was established by Cathy in 1984 on the campus of Berry College in Rome, Georgia. The foundation provides scholarships worth $16,000 each year to eligible Berry College students.

The foundation also provides a summer camp program—Camp WinShape—for boys and girls. Its philosophy is to challenge campers to put forth their best effort in all of their endeavors.

The WinShape Foster Care Program provides a loving, nurturing family environment for children who need it. In 1994, WinShare sponsored four foster homes in Georgia, and one each in Alabama, Tennessee, and Brazil.

Cathy also takes advantage of charitable opportunities that come around only once, such as sponsoring Quest Atlanta '96, an outreach organization that brought together churches, ministries, and other organizations during the 1994 Super Bowl in Atlanta. The success in reaching the community led Cathy to plan to do it again during the 1996 Olympics in Atlanta. The aim of Quest Atlanta is to make a positive impact on young people, visitors, business and government leaders, and almost every household in the metropolitan Atlanta area.[1]

Chick-Fil-A founder Truett Cathy enjoys using his time and resources to make life better for others.

Cathy's management of Chick-Fil-A illustrates the growing importance of ethical and socially responsible behavior of individuals and organizations in today's highly competitive environment. The concept of ethics and social responsibility has long been accepted in business. The Carnegie Foundation, with resources from Carnegie Steel, has endowed libraries and made numerous grants to colleges and universities since the turn of the century. Similarly, for many years the Ford Foundation, supported by Ford Motor Company, has provided consulting services for agricultural and management development programs in many emerging countries, such as India, Bangladesh, and Pakistan.

More recently, however, the concept and importance of social responsibility have changed significantly. Business firms have historically been asked to use their resources efficiently to produce goods and services that customers want and to sell them at prices customers are willing and able to pay. It was felt that if this were done effectively, profits would be made, and the material well-being of society would be ensured. This view meant that managers were permitted to optimize profits within the rules of the game set up by custom and the law. Now, it is recognized that what is legal and what is ethical are two quite different things. Just because something is legal does not mean that it is ethical and vice versa.

It is important for managers—or potential managers—to recognize the need to exercise individual, personal responsibility in dealing with others. As will be seen later in this chapter, managers should act ethically, regardless of what the law or rules and regulations say.

The Need for Social Responsibility

Because of the immense scope of the term *social responsibility*, it has been defined in many, widely differing ways. Essentially, however, **social responsibility** refers to management's obligation to set policies, make decisions, and follow courses of action—beyond the requirements of the law—that are desirable in terms of the values and objectives of society. Other terms for this basic concept include *social action, public affairs, community activities, social challenges,* and *social concern.* Notice the important distinction between acting legally—that is, following the letter of the law and adhering to company policies and procedures—and acting ethically from a personal and professional point of view.

Almost every managerial position today requires a willingness on the part of managers to accept their responsibility to society. In fact, many corporations have set up committees, special offices, or departments designed specifically for the purpose of analyzing the social and environmental responsibilities of the organization as a whole:

> Aetna Life & Casualty has a Corporate Social Responsibility Department.

> General Electric has a Public Issues Committee of the Board.

> INA, a major insurance firm, has the position of executive vice-president of legal and government affairs.

> GM has a full-time executive to handle environmental and safety issues.

While most business, public, and government organizations practice some form of social responsibility, many firms have unique programs for dealing with the

social responsibility
Management's obligation to set policies, make decisions, and follow courses of action—beyond the requirements of the law—that are desirable in terms of the values and objectives of society.

public's demand for socially responsible actions. Allied Corporation includes managers' community service in performance evaluations for bonuses. Procter & Gamble encourages its executives to participate in student groups, such as Junior Achievement. IBM sponsors a management training program for executives of not-for-profit organizations. The five-day program, led by IBM's own management development personnel, is designed to improve management development and leadership, planning, and finance.

Two Perspectives on Social Responsibility

There are many perspectives on the extent to which management should practice social responsibility. While few reputable management authorities argue against social responsibility in principle, there is considerable disagreement as to how far it should be taken. These perspectives can be viewed as a continuum, from *limited* (or restricted) to *unlimited* (or extensive). While some organizations may classify themselves as limited or unlimited, neither extreme of the continuum is effective; there must be a balance between the two. An organization with a completely limited view of social responsibility would not survive, if for no other reason than public condemnation, but most likely because of government regulation, for example, on pollution. On the other hand, an organization that has a totally unlimited view would not be effective in meeting other objectives, for example, profitability.

limited (or restricted) responsibility
Management should try to make a profit so that employees will benefit, the company will grow, and the public will benefit by having good, low-cost products, and the public will receive taxes and gifts.

Limited Responsibility   The best-known proponent of **limited** (or **restricted**) **responsibility** is Milton Friedman, a Nobel Prize laureate for economics. He argues that making business managers responsible both to business owners—for reaching profit objectives—and also to society—for enhancing the general welfare—represents a conflict of interest that has the potential of killing business as it is known today. According to Friedman, this will almost certainly be the result if business is continually forced to perform acts that are in direct conflict with private organizational objectives. Finally, he argues that managers are employees of the owners, not the public, and so should act for the owners. Moreover, the costs of social responsibility are passed on to consumers as higher prices, and this is "taxation without representation."[2]

Business writer Herbert London expressed this view well when he wrote, "Chairmen of companies should tell stockholders they are trying to make money, and if they do make a profit, employees will benefit, the company will grow, the public will have the product or service it covets, and contributions to the community in the form of taxes and gifts will increase. . . . Give the public what it needs and wants at a reasonable price and the rewards will be abundant."[3]

unlimited (or extensive) responsibility
Since business is such an important segment of society, it is responsible for helping maintain and improve the overall welfare of that society.

Unlimited Responsibility   The argument for **unlimited** (or **extensive**) **responsibility** begins with the premise that business is a major segment of society and exerts a significant impact on the way society exists. Moreover, since business is so influential, it is responsible for helping maintain and improve the overall welfare of society.

This view was well illustrated by Merck and Company, the New Jersey pharmaceutical company in 1987. Announcing the discovery of ivermectin (brand name, Mectizan), a "miracle drug" that would virtually rid the world of a disease threatening to blind millions in the Third World, Merck gave the rights to the patent to the World Health Organization. The drug offered a cure for "river blindness" to millions of people in more than 30 developing countries. The disease, spread by black flies that thrive near fast-flowing rivers, causes intense itching, weight loss, disfiguring skin irritations, and blindness. The drug—discovered by Merck scientists during research on animal parasites—was approved for human use by French drug officials on October 21, 1987, the day of Merck's announcement.[4]

Another example of a somewhat unlimited view of social responsibility was exhibited by NIKE, Inc., the largest shoe manufacturer in its industry, during the 1994 major league baseball strike. NIKE aired several TV commercials containing a reference to empty stadiums and a message at the end saying "Play ball, please." While NIKE did not side with either the players or the owners during the strike, it did plead with both sides to continue the sport. In a sense, NIKE was giving something back to the sport by making viewers socially aware of the problem.

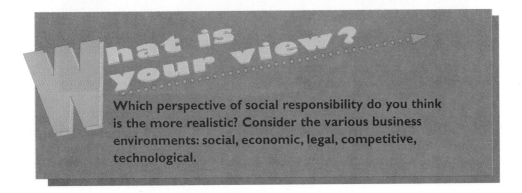

What is your view?

Which perspective of social responsibility do you think is the more realistic? Consider the various business environments: social, economic, legal, competitive, technological.

Social Responsibility and Profitability

Some authorities argue that business should perform socially responsible activities because profitability and growth go hand in hand with responsible treatment of groups such as employees, customers, and the community. In essence, this argument implies that being socially responsible is a means of earning greater organizational credibility and (perhaps) profit. As Ben Cohen, of Ben & Jerry's ice cream fame, once said, "By doing good, we will do well."[5]

The relationship between social responsiveness and profitability is not easy to establish, because (1) it is difficult to define socially responsible actions, and (2) it is practically impossible to measure the results of social responsiveness. For example, is management being socially responsible in replacing a dangerous machine with a newer and safer one, or might the action also improve productivity and profits and reduce taxes? The savings from reduced accidents (cost of health care and time lost also improve productivity and savings from reduced accidents by hourly employees) may justify the increased cost of the machine, making "social responsibility" an easy choice.

If we could clearly measure the benefits *and* costs of a proposed social program in precise financial terms, the decision for concerned managers would be easy: If total benefits exceed total costs, proceed with the program; otherwise, rethink the program. Unfortunately, there is no realistic way to objectively measure those costs and benefits. But there is some evidence that social responsibility does pay off financially. For example, practicing social responsibility has paid off for San

Labor's Olena Berg argues that steering investments to minorities creates jobs.

Francisco–based Parnasous Fund. It follows a socially conscious policy of not invest-ing in companies involved with alcohol, gambling, nuclear power, tobacco, or weapons. According to Lipper Analytical Services, the fund was up over 10 percent in 1992, compared to a scant 0.2 percent for the average stock fund.[6]

Assuming that such economically targeted investing (ETI) creates jobs, Assistant Labor Secretary Olena Berg, the nation's top federal pension regulator, has made a major push to steer more of the $2.1 billion private pension funds she supervises into inner-city, minority- and women-owned businesses. But private pension managers shrink away from investments aimed at anything other than earning the best return for pensioners. They worry that they will run afoul of the federal Employee Retirement Income Security Act (ERISA), which requires "prudent" investment of pension funds.[7]

Of course, some social programs may even reduce profits. For example, if a firm installs expensive antipollution devices and the costs cannot be passed on to consumers, its profits will probably be lower than before. When the Environmental Protection Agency (EPA) imposed further air pollution controls in 1987, motorists had to pay modest price increases, both on new automobiles and on gasoline, because it cost refineries about two cents more per gallon of gas to reduce smog-creating pollution.[8]

In a classic study of the relationship between corporate social responsibility and profitability, three reputable scholars were unable to corroborate the claims of either advocates or critics on the value social responsibility may have for industrial organizations. The literature dealing with this subject over an eight-year period and an in-depth questionnaire survey of 241 CEOs showed "no statistically significant relationship" between "concern for society" and "profitability."[9]

Although we can give no definitive answer as to whether or not social respon-sibility pays off financially, the following conclusions can be reached. First, it does help management in many ways. Second, if a business is to survive, it must act in a way that neither harms society nor reduces the economic value and financial integrity of the firm.

Perhaps the best answer to the relationship between social responsibility and profitability was found by Harvard Business School professors John Kotter and James Heskett. In studying 207 major U.S. companies, they found a relationship between the types of culture and profitability of those companies. Over an 11-year period, those companies that served the interests of all of their main constituencies—customers, employees, and stockholders—averaged an increase of 682 percent in sales. In contrast, those companies that satisfied only one or two constituencies had only a 166 percent increase.[10]

Emerging Views of Social Responsibility

The concept of social responsibility has evolved through four historical periods: (1) profit maximization, (2) trusteeship management, (3) activism, and (4) social responsiveness.[11] Because it is difficult to date these periods precisely, the time periods given are only approximations.

Profit Maximization Period

There seems to be no exact beginning to the period of profit maximization; its origins date back to antiquity. Nearly 5,000 years ago in Sumer (present-day Iraq), the government tried to enforce minimum wage regulations and improve employee working conditions. About 4,000 years ago, the Code of Hammurabi (named after the Babylonian king who instituted it) contained several laws relating to business, such as employer liability and minimum wages.

Later, during the Industrial Revolution, restrictions on business declined, especially in England. The principles guiding managers were John Locke's philosophy of ownership of private property—which was to be protected by government—and Adam Smith's belief that the well-being of society is enhanced when business acts on its own, guided by the "invisible hand" of the marketplace. The principles advocated by Locke and Smith were later incorporated into the U.S. Constitution.

These principles, plus the Protestant (work) ethic, which emphasizes hard work and industry, productivity, and thrift, guided U.S. business owner/managers from about 1800 to the early 1930s. Entrepreneurs like John D. Rockefeller, Andrew Carnegie, and Henry Ford concentrated on increasing efficiency to lower prices—so more people could afford their products—and to maximize profits for owners. Profits could often be used to foster additional economic growth and help society. Capitalists such as Rockefeller, Carnegie, and Ford were enlightened to the point of improving products, working conditions, and wages. Ford doubled wages in 1914—from $2.50 to $5.00 a day—in order to attract the best workers, improve productivity, and lower the price of his "Tin Lizzies" so more people could buy them.

Other capitalists, known as robber barons, were not as socially aware. Many of them believed that employees, like other resources, were to be hired, exploited, and then discarded when no longer productive. They felt they were not accountable to anyone, especially not to consumers. Railroad tycoon William H. Vanderbilt expressed this thought in 1882: "The public be damned. I'm working for my stockholders."[12] This attitude was reinforced by the supreme court of Michigan in 1919. When Henry Ford wanted to use his large pool of profits to reduce the prices of his cars so more people could afford to buy them, the court ruled against him, saying that "a business corporation is organized and carried on primarily for the profit of the stockholders."[13] This belief system had drastically changed by 1949 when C. E. Wilson, CEO of General Electric, testified before a congressional committee that corporate management has a responsibility to employees, consumers, and the general public, and that "stockholders have no special priority."[14]

This attitude, together with a concentration of wealth and power that permitted exploitation of employees and disregard of the public, led to the rise of unions and caused the public to demand government regulation. The Interstate Commerce Act (1887) prohibited unjust and unreasonable shipping rates as well as kickbacks and favorable rates to favored customers. The Sherman Anti-Trust Act (1890) restricted combinations and conspiracies to monopolize and restrict trade. The Pure Food and Drug Law (1906) was a direct result of Upton Sinclair's book *The Jungle,* which vividly described the unsanitary and unsafe working conditions in the meatpacking industry.[15]

Trusteeship Management Period

trustee management
Managers are concerned for employees, customers, and the community, while protecting stockholders' interests.

The second period, **trustee management,** began in the late 1930s following the Great Depression. The government and professional business managers began to show concern for employees, customers, and the community while protecting the interest of stockholders. There were two main reasons for the change. First, big business wanted to alter the public perception that it had caused the depression with its policies. Second, many of the old-line entrepreneurs, such as Henry Ford, had been replaced by professional managers. A few of the laws passed during this period to protect employees, customers, and investors include the following:

▶ The Wagner Act (1935), which gave employees the right to join unions and bargain collectively against management

▶ The Social Security Act (1935), which provided for unemployment insurance and old-age, survivors', and disability benefits

▶ The Wage and Hour Law (1938), which set minimum wages and maximum hours to be worked and restricted child labor

▶ The Wheeler-Lea Act (1938), which enlarged the power of the Federal Trade Commission (FTC) to prevent unfair competition and false advertising

▶ The Securities Act (1933) and Securities Exchange Act (1934), which gave a measure of protection to investors

Activism Period

The third period began with the activism of the early 1960s. Several streams of activities, or movements, during this period drastically and permanently changed the way managers operate. The main movements were in the areas of equal employment opportunity, environmental protection, and consumerism.

Equal Employment Opportunity The Civil Rights Act (1964), as amended, and a series of other **equal employment opportunity (EEO) laws** require that employment decisions not be based on race, color, religion, sex, national origin, age, disability, or being a Vietnam veteran. EEO will be covered in more detail later in this chapter and in Chapter 9.

equal employment opportunity (EEO) laws Laws and rulings that prohibit employment decisions based on race, color, religion, sex, national origin, age, disability, or being a Vietnam veteran.

Environmental Protection The Clean Air Act (1963) started the modern movement toward environmental control, although environmental laws go as far back as the Refuse Act of 1899. And private companies, such as International Paper, were practicing conservation as early as 1892. Since 1963, all aspects of the environment—air, solid waste, toxic substances, nuclear energy, and water—are to be included for protection. The National Environmental Policy Act (1969) set up the EPA to guard the public's interest.

Consumerism In 1962, President John F. Kennedy, alarmed by numerous claims of abuses by some marketers, sent a special message to Congress asking for protection of selected consumer rights, including freedom from products that could be hazardous to health or life, and fraudulent, deceitful, or grossly misleading information, advertising, labeling, and other practices. These and other rights became the basis of **consumerism,** the organized effort of independent, government, and business groups to protect consumers from poorly designed and produced products.

consumerism The organized efforts of independent, government, and business groups to protect consumers from poorly designed and produced products.

In 1966, Congress passed the Traffic and Motor Vehicle Safety Act, requiring manufacturers to notify new car purchasers of safety defects discovered after manufacture and delivery. The Child Protection and Toy Safety Act (1969) provided for

International Paper had been practicing conservation for over a century.

greater protection from children's toys with mechanical or electrical hazards. The Consumer Product Safety Act (1972) empowered the Consumer Product Safety Commission (CPSC) to set safety standards, require warning labels on potentially unsafe products, and order recalls of hazardous products.

Social Responsiveness Period

Because large modern businesses have become such power centers in the economic, social, and political realms, their managers should have a sense of social responsibility. Indications are that managers are now beginning to accept that responsibility by becoming more responsive to the needs of various groups, not just stockholders. The trade-off between maximizing profit for owners and assuming social responsibility is often reflected in an organization's objectives. In essence, the objectives are established to recognize what the firm believes to be the appropriate balance of interests of various stakeholder groups.

This balance was exemplified by Johnson & Johnson (J&J) during the "Tylenol scare." McNeil Consumer Products Company, a subsidiary of J&J, introduced Tylenol as a prescription drug for pain in 1955 when aspirin was found to be potentially harmful, especially to children. Later, as an over-the-counter drug, Tylenol was holding its own against competition, with a market share that increased 2 to 3 percentage points each year. By October 1982, Tylenol had acquired 37 percent of the painkiller market.

Then tragedy struck! Seven people in Chicago died from cyanide-laced Extra-Strength Tylenol capsules. Although it was proved that the tampering had been done on the retail level and not at the factory, by November Tylenol's sales had

Johnson & Johnson and McNeil Consumer Products CEO demonstrates new, safer Tylenol package.

dropped to 12 percent of the market. J&J's management immediately stopped production of Tylenol, recalled 22 million bottles of capsules, offered a $100,000 reward for information leading to the arrest of the guilty party or parties, and set up toll-free telephone lines to handle customer concerns. Because 80 percent of its customers bought Tylenol on the recommendation of their doctors, J&J also used telegrams, telephone calls, and visits by sales representatives to reassure physicians and pharmacies all over the country.

A three-way safety-sealed package was designed, and explained at news conferences and on talk shows, by the chairmen of J&J and McNeil Consumer Products Company. They demonstrated how safe Tylenol was and explained that the U.S. Food and Drug Administration had cleared J&J of any negligence or wrongdoing. Retailers and customers were reimbursed for any capsules thrown away, a 25 percent discount was given to retailers for Tylenol purchases at or above precrisis levels, and $1.00 discount coupons for the new safety-sealed capsules appeared in magazines, newspapers, and mailboxes.

J&J absorbed the entire cost of these activities—over $100 million—but the effort paid off. Within 15 months, Tylenol had recaptured over 30 percent of the total market and regained its leading market share.[16]

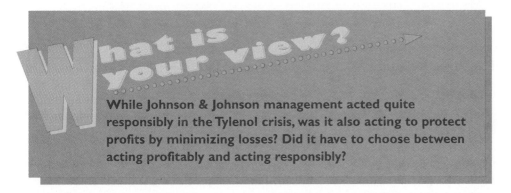

While Johnson & Johnson management acted quite responsibly in the Tylenol crisis, was it also acting to protect profits by minimizing losses? Did it have to choose between acting profitably and acting responsibly?

To what extent are U.S. managers socially responsive? A classic study of 116 corporate CEOs found broad and deep support for some basic social responsibility assumptions, as shown in Table 5.1. In 1992, the CEOs of 55 companies formed the Businesses for Social Responsibility to put these beliefs into practice. It planned to "spread the gospel" that corporate America can be "a pal to workers, a friend to the environment, a harbinger of government and social change, and still be profitable."[17]

Social Responsibility in Action

Social responsibility can best be illustrated in terms of specific action programs that management undertakes. These programs usually include—but are not limited to—activities in areas such as (1) employee relations, (2) public and community service, (3) environmental protection, (4) consumerism, (5) educational and medical assistance, (6) urban renewal and development, and (7) culture, the arts, and recreation.

TABLE 5.1 TOP MANAGEMENT SUPPORT FOR SELECTED SOCIAL RESPONSIBILITY ASSUMPTIONS

Assumptions About Social Responsibility	Percentage of Corporate Chief Executive Officers Agreeing with Each Assumption
Responsible corporate behavior can be in the best economic interest of the stockholders.	92
Efficient production of goods and services is no longer the only thing society expects from business.	89
Long-run success by a business depends on its ability to understand that is is part of a larger society and to behave accordingly.	87
Involvement by business in improving its community's quality of life will also improve long-run profitability.	78
A business that wishes to capture a favorable public image will have to show that it is socially responsible.	78
If business is more socially responsible, it will discourage additional regulation of the economic system by government.	71

Source: Based on Robert Ford and Frank McLaughlin, "Perceptions of Socially Responsible Activities and Attitudes: A Comparison of Business School Deans and Corporate Chief Executives," *Academy of Management Journal*, Vol. 27 (September 1984), p. 670.

Employee Relations

American managers are now more employee oriented than they were at any time prior to the 1960s. This is a reflection of the growing interest in and concern for employee rights, especially regarding safety and equal employment opportunity. Areas in which employee orientation is important include training, promotions, pay, and health and safety.

Current EEO regulations make it unlawful for any employer to discriminate against any person on the basis of race, creed, color, religion, sex, nation of origin, age, disability, or being a Vietnam veteran. These laws cover all aspects of employment, from recruiting to termination or retirement. Under some circumstances, managers do more than just *not* discriminate. If they have—or are seeking—a

affirmative action program (AAP) A program to actively seek out, hire, train, and promote minorities, women, Vietnam veterans, and the disabled.

government contract, they must have an **affirmative action program (AAP)** to actively seek out, hire, train, and promote minorities, women, Vietnam veterans, and the disabled. Such programs have occasionally resulted in reverse discrimination allegations and lawsuits.

As will be discussed in Chapter 9, an important aspect of employee relations is maintaining employee safety and health. While management has been involved in this area for a long time, the Occupational Safety and Health Act (1970) forced even speedier action.

A relatively new issue in employee relations is drug testing of current and prospective employees. While legislators and the courts are sorting out the legal aspects, some ethical problems remain. An even more controversial practice is testing employees and potential employees for antibodies to the HIV virus that causes AIDS.

Other areas of employee relations that will be discussed in Chapter 9 are sexual harassment, employment of the physically challenged, child care, and family leave. The U.S. Labor Department recently published research showing that 57 percent of women with children under 6 work outside the home. Recognizing the growing

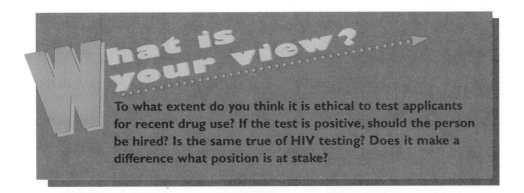

To what extent do you think it is ethical to test applicants for recent drug use? If the test is positive, should the person be hired? Is the same true of HIV testing? Does it make a difference what position is at stake?

role of women in the workforce, 137 progressive companies recently founded a cooperative organization to care for employees' children and elderly relatives. The American Business Collaboration for Quality Dependent Care, as it is named, has raised over $25 million to fund 300 such programs nationwide.[18]

Public and Community Service

Some business managers feel that their services should benefit the community as well as their employer. This concept is not new. What is innovative, however, is the extent to which employers are formalizing such programs to permit—or even require—their personnel to help in civic and community activities, such as the Girl Scouts, the Boy Scouts, and the Red Cross.

Employee volunteerism, which is the lifeblood of not-for-profit organizations, is now on the rise as profit-oriented businesses escalate their public service efforts. Some companies maintain employee skill banks for community groups, while others give workers time off to help out. Corporate volunteer councils also participate in joint projects in many cities.

Xerox has a Social Service Leave Program that pays employees full salary for a year while they are performing public service. Xerox's Peter Neidecker, a senior marketing executive who lived and worked in a plush area of Portland, Oregon, left it to live in the city's streets, alleys, night shelters, and soup kitchens, helping the poor and homeless. He found jobs for the unemployed, helped train people for work, held counseling sessions, and visited the poor.[19]

Another form of public service is making and paying for ads or announcements contributing to public safety and security. For example, Barber Milk Company, a Birmingham, Alabama, firm, puts National Child Safety Council messages on cartons of milk likely to be handled by children. Photographs and descriptions of missing children also appear on many grocery bags, orange juice cartons, and various other containers.

It is important to distinguish between genuine public service advertisements and cause-related marketing. For example, in 1990, Philip Morris received a 1990 Harlan Page Hubbard Lemon Award for its ads championing the Bill of Rights. According to the Coalition on Smoking and Health, it was a public relations effort to defeat government restrictions on tobacco promotion.[20]

The following profile of George Fraser shows how one entrepreneur truly benefited his people. He has devoted the last ten years to proving that "one person can make a difference."

Photos of missing children on milk cartons have helped in locating many of them.

PRACTICING MANAGER

Businessman, author, publisher, and leader in the black community—these are just a few of the terms that describe George Fraser, publisher of *SuccessGuide*, a directory of black entrepreneurs and businesspeople. He takes his leadership role so seriously that he even writes personal letters of encouragement to young people. When asked by a teenager's guardian to write the teenager a note to encourage him as he goes off to college, Fraser did not hesitate, although he had never met either of them.

As a child, Fraser had a somewhat unstable life. When he was in kindergarten, his mother became institutionalized with a mental illness. His father, unable to raise six children alone, sent the three youngest children to a foster home—George being one of them.

When George was a senior in high school, his father managed to bring the children back together again in Bedford-Styvesant—not as rough a neighborhood as it is today, but not exactly peaceful, even back then. After graduation, Fraser started classes at New York University, paying his way by mopping floors at La Guardia International Airport. He dressed well, observed successful people, and carried a dictionary to help him read the *Wall Street Journal*.

During the 1970s, Fraser moved from being a management trainee at Procter & Gamble to becoming a marketing executive with the company. Although he was busy with his work—raising money for the United Negro College Fund and doing other voluntary work—he felt something was lacking. So, by the early 1980s, he left Procter & Gamble for a three-year job as director of marketing and communications for United Way Services of Cleveland.

In 1987, Fraser left United Way for Ford, and was set to become Greater Cleveland's first black Lincoln-Mercury dealer when the bottom dropped out of the U.S. auto market. He decided then that it was a good time to take the "big leap" and do what he had been wanting to do for a long

GEORGE FRASER PROVES THAT ONE PERSON CAN MAKE A DIFFERENCE

time: devote the rest of his life to fixing some of the problems he saw surrounding him.

One of the problems he saw and tried to help correct was the negative image facing many African Americans today. A video made for Fraser's communications company, SuccessSource, Inc., states that "the vast majority of blacks do not sing or act, play pro basketball, sell drugs, go on welfare or rob convenience stores," yet this is a misconception believed by many in today's society.

Believing that one person can make a difference in the world, Fraser has been trying to change the false attitudes toward the black community. In 1988, he held his first SuccessNet (Success Through Networking) forum to help his people overcome their negative perception and achieve success. This led to his publishing *SuccessGuide*, a directory that lists thousands of black professionals and entrepreneurs for ten cities. It has 1.5 million readers annually.

His forums have included such inspirational speakers as Les Brown, James Earl Jones, John H. Johnson, Wally "Famous" Amos, and the late Arthur Ashe.

Fraser's most recent venture is his new book *Success Runs in Our Race: The Complete Guide to Effective Networking in the African-American Community*, which hit bookstores in July 1994.

Sources: George Fraser, "Ten Trends That Are Changing Black America: Happiness Comes from the Self-Respect That Forces Us to Accept Responsibility," *Vital Speeches of the Day*, April 15, 1994, pp. 411–416; Elissa Matulis Myers, "On Racism," *Association Management*, May 1994, p. 16; Dawn Baskerville, "Make That Move," *Black Enterprise*, June 1994, p. 66; George Fraser and Fonda Marie Lloyd, "Tapping into the Power of Networking," *Black Enterprise*, July 1994, pp. 62–68; and "Black Executive Extols Networking, Successes of Race," *Mobile (Alabama) Register*, July 17, 1994, p. 4F.

Environmental Protection

Environmental protection refers to maintaining a healthy balance between elements of the ecology—the relationships between living things, especially people—and their environment. These relationships are complex and fragile, for the real problem is how to maintain a balance between the use of natural resources now and the conservation of them for future generations.

But even when aware of problems, it is often difficult for managers to cope with them effectively. First, when operating internationally, they often have little control over the situation. Second, they may be unable to resolve the problem until further technological developments occur. Thus, a commitment to basic research and development in these areas may be a socially responsible activity. Finally, it may be difficult to balance ecological needs with economic ones. Although some producers, such as British detergent manufacturers, are trying to find that balance, for other industries the solutions are harder to find.

A socially responsible environmental protection program involves two steps: conserving natural resources and preventing pollution. Such programs can be difficult and expensive to implement.

Conservation **Conservation** means practicing the most effective use of resources, considering society's present and future needs. Conservation can be achieved by limiting the exploitation of scarce resources. For example, automakers are producing more fuel-efficient cars, and they are being driven less, so that petroleum use is increasing only slightly. Many states have instituted a refundable deposit on all beer and soda cans and bottles to encourage customers to return them to stores for recycling.

environmental protection Maintaining a healthy balance between elements of the ecology and the environment.

conservation Practicing the most effective use of resources, considering society's present and future needs.

Consumers are shopping "green," seeking out ecologically friendly products such as this phosphate-free detergent in London.

recycling Reprocessing used items for further use; a form of conservation.

Recycling—that is, reprocessing used items for further use—is another form of conservation. Many companies use recycled paper stationery. IBM prints its quarterly stockholders' reports on recycled paper. Reynolds Aluminum, which began its recycling program in 1968, and Alcoa, pay for the return of used cans, from which new aluminum products can be made at far less cost than from raw materials. As shown in Figure 5.1, 68 percent of all the aluminum beverage cans discarded each year in the United States are now being recycled.

While neither conservation nor recycling are long-term solutions to the increasing scarcity of depletable resources, many companies and industries are now cooperating in the effort. For example, engineers at AT&T developed a substitute for 1,1,1–trichloroethane, an ozone-depleting solvent used to clean circuit boards. The new method is called the cantaloupe technology because it contains a synthetic extract that appears naturally in the melon and some other fruits. AT&T is sharing cantaloupe, which has reduced 1,1,1 emissions to practically zero, with competitors for free.[21]

pollution The contamination or destruction of the natural environment.

Pollution Control   **Pollution**—the contamination or destruction of the natural environment—is one of the greatest problems facing the world today. Efforts to prevent or control air, land, water, and noise pollution are major goals of responsible companies.

The EPA is responsible for protecting the air and water, regulating chemical and toxic waste disposal, and seeing that these wastes are cleaned up when accidents or violations occur. The Nuclear Regulatory Commission (NRC) licenses nuclear power plants and sets standards for their construction and use. When there is an accident, such as the release of radioactive matter at Three Mile Island, the NRC sees that it is cleaned up and that measures are taken to prevent recurrence.

Many companies and governments have taken actions to reduce pollution. For example, in 1992, the *Eagle*, the first company-owned double-hull crude oil carrier, was added to Mobil Oil Company's fleet. It evolved from a design developed and patented by Mobil in 1968. This design minimizes oil spills, for if one hull is ruptured, the other one should contain the oil.

FIGURE 5.1
Recycling is growing in popularity.

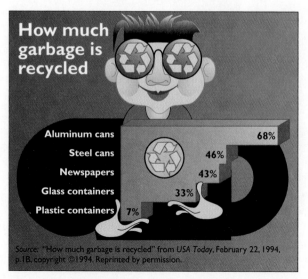

Sometimes, however, a cost-benefit analysis convinces management that antipollution measures are too expensive—or impossible to implement—and facilities are closed. For example, Phelps Dodge Corporation operated a copper smelter in Douglas, Arizona, for nearly 80 years. After failing to meet clean air standards for more than a decade, the company closed the smelter in 1987 rather than spend the millions of dollars required to meet regulations on sulfur dioxide emissions. The closure left many of the 347 employees and 13,000 town residents saddened—and left a $10 million hole in the town's economy.[22]

Consumerism Protection

While the old saying that "the customer is always right" may not be true, managers are now truly concerned about consumers' needs and wishes. The movement to protect the interests of consumers is a major force in the world of business and government. Over 500 state and local groups, as well as over 100 national ones, have sprung up around the nation to speak for—and support legislation to protect—consumers. And since President Kennedy's previously mentioned special message to Congress (see p. 147), consumers have more rights to know what is in products as well as more protection against mislabeling, false advertising, and harmful products.

In furthering this goal, industry and government often cooperate to protect the public. A classic illustration of this type of cooperation occurred in June 1993. Newspapers in New Orleans and Seattle carried reports of people claiming to have found syringes in Pepsi cans. Within a week, there were more than 50 such claims. True panic never occurred, though, because the claims were quickly found to be false. But the real reason for successful control of the situation was the effective cooperation between Craig Weatherup, CEO of PepsiCo, and David Kessler, commissioner of the Food and Drug Administration. They appeared together on several programs, such as *Nightline*, answering questions about product safety and showing how it was impossible for the syringes to have been introduced into the cans during production. The turmoil soon quieted, and the FBI made over 20 arrests of people for making false claims on product tampering.[23]

Educational and Medical Assistance

Business managers continue to cooperate with educational institutions to set up new programs and upgrade old ones. While graduates often contribute large amounts of money to colleges and universities, they may not realize that the business community, including their own employers and related foundations, gives almost as much.

Many employers, such as Truett Cathy in the Opening Case, also pay all or part of employees' tuition costs when they return to school to complete or supplement their education. Also, many companies are lending a helping hand to employees eager to ensure a good education for their children. Aluminum Company of America, for example, hands out more than 200 scholarships a year to employees' children.[24]

Employers also provide other forms of educational assistance, such as offering employees time off to help underprivileged children and providing educational facilities. For example, in 1982, Atlanta-based Rich's Department Store opened

Rich's Academy. Located on the sixth floor of the downtown store, the program was developed for high-risk teens seemingly headed for lives of crime or welfare dependency. When Rich's closed its downtown store, it joined other organizations to form what became known as Rich's Central, which continued the efforts of the earlier program.[25]

Other forms of employee benefits provided by companies are recreational facilities and on-site child care centers. G. T. Water Products, a Moorpark, California, manufacturer of drain-cleaning devices, offers a free on-site Montessori school from kindergarten through the twelfth grade for children of its 32 employees.[26] Scott Paper Company has created a complete line of seven products, a portion of whose sales always go to charity. A nickel of the purchase price of Helping Hand toilet paper, napkins, and other products is designated for groups such as the March of Dimes.[27]

Entrepreneurs and managers are concerned today with providing medical assistance to those who cannot afford it. MAP 5.1 illustrates this trend by explaining how McDonald's has been helping seriously ill children and their families.

Urban Renewal and Development

Many socially responsive companies also help with urban renewal and development. They do this by offering to rehabilitate run-down areas near their offices, stores, and plants, and by helping residents recover from natural disasters. Ralston Purina Company, the giant agribusiness firm, spent $4.5 million to help the city of St. Louis rehabilitate the area around its headquarters.[28]

Culture, the Arts, and Recreation

Companies have been contributing to culture, the arts, and recreation for a long time. Mobil Oil, for example, sponsors many cultural and news programs on public TV, and Texaco has sponsored radio broadcasts of the Metropolitan Opera since 1939. The Campbell Soup Company redeems labels from its soups and a variety of other foods for, among other things, playground equipment.

On a smaller scale, most companies—from mom-and-pop stores to large corporations—contribute in some way to hometown arts endeavors, from ballet recitals and arts workshops for children to performances by symphony orchestras and civic ballet companies. Because of recent changes in tax laws, however, corporate involvement and donations in these areas have decreased.

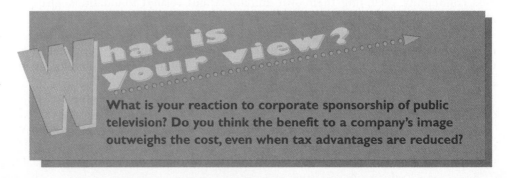

What is your reaction to corporate sponsorship of public television? Do you think the benefit to a company's image outweighs the cost, even when tax advantages are reduced?

MANAGEMENT APPLICATION AND PRACTICE 5.1

McDonald's Extends a Helping Hand Worldwide

Ronald McDonald House, a temporary lodging facility, is a home-away-from-home for families of seriously ill children being treated at nearby hospitals. It provides emotional support to parents and siblings of sick children, who also benefit by knowing their family is close by. For families traveling great distances to receive specialized medical care, the house provides a secure place to stay, a place where additional strength and stability are offered by other resident families in similar situations.

To date, there are more than 165 Ronald McDonald Houses in the United States and 11 other countries, including Australia, Austria, Brazil, Canada, England, France, Germany, Holland, New Zealand, Switzerland, and Sweden. Plans for establishing about ten more new Ronald McDonald Houses annually are under way, with the greatest number in foreign countries, including Brazil, Hong Kong, New Zealand, Sweden, and Switzerland. Since the Ronald McDonald House program began in Philadelphia in 1974, more than 1.5 million family members have benefited from the program.

The first Ronald McDonald House opened October 15, 1974, as a result of the perseverance and dedication of the Philadelphia Eagles and Jim Murray, their general manager, who rallied around teammate Fred Hill, a linebacker whose 3-year-old daughter, Kim, had leukemia. After Kim was treated at the Children's Hospital of Philadelphia, Murray, Hill, and his teammates were determined to do something to benefit families of other children who were hospitalized. Murray consulted with Kim's physician, Dr. Audrey Evans, a leading pediatric oncologist, who expressed a need for a home-away-from-home facility near the hospital. Ultimately, this led to a joint fund-raising effort by the Eagles and Philadelphia-area McDonald's restaurants to purchase and renovate the first house.

Each Ronald McDonald House is a community partnership—created by a team of concerned local citizens to meet the needs of their community. Before a local commitment is made to develop a house, several key supporting elements must be present: medical advisers from a hospital with need for such a house; a parent organization, made up of people whose children have been or are being treated at the same hospital; and local McDonald's restaurant owners.

Each house is owned and operated by a local not-for-profit organization formed to operate the Ronald McDonald House. Members and directors are unpaid volunteers. Many local and national companies provide support, through volunteerism, material donations, and monetary contributions. The local not-for-profit organization operating the house can qualify for a $25,000 start-up grant from Ronald McDonald Children's Charities (RMCC), of which the Ronald McDonald House is the cornerstone.

Since the first house opened, each Ronald McDonald House not-for-profit organization has received the active support of local McDonald's restaurants as major fund-raising partners. Over the past 20 years, local promotions by McDonald's restaurants nationwide have raised more than $45 million to support the Ronald McDonald Children's Charities.

The International Advisory Board (IAB), established in 1977, is the not-for-profit organization that provides direction to the international Ronald McDonald House Program. It assists local groups in

Ronald McDonald Houses help families of seriously ill children.

evaluating the need for a Ronald McDonald House and serves as a sounding board and communications coordinator for subjects of interest to local Ronald McDonald Houses. Serving on the board are representatives from the medical, business (McDonald's and others), and parent/volunteer group members.

Source: Conversations and correspondence with Henry Lienau, national coordinator, Ronald McDonald House Program, Ronald McDonald Children's Charities; and Ann Beattie, McDonald's/Ronald McDonald House.

The Growing Problem of Maintaining Ethics in Management

In general, being socially responsible requires a true concern for the well-being of others and the environment. This same well-being requires an ethical attitude on the part of individuals and an ethical code of conduct prescribed by organizations to which they belong. What we do and how we act must be in accordance with the standards established by society for the treatment of others.

But the real question is, Whose ethics are right? Who will decide what is right and wrong? There is no easy answer. Interest in ethics is increasing at a rapid rate. Ethics courses are now an integral part of the business curriculum of many colleges and universities, and business executives are also displaying more interest in the study of ethics. There are few management development programs that do not cover the subject to some degree. Figure 5.2 shows that maintaining ethical behavior is a worldwide issue, not one restricted to the United States.

ethics The standards used to judge the rightness or wrongness of a person's relations to others in terms of truth and justice.

Ethics are the standards used to judge the rightness or wrongness of a person's behavior toward others in terms of truth and justice. Just a few of the managerial activities related to ethical decisions are bribery, industrial theft and espionage, conflict of interest, false and/or misleading advertising, collusion, and fraud.

The discussion of these six issues is difficult because many of them may also involve legal issues. Unfortunately, what is legal is not always the same as what is

---

FIGURE 5.2
Ethical problems: An international issue. The top ethical issues facing businesses, according to more than 80 percent of the CEOs and senior managers surveyed by the International Survey on Corporate Ethics, which surveyed 300 companies worldwide.

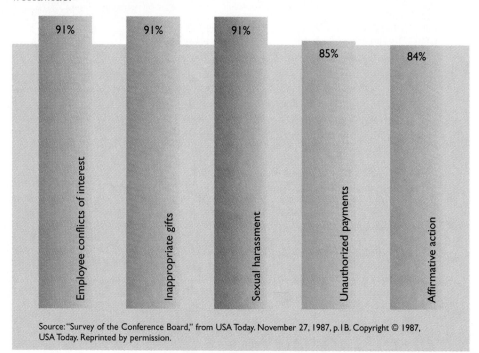

Source: "Survey of the Conference Board," from USA Today. November 27, 1987, p.1B. Copyright © 1987, USA Today. Reprinted by permission.

ethical. To be ethical, managers not only must *obey the law and applicable code(s) of conduct*, but must also *be personally ethical.*

For example, in 1989, junk bond czar Michael Milken, head of Drexel's Beverly Hills office, faced a 98-count federal indictment charging him with racketeering and other securities trading offenses. He admitted six felonies involving dealings with Ivan Boesky and Salomon Brothers. Accusing Milken of not going further for fear of increasing the risk of being caught, Judge Kimba M. Wood stated that Milken had the habit of "stepping just over to the wrong side of the law." She ordered him to serve ten years in jail and three years in full-time community service. The distinction Judge Wood made was that Milken stepped over the line from unethical to illegal behavior.[29]

Bribery

Bribery refers to offering something of value to a person to influence his or her judgment or conduct. Though it may be a part of the normal way of doing business in some foreign countries, bribery is considered illegal, or at least unethical, in the United States.

Yet the distinction between gift giving and bribery is often blurred. Consider, for example, a dye chemist at a leading textile mill who received an expensive chess set over a year's time. It was sent one piece at a time by a dye manufacturer, with accompanying advertising material that stressed "making the right move." The chessboard was sent at Christmas. Other factors of the relationship would have to be evaluated before a decision could be made as to whether this constitutes bribery or a gift.

One of the most difficult decisions managers operating abroad face is the question of making illegal payments. Should they engage in such activity where it is an accepted business practice? The answer is not always clear. The Foreign Corrupt Practices Act has now been modified to permit a certain amount of such payments if they are necessary to conduct business.

In 1975, it was disclosed that in order to sell the TriStar jet to Japanese airlines, Lockheed paid its Japanese agent $12 million to smooth the way to getting the contracts. Additionally, a $1.7 million payment was made to Japan's prime minister.[30] At the time, Lockheed's very existence was at stake because of its desperate financial situation, and it was following generally accepted business practices in Japan.

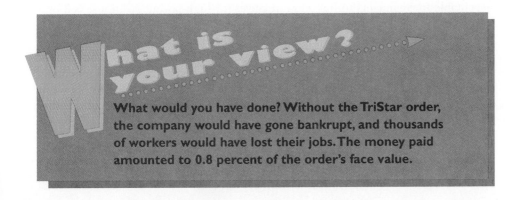

What is your view?

What would you have done? Without the TriStar order, the company would have gone bankrupt, and thousands of workers would have lost their jobs. The money paid amounted to 0.8 percent of the order's face value.

Industrial Theft and Espionage

In the past, corporate spies have been known to break into an office or plant and steal blueprints or formats for a new product or process. Now, such theft may be more subtle; a rival firm may hire a competitor's computer programmer by offering more money. But espionage is still a fact of business today. Gerber Products Company recently ended a 78-year-old tradition of conducting free public tours, partly because of fears of corporate spies stealing new technology secrets.[31]

It seems that as business becomes more global, industrial espionage is becoming more prevalent. Increasingly, economic intelligence gathering—from tracking technology trends to passing one company's business secrets to another company—is seen by businesses and governments as the key to their economic survival.

For example, the German newsmagazine *Der Spiegel* reported that in March 1993, more than a month before J. Ignacio Lopez de Arriortua left General Motors to join Volkswagen, he ordered copies made of secret GM documents. In May, GM filed an industrial espionage suit against its former purchasing chief and Volkswagen. Prosecutors in Darmstadt, Germany, said four boxes of documents were found in the apartment of two of Lopez's GM associates, who had defected with him to Volkswagen.[32]

Another aspect of industrial theft takes the form of patent infringement. In 1993, Litton Industries asked a federal judge to award it a $3.6 billion judgment when Honeywell was found guilty of patent infringement.[33]

Conflict of Interest

Conflict of interest is one of the most difficult ethical problems for managers to cope with because it occurs so often and in so many forms. It is easy for managers to rationalize an action that to them is good business but may be a conflict between company needs and personal needs. One form of this conflict occurs when a company issues its own stock to its employees' pension fund in order to conserve cash. It is legal for a firm to put up to 10 percent of its assets into such a fund. But the practice is questionable, for employees already rely heavily on the company for their pensions, and this type of investment may dilute their equity in the pension fund. The companies rationalize their action by assuming that the stock will grow in value and the pensions will benefit. Certainly it gives employees a powerful incentive to make the company more productive and profitable.

Some other interesting issues include questions such as these: Can a firm prevent its employees from dating or marrying employees of competing firms? Is it acceptable for managers to hire close relatives for high-paying positions? Is it ethical for an employee of a small company to use its WATS line to call his mother and not record the call on the telephone log? Is it "right" for an employee to take $10 worth of pencils from her employers to give to young people from a poor section of town who were playing paper-and-pencil games at a church weekend meeting?

Business managers are not the only ones who act unethically. As shown in Figure 5.3, more people think businesspeople have higher ethical standards than lawyers and members of Congress. Studies have found managers in other professions who sometimes act in a questionable manner.

The highly respected *New England Journal of Medicine* published a study of 60,000 imaging procedures ordered by 6,419 doctors. The researchers found that doctors

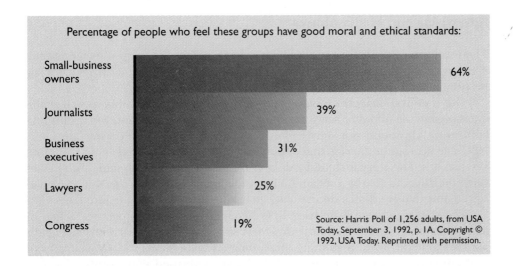

Percentage of people who feel these groups have good moral and ethical standards:

Small-business owners	64%
Journalists	39%
Business executives	31%
Lawyers	25%
Congress	19%

Source: Harris Poll of 1,256 adults, from USA Today, September 3, 1992, p. 1A. Copyright © 1992, USA Today. Reprinted with permission.

FIGURE 5.3
How ethical various groups are perceived to be.

who own X-ray machines and other imaging equipment "ordered 4 to 4.5 times more imaging tests than those who referred patients to radiologists." The resulting fees were 4.4 to 7.5 times higher per test for physicians who owned the equipment.[34]

In 1992, William Aramony, the CEO of United Way of America (UWA) since 1970, was accused of embezzlement and ethical mismanagement. He and two colleagues were charged in a 71-count federal indictment in 1994 of illegally spending $1.5 million on fancy homes, vacations, meals, and phony consulting fees. They denied the charges. The current UWA president said that corrective actions have been taken to prevent this happening again.[35]

In July 1994, the president of the American Federation of Government Employees placed its Local 12 in trusteeship when an audit showed funds missing—as much as $50,000 had been spent improperly.[36]

There are also ethical problems with the way some government agencies and officials operate. For example, John Shiler was fined $4,000 by the EPA in 1994 for killing a grizzly bear that was attacking him on his Montana sheep ranch. And Aspen, Colorado, has spent eight years and $8 million fighting EPA's demand that it spend $12 million to clean up 100-year-old lead deposits even though its citizens have below-average lead levels.[37]

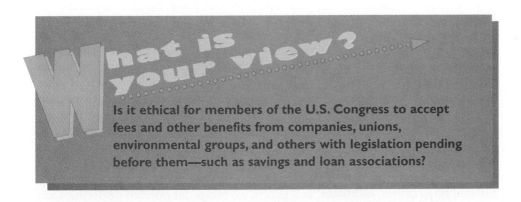

What is your view?

Is it ethical for members of the U.S. Congress to accept fees and other benefits from companies, unions, environmental groups, and others with legislation pending before them—such as savings and loan associations?

Advertising and Media Abuses

There is currently much concern about the ethics of advertising directed at children, especially during Saturday morning cartoon shows. In fact, Canada has a law prohibiting children's cereal ads for this reason.

Other ethical concerns include false and misleading advertising as well as the questionable use of public services primarily to gain publicity. False and misleading advertising are found not only in business but also in news reporting. In 1993, NBC's news program *Dateline* had to publicly retract a story it aired about GM's full-size pickups. The story included a demonstration of a pickup bursting into flames when hit from the side by a sedan. An investigation revealed that the NBC crew had rigged an explosive device on the truck to ensure it would explode into flames.[38]

Wal-Mart was recently accused by its leading discount competitor, Meijer, of false advertising. In a 1994 award, Wal-Mart signed an agreement with Michigan's attorney general "to stop running misleading advertisements." Many examples of misleading price advertising surfaced. Wal-Mart advertised that its price on Hills Bros. coffee was $1.45 lower than Meijer's. But Wal-Mart's offer was on a 34½-ounce can versus Meijer's 39-ounce can. Similarly, Wal-Mart failed to say that the reason its Dirt Devil hand-held vacuum was priced $15 less was because no attachments were included in the price.[39]

Collusion

collusion A secret agreement or cooperation between two or more people or organizations to help or harm another one.

Another worrisome ethical area is **collusion,** a secret agreement or cooperation between two or more individuals or organizations to help or harm another one. Collusion can also be found between employees within companies as well as with people outside the company.

A few years ago, *Wall Street Journal* financial writer R. Foster Winans, a broker, and several others were convicted of collusion. Winans had given the others advance information as to whether his column would contain favorable or unfavorable information about certain stocks. With this advance knowledge, the broker and other persons made $700,000 by anticipating the market's reaction to Winan's column. He received $30,000 as his share of the arrangement. He was tried and convicted of securities and mail fraud and of collusion. He was fined $5,000 and sentenced to 18 months in prison, 5 years' probation, and 400 hours of community service.[40]

Fraud

Another ethical problem for managers is fraud on the part of trusted employees. *Fraud* is the intentional misrepresentation of a material fact in order to induce another person to act on it, and consequently to part with some property of value, or to surrender some legal right. As you can see from Figure 5.4, over three-quarters of surveyed businesses were victimized by fraud in 1992. The most frequent types of fraud reported were misappropriation of funds, check forgery, credit card abuse, and false invoices.[41]

A classic example of fraud was perpetrated by 13 former employees of American Honda from 1979 to 1992. They were indicted for giving or receiving $10 million in bribes, kickbacks, and gifts in exchange for coveted dealerships and

FIGURE 5.4
Fraud is expensive.

sought-after car models. Honda says it has beefed up its ethics training and financial disclosure rules.[42]

Developing and Maintaining Ethical Standards ✗ 49

As will be shown throughout this text, an organization's culture has much to do with its ethical climate. If middle- and lower-level managers see top managers acting unethically and not following high standards, they will act accordingly. The firm's objectives state the ends to be achieved, but rewarding employees only on the basis of meeting objectives and ignoring the means sometimes encourage unethical behavior.

Although management does not want to acknowledge it, employees may be rewarded for doing things they know to be wrong. A study at Columbia University's business school found that 40 percent of 1,070 alumni from the classes of 1953 through 1987 had been "implicitly or explicitly rewarded for taking action they

"O.K. Whose turn is it to set the moral tone?"

Source: Drawing by Dana Fradon; © 1977 by The New Yorker Magazine, Inc.

considered ethically troubling." This was twice as many as were rewarded in some way for refusing to do wrong. Moreover, 31 percent of those who had refused to act unethically said they had been penalized for their choice.[43]

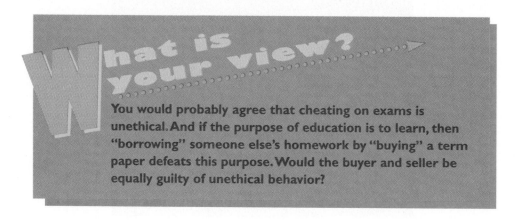

You would probably agree that cheating on exams is unethical. And if the purpose of education is to learn, then "borrowing" someone else's homework by "buying" a term paper defeats this purpose. Would the buyer and seller be equally guilty of unethical behavior?

Senior managers set the tone for the corporation, and they are the ones who should set high ethical standards. There is a real problem in maintaining ethical behavior on the part of managers today. The true problem, though, is in defining ethical behavior and establishing a more ethical workplace. Figure 5.5 presents five steps managers can follow to establish such an ethical climate.

FIGURE 5.5
Five steps toward establishing an ethical workplace.

Step One
State your corporate values in no more than three sentences. Make sure all employees understand what these values are and how they apply to daily activities. Publish the values so that your associates and customers also understand them.

Step Two
Act according to your published values. We are what we do, not what we say. For instance, do not overreport results, oversell your products or services, or sell employees short.

Step Three
Conduct ethical awareness training for employees. Allow them to see how your company's ethical system applies to everyday problems and gray areas. This is a slow process, and benefits may not be observed immediately, but do not give up.

Step Four
Outline specific responsibilities for decision making to ensure accountability. It is important that policies and lines of responsibility be clearly stated. Be willing to take action if your ethical code is violated.

Step Five
Encourage open discussion about controversial issues, ethical questions, and anything that might fall into gray areas. People must feel safe before they will speak openly.

Source: Adapted from Patricia Haddock and Marilyn Manning, "Ethically Speaking," *Sky Magazine*, March 1990, p. 130. This article has been reprinted through the courtesy of Halsey Publishing Co., publishers of Delta Airlines' *Sky Magazine*.

Analyzing Ethical Standards

Figure 5.6 provides a classical framework for analyzing the relationships between legal and ethical issues. Quadrant I shows management behavior that is both legal and ethical, because producing a high-quality product, at low cost, is ethically desirable and legally acceptable. Quadrant II shows behavior that might be regarded as ethical but is, nevertheless, illegal. Quadrant III illustrates legal but unethical behavior. Finally, polluting the environment and discriminating against minorities and women are both illegal and unethical, as shown in Quadrant IV.

It should be noted that there are risks accompanying these various categories of behavior. Ethical but illegal behavior can result in fines and/or imprisonment. Legal but unethical behavior can result in alienation of stakeholders, causing boycotts. Both risks accrue to behavior that is both illegal and unethical. But even actions that are both legal and ethical are not without risk, as laws and standards could change in the future. In cases where legal actions become illegal, laws are often made retroactive, with the result that firms pay fines for activity that was perfectly legal at the time it occurred but is no longer legal when discovered.

A second problem is the conflict between job demands and personal ethics. Consider Jeff Arnold, whose entrepreneurial interests are sparked when an independent programmer presents him with an exciting new software concept. It could be the perfect product for his wife's fledgling software development firm—if Jeff does not refer the idea to his boss.[44]

Many situations in today's business world cannot easily be labeled either right or wrong. Instead, as illustrated by the Lockheed case (p. 159), they fall into the gray area of maybe. To demonstrate how difficult these ethical dilemmas can be, try the ethics test in Learning Exercise 5.1 at the end of the chapter.

Another major difficulty, again illustrated by the Lockheed case, is that ethical standards differ in various cultures.

FIGURE 5.6
Framework for determining legal and ethical behavior.

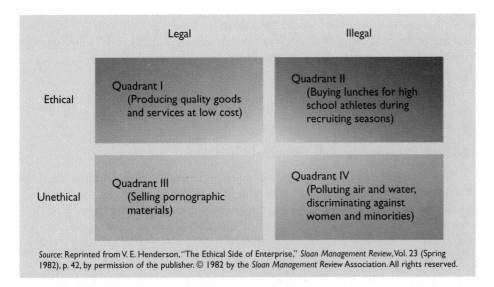

Source: Reprinted from V. E. Henderson, "The Ethical Side of Enterprise," *Sloan Management Review*, Vol. 23 (Spring 1982), p. 42, by permission of the publisher. © 1982 by the *Sloan Management Review* Association. All rights reserved.

Evaluating Ethical and Social Performance

While the public is demanding higher levels of social and ethical behavior, management faces the difficult task of implementing and evaluating that behavior. This requires new managerial skills and the use of social audits and codes of ethics.

Responsible Behavior Requires Improvements in Managerial Skills As the need for greater organizational effectiveness increases, the demand for more ethical and socially responsible behavior grows, and the managerial skills discussed in Chapter 1 must be improved to adapt to those changes.

Managers must become more knowledgeable about operations so that, particularly at the top level, the spokesperson for the organization will be able to give more truthful and meaningful information to external groups. Those managers will need to be persuasive, effective representatives in order to promote their organizations' best interests to outsiders.

Managers will need to develop a more cooperative problem-solving style. Instead of being confrontational, managers will find it beneficial to work with the social forces behind ethical and socially responsible changes, instead of working against them.

Finally, managers not only must have but also must exhibit more open-mindedness in their approach to social issues. They will need to see problems from other points of view, rather than from just their own short-run perspectives, in order to deal with increasing social pressures.

Using Social Audits and Codes of Ethics Some progressive firms measure their social performance by using a **social audit,** a formal procedure for evaluating and reporting on actions that have social implications. While there is no generally accepted format for these audits, subjects covered usually include equal employment opportunity and training, conservation and pollution control, educational assistance, and contributions to culture, the arts, and recreation.

In addition, many organizations and groups have adopted a **code of ethics,** a formal statement that serves as a guide to action in problems involving ethical questions. There are many such codes for regulating the behavior of professions or occupational groups, business associations, advisory groups, and individual organizations and managers. Such codes can be long and formal or as short as the Golden Rule: "Do unto others as you would have them do unto you."

One of the best codes of ethics is the Rotary International's code. Known as the Four-Way Test, it requires that four simple questions be asked:

▶ Is it the truth?

▶ Is it fair to all concerned?

▶ Will it build goodwill and better friendships?

▶ Will it be beneficial to all concerned?[45]

The Academy of Management is a unique organization of teaching professionals set up "to foster the general advancement of research, learning, teaching and practice in the management field." Consequently, it took the lead in encouraging ethical behavior in 1990 by adopting an official *Code of Ethical Conduct.* A summary of that code is shown in Figure 5.7. Membership in the Academy includes the individual's acknowledgment of and pledge to adhere to provisions of the code.

social audit A formal procedure for evaluating and reporting on actions that have social implications.

code of ethics A formal statement that serves as a guide to action regarding problems involving ethical questions.

SUMMARY*
THE ACADEMY OF MANAGEMENT
CODE OF ETHICAL CONDUCT
(APPROVED AUGUST 1990)

CREDO

We believe in discovering, sharing, and applying managerial knowledge.

PREAMBLE

Our professional goals are to enhance the learning of students, colleagues, and others and to improve the effectiveness of organizations through our teaching, research, and practice of management. We have five major responsibilities:

- To our students—Relationships with students require respect, fairness, and caring, along with recognition of our commitment to the subject matter and to teaching excellence.
- To managerial knowledge—Prudence in research design, human subject use, confidentiality, result reporting, and proper attribution of work is a necessity.
- To the Academy of Management and the larger professional environment—Support of the Academy's mission and objectives, service to the Academy and our institutions, and the recognition of the dignity and personal worth of colleagues is required.
- To both managers and the practice of management—Exchange of ideas and information between the academic and organizational communities is essential.
- To all people with whom we live and work in the world community—Sensitivity to other people, to diverse cultures, to the needs of the poor and disadvantaged, to ethical issues, and to newly emerging ethical dilemmas is required.

STUDENT RELATIONSHIPS

In our roles as educators, the central principles that underlie appropriate student-educator relationships are professionalism, respect, fairness, and concern.

ADVANCEMENT OF MANAGERIAL KNOWLEDGE

Academy member research should be done honestly, have a clear purpose, show respect for the rights of all individuals and organizations, efficiently use resources, and advance knowledge in the field.

THE ACADEMY OF MANAGEMENT AND THE LARGER PROFESSIONAL ENVIRONMENT

The Mission Statement of the Academy describes member benefits and professional opportunities which impose corresponding duties and service responsibilities.**

MANAGERS AND THE PRACTICE OF MANAGEMENT

Consulting with client organizations ("clients") has the potential for enriching the teaching and practice of management, for translating theory into practice, and for furthering research and community service. To maximize such potential benefits, it is essential that members who consult be guided by the ideals of competence, integrity, and objectivity.

THE WORLD COMMUNITY

As citizens of the world community, Academy members may have much to contribute in shaping global consciousness by their teaching, research, and service.

* This is a summary. The entire code appears in the December 1990 ACADEMY OF MANAGEMENT JOURNAL (VOL 33, NO 4 pp 901–8).
** The Mission of the Academy is stated in Article II of the Constitution of the Academy of Management that appears in the Academy of Management Handbook (April, 1989), page 28.

FIGURE 5.7

The Academy of Management's *Code of Ethical Conduct.*

In addition, many organizations have **ethical advisers,** older employees who have been with the firm for a long time and to whom employees can go for advice when they face ethical dilemmas. A variation of the ethical adviser is the full-time *corporate ethics officer.* In 1992, 65 people held this position in U.S. companies.[46]

ethical advisers
Longtime employees of a firm whom younger employees can consult when they face ethical dilemmas.

S U M M A R Y

When management acts in a socially responsible manner, it sets policies, makes decisions, and follows courses of action that are desirable in terms of the values and objectives of its customers, employees, and people in the community as well as its stockholders. Companies act responsibly because (1) if they do not, the people may take away their right to operate; (2) it is in their long-run best interest to do so; (3) if they do not, adverse legislation may result; and (4) it helps them maintain their credibility with the public.

Social responsibility has evolved through four stages. In earlier days, government and religious groups tried to force business owners/managers to act responsibly, but business was primarily operated for the benefit of owners. Most U.S. businesses grew as a result of applying the ethic of hard work, thrift, and savings to the principles of private property and unrestrained competition. But abuses by some shortsighted owners around the turn of the century led to legislation that protected customers.

This period of profit maximization ended with the Great Depression. Trusteeship management began by emphasizing concern for stockholders, employees, customers, and the community and gave meaning to that concern through the passage of many significant pieces of social legislation. However, primary emphasis was still on the owners.

The third phase developed during the 1960s and 1970s. It was a period of activism, with movements fostering equal employment opportunity, environmental protection, and consumerism.

The present stage includes—but is not restricted to—(1) maintaining effective but humane employee relations programs, (2) supporting public and community service, (3) ensuring environmental protection, (4) encouraging consumerism, (5) providing educational and medical assistance, (6) investing in urban renewal and development, and (7) subsidizing culture, the arts, and recreation.

There is a need for business managers to balance social responsibility and profits. While social responsibility may even increase profits in many cases, in others it may reduce them. In still other cases, however, companies are able to balance gains from effective operation with the costs of social action so that they incur no net losses. Although social responsibility is now generally accepted, some authorities think management's primary social responsibility is to make a profit for the owners. But the prevailing belief is that business must balance the interests of customers, employees, the public, and stockholders in order to survive.

A growing problem in maintaining managerial ethics involves what standards to use in judging the rightness or wrongness of a manager's relations to others. There is a growing interest in this subject among students, faculty members, business owners, managers, and the public. Just a few of the areas of concern are (1) bribery, (2) industrial theft and espionage, (3) conflict of interest, (4) advertising and media abuses, (5) collusion, and (6) fraud.

Many efforts are currently being made to develop some ethical standards of behavior. This chapter reviewed some of these efforts, especially those providing a framework for understanding socially responsible and ethical behaviors.

Management now faces the difficult task of implementing and evaluating socially responsible and ethical behavior. New skills are needed, and managers need to perform social audits and adhere to codes of ethical conduct. Recently, more and more ethical advisers and corporate ethics officers are being appointed in U.S. businesses.

KEY TERMS

social responsibility, 141
limited (or restricted) responsibility, 142
unlimited (or extensive)
 responsibility, 142
trustee management, 146
equal employment opportunity
 (EEO) laws, 147
consumerism, 147
affirmative action program (AAP), 150

environmental protection, 153
conservation, 153
recycling, 154
pollution, 154
ethics, 158
collusion, 162
social audit, 166
code of ethics, 166
ethical advisers, 167

DISCUSSION QUESTIONS

1. Discuss the rationale for management to be socially responsible.

2. Defend or refute Milton Friedman's concept of social responsibility.

3. Can management really practice social responsibility and still make a profit for the owners? In other words, do you think the odds favor trying to earn a profit or maintaining social responsibility? Explain.

4. How would you describe the evolution of the four stages of managerial social responsibility: profit maximization, trusteeship management, activism, and social responsiveness?

5. Explain the following statement: Management must be socially responsible to survive.

6. Describe or explain some of the managerial activities that involve ethical decisions.

7. How effective do you think social audits can be?

8. Your firm needs a new employee, and you have a friend who needs a job. You think the friend is qualified, but there are probably some better-qualified people available if the firm keeps looking. What would you do? Why?

9. What are some of the new skills required to cope with the increasing demands for more ethical and socially responsible behavior?

10. Do you think the authors are correct in saying that businesspeople do not act any more unethically than people in other areas, such as government, unions, and not-for-profit organizations? Defend you answer.

PRACTICING MANAGEMENT

5.1

case

Gerber Products—A Business with a Heart

For all his 20 years, Raymond Dunn, Jr. could not walk or talk. In fact, he could hardly breathe. But Raymond could do one thing: He could make people care—including a giant corporation that gave him sustenance.

Raymond lived with his parents, Raymond Sr., a car salesman, and Carol, a homemaker, in the Catskills town of Yankee Lake, New York. Raymond was born with a broken skull and a brain deprived of oxygen. His twisted, cramped body was only four feet tall and he never weighed over 38 pounds. He was severely mentally and physically retarded, blind, and mute. He could not move his arms or legs without help, and his warped spine had worn a dent in the pad of his wheelchair. The Dunns have no other children.

Raymond's allergies were so severe that he could not eat normal food. Since the age of 5, he had been unable to take any form of nourishment except Gerber's MBF, an expensive meat-based formula for allergic infants.

Life had always been difficult for the Dunns, but their problems seemed insurmountable when they received a letter from Gerber in July 1988 saying that it was running out of MBF. Faced with declining sales, Gerber had stopped making the brown liquid formula in 1985. The company had offered to reveal its formula and process for making MBF to any manufacturer who would supply Raymond, but none was willing or able to do so. So, according to George Purvis, Gerber's research director, "We scrounged around for every can of the stuff that was in existence." Since the expiration date on some of the cans had passed, Gerber obtained a waiver from the Food and Drug Administration and began delivering the cans to the Dunns.

In the meantime, Mrs. Dunn, whose life was already consumed with Raymond's care, desperately sought help by writing dozens of letters to business and political leaders, including President Bush, Donald Trump, and even the Princess of Wales. Unfortunately, however, Gerber remained her only hope. She says, "I felt somehow Gerber would not let Raymond die. I believed they wouldn't let me down because they're human beings in that corporation."

She was right. In 1990, Gerber's research division volunteers, who had been working with Mrs. Dunn, told their bosses they would be able to assemble the special equipment and ingredients (including beef hearts) needed to make the MBF. For a few days in April, other projects were put on hold, and one-quarter of the production space at Gerber Products's research center in Fremont, Michigan, was devoted to making the formula for Raymond. According to Purvis, "People worked on this on their own time. We all had our own jobs, but this was one we added on. I don't want to talk too much about it, as it was just something we could do, so we did it. It was a volunteer project, and the Dunns had nowhere else to turn."

The special run filled about 6,000 of the plant's 25,000 square feet of production space. Although the project cost Gerber about $15,000, the resulting supply of MBF was provided to the Dunns free of charge. The batch lasted two years, but when Raymond finished it, Gerber made more. When Raymond—who had become known as the "Gerber boy," died on January 17, 1995, there was still a year's supply on hand.

After Raymond's death, Dr. Sandra Bartholmey, a Gerber nutritionist, was surprised when someone asked why she and her colleagues devoted so much effort to a market of one. She replied, "It seemed like the right thing to do."

Mrs. Dunn plans to devote the energy she once spent on Raymond to raise money to build the Raymond Dunn Rainbow House, a facility for "medically fragile, technology-dependent children."

Sources: "Gerber Is a Lifesaver," *USA Today*, April 6, 1990, p. 2A; Rick Hampton, "Gerber Goes All Out for Allergic Teen-ager," *Mobile* (Alabama) *Register*, April 9, 1990, p. 6A; and Rick Hampson, "Raymond Dunn, 'Gerber Boy,' Dead at 20," *Mobile* (Alabama) *Press Register*, January 27, 1995, p. 2-A.

Gerber employees volunteered their time to help a sick child.

Questions

1. Do you think Gerber was being "socially responsible" to devote this much expense and effort to "a market of one"? Explain.

2. Should Gerber have publicized this activity? Explain.

3. Do you think Mrs. Dunn will be successful in raising money for the Raymond Dunn Rainbow House? Explain.

5.1

learning exercise

A Simple Ethics Test

Put your value system to the test in the following situations:

Scoring Code: Strongly Agree = SA   Agree = A   Disagree = D   Strongly Disagree = SD

	SA	A	D	SD
1. Employees should not be expected to inform on their peers.			✗	
2. There are times when a manager must overlook contract and safety violations in order to get on with the job.	✗			
3. It is not always possible to keep accurate expense account records; therefore, it is sometimes necessary to give approximate figures.			✗	
4. There are times when it is necessary to withhold embarrassing information from one's superior.		✗		
5. We should do what our managers suggest, though we may have doubts about it being the right thing to do.			✗	
6. It is sometimes necessary to conduct personal business on company time.		✗		
7. Sometimes it is good psychology to set goals somewhat above normal if it will help to obtain a greater effort from the sales force.		✗		
8. I would quote a "hopeful" shipping date in order to get the order.		✗		
9. It is proper to use the company WATS line for personal calls as long as it is not in use.			✗	
10. Management must be goal oriented; therefore, the end usually justifies the means.		✗		
11. If it takes heavy entertainment and twisting a bit of company policy to win a large contract, I would authorize it.		✗		
12. Exceptions to company policy and procedures are a way of life.		✗		
13. Inventory controls should be designed to report "underages" rather than "overages" in goods received. [The ethical issue here is the same as that faced by someone who receives too much change from a store cashier.]			✗	
14. Occasional use of the company's copier for personal or community activities is acceptable.			✓	✗
15. Taking home company property (pencils, paper, tape, etc.) for personal use is an accepted fringe benefit.			✗	

Score Key: (0) for Strongly Disagree, (1) for Disagree, (2) for Agree, (3) for Strongly Agree

If your score is:

0	Prepare for canonization ceremony	**11–15**	Good ethical values	**16–25**	Average ethical values
1–5	Bishop material	**16–25**	Average ethical values	**36–44**	Slipping fast
6–10	High ethical values	**26–35**	Need more moral development	**45**	Leave valuables with warden

Source: Adapted from Lowell G. Rein, "Is Your (Ethical) Slippage Showing?" *Personnel Journal*, vol. 59 (September 1980), p. 59. Reprinted with permission of *Personnel Journal*; all rights reserved. Copyright September 1980.

Question

1. What do you think is "right" or "wrong" with each of these actions? Explain your answers.

PART 2

Managing Strategies and Processes

> **Managers are responsible for the charting of the destiny of the firm and implementing the resulting strategies. The quality of that planning can be no better than the quality of managers who develop the plan.**
> —PAUL R. CONE AND RICHARD W. McKINNY

Part Two focuses on four fundamental management processes: (1) decision making, (2) strategic and operational planning, (3) organizational design and authority, and (4) human resource management. Chapter 6 discusses decision making, covering the steps in decision making, involvement of subordinates in decision making, and ways to stimulate creativity. Chapter 7 addresses strategic and operational planning, including the organizational mission, objectives, strategies, and approaches to putting plans into operation throughout the entire organization. Fundamentals in designing an organization as well as the processes of authority, power, responsibility, and accountability are found in Chapter 8. Organizational downsizing and reengineering are also discussed.

Chapter 9 reemphasizes that human resources are the most important element in any organization. Only through planning for, recruiting, selecting, training, developing, and compensating its employees can an organization be effective. Important changes in workplace laws and employee diversity are identified.

All the analyst really requires for the solution of a problem is, first, the painstaking assembly of all the phenomena; second, exhaustive patience; and third, the ability to comprehend the whole problem with a fresh and unbiased imagination.

—ELLERY QUEEN

Decision Making and Creative Problem Solving

LEARNING OBJECTIVES

After studying the material in this chapter, you should be able to:

- **Define** decision making.

- **Distinguish** between programmed and nonprogrammed decisions.

- **Identify** the steps in the decision-making process.

- **Explain** what variables help determine the extent to which a manager should involve subordinates in the decision-making process.

- **Describe** the concept of synergy and the processes of creative problem solving.

Peavey Electronics: World's Largest Seller of Power Amplifiers

Hartley Peavey is not alone at the top of his industrial empire: His wife, Melia, is there with him. They did not inherit their jobs; nor did they receive MBAs to prepare them for the business world; they just learned by doing, as they built Peavey Electronics from a small, Meridian, Mississippi, plant into a worldwide music and sound amplification giant—the world's largest seller of guitar amplifiers.

Hartley, with an undergraduate degree from Mississippi State University, describes the company as "the University of Peavey." Melia, who received a college scholarship but never used it, agrees, stating emphatically that she learned much more there than she ever could have in school.

She began working at Peavey in 1972, when it was just beginning to make waves, for $1.60 per hour—the minimum wage. She planned to work for a couple of years to save money to supplement her scholarship so she could major in psychology and sociology. Instead, she stayed at Peavey Electronics and has "loved every minute of it."

Melia credits her growth as a businessperson to Hartley's desire to have something of an "industrial Camelot," and to his willingness to allow people to do all they can. "He will give anybody a chance to do anything that they're capable of doing," she says. "I was 17 years old, female, with little education. I would never ever have been given the opportunities in another company that I was in this one. I didn't even know what an amplifier was!"

That was back when everybody had to do everything. Now, an organizational chart—if they had one—would show Hartley as president and Melia as vice-president, but at Peavey they do not care for titles. Instead, they act as co-presidents. Hartley does not like the routine details that come with running a business, while Melia is geared more in that direction. He is more than happy to let her watch the profit margin while he develops new products.

The Peaveys' goal is to build a $1 billion company. Estimates put it at, or very near, $500 million today, but all they will say is, "We're getting there." Obviously, Peavey Electronics is not a little mom-and-pop electric shop anymore. Instead, it is the country's top guitar maker, the world's largest manufacturer of power amplifiers, and producer of the best-selling guitar amp in the world (the Bandit 112 S). In all, it makes and/or packages about 2,000 different products and accessories. According to Peavey, that is a far cry from the early days when "Meridian wholesalers refused to supply me with Elmer's glue. They considered me a 'hippie.' I was 'that long-haired Peavey boy.'"

With over 1,000 U.S. dealers; outlets in 103 countries; two honors from the U.S. government for excellence in exporting; operations in Canada, England, and the Netherlands; plants in Decatur, Morton, and Leakesville, Mississippi; and corporate headquarters, main plants—a total of 29—training center, distribution center,

The Peaveys and some of their most popular products in the late 1980s.

and corporate hanger in Meridian, Peavey keeps dozens of people hopping. But because Peavey Electronics is theirs, Hartley and Melia stay actively involved in a hands-on fashion. Trade shows and conventions also keep them on the go, but one of the biggest and most important reasons for their travels is their "Being There" program, which puts Hartley and/or Melia face to face with Peavey dealers and customers. Hartley explains the program by saying, "Some competitors are quite willing to spend hundreds of thousands or millions of dollars for fancy brochures and ads but aren't willing to spend the most valuable commodity of all—their time—on dealers."

Peavey Electronics also demonstrates care for its employees in a way that most other companies do not—with a "no-layoff" policy. That policy was severely tested a few years ago when the economy took a dive and there was not enough work for all employees. "Rather than lay off hundreds of employees, we kept them busy sweeping streets, painting, cleaning roofs, and doing other such jobs. It ruined profits that year," Hartley adds, "but layoffs could have ruined families."

Hartley and Melia say they could not have kept the employees on the payroll had it not been for their policy of not borrowing money. That's right: Peavey Electronics does not borrow; nor does it seek or accept venture capital. "Everything is paid for out of cash flow," Hartley explains. "Our company is privately held for one reason: We sometimes do things because we think it's right, not because it puts the most dollars on the bottom line."

That is an example of the Peavey's policy of looking at the long-range effects of a decision or procedure instead of long-term profits. "Since day one, this company has been a great big poker game, for with every hand, all the chips are on the table."

From appearances, they are playing their cards right. In the first half of 1995, ovr 560 dealers, distributors, and resellers have visited the

Peavey Center for a week of training in various products and marketing strategy. The attendees have come from the domestic field as well as Latin America, Norway, Sweden, Italy, Syria, Central and South America, Canada, Australia, England, and Germany. This obviously means that there continues to be vigorous growth both domestically as well as internationally.

Some significant events in the development of Peavey Electronics are the following:

1964 First Peavey patent

1965 Peavey Electronics Corporation chartered

1968 First expansion, into a 6,000-square-foot building

1969 Begins exporting products

1972 Employment level reaches 100

1976 Introduces commercial sound power amplifiers (CS 800 TM) and commercial sound loudspeaker enclosures (SPI TM)

1978 Employment level reaches 500; introduces solid body electric guitars (T-4 TM and T-6 TM); awarded the Presidential "E" Award for Excellence in Exporting (U.S. Department of Commerce)

1979 Exports to the sixtieth country

1981 Employment level reaches 1,000

1984 Introduces world's first digital-powered amplifier (DECA 700 TM)

1985 Awarded the Presidential "E Star" Award for Excellence in Exporting (U.S. Department of Commerce)

1988 Employment level reaches 1,500; introduces first digital-signal-processing-based synthesizer that is upgraded via software, thus preventing obsolesence (DPM 3 TM)

1989 First private sector pilot site for Job Skill Education Program (JSEP), designed by the U.S. Army and decreed for nonmilitary training activities

1991 Selected as one of 20 U.S. companies to participate in the Japan Corporate Program, sponsored by the U.S. Department of Commerce; first occasion of a U.S. president recognizing a commercial sound equipment manufacturer with a personal visit: President George Bush visits Peavey

1992 Honored at the White House on network TV for workforce literacy efforts at the National Literacy Honors Award ceremony

1993 Employment level reaches 2,000[1]

This case illustrates several important concepts regarding decision making. First, it shows how the core values of decision makers influence the decisions they make. Second, it underscores the importance of examining the long-range effects of decisions. Third, it highlights how people with different personalities can use teamwork to come up with more effective decisions and results than could be achieved separately. Later in the chapter, you will have an opportunity to diagnose the problem-solving styles of Hartley and Melia Peavey.

Keep in mind that effective decision-making skills are a very important factor in advancing to higher levels of management. In a study by Norma Carr-Ruffino, 100 women managers identified problem-solving and decision-making skills as the second most important factor in reaching their present positions.[2]

Although the emphasis in this chapter is on decision making, we have also included some important concepts related to problem solving, as the areas are related. Some of the steps in problem solving are the same as those used in decision making. But while all problem solving involves decision making, not all decision making involves problem solving. In fact, many decisions involve choosing between attractive opportunities. As business organizations accelerate their use of ad hoc task forces, quality circles, and self-managing work teams, decision making and problem solving are integrated into the work of the teams.

> An example of the relationship between decision making and problem solving is a newspaper's daily "budget meeting." The problem to be solved is how to get a mass of information into limited space, especially on the front page. The editors must decide which stories are important enough to be featured (the top stories "above the fold"), which will be relegated to inside pages, and which dropped entirely.

All areas of management require decision making. In fact, it can be said that management *is* decision making, or that *to manage is to make decisions.* If you cannot make effective decisions, you will probably be ineffective as a manager. Because so many decisions are involved in planning, we have placed decision making in this section on planning.

Organizations are increasing the use of groups to deal with decision making and problem solving.

What Decision Making Is

Decision making is required of everyone, individuals as well as managers, and applies to taking advantage of opportunities as well as to solving problems. Each of us makes many decisions every day. We have to decide whether and when to get up, what clothes to wear, what to eat, where to go, and how to get there, in addition to the countless job or school decisions we face. Most of these decisions fall into the "routine" category and do not require a great deal of analytical effort. Occasionally, though, a choice comes along that involves much greater stakes.

> Sharon Jeffer was in a quandary as she left the office of Dr. Figures, the head of the
> university's accounting department. As a graduating senior, she was undecided
> about what type of accounting position to accept. An excellent student, she had
> received two offers from accounting firms, one from a bank, and another from a
> large utility. She had assured all of the prospective employers that she would let
> them know her decision within the week. Now she had just been offered a fifth
> alternative—an assistantship in the accounting department at the university to
> pursue work on her master's degree. She had said she would let Dr. Figures know
> within a week.

The decision Sharon makes will have a significant long-range impact on her life and therefore requires greater energy than the routine decisions she ordinarily makes. Her decision-making process will be similar to that used by managers in making important business decisions.

Managerial Decision Making

Managerial decision making can be defined as the conscious selection of a course of action from available alternatives to produce a desired result. Notice several aspects of this definition. First, decision making involves a *conscious* choice, not an unconscious or involuntary reaction. Second, there must be two or more *available* alternatives; otherwise there is no decision to be made. Third, the course of action selected leads to a *desired result.*

> **managerial decision making** The conscious selection of a course of action from available alternatives to produce a desired result.

Decision making is a way of life for managers, and the quality of the decisions made is a predominant factor in how upper management views a lower manager's performance. Books, movies, television series, and news documentaries dramatize decisions made by top managers, but middle and lower managers also face such decisions, as the following example shows.

> Gilbert, an environmental manager, had just ordered a shutdown and evacuation of
> his firm's nuclear research department. The shutdown involved the movement of
> over 110 persons and required at least 12 hours of corrective steps and tests before
> the area could be reopened. The cost of this decision was a minimum of $300,000,
> plus the load of paperwork, interviews, unfavorable publicity, and investigation by
> various federal and state officials. And there was a 30 percent chance that Gilbert's
> decision was an incorrect one. Still, on the basis of instrument readings and other
> evidence, Gilbert believed that everyone's safety was jeopardized by possible con-
> tamination in a radioactive area, and he could take no chances.

Employees As Decision Makers

Managers are not the only ones who make critical decisions in organizations. Air traffic controllers and aircraft inspectors, for instance, make life-and-death decisions daily. Computer maintenance technicians often make million-dollar decisions, secretaries decide who and what gets to their supervisors, and accountants decide what value to place on certain important assets. We can say that in an organization, every person's job—even the most routine one—involves some degree of decision making.

> J. Georg Bednorz and K. Alex Mueller, researchers at IBM's Swiss laboratory, began working on an idea so big that they were loath to share the details with IBM officials. When they mentioned to an IBM official their research to find a cheap, simple substance to conduct electricity with little if any resistance, they got a skeptical reaction. So they hunted quietly, telling a supervisor a half-truth and steering a curious visitor off the track. But their breakthrough with superconductors in January 1986 stunned the scientific world. It also earned them the 1986 Nobel Prize in physics.[3]

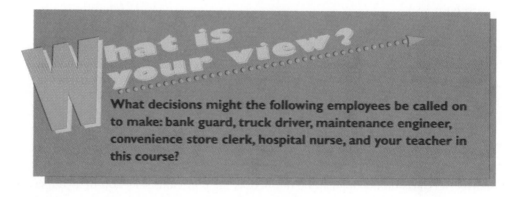

What is your view?

What decisions might the following employees be called on to make: bank guard, truck driver, maintenance engineer, convenience store clerk, hospital nurse, and your teacher in this course?

Programmed and Nonprogrammed Decisions

programmed decisions
Decisions that are routine and repetitive.

One broad method of classifying decisions is to examine whether or not a decision is programmed. **Programmed decisions** are those that are routine and repetitive. The manager (or organization), to facilitate decision making, has devised established, systematic guidelines for handling the decision situation. Examples of areas in which programmed decisions would be made include the following:

1. Decisions about how many items to reorder when the stock level in a grocery store reaches a certain count
2. Decisions about how to process a university student's request to drop or add a course
3. Decisions about how to admit new hospital patients
4. Decisions about the frequency of maintenance servicing of factory machinery and equipment
5. Decisions about what disciplinary action to take when an employee reports to work in an intoxicated condition

These examples are handled in a systematic way, and a decision framework (for example, a set of policies) has been established for the decision maker to follow.

Perhaps the handling of an intoxicated employee appears to you to be different from the other four examples. But if the company policy manual prescribes a given penalty for intoxication, the decision about the penalty the supervisor should impose tends to be a programmed or predetermined one.

Nonprogrammed decisions are those that occur infrequently and, because of differing variables, require a separate response each time. Examples of nonprogrammed decisions might include the following:

1. Whether to buy a new car, and which car to buy
2. Which job offer to select from the many received
3. Where to locate a new company warehouse
4. Whom to promote to the vacant position of plant manager at one of the company's plants
5. How to schedule workers' vacations, given their requests, so that the department can operate at 90 percent of capacity each week during the summer

nonprogrammed decisions Decisions that occur infrequently and, because of differing variables, require a separate response each time.

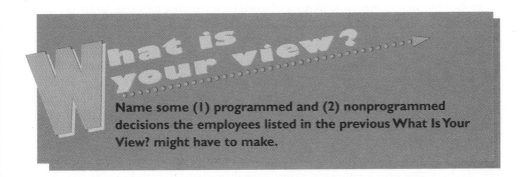

Name some (1) programmed and (2) nonprogrammed decisions the employees listed in the previous What Is Your View? might have to make.

Steps in Managerial Decision Making

The steps shown in Figure 6.1 represent the most common type of managerial decision-making model. It consists of the following steps:

1. Recognize that there is a problem to solve or an opportunity to seize
2. Develop alternative courses of action
3. Evaluate the advantages and disadvantages of each alternative
4. Select the preferred alternative and implement it
5. Evaluate the decision results and restart the process if the decision does not work

Feedback, in the form of evaluation results, permits a modification or a new decision if the original one is faulty. Learning Exercise 6.1, "The $100,000 Investment Decision," at the end of this chapter, can help you apply these steps in making a decision.

Step 1: Recognize a Problem or Opportunity

A frequent mistake is to observe a situation's symptoms and treat them as underlying causes. Let us look at a business example. Assume that you own a small business and your profits have been down sharply for the last several months. You would be

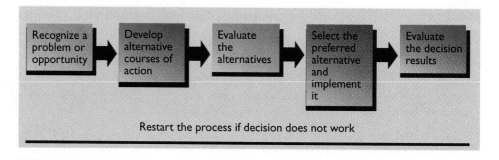

FIGURE 6.1
The decision-making process.

very naive to make assumptions about the causes without some investigation (unless there is some strong evidence that an obvious factor has caused the problem—for instance, a natural disaster or a competitor moving in next door). Possible causes might include the following:

1. Changes in the competitive situation (such as new competitors, disruptive competitor price policies, competitor product advantages)
2. Higher costs (increased rent, utilities, payroll, overtime)
3. Employee inefficiency (poor motivation, poor sales technique, pilferage)
4. Changes in traffic patterns (new thoroughfares, interstate highways, closed roads)
5. Seasonal shifts (many businesses, such as gift shops, ice cream parlors, and photography stores, routinely experience drops in sales—and profits—at certain times of the year)
6. Store policy (no credit, no returns on merchandise)

Effective decision makers are keenly aware of the importance of properly defining the situation and understanding it. This approach is at the heart of the Kepner-Tregoe decision-making method (shown in MAP 6.1), as applied to problem solving.

The following example illustrates recognition of both an opportunity and a problem, and how each was resolved.

A small consumer goods company in the Northeast sent representatives to Japan on a high-level trade mission sponsored by the U.S. Department of Commerce. The mission assumed a "looking around" attitude, rather than an "order writing" approach, and was well received.

The company's product was a picture cut in wood, with inlaid designs depicting scenes such as duck hunting. It has a "nice American feeling" and was very beautiful according to potential buyers as they looked at it on the display wall. After turning it over and looking at the back, however, the buyers lost interest.

When the company's potential Japanese partner was asked what the problem was, he answered, "This will never sell in Japan, because the back's not finished." Together, the manufacturer and the Japanese partner finished the back so it would not damage walls, and the product became a popular item.[4]

MANAGEMENT APPLICATION AND PRACTICE 6.1

The Kepner-Tregoe Problem-Solving Method

The Kepner-Tregoe method of problem analysis teaches that the first step in decision making, recognizing the problem, is the most important step. Getting a good definition of the real problem is critical for making an intelligent, valid decision about a solution. This method teaches that it is often easier to define what the problem is *not*, rather than what it *is*. Also, the problem—and its solution—is prioritized with other problems, to clarify its relative importance. The final step is searching for cause-effect relationships. In summary, the method includes the following:

1. Recognizing the problem

2. Defining what the problem is and is not

3. Prioritizing the problem

4. Testing for cause-effect relationships

5. Making the decision

This method has been taught to managers in some of the largest organizations in the world for the last quarter-century. One aspect of the difficulty in defining and understanding the problem is poor framing of the problem and/or alternatives. Decision makers often allow a problem to be "framed" by the language or context in which it is presented instead of exploring it from every angle. For example, at the Center for Decision Making at the University of Chicago, students were split into two groups to make a decision. One group was told that a business decision had an 80 percent chance of success; the other group was told that the decision had a 20 percent chance of failure. The first group gave the decision a green light, while the second group turned it down, even though both groups had actually been given the same information. The key variable was the form in which the data had been presented.

Source: Adapted from C. H. Kepner and B. B. Tregoe, *The Rational Manager* (New York: McGraw-Hill, 1985), and John McCormick, "The Wisdom of Solomon," *Newsweek,* August 17, 1987, p. 62.

Step 2: Develop Alternative Courses of Action

Once you have a clear definition and understanding of the situation, you are prepared to generate alternatives. Remember from the definition that if there is no choice of alternatives, there is really no decision to be made. The use of staff groups and the counsel of others may lead to the development of certain alternatives that the manager might not have been able to identify alone.

If there are many alternatives, it is sometimes beneficial to use a decision tree such as the one shown in Figure 6.2(a). A **decision tree** is a graphic tool for evaluating available alternatives. When a situation requires a decision, you look at the known available alternatives (A_1–A_4), then you evaluate the possible outcomes (O's), and select the alternative that promises the most favorable outcome.

An example of using a decision tree would be an investor who has $100,000 to invest for five years. Figure 6.2(b) identifies several alternatives and helps in assessing the pros and cons of each. In this example, the investor is considering five alternatives, ranging from a condo in a resort area to a money market fund. After conducting research on best-case and worst-case scenarios for each alternative, the investor will reach a decision, which may combine two or more alternatives.

Should a manager identify *all* feasible alternatives? Perhaps this sounds good in theory, but in practice it is frequently difficult to do, for several reasons. For one thing, managers do not usually have complete information at their disposal when making decisions. Although some books and courses in decision making advise the

decision tree Graphic tool for evaluating alternatives in decision making.

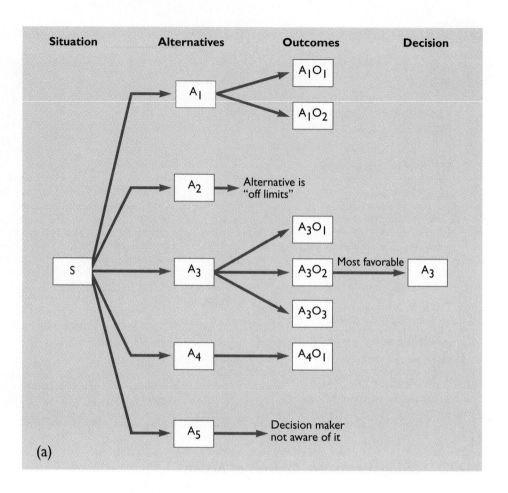

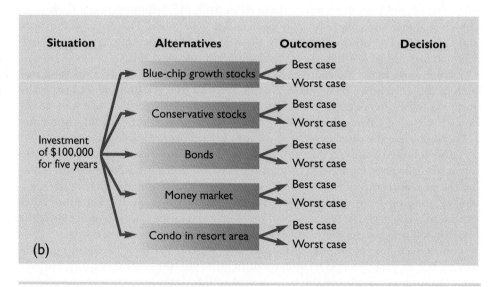

FIGURE 6.2

(a) A decision tree. (b) Example of using a decision tree.

decision maker to get "all the facts" before considering alternatives when making a decision, in reality this is not always possible. Managers can rarely make decisions based on complete information and perfect foresight because of lack of time and resources.

Herbert Simon, a noted management scholar, calls this concept *satisficing*, meaning that the decision maker selects an alternative that is reasonably good, although not necessarily the perfect or ideal one.[5] According to the concept of *bounded rationality*, Simon considered the range of satisfaction to be *maximizing* (most or greatest), *optimizing*, and *satisficing* (acceptable).

Even if the manager were able to think of every possible alternative, some could not be used, for the following reasons:

1. Some alternatives may be ruled out because they are too costly even to be considered.
2. The organization's physical facilities may eliminate certain alternatives from consideration.
3. The time constraints for making the decision may not allow a thorough search for alternatives.
4. Higher management may already have indicated to the decision maker that certain alternatives are "off limits"—A_2 in Figure 6.2a.

You need to keep in mind that the search for alternatives is greatly influenced by the way you go about defining or thinking about the situation. Suppose, for example, that a retailer's sales are down and the cause is found to be poorly motivated sales personnel. The available alternatives will focus on ways to motivate the present sales force—incentives, pep talks, trips to Hawaii, and the like. But let us take it one step further. Suppose the decision maker raises the fundamental question, "What function do my salespeople perform; why do I need them in the first place?" Now the retailer is able to get to the core of the situation. Some other available alternatives to be considered are (1) reaching customers not only through sales personnel but also through other methods, such as direct mail catalogs, and (2) the possibility of eliminating salespeople altogether and using only direct mail.

Nearly all managerial decision making requires a measure of **creativity,** which uses knowledge, evaluation, innovation, imagination, and inspiration to convert something into something else. The greater our knowledge, the more ideas we have; the wider our experience, the more imagination we have; and the freer our minds are to explore new ideas, the greater our creativity is. Then the new idea must be evaluated and developed into a useful alternative.

creativity Use of knowledge, evaluation, innovation, imagination, and inspiration to convert something into something else.

Step 3: Evaluate Advantages and Disadvantages of Alternatives

Assuming that alternatives have been derived, the next step is to evaluate them. A given alternative can have more than a single outcome (as shown earlier in Figure 6.2). It is important to understand not only the benefits of each alternative and how such benefits may influence the decision objective but also the potential negative side and costs of each alternative, as the following classic example illustrates.

Alfred Sloan, as head of GM, supposedly would defer any major decision on which his staff unanimously agreed. It is reported that on one critical decision, after hearing only favorable discussion of one alternative, he said, "Gentlemen, I take it we are all in complete agreement on the decision here?" They all nodded. "Then," he continued, "I propose that we postpone further discussion of this matter until our next meeting to give ourselves more time to develop some disagreement and perhaps gain some understanding of what the decision is all about." At the next meeting, the proposal was voted down.[6]

In evaluating alternatives, you cannot play "follow the leader." Instead, with extensive research and intensive analysis of the possible alternatives, you may find a profitable niche for yourself, as Progressive Corporation has done.

> According to CEO Peter B. Lewis, Progressive has scored big successes by signing up risky auto insurance customers, such as those who have been arrested for drunk driving, whom other firms routinely reject. Its secret is simple: It picks out the best candidates from those other insurers reject and charges them extremely high rates—though still lower than those of the few other firms, such as State Farm, that still take on the high risks.
>   Progressive chooses its clients with actuarial deftness rooted in obsessive fact gathering. After analyzing voluminous accident and arrest records, the analysts found that drunk drivers with children are least likely to mix gasoline and alcohol again. Also, while other insurers use the weight of the motorcycle as the basis for setting rates for motorcyclists, Progressive uses age. It found that middle-aged bikers are a pretty safe bet.[7]

One approach to evaluating alternatives is for one or more alternatives to be assigned to an individual, who then identifies the pros and cons and presents these to the decision maker. In this way, one person, or perhaps a team, will be responsible for fully exploring the decision potential of a given alternative.

As will be shown in Chapter 15, there are many types of management science tools, such as linear programming, queuing theory, network modeling, and regression analysis, that may be used to evaluate alternatives. But as will be shown later in this chapter, intuition can also be effective.[8]

> An example of intuitive decision making was the decision of Lodwrich Cook, CEO of Atlantic Richfield Company, the nation's eighth largest oil company, to hold the price increase of its gasoline to 4 cents per gallon early in the Persian Gulf crisis, while the other companies were raising prices substantially higher. Said Cook, "I felt it was the right thing to do."[9]

Step 4: Select the Preferred Alternative and Implement It

Once alternatives have been evaluated, it is important for managers to make a decision and implement it in a timely fashion. This fourth decision-making step causes difficulties for many managers. After getting the facts, managers may still not be able to decide, because the analysis and interpretation of the facts may make it more difficult to arrive at a clear-cut decision.

Some managers will not make a decision, even when they have all the facts. They straddle the fence, leaning one day in one direction, another day in the opposite. Once the decision is made, they may announce it in a half-hearted, almost apologetic manner. Such hesitancy may cause others to feel insecure and unsure of the decision maker's ability to make the right decision. It may also create greater resistance to the decision than if it were made quickly and decisively and announced confidently.

> Harold Barnes, owner and chief executive of Drexel Furniture Company, announced at a conference of financial reporters that a proposed merger with a larger firm noted for its progressiveness was "definitely on. Only the details have to be worked out."
>
> Three weeks later, at a meeting of Drexel's top and middle managers, he reported that "the merger is being studied but definitely has strong possibilities."
>
> The next day, a newspaper quoted him as stating that "at this point, the merger may not be in Drexel's best interests."
>
> His managers were upset, and one complained, 'I wish he'd hurry up and get it over with one way or another so we could let our people know something.[10]

How do managers actually make decisions? A recent survey of 349 managers at the level of executive vice-president and above by Pinnacle Group, a consortium of public relations firms, provides a hint.

> They hire consultants, badger assistants, and study management books, but when it comes right down to it, 43 percent of American executives say it's those old "gut feelings" they rely on most when making tough decisions.
>
> "You always suspect that many decisions are made based on gut feelings, but I didn't think many executives would actually admit it," said Darryl Lloyd of Darryl Lloyd Inc., a North Hollywood, California, public relations firm and Pinnacle member. Of those who do not rely on gut feelings, 37.2 percent indicated that they prefer to base decisions on staff recommendations; 30.9 percent turn to numbers or statistics; and 7.4 percent say they prefer to rely on consultants' opinions.[11]

Effective decision making does not stop when the decision is made. It also entails good follow-through and implementation by the parties involved. In fact, many good decisions may be ruined by ineffective implementation, but the decision maker is most often held responsible.

Step 5: Evaluate the Decision Results

After the decision is made and implemented, the job is not finished. Now you must perform the "control" function of management. That is, you must evaluate whether the implementation is proceeding smoothly and the desired results are being attained. If the decision turns out to have been a poor one, you are not bound by any rule to stick with it. You have perhaps heard the expression "don't throw good money after bad." In many cases, it is less costly for a manager to admit having made a poor decision and to reverse it than to try to save face by riding out a decision that does not accomplish its objective. This assumes, of course, that the decision is not irreversible. If it is irreversible, then you will have to stick it out and try to make it succeed.

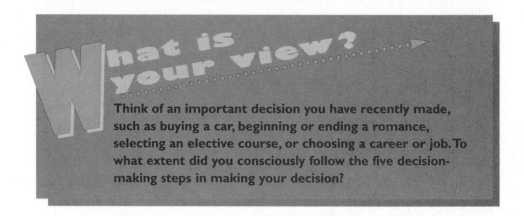

What is your view?

Think of an important decision you have recently made, such as buying a car, beginning or ending a romance, selecting an elective course, or choosing a career or job. To what extent did you consciously follow the five decision-making steps in making your decision?

As you may have discovered in answering the previous question, there are situations that arise every day that do not lend themselves to this decision model. In a crisis, the decision must be made quickly, and this approach may be too time-consuming or the subject may involve variables that do not lend themselves to a rational approach.

Approaches to Decision Making and Problem Solving

Two approaches that are particularly useful in both decision making and problem solving are the Myers-Briggs Type Indicator and the Vroom-Yetton Model. The Myers-Briggs Type Indicator is the better known and is used throughout the world.

The Myers-Briggs Type Indicator

Myers-Briggs Type Indicator (MBTI) A questionnaire focusing on measuring eight dimensions of one's personality type that helps identify an individual's decision-making style.

The 126-item **Myers-Briggs Type Indicator (MBTI)** helps identify an individual's personal style.[12] Although it measures eight dimensions of personality types, we will concern ourselves with only the four internal dimensions: (1) sensing versus (2) intuition and (3) thinking versus (4) feeling. These four are directly related to decision making and problem solving. (The Myers-Briggs concept is based on the work of scholar-physician Carl Gustav Jung, born in Switzerland and a contemporary of Sigmund Freud. Isabel Myers and her mother, Katherine Briggs, further refined and added to the basic theory.)

According to Myers-Briggs, people who rely primarily on *sensing*, or becoming aware of things through the five senses, tend to be patient, practical, and realistic. Those who rely primarily on *intuition*, tend to be impatient, idea and theory oriented, and creative. Although everyone uses both ways of perceiving, Myers-Briggs indicates that at an early age we develop a preference for one method over the other. Therefore, we tend to use our favorite approach and slight the one we enjoy less. Thus, people develop a set of traits based on whether they prefer sensing or intuition, as shown in the top half of Table 6.1.

TABLE 6.1 CHARACTERISTICS OF DIFFERENT PERSONALITY TYPES

SENSING AND INTUITIVE CHARACTERISTICS

Sensing Types	Intuitive Types
Dislike new problems unless there are standard ways to solve them.	Like solving new problems.
Like an established way of doing things.	Dislike doing the same thing repeatedly.
Enjoy using skills already learned more than learning new ones.	Enjoy learning a new skill more than using it.
Work more steadily, with realistic idea of how long it will take.	Work in bursts of energy powered by enthusiasm, with slack periods in between.
Usually reach a conclusion step-by-step.	Reach a conclusion quickly.
Are patient with routine details.	Are impatient with routine details.
Are impatient when the details get complicated.	Are patient with complicated situations.
Are not often inspired, and rarely trust the inspiration when they are.	Follow their inspirations, good or bad.
Seldom make errors of fact.	Frequently make errors of fact.
Tend to be good at precise work.	Dislike taking time for precision.

THINKING AND FEELING CHARACTERISTICS

Thinking Types	Feeling Types
Do not show emotion readily and are often uncomfortable dealing with people's feelings.	Tend to be very aware of other people and their feelings.
May hurt people's feelings without knowing it.	Enjoy pleasing people, even in unimportant things.
Like analysis and putting things into logical order. Can get along without harmony.	Like harmony. Efficiency may be badly disturbed by office feuds.
Tend to decide impersonally, sometimes paying insufficient attention to people's wishes.	Often let decisions be influenced by their own or other people's personal likes and wishes.
Need to be treated fairly.	Need occasional praise.
Are able to reprimand people or fire them when necessary.	Dislike telling people unpleasant things.
Are more analytically oriented—respond more easily to people's thoughts.	Are more people oriented—respond more easily to people's values.
Tend to be firm minded.	Tend to be sympathetic.

People who trust and prefer *thinking*, or using a rational, logical process to come to impersonal conclusions, are quite skillful in dealing with matters that require logic, objectivity, and careful examination of facts. On the other hand, those who trust and prefer *feeling*, or using innate processes that take into account one's own and others' values and beliefs, tend to be adept at working with other people and successful in applying skills in interpersonal and human relations. Such people are normally tactful and appreciative and have the ability to empathize with other people's problems and feelings. The bottom half of Table 6.1 compares thinking and feeling types.

The following examples contrast the decision-making styles of two former U.S. presidents.

Former President Carter has been said to have a sensing-thinking profile. A trained nuclear engineer, he was a "clean desk" executive: fastidiously neat in his handwriting, punctual, precise, logical, and rational in his decision making. A good listener and a fast reader, he was able to soak up and master masses of facts and data, which enabled him to display a dazzling command of facts and figures at press conferences and meetings with legislatures. However, it was apparently difficult for him to see substantive differences between sets of data, to recognize when ideas and objectives were in conflict, and to synthesize new facts with those he had stored away earlier.

Former President Reagan's style, by contrast, was intuitive-feeling, as many of his decisions were apparently made based on sheer instinct or intuition. Although he sometimes appeared to lack factual details, he seemed to have a grasp of the "big picture" and believed policies should be developed on the basis of principles. He was a master of public and human relations: Even most of his opponents liked him. As is characteristic of a feeler, Reagan hated to discipline anyone and rarely criticized aides, even for sloppy staff work that got him into political trouble.[13]

Although experience and growth opportunities can help develop weaker dimensions, most people have developed two of them more than others. The ideal is to maintain a balance by developing capability in all four. This is especially important for decision making, since all four dimensions can be valuable in the decision-making method described earlier.

Sensing, which helps in developing and facing facts as well as being realistic about the nature of the problem or opportunity, is helpful in Step 1, recognizing a problem or opportunity. *Intuition,* on the other hand, is used in areas where creativity is needed to see possibilities and develop opportunities. It is therefore helpful in Step 2, developing alternative courses of action.

Because *thinking* is impersonal and logically considers the consequences of cause and effect, it is helpful in Step 3, evaluating the alternatives. *Feeling* comes into play when it is necessary to consider the values and ethics of others and the impact of the final decision on them. This provides sensitivity in selecting the preferred alternative and implementing it.

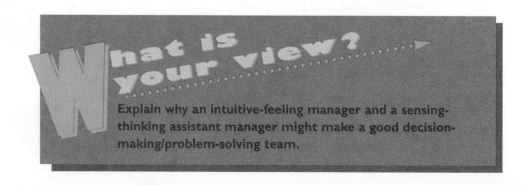

What is your view?

Explain why an intuitive-feeling manager and a sensing-thinking assistant manager might make a good decision-making/problem-solving team.

LINDA DEAN FUCCI

Linda Dean Fucci is senior vice-president and chief financial officer at AuburnBank in Auburn, Alabama. Her duties include investment portfolio management, shareholder relations, asset liability management, strategic planning, accounting procedures, budgeting, tax planning, and control. In 1994, her duties were expanded, and now the departments of data processing, marketing, and electronic services report to her. She was also promoted from secretary/treasurer to senior vice-president of the bank's holding company.

After graduating from Southern Union Junior College with a GPA of 4.0, she completed flight training to the level of commercial pilot and flight instructor. Linda has always regretted not completing a B.S. degree in business, but this lack has not been a barrier to her career achievement. For example, she graduated from Louisiana State University's Graduate School of Banking of the South—one of the premier schools in the country for bankers on a fast career track—in 1986 with a GPA of 2.73 (out of 3.0). In a graduating class of 353 bankers, she not only ranked ninth in academic achievements but also was elected class president. The Alabama Senate passed a resolution of commendation for that achievement. Her previous bank president, William Walker, singled her out in a speech at a state banking meeting as the best chief financial officer of any bank in the state.

Linda's decision-making style is intuitive-thinking. Although these two dimensions are her strongest, she is quite flexible. Through experience and effort, she has developed the sensing and feeling sides as well. In a confidential employee survey evaluating the effectiveness of the top-level Auburn National Bank officers, Linda received an excellent rating. Under the heading of "Additional Comments," one of the employees made this observation: "Linda is a great officer of the bank, representing us in a highly professional manner. She is a great manager and leader, earning a high degree of respect from her employees. She is my mentor. When I grow up, I want to be just *like her.*"

Asked to describe her management philosophy and core values, Linda responded with the following impromptu remarks:

Maybe because I came up through the ranks, I can remember what it was like to be at all different levels. I can remember being unsure of myself and how different reactions made me feel. I try not to reprimand when people make mistakes but to understand and teach. I try never to make them feel "stupid." I do not think that people make errors intentionally. . . .

I think that people need to feel important. Sometimes all it takes is a title. I do not like to call people "clerks." Doesn't "funds management assistant" sound better than "clerk"?

I try to provide my employees with as much knowledge as I can. I sincerely believe that shared knowledge is increased power. The more people in my department know, then the better they do their jobs and the better I, my department, and the whole organization look. I don't think anything makes me feel better than to teach someone something and then see them excel at putting it to use.

Once my employees have learned enough to progress to a given level, I try to leave them alone to get their jobs done. I know they will make some mistakes, but I also think they will learn more this way.

I try to give lots and lots of credit. Whenever I am praised for something done in my department, if others had a hand in it, I give them credit. On the other hand, I try not to pass on the blame. We deal with that back in the department.

I try always to be honest with the employees in my department.

I guess it all comes down to treating others the way I want to be treated; putting myself in their place and feeling how they feel; sensing what is difficult for them to say, to do, and trying to make it easier.

I believe in participative management. I have seen it work in our institution. People are experts in different areas, and the pooling of that expertise creates an exceptional organization. People work harder for a plan they have had a part in than a plan simply dictated to them.

Source: Discussions and correspondence with Linda Dean Fucci.

Otto Kroeger, an expert in Myers-Briggs, was asked to interpret former President George Bush's style. This type "tends to undertake too much, then somehow gets it done. Bush has high ideals, and he's a gracious, gentle person with a low need to be hard-charging, macho. He knows what he wants and he quietly goes about getting it."[14]

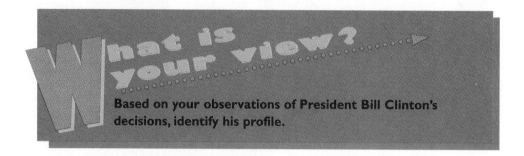

What is your view?

Based on your observations of President Bill Clinton's decisions, identify his profile.

Carl Jung saw type development as a lifelong, never-ending process. People grow and develop problem-solving and decision-making processes if they have the ability to learn from experience. In our Practicing Manager profile of Linda Fucci (intuitive-thinking), we saw an example of development of the sensing and feeling dimensions. As a result, she has the ability to use the appropriate dimension at the appropriate times, thus gaining good balance and wholeness in problem solving and decision making.

The Vroom-Yetton Model

Vroom-Yetton Model
A graphic method that attempts to identify when and to what extent employees should be involved in decision making.

The **Vroom-Yetton Model** provides guidelines on the extent to which subordinates are involved in decision making or problem solving.[15] This involvement may run the gamut from consensus decision making by a natural or self-managing work team, a committee, or an ad hoc task force to the manager making the decision with minimal or no involvement of others. The assistance of subordinates may occur at any of the decision-making steps.

The extent of employee involvement is a contingency call based on the situation, the quality of information available to the decision maker, the importance of subordinates' acceptance of the decision, and the time allowed to make the decision.

Participation   Table 6.2 defines five alternative participation styles, as developed by Vroom and Yetton. There are two autocratic approaches (A and B), two consultative approaches (C and D), and one group consensus approach (E). These five approaches represent the varying degrees of participation by others a manager uses in decision making.

Appropriate Style   A manager can use a decision tree (similar to the one in Figure 6.2) in determining which approach to use. One example of such a tree is shown in Figure 6.3. The questions shown at the top help the decision maker determine the characteristics of a given decision situation.

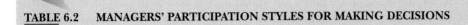

TABLE 6.2   MANAGERS' PARTICIPATION STYLES FOR MAKING DECISIONS

Participation Style	Description
A	You solve the problem or make the decision yourself, using the information available to you at the present time.
B	You obtain any necessary information from subordinates, then decide on a solution to the problem yourself.
C	You share the problem with the relevant subordinates individually, getting their ideas and suggestions without bringing them together as a group. Then *you* make the decision.
D	You share the problem with your subordinates in a group meeting, in which you obtain their ideas and suggestions. Then *you* make the decision.
E	You share the problem with your subordinates as a group. Together you generate and evaluate alternatives and attempt to reach agreement (consensus) on a solution. You can provide the group with information or ideas, but you do not try to press them to adopt "your" solution, and you are willing to accept and implement any solution that has the support of the entire group.

Note: A & B = autocratic, C & D = consultative, E = group consensus.

Source: Adapted and reprinted from *Leadership and Decision-Making,* by Victor H. Vroom and Philip W. Yetton, by permission of the University of Pittsburgh Press. © 1973 University of Pittsburgh Press.

FIGURE 6.3
Decision tree governing group problems.

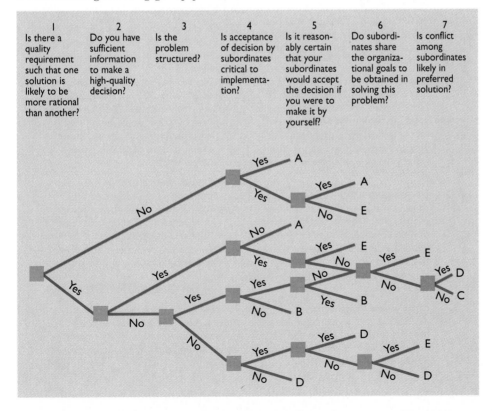

To use the model for a particular situation, you start at the left-hand side of the tree and work toward the right. When you encounter a box, answer the corresponding question and proceed to the next appropriate box. The decision style designation you finally reach will suggest which of the participation styles from Table 6.2 you should probably use.

There are other parts of Vroom's and Yetton's theory that are too detailed to present here. This classic model has been the subject of much attention and is being tested and evaluated by many management researchers.[16]

Two cases at the end of this chapter will give you an opportunity to put the model to use. Although a model such as the one just discussed can help in selecting the best decision-making method, a manager's personal style also has a major impact on the method chosen. (The following Tips box shows how to use the model in making the decision on a student banquet date.)

TipS 6.1

The Vroom-Yetton Model: Which Decision Style to Use

DECISION PROBLEM

As president of the Student Management Club at State University, you must make a decision concerning a date for the annual student banquet.

Q1 Is there a quality requirement such that one solution is likely to be more rational than another?

Ans Yes. One solution is likely to be more rational since there are various dates that will be unsatisfactory because of competing activities.

Q2 Do you have sufficient information to make a high-quality decision?

Ans No. You may have certain information on competing dates for some officially scheduled university activities, but there may be some other kinds of activities going on that you are unaware of.

Q3 Is the problem structured?

Ans Yes. Selection of a given date for a banquet to be held within the next month is a well-structured decision problem.

Q4 Is acceptance of the decision by your subordinates critical to implementation?

Ans Yes. If the subordinates (and others) don't show up, the banquet is a failure.

Q5 Is it reasonably certain that the decision would be accepted by your subordinates if you were to make it by yourself?

Ans No. You might accidentally select a date that would not be suitable to your subordinates. For example, the day you select could be one on which subordinates have a major exam or term papers due the following day.

Q6 Do members share the view that the banquet date is important?

Ans Yes. Members have shown good attendance at meetings and consider the banquet the highlight of the year. Awards are presented, next year's officers announced, and so on.

OPTIMUM DECISION STYLE

As president, you should share the problem with members as a group, with the group generating and evaluating alternatives, and should attempt to arrive at a consensus decision.

Creative Problem Solving

More and more organizations and individual managers are involving subordinates in decision making and problem solving, particularly using styles similar to D and E in the Vroom-Yetton Model. As a senior technician and union leader in a paper mill told one of the authors, "Management used to tell us what to do; now they ask us." One of the primary reasons for this trend is the concept of synergy.

The Concept of Synergy

Synergy means that the whole is greater than the sum of the parts. This concept is especially applicable in the use of teams and ad hoc task forces in problem solving. Assume that an ad hoc task force of five persons is presented with a complex problem that has an impact on the entire organization. If the team reaches a synergistic solution to the complex problem, then mathematically synergy can be defined as $1 + 1 + 1 + 1 + 1 = $ more than 5.

synergy The concept that two or more people working together in a cooperative, coordinated way can accomplish more than the sum of their independent efforts.

Increasingly, this type of synergy is being achieved by teams throughout the world. This emphasis on synergistic teamwork is recognized in the United States by Rochester Institute of Technology's College of Business and *USA Today's* Quality Cup Awards. These awards are presented in five categories to teams that have made outstanding contributions in products or services. The categories are manufacturing, service, nonprofit, government, and organizations with fewer than 500 employees. MAP 6.2 identifies the 1994 award winners in each category, and in Chapter 14 we examine in depth team development and empowerment strategies.

Developing Creativity

Scientists generalize that the right hemisphere of the brain captures our intuitive impulses. If we think of ourselves as problem solvers/decision makers, the right side of the brain generates ideas and is where imagination originates. Right-hemispheric functions are frequent catalysts for solution alternatives.

Alternatively, the brain's left hemisphere functions in logical, analytical, and linear ways, allowing the decision maker to evaluate his or her intuitive, imaginative alternatives. This is where judgment enters into the process. Although the brain has a multi-functional capacity, the decision maker may allow his or her preferred brain functioning to dominate and can allow left-side evaluation and analysis to encroach on "right-brain" intuitive ideas prematurely.

In order to gain the maximum benefit from ad hoc task forces, quality circles, self-managing work teams, or any problem-solving effort, the brain's left-hemisphere functions must be restrained initially. The key to doing so is to make use of the concept of deferred judgment. This is the idea behind brainstorming, and the secret is to develop right-hemispheric skills and to use them appropriately. After the ideas are generated, it is helpful to use analytical brain functions to evaluate and judge which insights are good, cost-effective, and so forth. Using right-hemisphere functions as thought generators and following them with left-brained functions result in powerfully effective "whole-brained" creativity. Three techniques that are

MANAGEMENT APPLICATION AND PRACTICE   6.2

Two Quality Cup Winners of 1994

SERVICE: Pacific Bell

WHAT THE TEAM DID
A Pacific Bell team reduced phone cable cuts 24%— saving $6 million in 1993.

WHAT A JUDGE SAID
"This was a very well-defined quality process at work."
—*Tom Johnson, professor, Portland State University*

Pacific Bell: Seated: Dale Bouguennec. From left, standing: John Gonzales, Bob Riordan, Don Stephens, Jerry Yim, Jerry Donnellan, Bob Smith, Paul Hirsch, Dan Brown, Ron Mana, Wayne Olson, John Negrete.

SMALL ORGANIZATIONS: Libralter Plastics

WHAT THE TEAM DID
Ten members fixed chaotic record-keeping and shaved inventory costs $240,000 a year.

WHAT A JUDGE SAID
"A perfect example of a supplier wanting to please its customers."
—*Ken Leach, consultant*

Libralter Plastics: Seated: Arlene Abdilla. From left, standing: John Woodhouse, Skip Jones, Ben Hart, Bo Markovic, Katherine Brandon, Tim Grove.

very useful in the idea generation process are brainstorming, the Crawford Slip Technique, and the nominal grouping technique.

Brainstorming

One of the most effective techniques in creative problem solving is brainstorming. **Brainstorming** refers to a group of individuals responding to a question, such as "How can we improve communication?" without evaluating the ideas as they are generated. The ideas are thrown out no matter how silly they may appear and without regard to the rank of individuals or the value of any idea. Sorting out the value of respective ideas comes later. Larry Hirschorn, management consultant and writer, has suggested four excellent guidelines when using this powerful technique:

brainstorming A group of individuals generating ideas without evaluating the ideas as they are generated.

1. The group favors quantity over quality.
2. Team members refrain from judging anyone's contributions; they can ask questions later, in the evaluation part.
3. Team members avoid censoring.
4. Pride of authorship is minimized; team members should feel free to offer variants and build upon one another's ideas.[17]

Brainstorming is especially useful in developing alternatives during Step 2 of the decision-making or problem-solving process. In most cases in creative problem solving, the team will draw from a number of alternatives in putting together the action plan. In addition to identifying possible solutions, brainstorming is also useful in these dimensions of creative problem solving:

▶ Defining all possible problems

▶ Redefining problems

▶ Determining all possible causes for a problem

▶ Listing all possible actions for implementing the chosen solution

Unfortunately, based on the observations of the authors, formally appointed committees and management meetings with subordinates rarely use brainstorming in their deliberations. For example, one of the authors recently observed a faculty committee spending the allotted time for the meeting (two hours) debating the pros and cons of the second idea presented. On the other hand, ad hoc task forces and problem-solving teams tend to use brainstorming in a more creative and effective manner.

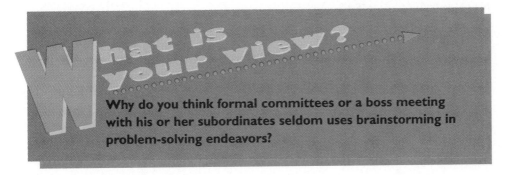

What is your view?

Why do you think formal committees or a boss meeting with his or her subordinates seldom uses brainstorming in problem-solving endeavors?

The Crawford Slip Technique

Crawford Slip Technique A problem-solving technique in which ideas are sorted by task forces that then make recommendations.

fluency The ability to let ideas flow out of your head like water over a waterfall.

flexibility The ability to use free association to generate or classify ideas in categories.

The **Crawford Slip Technique** was developed by Professor C. C. Crawford at the University of Southern California. It makes use of two elements that are important in achieving creativity—fluency and flexibility. **Fluency** is the ability to let ideas flow out of your head like water over a waterfall, and **flexibility** is the ability to use free association to generate or classify ideas in categories. Materials needed are a number of 3″ x 5″ scratch pads and a number of empty boxes distributed among the participants. The process starts by telling participants that they are about to engage in a new type of problem solving that will generate 50 to 100 new ideas.

For example, this technique was used with the top management of Baldor Electric Company, a very successful company listed on the New York Stock Exchange. Unfortunately, one of the large motors it produced was losing money. The following series of steps was initiated to deal with the problem.[18]

1. Participants were asked not to pause to evaluate ideas and not to generate such thoughts as "We've tried this before."
2. Every participant was given a pad of 3″ x 5″ slips of paper.
3. In this technique, the leader presents a problem in how-to form. In the case of Baldor Electric, the problem presented was, "How can we reduce costs on our 300 series motors without affecting quality?"
4. Each person would write down as many answers to the problem as time would permit. After an idea was written on a slip, it was placed in the idea bank (box) anonymously.
5. After ten minutes, the idea boxes were collected and task forces established. In the case of Baldor, there were three task forces, to whom the idea slips were distributed like cards dealt from a deck.
6. Each task force was charged with arranging the ideas in categories, using judgment (left side of the brain) to throw out weak ideas and then developing the good ideas and presenting recommendations to the larger group.

The chief executive officer of the company then judged what ideas were most relevant to solving the problem and decided to implement them. Please note that although there was considerable participation in the process, one person made the final decision. In many instances, this is a desirable approach in using participative management.

Nominal Grouping Technique

nominal grouping technique (NGT) A structured process in which small groups make suggestions in writing and then discuss all suggestions to reach a decision.

The **nominal grouping technique (NGT)** also makes use of brainstorming, and we have found the technique very effective in developing creativity and generating useful information. Nominal grouping is a structured group technique for generating ideas through round-robin individual responses, group sharing without criticism, and written balloting. The authors have found it to be exceptionally beneficial to use nominal grouping in working with organizations. Figure 6.4 identifies the steps in nominal grouping when it is used in this manner. The following example illustrates the steps in the process.

Steps in Nominal Grouping

Divide into groups of six or nine persons.

>   *Without* interaction, list the strengths you feel are associated with Question 1,
>   then list the problems for Question 2.   (Time: 6 minutes.)

Select a recorder.

>   a. The recorder asks each member, one at a time, to read from his or her card one strength associated with Question 1. *Example:* What are the strengths of this plant?
>
>   b. The recorder writes each strength exactly as it is read.
>
>   c. Those having the same strength should raise hands. The recorder checkmarks each strength once for each person raising a hand.
>
>   d. When all Question 1 strengths are recorded, the procedure is repeated for Question 2 problems. *Example:* What are the problems preventing this plant from reaching its potential effectiveness?

Discuss the two lists. Clarify, defend, elaborate, or add other items as needed.   (Time: 5 minutes.)

>   *Without* interaction, each member lists on an index card the *five* items he or she considers most important with reference to Question 1; do the same for Question 2.

The recorder collects and records the votes.

FIGURE 6.4
Steps in nominal grouping.

Two of the authors were asked to participate in a management development program for a branch plant of a corporation headquartered in our home state. The plant, located in another state, was struggling to achieve a break-even point, and the executive vice-president hired us to conduct management training sessions. The authors were rotating training sessions and the report after the first session was that the "canned management training was similar to placing a Band-Aid on a festering boil." During the break, the employees complained about issues and problems the training program did not directly address. A consultation with the executive vice-president resulted in a change in strategy for the next session. Using the nominal grouping process, the 25 participants (supervisors, managers, and staff personnel) were asked to respond to two questions:

1. What are the strengths of this plant?
2. What are the problems preventing this plant from reaching its potential effectiveness?

Twelve strengths were generated, and 55 problems were initially identified. Through nominal voting, the top five problems were prioritized; task forces from the participants were formed; and action plans were developed to solve the plant's more pressing problems.

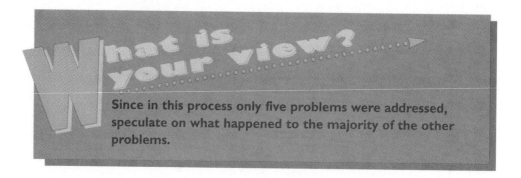

Since in this process only five problems were addressed, speculate on what happened to the majority of the other problems.

If your answer was, "They dissipated," you are correct.

Developing and implementing the action plans were catalysts in shifting the plant from a low performer to a high performer within a year. (More will be said about this process in Chapter 13.)

SUMMARY

This chapter focused on managerial decision making, which is the conscious selection of a course of action from among available alternatives to produce a given result. All employees, but especially managers, must make decisions.

Programmed decisions are routine and repetitive and enable management to develop a systematic way to make them. Nonprogrammed decisions occur relatively infrequently, and a separate decision must be undertaken each time.

The five steps in managerial decision making are (1) recognizing a problem or opportunity, (2) developing alternative courses of action, (3) evaluating the advantages and disadvantages of the alternatives, (4) selecting a preferred alternative and implementing it, and (5) evaluating the decision results.

The decision-making method used is also influenced by the decision maker's personal problem-solving type or style. According to the Myers-Briggs Type Indicator, individuals have two ways of perceiving information and two ways of evaluating it. The four combinations of sensing-thinking, intuitive-thinking, sensing-feeling, and intuitive-feeling have a definite influence on problem solving and decision making. Ideally, a balance will be developed by using all four dimensions in decision making.

To what extent should a manager involve others in the decision-making process? The Vroom-Yetton Model helps answer the question by examining the key characteristics of given decision situations and identifying various decision-making styles. A particular decision style can be selected on the basis of answers to questions about the characteristics of the given situation. Some techniques for involving others in creative problem solving are brainstorming, the Crawford Slip Technique, and the nominal grouping technique.

KEY TERMS

managerial decision making, 179
programmed decisions, 180
nonprogrammed decisions, 181
decision tree, 183
creativity, 185
Myers-Briggs Type Indicator (MBTI), 188
Vroom-Yetton Model, 192

synergy, 195
brainstorming, 197
Crawford Slip Technique, 198
fluency, 198
flexibility, 198
nominal grouping technique (NGT), 198

DISCUSSION QUESTIONS

1. Peter Drucker states that a big decision-making error managers frequently make is failing to get a handle on a problem. Often, managers plunge in prematurely. Why do you think many managers make this common mistake?

2. Discuss the following statement: It's better for a manager to try to carry out a poor decision for the sake of worker confidence. You can't build worker confidence by continually admitting the poor decisions you make.

3. What are the pros and cons of decisions made by groups such as committees and task forces as compared to decisions made by one person?

4. Is it possible for someone to be a good decision maker but a poor manager? Explain.

5. One manager says that she finds procrastination to be a big help in her decision making. Do you agree or disagree? Why?

PRACTICING MANAGEMENT

6.1

case

Coast Guard Cutter Decision Problem

You are the captain of a 210-foot medium-endurance Coast Guard cutter, with a crew of 9 officers and 65 enlisted personnel. Your mission is general at-sea law enforcement and search and rescue. At 2:00 this morning, while en route to your home port after a routine two-week patrol, you received word from the New York Rescue Coordination Center that a small plane had ditched 70 miles offshore. You obtained all the available information concerning the location of the crash, informed your crew of the mission, and set a new course at maximum speed heading for the scene to commence a search for survivors and wreckage.

You have now been searching for 20 hours. Your search operation has been increasingly impaired by rough seas, and there is evidence of a severe storm building to the southwest. The atmospherics associated with the deteriorating weather have made communications with the New York Rescue Coordination Center impossible. A decision must be made shortly about whether to abandon the search and place your vessel on a northeasterly course to ride out the storm (thereby protecting the vessel and your crew, but relegating any possible survivors to almost certain death from exposure) or to continue a potentially futile search and incur the risks it would entail.

Instructions: You have contacted the weather bureau for up-to-date information concerning the severity and duration of the storm. While your crew members are extremely conscientious about their responsibility, you believe that they would be divided on the decision of leaving or staying.

Review the decision processes in Figure 6.3 and Table 6.2 and decide which comes closest to what you would do if you were the captain in this situation. Circle your choice:

A   B   C   D   E

Source: Victor H. Vroom and Arthur G. Jago, *The New Leadership: Managing Participation in Organizations* (Englewood Cliffs, N.J.: Prentice Hall, 1988), pp. 42–43.

6.2

case

New Machines Decision Problem

You are the manufacturing manager in a large electronics plant. The company's management has always been searching for ways of increasing efficiency. They have recently installed new machines and put in a new, simplified work system, but to the surprise of everyone, including yourself, the expected increase in productivity was not realized. In fact, production has begun to drop, quality has fallen off, and the number of employee separations has risen.

You do not believe that there is anything wrong with the machines. You have had reports from other companies that are using them, and the reports confirm this opinion. You have also had representatives from the firm that built the machines go over them, and they report that the machines are operating at peak efficiency.

You suspect that some parts of the new work system may be responsible for the change, but this view is not widely shared among your immediate subordinates—four first-level supervisors, each in charge of a section, and your supply manager. The drop in production has been variously attributed to poor training of the operators, lack of an adequate system of financial incentives, and poor morale. Clearly, this is an issue about which there is considerable depth of feeling within individuals and potential disagreement among your subordinates.

This morning you received a phone call from your division manager. He had just received your production figures for the last six months and was calling to express his concern. He indicated that the problem was yours to solve in any way that you thought best, but that he would like to know within a week what steps you plan to take.

You share your division manager's concern with the falling productivity and know that your people are also concerned. The problem is to decide what steps to take to rectify the situation.

Instructions: Review the decision processes in Figure 6.3 and Table 6.2 and decide which comes closest to what you would do if you were the manager in the above situation. Circle your choice:

A   B   C   D   E

Source: Victor H. Vroom and Arthur C. Jago, *The New Leadership: Managing Participation in Organizations* (Englewood Cliffs, N.J.: Prentice Hall, 1988), p. 43.

6.1

learning exercise

Identifying Your Problem-Solving Style

Instructions: Indicate the response that comes closest to how you usually feel or act. If you really cannot choose, two answers being an absolute toss-up, leave that question unanswered. There are no correct or incorrect answers.

1. Which are you more careful about, (a) what people's rights are or (b) how people feel?

2. Which phrase do you feel best describes you, (a) having common sense or (b) having vision?

3. Are you more likely to be impressed by (a) principles or (b) emotions?

4. Which phrase best describes your preference as to how to get a job done, (a) using techniques that have proved effective in past situations or (b) experimenting with new and different approaches?

5. In making decisions, which is more important to you, (a) standards or (b) feelings?

6. Which do you think is worse, (a) not having a clear grasp of details or (b) not having a clear grasp of the big picture?

7. Do your friends see you as basically more (a) hardheaded or (b) warmhearted?

8. Are you basically more interested in (a) data or (b) ideas?

9. If another person says something that is incorrect, which would you normally do, (a) point out the error or (b) ignore it?

10. Which kind of person would you prefer as a roommate, (a) someone who's very practical, with both feet on the ground, or (b) someone who's always having new ideas?

11. Are you best described as (a) drawing conclusions in a logical, objective way or (b) drawing conclusions based on feelings or emotions?

12. In making decisions, are you more likely to decide based on (a) the real facts and data or (b) your hunches?

13. As a student, would you prefer taking (a) fact-oriented courses or (b) theory-oriented courses?

14. Which do you feel is the greater error, (a) to be too sympathetic or (b) to be too firm?

15. Assume that a party contains two rooms of people, and in each room are the same types of people. Which room would you be drawn to, (a) a room with sensible people or (b) a room with imaginative people?

16. Which of the following terms best describes you: (a) objective or (b) compassionate?

17. Which do you value more highly, (a) a strong sense of reality or (b) a strong imagination?

18. Which role has the greater appeal to you, (a) being a judge or (b) being a peacemaker?

19. In which of these activities have you more interest: (a) production or (b) design?

20. Would you describe yourself as (a) more firm than merciful or (b) more merciful than firm?

Score Sheet

Instructions: Record your answers to each question in the appropriate box. Then add the total number of checks in each column. If you have an equal number of points for Sensor and Intuitor, circle the Intuitor; if an equal number of points for Thinker and Feeler, circle the Feeler.

	a	b			a	b
2	✓	✓		1		✓
4	✓			3	✓	
6	✓	✓		5		✓
8	✓	✓		7	✓	
10	✓			9	✓	
12	✓			11		✓
14	✓	,		13	✓	
15		✓		16		✓
17	✓			18	✓	
19		✓		20		✓
TOTAL	6	4		TOTAL	5	5

S E N S O R	I N T U I T O R	T H I N K E R	F E E L E R

6.2   The $100,000 Investment Decision

learning exercise

Assume that a wealthy entrepreneur has provided a $2 million fund for the management department at your school, to be used in improving students' decision-making skills. The department has decided to use this course as the vehicle for student development in decision making.

Divide the class into teams of five to seven students. Each team is given $100,000 to invest for a period of five years. At the end of that period, a member of each team will have six months to liquidate the team's investment(s).

The $100,000 principal, along with 50 percent of profits, will be returned to the management department. The remaining 50 percent will be divided among team members. The department will cover any loss of principal up to $75,000.

Each team's assignment is as follows:

1. Following the steps of the decision-making process, reach a decision about what your investment(s) will be. Write out your reasoning for each step in the decision-making process and turn in the report to your instructor.

2. Be prepared to make a five- to ten-minute presentation to the rest of the class as to why your decision will reap the best return in five years.

At the end of the exercise, class members will vote on which team seems to have made the best investment decision(s).

chapter

7

Strategic and Operational Planning

Plan ahead—it wasn't raining when Noah built the ark.

—ANONYMOUS

Only a clear definition of the mission and purpose of the business makes possible clear and realistic objectives. . . . Strategy determines what the key activities are and strategy requires knowing "what our business is and what it should be."

—PETER DRUCKER

LEARNING OBJECTIVES

After studying the material in this chapter, you should be able to:

▸ **Explain** what planning is and give some reasons for doing it.

▸ **Show** how the time factor and management levels affect planning.

▸ **Define** strategic planning.

▸ **Explain** what an organization's mission is.

▸ **Identify** generic and master strategies.

▸ **Define** operational planning.

▸ **Explain** management by objectives (MBO) and describe the steps involved.

▸ **Differentiate** between and give examples of standing and single-use plans.

opening case

Sears, Roebuck: Back to Basics

Sears, Roebuck, founded in 1886 as a mail-order business, long enjoyed its status as America's no. 1 retailer and the epitome of the profitable, blue-chip American business enterprise. But the decades of the 1970s and 1980s created problems, namely the intrusion on Sears's turf by the successful broad and specialty discounters Wal-Mart and Kmart. The catalog business, long a Sears standout, encountered especially fierce competition, not only from rivals J. C. Penney and Montgomery Ward but also from the myriad specialty mail-order firms that cropped up in all lines of business.

In 1982, Sears was basically two very large businesses—the merchandising group, consisting of its retail and catalog operation, and its Allstate insurance group. That same year Sears tried a new approach and sought to diversify by acquiring Coldwell Banker, a residential and commercial real estate operation, and Dean Witter, a financial brokerage. The plan was to achieve synergy by linking the businesses. For example, Allstate would provide insurance annuities through Dean Witter; Coldwell Banker real estate agents would provide leads to Allstate agents; Coldwell Banker's commercial organization, which developed shopping centers, would be able to use Sears units as anchor stores.

However, Sears's performance was erratic, especially that of the merchandise group, which shortly thereafter saw Wal-Mart replace it as the no. 1 U.S. retailer. In 1991, amid much criticism that the company lacked "focus" and a game plan for the future, longtime CEO and Chairman Edward Brennan undertook a bold new plan to recapture Sears's lost magic. After a rigorous audit of the company's strengths, weaknesses, opportunities, and threats, and assessment of its target customers, Brennan announced the new "Sears" strategic plan:

1. Reemphasize merchandising, Sears's bread-and-butter business. This would be achieved by major store renovation and creation of new marketing programs in apparel and cosmetics, appliances, electronics, and auto centers.
2. Restructure by shutting down Sears catalog centers and 113 unprofitable stores; continue downsizing by eliminating 50,000 store positions.
3. Divest Dean Witter and Coldwell Banker's residential real estate businesses. Eighty percent of Dean Witter ownership would be given to Sears stockholders; 20 percent would be sold by Sears and used to pare down debt and help defray capital costs associated with modernization and expansion.

In 1992, the plan took effect—the company taking a one-time restructuring charge of $2.7 billion to cover the merchandise group's physical closings, early retirements, and so on.

But now for the good news. After only a year, the effects seemed very positive. Some store sales for the merchandise group increased 9 percent in 1993. Allstate's net income rose to a new record, and Sears's overall profit of $2.37 billion was the highest in its 107-year history. It seemed that Sears finally had it back in gear after two decades of aimless drifting.[1]

This case reflects the steps taken by Sears to regain its position as a progressive, growing company. Specifically, Sears's actions reflect what a major part of this chapter is about—strategic planning. But before examining strategic and operational planning, let us first examine some key aspects of the overall planning process.

Planning: Strategic and Operational

Planning can be broadly defined as the process of establishing objectives and determining how best to achieve them. Because planning establishes the backdrop for the subsequent management functions—organizing, leading, and controlling—it is often referred to as the primary management function.

planning The process of establishing objectives and determining how best to achieve them.

Basic Steps in Planning

As you will notice throughout this chapter, planning covers a wide variety of activities—from those that are highly complex, occurring over a long time and in uncertain environments, to those that are simple and occur over a short time in very predictable environments. Activities may range from Harley-Davidson's plans to increase production by 25 percent from 1993 to 1996 to a Sears cosmetics department manager's plan to recruit three part-time salespersons for an upcoming sale. The three basic planning steps are the same, as shown in Figure 7.1:

1. Setting an objective
2. Identifying and assessing present and future conditions affecting the objective
3. Developing a systematic approach by which to achieve the objective

Sometimes additional steps are included as part of planning. However, these steps really involve managerial functions other than planning:

4. Implementing the plan (organizing, leading)
5. Monitoring the plan's implementation (controlling)
6. Evaluating the plan's effectiveness (controlling)

These last three steps are not really planning steps; rather, they reflect the fact that as the primary management function, planning forms the basis for performing subsequent management functions. In this chapter, we shall focus on the basic three-step planning process (Steps 1, 2, and 3), but we will keep in mind that to be effective, planning must link closely with other managerial functions. Later in the chapter, a more specific strategic planning model is presented.

Setting Objectives The first step in planning—setting objectives—addresses the issue of what one hopes to achieve. Objectives may be set in performance areas such as profitability, market share, personnel to be recruited, and projects to be completed by a given date. A detailed discussion of objective setting, including areas in which objectives should be set and guidelines for setting objectives, is presented later in this chapter.

FIGURE 7.1
The three planning steps.

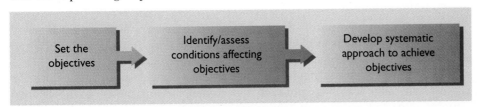

Identifying and Assessing Conditions Affecting the Objectives   The second planning step—identifying and assessing present and future conditions affecting objectives—recognizes the important variables that influence objectives, such as the purchasing power of consumers and the actions of competitors. Since planning involves the future, certain assumptions about important conditions occurring over the plan's time frame must be considered. General Motors, for instance, in its planning for the Saturn automobile, was required to make major assumptions, or accept certain premises, about conditions such as the public's demand for smaller cars; various government requirements regarding air bags, fuel economy, and emission controls; and so forth. The accuracy of such premises is critically important to effective planning.

> A central premise of Sears is that major shopping malls will continue to attract Sears's target customers, women from 25 to 54 years old and their families.
>   A major premise in Coca-Cola's plans for the late 1990s and beyond is that Europe will be the fastest-growing soft drink market around. This important premise has strongly affected Coke's plans, as it aggressively seeks to not only maintain but increase its already no. 1 European market share.[2]

Developing a Systematic Approach to Achieve the Objectives   The final aspect of planning—developing a systematic approach to achieve the objectives—is the step that addresses such issues as responsibilities for achievement and includes answers to such questions as who will do what, how, on what schedule, and with what results. The plan's complexity and importance are a principal factor in determining how formal and detailed this final step must be.

Where Planning Is Done

The question of how major planning work is done in an organization can be approached from several different angles. Planning may be *centralized* so that it is done by a single group, such as a corporate planning department. It is not unusual for large organizations to have over 50 employees in such departments.

In large organizations, *decentralized* planning may be used, whereby each division or department is responsible for planning all its own operations, with little if any guidance from the central planning unit. This is common in large-scale organizations with multiple product lines.

> At GE, primary responsibility for planning rests with the major sectors, such as medical systems, appliances, aircraft engines, and financial services. One of the early decisions then new CEO Jack Welch made in 1983 was to thin out the corporate planning department and decentralize the planning process.[3]

A disadvantage of a purely decentralized planning approach is the danger of overlaps or even conflicts in planning. Such problems may be avoided by a central planning unit that coordinates the plans of the decentralized divisions.

Under a modified arrangement, the central planning department does the original long-range planning, and each department and unit then does the detailed planning of its own activities needed to implement the long-range plan.

The planning policy to be followed generally depends on the type of enterprise that is to use the plans. It is important to note, however, that many plans—even long-term ones—originate at lower levels and work their way upward, as is the case at General Electric.

How the Time Factor Affects Planning

Time affects planning in three ways. First, considerable time is required to do effective planning. Second, it is often necessary to proceed with each planning step without full information concerning the variables and alternatives because of the time required to gather the data and calculate all the possibilities. Third, the amount (or span) of time that will be included in the plan must be considered.

Short-, Intermediate-, and Long-Range Plans

Short-range plans cover anywhere from a day to a year, **intermediate-range plans** have a time span of 1 to 3 years, and **long-range plans** involve activities 3 to 5 years ahead, with some plans projected 25 or more years into the future. In fact, paper companies such as International Paper and Weyerhaeuser are planning timber stands today that will be harvested around the year 2040 or later. Similarly, General Motors's Saturn was scheduled for introduction in 1990, but planning for it was begun eight years earlier.[4]

Since time ranges for planning differ so much from organization to organization, it is sometimes hard to say exactly whether a given plan is long-, intermediate-, or short-range. Also, plans change from long-range to intermediate-range to short-range as time passes. Long-range planning is now usually referred to as *strategic planning*.

Another time factor affecting planning is how often plans are to be reviewed or revised. This depends on the resources available and the degree of accuracy management seeks from planning in the first place. The usual relationship is this: *The longer the time span of the plan, the longer the period between reviews and revisions.* Conversely, *the more important the plan is to the organization's immediate success, the more closely it will be monitored.*

short-range plans
Plans covering a time span of one day to one year.

intermediate-range plans Plans covering a time span of one to three years.

These Douglas fir seedlings, which may take from 15 to 25 years to harvest, reflect Weyerhaeuser's long-range strategic planning.

long-range plans Plans covering a time span of three to five years and, in some cases, as much as 25 years.

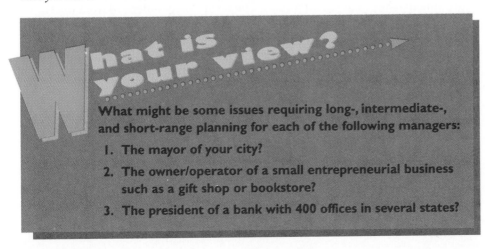

What is your view?

What might be some issues requiring long-, intermediate-, and short-range planning for each of the following managers:

1. The mayor of your city?

2. The owner/operator of a small entrepreneurial business such as a gift shop or bookstore?

3. The president of a bank with 400 offices in several states?

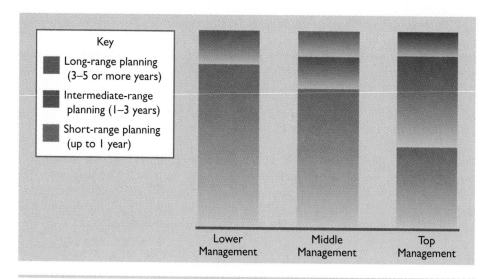

FIGURE 7.2
Time frame of planning changes at different organizational levels.

Notice in Figure 7.2 that lower-level managers tend to plan mostly for short periods—one day to one year. Middle managers plan primarily for the short run also but become involved in some intermediate-range plans of a year to three years or more. Top managers are more likely to be involved in intermediate- and longer-range plans—from one to five years or more into the future. These are, of course, generalizations, and there are many exceptions to this rule of thumb.

The Strategic Planning Process

The concept of strategic planning has become exceptionally important in management circles today, due in large part to the increasing complexities of both external and internal environments, which were discussed in Chapters 3 and 4, as well as to growing management sophistication. The term *strategy* is derived from the Greek word *strategos*, which means "a general." In ancient times, it meant the art and science of managing military forces to victory. Today, large and small businesses and not-for-profit organizations engage in strategy when choosing the best options for accomplishing their objectives.

strategic planning
Those activities that involve defining an organization's mission, setting its objectives, and developing strategies to enable it to operate successfully in its environment.

What Strategic Planning Is

Strategic planning includes those activities that involve defining the organization's mission, setting its overall objectives, and developing strategies to enable it to operate successfully in its environment. Strategic planning can be differentiated from other types of organizational planning by the following criteria:

MANAGEMENT APPLICATION AND PRACTICE 7.1

Strategic Planning in Global Telecommunications

The key players are positioning themselves to battle for multinational telecommunications business customers. MCI and British Telecom (BT) became the third recently announced strategic alliance, following one among Swiss, Swedish, and Dutch phone companies and one forged by AT&T. U.S.-based Sprint is also seeking a foothold, attempting to link with French and German telephone companies.

The MCI–British Telecom alliance, called Concert, will open with 700 to 800 employees and receive about $2 billion from its parent companies in the next few years. One billion will be used to buy telephone exchanges internationally and install and hire long-distance lines for international customers. Counting just BT equipment and customers, Concert immediately lays claim to 4,600 access points in some 30 countries for its clients to plug into.

Central to the Concert strategy is to provide its multinational clients standardized software and product offerings throughout the globe for voice and date communications. Analysts say the venture isn't likely to produce any short-term profits, but is a longer-term investment. As Michael Hepner, BT's chief executive, stated, "Multinational telecommunications are growing at a very rapid rate, and the total revenues that are flowing in are in the many billions. We're playing this game for serious money."

Source: Mary Lu Carnevale and Richard L. Hudson, "MCI's Alliance with British Telecom Clears Hurdle; Sprint Deal Faces Fight," *Wall Street Journal*, June 16, 1994, p. A3.

1. It involves decisions made by top management.
2. It involves ultimate allocation of large amounts of resources, such as money, labor, or physical capacity.
3. It has significant long-term impact.
4. It focuses on the organization's interaction with the external environment.[5]
   Note that all four of these are involved in the MCI–British Telecom alliance discussed in MAP 7.1.

Components of Strategic Planning

Figure 7.3 shows the basic components of **strategic management,** which includes not only the planning process but the implementation and control phases as well. This figure illustrates that strategic planning starts with a clear understanding of the organizational mission.

strategic management
Strategic planning, implementation, and control.

Second, organizational objectives must be established so that everyone knows what management wants to accomplish. Third, management identifies the strategic alternatives available to achieve those objectives. This step entails examining the organization's strengths and weaknesses, forecasting the future environment, and so on. Finally, to complete the planning process, strategic choices are made.

The manager profile of Ken Hoffman (p. 214) gives a good example of some strategic planning issues at a major division of Hartmarx, the large apparel maker.

Although we emphasize strategic planning in this chapter, managers must also be concerned with strategic implementation and control processes once strategic plans have been established.

PRACTICING MANAGER

Ken Hoffman, age 51, graduated from Loyola University in 1965 with a degree in liberal arts and a major in Latin. An excellent student as well as captain of the basketball team, he received an MBA from the University of Pennsylvania's Wharton Business School two years later and took his first job with Hartmarx as a management trainee. He has been with Hartmarx ever since, progressing through a series of early positions in advertising, sales, and marketing for Johnny Carson apparel and an executive vice-president and later president and CEO of M. Wile. Today, he is president and CEO of Hartmarx's flagship Hart Schaffner & Marx division, which manufactures and sells the industry-leading Hart Schaffner & Marx brand of men's clothing as well as Tommy Hilfiger, Austin Reed, Krizia, and others. Hoffman's division employs over 5,000 people.

KEN HOFFMAN, CEO, HART SHAFFNER & MARX

Hoffman feels a career key was his association with the start-up and initial success of the Johnny Carson clothing line. With Carson's visibility and the company's marketing expertise, "It was a fabulous learning experience," says Hoffman. "The suits were manufactured at M. Wile in Buffalo, which we had recently acquired. Arthur Gunzberg, M. Wile's former owner, stayed on as president and chief executive officer, and Arthur was my mentor. He knew the business inside and out—from buying, manufacturing, and cost control to selling—and he really took an interest in helping me learn."

As president of Hart Schaffner & Marx, Hoffman spends most of his time in the merchandise and sales area. He is also heavily involved in planning. "At Hartmarx, our division has a five-year strategic plan, which is rolled over each year. It starts with our three brand managers working out a five-year plan based on input from their sales managers and merchandise managers." This plan is presented to Hoffman and his chief financial officer, who discuss competition, volume, niche, changes in the market, and so on, and develop the numbers. The results are packaged into a single plan to present at the corporate level, where Hoffman, five other division presidents, and Hartmarx's chairman and president hear each division's plan and assess and modify each as needed. The cumulative package becomes the corporation's plan against which divisional performance is measured.

"An interesting concept," says Hoffman, "is what we call 'blue skying,' where we ask, during these strategic meetings and at other times as well, the 'what if?' questions, such as 'What if our competitor does this?', 'What if there's only one global currency and no trade barriers?', 'What if ...?' We get into some serious discussions of this nature that have definitely helped us prepare future strategies."

Hoffman has seen Hartmarx's mission change over the years. "When I joined Hartmarx, we were strictly in men's clothing—suits, sport coats, and slacks at both the retail and wholesale levels. We are currently a completely refocused company for two reasons: First, we are no longer in the retail business as we have sold our store group, the result being that they have become an extremely important independent customer. Second, our product emphasis has broadened to include all aspects of sportswear and golfwear in addition to tailored clothing."

The overall Hartmarx Corporation objective is to be the dominant quality apparel maker in the world. "Only a few years ago, our target market was the United States," says Hoffman. "But in today's global business climate, we must look ahead to the future, which includes world partnerships, licensing agreements, and joint ventures."

Hoffman feels his degree in liberal arts has been a big asset. "My job entails a lot of interacting variables, many affecting each other. I feel the broad background in liberal arts helped me greatly. People who think managing is strictly a numbers game are missing something."

Source: Discussions and correspondence with Ken Hoffman.

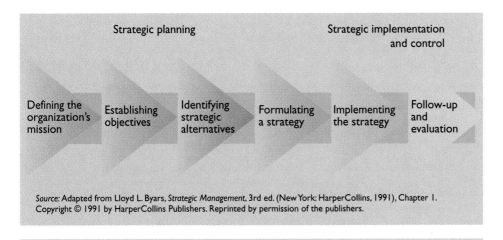

Source: Adapted from Lloyd L. Byars, *Strategic Management*, 3rd ed. (New York: HarperCollins, 1991), Chapter 1. Copyright © 1991 by HarperCollins Publishers. Reprinted by permission of the publishers.

FIGURE 7.3
Strategic planning as part of broader strategic management.

Organizational Mission, or "What Are We About?"

Organizations simply cannot survive if they do not know where they are going and what they are all about. An **organizational mission** defines the fundamental, unique purpose that the organization attempts to serve and identifies its products or services and customers. Thus, the mission identifies the organization's reason for existence—that is, what it stands for. Both profit-seeking and not-for-profit organizations need clearly stated and easily understood mission statements. Table 7.1 includes some sample mission statements.

organizational mission Definition of the fundamental, unique purpose that the organization attempts to serve and identification of its products or services and customers.

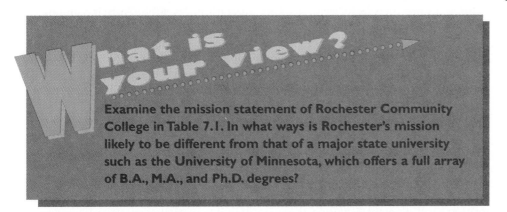

Examine the mission statement of Rochester Community College in Table 7.1. In what ways is Rochester's mission likely to be different from that of a major state university such as the University of Minnesota, which offers a full array of B.A., M.A., and Ph.D. degrees?

An organization's mission may change over time. BIC initially designed, manufactured, and distributed low-cost, high-quality disposable ballpoint pens. This product definition was broadened to "writing instruments" to include felt-tip pens and markers, and again later to inexpensive, high-quality items that could be mass produced and distributed through the same channels—to include disposable lighters, razors, and panty hose. Note that Sears (Opening Case) narrowed its mission substantially so as to refocus on its retail and insurance business.

TABLE 7.1   EXAMPLES OF MISSION STATEMENTS

Mary Kay Cosmetics, Inc.: "To achieve preeminence in the manufacturing and marketing of personal care products by providing personalized service, value and convenience to Mary Kay customers through our independent sales force."

Waste Management, Inc.: "To be the acknowledged worldwide leader in providing comprehensive environmental, waste management and related services of the highest quality to industry, government, and consumers using state-of-the-art systems responsive to customer need, sound environmental policy and the highest standards of corporate citizenship."

Rochester (Minnesota) Community College: "To [carry] out a commitment to lifelong learning. As an equal opportunity, open access institution, [the college] serves people with varying interests, aspirations, and abilities, reaching many who otherwise would not have the option to pursue higher education.

"Rochester Community College provides quality programs and services on an affordable, convenient basis. Helping people realize their potential, further their ambitions, and improve their lives is the purpose of Rochester Community College."

Sources: Company annual reports; excerpts from Rochester Community College mission statement.

An organization's resources are fundamental to the selection of appropriate fields of business. For instance, when the Salk and Sabin polio vaccines were perfected and the spread of polio halted, the Polio Foundation did not go out of business. Instead, it examined its resources and society's needs and formulated a new mission—financing research to prevent birth defects. We know the organization today as the March of Dimes.

credos or company creeds Outlines of the organization's beliefs or general guidelines that it will use in pursuing its mission.

Values, Beliefs, and Mission   An organization's mission statement often goes beyond defining its products or services, markets, and customers. Frequently, it contains an outline of the organization's beliefs or general guidelines that it will use in pursuing its mission. These are sometimes referred to as **credos** or **company creeds.** Perhaps the best-known example of a company creed is that of Johnson & Johnson, shown in MAP 7.2.

Overall Organizational Objectives

objectives The end results toward which organizational activities are aimed.

Objectives are the end results toward which organizational activities are aimed. Objectives are an important part of planning because they become the focal point for directing strategies. Organizations as a whole have a number of broad, long-term, overall objectives, among them profitability, market share, good labor relations, and others.

Examples of Organizational Objectives   Objectives go beyond and are more specific than answers to "What is our business?" At the same time, however, an organization's long-term ongoing objectives are usually stated in broad terms rather than in specific terms.

In the two examples that follow, note that some objectives are more general than others. But even though most of these statements are fairly general, they

MANAGEMENT APPLICATION AND PRACTICE 7.2

The Johnson & Johnson Credo

Perhaps no other organization's statement of beliefs, or what it stands for, has received as much attention as Johnson & Johnson's. First created in 1945 by General Robert Wood Johnson, son of the founder and himself CEO, the credo stemmed from the general's personal philosophy. In 1972, it was the theme of the corporate annual report; a series of ten "credo meetings" was held that same year to reinforce the credo to over 4,000 managers.

In 1975, Jim Burke, president, began a three-year series of "Credo Challenge Meetings," attended by over 1,200 managers, to test the credo's validity. Was it still applicable? Were changes needed? Was it still right for the company? And, perhaps most importantly, how could they ensure that it would be implemented? In 1979, a refined version was developed.

When Burke and the company faced the two Tylenol tamperings in 1982—and again in 1986—the credo was a dominant factor in J&J's decisive actions to recall all Tylenol products immediately, at a tremendous cost. As shown in Chapter 4, the company's response is considered a model of socially responsible corporate decision making.

Source: Courtesy of Johnson & Johnson.

Our Credo

We believe our first responsibility is to the doctors, nurses and patients, to mothers and fathers and all others who use our products and services. In meeting their needs everything we do must be of high quality. We must constantly strive to reduce our costs in order to maintain reasonable prices. Customers' orders must be serviced promptly and accurately. Our suppliers and distributors must have an opportunity to make a fair profit.

We are responsible to our employees, the men and women who work with us throughout the world. Everyone must be considered as an individual. We must respect their dignity and recognize their merit. They must have a sense of security in their jobs. Compensation must be fair and adequate, and working conditions clean, orderly and safe. We must be mindful of ways to help our employees fulfill their family responsibilities. Employees must feel free to make suggestions and complaints. There must be equal opportunity for employment, development and advancement for those qualified. We must provide competent management, and their actions must be just and ethical.

We are responsible to the communities in which we live and work and to the world community as well. We must be good citizens — support good works and charities and bear our fair share of taxes. We must encourage civic improvements and better health and education. We must maintain in good order the property we are privileged to use, protecting the environment and natural resources.

Our final responsibility is to our stockholders. Business must make a sound profit. We must experiment with new ideas. Research must be carried on, innovative programs developed and mistakes paid for. New equipment must be purchased, new facilities provided and new products launched. Reserves must be created to provide for adverse times. When we operate according to these principles, the stockholders should realize a fair return.

Johnson & Johnson

---

provide direction in the form of a set of end points toward which organizational strategy will be aimed.

Hewlett-Packard.   Hewlett-Packard (HP), founded in 1939, is a major designer and manufacturer of precision electronic equipment, including computers, calculators, medical and scientific instruments, and other products. The company's corporate objectives are summarized in these seven objectives:

Profit: To achieve sufficient profit to finance our company growth and to provide the resources we need to achieve our other corporate objectives.

Customers: To produce products and services of the greatest possible value to our customers, thereby gaining and holding their respect and loyalty.

Fields of interest: To enter new fields only when the ideas we have, together with our technical, manufacturing, and marketing skills, assure that we can make a needed and marketable contribution to the field.

Growth: To let our growth be limited only by our products and our ability to develop and produce technical products that satisfy real customer wants.

Our people: To help HP people share in the company's success, which they make possible; to provide job security based on their performance; to recognize their individual achievements; and to help them gain a sense of satisfaction and accomplishment from their work.

Management: To foster initiative and creativity by allowing the individual great freedom of action in attaining well-defined objectives.

Citizenship: To honor our obligations to society by being an economic, intellectual, and social asset to each nation and each community in which we operate.

Bloomin' Lollipops.   In September 1989, Michelle Statkewicz, Renee Sossaman, and their parents, Jiggs and Dot Martin, quit their jobs to start Bloomin' Lollipops. It opened in January 1990, after over six months of research and planning. The small business makes chocolate flowers, hard candy lollipops, and candy animals, which are placed in gift baskets for sale to gift shops, institutions, and the general public. Candy lollipop bouquets are available in a variety of colors and more than 50 different flavors, including lime, strawberry, grape, apple, lemon, watermelon, licorice, root beer, and piña colada. The owners have 150 or more career-, sports-, holiday-,

Even small businesses such as Bloomin' Lollipops need well-stated objectives.

and hobby-related molds with which to work. The Mobile, Alabama, business is booming, and the owners say several people from as far away as Texas are interested in obtaining franchises. Bloomin' Lollipops formulated the following statement of objectives:

We will make the best products, under environmentally sound conditions, deliver them to the customers as quickly as feasible, and charge a reasonable price—based upon our costs plus a satisfactory return on our investment of knowledge, time, and effort. We will set up satellite shops in Mobile and surrounding areas, and feed those shops from our kitchen. Afterward, we hope to franchise throughout the country.

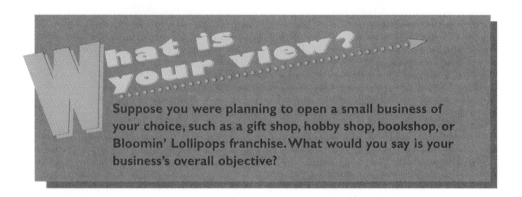

What is your view?

Suppose you were planning to open a small business of your choice, such as a gift shop, hobby shop, bookshop, or Bloomin' Lollipops franchise. What would you say is your business's overall objective?

Areas Needing Objectives Peter Drucker, while working as a consultant for GE, identified eight major areas in which businesses should set objectives. As shown in Figure 7.4, these areas are (1) market standing, (2) productivity, (3) physical and financial resources, (4) profitability, (5) innovation, (6) manager performance and development, (7) worker performance and attitudes, and (8) public and social responsibility.[6]

As you can see from Drucker's list, the eight areas in which objectives should be set require trade-offs in order to accomplish all of them. In other words, multiple goals require balancing, or accommodating, the wants, needs, and requirements of the many diverse stakeholders, such as stockholders, employees, customers, and community. Therefore, management should determine the optimum balance among these objectives, while allowing for flexibility still.

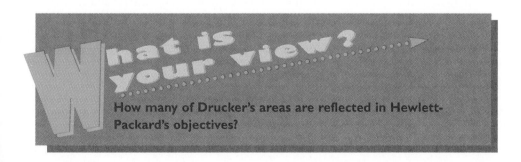

What is your view?

How many of Drucker's areas are reflected in Hewlett-Packard's objectives?

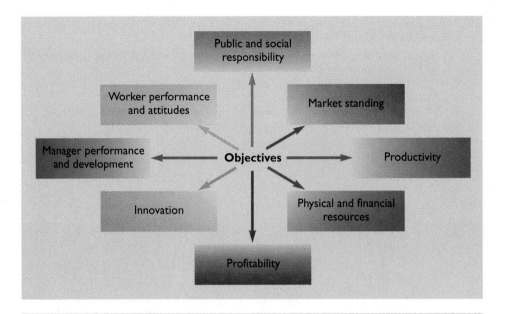

FIGURE 7.4
Areas that need objectives.

Identifying Strategic Alternatives

Strategic planning does not take place in a vacuum, but just consider the many variables that affect the organization. Thus, identifying key variables, being aware of their impact, and being able to predict their future potential impact are essential to effective strategic planning.

In Chapter 3 you learned that managers must set strategy within the framework of turbulent, complex, and unpredictable economic, sociocultural, technological, legal, and physical environments. They must also consider the internal environment, with its financial, authoritative, behavioral, and "political" complexities.

Incidentally, you—as a present or future manager—must consider these same external and internal factors when you choose a strategy to set and reach professional and personal goals.

Four Areas of Analysis   Figure 7.5 shows the four areas for analysis that an organization must consider. Before formulating strategies for meeting their objectives, planners must prepare the following information with which to work:

1. Analysis of internal organizational factors, such as management values, quality of personnel, competitive position and product line, and research and development.
2. Industry profile, which includes factors such as the industry's history, competitive forces, and financial condition.
3. Analysis of present external environmental factors, including political, economic, social, and technological forces.
4. Forecast of future external environmental factors, which involves predicting accurately the changes that are foreseen in present external environmental variables.

Area 1 **Internal organizational factors**	Area 2 **Industry profile**	Area 3 **Present external environment**	Area 4 **Future external environment**
Areas for analysis	Areas for analysis	Areas for analysis	Areas for analysis
1. Financial position 2. Organization structure 3. Quality and quantity of personnel 4. Quality and quantity of operative personnel 5. Competitive position and product line 6. Condition of facilities and equipment: manufacturing 7. Marketing capability 8. Research and development capability 9. Past objectives and strategies 10. Management values	1. History 2. Market practices and marketing structure 3. Financial condition 4. Competition 5. Operating conditions 6. Production techniques	1. Legal/political 2. Economic 3. Social 4. Technological 5. International	1. Legal/political 2. Economic 3. Social 4. Technological 5. International

Source: Adapted from Lloyd L. Byars, *Strategic Management*, 3rd. ed. (New York: HarperCollins, 1991), Chapters 2 and 3. Copyright © 1991 by HarperCollins Publishers. Reprinted by permission of the publishers.

FIGURE 7.5
Assessing internal and external environments.

Areas 1, 2, and 3 normally entail considerable overlap and can be performed simultaneously or sequentially. Area 4, forecasting future external environmental factors, is generally performed after the first three analyses have been completed.

SWOT (TOWS) Analysis One useful format for helping organizations to identify key internal and external variables as well as to pinpoint potential opportunities is SWOT analysis (sometimes called TOWS analysis). **SWOT (TOWS) analysis** is the process of systematically identifying an organization's Strengths, Weaknesses, Opportunities, and Threats, as shown in Figure 7.6.

Strengths are those resources or competencies that give a firm the upper hand over competitors. IBM's reputation for service is a clear strength; so are Wal-Mart's distribution system and low cost; Maytag's strengths include a reputation for high-quality, durable appliances. *Weaknesses* must also be acknowledged. Dow Chemical's

SWOT (TOWS) analysis The process of systematically identifying and analyzing an organization's strengths, weaknesses, opportunities, and threats.

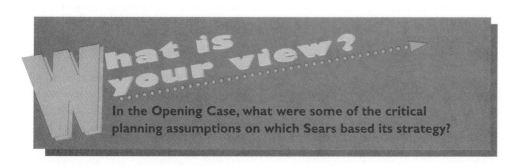

In the Opening Case, what were some of the critical planning assumptions on which Sears based its strategy?

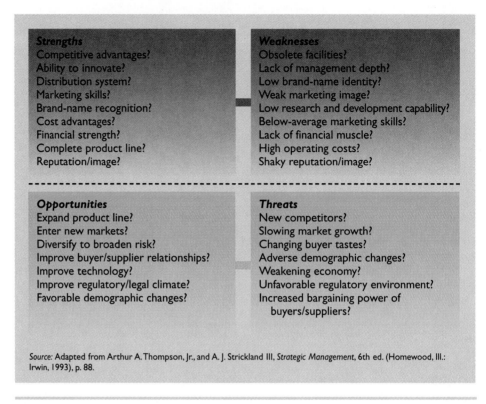

Source: Adapted from Arthur A. Thompson, Jr., and A. J. Strickland III, *Strategic Management*, 6th ed. (Homewood, Ill.: Irwin, 1993), p. 88.

FIGURE 7.6
The SWOT analysis checklist.

major weakness in the early 1980s was its unfavorable image as a result of its production of Agent Orange, the highly toxic defoliant used by the United States in Vietnam, and its stubbornness in resisting environmental controls. A weakness of Coors for years was its single Colorado brewing location, which prevented national distribution.

Opportunities offer potentially favorable happenings in the firm's environment. The opening of Europe's markets in 1992 has created opportunities for many international firms, such as Honda, Sony, and Citicorp.

> Thompson, S.A., the Paris-headquartered French conglomerate, was pursuing an objective of increasing its global presence in foreign markets. It seized an opportunity in 1987 when it purchased RCA's consumer electronics business from GE, instantly transforming itself into a global competitor.[7]

Threats are major unfavorable circumstances or impediments to a firm's present or future position. The movement to electronic information transfer and storage is seen as a threat to paper companies as well as publishers. The ability to access a complete encyclopedia on a single CD-ROM disk is not bright news for them. *USA Today*, initially scoffed at, became an overnight threat to local newspapers; many have responded by adding more color and expanding coverage of many features.

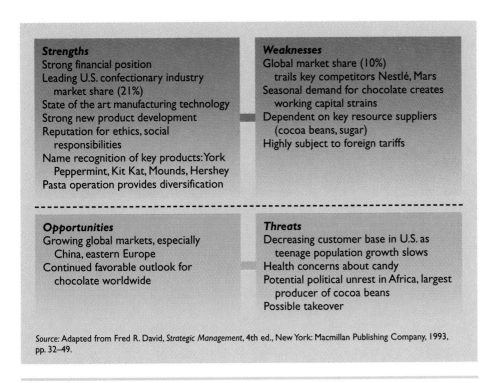

Strengths	Weaknesses
Strong financial position	Global market share (10%)
Leading U.S. confectionary industry	trails key competitors Nestlé, Mars
market share (21%)	Seasonal demand for chocolate creates
State of the art manufacturing technology	working capital strains
Strong new product development	Dependent on key resource suppliers
Reputation for ethics, social	(cocoa beans, sugar)
responsibilities	Highly subject to foreign tariffs
Name recognition of key products: York	
Peppermint, Kit Kat, Mounds, Hershey	
Pasta operation provides diversification	

Opportunities	Threats
Growing global markets, especially	Decreasing customer base in U.S. as
China, eastern Europe	teenage population growth slows
Continued favorable outlook for	Health concerns about candy
chocolate worldwide	Potential political unrest in Africa, largest
	producer of cocoa beans
	Possible takeover

Source: Adapted from Fred R. David, *Strategic Management*, 4th ed., New York: Macmillan Publishing Company, 1993, pp. 32–49.

FIGURE 7.7
SWOT analysis for Hershey Foods, 1991.

Figure 7.7, an example of SWOT analysis for Hershey's foods, gives a good idea of what it entails. SWOT analysis permits an organization to obtain a clearer picture of its strategic position. As a systematic analysis, it focuses on all major aspects of a firm's situation. But SWOT analysis consists of more than just formal list making. It is essential that weights, probabilities, and other evaluative measures be used to analyze the items identified.

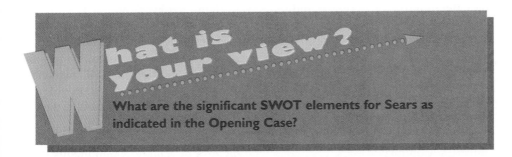

What is your view? ➤

What are the significant SWOT elements for Sears as indicated in the Opening Case?

Strategic Planning Matrixes Most large corporations have a number of products in one or more industries. It can be said, then, that each such company consists of a portfolio of several distinct smaller businesses, called strategic business units. A **strategic business unit (SBU)** consists of a unique company business that has its own mission, product or service lines, competition, customers, threats, and opportunities. Thus, each SBU has its own internal and external environments that must be assessed. For example, a large diversified corporation such as General Electric may

strategic business unit (SBU) A unique company business within a large corporation that has its own mission, product or service lines, competition, customers, threats, and opportunities.

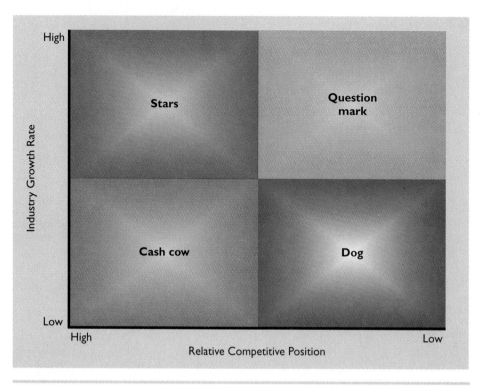

FIGURE 7.8
The BCG matrix.

have from 10 to 20 more SBUs. At a state university, colleges of arts, business, education, engineering, and science each have their own mission, faculty, students, and external environmental factors to monitor; each of these could be considered a separate SBU.

The Boston Consultant Group (BCG) matrix consists of a four-quadrant grid that is one of the most publicized techniques to help in strategic planning for diversified corporations.[8] As shown in Figure 7.8, the BCG matrix is based on two strategic variables: the industry's growth rate and the SBU's relative market share.

Stars are SBUs in fast-growth markets with large relative market share. In order to support their dominant position, substantial resources are required. Stars, however, offer excellent opportunities for future growth and profitability.

Question marks are SBUs in high-growth industries but with a small market share. They have appeal because of their high growth potential. However, in order to maintain their position in a growing industry, or to attempt to increase it, they normally require major financial outlays.

Cash cows are high-market-share SBUs that compete in mature, low-growth industries. Contrary to stars, cash cows typically do not require commitments of great financial resources. Thus, their profits can be "milked" and allocated to stars and question marks.

> F. W. Woolworth & Company has followed a strategy of using cash spawned from its variety stores (cash cow) to fund its present and future specialty store stars, such as Foot Locker (athletic shoes) and Champs (sporting goods).[9]

Dogs are SBUs with low market share, competing in industries with little growth. Their industry is mature and saturated and typically has strong competition with low profit margins. Dogs are sometimes referred to as cash traps because they invariably drain financial resources from healthier SBUs in the firm's portfolio.

A major advantage of growth/share analysis is its simplicity and the visual representation of the mix of SBUs within a company's portfolio.

The GE Strategic Planning Matrix is the nine-cell strategic planning grid originally used by GE.[10] As shown in Figure 7.9, the matrix resembles that of the BCG, except that the vertical axis, business strength, and the horizontal axis, industry attractiveness, consist of more than a single variable. Factors to be included are left to the judgment of the planners. The circle size represents the relative market size for each SBU; the shaded portion represents the proportion of market share the SBU has captured.

The GE matrix's advantage over the BCG approach is that it allows strategists to include more factors than the strictly two-factor BCG. A criticism is that it, like the BCG matrix, makes no allowance for changes in the business over time.

FIGURE 7.9
GE strategic planning matrix.

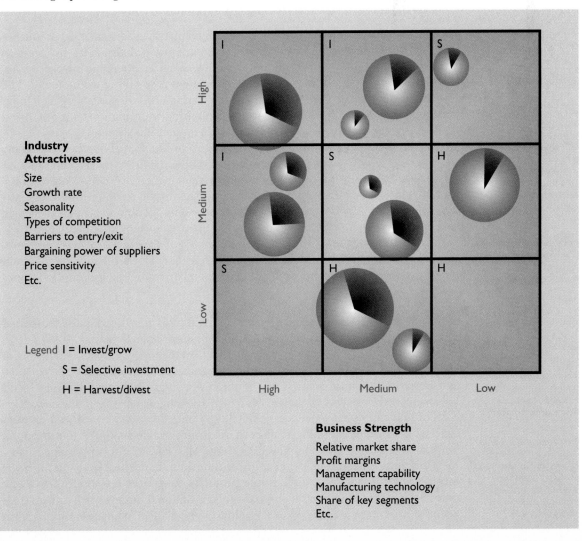

Some Strategic Options

strategy An alternative designed to achieve an organization's mission or objectives.

Thus far, we have discussed the major aspects of strategic planning that precede the final step of actually selecting a **strategy,** an alternative designed to achieve an organization's mission or objectives. Two broad types of strategies are discussed— generic strategies and master strategies.

The Generic Strategies   Basically, the firm's mission statement and objectives tell about the firm's purpose and what it seeks to achieve. How it can achieve this must be translated into a specific long-term or generic strategy. *Generic strategies* are so named because they can be adopted by any type of organization, be it a manufacturer or a high-tech or service organization. Based on Michael Porter's scheme (Chapter 3, p. 87), many planners believe a firm seeks a competitive advantage by following one of three fundamental generic strategies:

1. Striving for overall *cost* leadership
2. Striving to create and market unique products for varied customer groups through *differentiation*
3. Striving to have special appeal to one or more groups of consumers or industrial buyers, *focusing* on their cost or differentiation concerns[11]

cost leadership strategy A strategy to gain competitive advantage by producing goods and services more cheaply than the competition.

A **strategy of cost leadership** seeks to gain competitive advantage by producing goods and services more cheaply than the competition. A firm with this strategy seeks to exploit some fairly unique capability, such as dominant market share, access to supply sources, or the ability to implement cost-cutting technologies. The low-cost leader can then use its advantage by offering lower prices, attacking higher-cost competitors to gain market share, or benefiting from high profits. Southwest Airlines is a good example of a company that employs this strategy.

differentiation strategy Targets some unique product attribute that consumers see as advantageous over the attributes of competing products.

Differentiation strategy targets some unique product attribute that consumers see as advantageous over the attributes of competing products. Product quality, image, features, distribution channels, and supportive service networks are examples of vehicles for differentiation in attempting to win consumer loyalty. GM, for example, hopes that GM auto owners purchase only "genuine GM parts." Maytag seeks its differentiation in reliability and low maintenance of its appliances.

focus strategy Seeks to zero in on the needs of a particular market segment.

A **focus strategy** seeks to zero in on the needs of a particular market segment. Rolls-Royce (automobiles) seeks wealthy clientele; Fort Howard Paper specializes in paper products only for industrial and commercial customers. Commuter airlines are another example.

master strategies Provide the basis for coordinated, sustained efforts toward achieving the organization's long-term objectives.

Master Strategies   **Master strategies** provide the basis for coordinated, sustained efforts toward achieving the organization's long-term objectives.

concentration The strategy followed by a firm that operates with a single line of business.

Concentration is the strategy followed by a firm that operates with a single line of business, such as McDonald's or Polaroid. Advantages of concentration include relative simplicity of management, clarity of objectives, and a single organizational focus. Of course, there are certain dangers to a firm's putting all its eggs in one basket.

For much of its existence, Campbell Soup Company used a concentration strategy. But because of declining market share, it recently diversified into other food lines, such as Prego, Swanson, Vlasic, LeMenu, Mrs. Paul's, and Pepperidge Farm.[12]

horizontal integration Somewhat like concentration, but it normally involves acquiring another firm whose products or services are similar.

Horizontal integration is similar to concentration but differs in that it normally involves acquiring another firm whose products or services are similar. Thus, the objective is to increase market share through additional outlets, such as Circle K's acquisition of many 7-Eleven stores, Wal-Mart's purchase of Wholesale Club, or Peat

Marwick's merger with England's KMG Main Hurdman to form the world's largest accounting firm.

Vertical integration is the strategy of extending a business's scope by taking an activity or function backward toward sources of supply or forward toward the end user. Black and Decker, the power tool manufacturer, also has its own retail stores to sell and service its products. Knight-Ridder, a large newspaper publisher, also owns a papermaking operation that supplies the company's paper. Note in the SWOT analysis (p. 223) that a weakness of Hershey Foods is its dependence upon key resource suppliers. Were Hershey to acquire its own cocoa bean or sugar plantations, this would be a strategy of vertical integration.

Examples of forward integration include a book publisher's ownership of bookstores or a clothing manufacturer's establishment of its own retail clothing outlets. The major disadvantages of vertical integration are the increased complexity of management and the requirement of additional capital.

> A major reason for Matsushita Electric Industrial Company's purchase of MCA Inc. for $6.8 billion in late 1990 was to "guarantee itself the raw material—programming—for such innovative technologies as high-definition television."[13] MCA's movie and record properties should greatly enhance the Japanese company's position in the entertainment industry and help it sell more VHS-format VCRs.

Diversification is the strategy of entering a business or businesses different from the present one(s). The advantage is the protection afforded by dividing risks or by selecting industries that are countercyclical. **Related diversification** means retaining a common thread throughout the various different businesses, such as Weyerhaeuser's pulp, paper, lumber, newsprint, and timber businesses. **Unrelated diversification** means that the various businesses have few similarities. ITT follows a highly unrelated diversifying strategy: Its business segments include, among others, hotels (Sheraton), insurance (Hartford), telecommunications, fertilizers, and perfume. Acquisition of existing businesses is a very popular way to achieve diversification. The disadvantage associated with diversification, especially into unrelated fields, is the additional complexity of management.

Turnaround or **retrenchment strategies** are often used to nurse a poorly performing company back to health. Problems causing the negative performance, such as poor management, changing markets, increased competition, or outdated products, must be identified and addressed. Turnaround may focus on replacing management (frequently done!), paying attention to cost controls, disposing of unprofitable segments, or shifting resources from some segments to others. Chrysler Corporation, under Lee Iacocca's leadership in the 1980s, was one of the most visible examples of a successful turnaround/retrenchment strategy. Recent well-known turnaround failures are Eastern Airlines and Wang Laboratories, both of which ended in bankruptcy.

Divestment or **liquidation strategies** are taken when an organization's business is felt to have lost its appeal. In each case, it means a decision to sever the particular business entity. Divestment involves selling off the business or a component of it.

> In 1990, Whitman Corporation (originally Illinois Central Railroad, then Illinois Central Industries) planned to sell its Hussman Corporation, the world's leading producer of refrigeration equipment for the food industry. Proceeds of the sale

vertical integration The strategy of extending a business's scope by taking an activity or function backward toward sources of supply or forward toward the end user.

diversification The strategy of entering a business or businesses different from the present one(s).

related diversification The strategy of entering into different businesses that share a common thread.

unrelated diversification The strategy of entering into different businesses that have few similarities.

turnaround or retrenchment strategies Strategies used to nurse a poorly performing company back to health.

divestment or liquidation strategies Involve a decision to sever a business entity that has lost its appeal.

would be used to pay off some long-term debt and "pursue highly selective acquisitions" in the food and drink areas—to complement its Whitman's candy, Pet milk, and Pepsi-Cola products.[14] Often what is one company's albatross, because of mismanagement, poor strategic position, or changing market, may become another's silver lining.

Liquidation involves terminating the business's existence by either shutting it down or disposing of its assets, as Sears did with its catalog business.

Operational Planning

You have learned that strategic planning sets the organization's broad course and determines the organization's direction in adapting successfully to its external environment.

operational planning
Planning derived from strategic plans and designed to help achieve goals throughout the organization's operations.

Operational planning, by contrast, is planning derived from strategic plans and designed to help achieve goals throughout the organization's operation. Thus, these plans are called operational. Policies, programs, projects, and budgets are all types of operational plans.

The Role of Objectives in Operational Planning

Objectives are the end results, goals, or targets that an organization, department, or individual seeks to attain. They become the focal point toward which the specific who, where, when, and how questions of operational planning are addressed throughout all levels of the organization.

Management experts disagree often about management terminology, and the definition of an objective is one area of dispute. Some say objectives are broad and general, whereas goals are more specific; others say just the reverse. In this book, we use the terms interchangeably.

Objectives Permit Unified Planning   Earlier in this chapter, you saw at the broad, overall level some examples of objectives that were part of strategic planning. It is after these objectives are established at overall levels that lower levels base their own narrower, more specific objectives or goals on them. This framework creates a hierarchy of objectives. For example, assume that a hypothetical company, Hertex, has an overall 1996 profit objective of $3.2 million. A hierarchy of objectives for the sales function might look like this:

Hertex Inc.

1996	Overall profit objective:	$ 3,200,000
1996	Sales Division objective:	32,000,000
1996	Western Region sales objective:	14,000,000
1996	California State sales objective:	9,000,000
1996	California sales representative individual objective:	450,000

This cascading of objectives, with lower levels contributing toward the achievement of higher level objectives, enables performance at multiple organizational levels to be linked into a unified whole.

Objectives Provide Motivation and a Sense of Achievement   Realistic objectives serve as the basis for group and individual motivation. The Sales Division manager of Hertex gears his or her entire effort toward accomplishing the $32 million sales goal against which his or her performance will be measured. This is true throughout the entire hierarchy of objectives.

Research on objective setting at the individual worker level shows several important things. Researchers Edwin Locke and Gary Latham cite ten studies of keypunchers, typists, truck loaders, and soft drink cooler service workers that showed an increase in performance of 11 to 27 percent when specific objectives were introduced. Also, a comprehensive study of 70 goal-setting studies conducted between 1966 and 1984, covering over 7,000 workers, led the authors to conclude that *specific, difficult,* and *hard-to-achieve* goals increased performance significantly more than moderately high or easy "do your best" goals. However, performance *decreased* dramatically when goals were set so high that they were perceived as "impossible" to achieve.[15]

Lou Holtz, head coach of the Notre Dame "Fighting Irish," in his video *Do Right,* says that every individual needs goals to pursue in life. Only with a goal, he says, can you seek to make it happen. Holtz was turned on to goal setting by *The Magic of Thinking Big,* a book by David Schwartz, that his wife gave him when he was going through a particularly difficult time early in his career. Holtz read the book and realized that he had no goals in life. He sat down and wrote out a list of 100 things he wanted to achieve in life, such as climbing the pyramids, skydiving, and visiting a submarine. One item on that list was to be head coach at Notre Dame. Holtz credits this goal setting as a key factor in turning his life around and the basis for his success. He instills in all of his players the need to set personal objectives, not only in football, but in other aspects of their lives as well.[16]

Objectives Serve as a Basis for Control   Measurable objectives enable managers to perform the control function of management more effectively. As you will learn in Chapter 15, the control process involves (1) setting performance targets or standards, (2) measuring performance, (3) comparing actual performance with present standards, and (4) taking corrective action if needed. You will note that the first step of controlling, then, is having a goal or objective for which to shoot.

When information indicates that objectives are *not* being met, a manager must examine the situation and determine whether corrective action is necessary. If corrective action is needed, he or she must decide what form the action will take. But again, the corrective action is aimed at making the actual performance conform to the objective. The Tips box on the next page presents the general guidelines for setting objectives effectively.

Management by Objectives

Although it was used by Du Pont in the early 1920s, management by objectives (MBO) was first publicized by Peter Drucker in his book *The Practice of Management* in 1954.[17] MBO has grown to be quite popular, especially in larger organizations. It has certainly called much attention to the role of planning and setting objectives.

In general, **management by objectives** is a process that involves the superior and subordinate managers of an organization in jointly setting common goals,

management by objectives (MBO) Process whereby superior and subordinate managers jointly set overall organizational goals, define each individual's area(s) of responsibility in terms of the results expected, and use those measures as guides for operating the unit and assessing the contribution of each of its members.

Guidelines for Effective Objective Setting

Objective setting in the real world is often a poorly understood, poorly implemented process. Properly done, however, it leads to more effective management. The following guidelines—which apply to all management levels—will help you become more effective in setting objectives.

1. *Limit objectives to selected performance areas.* Many managers establish far too many objectives for their personnel. Since the nature of objective setting is to stimulate and direct attention and energy, critical objectives lose some of their luster when thrown in with many others. Instead of setting 15 objectives for your people, it is better to select 5 or 6 that address key performance areas that really count, such as profitability, quality, cost control, and/or customer relations.

2. *Be specific.* If you cannot count, measure, or describe an objective in some specific way, forget about it. Vague objectives not only are subject to misinterpretation by personnel but do not provide tangible satisfaction when they are achieved. Consider, for instance, this objective: "The Division X objective is to show good profitability in 1997." This statement is vague on several counts: (a) What is "good"

profitability? (b) What measure—return on assets, return on equity, return on sales, and so forth—will be used to determine profitability? (c) Will profitability be determined before or after taxes? A better statement would be this: "The Division X objective for 1997 is to earn a 20 percent return on average assets after taxes."

3. *Set challenging objectives.* Objectives should not be set so low that they can be met by "average" effort; nor should they be unrealistically high. For instance, it is unrealistic for Chrysler to set an objective of gaining 50 percent of the U.S. auto market by 1999. This not only would serve no useful purpose, it would also demoralize personnel who know there is no reasonable hope of achieving it.

4. *Keep objectives in balance.* Key performance areas tend to be interrelated, so managers must consider the impact objectives have on one another. For example, quality of work influences quantity of output; profitability and cost control may not always be consistent with customer service or maintenance of physical assets.

5. *Set realistic deadlines.* Objectives, properly set, should establish time frames for completion. This holds individuals accountable over a period of time and allows

for periodic assessment of their performance.

6. *Involve subordinates.* Since people are more committed to what they themselves establish, try to get them to set objectives and performance levels. As a manager, you are not necessarily committed to what they feel are reasonable objectives, but the level they establish will frequently surprise you. The major premise of MBO is based on this principle.

7. *Establish results-oriented objectives.* Since objectives are end results, they should be desirable levels of achievement within themselves. For example, the objective "to increase advertising by 10 percent in 1997" measures the amount spent on advertising, not the *end result* that the advertising is designed to achieve. A better objective would focus on the number of new customers, size of customer orders, or increased sales attributable to advertising, rather than the *level* of advertising itself.

8. *Follow up.* Do not wait until the end of the performance period to determine whether objectives are being met. Use intermediate performance reports or progress checks to see how your people are doing. If they are doing well, praise and reinforce their performance; if they are on the wrong track, coach them as needed.

defining each individual's major area of responsibility in terms of the results expected of him or her, and using those measures as guides for operating the unit and assessing the contribution of each of its members. The steps of the MBO process are shown in Figure 7.10.

Underlying Concepts of MBO   MBO's success is based on the underlying hypotheses that *if one is strongly attached to a goal, one is willing to expend more effort to reach it than if one were less committed to it.* It is also based on the concept that people prefer to be evaluated according to specific criteria that *they* perceive to be realistic and standards that *they* view as reasonably attainable. Under this method, people participate in setting the goals and identifying the criteria that will be used to evaluate and reward their performance. Some of the goals may be measurable in quantitative terms (such as sales—or production—volume, expenses, or profits), whereas others may be assessed qualitatively (such as customer relations, a marketing plan, or employee development).

Key Aspects of the MBO Process   There are five key parts of MBO that are critical to its success. Some of these are directly tied to the five steps outlined in Figure 7.10.

1. *Linking organizational goals.* Note that the first step in the MBO process enables the subordinate to understand his or her supervisor's objectives. An effective MBO program can produce a clear understanding of how division, department, section, and individual objectives are related.
2. *Forcing managerial planning.* In Steps 2 and 3 of the MBO process, employees are required to think their own jobs through. They are more likely to visualize the big, overall picture and to focus on the truly important performance areas. Instead of wasting their energies working on minor, less important activities, managers direct their efforts toward achieving the major performance targets they have established jointly with their superiors.
3. *Involving subordinates in objective setting.* Perhaps the unique feature of MBO is found in Step 3 of the process. Here subordinates play an active role helping to establish their own objectives. MBO assumes that individuals are more likely to be highly committed to objectives that they have had a hand in setting. Note that MBO does not give subordinates blanket privilege in setting their own objectives; the supervisor also provides his or her input. MBO emphasizes the jointness of the objectives and indicates that both parties can play an active role. The final decision for approval, of course, rests with the supervisor.
4. *Establishing specific, measurable performance objectives.* Important to MBO programs is the need in Step 3 for objectives that are specific and measurable—that is, ones that are concrete rather than ambiguous. Some examples of "weak" and "improved" statements of objectives are given in Table 7.2. Well-stated objectives facilitate the evaluation and reward processes, which are the final stages of the MBO cycle.

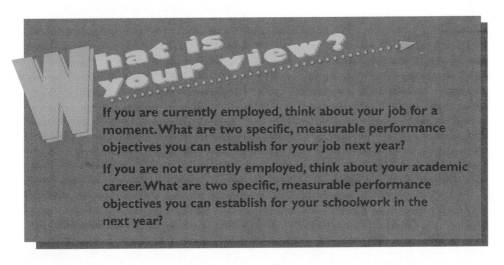

If you are currently employed, think about your job for a moment. What are two specific, measurable performance objectives you can establish for your job next year?

If you are not currently employed, think about your academic career. What are two specific, measurable performance objectives you can establish for your schoolwork in the next year?

5. *Increasing communication and interaction.* Properly executed, MBO establishes more direct, even daily communication between boss and subordinates. This is reflected in all five steps of the process.

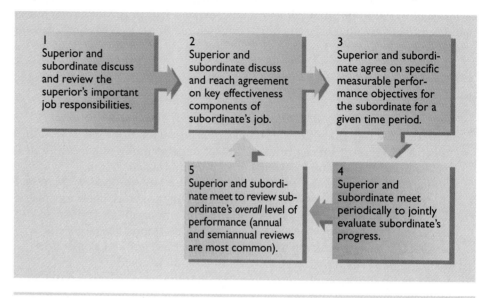

FIGURE 7.10
Steps in the MBO process.

TABLE 7.2   EXAMPLES OF MBO STATEMENTS OF OBJECTIVES

Weak	Improved
To improve communication with employees	To implement a system of weekly departmental meetings by the end of June
To stress individual development of my subordinates	To have each employee attend a professional development program of one day or more in his or her field during the year
To better the safety record in the department	To reduce lost work hours due to accidents from 1,200 to 1,020, or by 15 percent
To improve the quality of nursing service from the patient's standpoint	To average a score of 80 percent on the "quality of nursing service" questionnaires filled out by all hospital patients during the next year
To improve relationships and attitudes among my employees	To reduce the number of supervisory-related grievances filed in my department by 20 percent next year
To increase sales	To have each salesperson make ten additional sales calls per month and to gain a 10 percent increase in sales in the new territory by the end of the fiscal year

Figure 7.11 shows an actual MBO format used by one organization. Note that the subordinate is required to identify the basic objective and also must state the key action plans that will be taken toward completion of the objective. The supervisor's completed evaluation ultimately serves as the basis for determining the employee's annual performance rating and, ultimately, the merit increases or other rewards given by the organization.

Among the common problems encountered in MBO programs is the fact that for many managers, allowing subordinates to participate in objective setting runs

FIGURE 7.11

MBO in action. (Names of organizations and individuals are disguised.)

CHARITY HOSPITAL
MANAGEMENT OBJECTIVE STATEMENT (A)

Name: Larry C. Henderson **Title:** Human Resource Manager

Objective Number: 1 of 7 **Initials: (Supervisor)** A.R.H. **Initials: (Employee)** L.C.H.

Objective Statement (What)

To implement by Oct. 1, 1995 an In-House Physical Fitness Program that attracts 10% of hospital employees.

Action Plan (How) (give broad overview only)	Date Due	Responsibility Assigned To:
1. Create a PFP task force of persons from key departments to generate ideas, help plan PFP implementation.	March 1, 1995	Henderson
2. Interview a minimum of five responsible PFP directors in organizations that have established similar programs.	April 1, 1995	Henderson, Sanchez
3. Conduct written survey of all hospital employees to determine interest in various types of programs.	May 15, 1995	Henderson

CHARITY HOSPITAL
SEMIANNUAL PERFORMANCE EVALUATION (B)
Supervisor: Evaluate the employee's attainment of the work objectives shown on Form A. Your evaluation should be discussed with your employee.

Supervisor's Evaluation of Employee's Attainment of Work Objectives

Employee achieved objective well. Initial aerobics class, offered since September 1, has averaged 12% employee attendance during the week; the first lecture series was attended by 14%. Program has been well received, with many favorable comments encouraging expanded offerings.

Final Performance Rating (Check One)

☐ Unsatisfactory ☐ Satisfactory ☐ Competent ☐ Commendable ☒ Superior

Employee's signature (I acknowledge having read and discussed the comments and performance rating noted above.) *Larry C. Henderson*

Supervisor's Signature *Anna R. Hightower* **Date:** Jan. 18, 1996

Title: Assistant Administrator

contrary to their own styles and philosophy. Thus, they may resist implementing MBO properly. MBO can also be time-consuming, especially for managers with large numbers of subordinates. Paperwork may also increase because of managers' attempts to stay abreast of subordinates' progress. Finally, the need for specific, measurable objectives means objectives that are readily quantifiable, such as production volume, costs, or profits, may result in qualitative factors, such as employee attitudes and satisfaction, being ignored.

Standing Operational Plans

standing plans Operational plans that tend to be fixed for large periods of time and are designed to provide organizational stability.

Standing plans are operational plans that tend to be fixed for large periods of time and are designed to provide organization stability. They include (1) *policies*, or general statements that are guides to or channels of thinking and decision making by managers and subordinates; (2) *procedures* that establish a standing or routine method or technique for handling recurring activities; and (3) *rules and regulations* that state mandatory courses of action chosen from available alternatives. These plans, once established, continue to apply until they are modified or abandoned. They are thus fixed in nature and content.

policies General statements that serve as guides to managerial decision making and to supervising the activities of employees.

Policies   The term **policies** is used to define those broad, general statements that serve as guides to managerial decision making and to supervising the activities of employees. Some examples of policies are given in Figure 7.12. Sometimes policies are formally determined and announced; they may also be informally set by the

FIGURE 7.12
Some examples of policies.

Purchasing policy. "We will attempt to develop several sources of supply so as not to be totally reliant on only one."

Wage policy. "Wages shall be established and maintained on a level favorable to that found for similar positions within our industry and the community."

Marketing policy. "Only a limited number of dealers will be selected to distribute and sell the company's product lines in a given territory."

Hiring policy. "We are an equal opportunity employer."

Communications policy. "Managers should periodically hold group meetings with subordinates for the purpose of discussing objectives of the department, discussing new developments that may be of interest to or may affect subordinates, answering questions, and, in general, encouraging more effective and accurate communications within the organization."

Promotion policy. "We will attempt to fill vacancies by emphasizing promotion from within."

Open-door policy. "Every employee has the right to discuss with any higher-level manager any concerns he or she has about management actions or decisions."

actions of superiors, who may not intend for them to become policies. They may be written, unwritten, spoken, or even unspoken. As shown in Figure 7.13, they may be initiated at any level of the organization.

The purpose of policies is to provide stability, consistency, and uniformity throughout an organization, while at the same time allowing managerial flexibility. Thus, policies are intended as guidelines that do not, in fact, specify the exact action that managers should take in all circumstances.

Consider the promotion policy shown in Figure 7.13, "We will attempt to fill vacancies by emphasizing promotion from within." This policy guides managers' behavior by stating an expectation, but falls short of dictating that it be followed in *every* circumstance. Thus, managers should be preparing their personnel for advancement through training and upgrading their skills so that their candidacy will be seriously considered. If a manager has several times in the past recruited personnel from outside the organization, this pattern of behavior would show questionable support of company policy.

Once the broad organizational policies are set by the administration, the functional departments (such as production, sales, finance, and engineering) set forth their policies. These policies must conform and contribute to the ultimate organizational objectives. Functional departments usually establish policies pertaining to research, quality, distribution, procurement, and personnel, as well as planning and control policies.

A growing area of concern for management is establishing uniform personnel policies, especially those affected by public policy in the form of laws, court decisions, and administrative rules and regulations. Some new policy areas facing managers include providing equal employment opportunities for all groups, maintaining occupational safety and health, improving the quality of work life, providing comparable pay for comparable work, and securing employees' privacy.

FIGURE 7.13
Policies may originate at any organizational level.

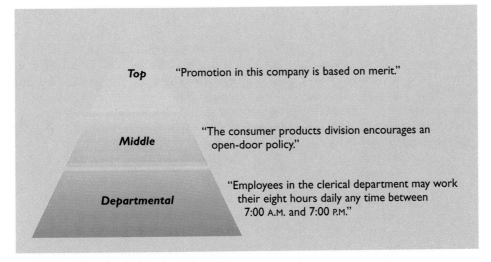

In short, policies are relatively permanent, general plans of action used to guide managerial decision making or other activities required to achieve organizational objectives. They are helpful in securing uniform performance and are used to guide management toward reaching the goal of efficient and effective operations.

Procedures   When it is important that certain steps be taken in a given sequence and that work be done accurately, management may establish detailed **procedures,** which establish a standard or routine method or technique for handling recurring activities.

procedures Detailed plans that establish a standard or routine method or technique for handling recurring activities.

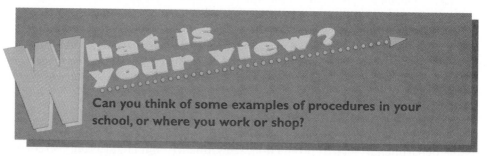

Can you think of some examples of procedures in your school, or where you work or shop?

Procedures should be designed to ensure that pertinent information flows to the people needing such data and that each person involved in the process understands just what he or she is to do with it. The transfer and manipulation of written information can be coordinated and simplified through the use of standard forms. Standardizing forms, in turn, leads to the standardization of information storage facilities. MAP 7.3 illustrates a fairly typical procedure—how to use time clocks and time cards—established through a series of steps.

Formal procedures are normally put in writing, especially those that require a number of steps or are complex or very important, or where it is essential to follow a specified sequence.

The most important advantages of procedures are that they (1) preserve managerial effort, (2) facilitate delegation of authority and placement of responsibility, (3) lead to development of more efficient methods of operation, (4) permit significant personnel economies, (5) facilitate control, and (6) aid the coordination of activities.

Rules and Regulations   The simplest yet usually the most detailed of all standing plans, **rules and regulations,** are guidelines that specifically state what can and cannot be done under given circumstances. Thus, they are used to implement other plans and are usually the result of a policy that requires strict adherence in *every* instance. When no variations are permitted, the plan becomes a rule or regulation, often carrying a negative outcome if it is violated. Some examples of rules and regulations are the following:

rules and regulations Guidelines that state specifically what can and cannot be done under any given circumstances.

No drugs permitted on the premises.

Hard hats must be worn in the plant at all times.

All customers' checks for over $25 must be approved by a department head.

A student may enroll for no more than 21 hours of course credit per semester.

MANAGEMENT APPLICATION AND PRACTICE 7.3

Procedures in Action: Using Time Clocks and Cards

The following procedures regarding time clocks and time cards have been adopted for all hourly and salaried nonexempt employees:

1. Time clocks are located in the three major entrances to the operations building; use the clock that has been assigned to you by your supervisor.

2. All hourly employees should punch in at the beginning of their work shift, punch out for lunch, punch in at the end of lunch, and punch out at the end of the work shift.

3. You must punch your own time cards. No one is allowed to punch in or out for another employee.

4. Time clocks will allow a 15-minute grace period at the beginning and end of the work shift, and a 15-minute grace period at the beginning and end of lunch. Should you punch in or out beyond the grace period, you are required to have the time card initialed by your supervisor at that time.

5. The computerized time clocks automatically calculate the number of hours worked. It is extremely important, therefore, that you punch in and out correctly.

6. Two time cards are issued to each employee at the beginning of each payroll period, one for each week of the payroll period.

7. Your time cards for each workweek will be signed and submitted to your supervisor for review and approval.

8. Supervisors should check each card for accuracy, sign each time card, and submit to Payroll for payment.

9. Rather than using time clocks, nonexempt salaried employees are to fill in their time cards manually, but are otherwise to follow the same procedures as hourly personnel.

Source: A manufacturing firm that desires anonymity.

Single-Use Plans

Organizations also use other types of operational planning that you might think of as one-time plans. The most prevalent formal types of **single-use operational plans** are programs, projects, and budgets.

Programs **Programs** are operational plans that involve the entire complex of activities necessary to carry out a given course of action. They compose objectives, goals, strategies, policies, rules and job assignments as well as the fiscal, physical, and human resources required to implement them. A distinguishing feature of this type of plan is the commitment (usually on a long-term basis) of these resources in the form of capital, development, and operating budgets.

A program usually includes a statement of objectives and a breakdown of the principal steps that must be taken to achieve the objectives—with the approximate timing of each—as well as the resources required to accomplish the stated objective. Considerable effort and expertise are required to design and implement a comprehensive program. Managers should therefore understand a program's nature and benefits so that they can decide whether its preparation is worth the expected expenditure of time, effort, and resources.

Major programs are usually found in an organization in the form of (1) the research, development, and initiation of new products or services; (2) the budget-

single-use operational plans Operational plans including nonrecurring programs, projects, and budgets, that serve a specific purpose for a limited period.

programs Operational plans that involve the entire complex of activities necessary to carry out a given course of action.

ing of sales, inventories, production requirements, and financial needs; and (3) the training and development of personnel to cope with some major change in the organization. Some examples of specific programs are the following:

1. Kmart's rebuilding program seeks to upgrade the physical appearance of its stores.
2. Procter & Gamble launched its new pain reliever Aleve with a massive promotion program costing $100 million.
3. General Motors has set aside huge sums for a program to prepare its obsolete workers for new jobs in areas such as servicing robots.

Projects   Frequently, individual segments of a general program are relatively separate and clear-cut, so they can be planned and executed as distinct **projects.** For example, an energy firm may have a program to reduce its reliance on imported petroleum from OPEC. Specific projects within the program may be to develop gasohol or extract oil from shale. Furthermore, each of these projects may have numerous subprojects.

Project planning is a flexible type of planning that may be adapted to a variety of situations. If operations can be easily divided into separate parts with a clear termination point, the project is a natural and effective planning device.

projects Plans for the execution of individual segments of a general program.

Budgets   Almost every individual, family, or organization uses some form of budgeting, either formally or informally. A well-planned budget serves as both a planning and a control device and should express realistic goals that can be achieved. Only when these goals are realistic and satisfactory will the budget serve as an effective measure of managerial performance.

A **budget** is a detailed operational plan or forecast of the results expected from an officially recognized program of operations, based on the highest reasonable expectations of operating efficiency. It is generally expressed in monetary terms.

By itself, a budget is merely a collection of figures or estimates that indicates the future in financial terms. **Budgetary control,** on the other hand, involves careful planning and control of all the activities of the organization in financial terms. It assumes a genuine desire on the part of management to keep as close to the previously charted course as possible, to check actual performance against the plans, and to use the budget as a road map to reach the previously established goals.

budget A detailed operational plan or forecast, generally expressed in monetary terms, of the results expected from an officially recognized program of operations.

budgetary control The careful planning and control of all the activities of the organization in financial terms.

SUMMARY

Planning involves three basic steps: (1) setting an objective or goal, (2) identifying and assessing present and future conditions affecting the objective, and (3) developing a systematic approach by which to achieve the goal. Planning can be centralized so that the major planning work of an organization is done from a central point. It can also be decentralized so that each division or department essentially does its own planning without a single central planning unit at the top of the organization. A combination of the two systems results in the central planning unit doing the original umbrella planning, with each unit working to complement the central unit's plans. Long-range plans cover periods of two to five or more years, intermediate-range plans vary from one to five years; and short-range plans consist of daily plans to those covering a year. Top managers typically devote a greater proportion of time to long-range plans, and lower managers typically are more involved in short-range plans.

An organization's overall objectives become the focal point for directing strategies. Businesses need organizational objectives in the key areas of market standing, productivity, physical and financial resources, profitability, innovation, manager performance and development, worker performance and attitudes, and public and social responsibility.

A number of important internal and external variables affect an organization's strategy. Planning premises, or assumptions about future conditions affecting the firm's environment, must be made. The firm's strengths, weaknesses, opportunities, and threats must also be analyzed.

The BCG matrix and the GE matrix are helpful in assessing strategies for the various SBUs in a diversified firm's lines of business. Low-cost leadership, differentiation, and focus are three generic strategies organizations may employ. Master strategies include concentration, horizontal integration, vertical integration, diversification, and divestment/liquidation.

Operational planning is derived from strategic plans and helps achieve goals throughout all parts of the organization's operation. Objectives play an important part in operational planning and are end results, goals, or targets sought that become the basis for operational planning. Objectives permit unified planning, provide motivation and a sense of achievement, and serve as a basis for control.

Management by objectives is the managerial process by which supervisors and subordinates jointly set performance objectives for each subordinate; the objectives thus established then become the basis for measuring and rewarding performance. MBO (1) links objectives set at different levels of management, (2) forces managers to plan, (3) involves subordinates in the goal-setting process, (4) provides increased communication between manager and subordinate, and (5) requires that specific, measurable performance objectives be established.

Standing operational plans, including policies, procedures, and rules and regulations, tend to be fixed in nature. Single-use operational plans, including programs, projects, and budgets, are nonrecurring.

KEY TERMS

planning, 209
short-range plans, 211
intermediate-range plans, 211
long-range plans, 211
strategic planning, 212
strategic management, 213
organizational mission, 215
credos or company creeds, 216

objectives, 216
SWOT (TOWS) analysis, 221
strategic business unit (SBU), 223
strategy, 226
cost leadership strategy, 226
differentiation strategy, 226
focus strategy, 226
master strategies, 226

concentration, 226
horizontal integration, 226
vertical integration, 227
diversification, 227
related diversification, 227
unrelated diversification, 227
turnaround or retrenchment
 strategies, 227
divestment or liquidation strategies, 227
operational planning, 228

management by objectives (MBO), 229
standing plans, 234
policies, 234
procedures, 236
rules and regulations, 236
single-use operational plans, 237
programs, 237
projects, 238
budget, 238
budgetary control, 238

D I S C U S S I O N   Q U E S T I O N S

1. How would you explain the relationship between management levels and the timing of planning?

2. What are short-, intermediate-, and long-range plans?

3. What is a SWOT (TOWS) analysis?

4. In what way(s) do the BCG and the GE planning matrixes differ?

5. What are the three generic types of organizational strategy?

6. What steps are involved in the process of management by objectives?

7. How do standing and single-use plans differ? What are some examples of each?

PRACTICING MANAGEMENT

7.1

case

Kmart Trying to Find Itself

Vowing to succeed in its head-to-heel battle with rival Wal-Mart, Kmart since 1990 has built 153 fashionable new discount stores and expanded or refurbished 800 existing ones in an ongoing $3 billion expansion program. To add balance, Kmart built a specialty retail group including Payless Drug, Waldenbooks, OfficeMax, Sports Authority, and Pace membership warehouse. Add to this Builders Square, Kmart's answer to Home Depot, and you get the picture: a company much more diversified than its rival. The only problem, though, is that Kmart has performed poorly compared to Wal-Mart, as shown below.

Wal-mart	(dollars in millions)	Kmart
32,602	1990 sales	32,070
1,291	1990 profits	756
67,345	1993 sales	34,156
2,333	1993 profits	534

The driving force of Kmart is Joseph Antonini, who holds the position of chairman, CEO, and president. In an effort to stimulate revenues and earnings, Antonini speaks in terms of Kmart's renewal, especially in its discount stores. Antonini lowered prices on thousands of items, such as health and beauty products, household goods, and detergents, to become more competitive with Wal-Mart. Kmart's "Look of the Nineties" stores—a more spacious, open look; color-coded department signs; pharmacy; and a music store—have been installed in over half the company's 2,400 locations. The apparel division has become the cornerstone of each store, including popular brands Wrangler, Hanes, L.A. Gear, and Britannia. But sales per square foot in all Kmart stores continued to drop for the third consecutive year. And Kmart cannot win a pricing battle with Wal-Mart, which has a huge 5 percent advantage on operating costs.

Kmart has undergone its own downsizing, announcing 1995 plans to eliminate 2,500 managerial and 6,000 operative jobs and to shut down 110 marginally to poorly performing discount stores.

While Antonini remains confident that the discount store division can turn itself around, Kmart has work to do in its other business lines too. Its Builders Square stores average $15 million in sales per store, compared to Home Depot's $40 million. Over the past two years, Builders Square turned tail and got out of the California, Atlanta, and Hartford markets. Home Depot has taken dead aim at San Antonio, Builders Square's headquarters, and Home Quarters, a division of Hechinger, is coming into Detroit, another critical area. Competition is really heating up. Kmart's Pace membership stores have been heavy losers; in 1993, Pace abandoned Dallas, selling its eight stores to Wal-Mart's Sam's Club after trying unsuccessfully to dislodge Sam's Club. Pace also sold out to Sam's in Chicago, Kansas City, St. Louis, and Toledo. A new management team at Pace is likely to sell off more stores and retrench, focusing on business customers.

A major positive sign has been the success of the Super Ks, which, at 167,000 square feet, are two-thirds larger than the normal Kmart. A full-line grocery store combined with specialty departments, pharmacies, video rentals, and complete discount store assortment, Super K sales have outstripped projections so greatly that 75 new stores were completed in 1994, with a projected 400 to 500 open by the year 2000.

Experts say Kmart still doesn't seem to have a clear strategy, but Antonini disagrees. Still, he seems to concede that he may be running out of time, with stockholders displeased with their company's performance.

Sources: Bill Saporito, "The High Cost of Second Best," *Fortune*, July 26, 1993, pp. 99–102; James B. Treece, "Is a New CEO on Kmart's Shopping List?" *Business Week*, October 3, 1994, p. 62; and Christina Duff, "Kmart to Close Stores, Cut 10% of Managers . . . ," *Wall Street Journal*, September 9, 1994, p. A3.

Questions

1. Based on this case and other available information, develop a SWOT (TOWS) analysis of Kmart.

2. Write a mission statement for Kmart, given the information presented.

3. What types of generic strategies do you see reflected in this case? Master strategies? Explain.

4. What are some of the important planning premises supporting a commitment to build 400 to 500 new Super Ks through the year 2000?

5. What are some similarities between Kmart and Sears, as described in the Opening Case? Differences?

chapter

8

Organization Design, Authority, and Power

LEARNING OBJECTIVES

After studying the material in the chapter, you should be able to:

▶ **Define** and explain basic concepts of organization.

▶ **Describe** the different types of organizations.

▶ **Explain** the variables in determining the span of management.

▶ **Explain** the role of delegation, what it is, and how it is done.

▶ **Discuss** some reasons for managers' reluctance to delegate authority, and explain why employees may not accept delegation.

▶ **Explain** the role and sources of authority.

▶ **Describe** what power is, where it comes from, and how it can be used most effectively.

▶ **Describe** responsibility and accountability and explain why they cannot be delegated.

▶ **Discuss** the rationale for companies engaging in downsizing, and appraise the pros and cons of the strategy.

▶ **Define** the concept of reengineering and discuss how it can improve organizational efficiency and effectiveness.

GE's Fight with Bureaucracy

In 1981, at the age of 45, Jack Welch took over the reins of General Electric (GE) from the popular and well-thought-of chairman and CEO Reginald H. Jones. Under Jones's leadership, earnings per share, adjusted for inflation, had risen an average of 4.9 percent a year as compared to 1.9 percent a year under his predecessor, Fred Borch. A major reason for the high regard for Jones was that GE had moved from a state of chronic cash shortage to one of tremendous financial strength. On the other hand, Jones's thirst for information and control led to the building of a bureaucracy, causing decisions to be reviewed at many levels.

Almost immediately after taking office, Jack Welch went to war with the bureaucracy that had developed during Jones's tenure. In the process, the world's tenth largest industrial corporation has been remade and—perhaps—revitalized. During this time, Welch has gained a reputation as a tough and ruthless manager. Noel Tichy, a consultant who often works for GE, says Welch stoked the fire beneath the corporate cauldron to avoid the boiled-frog syndrome. Tichy explained, "If you put a frog in a pan of water and turn up the heat gradually, the frog will just stay put 'til it dies. But try to put a frog into boiling water and it will jump right out—and survive."

A key question is, Has it been worth it? If you were to ask one of the over 100,000 workers whose jobs were eliminated through layoffs, attrition, or sales of businesses, you would get one answer. If you were to ask stockholders who have seen earnings per share rise from 4.9 percent under Jones to 7.6 percent under Welch, you would get another answer. What kind of man is it who has streamlined the company from 100 business units down to 14?

Welch was an only child whose father was a hardworking railroad conductor. Like many prominent leaders, he considers his mother the dominant influence in his life and his earliest role model. It was she, he says, who influenced his core values: "She always felt I could do anything. It was my mother who trained me. She wanted me to be independent. Control your own destiny—she always had that idea. Saw reality. No mincing words. Whenever I got out of line, she would whack me one. But always positive. Always constructive. Always uplifting." These core values have been translated into a GE strategy of ranking either first or second globally in the markets it serves. The strategy has succeeded, as 12 of GE's units are considered market leaders.

Today Jack Welch is considered one of the stars of American industry. His newsletter in GE's annual report is a much anticipated event by

Jack Welch went to war with General Electric's bureaucracy.

business leaders, stockholders, and scholars, who read it searching for creative ideas. In the 1993 annual report he states:

> We are betting everything on our people—empowering them, giving them the resources and getting out of their way—and the numbers tell us that this focus has not only pointed us in the right direction, but it is providing us with a momentum that is accelerating.
>
> With the objective of involving everyone, we use three operating principles to define the atmosphere and behavior at GE:
>
> *Boundaryless* . . . in all our behavior;
>
> *Speed* . . . in everything we do;
>
> *Stretch* . . . in every target we set.

Welch goes on to give us examples of boundaryless behavior—a woman in the appliance division of GE in Hong Kong helping NBC to develop a satellite TV service. On a broader scale is labor and management becoming partners to transform the unprofitable appliance parts complex in Louisville to profitability.

In the process of reorganizing, delayering, and reenergizing GE, Welch has not rested on past accomplishments but is continually on the warpath against inefficiencies caused by the excessive bureaucracy he inherited. The company's latest campaign, called Work Out, is designed to win the hearts and minds of all 300,000 GE employees worldwide. GE visualizes Work Out as a fluid and adaptable concept, not a program.

Work Out generally starts as a series of regularly scheduled "town meetings" that bring together large cross sections of GE's people from manufacturing, engineering, customer service, hourly, salaried, and higher and lower levels.

The initial purpose of these meetings is simple—to remove the more troublesome aspects of bureaucracy: multiple approvals, unnecessary paperwork, excessive reports, routines, and rituals. Ideas and opinions are often, at first, voiced hesitantly by people who never before had a forum—other than the water cooler—to express them. It has been found that after a short time, those ideas begin to come in a flood—especially when people see action taken on the ones already advanced.

With the desk largely cleared of bureaucratic impediments and distractions, the Work Out sessions begin to focus on the more challenging tasks of examining the myriad processes that make up every business, identifying the crucial ones, discarding the rest, and then finding a faster, simpler, better way of doing things. Next, the teams raise the bar of excellence by testing their improved processes against the very best from around the company and from the best companies in the world.

During Jack Welch's early years as CEO, a number of people called him one of the most unfeeling, ruthless CEOs in America. Today many people say he is a statesman and one of the most visionary of all America's CEOs. In 1989, *Financial World* selected him as CEO of the year. Is it possible that both viewpoints may be correct? Welch himself may provide the answer: "We have the ultimate chance at GE during the 1990s to create a corporate atmosphere where it's culturally acceptable to speak out—where telling the truth is rewarded and where bosses who yell at people for speaking are not."

T his chapter's Opening Case highlights General Electric's strategy in dealing with excessive size and bureaucracy. The rest of the chapter presents concepts important to all organizations in helping them become and remain effective.[1]

Organizing as a Management Function

organizations Groups of individuals with a common goal bound together by a set of authority-responsibility relationships needed to reach objectives.

Organizations, which are groups of individuals with a common goal bound together by a set of authority-responsibility relationships, are required wherever groups of people work together to reach common goals. One of management's functions is to coordinate available organizational resources for effective operations.

The term **organizing** has various meanings. It can be used to refer to the following:

organizing The management task of determining resources and activities required to achieve organizational objectives, combining them into a formal structure, assigning responsibility for achieving the objectives to capable individuals, and delegating to them the authority needed to carry out their assignments.

1. The way management designs a formal structure to use the financial, physical, material, and human resources of the organization most effectively.
2. How the organization groups its activities, with each grouping being assigned a manager with the authority to supervise group members.
3. The establishment of relationships among functions, jobs, tasks, and employees.
4. The way managers subdivide the tasks to be done in their departments and delegate the necessary authority to accomplish the tasks.

Formal Organization Structure

Better-managed organizations have a formal organization structure that is depicted in an organization chart. Such a chart shows several key aspects of organization, including division of labor or specialization, chain of command, unity of command, management levels, and bureaucracy.

synergy The concept that two or more people, working together in a coopera-tive, coordinated way, can accomplish more than the sum of their independent efforts.

We might say that the formal organization structure (as represented by the organization chart) reflects the type of game plan management has set up to reach the organization's objectives. But just as numerous game plans are never put into practice, formal organization charts often only remotely describe the important relationships that exist. Frequently, the pecking order of the informal organization is completely out of line with the formal organization chart. In such cases, the infor-mal organization (discussed in Chapter 10) carries greater weight, since it describes the way things actually get done.

Division of Labor or Specialization

division of labor The principle that dividing a job into components and assigning them to members of a group gets more accom-plished than would be possible if each person tried to do the whole job alone.

The goal of an organization is to achieve some purpose that individuals cannot accomplish by themselves alone. As the chapter's opening quotation from William Cornell indicates, groups of two or more people, working together in a cooperative, coordinated way, can accomplish more than any one of them could independently. This concept is called **synergy.** The cornerstone of organizing is **division of labor—** the principle that dividing a job into components and assigning them to members of a group allows more to be accomplished than if each person tried to do the whole job alone. To work successfully, division of labor requires **specialization,** whereby employees (and managers) carry out the activities for which they are best qualified and most adept.

We live in an era of specialization, in which employees, professionals, and managers must cooperate and coordinate their activities.

specialization The concept that employees (and managers) carry out the activities they are best qualified for and most adept at performing.

In a hospital with a staff of 300 there are doctors, nurses, technicians, food service personnel, receptionists, guards, laundry workers, custodians, clerks, and many other types of employees. When the job is divided into components, more can be accomplished by the total group than would be possible for even 300 doctors if each ran his or her own separate medical facility with no support personnel or assistance. Can you imagine how important it is for staff members to cooperate and how difficult it is to coordinate their activities?

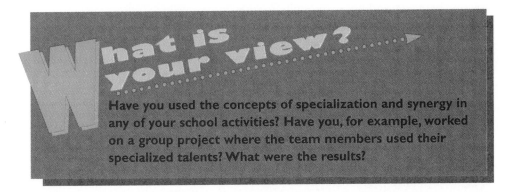

What is your view?

Have you used the concepts of specialization and synergy in any of your school activities? Have you, for example, worked on a group project where the team members used their specialized talents? What were the results?

Division of labor is effective because, since only a small part of a job is performed by each worker, workers need not have as many different skills, making them less expensive to employ and making job training easier. Moreover, the wasted motion that occurs when a person performs two or more parts of a job are minimized. Finally, division of labor usually leads to the invention of efficient equipment and machinery that increase productivity. For example, assembly line tools intended for one specialized task are simple and focused in design, permitting large-volume production.

How many straight pins could you and nine of your friends make in a day, assuming that you were using no automatic equipment? The answer depends on whether all of you would make entire pins or each would perform a specialized job—drawing the wire, rounding the body, sharpening the point, or shaping the head. Adam Smith argued the case for division of labor, or specialization, in his book *The Wealth of Nations,* published in England in 1776, when he addressed the issue of a small pin-making shop with ten workers. Each person, working independently to do the whole job, could have made no more than 20 pins daily, for a maximum of 200. But the shop, by employing specialization, produced about 4,800 pins daily.[2]

As you will see, however, severe behavioral consequences may result from the division of labor when it is carried to extremes. We will examine the consequences later in this chapter.

Chain of Command

chain of command
The authority-responsibility relationships that link superiors and subordinates throughout the entire organization.

The **chain of command** depicts the authority-responsibility relationships that link superiors and subordinates together throughout the entire organization. It flows from the chief executive down to the lowest worker in the organization. The upper portion of the scalar chain is shown in Figure 8.1, which depicts the top management of Boise Cascade Corporation.

Unity of Command

unity of command
The principle that each employee in an organization reports to and is accountable to only one immediate superior.

One of Henri Fayol's principles of management is **unity of command,** according to which each individual employee in an organization reports to and is accountable to only one immediate superior.[3] This means that the chain of command should be so clear that a subordinate will receive assigned duties and delegated authority from only one manager and be accountable to only one superior.

Unity of command is desirable because it simplifies communication and the placement of responsibility. Yet in today's complex organizations, many employees receive instructions from more than one manager. This is especially true when there is functional authority, as we show later in this chapter.

FIGURE 8.1
Chain of command of Boise Cascade Corporation.

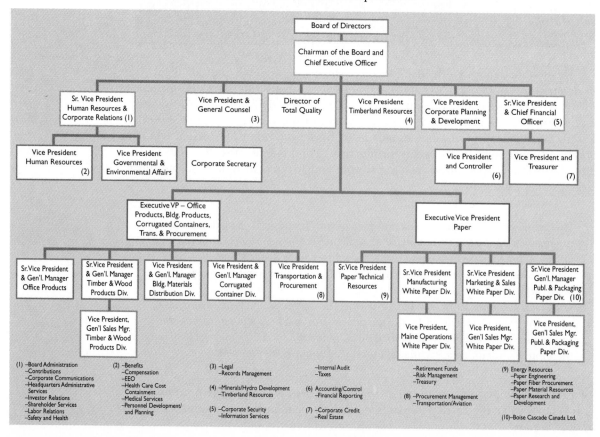

Management Levels

The levels of management that exist in a given structure, as well as the chain of command and reporting relationships, are also usually shown on an organization chart, as can be seen in Figure 8.1. Notice that the vertical lines from one level to another reflect different degrees of authority and responsibility.

Bureaucracy

You have probably heard various candidates for national and local office lambasting federal and state bureaucracies and bureaucrats. There are strong negative connotations associated with bureaucracy today. Let us now examine the meaning of this form of organization.

The concept of bureaucracy was advanced by the German writer Max Weber.[4] Under a **bureaucracy,** the organization's structure has the following characteristics:

1. Tasks are divided into very specialized jobs.
2. A rigorous set of rules must be followed to ensure predictability and eliminate uncertainty in task performance.
3. There are clear authority-responsibility relationships that must be maintained.
4. Superiors take an impersonal attitude in dealing with subordinates.
5. Employment and promotions are based on merit.
6. Lifelong employment is an accepted fact.

bureaucracy A highly specialized form of organizational structure designed to provide order and guidance, often characterized as highly restrictive and impersonal.

Most of us criticize unyielding bureaucracies, but in certain circumstances bureaucratic structures may be very effective, for they do provide order and guidance. Yet highly specialized tasks become monotonous, rules are often unnecessarily restrictive, managers cannot always be impersonal, and it is often difficult to identify clearly the more capable workers. Thus, management in the organization tends to become rigid, inflexible, and heavily reliant on **red tape,** or official routines and procedures marked by excessive complexity, resulting in unnecessary delay.

Often, as organizations become older and larger, they tend to become more bureaucratic. Notice that GE, as described in the Opening Case, has taken action to prevent that malaise.

red tape Official routines and procedures marked by excessive complexity, resulting in unnecessary delay.

Types of Organizations

Any understanding of organizational design requires an explanation of the most popular types of organizations. Two types are (1) the line organization and (2) the line-and-staff organization.

The Line Organization

In general, the **line organization** refers to those departments of an organization that perform the activities most closely associated with its mission or purpose. For example, in the military, the line organization consists of the combat units—infantry, artillery, and so forth.

line organization Those departments of an organization that perform the activities most closely associated with its mission or purpose.

Line officers are the ones who command troops in operations.

If the objective of the organization is to produce and sell goods, then the line organization would consist of at least the presidents, a production manager, a sales manager, and a finance manager, together with the employees who perform production, sales, and finance work. Figure 8.2 presents the organization chart of a small manufacturing company that operates as a pure line organization. As shown, individuals in each department perform the primary activities of the enterprise—production, sales, and finance. Each person has a reporting relationship to only one superior, so there is unity of command.

The Line-and-Staff Organization

Suppose the small line organization shown in Figure 8.2 grows to the point where it makes sense to hire certain persons who do not directly perform production, sales, or finance activities. Instead, they assist the line managers or departments to operate more effectively. Perhaps the position is that of an accounting specialist who will perform services such as keeping the books, preparing cost reports, and billing customers. Another position might be that of a personnel specialist, who will deal with recruiting, interviewing, and screening of potential job candidates. Another specialist might be an industrial engineer, who will aid the line organization by seeking to find improved work methods and practices. Another might be a purchasing specialist, who will follow through and serve the line by handling all the orders for materials, equipment, and supplies. And another might be a maintenance specialist, who will aid the line departments by servicing and maintaining equipment. These new personnel, who do not perform line activities, are referred to as staff.

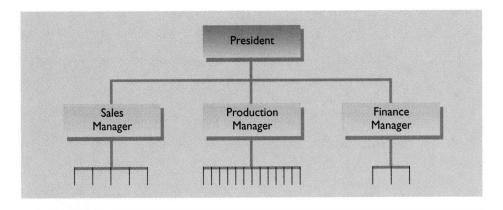

FIGURE 8.2
A simple line organization.

This organization structure will reflect the presence of staff as well as line, as shown in Figure 8.3. Notice that an additional staff position, legal, is also shown. The result is what is called a **line-and-staff organization,** in which staff positions have been added to serve the basic line departments and help them accomplish the organization's objectives more effectively.

Essentially, *staff employees* or *staff departments* are those that are not directly involved in the organization's or department's mainstream activities. For example, maintenance specialists do not create a product or sell it or account for profit or loss. Neither do purchasing agents, computer programmers, industrial engineers, public relations people, or personnel specialists. These specialists are not line personnel unless the company is a public relations or engineering firm, an advertising agency, a computer programming service, or the like.

Why do we make such a distinction between line and staff activities? First, since line activities represent the fundamental activities of the organization, management must be especially aware of the need to preserve the integrity and influence of those departments. To restrict the performance of line departments by granting too much authority or influence to staff can ultimately erode the departments' morale and efficiency.

Sometimes it is difficult to tell whether a department or position is line or staff. Some departments are so intimately related to obvious line work that they are considered part of the line. To make the distinction, you must ask the question, What is the business of the firm? Line activities are the organization's fundamental reason for existence—the bread-and-butter activities, so to speak.

line-and-staff organization An organization structure in which staff positions are added to serve the basic line departments and help them accomplish the organization's objectives more effectively.

Ordinarily, maintenance is considered a staff function in a manufacturing facility; the company is not in the business of providing maintenance. With an airline, however, airplane maintenance is so critical that it is considered a line activity.

Auditing, for instance, is normally considered staff in most organizations, but when a junior partner at Price Waterhouse, the well-known accounting firm, undertakes an auditing service for a customer, he or she is engaged in a line activity.

An editor at a publishing house is doing a line activity, but an editor at a manufacturing plant, editing the employee newsletter, is doing a staff function.

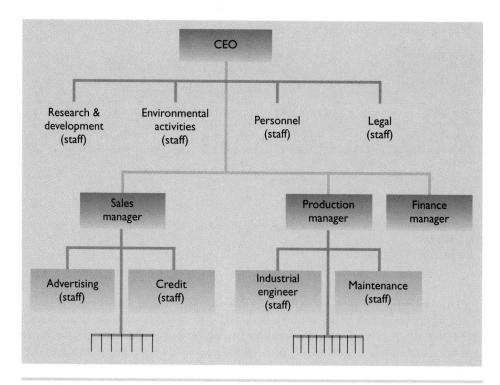

FIGURE 8.3
A simplified line-and-staff organization. (Staff positions are indicated by green lines.)

personal staff
Employees who provide advice, help, and service to an individual manager.

specialized staff
Employees who advise, counsel, assist, and serve the line and all elements of the organization.

The two main types of staff are personal staff and specialized staff. **Personal staff** is created to provide advice, help, and service to an individual manager. Sometimes referred to as the "assistant to" or "staff assistant," this person works on a variety of tasks for the manager.

Specialized staff, on the other hand, advises, counsels, assists, and serves the line and all elements of the organization. It is referred to as "specialized" staff because its function is narrow and the employees are viewed as experts; the specialists' expertise is made available throughout the organization. Examples of specialized staff include personnel specialists, safety specialists, legal specialists, and environmental control specialists. Specialized staff may report to various levels of the organization, such as the corporate level, the division level, or the decentralized facility level.

Span of Management

span of management (control, authority)
The number of subordinates reporting to a given manager.

The principle of **span of management,** sometimes referred to as the span of **control** or span of **authority,** has to do with the number of subordinates a manager can effectively supervise. According to the theory of the *span of management,* there is a limit to the number of subordinates a manager can effectively supervise.

The span of management theory is based on the work of V. A. Graicunas, a noted French consultant who wrote in 1933 that a given manager's span of management could be computed as follows: $R = n(2^{n-1} + n - 1)$, where $R =$ the number of relationships, and $n =$ the number of subordinates. Because a manager has three potential types of relationships—direct, group, and cross—his or her span increases as new subordinates are added. Direct relationships are the same as the chain of command, group relationships are those occurring in meetings between manager and subordinates, and cross relationships are those occurring between manager and two or more subordinates and any person outside the chain of command. Thus, 2 subordinates = 6 potential relationships, 3 subordinates = 18 potential relationships, and 18 subordinates = 2,359,602 potential relationships.[5]

In another study, Robert Dewar and Donald Simet found that the optimum span of management depends on several variables, including the size of the organization, technology, specialization, and routines or activities.[6] In general, the optimum span depends on the supervisor's "burden": The greater the burden, the smaller the span; the smaller the burden, the greater the span. MAP 8.1 is an example of the span of management being increased through eliminating two tiers of middle management.

Use of Different Spans at Different Levels

Does the span have to be the same throughout the organization? The answer is, "Certainly not!" In fact, the span may vary widely. Generally, the span of management becomes narrower as one moves from the bottom to the top of the organization. At the first-line management level, spans are much broader, possibly exceeding 30 to 40 subordinates when the work is routine, repetitive, unskilled, standardized, and manual.

Spans, Levels, and Employee Satisfaction

We have found from our studies of the effect of hierarchical levels on employee satisfaction that employees at higher levels of organizations are more satisfied than employees at lower levels. Also, higher-level managers in tall, steep organizational structures are more satisfied than higher-level managers in flat organizational structures. Conversely, lower-level managers in flat organizational structures are more satisfied than lower-level managers in tall ones.

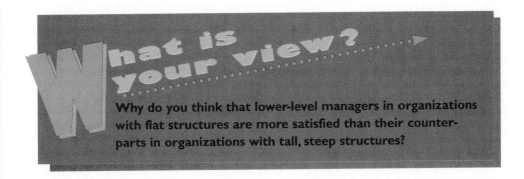

What is your view?

Why do you think that lower-level managers in organizations with flat structures are more satisfied than their counterparts in organizations with tall, steep structures?

MANAGEMENT APPLICATION AND PRACTICE 8.1

Toyota Cuts Middle-Management Fat

Until August 1989, 25-year-old Toyota Motor Company employee Hiroshi Hashimoto fit neatly into an orderly corporate structure. He reported to a section chief, who reported to a division chief, and so on up to the CEO.

In the normal course of things, Mr. Hashimoto expected to ascend to section, or even division, chief. But Toyota abruptly eliminated two tiers of middle-ranking positions. Far from being discouraged, Mr. Hashimoto was delighted by the change. "Before, the *kacho* [section chief] just gave instructions. From now on, we can ask him to move the pencil a bit, too. Now I feel that we're people working together."

Toyota made the move because it had become bogged down by the swollen number of middle-aged, white-collar worker who were receiving automatic seniority promotions. But with the reorganization, about 1,000 people were reassigned, primarily to lower-level jobs. This reorganization had the double effect of eliminating inefficient layers of bureaucracy and preventing top-heaviness in management. It should also help the company deal with a decreasing number of workers.

Toyota's move was one of the most dramatic efforts yet in Japan to get out of the traditional seniority-promotion system. In addition to eliminating the titles of 1,000 middle managers, the reorganization flattened out some vertical management structures to lower the number of people and bureaucratic levels involved in key business decisions and strategic planning. The company's officials think that quick decision making is important, especially when trying to get new car models off the drawing board, into production, and into showrooms.

According to Yoshihisa Murasawa, a vice-president of the consulting firm of Booz-Allen & Hamilton (Japan) Inc., "By eliminating titles, the organization becomes more flexible. Business is becoming much more complex, and it was too easy for decisions to fall between different sections in the same company."

Source: Yumico Ono and Marcus W. Brauchli, "Japan Cuts the Middle-Management Fat," *Wall Street Journal,* August 8, 1989, p. B1.

Factors Affecting Span

How can you determine the correct span of management for a given management position? While there is no definite answer that fits all situations, the following *contingency approach* (see Chapter 2) can be used to make the decision.

1. *Similarity of functions:* The more similar the functions performed by the work group, the larger the span.
2. *Geographic proximity:* The closer a work group is located physically, the larger the span.
3. *Complexity of functions:* The simpler and more repetitive the work functions performed by subordinates, the larger the span.
4. *Degree of direct supervision required:* The less direct supervision required, the larger the span.
5. *Degree of supervisory coordination required:* The less coordination required, the larger the span.
6. *Planning required of the manager:* The less planning required, the larger the span.
7. *Organizational assistance available to the supervisor:* The more assistance the supervisor receives in functions such as training, recruiting, and quality inspection, the larger the span.

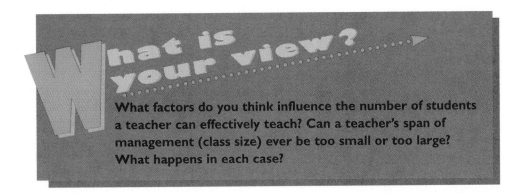

What factors do you think influence the number of students a teacher can effectively teach? Can a teacher's span of management (class size) ever be too small or too large? What happens in each case?

There is no magic formula for determining the correct size of a manager's span. Thus, the contingency approach, in which span size varies depending upon the particular situation, makes the most sense.

Departmentalization

There are several ways in which organizations decide on the organizational pattern that will be used to group the various activities to be performed. The organizational process of determining how activities are to be grouped is called **departmentalization.** Following are examples of several forms of departmentalization.

departmentalization The organization process of determining how activities are to be grouped.

1. *Function*—sales, accounting, production, customer service, or credit department
2. *Product or service*—a bank's loan department, a hospital's coronary care unit, a state highway department
3. *Territory*—Southwest Division, Northern Zone, International Operations
4. *Customer*—industrial sales, retail sales, governmental sales, consumer sales
5. *Process*—cutting department, relay assembly group, mailroom
6. *Matrix*—used by many high-technology, energy-oriented, and consulting firms.

It should be noted that most organizations use a combination of these forms; that is, most organizations will use more than one of these approaches in their groupings. However, most organizations use the functional approach at the top and others at lower levels. Because three of these forms are more complex and used extensively, we provide elaboration regarding functional, product, and matrix departmentalization.

Functional Departmentalization

Functional departmentalization groups together common functions or similar activities to form an organizational unit. Thus, all individuals performing similar functions are grouped together, such as all sales personnel, all accounting personnel, all nurses, all computer programmers, and so on. Figure 8.4 shows how functional departmentalization would be used at the top management level in dividing the three major business functions—production, sales, and finance.

functional departmentalization A form of departmentalization that groups together common functions or similar activities to form an organizational unit.

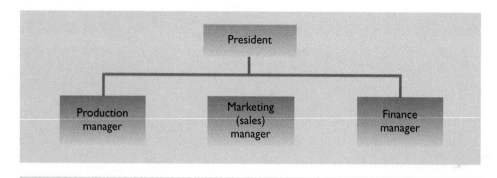

FIGURE 8.4
Functional departmentalization at the top-management level.

Advantages of the Functional Approach   The primary advantages of the functional approach are that it maintains the power and prestige of the major functions, creates efficiency through the principles of specialization, centralizes the organization's expertise, and permits tighter top-management control of the functions. For example, having all library-related activities on a college campus reporting to a common "library director" permits unified library policy to be carried out.

This approach also minimizes costly duplications of personnel and equipment. Having all computers and computer personnel in one department is less expensive than allowing several departments to have and supervise their own computer equipment and personnel.

Disadvantages of the Functional Approach   There are also many disadvantages to a functional approach. Some of these are that responsibility for total performance rests only at the top, and, since each manager oversees only a narrow function, the training of managers to take over the top position is limited. Organizations attempt to remedy this by transferring managers so that they become "rounded," with experience in several functions. Coordination between and among functions becomes complex and more difficult as the organization grows in size and scope. Finally, individuals identify with their narrow functional responsibilities, causing subgroup loyalties, identification, and tunnel vision.

Product Departmentalization

product departmentalization A form of departmentalization that groups together all the functions associated with a single product line.

At some point, the problems of coordination under a functional approach become extremely complex and cumbersome, especially when rapid, timely decisions must be made. The functional approach is slow and cumbersome because there is no single manager accountable for all the given activities, with the result that considerable coordination and communication are required before decisions can be reached. Consequently, some products that top management feels have the most potential may not receive the attention they deserve. And no one person is accountable for the performance of a given product line. What can be done to resolve this dilemma? One solution for many organizations is to shift to smaller, more natural semiautonomous miniorganizations built around specific products, each with its own functional capabilities. This is known as **product departmentalization,** in which all the functions associated with a single product line are grouped together.

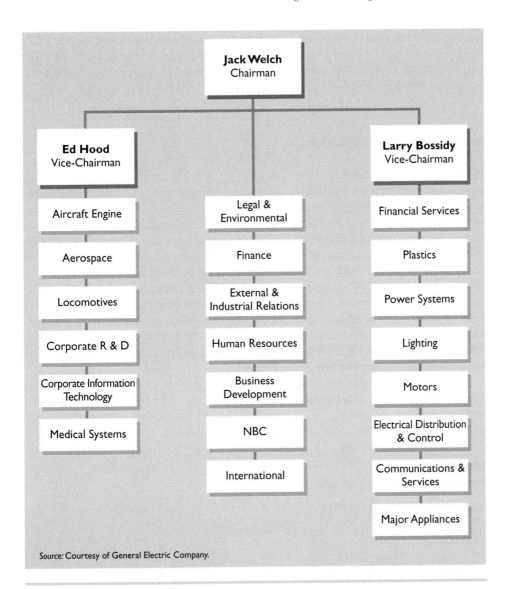

FIGURE 8.5
GE organization chart at the end of 1990.

Figure 8.5 demonstrates the grouping of major business activities of General Electric at the end of 1990. Each general business group is broken down into various products, each with its own activities, such as manufacturing, sales, finance, and engineering. In essence, each group is run as one of a network of smaller companies within the policy guidelines and controls established by top management.

Some of the advantages of product departmentalization are that attention can be directed toward specific product lines or services, coordination of functions at the product division level is improved, and profit responsibility can be better placed. Also, it is easier for the organization to obtain or develop several executives who have broad managerial experience in running a total entity.

Some of the disadvantages of product departmentalization are that it requires more personnel and material resources, it may cause unnecessary duplication of resources and equipment, and top management assumes a greater burden of establishing effective coordination and control. What a disaster it would be for GM's next economy-priced Chevrolet to have a body style almost identical to GM's top-priced Cadillac Seville. Top management must use staff support to create and oversee policies that guide and limit the range of actions taken by its divisions.

Matrix Departmentalization

matrix departmental-
ization A hybrid type
of departmentaliza-
tion in which person-
nel from several
specialties are brought
together to complete
limited-life tasks.

Matrix departmentalization is a hybrid type of departmentalization in which personnel from several specialties are brought together to complete limited-life tasks. It usually evolves from one or more of the other types of departmentalization and is used in response to demands for unique blends of skill from different specialties in the organization. The matrix structure is used not alone but in conjunction with other types of departmentalization. Say, for example, that a company had to complete a project requiring close, integrated work between and among numerous functional specialties. The project could be designing a weapons system or building a prototype for a supersonic aircraft. The traditional approaches to organization we have discussed do not easily provide for the flexibility to handle such complex assignments, which involve expertise from numerous functional areas of the organization. As shown in Figure 8.6, a project manager is given line authority over the team members during the life of the project.

The matrix organization provides a hierarchy that responds quickly to changes in technology. Hence, it is typically found in technically oriented organizations, such as Boeing, General Dynamics, NASA, and GE, in which scientists, engineers, or technical specialists work on sophisticated projects or programs. It is also used by compa-

FIGURE 8.6
Example of matrix departmentalization.

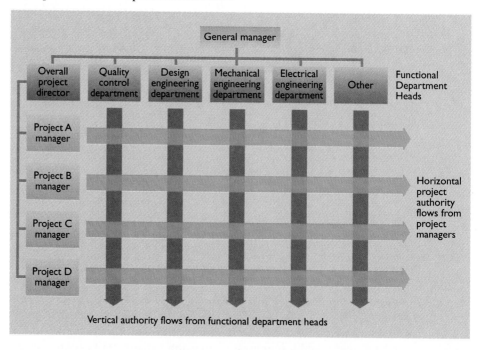

nies with complex construction projects. Under this system, team members' functional departments maintain personnel files, supervise administrative details, and assemble performance reports while their members are on assignment.

Advantages of the Matrix Approach   One advantage of the matrix approach is that it permits open communication and coordination of activities among the relevant functional specialists. Another advantage is that its flexibility enables the organization to respond rapidly to change. This response to change is the result of a self-imposed and professional desire to respond—not a response to a hierarchically managed change effort. The use of this approach is essential in technologically oriented industries.

Disadvantages of the Matrix Approach   One disadvantage of matrix departmentalization relates to the lack of clarity and coordination in assigned roles. Conflict may occur when the requirements of the project team result in decisions contrary to the philosophy and viewpoint of the home office. For example, a project team might want the authority to make most decisions on site, while the home office wants tight control. Another possible source of conflict is the assignment of team members to more than one project; someone must determine how to allocate such team members' time on each project. Such situations require *facilitators*, who intervene to resolve clashes resulting from conflicting priorities.

> Jean Johnson was a professor of management at Mid-Atlantic University. For the past year, she had been teaching in the management department and working half-time on an interdisciplinary project to improve the university computer system. For the life of the project, she had two bosses—the project director and the chairman of the management department. Until recently, this dual reporting had not caused any problem, but within the last month, the chairman of the management department had been putting increasing pressure on Jean to teach an additional course for the fall term. A professor had resigned suddenly, leaving the department shorthanded. The dilemma was that the computer study was nearing completion and required a major commitment of time and effort from all project members.

In a matrix structure, who will decide on the members' advancement and promotion? Moreover, who will assign them to their next projects? Normally, the functional department head will make these decisions, based in part on reports received from project managers for whom the persons have worked. But functional specialists are often caught in the middle in disputes and torn between loyalties to project managers and to their functional department heads.

Finally, there are disadvantages relating to the temporary nature of assignments under this form of departmentalization. Psychologically, one may never feel that one has "roots" while drifting from one project to another—perhaps unrelated—project. Moreover, the close personal ties formed while working on a project team may be severed at the project's completion, in which case an individual's reassignment requires establishing a new set of working relationships with strangers.

Special Managerial Abilities Required   Because of the complexities of the matrix approach, managers should have special abilities in order to be successful. They should be adept at teamwork and coordination but also be competitive, they should have the intrapreneurial viewpoint and have persuasive and negotiating skills, and they should be opportunistic, fast reacting, and visionary.

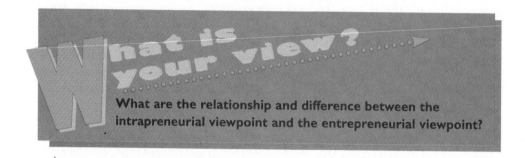

What are the relationship and difference between the intrapreneurial viewpoint and the entrepreneurial viewpoint?

The Role of Delegation

delegation The process by which managers distribute and entrust activities and related authority to other people in the organization.

Delegation is the process by which managers distribute and entrust activities and related authority to other people in the organization. *Authority* is the right to do something, or to tell someone else to do it, in order to reach organizational objectives. *Responsibility* is the obligation that is created when an employee accepts the manager's delegation of authority. Delegation occurs when the following actions take place:

1. The manager assigns objectives or duties to a lower-level employee.
2. The manager grants the authority needed to accomplish the objectives or duties.
3. The employee accepts the delegation, whether implicitly or explicitly, thereby creating an obligation or responsibility.
4. The manager holds the employee accountable for results.

Reasons for Delegation

There are many reasons for delegating. For one, delegating tasks enables managers to accomplish more than if they attempted to handle every task personally. Also, delegation allows managers to focus their energies on the most crucial, high-priority tasks and the things they need to do, such as long-range planning or coordinating with other departments. MAP 8.2 shows how one Canadian entrepreneur has developed an outstanding organization by delegating.

Delegation also allows subordinates to grow and develop, even if this means learning from their mistakes. Failure to delegate may result in a lack of personnel prepared to assume managerial responsibilities in the future.

When Robert Ingalls, founder of Ingalls Industries, died of a stroke, his once proud shipbuilding company ran into heavy seas and began to flounder. Ingalls's son had not been prepared to assume command, and the organization went steadily downhill until the shipbuilding subsidiary was later purchased at a very low price by Litton Industries.

MANAGEMENT APPLICATION AND PRACTICE 8.2

Using Delegation to Rebuild a Company

From his sixteenth-floor office in the Calgary headquarters of Alberta Trailer Company, Ltd. (ATCO), Ronald Southern manages a commercial empire that stretches far beyond the snow-topped Rockies that span the horizon.

ATCO manufactures transportable buildings used in the construction industry and as temporary offices and schoolrooms in Canada, the United States, and the Middle East. The company engages in oil and natural gas exploration and is also a major gas and electrical power producer in Western Canada.

Southern built on the base that his father, Donald, began in 1947 with $4,000 to build trailers and, later, transportable home and buildings. Donald Southern died in March 1990 at the age of 80. Now a diversified enterprise with more than $3 billion in assets and around 5,500 employees, ATCO has recovered from the serious blow it suffered early in the 1980s, when a combination of factors undermined ATCO's profitability. Canada's soaring interest rates and Ottawa's national energy policy—which kept Canadian oil prices well below world levels—slowed Alberta's energy industry. According to Southern, his company was then "on the ropes."

Southern battled to restore the company's fortunes by introducing operating economies, selling some assets, and imposing demanding performance goals. In the rebuilding process, Southern repatriated an electrical utility firm and two key Alberta natural gas companies from U.S. ownership. He also resisted selling control of the firm to "outside" buyers, preferring to keep this major Canadian corporation in his native province.

He also redefined his role as chairman by delegating some of his activities to ATCO's senior vice-president and chief financial officer, Cameron Richardson. Richardson in turn delegated more to ATCO's 38 regional managers, who for three years commuted to Calgary once a month for planning and reporting meetings. Southern says the process "unleashed a whole new level of capability, innovation, and determination." In the end, too, it was worth the expense, as ATCO emerged a more efficient and profitable firm.

Source: Adapted from "Maclean's Honor Roll: High-Class Performers," *Maclean's*, December 31, 1990, p. 28.

Effective delegation is a major difference between successful managers and unsuccessful ones, as the following example illustrates:

When Cam Starrett, vice-president for personnel and administration at Maxwell-Macmillan group, moved to Macmillan in 1989, she reduced her staff from 40 to 29 and management layers from six to three.

Under the old arrangement, supervisors reported to an assistant manager, who reported to a manager, and so on through a chief manager, a director, and finally a vice-president. Each person's duties were clearly spelled out, and anything that fell between job descriptions ended up back on the boss's desk. The result, according to Ms. Starrett, was that "everybody became very adept at upward delegating." She reversed the procedure, delegating more decision making down the ranks, while insisting on teamwork.

Ms. Starrett says the new approach produced "richer" strategic thinking and a quicker response. For such an arrangement to work, though, you need people who are flexible and want to get involved.[7]

Delegation is also important because managers do not always have the information needed to make decisions. They may see "the big picture" but not know enough about the problem to act intelligently. Operations in another country, particularly, require delegation, as the home office cannot know all the variables involved.

In its takeover bid for NCR, AT&T wanted to acquire control of NCR's computers and automated teller machines, which would strengthen what was a weakness in AT&T's product line. Since NCR was already a major competitor in Europe, AT&T also wanted to use NCR's large customer base—particularly in the retail and finance markets—to increase its international operations.

Robert Allen, AT&T's CEO, promised that, if the deal went through, AT&T would fold its computer business into NCR and give the new management of the European operations a free hand in running the business.[8]

Why Managers Fail to Delegate

Although delegation is critical to effective management, some managers fail to delegate or delegate weakly. Some of the more important reasons for this are that managers may

feel more powerful if they retain decision-making privileges for themselves;

not care to face the risk that employees will exercise authority poorly;

believe that they can do it better themselves, feeling that employees lack the ability to exercise good judgment;

feel that workers would prefer not to have broader decision-making latitude;

fear that employees will perform tasks so effectively that their own positions will be threatened; or

be reluctant to become involved with more detailed operations of the business.

In some cases, a manager may not be reluctant to delegate, but, in fact, becomes more involved in everyday activities.

When Dale Ward became chief executive of National Intergroup Inc.'s Ben Franklin retail chain, he cut out a whole layer of senior vice-presidents and gave more autonomy to regional vice-presidents. But then he also had to become more involved in day-to-day operations, dropping in at meetings to suggest marketing

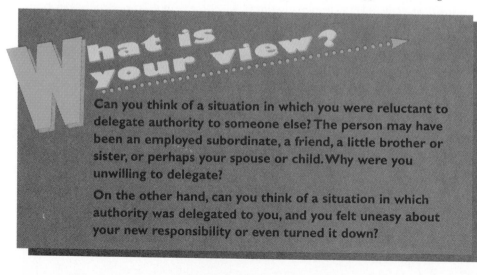

What is your view?

Can you think of a situation in which you were reluctant to delegate authority to someone else? The person may have been an employed subordinate, a friend, a little brother or sister, or perhaps your spouse or child. Why were you unwilling to delegate?

On the other hand, can you think of a situation in which authority was delegated to you, and you felt uneasy about your new responsibility or even turned it down?

strategies and spending more time with suppliers than his predecessor had. He says managers previously "didn't dare trust the chief executive with any problems. But if you're cutting staff, you've got to be more involved in everyday matters. You don't want to do your subordinates' jobs, but you have to show them you know how to sweep the floor."[9]

Why Employees May Not Welcome Delegation

Not all barriers to effective delegation come from managers, however. Employees themselves may resist accepting delegation for many reasons. First, delegation adds to their responsibilities and accountability. Second, there is always the chance that they will carry out their assignments poorly and receive criticism. Third, some employees lack self-confidence and feel a great deal of pressure when granted greater decision-making authority and/or additional duties or tasks. Finally, delegation can mean increased stress on employees. They become more visible, and everybody is required to be more productive.

> When the Corning Inc. plant at Blacksburg, Virginia, switched from producing glass to making auto pollution control parts in 1988, it reduced the layers of management to two levels from the previous four or five. Robert Hoover, the plant manager, and six other managers had to oversee about 170 workers. Hoover started a work simplification program by eliminating a lot of paperwork and other time-consuming tasks. Although all managers at other Corning plants must write quarterly reports, he is the only one at Blacksburg who does so.
>
> The plant is organized around five key jobs that all hourly employees must learn. In the process, they spend a fifth of their time in training. They now handle many of the jobs previously done by their foreman, from scheduling overtime and vacations to handling bottlenecks on the line and tracking quality. But having just one layer of management between Hoover and the workers puts more stress on everyone. "There aren't enough layers to protect just average performance," says Hoover.[10]

As has been shown, or implied, there are at least four factors involved in delegating: authority, power, responsibility, and accountability. These interact to make delegating effective—or ineffective.

The Role of Authority

Since authority is constantly being used, its nature and role should be well understood. As mentioned earlier, **authority** is the *right* to do something, or to tell someone else to do it, in order to reach organizational objectives. If no one in an organization had authority, employees could come to work and leave when they wanted to; they could carry out their assignments any way they wanted to, rather than the way prescribed by higher authority. Without a system of authority, an organization could not function. The following are some examples of higher authority in action.

authority The right to do something, or to tell someone else to do it, in order to reach organizational objectives.

A police officer gives a motorist a ticket for driving 45 mph in a 30-mph zone. The officer's authority derives from the city council.

In 1978, Henry Ford, as chairman of Ford Motor Company, fired Lee Iacocca as its president. Ford's authority came from the company's board of directors, which got its power from the stockholders.

The department manager at Macy's assigned the work shifts for her personnel during the Christmas holidays. Her authority was delegated by the store manager.

In each of these examples, an individual exercised the right to exert authority over others. That authority came with the position and resulted from delegation by a higher-level manager.

Sources of Authority

Basically, there are two contradictory views regarding the source of a manager's authority: the formal theory and the acceptance theory.

formal theory of authority The concept that a manager's authority is conferred; it exists because someone was granted it.

Formal Authority View   According to the **formal theory of authority,** authority is conferred; authority exists because someone was granted it. This view traces the origin of authority upward to its ultimate source, which for business organizations is the owners or stockholders. The head nurse in a hospital has authority granted by the nursing director, who has been granted it by the hospital board, which has been granted it by the stockholders (if a private hospital) or the public (if a public hospital). The formal theory is consistent with the definition of authority we presented in the previous section.

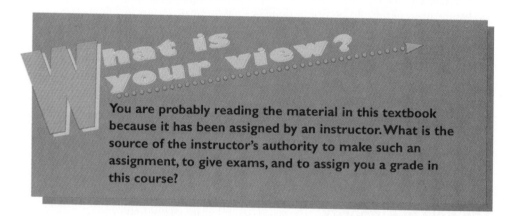

What is your view?

You are probably reading the material in this textbook because it has been assigned by an instructor. What is the source of the instructor's authority to make such an assignment, to give exams, and to assign you a grade in this course?

acceptance theory of authority The concept that a manager's authority originates only when it has been accepted by the group or individual over whom it is being exercised.

Acceptance of Authority View   The **acceptance theory of authority** disputes the idea that authority can be conferred. Acceptance theorists (chiefly behaviorists) believe that a manager's authority originates only when it has been accepted by the group or individual over whom it is being exercised. Chester Barnard stated this position when he wrote, "If a directive communication is accepted by one to whom it is addressed, the authority for him is confirmed or established."[11] Thus, acceptance of the directive becomes the basis of action. Disobedience of such a communication by an employee is a denial of its authority for him or her. Therefore, under this definition, the decision about whether an order has authority lies with the persons to whom it is addressed and does not reside in "persons of authority" or those who issue those orders, as the following example implies.

> Jan was a manager in a large publishing company that had initiated a participative management by objectives process (see Chapter 7). Jan's immediate supervisor asked her to set objectives for her area and develop a one-year plan to accomplish those objectives. Jan consulted her employees and developed what she perceived as difficult but attainable objectives.
>
> When her boss reviewed the objectives, he discovered he disagreed and revised them drastically. He then called Jan in and dictated that she accept the altered objectives. Jan responded that the objectives would be impossible for her staff to achieve, and she could not in good conscience agree to them. At this point, Jan refused to accept her boss's authority, and although her boss eventually capitulated, it caused some future difficulties in their relationship.[12]

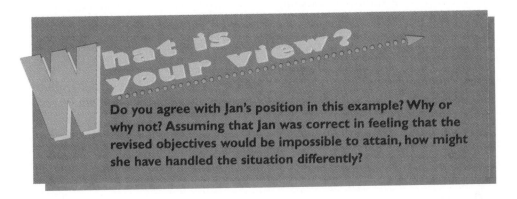

What is your view?

Do you agree with Jan's position in this example? Why or why not? Assuming that Jan was correct in feeling that the revised objectives would be impossible to attain, how might she have handled the situation differently?

We have defined authority in line with the position taken by the formal theorists—that authority is a right a manager has been formally granted by the organization. As we will shortly point out, though, the acceptance theorists seem to confuse authority with power or leadership, which involves the ability of a manager to influence employees to accept his or her authority.

The behaviorists do, however, make the point that *to be effective*, managers are certainly very dependent on acceptance of their authority, as the following classic example illustrates.

> In the early 1950s, Howard Hughes's capricious leadership chased from Hughes Tool Company many outstanding managers and scientists who refused to accept his authority. Many of them achieved outstanding success, and one, Tex Thornton, founded Litton Industries, today one of the nation's top industrial firms.
>
> The scientists refused to accept Hughes's authority because one day he would tell them to proceed with a project and the next day change his mind and reverse his decision.

In Chapter 12, we will examine some of the ways in which managers can gain acceptance of their authority through the use of effective leadership.

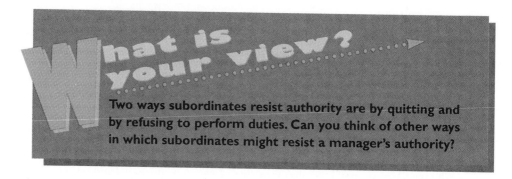

Two ways subordinates resist authority are by quitting and by refusing to perform duties. Can you think of other ways in which subordinates might resist a manager's authority?

Types of Authority

Another aspect of authority is the distinction between types of authority, namely, line, staff, and functional. Managers in all types or organizations may at one time or another use each of these kinds of authority. For example, the personnel manager uses line authority in dealing with subordinates in the personnel department, staff authority in advising top management about personnel matters, and functional authority when dealing with personnel questions—such as EEO—in the rest of the organization.

line authority
Authority that managers exercise over their immediate subordinates.

Line Authority   The authority that managers exercise over their immediate subordinates is known as **line authority.** It is command authority and corresponds directly to the chain of command. It is directed downward through the organizational levels. As shown in Figure 8.7, both line and staff department managers exercise line authority over their immediate subordinates. In fact, all managers exercise line authority over their employees.

FIGURE 8.7
Staff and line department heads have line authority within their departments.

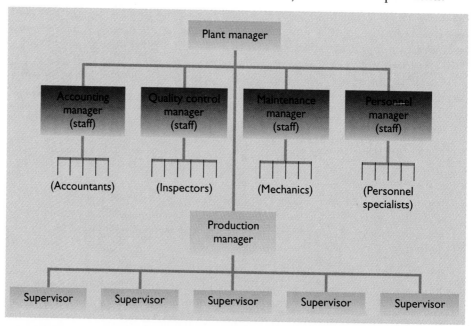

Staff Authority The right possessed by staff units or specialists to advise, make recommendations to, or counsel line personnel is called **staff authority.** It does not give the staff members the authority to dictate to the line or command them to take certain actions. In fact, it is frequently directed upward, toward those above the staff members. This is the most common type of staff relationship with the line departments and is dependent on staff's degree of influence.

Functional Authority The strongest relationship staff can have with line units is **functional authority.** When granted functional authority by top management, a staff specialist has the right to command line units in matters regarding the functional activity in which the staff specializes. Some examples of different staff specialists exercising functional authority are as follows:

1. A safety specialist may have authority to command line laboratory managers to shut down a lab when noxious fumes reach a certain level.
2. The quality control inspector may have authority to require production departments to redo a production run that does not meet standards.
3. The legal department may be able to modify or alter the wording of all contracts that obligate the organization to outside entities such as dealers, suppliers, or contractors.
4. Personnel departments may have functional authority to tell managers of other departments how to implement Equal Employment Opportunity (EEO) and affirmative action programs (AAPs).

As shown in Figure 8.8, functional authority, when granted to staff units, may violate the principle of unity of command and in so doing cause many organizational

staff authority The right of staff units or specialists to advise, make recommendations to, or counsel line personnel.

functional authority The right of staff specialists to command line units in matters regarding the functional activity in which the staff specializes.

FIGURE 8.8
Organization chart showing staff and functional authority of staff specialists.

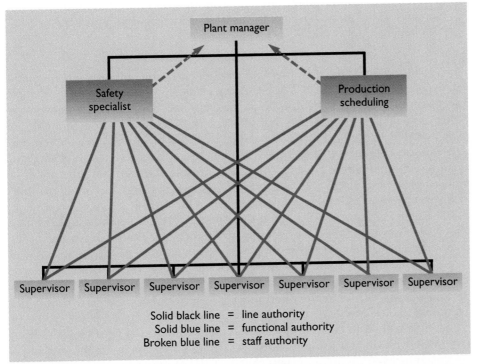

Solid black line = line authority
Solid blue line = functional authority
Broken blue line = staff authority

conflicts. As you may recall, the unity of command principle maintains that an employee should receive orders and assigned duties from only one manager. The *overuse* of functional authority also undermines the integrity of the line departments that are held accountable for results. For this reason, functional authority should be granted to staff to be exercised only in crucial situations.

The Role of Power

The manager's possession of authority is not always sufficient in itself to ensure that subordinates will respond as the manager desires. In such cases, a manager must use some other approach, as the following example illustrates.

> Mary Fleming was named supervisor of the no. 2 paper machine at the Northern Mill of a large national company.[13] She was the first female supervisor to be named to such a traditionally male position. The position carried much authority with it, but Mary was intelligent enough to realize that her authority alone would not get her workers to accept her and meet performance standards.
>
> Several of the employees tested her immediately by taking extended work breaks and making some snide remarks within her hearing range about the department's "skirt supervisor." Mary ignored this behavior the first few days and felt that the worst thing she could do was to overreact and come on too strong. But the resistance persisted. Mary had a meeting with Carl White and Pete Anthiem, the two senior members of the department, and asked for their advice about handling the situation. White and Antheim seemed flattered by being consulted and told Mary they'd handle the situation. The problems never recurred, and six months after the incident, Mary's group was highly supportive of her leadership, and the "female department head" issue had been forgotten.

power The ability to influence individuals, groups, decisions, or events.

We will now study this example with an eye toward the authority-power combinations illustrated in Figure 8.9. Mary used a leadership strategy that played a key role in getting her into Quadrant 3, where she had both authority and power. **Power** is the ability to influence individuals, groups, events, and decisions and is closely related to leadership. In an earlier example in this chapter—where Jan refused to accept impossible objectives dictated by her boss—we see an example of Quadrant 2 in operation. Jan's boss had considerable authority but little power to influence Jan to accept his edict. In other cases, staff personnel have little authority but much power to influence line managers (Quadrant 4).

The belief of Sir Dahlberg Acton that "power tends to corrupt, and absolute power corrupts absolutely" is widespread in today's culture. In recent years, however, there has been an increasing awareness that power is not necessarily all bad—that the use of power may be essential for the effective accomplishment of individual, organizational, and social goals. In fact, interest has been revived in Niccolò Machiavelli's seventeenth-century classic treatise on power, *The Prince*. According to Machiavelli, leaders can be effective by (1) winning people's love or (2) acting forcefully to make people respect them.[14] Interest in power has also been generated by David McClelland's research (covered in Chapter 11) showing that a high need for power is an important characteristic of successful managers.

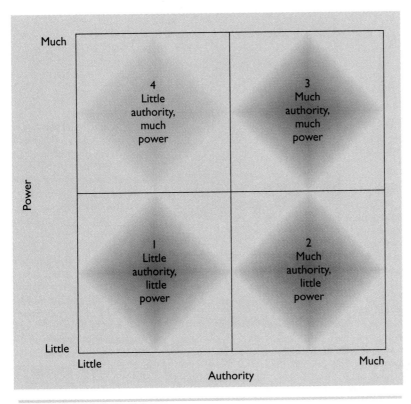

FIGURE 8.9
Authority-power combinations.

How Power Is Obtained

As shown by J. R. P. French, Jr., and Bertram Raven in one of the earliest—and still most useful—studies, there are many sources from which power can be obtained.[15] Six of these sources have been translated into types of power, classified as follows:

1. **Reward power** arises from the number of positive rewards (money, protection, and so forth) that a leader is perceived as controlling.
2. **Coercive power** results from people's perceived expectation that punishment (being fired, reprimanded, and so on) will follow if they do not comply with the orders of a leader.
3. **Legitimate power** develops from internalized values that dictate that a leader has an inherent right to influence subordinates. According to this view, one has an obligation to accept that influence simply because a person is designated boss or leader.
4. **Control-of-information power** derives from the possession of knowledge that others do not have. Some people exercise this type of power by either giving or withholding needed information.
5. **Referent power** is based on people's identification with a leader and what that leader stands for or symbolizes. Personal charisma, charm, courage, and other traits are important factors in the exercise of referent power.
6. **Expert power** results from a leader's expertise or knowledge in an area in which that leader wants to influence others. The Practicing Manager of NBC's Brandon Tartikoff illustrates this type of power.

reward power Power arising from the number of positive rewards that people perceive a leader as controlling.

coercive power Power arising from perceived expectations that punishment will follow noncompliance with a leader's orders.

legitimate power Power developed from internalized values dictating that a leader has an inherent right to influence subordinates.

control-of-information power Power derived from the possession of knowledge that can be communicated or withheld at will.

referent power Power derived from identification with a leader and what that leader stands for or symbolizes.

expert power Power derived from a leader's expertise or knowledge in an area in which that leader wants to influence others.

PRACTICING MANAGER

BRANDON TARTIKOFF, NBC ENTERTAINMENT GROUP

At age 41, Brandon Tartikoff, newly appointed chairman of the NBC Entertainment Group, was already a legendary figure in the television industry. In a field where job security is almost nonexistent, Tartikoff had spent the previous decade employing his programming wizardry to catapult NBC from the ratings pit to the no. 1 spot. Serving as president of NBC Entertainment throughout the 1980s, he injected humor and creativity into an otherwise treacherous job and seemed truly to enjoy himself as he produced some of the finest television programming the industry had yet seen.

In 1980, the year Tartikoff took control of NBC's programming, the network was consistently placing a miserable third in the ratings. After being honored at a Jaycees banquet as one of America's "Ten Outstanding Young Men"—along with a pilot who had rescued people from a war zone; a doctor who had discovered a possible cure for one form of cancer; the president's budget director, David Stockman; and Darryl Stingley, a football player who had been paralyzed—Tartikoff remarked, "And there I was—a guy whose main contribution to society that year was deciding how to prop up *B.J. and the Bear* and *Sheriff Lobo*." From that moment forward, he dedicated himself to putting on at least a few programs that he could really be proud of, and the results of his dedication were such classics as *Hill Street Blues, The Cosby Show, Cheers,* and *St. Elsewhere.*

Tartikoff's philosophy is that programs should be considered according to their audience appeal, and once they have been effectively positioned in a successful time slot, they should be kept there. To secure those time slots in 1983, his strategy was an all-out blitz on the 8:00 P.M. to 10:00 P.M. period. Tartikoff knew that the network that wins the 9:00 P.M. competition generally wins the night's audience—and ratings.

Although Tartikoff is serious about his work, one of his strengths is his ability to step back and look at his position objectively and with a bit of humor. In fact, he opened a season premier of *Saturday Night Live* with a monologue spoofing his own job, proving that he can be genuinely funny.

Tartikoff can be very serious, however, when it comes to saving his network's ratings. When he became president of NBC Entertainment, he showed no fear of killing unsuccessful shows, and the ax began to fall. Thanks to his leadership, NBC firmly held the top spot in the prime-time ratings from 1985 through 1990 and achieved profits up to $500 million a year.

Despite his success as chairman of the NBC Entertainment Group in mid-1991, Tartikoff left NBC to become chairman of Paramount Pictures. After just 18 months on the job, he resigned following a car accident that seriously injured his 8-year-old daughter. He and his wife, Lilly, moved with her for rehabilitation therapy to New Orleans, and for a time Brandon devoted full time to his family.

After his daughter's condition improved and after producing some shows for New Orleans TV, he accepted a position in June 1994 as chairman of New World Entertainment Ltd., which will provide programming for Fox Broadcasting and other television networks.

Sources: Monica Collins, "The Boys of Autumn: Masterminds Behind the New TV Season," *TV Guide,* September 1, 1990, pp. 7–8; Bill Carter, "Tartikoff Show Goes On, but Its Script Is Changing," *New York Times,* July 23, 1990, p. 6C; Kevin Goldman, "NBC Entertainment Appoints Tartikoff as Chairman, Littlefield as President," *Wall Street Journal,* July 18, 1990, p. A4; "NBC's Tartikoff Unveils Plan B," *Broadcasting,* July 4, 1988, p. 29; "Paramount Snags Tartikoff," *USA Today,* May 2, 1991, pp. 1A, 1D; *Time,* January 24, 1994, p. 60; and *Advertising Age,* June 20, 1994, p. 4.

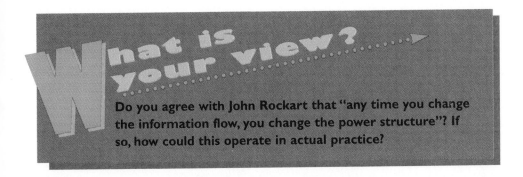

Do you agree with John Rockart that "any time you change the information flow, you change the power structure"? If so, how could this operate in actual practice?

Do not infer from this discussion that a given manager draws upon all of these types of power. Rather, each manager finds his or her own source of strength from many of these types. Table 8.1 gives some examples of these types of power.

How Power Can Be Used

Some managers believe that if a manager has power and shares it with others (delegates it), it is diminished. Actually, the best way to expand power is to share it, for power can grow, in part, by being shared. Sharing power is different from giving it or throwing it away—delegation does not mean abdication.

Effective managers have a high need for power, but that need is oriented toward the benefit of the organization as a whole. In addition, the need for power

TABLE 8.1   EXAMPLES OF POWER SOURCES

Situation	Source of Power
1. Jones volunteers for weekend work because supervisor promises him a highly desirable job assignment.	Reward
2. Supervisor directs employee to comply with company policy or be fired. Employee complies.	Coercive
3. Visitor stops car at the company gate in response to a uniformed security officer's upraised hand.	Legitimate
4. Graduate assistant quiets the class, telling them that the professor is out of town, and since he (the assistant) wrote the final exam, he will now review how to study for it.	Control of information
5. Company president and founder is hard-driving, innovative, and outspoken; puts in 75 hours a week on the job; and has a charismatic personality and the ability to inspire others.	Referent
6. Crucial piece of equipment breaks down. Junior machinists quickly follow the orders barked out by a senior mechanic, Wilson, widely respected as one of the most knowledgeable in the industry.	Expertise

is stronger in these managers than the need to be liked by others. Thus, as a manager, you must be willing to play the influence game in a controlled way. This does not imply that you need to be authoritarian in action. On the contrary, it appears that power-motivated managers make their subordinates feel stronger rather than weaker. A true authoritarian would have the reverse effect, making people feel weak or powerless.

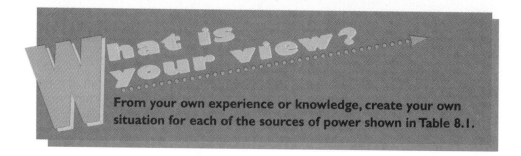

What is your view?

From your own experience or knowledge, create your own situation for each of the sources of power shown in Table 8.1.

Limits on the Use of Authority and Power

All organization members have certain restrictions or limitations placed on their authority. The president of the United States cannot legally declare war; only Congress has that authority. The chief executive officers of major corporations, even though they may be very powerful, lack absolute authority. Some of these limits are imposed by external factors, such as agencies of federal, state, and local governments; contracts with dealers and suppliers; and collective bargaining agreements.

Internal factors may also limit managerial authority. These include the organization's charter and bylaws, policies, rules, procedures, budgets, and position descriptions. A vice-president may have the authority to spend, say, $250,000 without consulting the company president, whereas a first-line supervisor may be permitted to spend only $100 for needed supplies without first clearing it with the department head.

The scope of authority is broader at the top of an organization and narrower at the lower levels of the chain of command. Yet there are restrictions or limits on the authority of even the stockholders. For example, they can do only those things permitted by the corporation's charter, and they cannot do things that are illegal—such as refusing to pay valid taxes.

responsibility The obligation that is created when an employee accepts a manager's delegation of authority.

accountability The fact that employees will be judged by the extent to which they fulfill their responsibilities.

The Role of Responsibility and Accountability

Responsibility is the obligation created when an employee accepts the manager's delegation of authority. Another frequently used term is **accountability,** which refers to the fact that employees will be judged by the extent to which they fulfill their responsibilities. Being accountable implies that one's supervisor can confer either punishment or reward, depending on how well one has exercised the responsibility to use the delegated authority.

Delegation of Responsibility and Accountability

Can a person escape his or her own responsibility or accountability by shifting it to another person? The following example furnishes a partial answer:

> Bill Jones walked into his professor's office very upset about the F he had received on his term paper. He had put a lot of work into the paper and felt it deserved at least a B.
>
> Dr. Hanna explained, "You knew the date the paper was due and that the penalty for lateness was one letter grade for each day it was late. Your paper was a B—a good solid paper, Bill—but I received it four days late. This gave you a grade of F. I'm sorry that you couldn't get it in on schedule."
>
> Bill explained that Edith Evans, a secretary at the university, had typed the paper and said she would give it to Dr. Hanna on the due date. Bill argued that he should not have been penalized by Dr. Hanna, since the paper's lateness was not his fault but the secretary's.[16]

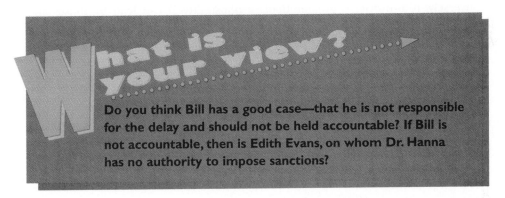

What is your view?

Do you think Bill has a good case—that he is not responsible for the delay and should not be held accountable? If Bill is not accountable, then is Edith Evans, on whom Dr. Hanna has no authority to impose sanctions?

If you agree with Bill, you have overlooked a major organizational principle: No one can assume—or accept—another person's responsibility for performing a duty. Delegating your authority to another person does not relieve you of the original responsibility and accountability. Authority flows down, and accountability and responsibility flow up. The exception would be in a matrix structure, where horizontal flows are involved.

Equality of Authority and Responsibility?

An important principle of organization is that individuals should be assigned or delegated sufficient authority to carry out their responsibilities. For example, if a manager's responsibility is to maintain a certain production capacity, he or she must be given sufficient latitude to make decisions that affect production capacity.

Equality of responsibility and authority is good in theory, but it is difficult to achieve in practice. In fact, many experts argue that in today's management world, it is unrealistic even to attempt to achieve it. Some reasons for this are government laws and regulations, the presence of unions, and the network of dependence that exists in organizations. Most managers—even efficient ones—have more responsibility than authority.

"As you see we have a highly centralized organization."

Sam Jenkins recently retired from a staff position in human resources with International Paper Company (IP). Among Sam's responsibilities was the charge to develop and improve management skills of IP managers ranging from supervisor to mill manager. Yet Sam was given no special authority—not even functional authority—in carrying out this responsibility. His only asset was his ability to sell his ideas to mill managers. In this regard, he was a master and had tremendous influence and power resulting from ideas rather than authority.[17]

Another major reason for inequality of authority and responsibility is the reluctance of higher-level managers to delegate authority to their subordinates. It is similar to saying, "You're responsible for getting results, but I'll call all the shots." It is fundamental that people have a range of authority to exercise judgment and latitude in making decisions about those major results for which they will ultimately be held responsible and accountable.

There are two frequent violations of the principle of equality of authority and responsibility that lead to ineffective management. First, giving a person little authority but much responsibility can result in frustration and inefficiency. Conversely, if authority is greater than responsibility, it can lead to abuses and arrogance.

The Role of Decentralization and Centralization

Another important factor leading to effective management is the degree of decentralization of authority within the organization. Actually, authority can be centralized or decentralized.

Decentralization Versus Centralization

The concept of decentralization, like the concept of delegation, has to do with the degree to which authority is concentrated or dispersed. Whereas *delegation* usually refers to the extent to which individual managers assign authority and responsibility to people reporting directly to them, *decentralization* is a broader concept and refers to the extent to which upper management delegates authority downward to divisions, branches, or lower-level organizational units.

centralization Concentration of power and authority near the top, or at the head, of an organization.

decentralization Dispersion of power and decision making to successively lower levels of the organization.

Centralization is concentrating the power and authority near the top, or in the head, of an organization. **Decentralization** is dispersing the power and decision making to successively lower levels of the organization (see Figure 8.10). *No organization is completely centralized or decentralized; the extent ranges along a continuum from high centralization to high decentralization.*

In Operation Desert Storm, two U.S. Army generals ran a war that started out being fought almost entirely by fliers from the U.S. Air Force, Navy, and Marines, along with Coalition forces from England, France, Kuwait, and Saudi Arabia. Navy jets flew from their own carriers, using Air Force fields for refueling and rearming between missions. According to the two generals—General Colin L. Powell, chairman of the Joint Chiefs of Staff, and General H. Norman Schwarzkopf—the Air

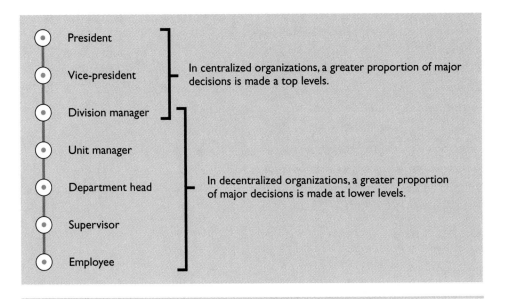

FIGURE 8.10
Centralization-decentralization and the chain of command.

Force, Navy, Marine, and Coalition pilots had a "superb integrated performance with the Army in the war."

This was a drastic change from the Vietnam War, during which the Air Force would not even tell Army officers what targets they were planning to bomb in their areas.

Legislation passed between the wars stripped power from the rival service chiefs in the Pentagon and gave it to a single, unified commander in the field. It also gave the chairman of the Joint Chiefs more power to deal directly with the president and the commanders in the field.[18]

Factors Affecting the Degree of Decentralization and Centralization

The extent of decentralization or centralization within a given organization depends on several interrelated factors, as shown in Table 8.2. These are as follows:

1. The management philosophy of the organization
2. The history of organizational growth
3. The geographic dispersion of the organization
4. The availability of effective controls
5. The quality of managers at different levels
6. The diversity of products or services offered

Need for a Contingency Approach

Several factors affect the degree of centralization and decentralization in an organization. Moreover, the degree may vary among different divisions or departments of the organization and must change according to the organization's internal and

TABLE 8.2	FACTORS AFFECTING DEGREE OF CENTRALIZATION	

Condition Favorable for Centralization		Condition Favorable for Decentralization
No	Is top management's philosophy consistent with strong delegation?	Yes
No	Has organization grown externally through merger and acquisition?	Yes
No	Is organization widespread geographically?	Yes
No	Are effective controls available to monitor lower levels?	Yes
No	Is there an adequate number of highly qualified managers?	Yes
No	Does organization have a diverse product/service line?	Yes

external environment. Thus, a contingency approach is the most logical approach for organizations to follow.

> GM has been known for its bureaucratic squabbles and rigid lines of authority. In 1984, then chairman Roger B. Smith started trying to revitalize the company by breaking down the rigid divisions between the company's car operations. He lumped Chevrolet, Pontiac, and GM Canada into one division and Buick, Oldsmobile, and Cadillac into another. This process started managers from the different car lines meeting to share ideas and to work toward greater cooperation.
>
> But GM's ponderous bureaucracy was still a major stumbling block to carrying out Smith's plan. In 1990, despite massive employee cutbacks, GM still had 36 vice-presidents, one more than it had had in 1980, before the reorganization started.
>
> It is no accident that the three GM divisions that have had the highest performance, productivity, and profitability are ones that are physically and organizationally distant from headquarters. For example, GM Europe is an ocean away from Detroit, GMC Truck was a "poor relation" that was virtually ignored by top brass for many years, and Saturn has proved to be effective because of geographic separation, since it operates in Spring Hill, Tennessee, as an independent subsidiary.
>
> Managers from General Motors of Europe Ltd. are particularly proud of their outstanding performance. At GM's annual conference for its top 950 executives, they told how a combination of better cars and increased productivity had transformed the European division from a perennial money loser into GM's most profitable car operation.[19]

Historically, recessions see many companies cutting losses by reducing the number of staff personnel in corporate headquarters. The result is frequently a move toward greater decentralization.[20] This allows lower line units to carry out functions previously carried out by staff personnel in corporate headquarters.

While decentralizing staff tasks, like planning or finance, may cut costs by eliminating huge departments, savings are not guaranteed. In fact, research conducted by A. T. Kearney found that a centralized finance department costs about 1.3 percent of revenue, while a decentralized one costs around 2.7 percent.[21]

The Role of Downsizing

In a 1988 article, management theorist Peter Drucker predicted that by the year 2008, a typical business would have half as many levels of management and only a third as many managers as typical business did in the late 1980s.[22] As indicated earlier in this chapter, many companies have already made that prophecy come true, years ahead of schedule. An excellent example is Citicorp's Diners Club.

> James Emhoff, president of the Diners Club unit of Citicorp, slashed layers of management between himself and first-line supervisors from eight to four and restructured many jobs in an effort to serve customers better. Now the company's biggest customers receive customized products and services, and their complaints are handled faster. Emhoff now oversees eight managers—twice as many as before—and his mangers work harder then they did under the previous system.[23]

Ways to Downsize

Although large organizations can slim down in many ways, a favorite way to increase efficiency is to reduce corporate staff, which is called **downsizing.** David Clarke, president of Hanson Industries, believes that maintaining a streamlined organization is second in importance only to creating an excellent product at the right price.[24] Clarke practices what he preaches, for shortly after taking over the company, he eliminated not only superfluous internal staff specialties but also the use of 30 outside consultants. The latter move alone saved $2 million.

downsizing Increasing efficiency by reducing corporate staff.

Many companies are changing the role of the corporate headquarters from that of a command group to that of a performance monitor. The new trend is to conceive of the corporate center as a small merchant bank or holding company, investing capital among various enterprises. Then it monitors the profitability of each against projections, replaces underachieving top managers, and constantly searches for new investment opportunities.[25]

Another way of downsizing is to concentrate on one—or a few—product(s) and eliminate marginal or unprofitable units. This is what was done at one giant firm after the death of its legendary founder.

> When Ray R. Irani took over the reins of Occidental Petroleum Corporation in early 1991, he wanted to make it clear that the changes he planned were not meant to reflect on the Armand Hammer legacy. Circumstances change, he said, and so "the new Oxy" would concentrate on oil and chemicals, sell $3 billion in assets, take a $2 billion charge against earnings, and cut the dividend from $2.50 to $1.00 a share. Many of the money-losing businesses up for sale were Dr. Hammer's favorites, including a Soviet petrochemical project, Chinese coal mining, Arabian horses, Black Angus cattle, and the film production company whose perennial star was Dr. Hammer himself. But profitability is the name of the game, and the new CEO could not afford to be sentimental.[26]

Pros and Cons of Downsizing

Evidence is clear that in the three decades from the end of World War II into the 1970s, many large North American companies became increasingly bureaucratic, with excessive levels of hierarchy and support staff.

One of the major benefits of downsizing is the tremendous cost reductions that occur almost immediately. Perhaps even more important are the improvements that occur in the way the organization is managed. There are increasingly faster turnaround time in decision making and usually improved communication in all directions. Moreover, the organization is more responsive to customers and provides faster product delivery. Downsizing also removes the tendency for each level to justify its existence by close supervision and by frequently asking for reports and data from lower levels. Thus, without excessive interference and the stifling of creativity at lower levels, line managers have more opportunity to develop and use their authority to make decisions affecting the bottom line. In the final analysis, all of these things translate into higher profits.

On the other hand, there are some cons that could wreck the higher-profit prospect. For example, some companies can be very insensitive when they decide to downsize, with the result that loyal, effective managers are sometimes suddenly told that they are no longer needed. A heavy-handed approach can lead to morale problems with remaining employees for years to come. Some other potential disadvantages are increased workloads and diminished chances for promotion for those remaining. Finally, the remaining managers must develop skills in team building. In tall, narrow organizational structures, middle managers and supervisors are accustomed to carrying out orders, and now they must operate differently.

Ways to Get Beyond Downsizing

Without question, downsizing has a negative impact on employee morale, and according to an American Management Association survey, just 45 percent of firms that have downsized have seen corporate profits increase.[27] Thus, it is important to look on downsizing not as an end in itself but as a means to an end. The way to get back to health is to focus on the remaining employees by developing a strategy of support for survivors and a strategic plan for growth and development for the organization.

However, it is important not to go back to a traditional management and organizational design based on principles of command, control, and compartmentalization.[28] Two ways to negate these dangers are the development of effective work teams (discussed in Chapter 14) and a process called *reengineering*, which we discuss next.

reengineering "It means starting over.... It means asking and answering this question. If I were recreating this company today, given what I know and given current technology, what would it look like?"

Reengineering

Reengineering is a reaction to the way many organizations do work today using the traditional methods of command, control, and compartmentalization. In a world of rapid change, firms that focus on division or specialization of labor with a resulting fragmentation of work end up with vertical structures built on narrow pieces of a process. Consequently, decisions are slow, and people look upward to their departments and bosses for answers, rather than getting information from internal and external customers to solve problems and get answers. [29]

When Michael Hammer and James Champy, two of the world's leading experts on reengineering, were asked for a quick definition, they gave this answer: "It means starting over. . . . It means asking and answering this question. If I were recreating this company today, given what I know and given current technology, what would it look like?"[30]

Their more formal definition of reengineering is "the fundamental rethinking and radical redesign of business processes to achieve dramatic improvements in critical, contemporary measures of performance such as cost, quality, service, and speed."[31]

Reengineering can be very expensive, and so firms should not use it for everything. If you have an unprofitable business, it may be better to close it, or if quality is a problem, focus on improving the quality rather than starting over. The general guideline is to save reengineering for big challenges that really matter, such as new product development or customer service. Although by one estimate, 50 percent of reengineering efforts fail to achieve the goals set for them, when it is done properly, reengineering has a big payoff. For example, Union Carbide used reengineering to save $400 million in three years.[32]

As Hammer and Champy have documented, the following types of changes occur when a company has successfully reengineered business processes:

▸ Work units change from functional departments to process teams.

▸ Jobs change from simple tasks to multidimensional work.

▸ People's roles change from controlled to empowered.

▸ Job preparation changes from preparation to education.

▸ Focus of compensation shifts from activity to results.

▸ Advancement criteria change from performance to ability.

▸ Values change from protective to productive.

▸ Managers change from supervisors to coaches.

▸ Organizational structure changes from hierarchical to flat.

▸ Executives change from scorekeepers to leaders.

SUMMARY

This chapter has focused on the organizing function of management.

First, some basic concepts of organization were discussed. A formalized organization structure, often shown on an organization chart, represents the official organizational game plan for accomplishing work. Several key aspects of organizing shown by a formal organization chart are chain of command, unity of command, departmentalization, levels of hierarchy, span of management, and division of work.

Bureaucracy is a specific form of organization, characterized by a high degree of division of labor (or specialization), rigorous rules, clear authority-responsibility relationships, impersonal attitudes toward subordinates, employment and promotions based on merit, and lifelong employment. It tends to become rigid, inflexible, and burdened with red tape.

The types of organizations were then discussed. The line organization was shown to consist of those departments that directly accomplish the organization's objectives of producing and selling a product. The addition of staff specialists who also interact with line personnel results in a line-and-staff organization. Staff departments ordinarily advise, recommend, counsel, and serve line departments.

The principle of span of management states that there is a limit to the number of subordinates a manager can effectively supervise. Generally, spans are broader at lower levels of management and narrower at the top. Factors affecting span size include the similarity of the function supervised, the geographic proximity of subordinates, the degree of direct supervision required, the degree of coordination necessary, and the managerial assistance available to the supervisor.

Organizations departmentalize their activities along several lines, using one of the following approaches: (1) functions, (2) product, (3) territory or geography, (4) customer, (5) process or equipment, and (6) matrix departmentalization. The matrix form is a hybrid in that it is a temporary structure designed to use personnel specialties from various functional areas of the organization.

Delegation can be used to make organizations more effective. Delegation is the process by which a manager assigns authority and activities downward in the organization. Some reasons for delegating are that it allows managers to focus their energies on the most critical, high-priority tasks; it enables subordinates to grow and develop; and it enables managers to accomplish much more than if they attempted to do all the tasks themselves. Managers fail to delegate for many reasons, including fear of employee failure or the desire to retain their own power by keeping on top of all activities. Some employees resist delegation because it means added responsibility and because they lack the self-confidence to handle a larger decision-making role.

Authority is defined as the right to do something or tell someone else to do it in order to reach organizational objectives. The legitimacy of a manager's authority is received from formal delegation by higher levels. The acceptance theory disputes that formal view, arguing that authority exists only when it is accepted by others.

The three basic types of authority used by managers are (1) line authority, which is the right to tell someone what to do; (2) staff authority, which is the right to advise someone on what *should* be done, or how it is to be done; and (3) functional authority, which gives a staff person a limited amount of line authority over a specialized function.

Power is the ability to influence others; it exists as a corollary of the concept of authority. There are a number of types of power: reward, coercive, legitimate, control-of-information, referent, and expert. Effective managers seem to possess a strong need for power, but they orient their use of power toward the goals of the organization rather than solely for their personal, selfish needs.

There are limits to every manger's ability to delegate authority. The scope of delegated authority is broadest at top-management levels and narrowest at the lower levels of the chain of command. When managers are granted authority—or acquire power—they soon find that responsibility and accountability follow. But even though managers may delegate their authority, they cannot escape their responsibility and accountability to their own superiors.

Centralization and decentralization in an organization refer to the extent to which delegation has been granted to lower levels of the organization. The degree of centralization and decentralization is affected by (1) top-management philosophy, (2) the history of the organization's growth, (3) the geographic dispersion of the organization, (4) the availability of effective controls, (5) the quality of managers, and (6) the diversity of products and services offered.

The role of downsizing is to cut down on cost and bureaucracy and increase efficiency. Downsizing can be achieved by reducing management levels, reducing the role of headquarters, and/or disposing of ineffective or marginal units. Reengineering, by comparison, involves fundamental rethinking and radical redesigning of business processes.

KEY TERMS

organizations, 246
organizing, 246
synergy, 246
division of labor, 246
specialization, 247
chain of command, 248
unity of command, 248
bureaucracy, 249
red tape, 249
line organization, 249
line-and-staff organization, 251
personal staff, 252
specialized staff, 252
span of management (control, authority), 252
departmentalization, 255
functional departmentalization, 255
product departmentalization, 256
matrix departmentalization, 258
delegation, 260

authority, 263
formal theory of authority, 264
acceptance theory of authority, 264
line authority, 266
staff authority, 267
functional authority, 267
power, 268
reward power, 269
coercive power, 269
legitimate power, 269
control-of-information power, 269
referent power, 269
expert power, 269
responsibility, 272
accountability, 272
centralization, 274
decentralization, 274
downsizing, 277
reengineering, 278

DISCUSSION QUESTIONS

1. In a large department store, three different shoe departments—men's, women's, and children's—are located in the parts of the store devoted to these three types of customers. Should these three departments report to a single shoe manager, or should they report to the men's department manager, women's department manager, and children's department manager? What are the pros and cons of each reporting relationship?

2. From an employee's standpoint, what are the pros and cons of the supervisor having a very large span of management—say, 25 to 30 persons? What are the pros and cons of a very small span—6 to 8 persons?

3. Is bureaucracy all bad? What are some advantages of bureaucracy?

4. "The best way to make sure something gets done is to put two people in charge of it instead of one." Discuss the statement.

5. If a formal chart is needed to show how the organization is supposed to work, why is it that so many small- and medium-size organizations do not have formal charts drawn up?

6. Suppose a supervisor who reported to you had excellent managerial potential but refused to delegate to subordinates. In fact, several of the subordinates mentioned this to you. What steps might you take to help your supervisor become a more effective delegator?

7. Perhaps against your better judgment, you accept a staff person's recommendation and make a decision to purchase some expensive new equipment that has just come on the market. It turns out that the equipment is inferior and does not work as well as what you had before. In explaining the situation to your boss, you say, "It's not my fault. Henderson recommended that I buy it, and he's our resident expert. If I were you, I'd really knock him down a peg or two. He cost me about $3,800 with his most recent recommendation. He's accountable, not me." Are you correct in saying that you're not accountable? Discuss.

8. Of the six power sources, which do you feel is the most effective? Least effective? Why?

9. Can authority and responsibility really be equal in practice? Explain.

10. In a large auto manufacturer such as General Motors, which is organized by divisions, to what extent can auto design be decentralized to the various divisions?

11. Where should admissions be administered in a university? Should each college set its own admissions criteria, or should admissions be centralized in a single, central admissions office? Discuss.

12. If a firm decides it must engage in downsizing, discuss ways it may offset the negative consequences.

PRACTICING MANAGEMENT

8.1 Drawing an Organization Chart

learning exercise

Following are the names of certain positions in a manufacturing company. Draw an organization chart showing the reporting relationships.

vice-president of finance	treasurer
board of directors	environmental engineer
industrial relations specialist	president
safety director	director of engineering
design engineer	production scheduling specialist
controller	recruiting interviewer
credit manager	budget director
sales manager	vice-president of marketing
chief accountant	and sales
advertising manager	accounting clerks (3)
customer service representative	vice-president of personnel
plant superintendent	shipping and receiving
maintenance planning specialist	superintendent of maintenance
director of quality control	assistant to the president
regional sales managers (3)	general supervisors (4)
sales personnel (12)	project engineering
vice-president of engineering	production supervisors (24)
and research and development	director of plant security
research director	vice-president of manufacturing
purchasing director	

8.2 Reducing Costs in a Consulting Firm

learning exercise

Divide the class into groups of five or six students, each group representing the managing partners of a consulting firm. Have them discuss the following situation and report back to the class what their plan is, how they would communicate it to employees, and how they would enforce their decision.

There are 1,800 employees in your organization, and for the past year, sales and profits have been down. In fact, for the past six months, the firm has been operating at a loss.

Two months ago, a holding company acquired your firm in a friendly takeover. Its philosophy is to treat your consulting organization as a semiautonomous division of the holding company, providing only general guidance and managing by results.

The holding company CEO has asked your group, the managing partners, to develop a plan to reduce costs. It is important to note that 90 percent of your budget goes to salaries. Along with your plant, the holding company CEO wants to know how you will communicate the plan to employees and how you will enforce your decision.

Managing Human Resources *and* Diversity

LEARNING OBJECTIVES

After studying the material in this chapter, you should be able to:

- **Explain** the dominant role played by human resources in today's organizations.

- **Discuss** the growing diversity of human resources, especially the growing reliance on women and minorities.

- **Describe** some of the more important laws providing equal employment opportunity for diverse groups.

- **Discuss** the importance of planning human resource needs and explain how to do so.

- **Describe** the most effective procedure for recruiting and selecting employees.

- **Discuss** the need for and some methods of training and developing employees.

- **Explain** the role of employee appraisals.

- **Describe** some compensation problems, especially the growing role of employee benefits.

- **Discuss** how employee health and safety can be maintained.

- **Explain** how industrial relations can be handled effectively.

Corporate Women—Breaking Through to the Top

According to writer Laurie Baum, there are "few women in America with wide-ranging, high-level line responsibilities at a major corporation, performing tough, general management jobs." Yet it is from this small group that many major companies will select the next generation of CEOs and other top managers. This group is in the vanguard of a new era for women managers. For example, 40 percent of women are now in executive management and administrative jobs, as compared to 20 percent in 1972. The number of women in those positions increased by about 95 percent in just the last decade.

More important than their increasing numbers is the fact that women managers are now moving beyond staff and midlevel management jobs, where they staked their claims in the 1960s, 1970s, and early 1980s. For example, a poll of 201 male CEOs of the nation's largest companies found that the number of top-level female officers increased 62 percent from 1988 to 1993, while the number of middle managers who are women increased 92 percent.

There are several reasons for the rapid progress of these managers. First, they are better educated and more determined to advance. Second, the broad economic shift from manufacturing to services—which more readily accept women as managers—provides more opportunities to land top jobs. Third, many male managers working their way up in American business are accustomed to having women as peers, having gone to school and worked with women as colleagues and supervisors. Finally, the wave of restructurings, spin-offs, and leveraged buyouts—with huge personnel reshufflings, breaking up long-entrenched male cultures—favors women's progress.

For example, before International Harvester (now Navistar International Corporation) ran into financial problems in the late 1970s, female managers were found in only narrowly defined, specialized areas. But after divisions were disposed of, a new corporate culture developed. One result of this change was that Roxanne J. Decyk, who is 37 years old, has a law degree from Marquette University, and started as corporate secretary in 1981, became one of Harvester's top executives. After several promotions, she became senior vice-president for distribution in June 1989. She then moved to Amoco Chemical Company, where she is now vice-president of marketing and sales, polymers. She has also served on the board of directors of both Harris Bank in Chicago and Material Sciences Corporation in Elk Grove, Illinois.

Roxanne J. Decyk, vice-president of marketing and sales, polymers, Amoco Chemical Company.

But women still face many hurdles in climbing the corporate ladder. They still encounter old-fashioned prejudice and resistance at some companies. For example, the previously mentioned survey that found only 16 percent of the respondents thought it likely that their company would have a female CEO in ten years. Also, women still earn about 42 percent less than their male counterparts. Finally, according to Laurie Baum, "Many women simply don't want to make the family sacrifices generally required in the highest ranks of America."

If this estimate of progress for women managers is true, what does it portend for staffing and managing human resources in the future?[1]

This case illustrates the importance—and changing nature—of one of the major problems facing management today: managing human resources and diversity. How effectively managers perform this activity will determine their success or failure. This chapter looks at the most important aspects of managing human resources and diversity.

The Dominant Role of Human Resources

Corporate annual reports often include a statement to the effect that "people are our most precious asset." And according to David Glass, who succeeded Sam Walton, the legendary founder of Wal-Mart, as CEO, "For our company, it is absolutely true that our people make the difference."[2] Finally, the great industrialist Andrew Carnegie once said, "Take away all our factories, our trade, our avenues of transportation, and our money, but leave me our organization, and in four years, I will have reestablished myself." By this he meant that an organization is not the factories, trade, transportation, money, or other financial and physical resources. Rather, *an organization is made up of the people or human resources who are linked together in a formal structure, guided by managerial leadership.* People are vital to an effective organization, as shown by the Practicing Manager profile of Ronald Allen.

Effective management of human resources cannot be done with a quick, simple, one-shot approach. Instead, it is a continuous activity, requiring the best efforts of capable people. Increasingly, CEOs are saying, "Check it out with our human resource people" before instituting new programs, locating a new facility, or making other major decisions.

Human resource management (HRM)—that is, planning employment needs; recruiting, selecting, training, and developing capable employees and placing them in productive work environments; and rewarding their performance—is a very important aspect of management. It has increased in significance with the impact of labor unions, the equal employment opportunity movement, growing government regulation, escalating technology, and other major developments discussed in Chapter 3. High-tech demands are causing great concern for management, because skill requirements are increasing more rapidly than employees with those skills are becoming available. Also, many current—and prospective—employees are becoming obsolete for lack of needed education and training.

The model for managing human resources recommended in this book is shown in Figure 9.1. Notice that HRM is performed in two different types of environments: (1) the external environment, consisting of all the factors outside the organization that directly or indirectly affect it and (2) the internal environment, made up of all the elements within the organization.

The HRM activity must be performed by all managers, whether they run the largest corporations or are the owners of small businesses, whether they manage private or public corporations, or whether they operate for profit or not-for-profit. HRM is a shared responsibility. Top management is responsible for developing overall HRM policies. From there, the responsibility for carrying out those policies flows down through operating managers to first-line supervisors. But these managers cannot handle the function alone; they need the help of the human resource department staff.

human resource management (HRM) Planning personnel needs; recruiting, selecting, training, and developing capable employees; placing them in productive work environments; and rewarding their performance.

PRACTICING MANAGER

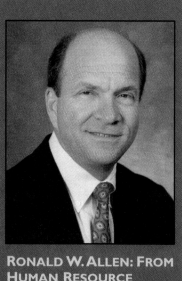

RONALD W. ALLEN: FROM HUMAN RESOURCE MANAGER TO CEO

In August 1987, Ronald W. Allen, at age 46, became the youngest CEO Delta Air Lines, Inc., ever had. His impressive management of its human resources prepared him to run what was then the country's best-run airlines as chairman of the board, president, and CEO.

After joining Delta in 1963 as a part-time methods analyst intern in the methods and training department, Allen was promoted through the ranks —following Delta's policy of promoting from within. Before becoming CEO, he served as administrative assistant, personnel; director, methods and training; assistant vice-president, administration; vice-president, administration; senior vice-president, personnel; member of the board of directors; senior vice-president for administration and personnel; and president.

Allen works with other Delta top managers in a smoothly functioning team. This consistency in management did not come about by accident, however. In the late 1960s, C. E. Woolman, long-time head and strong-willed aviation pioneer of Delta, began shifting the burdens of management to the nucleus of top officers, including Allen. He impressed upon them the value of Delta's employees to its success, and taught them to use teamwork and consensus in managing those human resources. On Woolman's sudden death in 1966, the team continued with little disruption and has continued to function smoothly as a unit.

Allen and Delta's other managers maintain an open-door policy and work diligently to keep the lines of communication open at all times. Top management meets with all employees in groups of 25 to 30 at least once every 18 months. After a formal briefing on current company activities and their results, the meeting is opened for questions, complaints, and suggestions.

In keeping with Delta's open communication policy, top management is also kept updated on all important activities. Clearly defined responsibilities and short communication lines make for a smooth-running management team. Allen and his colleagues have been described as having taken the concept of interchangeability of parts and applying it to Delta's management policies. As a cohesive, workable whole, these policies have made Delta outstanding in its industry. In fact, Delta was recently found to be one of the "top 10 best places to work in the United States," based on pay and benefits, opportunities for advancement, job security, company pride, and friendly relations among colleagues. (This reputation may since have become tarnished, however, as Delta was forced to eliminate several thousand employees in 1994 in order to compete with lower-cost carriers.)

Allen is an affable, outgoing manager whose aggressiveness has resulted in Delta's becoming the official airline of Disneyland and Walt Disney World. He has served on the board of directors of the Coca-Cola Company, NationsBank Corporation, Presbyterian College, the U.S. Chamber of Commerce, and others.

Sources: Communication with Ronald Allen and Delta Air Lines, Inc.; various Delta Air Lines, Inc., annual reports; Sarah Smith, "America's Most Admired Corporations," *Fortune*, January 29, 1990, pp. 58, 92; Brian Dumaine, "How to Manage in a Recession," *Fortune*, November 5, 1990, pp. 58–72; and Robert Levering and Milton Maskovitz, *The 100 Best Places to Work in America* (New York: Doubleday, 1993).

Growing Diversity of Human Resources

The Dictionary of Occupational Titles listed around 17,500 jobs when it was first published in 1939. Since then, it has added over 18,000 new job titles, mostly in new fields, such as computers, electronics, and space exploration. From 1977, when the fourth edition was published, until 1991, when it was revised, 208 titles were added, and 1,609 were modified.[3]

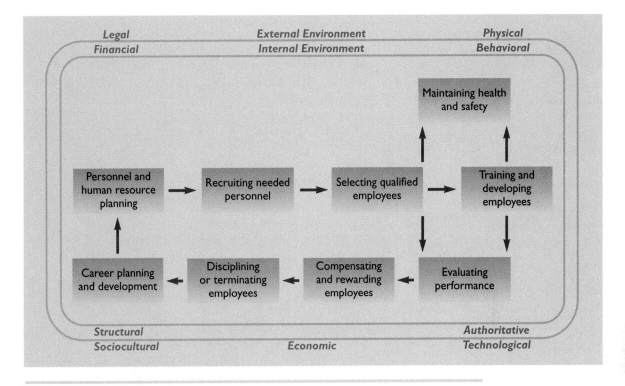

FIGURE 9.1
A model human resource management system.

There have been two significant changes in U.S. employment during recent decades. First, the proportion of workers producing goods has decreased relative to those performing services. Second, the workforce has become much more diverse.

Shift from Goods-Producing to Service-Producing Jobs

As Figure 9.2 indicates, there has been a definite shift away from goods-producing and toward service-producing jobs during the past two decades. In fact, nearly 92 percent of the 33 million new jobs created during the last 15 years were in services. Retail and wholesale trade, together with finance, insurance, and real estate, creates around 2 million new jobs each year.[4]

It is expected that fully 81 percent of all U.S. civilian employees will be performing services by the year 2005. And while the total number of jobs is expected to grow by 21 percent, the number of service-producing jobs should escalate by around 27 percent, while goods-producing jobs will grow by only 1 percent.

Over the last century, there has also been a marked shift from blue-collar to white-collar jobs, especially from operative types of jobs to technical and professional positions. Around 52 percent of all jobs are now white-collar positions, and this proportion is expected to increase to around 53 percent by the year 2005.

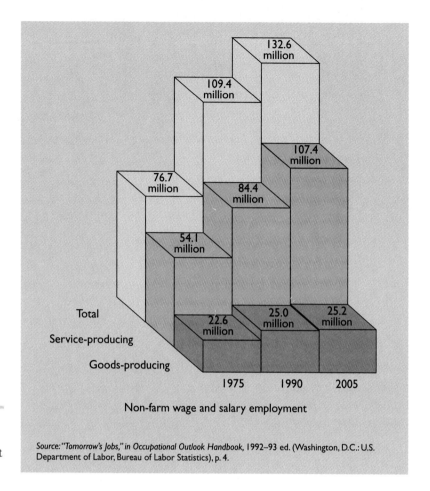

FIGURE 9.2
Industries providing services will account for nearly four out of five jobs by the year 2005.

Source: "*Tomorrow's Jobs,*" *in Occupational Outlook Handbook,* 1992–93 ed. (Washington, D.C.: U.S. Department of Labor, Bureau of Labor Statistics), p. 4.

Need for a More Diverse Workforce

As a result of this changing nature of employment, the U.S. Department of Labor's Bureau of Labor Statistics predicts that future managers will have to deal with a very *diverse* group of employees. As shown in Figure 9.3, in the year 2005, 12 percent of workers will be black, 11 percent will be Hispanic, and 4 percent will be Asian, Native American, and members of other groups. White men will account for only 38 percent of the workforce (down from 43 percent in 1990), and white women will remain at 35 percent.

As diversity increases, managers' jobs will become more difficult and challenging. It will become even more important to know—and know how to apply—the laws dealing with minorities and other special groups, as will be shown later in this chapter.

There Will Be More Minorities   While the racial mix of today's employees, as shown in Figure 9.3, is changing, the real progress has been in the improved position of these employees in the white-collar, professional, technical, and managerial ranks. For example, in 1991, 6.3 percent of white-collar, 6.7 percent of professional, 8.9 of

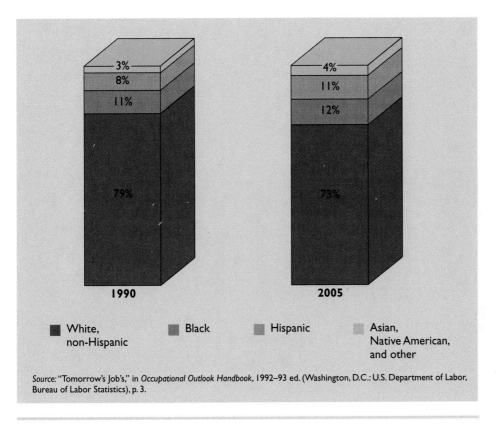

79%   73%

1990   2005

■ White,   ■ Black   ■ Hispanic   ■ Asian,
non-Hispanic   Native American,
                                            and other

Source: "Tomorrow's Job's," in *Occupational Outlook Handbook*, 1992–93 ed. (Washington, D.C.: U.S. Department of Labor, Bureau of Labor Statistics), p. 3.

FIGURE 9.3
Distribution of the labor force, by race and ethnic origin.

technical, and 6.3 percent of managers were black. These figures indicate a slow—but steady—upward trend.

There Will Be More Women   The progress made by women in the U.S. workforce is shown in Figure 9.4. Notice that only 30 percent of employees were women in 1950, but now over 46 percent are, and this percentage is expected to increase to about 48 by the year 2000. One reason for this trend is that about seven out of ten new jobs in the late 1970s were filled by women. This trend is now weakening. In 1960, there were 8.1 million working mothers; today there are over 21 million. From 1975 to 1991, the percentage of women with children under age six who were in the workforce increased from 39 to 59.[5]

The jobs women hold are also being upgraded. Although women are still concentrated in "women's jobs," they are beginning to move into higher-level positions.

Need for Improved Management of Diversity

This discussion indicates a growing need in business schools and management training programs for intensive instruction in how to function effectively in a diverse workforce, where the impact of diverse cultures is so important. There also

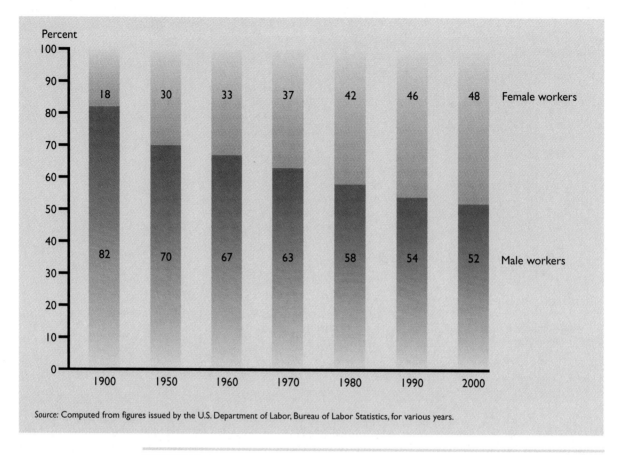

Source: Computed from figures issued by the U.S. Department of Labor, Bureau of Labor Statistics, for various years.

FIGURE 9.4
Women's share of jobs is increasing.

needs to be a changed management attitude toward women. These problems will require even more attention in the near future.

Human Resources and the Legal Environment

equal employment opportunity (EEO) laws Rulings that prohibit employment decisions based on race, color, religion, sex, national origin, age, or disability.

Almost every aspect of HRM—from personnel planning to retirement—is now affected by **equal employment opportunity (EEO) laws,** which prohibit employment decisions based on race, color, religion, sex, national origin, age, or disability. (We are putting this discussion early in the chapter so that you can refer to it as you study the various subjects involved in HRM.)

It might surprise you to learn that until the early 1960s, employment discrimination was generally accepted. Most managerial and other desirable jobs were held by white males. Women, minorities, the aged, and the disabled were placed in low-status jobs—and remained there. Now, for moral, economic, and legal reasons, EEO is generally accepted.

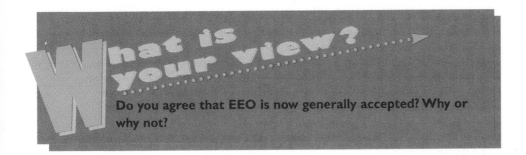

Do you agree that EEO is now generally accepted? Why or why not?

Laws Providing Equal Employment Opportunity

The specific requirements of the most significant EEO laws are shown in Table 9.1. It is important to recognize that the laws apply to all employment practices, including—but not limited to—(1) hiring and firing; (2) wages, terms, conditions, and privileges of employment; (3) classifying, assigning, and promoting of employees; (4) assigning the use of facilities; and (5) training or retraining.

Title VII of the Civil Rights Act of 1964 is probably the most far reaching of these laws, as *it prohibits discrimination by employers with 15 or more employees in any employment activity* on the basis of race, creed, color, religion, sex, or nation of origin. We will now examine just how these laws protect women, minorities, older workers, the disabled, and Vietnam-era veterans.

Women and Minorities EEO effectively began when Congress passed the *Civil Rights Act* in 1964.[6] That law was followed by the issuance of various executive orders and laws. The most significant of these was *Executive Order 11246*, as amended, which prohibited such discrimination by government contractors with 50 or more employees. As a result of these and other laws, business employers now have to do more than just see that their employment practices are not unfair. If they have government contracts of over $50,000 a year, they must develop an **affirmative action program (AAP)** that spells out direct and positive actions management will take to search for, recruit, select, develop, promote, and reward women, minorities, and other groups that formerly would have been deprived of employment opportunities. AAPs are also required for the disabled and for Vietnam veterans. *The Civil Rights Act of 1991* greatly modified and strengthened Title VII, the Americans with Disabilities Act, and various other laws. It allows for punitive and compensatory damages in cases of intentional discrimination and permits more extensive use of jury trials.

Older Workers During the 1960s, there was a decline in the hiring—and an increase in the forced retirement or discharge—of older workers. An employer could discriminate not only by *not hiring* such persons but also by *not providing training and advancement opportunities* for those already employed, or by *forcing them to take lower-level jobs or early retirement.* To protect older workers, Congress passed the *Age Discrimination in Employment Act (ADEA)*, in 1967. It prohibits discrimination against employees who are age 40 and above—which in effect eliminates mandatory retirement (except for airline pilots, firefighters, police officers, and prison guards). The law was slow being enforced until 1990.

affirmative action program (AAP)
Program set up by a business to take direct and positive actions to increase employment opportunities for women, minorities, and other underutilized groups.

Affirmative action requires recruitment at minority and women's schools.

TABLE 9.1   LAWS PROVIDING EQUAL EMPLOYMENT OPPORTUNITY

Laws	Basic Requirements	Coverage	Enforcement Agencies
Section 1981 of Civil Rights Act of 1866	Prohibits racial discrimination in employment	All private employers, labor unions, and employment agencies	Judicial system
Title VII of Civil Rights Act of 1964	Prohibits employment discrimination based on race, color, religion, sex, or national origin	Private employers engaged in interstate commerce with 15 or more employees, labor unions, employment agencies, federal government workers, and state and local government workers	Equal Employment Opportunity Commission (EEOC)
Executive Order 11246 of 1965, as amended	Prohibits employment discrimination based on race, sex, color, religion, or national origin, and requires contractors employing 50 or more workers to develop affirmative action plans (AAPs) when contracts exceed $50,000 a year	Federal contractors and subcontractors holding contracts of $10,000 or more	U.S. Department of Labor's Office of Federal Contract Compliance Programs (OFCCP)
Age Discrimination in Employment Act of 1967, as amended	Prohibits employment discrimination against persons over age 40	Same as those under Title VII, except that private employers with 20 or more employees are covered	EEOC
Vocational Rehabilitation Act of 1973	Prohibits employment discrimination against otherwise qualified handicapped persons, requires reasonable accommodation, and requires development of AAPs	Federal contractors and subcontractors holding contracts in excess of $2,500, organizations that receive federal assistance, and federal agencies	OFCCP
Vietnam Era Veterans' Assistance Act of 1974	Requires contractors to develop AAPs to recruit and employ qualified disabled veterans and veterans of the Vietnam War	Federal contractors and subcontractors holding contracts in excess of $10,000	OFCCP
Immigration Reform and Control Act of 1986	Prohibits recruiting, hiring, or referring aliens who are not eligible to work in the United States; prohibits employment discrimination based on national origin or citizenship	Private employers, labor unions, and employment agencies	U.S. Department of Justice's Special Counsel for Unfair Immigration-Related Employment
Americans with Disabilities Act of 1990	Prohibits employment discrimination against qualified individuals with a disability and requires reasonable accommodation	Same as Title VII	EEOC
Civil Rights Act of 1991	Amends Title VII and the Americans with Disabilities Act to allow for punitive and compensatory damages in cases of intentional discrimination and more extensive use of jury trials	Same as Title VII	EEOC

Source: Leon C. Megginson, Geralyn M. Franklin, and Jane Byrd, *Human Resource Management* (Houston, Tex.: Dame Publications, 1995), Table 3.1, pp. 58–59.

On December 7, 1990, a federal judge found Quasar, a unit of Matsushita Electric, guilty of age and racial discrimination against American employees. Quasar was ordered to pay $2.5 million in damages to three former employees—all over age 50—who had filed age and racial discrimination charges against it after they and 63 other U.S. managers were fired in 1986 but no Japanese managers were fired.[7] This decision effectively determined how the law would later be enforced.

The Disabled The *Vocational Rehabilitation Act (VRA)*, passed in 1973, prohibits employers with federal contracts from discriminating against the disabled. Job opportunities—including special facilities, if needed—must be provided. A **disabled person** is defined as anyone who has a physical or mental disability that substantially restricts major normal activities such as physical movement or learning, seeing, speaking, or hearing.

disabled person Anyone with a physical or mental disability that substantially restricts major normal activities such as physical movement learning, walking, seeing, speaking, or hearing.

Deaf workers have traditionally been hired by the printing industry as compositors and printing press operators because they are not easily distracted, and the noise of high-speed presses and other machinery does not bother them.

The *Americans with Disabilities Act (ADA)*, passed in 1990, expanded the scope and coverage of the VRA. In essence, the ADA prohibits discrimination on the basis of disability in hiring, promotion, and all other terms, conditions, and privileges of employment. The ADA applies to virtually all employers with 15 or more employees, not just government contractors. But unlike the VRA, it does not require employers to develop AAPs.

Vietnam-Era Veterans The *Vietnam-Era Veteran's Assistance Act of 1974* provides for job counseling, training, and placement service for Vietnam-era veterans. In addition, it requires firms with federal contracts to have AAPs for recruiting and hiring Vietnam-era veterans.

Enforcement of EEO Laws

While enforcement of EEO laws is spread over several agencies, the most important ones are the **Equal Employment Opportunity Commission (EEOC)** and the **Office of Federal Contract Compliance Programs (OFCCP).** The EEOC has overall responsibility for coordinating enforcement. The OFCCP, which is in the U.S. Department of Labor, enforces those laws requiring AAPs. A set of *Uniform Guidelines on Employee Selection Procedures* that helps employers comply with EEO provisions is used by all federal agencies.[8] As indicated above, several laws require affirmative action programs.

Equal Employment Opportunity Commission (EEOC) and **Office of Federal Contract Compliance Programs (OFCCP)** Agencies with primary responsibility for enforcing EEO laws.

Affirmative Action Programs (AAPs) In general, an *affirmative action program (AAP)* should include (1) making concerted efforts to recruit and promote women, minorities, the disabled, and veterans—including recruiting through state employment services and at minority and women's colleges; (2) limiting the questions that may be asked on employment applications and interviews, as shown in Figure 9.5; (3) determining available percentages of women, minorities, and the disabled in the local labor force; (4) setting up goals and timetables for recruiting women,

Here is an up-to-date summary of ten of the most dangerous questions or topics you might raise during an interview.

1. *Children.* Do not ask applicants whether they have children, or plan to have children, or have child care.

2. *Age.* Do not ask an applicant's age.

3. *Disabilities.* Do not ask whether the candidate has a physical or mental disability that would interfere with doing the job.

4. *Physical characteristics.* Do not ask for such identifying characteristics as height or weight on an application.

5. *Name.* Do not ask a female candidate for her maiden name.

6. *Citizenship.* Do not ask applicants about their citizenship. However, the Immigration Reform and Control Act does require business operators to determine that their employees have a legal right to work in the United States.

7. *Lawsuits.* Do not ask a job candidate whether he or she has ever filed a suit or a claim against a former employer.

8. *Arrest records.* Do not ask applicants about their arrest records.

9. *Smoking.* Do not ask whether a candidate smokes. While smokers are not protected under the Americans with Disabilities Act (ADA), asking applicants whether they smoke might lead to legal difficulties if an applicant is turned down because of fear that smoking would drive up the employer's health care costs.

10. *AIDS and HIV.* Never ask job candidates whether they have AIDS or are HIV-positive, as these questions violate the ADA and could violate state and federal civil rights laws.

Source: Adapted from Janine S. Pauliot, "Topics to Avoid with Applicants," *Nation's Business,* July 1992, pp. 57–58, by permission, *Nation's Business,* July 1992. Copyright 1992, U.S. Chamber of Commerce.

FIGURE 9.5
Topics to avoid when interviewing applicants.

minorities, the disabled, and veterans; and (5) avoiding testing unless it meets established guidelines at the time of publication of this book, the whole question of affirmative action was being addressed by Congress, the President, and the U.S. Supreme Court.

Rights of Religious Minorities   The EEOC's rules on enforcing accommodations for religious minorities are particularly troubling to managers. First, they require employers to go out of their way to avoid assigning employees to work on any day that violates their religious beliefs. Second, the definition of religion includes "sincerely held moral or ethical beliefs." This part of the Civil Rights Act seems to be harder to administer than the other provisions because of its nebulous nature.[9]

Sexual Harassment

A growing problem in managing diversity is dealing fairly and legally with charges of sexual harassment. According to the *Uniform Guidelines,* sexual harassment is an unwelcome sexual advance, request for sexual favors, and other verbal or physical conduct—by either sex—that involves the victim's employment. For example:

In its company handbook, Honeywell considers *verbal harassment* as "everything from whistling and catcalls to unwanted sexual compliments, and spreading lies about someone's sexual conduct. *Non-verbal harassment* includes blocking a person's path, following someone, looking at someone suggestively, and displaying suggestive visual materials. *Physical harassment* is unwanted touching of one's clothes, hair, and body." The handbook makes no distinction between men and women, or between bosses and co-workers.[10]

Planning Human Resource Needs

Managers should not wait to seek competent people until they are needed to fill specific positions. Instead, management must make a concerted effort to plan for future needs and to decide where to find the right people to fill those needs. This effort requires **human resource planning,** which includes all activities needed to provide for the proper types and numbers of employees to reach the organization's objectives.

There are two basic aspects of human resource planning: (1) determining job needs, including the jobs to be performed, the abilities needed by employees to do the jobs, and the number of employees that will be needed, and (2) developing sources of supply of potential employees.

Determining Job Needs

How do employers actually go about creating an effective workforce? Simply stated, based on the organization's objectives and plans, they determine the types of jobs to be performed and the skills needed to perform them. They also determine the total number of employees needed for a given period in the future and estimate how many new people must be hired and when they will be needed. Finally, some type of action program for filling the needs must be set up.

Determining Types of Jobs and Skills Needed This step begins with management deciding on its goals and objectives, as discussed in Chapter 7. What does the organization plan to do? What new products or services are going to be introduced? Are new markets or clientele going to be opened up? The answers to these and related questions will influence the number and types of people to be hired.

The actual determination of the jobs and skills needed starts with some form of **job analysis,** which is the process of gathering information, determining the elements of each job through observation and study, and presenting the results in written form. From these data, management prepares **job descriptions** that outline the skills, responsibilities, knowledge, authority, environment, and interrelationships involved in each job. Figure 9.6 is a particularly good example of a job description.

Job descriptions are then written up as job specifications that become the basis for hiring new people. **Job specifications** are written statements about each job and the qualifications required of a person to perform the job successfully. Job specifications must be job related and have *validity*, in that they measure the qualities that ensure and predict success on the job. These qualifications are becoming more rigorous as we become more technologically oriented, as humorously presented in this cartoon.

human resource planning The activities needed to provide for the proper types and numbers of employees to reach organizational objectives.

job analysis The process of gathering information and determining the elements of each job, by observation and study, and presenting the results in written form.

job descriptions Outlines of the skills, responsibilities, knowledge, authority, environment, and interrelationships involved in each job.

job specifications Written statements about each job and the qualifications required of a person to perform the job successfully.

"I can remember when all we needed was someone who could carve and someone who could sew."

Source: *Phi Kappa Phi Journal, Spring 1985, p. 14.*

Chief Quality Control Engineer		*156.132*		
Job Title		Job Code		
Manager of Quality Control		*Quality Control*		
Title of Immediate Supervisor		Department		
7	*Louisville*	*Exempt*		*March 26, 1991*
Bldg.	Plant	Status		Date
Kathy Johnson	*Robert Myers*	*16*	*751*	*1/2*
Written by:	Approved by:	Grade	Points	EEO/AAP

SUMMARY

Supervises six salaried quality control personnel; plans, organizes, coordinates, and administers manufacturing activities.

JOB DUTIES

1. Establishes and maintains supplier contacts to assist in solving quality problems by evaluating contacts' quality capabilities, facilities, and quality systems. (10%)
2. Establishes and reviews goals, budgets, and work plans in the areas of quality, cost schedule attainment, and operator/equipment utilization. (10%)
3. Reviews product and process designs, identifying problems that might result in customer dissatisfaction or failure to meet established goals or allocated costs. (20%)
4. Specifies quality control methods and processes to support quality planning. Provides cost estimates and procures necessary tools and equipment to support overall project schedule. (10%)
5. Supplies input to manufacturing engineers on producibility and other quality matters. (20%)
6. Provides feedback on quality levels and costs during test runs and during production to measure system effectiveness. (10%)
7. Supervises six to eight salaried personnel assigned to the quality control engineering area. Trains new personnel in proper procedures and policy. Completes performance appraisals of subordinates. (20%)

Source: Reprinted by permission of Merrill, an imprint of Macmillan Publishing Company, from *Personnel: Human Resource Management,* 3rd. ed., by Michael R. Carrell, Frank E. Kuzmits, and Norbert F. Elbert. Copyright © 1989 by Merrill Publishing.

FIGURE 9.6
A sample job description.

Determining Human Resource Needs   Next, management must decide how many employees are required to perform the jobs and what skills and abilities they will need. This is done by estimating the organization's overall needs in terms of occupational specialties, job skills, personal characteristics, and number of new employees needed.

Then management must do some type of inventory to see how many people it has who can perform those jobs. This inventory enables management to match the skills of the people in the organization with its overall human resource needs.

The difference between the overall needs and present employee inventory is the number and type of workers to be filled by recruitment. In addition to the number and type of people needed, other factors, such as occupational choices, experience, age, sex, race, and expected retirements, terminations, and transfers, should also be considered.

Setting Up an Action Program   Management can start some type of action program to recruit and select employees once it knows the net need for new people. An *action program* involves all the human resource functions needed to fill the organization's human resource needs and objectives, including recruiting, selecting, developing, maintaining, and rewarding employees.

Developing Sources of Supply of Employees

In general, the larger the number of sources of supply you use, the greater the chances of finding a person with the needed qualities. Most effective managers, realizing this, develop and maintain many different sources of supply. In addition, many human resource managers maintain an ongoing relationship with college and university faculties in order to know when capable graduates are available.

> For example, the accounting firm of Lawton, Burton & Bunge (LB&B) has developed excellent rapport with the accounting faculties at universities in the area. It sponsors social functions, provides guest speakers for classes, and even flies faculty members to its main office for tours or special occasions. Each year LB&B has had no problem hiring the top accounting graduates in its area.

There are essentially only two sources from which employees can be recruited to fill specific jobs—from within the organization and from outside. Managers usually prefer to use the *internal source* because it tends to motivate present employees better. If you do an effective job for your employer and are then promoted to a higher-level job, your morale is boosted and you tend to be motivated. Furthermore, as you see others promoted internally, this also encourages you, as you too could get a promotion. Promotion from within is "the gospel" at Delta Air Lines, as the earlier profile of Ronald W. Allen illustrates. Only specialists are hired from the outside.

Some jobs, however, do require going outside to find the right people. When a new technological development is introduced, management must look outside if present employees cannot be trained to do the job. Also, if the internal source is used exclusively, there is the risk of "inbreeding." Everybody will be familiar with the way everybody else thinks, and there will be few new ideas. Therefore, most organizations use a combination of promoting from within and hiring from without, but there are exceptions.

Internal Sources   There are three methods of obtaining employees internally. First, they can be obtained through **upgrading,** whereby the employee currently holding the position is educated, trained, or developed to perform the job better or differently, as the situation demands.

> For example, a large church changed from doing accounting by hand to doing it by computer. The business administrator sent the current bookkeeper to a computer school rather than going outside to hire someone else.

Second, jobs can be filled by **transferring** or moving employees from less desirable or less rewarding jobs in the organization to others that better satisfy their needs. Third, jobs can be filled by **promoting** employees from a lower-level job to a

upgrading Educating, training, or developing current employees to perform the same job better or differently, as the situation demands.

transferring Moving employees from less desirable or less rewarding jobs in the organization to others that better satisfy their needs.

promoting Moving employees from a lower-level job to a higher-level one.

higher-level one. This usually carries with it a higher salary, a new job title, and added duties and responsibilities. This form of reward serves as an effective motivator.

External Sources   When outside recruiting is required, the supply source to be used will depend on the job to be filled, the type of employee(s) desired, and job market conditions. Some of the more popular external sources of employees are (1) former employees who left with a good record, (2) personal applications, (3) friends and relatives of present employees, (4) competing firms, (5) labor organizations, (6) private and public employment agencies, (7) schools and colleges, (8) migrants and immigrants, and (9) part-time employees.

temporaries Part-time employees who want to work for only a limited time during each week.

Employers are now using many part-time employees or **temporaries,** such as students, retirees, and parents with school-aged children who want to work for only limited hours each week. Also, many organizations hire employees from outside businesses that specialize in performing a given service. A major motivation for using temporaries is the many rules and legal decisions pertaining to unlawful discharge. Using temporary workers (with no long probationary period) helps managers avoid some of these problems.

This method is particularly useful in clerical, custodial, and maintenance operations for which an employee with a given specialty can be hired by the hour or day, as the situation dictates. The Bureau of Labor Statistics estimated that there were 6.3 million people working part-time in the summer of 1993.[11]

An increasingly important source of temps, as temporary workers are often called, is *employee leasing*, whereby an outside company hires a client company's employees, provides them with insurance and other benefits, and then leases them back to the company. While the temps work for the client company, they are employees of the leasing company. This type of employee is particularly important to small firms. As shown in Figure 9.7, there were around 1.6 million such employees in 1993.

FIGURE 9.7
Number of temporary workers in 1993.

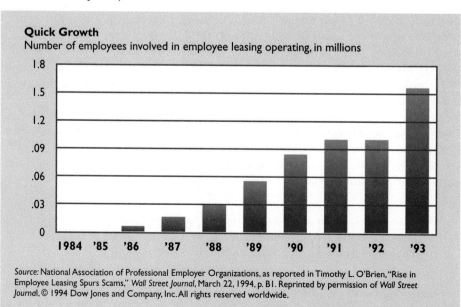

Quick Growth
Number of employees involved in employee leasing operating, in millions

Source: National Association of Professional Employer Organizations, as reported in Timothy L. O'Brien, "Rise in Employee Leasing Spurs Scams," *Wall Street Journal*, March 22, 1994, p. B1. Reprinted by permission of *Wall Street Journal*, © 1994 Dow Jones and Company, Inc. All rights reserved worldwide.

Recruiting and Selecting Employees

You are probably familiar with the method of recruiting athletes for college sports. The coaches or managers determine what positions must be filled, look over potential players in selected high schools and junior colleges, decide which players they want, and then go out and recruit them. Essentially, this is what industry does when it seeks candidates for top jobs; in fact, there are "headhunter" employment agencies whose sole function is to find corporate executives, sometimes "stealing" them from other companies.

Recruiting Personnel

Recruitment refers to reaching out and attracting a pool of potential employees from which to select the ones needed to satisfy the organization's needs. Recruiting, then, involves attracting the right number of people with the abilities needed to fill the available jobs.

> **recruitment** The process of reaching out and attracting a pool of potential employees from which to select the ones required to satisfy the organization's needs.

The methods used to recruit personnel vary with different employers, in different industries, and in different localities. Some managers wait until they need a new worker and then put a sign in the window. Others, using a more aggressive approach, go out seeking and searching for potential employees. The usual methods of recruitment involve *employee referrals, advertising, college recruiting,* and *use of computerized databases.*

Employee Referrals If used properly, **employee referrals** are an excellent method of recruiting personnel. Since current employees know the job to be filled and the personal abilities needed to fill it, they may be able to recommend a relative or friend who would make an excellent employee. In fact, many firms give bonuses to employees who attract new employees.

> **employee referrals** Recommendations by current employees of friends or relatives who have the qualifications to fill specific jobs.

An example of an employee referral program is the one used at Loral Electronics. One of its divisions offers a $5,000 bonus for finders of engineers with a minimum of four years of experience. One General Electric (GE) unit pays a $500 finder's fee and gives the finder a "GE name-dropper" T-shirt.

Advertising The most common form of recruiting is the use of want ads in newspapers. In fact, Sears, Roebuck and Company began when Alvah Roebuck answered the following want ad placed by Richard Sears in the *Chicago Daily News* of April 11, 1887. The rest is history![12]

> **WATCHMAKER WANTED**
> with references, who can furnish
> tools. State age, experience, and
> salary required.
>   T39, *Daily News*

The most common—and least expensive—forms of advertising are newspaper display and want ads. No other method is so flexible, relatively inexpensive, and effective. However, other media can be employed, such as trade, specialty, and professional journals. Radio, television, billboards, cinema slides, and recordings at special events, such as professional meetings and conventions, are also used. Even TV is now being effectively used for employee recruitment.

> For example, on March 1, 1993, when The Career Television Network (TCTN) began broadcasting job opportunities nationwide on CNBC, the cable television arm of NBC, newspaper want ads ran headlong into the video age. TCTN, the first nationwide job opportunity video network, airs daily for one hour, Monday through Friday. An anchor introduces up to five new job openings each hour. The program also includes interviews with people currently employed with the company and features the advantages and benefits of working for the employer.[13]

College Recruiting   College graduates provide the best source of scientific, technical, professional, and managerial employees. In fact, colleges are the major source. Therefore, large, successful firms do some type of campus recruiting. The recruiters' activities are usually coordinated by each school's placement officer.

Computerized Databases   You are probably familiar with computer dating services that attempt to match individuals. Computers can be used in a similar way to match jobs and people. In addition to companies, such as Citibank, which uses a computerized position-employee matching system, an increasing number of job-hunting computer owners are using their phones to plug into listings of job openings provided by enterprising entrepreneurs.

> For example, KiNexus, a Chicago-based database firm, already has more than 175,000 résumés on file. According to Albert Copland, its director of communications, "Ten years from now this will be the primary method for recruiting. I liken it to word-processing software; 10 years ago, very few people used it."[14]

Selecting the Right Person for the Job

selection The process of choosing from a group of potential employees the specific person to perform a given job.

Selection is choosing the specific person to perform a given job from among a group of potential employees. In theory, selection is simple. As shown earlier, management decides what the job involves and what abilities an individual must possess to perform the job effectively. The manager then looks at the applicants' past performance records and selects the one whose abilities, experiences, and personality most nearly conform to the job requirements. Unfortunately, selection is not that simple. It is much more complicated than it appears, and it is very important, for hiring the "right" person for the "right" job can greatly improve employee performance.

As *past performance is still the best indicator of future performance*, what a person has done in the past, as evidenced by school records, work experience, and extracurricular activities, is the best predictor of what he or she will probably do in the future.

What to Look For   It is impossible to state exactly what to look for in a potential employee. Yet there are some factors that tend to affect an employee's performance, including (1) *personal background,* (2) *aptitudes and interests,* (3) *attitudes and needs,* (4) *analytical and manipulative abilities,* (5) *skills and technical abilities,* and (6) *health, energy,* and *stamina.*

Notice that only one of these variables deals with job specialization. The others deal with the applicant's attitudes, values, thinking ability, and relationships with people. Those are the factors that most nearly lead to success, especially in supervisory people, as the following example shows:

> Hugh Aaron, of Belfast, Maine, explains the success of his plastics material business as follows: "[We sought] people who were intelligent, flexible, reliable, with a good basic education, and the ability to communicate well. Family people, . . . with responsibilities, were preferred. Some, of course, had to have sufficient motor skills to perform certain tasks."[15]

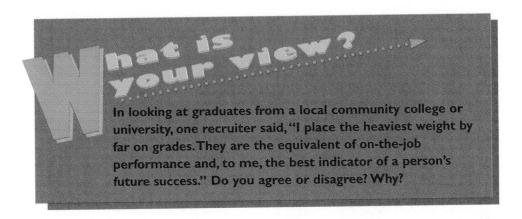

In looking at graduates from a local community college or university, one recruiter said, "I place the heaviest weight by far on grades. They are the equivalent of on-the-job performance and, to me, the best indicator of a person's future success." Do you agree or disagree? Why?

Selection Procedure   The actual selection of people is a continuous process and can never be thought of as totally completed. The procedure shown in Figure 9.8 illustrates one way of choosing people. The usual steps are (1) preliminary interview, (2) biographical inventory, (3) testing, (4) in-depth interview, (5) checking of performance references, (6) physical examination (if legally permitted), and (7) personal judgment.

Preliminary Interview.   During the preliminary interview, less capable applicants are rejected because of poor appearance, physical disabilities that would prevent them from doing the job for which they are applying, or an apparent lack of serious interest in the job. It is at this point that management may begin to run afoul of the EEO laws. Figure 9.5 shows some topics to avoid when interviewing applicants. Merely asking these questions is not illegal, but discrimination based on them is.

Biographical Inventory.   Probably the most frequently used step in the selection procedure is looking for evidence of past performance in a person's record. This information can be found from an application form, a personal data sheet or résumé, work records, school records, military records, and similar biographical sources.

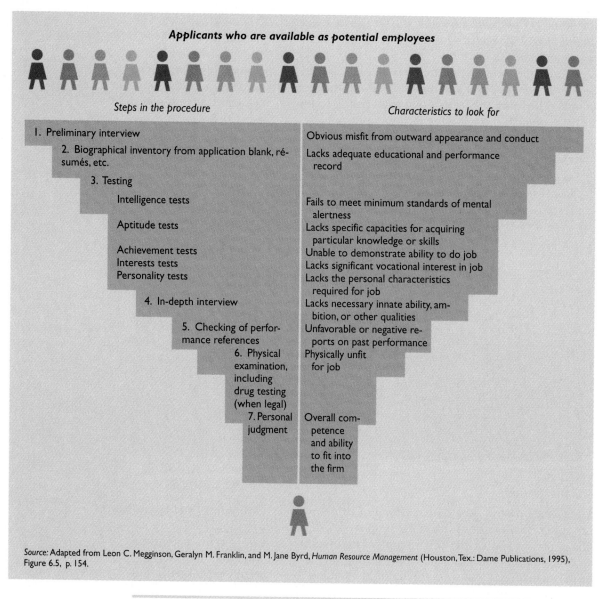

Source: Adapted from Leon C. Megginson, Geralyn M. Franklin, and M. Jane Byrd, *Human Resource Management* (Houston, Tex.: Dame Publications, 1995), Figure 6.5, p. 154.

FIGURE 9.8
Suggested procedure for selecting employees.

Testing.   Testing provides the only objective basis for gathering information about the applicant. According to a definitive study by *Personnel Administrator* magazine, the most popular kinds of preemployment tests are as follows: physical, 42 percent; drug, 25 percent; personality, 19 percent; and aptitude, 14 percent.[16] Achievement, ability, and/or performance tests are also quite popular.

Use of the polygraph, or "lie detector"—except by governments, firms doing sensitive contract work for the Department of Defense, the CIA and FBI, pharmaceutical firms handling controlled substances, and security guard services—is largely prohibited by the *Employee Polygraph Protection Act* of 1988. Only 2.7 percent

MANAGEMENT APPLICATION AND PRACTICE 9.1

Typical Questions Asked During an Employee Interview

Indicated below is a general classification of those questions that, in one form or another, were reported as being used by three or more companies. These were indicated as the most helpful questions asked by employers during the initial interview with graduating college seniors as reported by 170 companies.

	Number of Companies
1. What are your long-range goals? Ambitions? Future plans? Basic objectives? What do you want to be doing in 5, 10, 15 years from now? What are your immediate objectives?	93
2. Why did you choose your field of special study? How have you prepared yourself for work in your chosen field? What subjects have you enjoyed most? Least? Do you have plans for graduate study?	74
3. What type of work do you want to do? Why? Why do you think you qualify for this type of work? In what type of job would you like to start?	60
4. Why do you think you might like to work in our type of industry? Our company? Why did you select this company? What can you contribute to a company such as ours?	53
5. What were your extracurricular activities? What have you gained from your activities? What leadership office(s) have you held? What are your hobbies—your interests out of school?	40
6. What is your scholastic record? Where do you stand in your class? Explain your academic record. In what courses have you earned your best grades? How well did you apply yourself in your studies?	37
7. Do you like to travel? Are you willing to travel? To relocate? Have you geographic preferences? Would you like to live in our community?	36
8. What are your major strengths and weaknesses? Your accomplishments to date? Major achievements in college? Any plans for improvement?	30
9. What work experience have you had? Summer jobs? Part-time work? What experiences did you like the best? Why?	28
10. What do you know about our company? What questions would you like to ask? Is the size of the company important to you?	15

Source: Victor R. Lindquist, *Employment Trends for College Graduates in Business*, Northwestern Endicott Report (Evanston, Ill.: Placement Center, Northwestern University, n.d.).

of companies in the *Personnel Administrator* survey said they gave lie detector tests to job candidates.[17]

In-Depth Interview. During the in-depth interview, all the information about the applicant is brought together at one point. The interview is an effort to get information about the person's attitudes, feelings, and abilities. It is the only two-way exchange of information between the potential employee and management. See MAP 9.1 for some typical questions asked during these interviews.

Performance References.   By checking with previous employers, you may be able to obtain useful information about the applicant's past performance. But care must be taken to protect the individual's personal rights. One problem is that some former employers—especially large companies—often avoid giving any type of reference for fear of being sued. Therefore, managers need to learn to "read between the lines" and gather information in more creative ways or have disclaimer forms.

Physical Examination.   A physical examination was once required of all job applicants, but the Americans with Disabilities Act (ADA) has limited its role in hiring the disabled. Now, employers cannot require a physical exam before a preliminary job offer is made.[18] Nor can they ask questions about the applicant's medical history.[19] The only valid questions must deal with the applicant's ability to do the essential functions of the job.

Two burning issues now challenging employers are (1) testing and treatment for drug and alcohol abuse and (2) testing and treatment for AIDS (acquired immune deficiency syndrome). These two problems will challenge managers for years to come, and solutions to them are nowhere is sight.[20] Under certain situations, and for certain jobs, drug testing can be done.

Personal Judgment.   When all else has been done, and these procedures have been used, some manager(s) must make a personal decision to accept or reject the applicant for employment. In the final analysis, this decision may come down to the question of whether the manager thinks the applicant will fit in and work well with others in the organization.

In addition, most large firms, such as GE, Ford, and IBM, have established methods of identifying managerial talent in their operating employees. One of the more effective ways of selecting managers is the use of assessment centers. Basically, an **assessment center** is a place where applicants for a given position spend a period of time taking tests and doing exercises in order to determine whether they have the skills to succeed in a management position. Assessment usually consists of personal interviews; the completion of various language skills, interest, and personality tests; and participation in exercises such as case analyses and in-basket simulations. Panels of trained experts observe applicants' performance and assess the extent to which it reflects their analytical, interpersonal, communications, and problem-solving skills. As assessment centers involve groups, and measure the person's individual behavior in the group, they provide better results than pencil-and-paper tests.

assessment center A place where applicants spend a period of time taking tests and doing exercises in order to determine whether they have the skills to succeed in a management position.

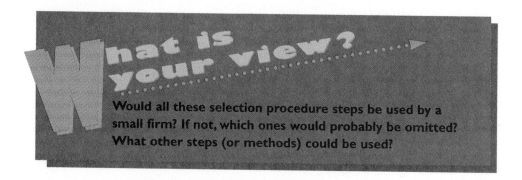

Would all these selection procedure steps be used by a small firm? If not, which ones would probably be omitted? What other steps (or methods) could be used?

Training and Developing Employees

New employees usually already have the education and training needed to perform the basics of a new job. They are a product of an educational system and experience that have given them a certain level of ability and competence. Managers must begin with that level of development and build on it through additional training and development. For purposes of this discussion, **training** is defined as attaining specific, detailed, and routine job skills and techniques. **Development** is the broad scope of improvement and growth of abilities, attitudes, and personality traits.

training The process of attaining specific, detailed, and routine job skills and techniques.

development The broad scope of improvement and growth of abilities, attitudes, and personality traits.

Reasons for Training and Development

Training and development are important for both the individual and the organization. An organization that wants to grow and develop must have people who grow and develop. In fact, employers inevitably pay the cost of developing employees—in the form of poor work, waste, grievances, absenteeism, and labor turnover—even if they have no formal training program.

In general, today's workers need higher levels of training and education than previous workers in order to hold down more technically oriented jobs. A person who was an effective electrician a few years ago probably needs to learn how to become an electronics technician. And the formerly capable accountant needs to understand computer programming and capabilities.

As you can see, learning is a lifelong process, and training and development should be also. As the Red Queen admonished Alice in *Through the Looking Glass*, "It takes all the running you can do, to keep in the same place." Margaret Mead, the noted anthropologist, said the same when she wrote, "No one will live all his life in the world into which he was born, and no one will die in the world in which he worked in his maturity. . . . Learning . . . must go on not only at special times and in special places, but all through production and consumption."[21] Thus, we no longer assume that learning stops when people leave school. Employees—and their employers—must keep on training and developing if they hope to be able to adapt and adjust to the changes that will continue to occur, as the following example illustrates.

> Hugh Aaron (see previous example) and his employees had a "willingness to adapt and learn again and again." Their training was designed to teach employees "to expect change and use their natural and acquired capacities to adapt to it."[22]

Orientation of New Employees

Training actually begins with orientation. After being selected, the employee is placed on the job and introduced to the organization through some form of orientation. This process is important because a new job is difficult and frustrating for a new employee. The new employee may be qualified for the job, but the new situation is different and strange, and poor orientation can squelch enthusiasm and effort right from the start.

Research has shown that an effective orientation program can (1) reduce labor turnover, (2) reduce employee anxiety and uncertainty, (3) save time of fellow employees and supervisors, and (4) instill more positive work values and improve the motivation and job satisfaction of the new worker.[23]

The orientation process can be a simple introduction to present employees or a lengthy process of informing the employee about the employer's organization and its policies, procedures, and employee benefits.

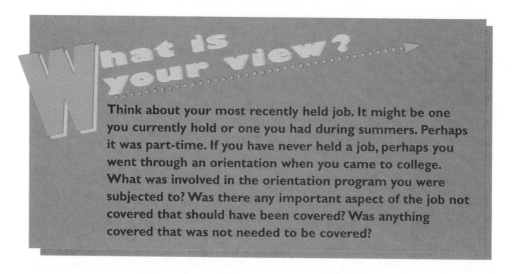

What is your view?

Think about your most recently held job. It might be one you currently hold or one you had during summers. Perhaps it was part-time. If you have never held a job, perhaps you went through an orientation when you came to college. What was involved in the orientation program you were subjected to? Was there any important aspect of the job not covered that should have been covered? Was anything covered that was not needed to be covered?

Training and Development Methods

There are so many methods used for training and developing employees that it is not feasible to discuss all of them. Generally, nonmanagerial employees are trained on the job, while managers are trained both on and off the job.

on-the-job training (OJT) Learning the job by actually performing it under the guidance of an experienced person.

On-the-Job Training Methods   **On-the-job training (OJT)** is the most frequently used method to train new employees. Employees learn by actually performing the work under the guidance of an experienced worker or supervisor. Through advice and suggestions, the more experienced employee teaches the new one effective work methods.

The most frequently used on-the-job methods are (1) *coaching*, whereby superiors or fellow employees provide guidance and counsel to new workers in the course of their regular job performance; (2) *planned progression*, or moving subordinates through a well-ordered series of jobs into increasingly higher levels of the organization; (3) *job rotation*, or moving people through a series of highly diversified and differentiated jobs in different areas; and (4) *temporary or anticipatory* assignments, in which the subordinate serves in management positions for short periods.

mentor A person who will systematically develop and promote a subordinate's abilities through intensive tutoring, coaching, and guidance.

An important aspect of on-the-job training is providing a **mentor**—an individual who will systematically develop and promote a subordinate's abilities through intensive tutoring, coaching, and guidance. Often women and minorities, still breaking into fields previously dominated by white males, are the ones most in need of mentors. Unfortunately, they also have more difficulty finding them.[24]

apprenticeship training Combining OJT and classroom instruction to learn jobs requiring long periods of study to acquire specific skills.

Apprenticeship training combines both OJT and classroom instruction to learn jobs requiring long periods of study to acquire specific skills. The method is

A worker is being trained to test computer chip boards.

used mostly in the construction trades, where those seeking to become machinists, carpenters, and plumbers learn the trade while serving as assistants to skilled workers and also by attending classes to learn the theory of the job. An effort is now being made to expand this method to nontraditional fields like finance and health care.[25]

Vestibule training is used to train large numbers of workers to use new equipment—in a hurry. Vestibule schools (or training areas) are replicas of the actual work area except that only training occurs; no actual production takes place, as in OJT. New employees learn how to do the job using machines they will later use on the job. The transition from training to producing is relatively easy.

Programmed learning, sometimes referred to as *learning machines,* involves presenting material in a sequential order on film, through printed matter, or by computer. Learners progress at their own speed until they learn the material.

Developing Managers While employee training has been done for centuries, management development came into its own only after World War II. Management development can occur either on the job, as previously discussed, and/or off the job. On-the-job management development occurs much as OJT does for other employees, except apprenticeship and vestibule training are rarely used.

vestibule training
Learning to do the job in an adjacent area using actual machines and methods used on the job.

programmed learning
Learning in which material is presented in sequential order on film, through printed matter, or on computer, so that learners can progress at their own rate.

executive development program
Generalized programs in which managers participate using case analysis, simulation, and other learning methods.

laboratory training A program in which a person learns through interacting with others in a workshop environment to be more sensitive to other people and more aware of his or her own feelings.

organization development (OD) A program that emphasizes change, growth, and development of the entire organization.

Off-the-job development usually takes place in (1) **executive development programs** at universities or other educational institutions, where managers participate in generalized programs using case analysis, simulation, and other learning methods; (2) **laboratory training,** where, in an unstructured training program, one learns to be more sensitive to other people and to become more aware of one's own feelings; and (3) **organization development (OD),** which emphasizes change, growth, and development of the entire organization.

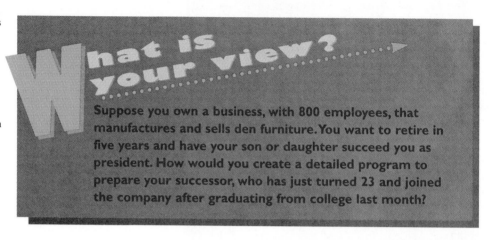

What is your view?

Suppose you own a business, with 800 employees, that manufactures and sells den furniture. You want to retire in five years and have your son or daughter succeed you as president. How would you create a detailed program to prepare your successor, who has just turned 23 and joined the company after graduating from college last month?

Role of Performance Appraisal

performance appraisal (merit rating, efficiency rating, employee appraisal) The process used by an employer to determine how effectively an employee is doing a job.

Performance appraisal (also called **merit rating, efficiency rating,** and **employee appraisal**) is the process an employer uses to determine how effectively an employee is doing the job. Figure 9.9 illustrates an effective appraisal process. Notice that employees have (1) personal qualities that lead to (2) job behaviors that

FIGURE 9.9
How performance appraisals operate.

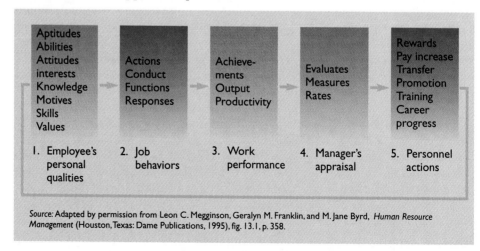

Aptitudes Abilities Attitudes interests Knowledge Motives Skills Values	Actions Conduct Functions Responses	Achieve- ments Output Productivity	Evaluates Measures Rates	Rewards Pay increase Transfer Promotion Training Career progress
1. Employee's personal qualities	2. Job behaviors	3. Work performance	4. Manager's appraisal	5. Personnel actions

Source: Adapted by permission from Leon C. Megginson, Geralyn M. Franklin, and M. Jane Byrd, *Human Resource Management* (Houston, Texas: Dame Publications, 1995), fig. 13.1, p. 358.

result in (3) work performance. Therefore, a manager needs to (4) appraise those qualities and behaviors in order to estimate performance as a basis for (5) taking some type of action. Real performance improvements do not result as much from the appraisals themselves as they do from the follow-up discussions managers have with employees to explain the evaluation and resulting personnel action.

> For example, Procter & Gamble product-marketing managers are evaluated on success in increasing unit volume and controlling costs. After the evaluation, the managers' supervisors explain to them the results of the evaluation, as well as the criteria used in making the evaluation.

Many of the more progressive companies—such as Amoco, Cigna, and Du Pont—are now using subordinates' ratings of how their bosses manage in order to make their operations less hierarchial and more competitive.[26]

As shown in Figure 9.10, the typical performance appraisal system requires a manager to rate each employee's performance according to preestablished performance criteria over a given period of time (normally six months or a year). Note the focus on ways the employee can grow and develop in his or her present position. Performance appraisal systems also provide a basis for coaching and planning progression as well as a means for determining merit increases, transfers, and dismissals. Performance appraisals must be objective and job related if they are to be accepted by the EEOC.

Compensating Employees

> *He got a fair raise; or, to be precise,*
> *Just half what he estimated*
> *He well deserved—and easily twice*
> *What the boss believed he rated.*
>
> —GEORGE S. GALBRAITH

This doggerel[27] helps explain why the question of **compensation**—that is, providing employees with a financial reward for work performed and as a motivator for future performance—is one of the most difficult and perplexing employee issues with which management has to deal. Although wages must have some logical and defensible basis from management's perspective, they involve many emotional factors from the point of view of employees.

Compensation takes two forms—wages and benefits. **Wages,** which are the monetary reward one receives for working for someone else, take the form of an hourly rate, salary, bonus, tips, and/or commission. **Salaries** are usually paid for services requiring special training or abilities, in a fixed amount, and for longer periods of time—usually a month. **Employee benefits** are a present or future benefit to supplement the cash payments or wages or salary a person is entitled to because of being an employee. They take the form of benefits such as paid holidays, vacations, insurance, and pensions, and are not based on the employee's performance.

compensation
Providing employees with a financial payment as a reward for work performed and as a motivator for future performance.

wages The monetary reward one receives for working for someone else.

salary The compensation usually paid for services requiring special training or abilities, in a fixed amount, and for longer periods—usually a month.

employee benefits A present or future benefit to supplement the cash payment or wages or salaries a person is entitled to because of being an employee.

Employee Name _Fred Willis_____   Position _Chief Engineer, Materials Research_

Period covered by evaluation: from _1/1/81_ to _7/1/81_

	(1) Unsatisfactory	(2) Meets Minimum	(3) Average	(4) Above Average	(5) Outstanding	Score
1. Quality and thoroughness of work		✓				2
2. Volume of work				✓		4
3. Knowledge of job, methods, and procedures				✓		4
4. Initiative and resourcefulness				✓		4
5. Cooperation, attitude, and teamwork			✓			3
6. Adaptability and ability to learn quickly					✓	5
7. Ability to express self clearly in speaking and writing			✓			3
8. Planning, organizing, and making work assignments		✓				2
9. Selection and development of subordinates		✓				2
10. Morale and loyalty of subordinates			✓			3

Total Score   32

What steps can this employee take to improve his work?

Employee is an eager, innovative, resourceful person whose eagerness sometimes causes him to sacrifice quality of work. While highly talented, he must learn to delegate more technical work to subordinates and assume more managerial tasks himself.

Other comments:

Employee has been in position about 7 months. This is his first managerial job and some problems in making the adjustment were expected. He is successful in meeting targeted goals and objectives.

Total score:
10–15   Unsatisfactory
16–25   Meets minimum
26–35   Average
36–45   Above average
46–50   Oustanding

Supervisor's signature _Paul Batson_____
Title _Head Engineering Research_____
Employee's signature _Frederick R. Willis_____
Approved by _Ann Walhelm_____
Title _Director, Research and Development_____

FIGURE 9.10
Sample employee evaluation form.

Role of Compensation

Compensation is very important to individual employees because it is a measure of their worth to themselves, fellow workers, families, and society. Employees' absolute level of income determines their scale of living, and their relative income indicates their status and prestige. Compensation is quite important to the organization, for the amount it pays its employees in the form of wages and benefits is usually its most important (and frequently greatest) cost item.

The government is also interested in compensation, as about 80 percent of the nation's income is derived from this source. Finally, employee income is the largest part of the purchasing power used to buy the goods and services produced by business firms.

Importance of Income Differentials

Employees usually judge the fairness of their pay by comparing it with that of other employees. Whether or not they think their income is fair will depend on how they see its value relative to that of others. Most employee dissatisfaction is over differences in pay between jobs and individuals.

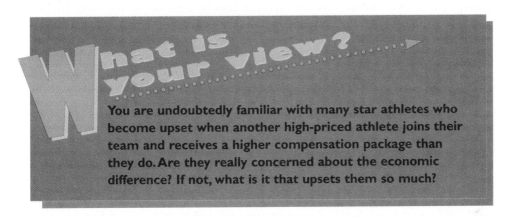

What is your view?

You are undoubtedly familiar with many star athletes who become upset when another high-priced athlete joins their team and receives a higher compensation package than they do. Are they really concerned about the economic difference? If not, what is it that upsets them so much?

Acceptable Differences   In general, employees will accept pay differences based on greater responsibility, ability, knowledge, productivity, job differences, or managerial activities. But they tend to resent differences that cannot be justified on the basis of one of these factors. For example, college professors tend to be unconcerned if they earn less than plumbers, electricians, truck drivers, or bricklayers. But they will become upset if the professor down the hall, with less experience and fewer publications, gets a larger salary increase than they do.

Unacceptable Differences   Differences in pay based on factors such as race, ethnic group, and sex are now prohibited by law and public policy, including the EEO laws discussed earlier in this chapter. In addition, the *Equal Pay Act of 1963* makes it illegal to pay women less than men for the same general type of work.

A major current compensation issue is whether comparable pay should be given for jobs of comparable worth. Compensation for comparable worth means paying employees for a given job according to points arrived at by a formula that considers the education, effort, skill, and responsibility required for the job. **Comparable worth** means going beyond paying equal salaries for equal jobs—which is required by law—as it requires equal salaries for women performing jobs that are different from but just as demanding and valuable as those performed by men.[28]

comparable worth
Paying equal salaries to women for performing jobs that are different from but as demanding and valuable as those performed by men.

How Income Is Determined

Management's compensation policies and practices are determined by the interaction of three factors: what it is *willing* to pay, what it is *required* to pay, and what it is *able* to pay.

What Management Is Willing to Pay   It is no exaggeration to say that most managers want to pay "fair" salaries. Yet managers also feel that employees should do "a fair day's work for a fair day's pay." They therefore try to improve employee performance and output, so that higher wages and salaries can be paid.

What Management Is Required to Pay   In the short run, wages and salaries are based on external pressures from governments, unions, and community and industry wage patterns.

Government Factors.   Many state and federal laws in addition to the ones already discussed deal with employee income. The best known is the *Fair Labor Standards Act of 1938*, which sets the minimum ages and wages for employees and the maximum number of hours (40) they may work per week without receiving overtime premium pay. In 1995, the minimum wage was $4.25 per hour, where it will remain until Congress raises it. Under the law, there are restrictions on when, where, and for how long workers under 18 can work.

Unions.   Unions have a great effect on wages and salaries, whether or not the employer is unionized. Through legislative lobbying, strikes, and other activities, unions tend to increase the wages of their members and others.

Community and Industry Wage Patterns.   An organization's wage and salary practices must conform to wage patterns in its community and in its industry. For example, local hospitals must pay about the same as other hospitals in order to hire nurses, and banks pay about the same for tellers. This conformity is caused by competition, as well as activities of trade associations.

Certain occupations also have relatively the same earnings. Doctors, lawyers, and other professionals tend to have fee structures that are generally the same for everyone in the profession.

What Management Is Able to Pay   Regardless of short-term wishes or pressures, in the long run, a private employer can only pay salaries based on employee output—despite other factors. There must be income before there can be wages. There must be profits for the owners if wages are to continue to be paid. *Real wages* of employees are based on employee productivity. In the last few years, salaries and wages have risen at about the same rate as the cost of living, primarily because of competition from foreign producers, who tend to pay lower wages.

How Employees Are Paid

At one time, employees were paid in cash at the end of the day on the basis of the number of hours worked or units produced. Many are still paid an *hourly wage* but receive it in a check at the end of the week. This is called *time* (or *day*) *wages*. Other employees are paid a fixed salary per week, month, or year.

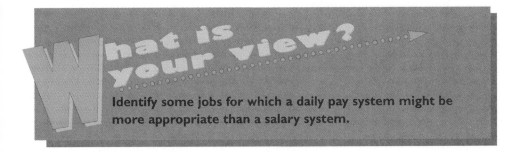

Identify some jobs for which a daily pay system might be more appropriate than a salary system.

About 25 percent of production employees and many sales representatives are also paid some form of **incentive wage,** whereby their earnings are directly related to the amount they produce or sell above a predetermined standard. For example, the people who sell refreshments at sports events are paid according to the number of units they sell. Automobile and real estate salespersons receive a percentage of their sales as a commission. Food service personnel receive tips, and some sales reps get a bonus for meeting a quota.

Many firms have a **profit-sharing plan** under which employees receive a definite, prearranged percentage of the firm's profits as extra income. According to the American Productivity Center in Houston, this method was used by 32 percent of a group of 1,600 firms surveyed in the mid-1980s.[29]

Growing Importance of Employee Benefits

One of the fastest-growing segments of compensation is the amount spent on *employee benefits* above and beyond basic salary. Originally called "fringe benefits," these now cost over a third of an organization's payroll. Some of these are *legally* required, while others are *voluntarily* granted by employers.

Legally Required Benefits   Chief among those legally required benefits is **social security,** a federal government–sponsored program that provides for retirement pay, disability pay, and survivors' benefits. These benefits come out of a fund paid into by employees, employers, and self-employed persons. **Unemployment compensation,** which is financed by a tax on employers, provides some financial support to employees who are laid off for reasons they cannot control. **Workers' compensation,** which is also financed by employers, provides financial support to employees for work-related illness or injuries.

A relatively new required program was mandated by the *Family and Medical Leave Act of 1993 (FMLA).* The FMLA requires employers with 50 or more employees working within a 75–mile radius to offer employees up to 12 weeks of unpaid leave during a 12–month period for (1) birth of a child; (2) placement of a child for adoption or foster care; (3) care for a spouse, child, or parent with a serious health condition; and (4) the employee's serious health condition. Employees with less than one year of service or those who have worked less than 1,250 hours in the past year may be excluded. Certain other restrictions apply.[30]

An employee who takes leave under the FMLA must be returned to either the same or a comparable position at the end of the leave. In addition, employers must continue health care coverage while the employee is on leave. If the employee fails to return to work for reasons other than a serious health condition, the employer

incentive wage Wages directly related to the amount an employee produces or sells above a predetermined standard amount.

profit-sharing plan A plan whereby employees receive a definite, prearranged percentage of the firm's profits as extra income.

social security A federal government–sponsored program that provides for retirement pay, disability pay, and survivors' benefits.

unemployment compensation A program that provides some financial support to employees who are laid off for reasons they cannot control.

workers' compensation A program that provides financial support to employees suffering a work-related illness or injury.

TABLE 9.2   SOME OF THE MOST POPULAR EMPLOYEE BENEFITS

LEGALLY REQUIRED

Social security/Medicare	Workers' compensation
Unemployment insurance	Family and medical leave

VOLUNTARY, PRIVATE

Health and accident insurance	Life and disability insurance	Sick leave	Income maintenance	Pay for time not worked
Eye care and eyeglasses	Accidental death and dismemberment	Includes maternity leave	Severance pay	Holidays
Chiropractic care	Group term life insurance		Supplemental unemployment benefits (SUBs)	Personal time
Dental and orthodontic care	Long-term disability		Pensions	Sabbatical leaves
Health maintenance—diagnostic visits/physical exams				Union activities
Major medical/hospitalization				Vacations
Psychiatric and mental care				
Accident and health insurance				

Employee services and others

Alcohol and drug rehabilitation	Legal assistance
Auto insurance	Liability coverage
Child care and day care centers for other family members	Matching gifts to charitable organizations or schools
Christmas bonuses	Matching payroll deductions and savings plans
Clothing and uniforms	Moving and transfer allowances
Company car	Personal counseling and financial advice
Credit unions	Recreation center
Discount privileges on organization's products or services	Service awards
Loans and financial assistance	Stock purchase and profit-sharing plans
Food services and cafeteria	Transportation and parking
Group tours and charter flights	Tuition for employee and/or family members
Gymnasium and physical training center	

Sources: Various government and private publications.

may recover from the employee the premium paid for the health insurance coverage during the leave.

Voluntary Benefit Programs   There are also many *voluntary benefit* programs, and they take many forms, as shown in Table 9.2. The most popular ones include pay for time not worked—such as holidays, personal time off, and sick leave—pay for overtime and special activities, retirement pay, company-financed health and life insurance, legal services, dental services or insurance, educational benefits, and discounts on purchases of goods and services. An increasingly popular program is on-site childcare centers.[31] Also, provision is now being made for elder care. Management feels that these voluntary benefits are essential for attracting and retaining employees.

Maintaining Employee Health and Safety

An increasingly important activity for human resource managers is maintaining employee health and safety. For example, there were 3,000 on-the-job deaths reported to the Occupational Safety and Health Administration (OSHA) during a recent year.[32] And each year, on the average, 2.4 million workers are seriously injured, at a cost of over $12 billion in lost wages, reduced output, and other losses.[33]

While business is doing much to improve this situation, the *Occupational Safety and Health Act of 1970* quickened the pace by establishing a regulatory agency, the **Occupational Safety and Health Administration (OSHA),** to establish and enforce safety standards. The law has forced employers and employees to provide even safer and more healthful working conditions and to be more responsible for these activities.

OSHA (1) develops standards, (2) conducts inspections to see that standards are being met, and (3) enforces standards by issuing citations and imposing penalties for violations. Its inspectors are now concentrating on those industries with the highest accident rates.

Occupational Safety and Health Administration (OSHA) Federal agency that sets and enforces safety and health standards.

Handling Industrial Relations

Although there were unions in the United States before the American Revolution, they have become major power blocks only in the last 60 years or so. Directly or indirectly, managerial decisions in almost all organizations are now influenced by the effect of unions. Managers in unionized organizations must operate through the union in dealing with their employees instead of acting alone. Decisions affecting employees are made collectively at the bargaining tables and through arbitration, instead of individually by the supervisor when and where the need arises. Wages, hours, and other terms and conditions of employment are largely decided outside of management's sphere of discretion.

Legal Bases of Industrial Relations

The basic U.S. labor law is the *National Labor Relations Act (NLRA)*—commonly called the *Wagner Act*—passed in 1935, which protects employees' rights to engage in union activities. It is difficult to condense the provisions of the NLRA into a few statements. But it essentially does three things: (1) permits workers to form or join unions of their own choosing without fear of prosecution under the antitrust laws, (2) limits the rights and discretion of management by having working conditions determined bilaterally at the bargaining table rather than unilaterally at the place of occurrence, and (3) limits the rights of unions to illegally interfere with employees and employers in the exercise of their rights. The law is administered by the **National Labor Relations Board (NLRB).**

National Labor Relations Board (NLRB) The principal agency that enforces the federal laws dealing with industrial relations.

The NLRA has been amended by the *Labor-Management Relations Act (LMRA)*—also called the *Taft-Hartley Act*—passed in 1947 and by the *Labor Management Reporting and Disclosure Act (LMRDA)*—or the *Landrum-Griffin Act*—passed in 1959. *Title VII of the Civil Service Reform Act (CSRA)*, passed in 1978, gives federal employees protection similar to that provided by the NLRA, as amended. State laws are also in existence to cover state and municipal employees.

Union Objectives

The main reason unions are needed is that it is difficult for individual workers to influence decisions of the large groups, such as large companies and governments, that affect them. Therefore, workers must act as groups, not as individuals.

Unions have consistently had four practical objectives for their members: (1) higher pay; (2) shorter hours of work per day, week, or year; (3) improved physical, social, and psychological working conditions; and (4) improved personal and job security. In order to meet this last goal, unions usually oppose mechanization and automation if they threaten the job security of their members. There are times, though, when not to automate may cause an employer to go bankrupt. Then a compromise must be worked out.

> For example, the machinist union recently ratified an agreement with Pratt & Whitney and the state of Connecticut that avoids plant closings and saved 2,300 jobs through productivity improvements and tax incentives.[34]

How do unions accomplish their objectives? The usual methods are (1) collective bargaining; (2) processing of grievances, conciliation, mediation, and arbitration; (3) strikes and the threat of strike; and (4) boycotts.

Changing Union Membership

For some time now, union membership has been declining, although slowly. In 1935, there were 3.5 million union members; by the end of 1980, there were 22.3 million members; and by the end of 1992, the figure was estimated to be slightly over 16.4 million.[35]

Although the number of union members is still quite large and is a potent economic and political force, the percentage of all employees who are union members has declined over the last five decades. The figure grew from about 12 percent in 1930 to around 35.5 percent by 1945. Yet by 1995, only 15.5 percent of the total labor force were union members, and unions represented only about 10 percent of the private sector labor force.[36]

Union leaders are now varying their organizing efforts in order to cope with changes in the workforce discussed earlier. They are expanding their organizing budgets and efforts to attract (1) public employees, such as police and firefighters; (2) professionals, such as teachers, medical personnel, athletes, dentists, and lawyers; (3) persons in the service industries; (4) agricultural workers; (5) white-collar employees; (6) women; (7) minorities; and (8) young workers. In fact, the main source of union growth since the 1960s has been public employees. As a result, nearly 37 percent of all public employees are unionized.[37]

Growing Labor-Management Cooperation

A hopeful trend seems to be developing in industrial relations. Negotiations and relationships between the parties are being modified because of fundamental changes in our economy. New problems and pressures on management—such as greater domestic and foreign competition, structural and technological changes, judicial decisions, deregulation, spiraling health care costs, and changing political necessities and social values—are requiring managers to reevaluate concessions formerly made to unions. Unions, in turn, are losing some of their economic and political clout, and their members are becoming more educated and sophisticated; thus, union leaders are having to make more concessions in order not to lose more jobs—and members.

What we are seeing is that both union leaders and managers are being pressured to work with each other in order to preserve jobs and increase productivity.

The entry of a union into an organization affects HRM in many ways. It starts a series of emotional, economic, and procedural events that change the way management operates. The first thing managers should do is to improve all aspects of the HRM function—especially listening to employees to see what their gripes are, and then doing something to correct those complaints.

S U M M A R Y

While effective employees are needed if an organization is to succeed, a productive work group does not just happen. Instead, human resource management is essential to achieve successful performance in organizations.

Management must plan for its human resource needs. It must decide how many workers of each type are needed and where they can be recruited. In general, workers for new jobs and those in the lower levels are recruited from outside the organization. Higher-level jobs are filled by upgrading, transferring, or promoting present employees. The skills required to perform future jobs will generally involve math and language areas to a greater extent than today.

Individual employers must compete with others for new employees; new employees are, after all, a scarce resource. Therefore, managers need to study the national labor market to see what the overall supply and demand picture looks like. In general, the newer jobs are in the service-performing industries rather than the goods-producing ones. In fact, around 75 percent of all workers now perform services, while only about 25 percent produce goods.

Another trend is the increasing number of workers who were previously not employed in the better jobs. The modern workforce has more women, especially as high-level managers, and minorities. During this decade, nearly 90 percent of workforce growth will come from women and minorities.

Employers must now have well-defined action programs to actively recruit minorities, women, veterans, the disabled, and older persons. The most common forms of recruiting are advertising, college recruiting, and employee referrals.

The usual procedure for selecting employees involves some combination of preliminary screening or interviewing, studying past performance, testing, in-depth interviewing, and checking references. Finally, a personal value judgment must be made as to whether or not to hire the candidate.

Both new and old employees should be trained and developed. Otherwise, the organization pays a high price in the form of poor performance, complaints and grievances, absenteeism, and labor turnover. Performance appraisal is useful in deciding who needs training, who will be promoted, and how much an employee will be paid.

Employee compensation is quite significant to employees, employers, and the nation. Management should try to set its wage rate high enough to attract capable employees, yet low enough to allow the price of the firm's product to be competitive. Also, the owners must make a profit.

The health and safety of employees are now requiring much of management's time, effort, and money. While union membership is declining, handling industrial relations is very important to both management and employees. The trend is away from conflict and toward greater accommodation and cooperative relationships.

KEY TERMS

human resource management (HRM), 287
equal employment opportunity (EEO) laws, 292
affirmative action program (AAP), 293
disabled person, 295
Equal Employment Opportunity Commission (EEOC), 295
Office of Federal Contract Compliance Programs (OFCCP), 295
human resource planning, 297
job analysis, 297
job descriptions, 297
job specifications, 297
upgrading, 299
transferring, 299
promoting, 299
temporaries, 300
recruitment, 301
employee referrals, 301

selection, 302
assessment center, 306
training, 307
development, 307
on-the-job training (OJT), 308
mentor, 308
apprenticeship training, 308
vestibule training, 309
programmed learning, 309
executive development programs, 310
laboratory training, 310
organization development (OD), 310
performance appraisal (merit rating, efficiency rating, employee appraisal), 310
compensation, 311
wages, 311
salary, 311
employee benefits, 311
comparable worth, 313

incentive wage, 315
profit-sharing plan, 315
social security, 315
unemployment compensation, 315
workers' compensation, 315

Occupational Safety and Health
Administration (OSHA), 317
National Labor Relations Board
(NLRB), 318

D I S C U S S I O N   Q U E S T I O N S

1. Is human resource management (HRM) really as important as the authors claim? Explain.

2. (a) What are some of the laws providing for equal employment opportunity? (b) What employers are covered by each? (c) What protection does each provide, and for whom is it provided?

3. What is an AAP? Explain.

4. What is human resource planning, and why is it so important to management?

5. (a) What are the most important internal sources of supply of employees? Explain. (b) What are the most important external sources of supply?

6. Explain what types of jobs will provide an increasing number of employees during this decade.

7. (a) What is recruitment? (b) What are some of the methods used to recruit personnel?

8. (a) What is selection? (b) What are the usual steps in the selection procedure?

9. (a) Why are employee training and development so important? (b) What are some of the more popular ways of developing managers? Explain.

10. (a) Why is performance appraisal so important? (b) How is it done?

11. (a) What are some acceptable income differentials? (b) Unacceptable? (c) What is being done to remove the unacceptable ones?

12. What three factors help determine management's compensation policies and practices? Explain.

13. Why are employee health and safety such important issues?

14. At many companies, employees are counseled to "avoid the personnel department" if they really want a promotion or lateral transfer. Why do you think this happens?

PRACTICING MANAGEMENT

9.1 case   Underutilizing a National Resource

Robert Musser, a human resource professional with 25 years of experience, lost his job with Microdot in June 1989 as a result of a plant closing. Since that time, he has been diligently searching for another human resource position—including submitting numerous applications to many firms—without success. In the meantime, he has been working part-time as a consultant. He belongs to a peer group of unemployed human resource professionals, all in their fifties, who provide emotional support for one another. One of the authors asked him if he thought he had been discriminated against in his job search. He stated that as a result of so little response to his job applications, he had streamlined his résumé by deleting some of his earlier jobs and listing only the last 13 years of work experience with Microdot. Shortly thereafter, he received four interviews with different companies. However, once they observed his gray hair, they began probing his earlier work experience. Mr. Musser did not get a job offer as a result of any of these interviews, which, he felt, supported the thesis that some companies are very reluctant to hire professionals beyond a certain age. But he says he is a survivor and will continue his job search, confident that he will obtain a job in his field.

He also believes that women are hired in preference to experienced males because they are willing to accept less money. He based this theory on the fact that when he first joined the Detroit Personnel Association, 23 years ago, there were 250 members, only 8 of whom were women. Today, there are 650 members and 65 percent of them are women.

In no way is Mr. Musser indicating that women and younger people should not be hired. Instead, he is saying that companies are overlooking a national, viable, rich resource by not hiring older, experienced professionals who not only are more sensitive to the daily challenge of the human-resource function but, in view of their experience, are less likely to commit mistakes that could lead to costly litigation.

Source: Conversations and correspondence with Mr. Robert Musser, Fenton, Michigan.

Questions

1. From the information presented, do you think employers are discriminating against Mr. Musser? Why or why not?

2. What consideration should an employer give to a professional's 25 years of experience?

3. Can an employer legally refuse to hire Mr. Musser because of his age? Explain.

4. What would you do now if you were Mr. Musser? Explain your answer.

9.1 learning exercise   Whom Do You Promote?

Suppose that your company recently developed a plan to identify and train top hourly employees for promotion to a first-line supervisory position. As a part of this program, your boss has requested a ranking of the six hourly workers who report to you with respect to their promotion potential. Given their biographical data, rank them in the order in which you would select them for promotion to first-line supervisor; that is, the person ranked no. 1 would be first in line for promotion.

Biographical Data

1. Sam Nelson—white male, age 45, married, with four children. Sam has been with the company for five years, and his performance evaluations have been average to above average. He is well liked by the other employees in the department. He devotes his spare time to farming and plans to farm after retirement.

2. Ruth Hornsby—white female, age 32, married, with no children; husband has a management-level job with the power company. Ruth has been with the company for two years and has received above-average performance evaluations. She is very quiet and keeps to herself at work. She says she is working to save for a down payment on a new house.

3. Joe Washington—black male, age 26, single. Joe has been with the company for three years and has received high performance evaluations. He is always willing to take on new assignments and to work overtime. He is attending college in the evenings and someday wants to start his own business. He is well liked by the other employees in the department.

4. Ronald Smith—white male, age 35, recently divorced, with one child, age 4. Ronald has received excellent performance evaluations during his two years with the company. He seems to like his present job but has removed himself from the line of progression. He seems to have personality conflicts with some of the employees.

5. Betty Norris—black female, age 44, married, with one grown child. Betty has been with the company for ten years and is well liked by fellow employees. Her performance evaluations have been average to below average, and her advancement has been limited by a lack of formal education. She has participated in a number of technical training programs conducted by the company.

6. Roy Davis—white male, age 36, married, with two teenage children. Roy has been with the company for ten years and received excellent performance evaluations until last year. His most recent evaluation was average. He is friendly and well liked by his fellow employees. One of his children has had a serious illness for over a year, resulting in a number of large medical expenses. Roy is working a second job on weekends to help with these expenses. He has expressed a serious interest in promotion to first-line supervisor.

Source: This exercise was prepared by Carl C. Moore, University of South Alabama, for Donald C. Mosley, Leon C. Megginson, and Paul H. Pietri, Jr., *Supervisory Management: The Art of Empowering and Developing People*, 3rd ed. (Cincinnati: South-Western Publishing, 1993), pp. 90–92. Produced with the permission of South-Western Publishing Co. Copyright 1993 by South-Western Publishing Co. All rights reserved.

Questions

1. What factors did you consider in developing your rankings? (It should be pointed out that the supervisor's rankings will reflect what top management really wants. Therefore, in ranking people for a job, you must know what management wants the person in that job to do.)

2. What was the most important factor you considered?

3. What information in the biographical data, if any, should not be considered in developing the rankings?

PART 3

Leading and Developing People in Organizations

As shown in Part Two, success in management comes from effective planning and decision making, choosing capable people, assigning them definite work to do, granting them adequate authority, and holding them responsible for the use of that authority. Yet an organization and its plans will be ineffective until the leadership function is performed. This function sets the organization in motion, giving it life and meaning.

While human resources are an organization's most precious asset, leading those resources is the very heart of management.

From a practical point of view, leading involves communicating and motivating employees, exercising leadership, managing change and conflict, and having employees work effectively as members of a team. Communicating with people is covered in Chapter 10; motivating employees is discussed in Chapter 11; the various aspects of managerial leadership are examined in Chapter 12; managing change and conflict is addressed in Chapter 13; and team development is the focus of Chapter 14.

> Any use of human beings in which less is demanded of them and less is attributed to them than their full status is a degradation and a waste.
> —NORBERT WIENER

Communicating *for* Results

> *Meanings are not in words, but in us.*
> —SENATOR S. I. HAYAKAWA

LEARNING OBJECTIVES

After studying the material in this chapter, you should be able to:

- **Recognize** the important role communication plays in practicing management.
- **Identify** the four basic flows of formal organizational communication.
- **State** the purpose served by informal communication.
- **Describe** the major elements in a communication model.
- **Describe** the main types of nonverbal communication.
- **Explain** some of the new technological developments that permit managers to communicate electronically.
- **Show** how certain organizational and interpersonal factors act as barriers to effective communication.
- **Discuss** how feedback and effective listening help communication effectiveness.

Getting Communications
On-Line at Whirlpool

Whirlpool Management Journal (WMJ) is a 44- to 60-page bimonthly published by Whirlpool's corporate communications department. It's a far cry from the typical in-house company magazine for managers, and by design. According to Bruce Berger, Whirlpool's vice-president for corporate affairs and editor of *WMJ*, when Whirlpool embarked on its mission to restructure itself and strive to become the global appliance leader, its communications programs required a major overhaul. Communication channels needed to be opened up and shifted from top-down toward upward and horizontal flows. The company's older communications programs just weren't up to the task.

Berger headed up a five-person team from inside and outside the company whose job it was to begin work on the new, multidimensional communication effort. The team did extensive research, including studies of Malcolm Baldridge Award winners Federal Express, AT&T, Xerox, and others. Other data-gathering approaches included employee surveys, in-depth interviews, and focus group meetings. The notable finding was that Whirlpool's formal communications just weren't on track.

Large-scale changes have been made in *WMJ*, which is directed toward company personnel. Gone are the extensive use of full-color graphics and pictures, cheerleading by top managers, and coverage of company events. Today's *WMJ*:

▶ Encourages managers to think critically about business issues such as quality, globalization, and diversity

▶ Encourages in its "Point of View" section formal debate on company policies and procedures

▶ Interviews government and industry leaders on current issues and philosophies

▶ Discloses results of opinion surveys of Whirlpool managers

▶ Has outside contributors, such as Edwin Newman, take aim at corporate doublespeak and language abuses

▶ Describes candid customer service stories, both successful and unsuccessful

Vision, an employee-aimed publication, was strictly a top-down vehicle; only 20 percent of employees rated it as valuable and believable. Today's *Vision*, completely overhauled, is managed and content-directed by the 20,000 manufacturing employees who make up its readership.

Written media, as reflected by *WMJ* and *Vision*, are but one phase of the new Whirlpool communication approach. The company has also made significant progress in face-to-face training modules for Whirlpool's global communications and progress in developing specific communication accountabilities for all managers. As Berger states, though, "This is not something we ever imagined could be accomplished in one year, three years, or even five. We still have a long way to go."[1]

A s this case illustrates, communication plays an integral role in organizational effectiveness. When communication is effective, it tends to encourage better individual and organizational performance and to result in higher job satisfaction. But communicating effectively cannot be left to chance, as poor communication is a problem that plagues all organizations and individual managers.[2] In this chapter, you will gain a better perspective on the communication process and on actions managers and organizations can take to communicate more effectively.

What Is Communication?

The term *communication* is relatively new to organizations. *Communication* itself was not an important part of management's vocabulary until the late 1940s and early 1950s. But as organizations became more "people conscious" with the beginning of the behavioral approach to management (see Chapter 2), communication became one of management's chief concerns, as shown in an interview of Jack Welch, CEO of General Electric, for the *Harvard Business Review*. When asked, "What makes a good manager?" Welch responded largely in terms of managers' communication practices: "They go up, down, and around their organization to reach people . . . countless hours of eyeball to eyeball, back and forth. . . . It's not pronouncements on a videotape; it's not announcements in a newspaper. It is human beings coming to see and accept things through a constant interactive process."[3]

Communication is the process of transferring meaning from one person to another in the form of ideas or information. It uses the chain of understanding that links the members of various units of an organization at different levels and in different areas. An effective interchange involves more than just the transmission of data. It requires that the sender and receiver use certain skills—speaking, writing, listening, reading—to make the exchange of meaning successful. In spoken conversation, a true interchange of meaning encompasses shades of emphasis, facial expressions, vocal inflections, and all the unintended and involuntary gestures that suggest real meaning.

communication The process of transferring meaning from one person to another in the form of ideas or information.

A large part of the typical manager's time is spent in some form of communication—reading, listening, writing, or speaking. It has been estimated that around 80 percent of a manager's time is spent in verbal communication.[4] Despite its importance, though, there is much evidence that communication is not handled effectively in organizations.

> Of the 30,000 managers, professionals, and clerical personnel surveyed by Opinion Research Corporation over a four-year period, 60 percent felt that their organizations were not doing a good job of keeping them informed about company matters. Moreover, fewer than 30 percent felt that their companies were willing to listen to their problems.[5]

Formal Communication Channels in an Organization

You can better understand organizational communication if you examine the basic directions in which it moves. **Formal communication channels** are the prescribed means by which messages flow inside an organization. The three basic channels are downward, upward, and lateral or horizontal.

formal communication channels The prescribed means by which messages flow inside an organization.

Downward Communication

downward communication Communication that follows the organization's normal chain of command from top to bottom.

Communication that follows the organization's formal chain of command from top to bottom is called **downward communication**. It tends to follow and reflect the authority-responsibility relationships shown in the organization chart. Some examples of downward communication are

1. Information related to policies, rules, procedures, objectives, and other types of plans
2. Work assignments and directives
3. Feedback about performance
4. General information about the organization, such as its progress or status
5. Specific requests for information from lower levels

What specifically do employees want to know from their managers in the form of downward communication? Research by the Hay Group for Management Database found that they wanted to know about pay and benefit programs, the company's plans for the future, how to improve performance, and how their work fits into the total picture.[6]

Downward messages may be either written or oral. They are typically provided by the immediate supervisor or other manager; employee booklets or handbooks; bulletin boards; memos, reports, or other documents; conferences, meetings, and speeches; and in small groups or person to person. Top management traditionally concentrates most of its communication effort on downward communication.

Research indicates that employees rate their supervisors as the preferred source of communication.

But even CEOs and top managers can get into the act on a large-scale basis, given the advanced state of electronic communication:

> Four Sundays a year, Home Depot's CEO, Bernard Marcus, and its president, Arthur Block, don their orange aprons and stage the "Breakfast with Bernie and Arthur" show. The 6:30 A.M. pep rally/revival program is broadcast live over Home Depot's closed-circuit television network to most of the company's 45,000 employees.[7]

A study of over 10,000 U.S. and Canadian employees was made by the consulting firm of Towers, Perrin, Foster & Crosby to determine the actual sources from which employees received communications about organizational matters and the sources they preferred. Supervisors were rated tops as both actual and preferred sources of information by 92 percent of the respondents. This result was similar to the 91 percent of AT&T employees at one location who also identified their immediate bosses as their preferred source for information.[8]

Upward Communication

Feedback of data or information from lower levels to upper-management levels is called **upward communication**. It includes

1. Performance-related reports indicating results, progress, or problems
2. Requests for assistance, information, or resources
3. Expression of attitudes, feelings, and gripes that influence performance directly and indirectly
4. Ideas and suggestions for improvements and problem solving

> **upward communication** Communication that is feedback of data or information from lower levels to upper-management levels.

Suggestion systems are an excellent source of upward communication. In a study of 900 organizations, the National Association of Suggestion Systems found that $160 million had been paid to employees for adopted suggestions that had saved their companies $2.2 billion,[9] and it is estimated that since the late 1980s, Toyota Motors has averaged almost 50 formal ideas/suggestions per employee yearly, with over 90 percent of these adopted by management.[10] Since the cornerstone of total quality management programs (Chapter 14) is employee involvement, upward communication has become more important in today's organizational setting, as pointed out in the case of Whirlpool at the opening of this chapter.

Lateral or Horizontal Communication

Lateral or **horizontal communication** includes the following:

1. Communication among peers within the same work group
2. Communication between and among departments on the same organizational level

> **lateral (horizontal) communication** Communication that is coordinative in nature and involves peers within the same work group and departments on the same organizational level.

This form of communication is essentially coordinative or problem-solving in nature and results from the concept of organizational *specialization*. That is, if you are to function effectively in your own job, you will most likely need to interact with and be dependent on other organizational units. Moreover, organizations today seek to use the abilities of specialists by creating special project teams, task forces (recall the matrix form of organization discussed in Chapter 8), or committees that pull together representatives from various specialties. Communication helps coordinate these lateral activities.

> At Motorola, cross-functional teams have helped reduce from three or four years to 18 months the time needed to open in Austin, Texas, one of the most sophisticated microchip plants in the world. Lateral communication was critical to this effort.[11]

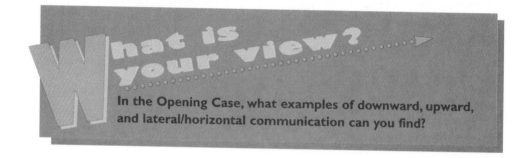

What is your view?

In the Opening Case, what examples of downward, upward, and lateral/horizontal communication can you find?

Role of Informal Communication

informal communication Communication flows that travel along channels other than those formally designed by the organization.

Informal communication, which is communication other than through formal channels, is also an important part of an organization's communication flow.

Informal communication serves a variety of purposes, including:

1. Satisfying personal needs, such as the need for relationships with others
2. Countering the effects of boredom or monotony
3. Attempting to influence the behavior of others
4. Providing a source of job-related information that is not available through formal channels

grapevine The best-known type of informal communication within an organization, the grapevine involves transmission of information by word of mouth without regard for organizational levels.

The best-known type of informal communication is referred to as the **grapevine,** which involves transmission of information by word of mouth without regard for organizational levels, and, like its namesake, is twisted, tangled, and hard to follow. Yet research has demonstrated that communication grapevines function rapidly, selectively, and effectively. The previously mentioned study of U.S. and Canadian employees ranked the grapevine as the second major source of information.[12]

We tend to think of the grapevine as being inaccurate. Yet research on grapevine activity shows that "in normal work situations well over three-fourths of grapevine information is accurate."[13] Moreover, it is often perceived by employees as more credible than information passed through formal channels.[14]

> A study by *CPA/Administrative Reports* tends to corroborate these findings. It found the office grapevine to be 75 to 95 percent accurate, providing managers and staff with better information than formal communications. This medium is also being

used more extensively because corporate restructuring and takeovers are making people more nervous—and therefore more receptive to rumors.[15]

How the Communication Process Operates

People, not organizations, communicate. An organization's communication system therefore reflects a variety of individuals with different backgrounds, education levels, beliefs, cultures, moods, and needs. When individuals in an organization communicate, what exactly takes place? Let us examine a basic communication model so that we will be better able to understand why communication fails so frequently and what actions managers can take to improve their communication effectiveness.

Many different models of communication exist, depending on the context of communication involved. We will concentrate on the interpersonal communication model shown in Figure 10.1. This model illustrates the six most important elements involved in communication between and among organization members:

1. The source of the communication message
2. Encoding the message
3. Transmitting the message
4. Receiving the message
5. Decoding the message
6. Sending feedback to the source

Later in the chapter, we will discuss how communication barriers affect various stages of the communication model.

FIGURE 10.1
Steps in the communication process.

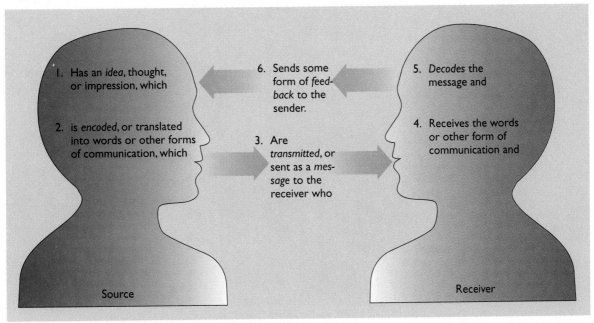

The Source: Steps 1–3

The *source*, or originator of the message, takes the first step in the communication process. The source controls the type of message sent, the form in which it is sent, and frequently the channel through which it passes. The intended communication is based on satisfying some need in which someone else (a receiver) plays some role. Some event stimulates the need for transmitting ideas, information, or feelings to someone else. The stimulation creates a desire to communicate and helps provide a need or purpose for the communication, whether it reflects a need to provide information, to offer advice, to solicit an opinion, to create a given impression, or to take a given action.

The second step—*encoding*—involves choosing some verbal or nonverbal communication that is capable of transferring meaning, such as spoken or written words, gestures, or actions.

One must think not only of what is going to be communicated but also of *how* it will be presented to have the desired effect on the receiver. Thus, the message must be adapted to the level of understanding, interest, *and* needs of the receiver to achieve the desired consequences. It is also important, however, to consider possible unintended consequences and to present the message so that these are minimized or avoided. That is, effective managers need to understand human nature and develop sensitivity not only to the meaning of words but also the effects those words might have on others.

Encoding is sometimes done by someone other than the original sender. For example, a secretary may write down a phone message to present to the receiver. In such a case, the intermediary becomes another receiver through whom the message is filtered, and the sender must be even more careful to make the message clear.

Written communications are often transmitted to employees through bulletin boards.

TABLE 10.1   ADVANTAGES OF ORAL AND WRITTEN MESSAGES

Oral	Written
1. Allows nonverbal communication—tone of voice, inflection, body language	1. Provides a record
2. Is transmitted rapidly	2. Allows greater attention to organization and wording of message
3. Lends itself to more immediate feedback—questions, clarifications	3. Enables receiver to interpret at own pace

The third step—*transmitting*, or sending the communication from the source to the receiver—reflects the communicator's choice of medium or *distribution channel.* Oral communication may be transmitted thorough many channels—in person, by telephone, by audio- or videotape. It may take place privately or in a group setting. In fact, one of the most important decisions the source has to make is determining the appropriate channel for transmitting a given message.

Table 10.1 shows that, in addition to its speed, a fundamental advantage of oral, person-to-person communication is the opportunity for interaction between source and receiver. A main disadvantage is lack of permanence: There is no record, except in some more modern instances, such as tapes.

Written communication may be transmitted by means such as memos, letters, reports, notes, bulletin boards, company manuals, and newsletters. Written communication has the advantage of providing a record for future reference, but the major disadvantage is that it does not allow spontaneous, face-to-face feedback.

Some companies are now encouraging the use of electronic mail (E-mail) to reduce the level of paper communications. Additionally, E-mail has made written messages easier to send and has facilitated more spontaneous feedback.

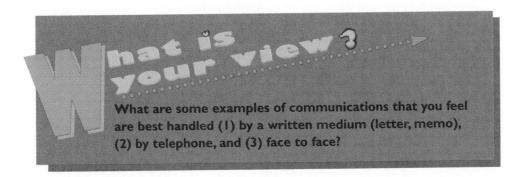

What are some examples of communications that you feel are best handled (1) by a written medium (letter, memo), (2) by telephone, and (3) face to face?

The Receiver: Steps 4–6

The fourth step is *receiving* the message. People receive messages through their five senses—sight, hearing, taste, touch, and smell. Full transmission has not occurred unless a party actually *receives* a message. Many important attempts at communication have failed because the message never got to its intended receiver.

The fifth step of the communication process is *decoding*, which involves providing meaning to the message by the receiver or his or her representative. This meaning is a product of such variables as the receiver's heritage, culture, education, environment, prejudices, and biases, as well as distractions in the surroundings. There is always the possibility that the source's message, when decoded by the receiver, will yield a meaning far different from the one the sender intended. The receiver thus shares a large responsibility for communication effectiveness, for *communication is a two-way street*. Managers and subordinates may occupy both source and receiver roles throughout an interaction.

feedback The responses the receiver gives by further communicating with the original sender.

Step 6 of the process is **feedback**—the responses the receiver gives by further communicating with the sender. Communication is thus a continuous and perpetual process. A person communicates, the receiver responds by further communicating with the original sender or another person, and so forth.

Management might distribute a policy bulletin to a group of supervisors, but until there is a response in the form of questions, agreement, comment, or behavior, or until there has been a check to see whether the policy is being followed, management does not know how effective the statement has been.

Communication is an *exchange*. If it is to be successful, information must flow *back and forth*, from sender to receiver and back again, or at least the sender must have some knowledge of the receiver's reaction. Although the term *feedback* may be new, its importance is not.

Role of Nonverbal Communication

Nonverbal communication plays an important role in the communication process. Nonverbal communication is not limited to face-to-face messages, either. A written message communicates by its appearance—whether it is neatly typed or scrawled by hand, on cheap or expensive paper, letterhead or plain, printed by a laser printer or a cheap dot matrix, and so on.

nonverbal communication Transmission of meaning without the use of words.

Nonverbal communication, or the transmission of meaning without the use of words, frequently carries more weight in a message outcome than verbal communication. Facial expressions, clothes, posture, tone of voice, or body movements may loudly or subtly communicate messages. In fact, nonverbal messages cannot be as readily disguised or controlled as verbal ones, and often contradict verbal messages.

A classic study found that as much as 55 percent of the content of a message is transmitted by body posture and facial expression; around 38 percent is derived from inflection and tone of voice; and *only 7 percent of the meaning is derived from the words themselves.*[16]

William Gould, a partner of Gould & McCoy Inc., a New York executive search firm, recommends that new corporate leaders spend their first few months being visible but quiet, and doing a lot of listening. They can declare their leadership by their manner, tone, and meaningful gestures.

Nonverbal communication plays a particularly important role in interactions with people from other cultures. Tips 10.1 illustrates the importance of nonverbal communication between and among persons from Western and Asian cultures.

ipS 10.1

Communicating in Asia

A common problem cited by many Western businesspeople is communicating effectively with their business counterparts in Japan, the Philippines, Hong Kong, Singapore, Taiwan, and other Pacific Rim countries. Here are some—mostly nonverbal—tips that will help Western businesspeople visiting Asia.

1. *Dress conservatively.* Throughout Asia, the traditional uniform is business suits for men and plain dresses for women. Women should definitely avoid pantsuits. In Japan, shoes are commonly removed when you visit someone's home or dine out. Thus, make sure your socks are in good shape.

2. *Avoid physical contact.* In Europe, you may not blow a deal by slapping a potential foreign partner on the back, but in Asia, you are asking for trouble. Most Asians feel uncomfortable with other than minimal physical contact. Definitely do not pat an Asian's head, as the head is viewed as the dwelling place of the soul. Moreover, since feet are seen as the lowliest part of the body, do not cross your legs while sitting, because exposing or pointing your shoe sole at an Asian is a social faux pas.

3. *Follow certain conventions when greeting people.* Ordinarily, a simple nod and handshake suffice. Bowing at the waist is appreciated but not expected of foreigners. Stick to surnames and titles. An exchange of business cards at a first encounter is essential; try to have your name, company, and title printed in the local language. Use both hands to present and receive cards. Above all, pay close and obvious attention to the card upon receiving it, rather than immediately pocketing it.

4. *Gift giving is commonplace, but be careful.* In Japan, err on the side of something more expensive. But outside Japan, giving something too personal or expensive puts pressure on your counterpart to respond in kind. Learn the culture of the country. In China,

for example, white carnations suggest mourning; clocks are associated with dying. Use both hands when presenting and receiving gifts. Do not open your gift in the giver's presence; it is the thought that counts.

5. *Be prepared for male chauvinism.* Chauvinism is a way of life in Asian business, more so than in the West. While much is unintentional, attempts to overcome it may make your Asian counterparts uncomfortable. When negotiating with the Japanese, one U.S. female executive was surprised to see all questions directed to her less senior male colleague. Each time, he would look to her and say, "You'll have to talk with her." Female managers should clearly spell out their rank and responsibilities prior to a meeting so that Asian counterparts clearly understand rank and status.

6. *There are some no-no's.* Do not tell jokes, especially long and involved ones. Also, do not talk politics, especially in a host's home. Remember that to Asians, face-saving is extremely important; most will avoid a direct "no." Thus, when one responds to your sales pitch with something like, "It is difficult," or "We will consider it in a forward-looking manner," interpret this as a polite "no."

7. *Drinking is a national sport in Asia; Western business acquaintances are expected to play.* Rejecting an offer of a glass of sake can negate all the positive steps you have taken to develop a healthy relationship.

The importance of understanding foreign cultures is recognized by many organizations, which automatically require executives to attend training courses prior to overseas assignments. The Westerner who fails to appreciate the important communication variables invites failure in relationships with foreigners.

Source: Rick Tetzeli, "How to Act Once You Get There," *Fortune*, Special Issue: *Asia in the 1990s*, Fall 1990, pp. 87–88.

There are several forms of nonverbal messages. The most important are (1) sign language, (2) action language—how we move and look (3) object language—physical items such as what we wear, and (4) paralanguage—how we sound.

Sign language takes the form of nonverbal messages that literally replace words. For example, road crews may use flags to signal motorists to slow down, halt, or proceed; a nod of the head indicates "yes," a shake, "no"; a military salute demonstrates respect for a higher-ranking officer.

> The battle of Trafalgar in 1805—which led to the downfall of Napoléon—was won by Admiral Horatio Nelson because he had a secret weapon—signal flags. This technique for communicating over long distances, invented by the Royal Navy, revolutionized naval warfare.[17] "Flags," such as No Smoking signs, are still being effectively used today.

Action language consists of those body movements or actions that are not specifically intended to replace words but nevertheless transmit meaning. Rising and walking toward the door indicate readiness to terminate a conversation; shrugged shoulders and uplifted palms may indicate "I don't know." Walking at a quick pace communicates that one is in a hurry. A sharply pointed finger may convey a scolding. A blank stare on the face of the person you are speaking to may communicate that his or her mind is elsewhere (or that he or she would like to be!) or that the person does not understand what you are talking about.

Object language consists of physical items such as art, graphs, charts, clothes, furniture, physical possessions, or other *things* that convey messages. Thus, a classroom communicates a certain atmosphere of formality or informality. Awards displayed in an office indicate the occupant's accomplishments, while the size, furnishings, and location of the office indicate the occupant's status and perhaps tell something about his or her personality and interests. Even the arrangement of furnishings can act as object language. Some objects worn by individuals—clothing, jewelry, and other accessories—communicate strong messages to others. Clothing with signatures and logos (such as an alligator, polo player, or swan) is an example of object language. IBM, known for years for the conservative attire of its employees, believes that its success is directly related to its image of "competence," and that the conservative attire of its personnel is vital to this image. Even IBM's "customer engineers" (service personnel) arrive in a car (not a truck) wearing formal business clothing.

You have heard the expression "It's not what you say, it's the way you say it." *Paralanguage* is related to vocal sounds that influence how words are expressed. Paralanguage may be things such as pitch, tone, volume, pace, and other delivery-related factors.

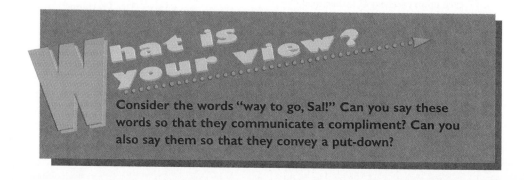

What is your view?

Consider the words "way to go, Sal!" Can you say these words so that they communicate a compliment? Can you also say them so that they convey a put-down?

Communicating Electronically

The merging of space-age telecommunications technologies with advanced computer techniques has led to innumerable ways of gathering, using, and disseminating information, including such useful new information processing technologies as (1) personal computers, (2) electronic mail, (3) teleconferencing, and (4) computer networking.

Personal Computers

In the past, managers tended to rely on highly trained specialists to do their computing. Thus, managers were consumers of computerized information rather than generators of it. Programmers with access to large, complex computers would provide managers with information needed to make decisions. Managers also had to rely on technical and clerical staffs to perform duties such as collecting the data and information to be processed, calculating statistical summaries, and doing other analyses.

While these specialists still do much of the computing, rather than being in printed form, the information is now available more immediately to managers on their own PCs, which are linked to a main terminal. Not only can managers receive information from other sources as they need or want it, but they can generate their own data or manipulate data as they desire.

Their PCs may include programs that provide word processing capabilities; a variety of serving facilities (such as archives, data banks, learning support systems, and printers); files for incoming messages, authorizations, and schedules; a personal library; and work-related information regarding relationships with others within and outside the organization.

Electronic Mail

Electronic mail (E-mail), which involves transmitting information to other users by means of a computer and appropriate software, eliminates the need to handle documents physically, thereby reducing turnaround time for written messages. Office communications, then, can be handled via high-speed printers, keyboard entries, or video display terminals (VDTs). IBM CEO Louis Gerstner indicated that he received from IBM employees 200 to 250 E-mail messages per day during his first few weeks on the job in 1993. As Gerstner stated, "I take them home and read them. . . . [M]ost are from people suggesting things . . . [and] many give me opinions on IBM's strengths and weaknesses."[18]

electronic mail (E-mail) Transmission of information to other users by means of a computer.

Teleconferencing

The use of electronic devices can even permit several individuals in different locations to hold a conference. By **teleconferencing,** people can be actively involved in many projects and belong to many interest groups. Meetings and exchanges of information—including international conferences—can take place within or outside the organization.

teleconferencing Use of electronic devices to permit several individuals in different locations to hold a conference.

The A. L. Williams Insurance Company uses a closed-circuit TV network to help managers keep in touch with its branch offices.

videoconferencing A type of teleconference in which members at remote locations can see each other through video cameras and monitors.

Videoconferencing is a type of teleconference in which members at remote locations can see each other live by means of camera and monitor hookups.

Boeing completed development of its 757 aircraft ahead of schedule partly because it had four video sites linking different parts of its widely dispersed Seattle facilities. This enabled hundreds of executives, pilots, and technicians to make more rapid design decisions.[19]

Computer Networking

Strictly speaking, networking is not a single distinct technology, but a combination of several of those just described. *Networking* involves connecting computers in such a way as to allow users to share programs, exchange information, and have access to common databases. One of the most popular networks is Ethernet. Local area networks (LANs), in which computer users in a single location are linked in a network within a restricted geographic area, are also often used.

Barriers to Effective Communication

While managers may spend 80 percent of their time communicating, communication frequently fails to achieve its intended objectives because of "noise." These barriers are usually thought of as either (1) organizational barriers or (2) interpersonal barriers.

Noise is any interference or barrier that impedes communication effectiveness. Noise may interfere with communication at various stages of the process, such as a source having negative perceptions about the receiver; sending a poorly organized, verbose message or a too brief message; using a poor channel; or a receiver's inattentive listening or fear of giving honest feedback to the message source.

Organizational Noise

Organizations, by their very nature, tend to inhibit effective communication. A communication consultant can examine the organization chart of a firm and immediately see that communication barriers exist. Four organizational barriers are (1) organizational levels, (2) managerial authority, (3) specialization, and (4) information overload.

Organizational Levels   As pointed out earlier, when an organization grows, its structure expands, creating many communication problems. If a message must pass through added levels—among increased numbers of people or departments—it will take longer to reach its destination and will tend to become distorted along the way.

As a message goes through various organizational levels, it passes through several "filters." Each level in the communication chain can add to, take from, modify, or completely change the intent of a given message.

One explanation for this tendency is that messages are usually broader and more general at higher levels of management and must be made more specific as they filter down to lower levels. If the broad message is misinterpreted, then the specifics that are added may be incorrect.

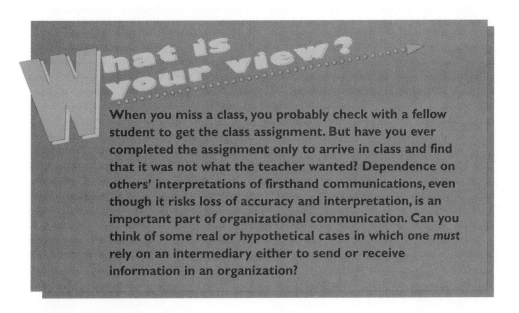

What is your view?

When you miss a class, you probably check with a fellow student to get the class assignment. But have you ever completed the assignment only to arrive in class and find that it was not what the teacher wanted? Dependence on others' interpretations of firsthand communications, even though it risks loss of accuracy and interpretation, is an important part of organizational communication. Can you think of some real or hypothetical cases in which one *must* rely on an intermediary either to send or receive information in an organization?

Managerial Authority   Authority is a necessary feature of any organization. Yet the fact that one person supervises others creates a barrier to free and open communication. Many bosses feel that they cannot fully admit problems, conditions, or results that may make them look weak. Many subordinates, on the other hand, avoid situations that require them to disclose information that might make them appear in an unfavorable light. As a result, there often is a lack of openness between managers and subordinates. Job problems, frustrations, below-standard work, disagreements with the superior's policies, and other types of unfavorable information tend to be withheld or changed to look more favorable.

> In lamenting Kmart's problems in competing with Wal-Mart stores, critics blame the poor physical appearance of many Kmart stores, a weak distribution system that often results in stores running out of merchandise, and the CEO's communication style. The boss, CEO Joseph Antonini, supposedly hates bad news, and the culture is to tell the chairman what he wants to hear. There has been a lot of bad news recently, though, and Antonini has been under fire by stockholders for Kmart's poor financial performance.[20]

Specialization   Although specialization is a fundamental part of organizations, it also creates problems, for it tends to separate people even when they work side by side. Different functions, special interests, and job jargon can make people feel that they live in different worlds. The result can prevent any feeling of community and make understanding very difficult.

> John Scully left PepsiCo to become Apple Computer's CEO in 1983. Scully describes a meeting at Apple at which he presided after only a few days on the job: "The conversation would become littered with technical talk; . . . it was almost as if some of them spoke a foreign language: Winchester disks, seek times, . . . , the IWM chip. I feverishly scribbled the words and acronyms down in a little notebook—just as I did in Europe and Latin America when I heard words in Spanish or German and tried to do business in the native language [when I worked] at Pepsi's International Foods division. Later, I'd look up the words in a small pocket dictionary. . . . I laughed when I discovered that the IWM chip really meant the 'Incredible Woz Machine,' the disk drive controller chip designed by Apple cofounder Steve Wozniak. It was a whole new vocabulary for me."[21]

jargon Technical vocabulary used by various specialists.

A common problem created by specialization, as this example shows, is the **jargon** or technical vocabulary used by various specialists. Much resistance to data processing is caused by the technical language that its specialists use. Bureaucracy can often lead to seemingly meaningless gobbledygook, as shown in Figure 10.2. Yet jargon can be quite effective among members of a group and in special situations.

> At William M. Mercer-Meidinger, Inc., a New York consulting firm, a specialist in firing people is designated an expert in "structuring employee terminations" and uses terms such as *outplacement* and *replacement* to soften the impact on those being fired.[22]

Even deeper than the problem of language, however, are the differing perceptions and conflicting frames of reference involved when sales, credit, production, quality control, finance, personnel, and research departments interact with one another. These departments have their own specialized interests, attitudes, and

A plumber of foreign extraction wrote the National Bureau of Standards and said he found that hydrochloric acid quickly opened plugged drainage pipes and inquired if it was a good thing to use. A scientist at the Bureau replied:

Dear Sir:

While the efficacy of hydrochloric acid is undoubtedly indisputable, dysfunctional coincidental effects render its commercial utilization in said writer's case a hazardous undertaking which this office cannot endorse.

The plumber wrote back thanking the Bureau for telling him that hydrochloric acid was good to use. The scientist was disturbed about the misunderstanding and brought the situation correspondence to his boss—another scientist—who wrote the plumber:

Dear Sir:

Hydrochloric acid, while a highly efficacious atomistic debilitator, imposes a strongly noxious residue when interacting with metallic-based substances, introducing permanencial structural damage and eliciting a definitive negative endorsement of your request.

The plumber wrote back that he agreed with the Bureau—the hydrochloric acid really seemed to "clean out pipes real good"—and thanked the Bureau for its helpfulness. Greatly upset about their communication breakdown, the two scientists brought the problem to the top boss, who was *not* a scientist. He shook his head in dismay and wrote the plumber:

Dear Sir:

Don't use hydrochloric acid. It eats the hell out of pipes!

Shortly thereafter, the Bureau received another letter from the plumber. It read:

Dear Sir:

Thanks! But I found that out for myself.

Source: Excerpted from *Power of Words*, copyright 1954, 1953 and renewed 1982, 1981 by Stuart Chase, reprinted by permission of Harcourt Brace Jovanovich, Inc.

FIGURE 10.2
Cut the jargon!

ways of looking at things that frequently create strains between individuals and departments.

Information Overload   Managers sometimes operate on the assumption that "more communication is better communication." They therefore provide employees with such enormous amounts of information that they are overwhelmed with data they do not understand or cannot use effectively. This results in *information overload*, in which employees receive more communications than they need or can process. This problem is compounded by the electronic communication technology discussed earlier. As a result of information overload, the recipient may be confused and uncertain—and this can lead to inaction.

Interpersonal Noise

Even if organizational communication barriers did not exist, managers would still face the possibility that their messages would become distorted. Many mis-communications are caused not by organizational factors but by human and language imperfections. Managers need to be aware of interpersonal barriers such as (1) differing perceptions, (2) status of the communicator, (3) poor listening, (4) imprecise use of language, and (5) differences in language.

perception A complicated process by which we select, organize, and give meaning to the world around us.

Differing Perceptions **Perception** is the complicated process by which we select, organize, and give meaning to the world around us. Experience is a major influence on what we perceive; we expect to see a train when we hear a train whistle, and we may automatically become defensive when called into the boss's office—or asked to see the professor after class. The different experiences each of us has had account for the varied interpretations of communication events and actions in organizations.

stereotyping The perpetual tendency to generalize about a group of people who share a common characteristic.

Stereotyping is the perceptual tendency to generalize about a group of people who share a common characteristic. Thus, we have stereotypes for certain groups and nationalities, union leaders, politicians, engineers, and even teachers and students. We then treat members of each group according to our perceptions of that stereotype, and this strongly influences our communications with them.

Status of the Communicator Another major communication barrier is the tendency to size up, evaluate, and weigh a message in terms of the characteristics of the person who sends it, especially his or her *credibility*. Credibility is based on the person's "expertness" in the subject area being communicated and on the receiver's degree of confidence or trust that the person will communicate the truth. The profile of R. David Thomas (page 347) illustrates this point.

When employees perceive managers as having a high credibility rating, they are more likely to accept their messages. It follows, then, that managers must be viewed by their followers as credible and trustworthy. Otherwise, attempts to motivate, persuade, and direct work efforts are greatly handicapped from the start.

Poor Listening If they are to succeed at managing and communicating with others, managers must also learn to listen effectively. If managers do not listen, how can they know what others are thinking and know their needs, wants, wishes, and ideas? Some irritating listening habits are shown in Table 10.2 and include (1) listening only on the surface, with little attempt to consider seriously what the other person is saying; (2) giving the impression, through either speech or manner (glancing at watch, staring into space, fidgeting), of eagerness to end the conversation; and (3) showing signs of annoyance or distress over the subject matter being discussed.

More basic than good listening itself are managers' attitudes toward listening. Are they willing to spend time with employees? Do they make themselves available?

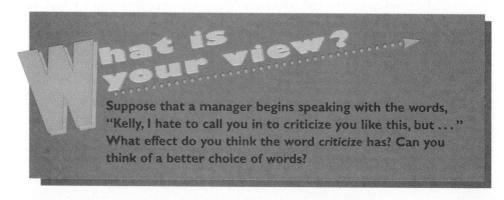

What is your view?

Suppose that a manager begins speaking with the words, "Kelly, I hate to call you in to criticize you like this, but ..." What effect do you think the word *criticize* has? Can you think of a better choice of words?

TABLE 10.2   IRRITATING LISTENING HABITS

1. He doesn't give me a chance to talk. I go in with a problem and never get a chance to tell about it.
2. She interrupts me while I'm talking—never lets me complete more than a couple of sentences before interrupting.
3. He never looks at me while I'm talking. I don't know for sure whether he's even listening or not.
4. She constantly fidgets with a pencil or a paper, studying it rather than listening to me.
5. He never smiles. I'm somewhat apprehensive about talking to him.
6. She always gets me off the subject with her questions and comments.
7. Whenever I make a suggestion, he throws cold water on it. I've quit trying to give him suggestions, ideas, or help.
8. She's always trying to anticipate what I'm going to say next and jumps ahead of me to tell me what my next point is.
9. He rephrases what I say in such a way that he puts words into my mouth that I did not mean.
10. Occasionally, she asks a question about what I've just told her that shows she wasn't listening.
11. He argues with almost everything I say, often even before I've had a chance to state my case.
12. When I'm talking, she finishes sentences for me.
13. He acts as if he's just waiting for me to get through talking so he can interject something of his own.
14. When I have a good idea, she always says, "Yes, I've been thinking about that too."
15. He overdoes trying to show me he's following what I'm saying—too many nods of the head, yeahs, uh-huhs.
16. She tries to insert humorous remarks when I'm trying to be serious.
17. He frequently sneaks looks at his watch or his clock while I'm talking.
18. When I come in, she doesn't put down what she's doing and turn her attention completely to me.
19. He often acts as if I'm keeping him from doing something "important."
20. She asks questions that demand agreement. For example, she makes a statement and then says, "Don't you think so?" or "Don't you agree?"

Source: Adapted from Larry R. Smeltzer and Donald F. Leonard, *Managerial Communication* (Burr Ridge, Ill.: Irwin, 1994), p. 32.

Are they willing to risk the potential discomfort of learning about a subordinate's personal problems?

Imprecise Use of Language   One of the biggest mistakes we make in communicating is to assume that all meaning lies in the words we use. For example, a supervisor may ask a subordinate to "clean up around here" or "get on this job as soon as you can." These instructions are quite vague and subject to broad interpretation.

A study of the *Oxford English Dictionary* reports an average of 28 separate meanings for each of the 500 most used words in the English language.[23] Furthermore, words can arouse differing feelings, emotions, and attitudes within people.

Sometimes words are deliberately misused in order to convey an erroneous message. When detected, this may lead to questions about the originator's ethical behavior:

Pan American Airlines was one of ten companies to win a Harlan Page Hubbard Lemon Award in 1990 for "the most misleading, unfair, or irresponsible ad campaigns." Pan Am claimed its transatlantic fleet of planes was among the youngest—and, by implication, the safest—in the air. According to the Aviation Consumer Action Project, the company shaved four years off its fleet's age by counting recently overhauled planes as "new."[24]

Differences in Language and Culture   Another barrier results from the diversity of cultures and languages found in many of today's work groups.

The increasingly diverse culture that influences organizations often leads to quite different styles of communicating and subsequent perceptions and interpretations of what we see and hear. As an example, Table 10.3 shows that negotiating styles of American and Japanese managers are apt to differ greatly. With the increase in multinational businesses and the purchase of U.S. businesses by other nations, giving instructions, receiving feedback, and making decisions become more difficult.

When Japan's Sanyo Electric Company bought a TV factory in Forrest City, Arkansas, it tried using "consensus management." An operating committee of three Americans and three Japanese was formed to solve problems and improve performance. As only one Sanyo executive spoke fluent English, an interpreter was required at each meeting. After two years, Sanyo dropped the program and began relying increasingly on the American managers.[25]

TABLE 10.3   Contrasting Negotiating Styles of American and Japanese Managers

U.S. Negotiating Style	Japanese Negotiating Style
Speaks directly	Speaks indirectly
Is assertive	Is nonassertive
Speaks to the point	Uses ambiguity
Uses hard sell	Uses soft sell
Focuses on short term	Focuses on long term
Is argumentative	Is nonargumentative
Acts in a confrontational way	Acts in a conciliatory way
Favors verbal	Favors nonverbal
Is verbose	Is suspicious of words
Avoids silence	Ample use of silences and pauses
Values eloquence	Values humility
Makes direct eye contact	Avoids direct eye contact
Uses expansive gestures	Uses small gestures
Employs relatively informal style	Employs relatively formal style
Uses dramatic, animated style	Uses restricted, quiet style
Projects speaking voice	Restrains voice
Challenges other negotiators	Seeks to save face of all involved
Favors decision by majority vote	Wants complete consensus

Source: John M. Penrose, Robert W. Rasberry, and Robert J. Myers, *Advanced Business Communication* (Belmont, Calif.: Wadsworth Publishing, 1993), p. 13.

R. David Thomas, equipped with a tenth-grade education and a keen business sense, has come a long way from his days of working behind a lunch counter in Knoxville, Tennessee. Thomas now sits atop Wendy's Old Fashioned Hamburgers, the nation's third largest hamburger empire, boasting gross sales of over $4.2 billion. Founder of Wendy's International, Incorporated, "Wendy's dad" has become a familiar face to millions of Americans after appearing in many of his company's television commercials. These factors have given him a high degree of credibility with consumers and Wendy's employees.

R. DAVID THOMAS, WENDY'S INTERNATIONAL

Who can forget Wendy's 1984 "Where's the Beef?" advertising campaign? It was one of the most memorable and successful campaigns in the history of television advertising. Thomas, a sincere, easygoing man, has managed to translate his own down-home, no-frills attitude into a powerful business marketing tool, charming the public into sampling his Hometown, U.S.A., cooking at one of over 4,500 Wendy's restaurants around the globe. Since, then, Thomas himself has appeared on camera, giving customers a simple, honest sales pitch about how good his hamburgers really are. One of his most effective messages—conveyed in his homespun manner—is "Our hamburgers are the best in the business, or I wouldn't have named the place after my daughter."

Thomas's interest in the restaurant business began at the age of 12, when he took a job at a diner in Knoxville. He dropped out of high school after the tenth grade to pursue his career in the restaurant industry. Thomas worked as a short-order cook for several years, then accepted a job from a friend in Columbus, Ohio, who owned four Kentucky Fried Chicken restaurants, which were on the verge of collapse. Thomas's ingenuity and hard work saved the restaurants, and made him a millionaire by the age of 35.

The first Wendy's Old Fashioned Hamburgers restaurant opened in 1969 in Columbus, Ohio. Thomas named the business after his daughter, Melinda Lou, known to her brother and sisters as Wendy, because Melinda Lou was too difficult for them to say. The red-haired, freckled little girl pictured on every Wendy's sign is now married and with her husband owns and operates several Wendy's restaurants in Texas.

Thomas's empire grew quickly, to its current size of more than 4,500 restaurants in the United States and 33 other countries. But success has not spoiled Wendy's dad. Thomas's unaffected style has not changed since the day he opened the very first Wendy's. His attitude, unconstrained by the trappings of success in our corporate culture, is evident in his relations both with the public and with employees of the chain. Thomas is a firm believer in communicating and specializes in personal visits to his restaurants, circulating among customers and employees with a jovial "Hi, I'm Wendy's dad." He examines each location for cleanliness, efficiency, quality of food, and overall customer satisfaction. Thomas likes to keep his fingers on the pulse of his company's lifeblood, and he is compassionate. Himself an adoptee, Thomas has developed an adoption assistance benefit for his employees that offers up to $4,000 for adoption expenses for each child.

In an ironic twist, Thomas—the high school dropout and G.E.D. recipient—serves as member of the board of advisors at Duke's Fuqua School of Business, where he shares his business acumen with up-and-coming entrepreneurs. He offers students exposure to the entrepreneurial spirit of America, imparting knowledge that cannot be gleaned from textbooks—attained as it was through the experience of success and failure in the business world. Despite his own educational background, the burger magnate emphasizes the importance of higher education in order to succeed in today's business market. "Wendy's dad" says his focus has remained unchanged over the past 20 years—he still wants to provide customers with the best product and service on the market. Thomas says his life's credo is "not to take himself too seriously."

Source: Correspondence with Wendy's International Incorporated; Cindy Brownfield and Todd Gutner, "Dave's World," *Forbes*, January 3, 1994, p. 149; Milford Prewitt, "Dave Thomas: A Folksy Man with a Vision," *Nation's Restaurant News*, October 12, 1992, p. 44; "Just a Hamburger Cook at Heart," *Destin (Florida) Log*, September 2, 1989, pp. 1A, 8A; and Stuart Elliott, "Wendy's Could Star in Ads," *USA Today*, October 18, 1989, p. B1.

Using an interpreter has its drawbacks because you can never be sure how the interpreter is translating what you are saying, you can never communicate one-on-one with employees, and the interpreter may be viewed by other workers as having more authority than is actually the case. As an alternative, you can learn the language spoken by most of your employees, as the following example shows.

> When Stephen Miller took over as president of the Willette Corporation, a small manufacturing firm in New Jersey, after his father's retirement, he found that all of his plant personnel were Spanish-speaking and he had a great deal of difficulty communicating with them. He tried using an interpreter but found that to be an unsatisfactory solution. So he decided to learn to speak Spanish and enrolled in an intensive crash course. As a result, he is able to speak with his employees and also to post notices on the company bulletin board in both Spanish and English. One unanticipated benefit for him, although not always for the workers, is that he is also able to understand what they are saying to one another in the plant.

How to Increase Communication Effectiveness

So far, we have pointed out several causes of communication problems and the difficulty of effective communication. Now we would like to present some ways in which managers can increase their communication effectiveness. These techniques are essentially ways to overcome some of the difficulties presented.

Be Aware of the Need for Effective Communication

Because of the many organizational and interpersonal barriers, effective communication cannot be left to chance. Managers must first appreciate the important role communication plays, for only then can steps be taken to increase communication effectiveness. Note that Whirlpool (Opening Case) recognized the need to overhaul its communication processes to bring them into step with the company's new culture.

As evidence of top management's recognition of the importance of communication, many large organizations today employ "communication specialists." These specialists attempt to improve communication by helping supervisors solve internal communication problems; by devising company communication strategy regarding layoffs, plant closings or relocations, and terminations; and by measuring, through interviews or surveys, the quality of communication efforts.

Several other changes reflect management's constant search for improved communication effectiveness. For example, Texas Instruments, Westinghouse, British Petroleum, and other firms have adopted videotaped television broadcasts to present information to employees. Bethlehem Steel had only one newsletter in 1973; later it had 23 different publications tailored to the needs of its individual plants.

Top management is also acknowledging the key communication linkage represented by first-line supervisors in their organizations. After all, it is this level that works directly with the great bulk of operative employees. In one company, the plant manager meets for a half-hour every week with six to eight of the company's first-line managers, discusses key issues with them, and gets their input. The discussions range from dealing with rumors to company profitability, new equipment, problems with line-staff departments, and handling supervisory difficulties faced by the supervisors. The plant manager, by example, encourages each supervisor to have similar meetings with his or her own personnel.

Create an Open Communications Environment

Another important means of improving communication is to open the environment to two-way communications. Managers can do at least two things to encourage an open, two-way communications environment: (1) ensure that their own communications style is feedback oriented and (2) use participative management.

Managers must take an active role in soliciting information from others and creating a favorable environment for feedback. For example, after communicating a job assignment, you might ask, "Do you understand?" or "Do you have any questions?" or "Did I leave anything out?" But these questions do not encourage answers; a more direct approach would be to say, "This is quite important, so, to make sure we understand each other, tell me what you are going to do." Frequently, this produces clarification of points that a subordinate might otherwise be unwilling or afraid to mention. Remember, though, that you must also provide subordinates with pertinent feedback. One approach to doing this is shown in Tips 10.2.

Participative management requires two-way communication. A manager who allows employees to make decisions or express opinions receives helpful responses from them. These responses serve as a form of feedback that helps the manager better understand the employees' thinking. Also, the opportunity to participate makes employees feel a great responsibility to "make things go right."

> General Electric uses special programs to enhance its communications. One such program is its "Work Out" program, designed to improve the way work gets done throughout the company. Under the program, each business unit assembles 50 to 100 employees eight to ten times a year to tell the division's upper management how they perceive things—what they like and dislike, what bothers them, and ways their jobs could be improved. At the GE Medical Systems Division, one five-day Work Out session ended with individuals and functional teams signing almost 100 written contracts to implement improved new work procedures. As GE CEO Jack Welch points out, the norm in most companies is *not* to bring up critical issues with the boss, especially in a public setting. But at GE, the objective is to create more fulfilling and rewarding jobs. GE credits Work Out and its other communications programs with helping keep the company competitive.[26]

For effective two-way communication to occur, a high level of trust between a manager and subordinates is essential. Numerous research studies have confirmed that low trust is directly correlated with subordinates' tendency to distort the flow of upward communication. This is especially true where the superior is seen as having substantial influence over subordinates' careers.[27]

ipS 10.2

Giving Negative Feedback with Sensitivity: The "I" Message

One action requiring considerable tact and diplomacy is addressing behavior of others that a manager wants to change. Some managers put off such a discussion because it's distasteful. Others do it in a blunt, threatening way that may cause resentment. Too often, when we have a problem with someone else's behavior, we tend to *blame, lecture, put down, warn,* or *coerce* people to get them to change. The result often is no change, a halfhearted change, or resentment by employees at having been called on the carpet.

Using an "I" message, though, may help managers achieve their goal of (1) changing the behavior and (2) doing so in a way that salvages the other party's ego. There are three major parts of an "I" message:

Feelings: Indicate how you feel about the *effects* of the behavior (angry, embarrassed, frustrated, and so on).

Behavior: Identify the behavior (absenteeism, not arriving at appointments on time, not meeting quotas, and so forth).

Effect: Spell out the end result of the behavior (poor example for others, fail to meet quotas, puts you behind schedule, you drop what you're doing, and so on).

Sending an "I" message provides feedback in a nonthreatening, objective way. It represents a type of *appeal* rather than a *demand* that an employee change. Note the "You" and "I" messages below. No one likes being told his or her behavior is a problem; however, framing your displeasure in an "I" message addresses the problem more openly and tactfully, with less likelihood of employee resentment.

"You" Message	*"I" Message*
1. "You neglected to proofread that report. You should know better than to let a report go out like that."	1. "I was really upset when I noticed the typographical errors in the report. It makes our unit look unprofessional."
2. "You've got to be on time for meetings by being better organized. You know how important meetings are."	2. "When you're late for meetings, it bothers me that the message sent to others is that you consider them unimportant."
3. "Everybody would rather sell a customer than spend time on refunds. But giving refunds is store policy, so you have no choice but to do it."	3. "When I hear customers complain about your unwillingness to accept their returns, I get concerned about your not complying with policy."

Source: Adapted from Thomas Gordon, *Leader Effectiveness Training* (Chicago, Ill.: Dryden Books, 1977), pp. 92–107.

Practice Effective Listening

Poor listening techniques plague many managers, just as they plague many of us in our nonwork relationships with others. We are more likely to be interested in ourselves, to be thinking about what we are going to say, instead of really hearing what others tell us. Moreover, although most of us have had some formal training in writing and speaking, few have had training in effective listening.

Keith Davis and John Newstrom have developed ten guides to more effective listening. These suggestions are summarized in Table 10.4.

TABLE 10.4   TEN GUIDES TO MORE EFFECTIVE LISTENING

1. *Stop talking!* You cannot listen if you are talking. Polonius (in *Hamlet*): "Give every man thine ear, but few thy voice."
2. *Put the talker at ease.* Help a person feel free to talk. This is often called a permissive environment.
3. *Show a talker that you want to listen.* Look and act interested. Do not read your mail while someone talks. Listen to understand rather than to oppose.
4. *Remove distractions.* Do not doodle, tap, or shuffle papers. Would it be quieter if you shut the door?
5. *Empathize with talkers.* Try to help yourself see the other person's point of view.
6. *Be patient.* Allow plenty of time. Do not interrupt a talker. Don't start for the door or walk away.
7. *Hold your temper.* An angry person takes the wrong meaning from words.
8. *Go easy on argument and criticism.* These put people on the defensive, and they may "clam up" or become angry. Do not argue. Even if you win, you lose.
9. *Ask questions.* This encourages a talker and shows that you are listening. It helps to develop points further.
10. *Stop talking!* This is the first and last, because all other guides depend on it. You cannot do an effective listening job while you are talking.

    Nature gave people two ears but only one tongue, which is a gentle hint that they should listen more than they talk.

    Listening requires two ears, one for meaning and one for feeling.

    Decision makers who do not listen have less information for making sound decisions.

Source: Adapted from Keith Davis and John W. Newstrom, *Human Behavior at Work: Organizational Behavior*, 9th ed. (New York: McGraw-Hill, 1993), p. 109. Used with permission.

S U M M A R Y

Communication is a most important part of managing. The typical manager spends a large percentage of the workday in some form of communication with others. Communication is linked closely to the managerial functions of planning, organizing, leading, and evaluating.

Downward communication consists of policies, rules, procedures, and the like, that flow from top management to lower levels. Upward communication consists of the flow of performance reports and other information from lower to higher levels. Lateral or horizontal communication is essentially coordinative and occurs between and among individuals or depatments on the same level.

Information as well as formal channels are important to organizational communication. The grapevine, a form of informal communication, is not only inevitable but usually quite effective.

The components of a communication model are the source, encoding the message, transmitting the message, receiving the message, decoding the message, and feedback. Noise, however, may interfere at any stage of the process.

Important messages are passed by nonverbal as well as verbal means. Nonverbal communication includes sign language, action language, object language, and paralanguage.

Electronic communication involves using telecommunications and computer technologies to improve and speed up the communication process. Useful methods include personal computers, electronic mail, teleconferencing, and computer networking.

Some organizational barriers to communication are organizational levels, managerial authority, specialization, and information overload. Interpersonal barriers include differing perceptions, the status of the communicator, poor listening habits, imprecise use of language, and differences in language.

To improve the effectiveness of organizational and interpersonal communication, organizations must first develop and maintain awareness of the need for effective communication. The use of feedback and proper listening techniques are among the effective communication tools at a manager's disposal.

KEY TERMS

communication, 329
formal communication channels, 329
downward communication, 330
upward communication, 331
lateral (horizontal) communication, 331
informal communication, 332
grapevine, 332
feedback, 336

nonverbal communication, 336
electronic mail (E-mail), 339
teleconferencing, 339
videoconferencing, 340
jargon, 342
perception, 344
stereotyping, 344

DISCUSSION QUESTIONS

1. Explain the steps in the communication process.

2. A recent survey of 101 chief executive officers of banks conducted by one of the authors showed that almost half (43 percent) felt that the biggest communication flow problem was lateral/horizontal. Why do you think these bankers selected this flow rather than upward or downward communication as their most important problem?

3. (a) What are the four forms of nonverbal communication discussed in the text? (b) Explain each.

4. Name and explain the three organizational barriers to effective communication.

5. Recently, an employee of an industrial firm received a severe electric shock while performing a job in the field. A paramedic team rushed to the scene and administered artificial respiration, but en route to the hospital emergency center, the patient lost his vital signs. Upon arrival at the hospital, he was pronounced dead, and his body was "released to the morgue"—the common hospital terminology used. In all the excitement of the accident, no one had

called the employee's spouse, who heard about the accident shortly after it happened. When she called the company, the company spokesperson said he knew nothing of the accident. Quickly investigating, he placed a call to the hospital and learned the employee's status. He then called the employee's wife and told her that her husband was apparently in good shape, as a hospital spokesperson had said that the employee had been "released." Explain this communication breakdown, using the six-stage communication model presented in the chapter. Upon whom would you place blame? Why?

6. When he was the owner and CEO of Apple Computer, Steven Jobs often dressed very casually at work, frequently wearing jeans; a coat and tie were exceptions rather than standard attire. Jobs said it was just his personal style. What form of nonverbal communication is involved here? What do you think about this type of dress for the top official in a major company? Discuss.

7. Think of the best and worst listeners you personally know. What are their characteristics?

8. (a) What are five interpersonal communication barriers discussed in the chapter? (b) Explain each.

9. How can feedback be used to improve communication?

PRACTICING MANAGEMENT

10.1

case

The Ineffective Committee

The Evans Company,* a Fortune 500 company plagued by increasing costs and labor unrest at its major plant site, decided to go to its employees for assistance. Members of top management were proud of their brainchild, the "Productivity Improvement Committee Concept," or "PIC," as it was called. They had high hopes that the PIC, based on the Japanese quality circle approach, would result in not only increased efficiency but also improved morale at the plant.

Basically, the PIC would be implemented in the following manner. Each department of the plant would become a productivity improvement committee (PIC), with all employees in the department serving on it. Committee leadership was to consist of three people per department. One leader was the department supervisor, another the union shop steward, and the third an employee elected by members of the department. The number of committee members varied from 6 to 31 people, depending on the number of people in the department. Each committee was to meet for 30 minutes a week and address situations in which improvements could be made. The committee's recommendations went directly to the plant manager.

After a month of functioning, only three recommendations had been generated by any of the 18 PICs. Of these, none was judged feasible by the plant manager, who was disappointed with the poor quality of the suggestions. Accordingly, he named another committee, consisting of the union president, the director of human resources, and the head of engineering, to investigate the PIC situation. After meeting with PIC leaders, this committee presented the plant manager with a list of five reasons the PIC concept was not working as presented.

1. Fear among employees and leaders that people would lose jobs as a result of the PIC program

2. Inexperience of leaders in conducting PIC meetings

3. Feeling that top management would not seriously consider PIC recommendations

4. Difficulty of resolving matters within the 30-minute PIC format

5. Lack of understanding among employees and leaders as to what their role was as PIC members.

Questions

1. What barriers to communication do you see reflected in the five reasons given for failure of the PIC?

2. What changes, if any, would you recommend in the PIC format?

3. Assume that you are the plant manager. What action will you take based on the five reasons given for failure of the PICs?

* Company name disguised.

10.1   Developing a Communication Strategy

learning exercise

Assume that you are a branch manager for a large national organization. The branch for which you are responsible has 120 employees. There are two levels of managers—department heads and supervisors—between you and most of the employees. All employees work at the branch location. For each of the situations shown, develop in writing a communication plan or strategy for dealing with each, and clearly support your reasons for selecting the strategy you recommend.

1. You have just learned from your regional manager via a telephone call that your company has been bought by a firm from Saudi Arabia. The sale will be announced to the financial community within the hour. The regional manager knew little of the details but wanted you to get the word to your people as soon as possible.

2. One of your new department managers has been badly off the mark in keeping the departmental budget under control. A report from the branch controller's department showed that two months ago the department head exceeded the budget for items such as supplies and equipment, overtime, maintenance and repairs, and telephone by 40 percent. You said nothing, since it was the department head's first month in the new position. But this time you feel that you must take some action, for last month the department's budget was exceeded by 55 percent. Other departments did not have this difficulty.

3. You must communicate a new overtime system that will be installed, effective in four weeks. In the past, supervisors would get in touch with workers—by seniority—either in person or by telephone to make sure that the most senior workers would have first opportunity for overtime work. This proved slow and ineffective, since some senior workers failed to decline overtime. The new system will give each supervisor more flexibility in overtime assignments by getting monthly advance overtime commitment from workers. You know that your department managers and supervisors definitely prefer the new system and feel that most employees will too, although several of the more senior people will probably get upset.

4. You learn that your own boss, who held your position several years ago, has been bypassing you and communicating directly with two of your department managers. The managers have reported to your boss several negative things about you, for which you received a slight reprimand. You were caught by surprise, because although the facts reported to your boss were true, he did not get the total explanation, which would have put you in a favorable rather than unfavorable light. You will clear up this bypassing matter with your boss, who is due for a branch visit in two days.

Motivating Employees

Give me enough medals and I'll win you any war.
—NAPOLÉON BONAPARTE

Always dream and shoot higher than you know you can do. Don't bother just to be better than your contemporaries or predecessors. Try to be better than yourself.
—WILLIAM FAULKNER

LEARNING OBJECTIVES

After studying the material in this chapter, you should be able to:

▶ **State** the purposes of motivation in organizations.

▶ **Discuss** why the study of motivation is important.

▶ **Describe** how human behavior affects motivation.

▶ **Explain** how some popular theories of motivation operate.

▶ **Recognize** that money is involved in many aspects of motivation.

▶ **Understand** that motivation is more than mere techniques; it is a philosophy with ethical implications.

▶ **Understand** what motivation strategies are important in today's business environment.

The Role of Management Expectations

One of the most comprehensive illustrations of the effect of managerial expectations on productivity is recorded in studies of the organizational experiment undertaken by Alfred Oberlander, manager of Metropolitan Life Insurance company's Rockaway district office. Observing that outstanding agencies grew faster than average or poor ones and that new insurance agents performed better in outstanding agencies than in average or poor ones, regardless of their sales attitude, Oberlander decided to group his superior agents in one unit to stimulate their performance and to provide a challenging environment into which to introduce new salespeople.

Oberlander assigned his six best agents to work with his best assistant manager, an equal number of average producers to an average manager, and the low producers to the least able manager. Then he asked the superior group to produce two-thirds of the premium volume achieved by the entire agency the previous year. He describes the results as follows:

> Shortly after this selection had been made, the people in the agency began referring to this select group as a "super-staff" because of their high *esprit de corps* in operating so well as a unit. Their

production efforts over the first 12 weeks far surpassed our most optimistic expectations . . . proving that groups of people of sound ability can be motivated beyond their apparently normal productive capacities when the problems created by the poor producer are eliminated from the operation.

Thanks to this fine result, our overall agency performance improved by 40 percent and it remained at this figure.

At the beginning of [the next year] . . . when, through expansion, we appointed another assistant manager and assigned him a staff, we again used this same concept, arranging the agents once more according to their productive capacity.

The assistant managers were assigned . . . according to their ability, with the most capable assistant manager receiving the best group, thus playing strength to strength. Our overall agency production again improved by about 25–30 percent, and so this staff arrangement remained in place until the end of the year.

[Two years later] . . . , we found upon analysis that there were so many agents

---

This case, a *Harvard Business Review* "classic," highlights several important concepts about motivation. First, managers' expectations and the way they communicate them influence employee performance. In addition, managers' self-image affects not only their own motivation but also how effectively they motivate others. If a manager's expectations are high and there is a supportive climate, productivity is likely to be high; if expectations are low, productivity is likely to be poor.

Purposes of Motivation

Motivation has to do with understanding the "why" of human behavior. If we have some knowledge of why people do what they do, we can do a better job of understanding, predicting, and influencing that behavior. Why do some people work

. . . with a potential of half a million dollars or more that only one staff remained of those people who were not considered to have any chance of reaching the half-million-dollar mark.

Although the productivity of the "superstaff" improved dramatically, the productivity of the members of the lowest unit, "who were not considered to have any chance of reaching the half-million-dollar mark," actually declined, and attrition among them increased. The performance of the superior agents rose to meet their managers' expectations, while that of the weaker ones declined as predicted.

The "average" unit, however, proved to be an anomaly. Although the district manager expected only average performance from this group, its productivity increased significantly because the assistant manager in charge of the group refused to believe that she was less capable than the manager of the superstaff or that the agents in the top group had any greater ability than the agents in her group. Stressing to her agents that everyone in the middle group had greater potential than those in the superstaff, lacking only their years of experience in selling insurance, she stimulated them to accept the challenge of outperforming the superstaff. As a result, the middle group increased its productivity by a higher percentage each year than the superstaff (though it never attained the dollar volume of the top group).

Just as Eliza Doolittle's image of herself as a lady did not permit her to accept others' treatment of her as a flower girl, the self-image of the manager of the "average" unit did not permit her to accept others' treatment of her as an "average" manager. Instead, she transmitted her own strong feelings of competence to her agents, created mutual expectations of high performance, and greatly stimulated productivity.[1]

Met Life head office, Aurora.

hard and others coast? Why do some leaders have high-producing units and others, with employees of comparable background, have low-producing ones? Why are some organizations noted for a culture in which employees are highly motivated and enjoy work, whereas others are noted for high turnover rates? Although a number of factors affect employee performance, a primary variable is **motivation,** the process of inducing a person or a group of people, each with distinct needs and personalities, to achieve the organization's objectives, while also working to achieve personal objectives.

Motivation is as individual as human personality and behavior, so you will probably find that your classmates, having different backgrounds, needs, and aspirations, ranked the items differently. But certain underlying principles and theories of motivation enable managers to better understand and predict people's responses to performing their tasks, despite the uniqueness of human beings. We expose you to these underlying concepts of motivation in this chapter.

motivation The process of inducing a person or a group of people, each with distinct needs and personalities, to achieve the organization's objectives, while also working to achieve their own objectives.

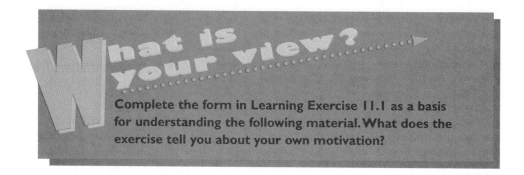

Complete the form in Learning Exercise 11.1 as a basis for understanding the following material. What does the exercise tell you about your own motivation?

There are at least three primary purposes of managerial motivation, each requiring different approaches, tactics, and incentives:

1. To encourage potential employees to join the organization
2. To stimulate present employees to produce or perform more effectively
3. To encourage present employees to remain with the organization

The first and third purposes were covered in Chapter 9; here we concentrate on the second motivational objective—improving employee performance. As you prepare yourself to manage in an organization, however, you will need to keep all three of these objectives in mind.

Motivation Is the Essence of Management

Managers are *continually* generating either positive or negative responses from employees. Performance results when managers obtain a positive response; it does not occur when the response is negative. The real question is what type of environment managers can provide in order to stimulate improved performance and employee development most effectively.

> Max De Pree, retired CEO of Herman Miller, a leading office furniture company, emphasized this point when he said, "Most people come to work well prepared, well motivated, and wanting to reach their potential." He added that one of the primary issues for the 1990s will be for managers to understand that their job is to liberate and enable workers to reach their potential.[2]

There is no question that one of the primary challenges facing organizations is improving employee performance. This challenge was highlighted in a study in which fewer than one of every four U.S. employees felt they were working at full potential. Half said they put no more effort into their job than was necessary to keep it. The vast majority—75 percent—said they could be significantly more effective than they were.[3]

Just imagine what would happen to performance and productivity if that 75 percent became significantly more effective. Perhaps Tom Peters and Nancy Austin were correct when they observed that a group of 100 motivated people "can do the same work, faster and of higher quality, than several thousand are able to accomplish."[4]

Quad/Graphics employees are more productive because they own the company, share in profits, and assume responsibility for their own performance.

Other studies, such as the one in the Opening Case, have shown that if people are allowed greater involvement in decisions affecting their work, productivity improves.

> Quad/Graphics, a successful Pewaukee, Wisconsin, printing firm, allows each division to set its own operational goals. Most employees participate in decision-making processes and assume responsibility for managing their own work. Employees own the company's stock, share in profits, have excellent benefits, and choose to work a three-day, 36-hour workweek (three 12-hour shifts, four days off). With this new arrangement, productivity increased 20 percent.[5]

Motivation, Ability, and Performance

The relationship among motivation, ability, and performance would be simple were productivity a function of ability alone, since employees' output would vary directly with increases in their abilities. However, because employees have the freedom of choosing to perform effectively, ineffectively, or not at all, motivation is necessary to increase output. Thus, performance is to a large extent a function of both ability and motivation, as the following example illustrates.

> Jim Jackson entered college with a score of 29 on his ACT. His performance in the first semester resulted in four Fs and one D. At that time, he dropped out and

spent two years in the Airborne Infantry. He then returned to college, and in his initial semester his performance resulted in four As and one B.

This example highlights the fact that, although teachers and managers can certainly create a climate of positive motivation, in the final analysis motivation comes from within each person.

Motivation occurs through the interaction of intrinsic and extrinsic rewards with employee needs, as modified by the employee's expectations. Managers can motivate employees toward improved performance by creating a positive climate where people can be motivated from within.

What Motivation Involves

Many people believe management can never become a science, because managers have to deal with (1) human behavior that often seems unpredictable and irrational and (2) human beings, who often act from emotions rather than with reason. Without denying that people do sometimes act emotionally, we still contend that most human behavior is rational and relatively predictable (except for that of the mentally ill). Therefore, human behavior should seem less irrational and unpredictable if we understand the *why* of it.

We would like to make three basic assumptions about human behavior as it affects motivation. First, *human behavior is caused;* second, it *is goal directed;* and third, it *does not occur in isolation.* This means that our behavior may be caused by the way we perceive the world and is directed toward achieving a certain goal or goals. Therefore, as shown in Figure 11.1, the motivational process is basically one of causation. *Employee needs* (motives) cause an inner *desire* to overcome some lack or imbalance. Some form of *managerial incentive* is applied that motivates us to respond and behave so that performance results. Thus, our needs are satisfied, and the organization attains its desired output. Understanding this process contributes to success in seeing that organization members contribute their joint efforts to generate productivity.

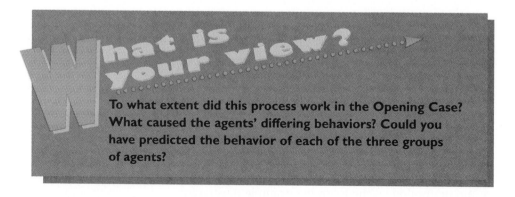

What is your view?

To what extent did this process work in the Opening Case? What caused the agents' differing behaviors? Could you have predicted the behavior of each of the three groups of agents?

Motivation provides the best potential source of increased productivity and profitability. It implies that employee abilities will be used more efficiently, which in turn should lead to improved job satisfaction as well as increased productivity.

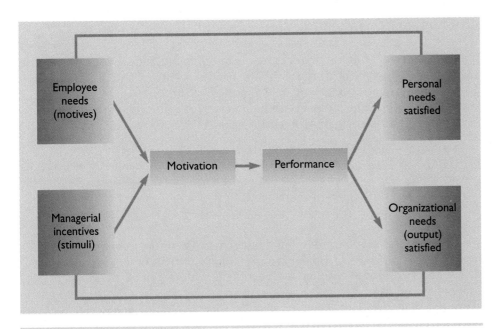

FIGURE 11.1
Motivation is goal directed.

Shortly we will examine various popular theories of motivation. Theories of motivation help explain the "why" of human behavior, and, although no one theory has all the answers, collectively they help managers create an environment in which individuals and groups work to achieve the organization's objectives while also working to achieve their own objectives.

Some Popular Theories of Motivation

Although theory is often viewed as abstract and unrelated to the real world, good theory provides a basis for understanding, explaining, and predicting what will happen in the real world. In fact, sociologist Kurt Lewin once said that nothing is more practical than good theory.[6] Moreover, whether they realize it or not, students and managers, working with and through other people, must operate from some theory. For discussion purposes, the prevailing theories of motivation can be classified into two categories—*content* and *process*.[7]

Content theories (sometimes called **need theories**) are concerned with the question of *what causes people to act.* This question leads to an identification of needs, incentives, and perceptions. The most popular of the content theories are (1) psychologist Abraham Maslow's hierarchy of needs, (2) researcher and author David McClelland's need-for-achievement theory, and (3) Frederick Herzberg's motivation-maintenance theory.

Process theories try to explain the process by which behavior is energized, directed, and related to performance and satisfaction—in other words, "What can I do to influence the behavior of others?" The currently accepted process theories are (1) expectancy theory, (2) reinforcement theory, and (3) equity theory.

content (need) theories
Theories of motivation that are concerned with the question of what causes behavior.

process theories
Theories of motivation that deal with how behavior originates and is performed.

Content Theories of Motivation

Content theories of motivation focus on the question of *what causes behavior to occur and stop.* The answers usually center on the needs, incentives, and perceptions that drive, pressure, spur, and force people to perform. The needs and perceptions are internal to the individual; the incentives are external factors that give value or utility to the goal or outcome of peoples' behavior.

hierarchy of needs
Psychologist Abraham Maslow's concept that human needs may be arranged in a hierarchy of importance progressing from a lower to a higher order, and that a satisfied need no longer serves as a primary motivator of behavior.

Maslow's Hierarchy of Needs   Maslow based his concept of a **hierarchy of needs** on two principles.[8] First, *human needs may be arranged in a hierarchy of importance* progressing from a lower to a higher order of needs, as shown in Figure 11.2. Second, *a satisfied need no longer serves as a primary motivator of behavior.*

How It Functions.   Maslow points out that needs can be thought of as being ranked in a hierarchy in which one need is more important than others—until it is satisfied. Once that need is satisfied, the next higher one becomes predominant. The order, however, can be reversed and even swing back and forth. Also, culture can affect the structure. For example, in many societies, social needs may be more important than ego or self-esteem.

Once satisfied, a given need no longer motivates behavior, for only when one is deprived of something and therefore craves it can it be used as an incentive. (The threat of deprivation is also an incentive.) This concept is significant, for it effectively limits the use of certain incentives and restricts the use of others.

Now let us look at the hierarchy of needs, as shown in Figure 11.2, and then elaborate on each of the levels.

1. *Physiological needs.* At the lowest level, but of primary importance when they are not met, are our physiological or biological needs. "Man does not live by bread alone," says the Bible, but anything else is less important when there is no bread. Unless the circumstances are unusual, the need we have for love, status, or recognition, for example, is inoperative when our stomachs have been empty for a while. When we eat regularly and adequately, however, we cease to regard hunger as an important motivator. The same is true of other physiological needs, such as those for air, water, rest, and exercise.

2. *Safety needs.* When the physiological needs are reasonably well satisfied, safety and security needs become important. These protect us against danger, threat, or deprivation. When we feel threatened or dependent, our greatest need is for guarantees, for protection, for security. For example, many employees join unions to ensure against unilateral, arbitrary management actions.

Most employees are in a dependent relationship in their work environment. Therefore, they may regard their safety needs as very important. Arbitrary management actions (such as favoritism or discrimination) and unpredictable application of policies can be powerful threats to the safety needs of any employee at any level.

3. *Social needs.* Social needs include the need for belonging, association, acceptance by colleagues, and giving and receiving friendship and love. When people's social needs—as well as their safety needs—are not satisfied, they may behave in ways that tend to stymie motivation and defeat organizational objectives. They become resistant, uncooperative, and even antagonistic. But this behavior is a consequence of their frustration, not a cause.

Social needs can be addressed in a number of ways at work.

4. *Esteem needs.* Above the social needs—in the sense that they do not become motivators until lower needs are reasonably well satisfied—are the esteem needs. These needs are of two kinds: (1) those that relate to one's self-esteem—needs for self-confidence, independence, achievement, competence, and knowledge—and (2) those that relate to one's reputation—needs for status, recognition, appreciation, and the deserved respect of one's colleagues.

Unlike the lower-order needs, these are rarely fully satisfied, since people seek indefinitely for more satisfaction of these needs. The typical organization offers few opportunities for the satisfaction of these egotistic needs to people at lower levels in the hierarchy. The conventional method of organizing work, particularly in industries involved in mass production, gives little consideration to this aspect of motivation.

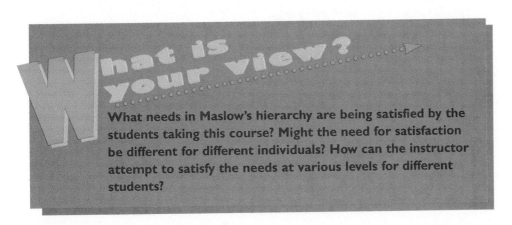

What is your view?

What needs in Maslow's hierarchy are being satisfied by the students taking this course? Might the need for satisfaction be different for different individuals? How can the instructor attempt to satisfy the needs at various levels for different students?

5. *Self-actualization needs.* Finally, there are needs for self-actualization, which include seeking self-fulfillment, realizing one's own potential, continuing self-development, and being creative in the broadest sense of that term. It is clear that the quality of work life in most organizations gives only limited opportunity for fulfilling these needs. Although companies are making greater strides, many still do not provide an environment that allows workers to achieve self-fulfillment.

How Managers Can Use This Theory.   Figure 11.2 provides some practical examples of how the needs hierarchy can be used in management motivation. The first three levels are self-explanatory; this chapter, Chapter 12 (on leadership), and Chapter 13 (on organizational change) provide greater insight into tapping the higher-level needs.

Maslow's theory should be regarded as only a general guide by managers, for it is a theoretical concept, not an absolute explanation of human behavior. There are therefore some important qualifications of which you should be aware.

FIGURE 11.2
Maslow's hierarchy of needs, in theory and as applied to managerial motivation.

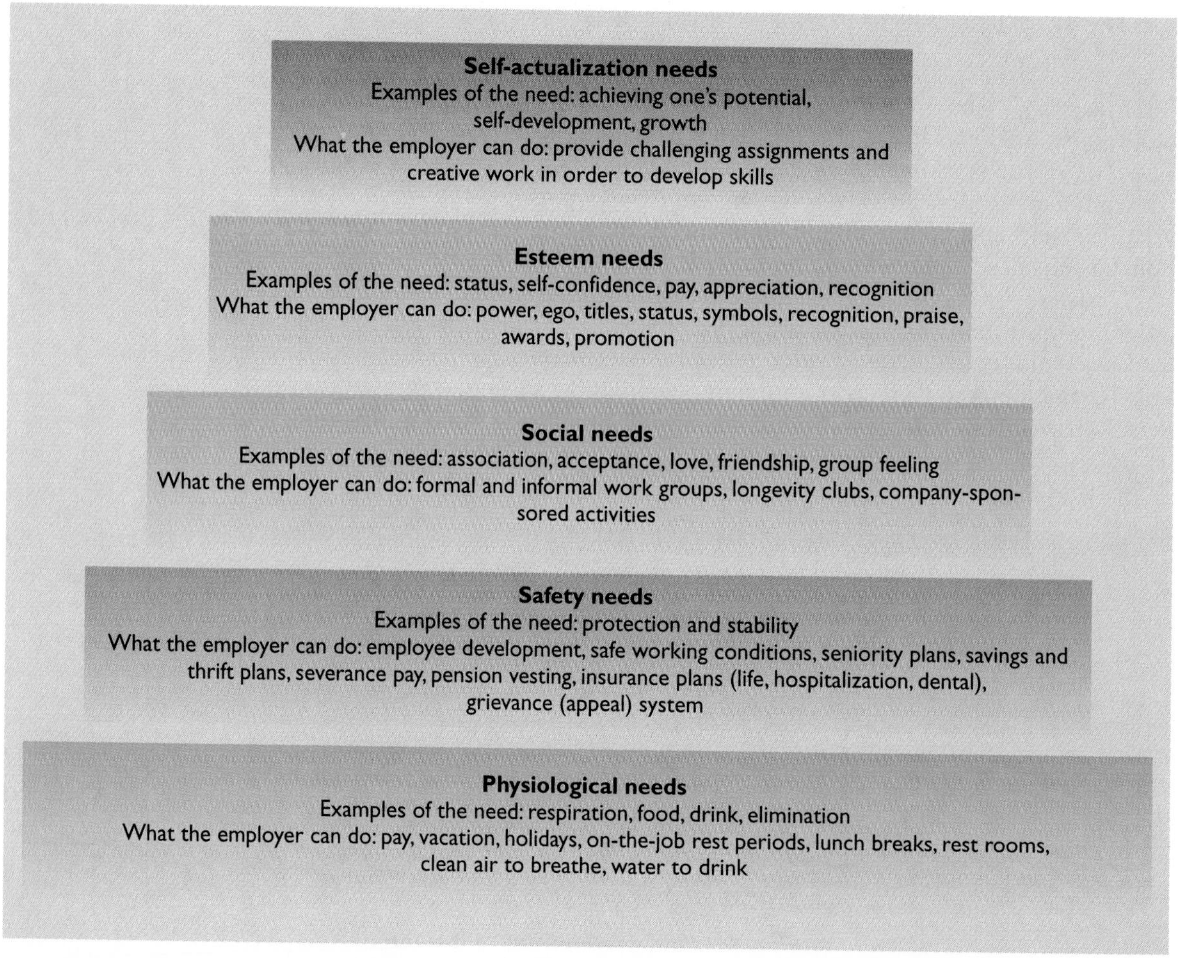

Self-actualization needs
Examples of the need: achieving one's potential,
self-development, growth
What the employer can do: provide challenging assignments and
creative work in order to develop skills

Esteem needs
Examples of the need: status, self-confidence, pay, appreciation, recognition
What the employer can do: power, ego, titles, status, symbols, recognition, praise,
awards, promotion

Social needs
Examples of the need: association, acceptance, love, friendship, group feeling
What the employer can do: formal and informal work groups, longevity clubs, company-sponsored activities

Safety needs
Examples of the need: protection and stability
What the employer can do: employee development, safe working conditions, seniority plans, savings and
thrift plans, severance pay, pension vesting, insurance plans (life, hospitalization, dental),
grievance (appeal) system

Physiological needs
Examples of the need: respiration, food, drink, elimination
What the employer can do: pay, vacation, holidays, on-the-job rest periods, lunch breaks, rest rooms,
clean air to breathe, water to drink

PATRICIA G. LYNCH,
U. S. ARMY CORPS OF
ENGINEERS

PRACTICING MANAGER

Patricia G. Lynch, an employee development specialist for the Portland, Oregon, district of the U.S. Army Corps of Engineers, grew up in Huntington, West Virginia. Her father, a bricklayer, has been secretary-treasurer of the local union for as long as Pat can remember. Her mother, now deceased, was a homemaker and active in county and state politics. Pat has one older brother who still lives in Huntington.

From a motivational standpoint, Pat's profile is interesting in that the expectations her early role models had for her have played a large part in her life. She dropped out of Marshall University to get married. Her husband was in the U.S. Navy but later went to work for the Corps of Engineers. After 20 years of marriage and three children, Pat and her husband divorced in 1980. The following period was a difficult time for her because, among other things, she had the primary responsibility for supporting three boys on a much lower income than before. We can gain some insight into how she handled this crisis from her background.

Pat's earlier role models were men, two of whom were teachers. Although she had a good mind, she feared tests and did only fairly on them. Pat remembers that one of her elementary teachers, Mr. Shirley, "would keep me in at recess and question me about material that was going to be on the test. Although I didn't know what he was doing, he later told me he had given me the test and I had passed with flying colors. He convinced me that I could put the same answers on paper and do just as well."

Another role model was her high school biology teacher, Mr. Lyle Plymale. Pat says that "this man was very knowledgeable in his field and never had a 'bad' student. He always found strong points in all students and helped them develop their potential. He had high expectations of them, and they responded by delivering good work. I learned from him what possibilities and capabilities were all about."

During their marriage, Pat's husband moved about every two years in pursuit of his career. At one point, while living in North Dakota, Pat started a successful small business. After two years as an entrepreneur, when the family moved to Vancouver, Washington, Pat went to work for the Corps of Engineers. Soon afterward, she was divorced and during this time of crisis she was motivated to use her management skills to organize a network of divorced women. This network "established a babysitting service, learned to recycle clothes, and developed a list of merchants that provided reasonable and honest car service, electrical service, hardware equipment, and so forth," and generally provided help and companionship for the divorced women. Pat's career at the Corps now demands most of her energy and talent, leaving her no time for outside activities, but the network she initiated is still functioning.

Since joining the Corps in 1978, Pat has been promoted from Employee Development Clerk, to Employee Development Specialist. In March 1993 she was appointed Acting Chief of the Training and Development Branch. Her past six performance evaluations have been rated in the Exceptional category. In addition, she has received several letters of commendation.

As the Training Officer, she manages the training function servicing 1400 employees at all levels of the organization. Her goal is to have training that is customer driven, competency based, and focused on achieving mission goals and objectives in an organization that is under ongoing and continuing change.

Pat is especially proud of two achievements: (1) the design and development of a women's leadership program for GS-9s and above and (2) the design and development of the district's Learning Resource Center (LRC). The audio/video portion of the LRC was transferred to the District Library in 1994, where it would have more visual exposure. Redge Martin, her former boss, singled her out for her "leadership role in the implementation of team building and partnering workshops in the District." He said that Pat is the human resource office's liaison to ensure the coordination of skills training needed to provide the linkage of management's and the construction partners' goals in achieving a quality partnership with customers. In fact, it was while serving as outside consultant for a partnering program that Pat came to our attention.

Source: Correspondence and discussions with Patricia G. Lynch, Redge Martin, and others.

For one thing, there are many exceptions to the theory—for example, "starving artist" types, who make sacrifices in their personal comfort while trying to achieve self-actualization through creating their works. Moreover, some people are much less security oriented or achievement oriented than others.

Furthermore, the two highest levels can hardly ever be fully satisfied, for there are always many new challenges and opportunities for growth, recognition, and achievement. In creative organizations, people may remain in the same job position for years and still find a great deal of challenge and motivation in their work.

Maslow's theory indicates that when the lower-level needs are relatively well satisfied, they cease to be important motivators of behavior. When they are threatened, however, these needs may suddenly become important again.

Take a look at the Practicing Manager profile of Patricia Lynch and see what needs motivate her.

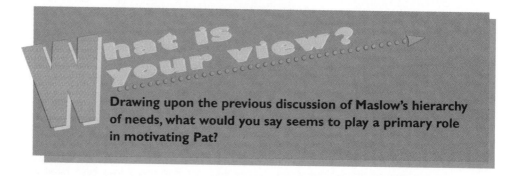

What is your view?

Drawing upon the previous discussion of Maslow's hierarchy of needs, what would you say seems to play a primary role in motivating Pat?

Maslow's theory can be used to explain and predict not only *individual* but also *group* behavior. This is especially true for those whose work is closely related to that of others and brings them into contact with others. It can also explain what happens as people's desire for the good life increases. When people are operating below or near subsistence level, they will be motivated to work for low wages and even be satisfied with poor working conditions. They may even be satisfied to continue under such conditions—for a while. But once they are made aware that there is more to life, they naturally want, expect, and demand more. The so-called carrot-and-stick approach does not work very well once a person moves beyond the subsistence level.

> A classic example of this tendency is what happened in South Korea. When the country was quite poor, people were willing to work long, hard hours for a pittance. As it became an industrialized nation, however, and achieved prosperity, workers wanted more of the better life—and many went on strike to get it.

McClelland's Achievement Theory   At a management conference in Helsinki, a Finnish bank officer was asked to name the most influential book he had read dealing with management. He replied, "*The Achieving Society*, by David McClelland." In this book, McClelland concluded that a country's economic development depends on the extent to which its citizens have a *need for achievement*.[9] Research by McClelland and others indicates that there is a high positive correlation between the need for achievement and effective performance and executive and entrepreneurial success. In the aggregate, how successful executives and entrepreneurs are helps determine a country's economic development. McClelland also discovered that this need *can* be developed in mature people, for an individual's drives or motives are not fixed as a result of childhood experiences.

Characteristics of the Achievement Oriented. Achievement-oriented people have certain characteristics that can be developed. In general, such people

1. Enjoy *moderate risk taking* as a function of skill, not chance; enjoy a *challenge;* and want *personal responsibility* for outcomes.
2. Tend to set *moderate achievement goals* and take calculated risks. One reason many companies have moved into a management by objectives (MBO) program is that there is a positive correlation between goal setting and performance levels.
3. Have a *strong need for feedback* about how well they are doing.
4. Have *skill in long-range planning* and possess *organizational abilities.* Both successful students and successful managers are adept at looking at future objectives and considering alternative ways of reaching those objectives. Many companies recruiting college graduates look very carefully at their extracurricular activities and particularly their leadership positions in student organizations. They know from experience that this activity enhances their organizational abilities and leadership skills.

The Need for Affiliation and Power. More recently, McClelland has gone further with his research and studied the needs people have for affiliation and power.[10] Since the need for affiliation is essentially the same as Maslow's social need, we will focus on the power need. Although all of us have degrees of all three needs—achievement, affiliation, and power—one is usually stronger than the other two. While the word *power* has a negative connotation for many people, it should be kept in mind that power is closely related to leadership and results in influencing people, events, and decisions within an organizational framework.

McClelland's research has found that managers with a high need for power in the majority of instances use it for the benefit of the organization rather than for self-aggrandizement. They use power to increase the power of others through participation, support, and the positive reinforcement of accomplishments. They view their role as managers as a way to expand power for themselves and for other members of the organization rather than as a way to hoard power. Tips 11.1 offers some hints for increasing power.

> One classic study discovered that male managers with a higher need for power had more productive departments than managers with a high need for affiliation.[11]

Herzberg's Motivation-Maintenance Theory In general, employees tend to focus on lower-level needs, particularly security, in their first jobs. After those are satisfied, however, they try to fulfill higher-level needs, such as initiative, creativity, and responsibility. It is by appealing to those needs that real achievement in efficiency, productivity, and creativity can be made, although managers do not always do this.

Several motivation research experiments, including those of Frederick Herzberg, have demonstrated the importance of these higher-level needs as motivators. His two-factor theory of motivation is really a transitional theory between describing needs and understanding how behavior can be influenced. Herzberg's

TipS 11.1

How to Increase Your Power

What could be more American than football? What could be more international than the accumulation of power? In his article "Power," Tom Peters, coauthor of *In Search of Excellence*, gives advice on how to build up "27 to 7 leads" so that your career won't be "lost in the last 30 seconds because of an unlucky bounce, a referee's bad call."

Peters's advice focuses on small, practical, detail-oriented steps that can be taken to greatly improve one's own power. His focus is on "thank-you notes and on not being a jerk." And he warns the reader to "remember that business is a human game." Although each piece of advice seems logical, even obvious, it is often overlooked by both employers and employees. However, his advice can turn a practicing manager's mere survival into success. Below is a condensed list of over 40 of Tom Peters's sterling suggestions.

1. Don't forget the power of sending handwritten thank-you notes.

2. Give credit, appreciation, applause, approval, and respect liberally.

3. Gently remind people of how much you have done for them.

4. Praise in public, punish in private.

5. Show up, preferably in person.

6. It's the little stuff.
   a. Stand behind people in their time of stress.
   b. Accumulate the small wins.
   c. Remove the little obstacles out of your subordinates' ways.
   d. Soak yourself in details and knowledge to outdo your competitors, but obsess about the small stuff in private.
   e. Don't forget the little people who have the best information and could dash your hopes of success if they become resentful.

7. A thick Rolodex shows great power through the network of people you've created. Don't miss cocktail parties or power lunches that can foster networking.

8. Work the phones and return phone calls fast.

9. Build credibility from the outside in. When the customer loves you, internal politics can be avoided and you become indispensable.

10. Be committed, persistent, and sincere.

11. Perception is reality, so dress the part and look popular at your next speaking engagement, even if it means holding the event in a phone booth rather than an auditorium.

12. Hold your tongue. "Smart" comments will haunt you.

13. As smart as an MBA may be, there are no right answers.

14. Fighting drains energy without gaining supporters. So seize opportunities with the knowledge of when a retreat is necessary.

15. Finally, when you're working on "the main event" of your career, shut off all distractions, even if that means breaking some of the previous rules.

Source: Tom Peters, "Power," excerpted from his *The Pursuit of WOW* in *Success*, November 1994, pp. 32–44.

factors are not needs but work conditions that can be altered by management to provide more or less satisfaction or dissatisfaction.

Job Satisfaction.   In the initial study, Herzberg and his associates conducted in-depth interviews with over 200 engineers and accountants.[12] These professionals were asked—as you were— to recall events or incidents from the past year that had made them feel unusually good or bad about their work. They were also asked to speculate on how much the events had affected their performance and morale.

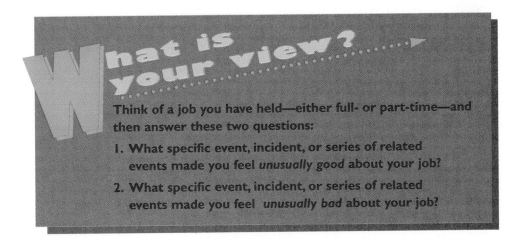

Think of a job you have held—either full- or part-time—and then answer these two questions:

1. What specific event, incident, or series of related events made you feel *unusually good* about your job?

2. What specific event, incident, or series of related events made you feel *unusually bad* about your job?

The interviews were assessed, and in almost all cases, the factors causing job satisfaction had a stimulating effect on performance and morale, whereas the factors causing job dissatisfaction had a negative effect. Another important finding was that *the positive factors were all intrinsic to the job content, whereas the negative factors were all extrinsic.* That is, when people felt good about their jobs, it was usually because they were doing their work particularly well or were becoming more expert in their professions or being recognized for good performance. Favorable feelings were related to the specific tasks performed, such as designing a bridge, meeting a deadline, or making a big sale, rather than to background factors, such as money, security, or working conditions. Conversely, unfavorable feelings resulted from some disturbance in the work context that caused people to feel that they were not being treated fairly, such as poor wages, unsafe conditions, poor relations with superiors or co-workers, or fear of losing their jobs.

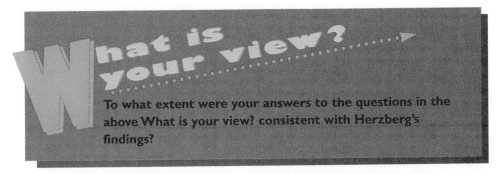

To what extent were your answers to the questions in the above What is your view? consistent with Herzberg's findings?

Motivators and Maintenance Factors. On the basis of these findings, the researchers made a distinction between what they called *motivators* and what they called *maintenance factors,* as shown in Table 11.1. **Motivators,** or **motivating factors,** have an uplifting effect on attitudes and lead to improved performance. **Maintenance factors** (sometimes called **hygiene factors**) are significant only in their absence, which causes increased dissatisfaction; their presence merely prevents dissatisfaction. These factors can be compared to dental hygiene. Brushing our teeth regularly does not *improve* them, but it helps to *prevent* further decay.

motivators (motivating factors) Factors primarily concerned with work *content* issues, which have an uplifting effect on attitudes or performance by creating satisfaction.

maintenance (hygiene) factors Factors primarily concerned with work *context* issues, which cannot motivate but do contribute to dissatisfaction if not present.

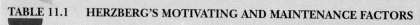

TABLE 11.1   HERZBERG'S MOTIVATING AND MAINTENANCE FACTORS

Motivating Factors	Maintenance Factors
Opportunity for achievement	Company policies and administration
Responsibility	Quality of technical supervision
Recognition	Interpersonal relationships with superiors, peers, and subordinates
Advancement	
Creative and challenging work	Salary
Possibilities for personal growth on the job	Job security
	Working conditions
	Employee benefits
	Job status
	Personal life

These two sets of factors parallel Maslow's concept of a hierarchy of needs. The *motivators* relate to the highest levels (esteem and self-actualization), and—as shown in Figure 11.3 and Table 11.1—the *maintenance factors* relate to the lower-level needs, primarily the security needs and, to a large extent, social relationships.

What this indicates is that employees *expect* to be treated fairly by their managers, to have decent working conditions and pay comparable to that of people doing simi-

FIGURE 11.3

Comparison of Maslow's hierarchy theory with Herzberg's motivation-maintenance theory.

Maslow's needs hierarchy theory	Herzberg's motivation-maintenance theory
Motivational factors	
Self-fulfillment/self-actualization	Creative and challenging work
	Achievement
Ego/esteem	Possibility of growth
	Responsibility
	Advancement
	Recognition
Maintenance factors	
Ego/esteem	Status
Social/belonging	Interpersonal relations
	Superior
	Subordinates
	Peers
	Supervision
	Company policy and administration
Safety/security	Job security
	Working conditions
	Salary
Physiological/biological	Personal life

lar work, and to have company policies consistently and equitably applied to all employees. When these expectations are not met, employees are demotivated (or negatively motivated), usually resulting in inefficiency and a high turnover rate. But fulfilling these expectations does not necessarily motivate employees, for, as Maslow's theory maintains, it is only when the lower-level needs are satisfied that the higher-level needs can be used most effectively in motivating employees. The key is for managers to make sure that maintenance factors are provided for and to create an environment that taps the motivating factors. Tips 11.2 explains some of the things a manager can do to motivate employees with the two-factor theory.

Evaluation of the Theory. After the original study, critics of Herzberg's theory were quick to point out that, although the findings might apply to professionals who sought creativity in their work, they would not apply to other groups of employees. Herzberg, however, found similar results in 12 studies involving various groups.[13] Similar studies by different investigators in different countries *using the same research method* have shown surprisingly similar results (although with minor variations).

In a study conducted in New Zealand using Herzberg's methodology, findings similar to those of previous studies were obtained.[14] One employee, when asked for one of the most dissatisfying job experiences, stated that it was the quality of job supervision. His answer supports the role of supervision as a maintenance factor:

> *I was given complete responsibility for performance on a temporary job. I was to "report back at a later date and tell the boss how I was getting on." When a couple of hours later the boss came down and asked me how I was doing, I was glad he appeared to be taking an interest. But when he came back again every two or three hours, I got fed up and looked for ways of palming the job off on someone else. I wondered why I was given the job in the first place if the boss thought I couldn't do it right.*

TipS 11.2

How to Use the Two-Factor Theory to Motivate Employees

Some practical things managers can do to create a motivating environment include

1. Sending employees to training courses for skill upgrading and management development

2. With new and untrained employees, assigning experienced employees to assist in training and development

3. With trained and motivated employees, delegating authority and supervising by results rather than using close supervision

4. In dealing with complex problems or special projects, calling employees in and getting their ideas

5. Assigning employees to special ad hoc task forces for developing recommendations on key issues

6. Complimenting and recognizing employees for good work

Colgate-Palmolive Company has a program to recognize outstanding employees. The winners of its "You Can Make a Difference Award" are given a week-long tribute, including being introduced at the annual meeting and receiving $3,500 in stock, a gold medal, and an embroidered blazer.

Source: "We Love You: More Companies Reward Workers Who Go That Extra Mile," *Wall Street Journal*, May 2, 1989, p. 1.

I started taking longer on the job than I should have and couldn't have cared less if what I was doing was right or wrong, since this boss was constantly checking to see if I made any mistakes.

The experience of Sony Corporation's U.S. subsidiary in Park Ridge, New Jersey, tends to confirm the theory. Product specialists who answer calls from customers are given bonus points not for taking more calls but for the *quality* of their conversations. They are motivated for the hard work by "nothing more than the job itself and any promotions it brings."[15]

On the other hand, studies *using a different research method* have, in the majority of instances, failed to support Herzberg's theory.[16] This fact has led some researchers to conclude that the theory is "method-bound"; that is, when Herzberg's research method is followed, the theory is supported; when his method is not followed, the theory fails. In other words, you are more likely to mention something that *you did* when asked about a satisfying experience. You are more likely to mention something *you could not control* when identifying a dissatisfying work experience.

A survey of 3,500 workers by the Wyatt Company found results contrary to the theory. The top four factors these workers valued in a job were (1) a boss they could respect, (2) satisfying work, (3) satisfactory pay, and (4) opportunities for advancement. These were top priorities for both men and women. Notice that the first and third of these factors are maintenance factors, which, according to Herzberg, are not supposed to motivate.[17]

Herzberg's theory is valuable as a general guide to understanding motivation at work. Two weaknesses are the conclusion that money is always a maintenance factor and that recognition and achievement are always motivators. Later, we develop the thesis that money can be a powerful motivator when it is used as a recognition of and reward for achievement. Money also has symbolic meaning. In addition, lack of recognition can cause considerable dissatisfaction when one is convinced that one's performance deserves recognition and it is not forthcoming.

expectancy theory A theory of motivation stating that individuals are predicted to be high performers when they see (1) a high probability that their efforts will lead to high performance, (2) a high probability that high performance will lead to favorable outcomes, and (3) that these outcomes will be, on balance, attractive to them.

Process Theories of Motivation

The previous theories focus on the *needs* that drive or spur behavior and the *incentives* that attract or induce behavior. The *process theories* focus on how behavior is energized and directed and how it is related to performance and satisfaction. We will look at (1) expectancy theory, (2) reinforcement theory, and (3) equity theory.

Expectancy Theory   Some of the most important modern process theories of motivation rely on what is called **expectancy theory.** This concept says that individuals are predicted to be high performers when they see (1) a high probability that their efforts will lead to high performance, (2) a high probability that high performance will lead to favorable outcomes, and (3) that these outcomes will be, on balance, attractive to them.

Expectancy theory states that much work behavior can be explained by the fact that employees determine in advance what their behavior may accomplish and the value they place on alternative possible accomplishments or outcomes.

Notice in the Opening Case that the supervisors of both the "superstaff" and the "average" unit motivated their agents by instilling in them the idea that they were superior performers—and they performed accordingly.

Another example is the point system Eastman Kodak Company's International Biotechnologies unit uses to motivate employees to give better customer service. Workers earn one point for every phone call received and two for each follow-up call. Employees showing the most improvement from month to month can trade in their points for a prize: paid time off. Many employees earn up to four hours off.[18]

Some writers have termed this a "payoff" or "what's in it for me?" view of behavior. Yet this approach does partially explain how behavior is energized, resulting in increased performance and satisfaction. For example, if you expect hard work and performance to lead to superior pay and a promotion, you will place a high value on both receiving superior pay and eventually earning a promotion. In this situation, assuming that you have the ability to do the work, you would probably be inclined to put forth a strong effort to receive the superior pay and promotion.

According to Victor Vroom, people are motivated to work if they (1) expect increased effort to lead to reward and (2) value the rewards resulting from their efforts.[19] Thus, from management's point of view, Vroom's value-expectancy theory produces the following results:

$$\text{Motivation} = \begin{bmatrix} \text{Expectancy that} \\ \text{increased effort will lead} \\ \text{to increased rewards} \end{bmatrix} \times \begin{bmatrix} \text{Value to the individual} \\ \text{of the rewards resulting} \\ \text{from his or her efforts} \end{bmatrix}$$

Employees work harder for paid time off.

Let us take a look at how Vroom's theory operates. Suppose that Bill's boss says, "If you are able to complete the maintenance work by this Saturday, Bill, I'll recommend you for promotion to supervisor. I realize that it will mean your putting in some overtime, but think about it, and let me know your answer." There are two important factors involved: (1) the *value* Bill places on being promoted to supervisor (suppose the last thing in the world he wants is a promotion!) and (2) Bill's *expectancy* that (*a*) he will be able to realistically complete the work by Saturday and (*b*) if he completes the work, he will actually be named supervisor. (In other words, does Bill's supervisor really have the influence to get him promoted?) The answers to these questions explain Bill's decision whether to exert the necessary effort to complete the work by Saturday.

From our research and consulting, we have found that if there is a high likelihood of successfully completing an assignment and receiving a desirable reward, a person is more likely to be motivated to perform the job well. Therefore, a manager who understands employees' needs and abilities can influence their performance by setting challenging but attainable goals and providing suitable rewards.

Another finding is that *motivation is more powerful when a person is internally motivated.* In the example just presented, Bill's internal motivation will be activated if Bill wants a promotion and believes his boss can really get him promoted if he works hard.

Reinforcement Theory   Another theory of influencing and changing work behavior is *reinforcement theory*, largely based on the work of psychologist B. F. Skinner.[20] Other terms used to describe this approach are *positive reinforcement* and *behavior modification.* Many managers have been using some of its principles for a long time, but only recently has there been a systematic examination and application of the principles in work settings.

Source: Copyright 1971. Reprinted with special permission of King Features Syndicate, Inc. World Rights reserved.

Reinforcement theory, which is based primarily on the *law of effect*, states that behavior followed by satisfying consequences tends to be repeated, whereas behavior followed by unsatisfying consequences tends not be repeated.[21] In this way, behavior is influenced or shaped in the way the environment (the organization) desires.

Skinner distinguishes between *reinforcement*, the presentation of an attractive reward following a response or the removal of an unpleasant or negative condition following a response, and *punishment*, providing unpleasant consequences for undesirable behavior. Thus, reinforcement theory is a method of motivation in which favorable behavior is eliminated by unsatisfying consequences. Suppose a worker's attendance has been spotty recently. Reinforcement theory can work in two ways:

1. You can *reinforce* (praise, reward) the worker's favorable behavior (showing up on time), thereby encouraging him or her to repeat it.
2. You can *discourage* (scolding, written disciplinary warning) the worker's unfavorable behavior through punishment, thereby encouraging him or her not to repeat it.

Training, development, and growth occur through positive reinforcement or focusing behavioral responses on what should be done. As shown in Chapter 7, MBO is based on this principle, for it relies heavily on the behaviorist model of motivational principles.

The theory does seem to operate when standards are clearly set, and improvement results from the frequent application of positive feedback and from recognition for satisfactory behavior. It is assumed that the employees' desire for the rewards of positive feedback and recognition will in large measure motivate them to perform satisfactorily in anticipation of such rewards.

> This method is used by Mary Kay Ash, founder of Mary Kay Cosmetics Inc., to motivate her independent saleswomen—called beauty consultants. She gave away $6 million in sales incentives to some of the 25,000 women attending a recent convention in Dallas. Among the rewards were 523 pink Cadillacs, 225 all-expense-paid European trips, 1,981 diamond rings of 1 to 3.5 carats each, 102 mink coats, 2,693 Pontiacs and Oldsmobiles, and five "fantasy gifts" worth $5,000 each. That type of reinforcement has made her company number two (after Avon) in door-to-door cosmetics sales.[22]

Positive reinforcement, when properly applied, can be very powerful in influencing motivation. When positive reinforcement consists of praise, it is essential that it be sincere and based on a behavior or outcome that deserves tribute. If you attempt to flatter someone insincerely, the praise can backfire.

A knowledge of motivation theory is helpful in providing managers with the ability and tools to create a positive motivational environment. This same knowledge, however, also provides managers with the ability to manipulate people in an unethical manner, as shown in MAP 11.1.

To be most effective, praise should be as specific as possible. A compliment on a particular task done well is much more satisfying than a generic "You're doing a great job!" Effective praise, however, has many advantages over other reinforcements. As one authority notes, "It costs nothing and is almost universally applicable. A manager who is unsure of where to begin can safely use praise as the first step

reinforcement theory
A method of motivation in which favorable behavior is reinforced by satisfying consequences and unfavorable behavior is eliminated by unsatisfying consequences.

MANAGEMENT APPLICATION AND PRACTICE   11.1

Unethical Applications of Motivation Theory

A manager attempted to gain influence and manage her boss primarily through positive reinforcement. Actually, this technique can be a powerful force, and for over a year it worked very effectively. Eventually, however, it dawned on the boss that the subordinate manager was manipulating him by providing compliments and positive strokes both when they were deserved and when they were not. Everything he did seemed to be deemed worthy of positive strokes. In this case, the tactic backfired, as the subordinate manager lost credibility with her boss, sacrificing her influence and ultimately her position as well.

In another situation, a company president manipulated a union representing his employees by using expectancy theory. During a recent recession, the president agreed not to lay off workers if the union would agree to a pay reduction. Moreover, he promised the employees that, after the company had recovered from the recession and reached a certain level of income, the pay would be restored and a bonus system for all employees introduced.

Once the recession was over, the pay *was* restored, and a bonus system *was* introduced, but only for top executives. In this case, the president's decision was comparable to the farmer who killed the goose that laid the golden eggs. The union went on a prolonged strike, and the board removed the president and replaced him with someone from outside the organization.

toward increasing employee productivity. Even praise poorly given may have a positive effect on an individual's behavior."[23] In MAP 11.2, which highlights motivational practices at America's best-managed companies, note the importance of creating a climate of positive reinforcement.

equity theory
Predicts that people will compare (1) the *inputs* they bring to the job in the form of education, experience, training, and effort with (2) the *outcomes* (rewards) they receive as compared to those of other employees in comparable jobs.

Equity Theory   Another theory that has received support from research studies is **equity theory** (or, as some term it, the *inequity theory*). This theory predicts that people will compare (1) the *inputs* they bring to the job in the form of education, experience, training, and effort with (2) the *outcomes* (rewards) they receive as compared to those of other employees in comparable jobs.[24]

The belief, on the basis of comparison, that an inequity exists, in the form of either underpayment or overpayment, will have possible adverse motivational and behavioral effects on performance. It should be kept in mind that the key factor is whether an inequity is *perceived*, not whether it actually exists.

An associate professor was satisfied with her status and income, even though she knew she could receive a higher salary elsewhere. This fact did not bother her, because the cost of living was much lower in the small university community where she lived, the lifestyle and quality of life were attractive, and she was making contributions to her field through publications.

Things were fine until she heard that another associate professor was earning a much higher salary than she was. She was greatly upset because she considered herself a much better teacher and had contributed more in her field in publications than he had. A discussion with the department head failed to resolve the "inequity" by providing an increase in salary. She therefore sought another position and left the university the next year.

MANAGEMENT APPLICATION AND PRACTICE 11.2

Motivational Practices at America's Best-Managed Companies

Many organizations and their managers are quite adept at penalizing employees for mistakes or poor performance. The best-selling book *In Search of Excellence: Lessons from America's Best-Run Companies* concluded that "the dominant culture in most big companies demands punishment for a mistake no matter how useless, small, invisible." The book goes on to say that the dominant culture in the *best-managed companies* is just the opposite. These companies develop "winners" by constantly reinforcing the idea that employees are winners. The performance targets are set so that they provide a challenge—but are attainable. The effective manager continually gives recognition for effective employee performance.

Organization psychologists have long been advocating certain company actions to increase the motivation of individuals. According to one authority, many of America's best-managed companies have implemented these actions, which include (1) tying extrinsic rewards (such as pay) to performance; (2) setting realistic and challenging goals; (3) evaluating employee performance accurately and providing feedback on performance; (4) promoting on the basis of skill and performance rather than personal characteristics, power, or connections; (5) building the skill level of the workforce through training and development; and (6) enlarging and enriching jobs through increases in responsibility, variety, and significance. These actions demonstrate the practicality of the theories presented in this chapter.

On a more all-encompassing note, an article on employee practices at the best-managed companies shows that these companies place considerable emphasis not only on the rights and responsibilities of employees but also on the value of employee contribution through participative management. Specifically, these companies provide stakeholder status for unions, employee stock ownership, a fair measure of job security, lifelong training, benefits tailored to individual needs, participation in decision making, freedom of expression, and incentive pay.

Although the equity theory seems to explain motivation in some situations, most of us can identify some individuals who don't conform to the equity theory model.

For example, an international accounting firm manager in New Zealand told the following story. Two accountants were hired at the same time, and at the end of the year, one was given twice the raise of the other, based on her performance. When the high-performing accountant discovered that her raise was twice what her friend had received, she talked privately with her manager and requested that her raise be lowered to the same level as her friend's.

The Role of Money as a Primary Motivator

The role of money as a primary motivator has long been a subject of debate, especially since Herzberg's research. Let us examine the debate by first making the case that money is *not* a primary motivator and then the case that it *is* a primary motivator.

Money Is Not a Primary Motivator

In Herzberg's motivation-maintenance theory, money was found to be a mainte-nance (hygiene) factor that prevented losses of efficiency was but was not a moti-vator in and of itself. In essence, the lack of money could be a demotivator, but more money (pay) does not necessarily increase motivation.

Most of us are aware of people who have values that are at odds with material-istic concerns. Many people, because of these values, choose professions that pay much less than other occupations. Missionaries, Peace Corps workers, social work-ers, nurses, and elementary and high school teachers come to mind. Along these lines are people who turn down promotions and transfers to other locations with considerably higher salaries because of family considerations or preference for a certain location.

We can also cite examples of certain professions and business organizations where the pay is high but output is not close to its potential. Again, there seems to be no correlation between pay and performance.

Alfie Kahn, an expert on pay systems, has for quite some time challenged the underlying assumptions behind incentive pay plans. Among other points, he indi-cates "research suggests that, by and large, rewards succeed in securing one thing only—temporary compliance. When it comes to producing lasting changes in atti-tude and behavior, however, rewards, like punishment, are strikingly ineffective. Once the rewards run out, people revert to their old behaviors."[25]

Finally, a study done by Korn/Ferry International and the UCLA Graduate School of Management found that love of work—not money—motivates top exec-utives. The study was of vice-presidents of major companies and clearly found that money was secondary to love of work.[26]

Money Is a Primary Motivator

It should be pointed out that in the UCLA study, the average salary of the vice-pres-idents was $215,000 a year, so they already had plenty of money. As Maslow's theory demonstrates, for people struggling to satisfy lower-level needs, money *is* a primary motivator.

> While conducting a management development program at Southeast Paper Company in Dublin, Georgia, a consultant heard supervisors challenging the Herzberg finding that money is a hygiene factor and not a motivator. They indi-cated that money was a primary motivator not only for them but for all the employ-ees in their facility. They cited as evidence a recently instituted bonus system tied to production quotas. After the bonus system was introduced, production increased dramatically and remained at a high level, resulting in more money for employees.

Related to this example is Wal-Mart, which uses money—along with other incentives—to motivate its employees, almost all of whom are stockholders. Employees earn bonuses, based on their store's profits, which generates a strong team spirit. Some have become quite wealthy, and Wal-Mart's profits jumped 32 percent in 1989. By 1990, it had passed Kmart as the number two retailer, and in 1991, it passed Sears as number one. Since 1962, Wal-Mart has become the world's

What motivation theory best helps to explain what
happened in the Southeast Paper Company plant?

largest retailer, is present in 47 states, and now includes an International Division. At the end of 1994, the joint agreement with Mexican partner CIFRA was strengthened, resulting in a total of seven warehouse clubs, two supermarkets, ten discount stores, two combination stores, and two supercenters. More store expansions are planned in Mexico. One hundred twenty-two stores were acquired from Woolworth Corp. in Canada. Wal-Mart believes in employee team spirit. Through the "Yes We Can, Sam" suggestion program, 650 employee ideas were implemented. Incentive programs and stock ownership plans are also used to foster a sense of ownership and commitment.[27]

Edward Lawler III, an expert on motivation, maintains that his work, as well as that of others, continues to show that money can be an important motivator when a "line of sight" exists for individuals. By line of sight, he means that individuals view the reward as important and can see a direct relationship between their effort and the reward.[28] This conclusion underlies the expectancy theory of motivation. In our culture, money serves as a symbol of success and achievement. For many of us, it is a way of "keeping score," giving us feedback on how well we are doing.

Unfortunately, during this period of downsizing and restructuring, a group that has been slighted in the motivational practices of a number of large companies has been middle managers. In many downsizing and merger situations, many high-performing managers lose out on promotional opportunities. Professor Michael Gibbs studied two types of motivations available to large companies—promotion-based motivation and within-the-job motivation, such as raises and bonuses. He found promotion to be a primary motivational tool but discovered that when people were passed over for promotion, pay raises were not closely related to performance evaluations. As might be expected, over time this situation had a demotivating effect on the passed-over middle managers, who continued to receive high performance evaluations but only slight or no pay raises.[29]

The Current Motivational Challenges

Three forces are having a major impact on and increasing the challenge of creating a motivational climate in today's workplace: worker diversity, a shift to a more service-based economy, and the globalization of the marketplace. These forces have led to brutal competition. As a result, the old employee contract of worker loyalty for job security is no longer operative. For example, in 1980–82, 79 percent of management and 75 percent of nonmanagement felt "good" or "very good" about job security. In 1992–94, the percentage reporting their job security was "good" or "very good" had dropped to 55 percent for management and 51 percent for nonmanagement.[30] The new contract that appears to be emerging is spelled out in MAP 11.3.

MANAGEMENT APPLICATION AND PRACTICE   11.3

What Companies and Employees Owe One Another

The encouraging news is that certain companies are crafting a new deal that works—sometimes. It makes no one feel warm and fuzzy, but it seems to minimize debilitating fury and anxiety. In its most naked form, it goes like this: "There will never be job security. You will be employed by us as long as you add value to the organization, and *you* are continuously responsible for finding ways to add value. In return, you have the right to demand interesting and important work, the freedom and resources to perform it well, pay that reflects your contribution, and the experience and training needed to be employable here or elsewhere."

For some companies and some workers, that is exhilarating and liberating. It requires companies to relinquish much of the control they have held over employees and give genuine authority to work teams.

Companies must work harder than ever to make themselves attractive places to work. Employees become far more responsible for their work and careers: No more parent-child relationships, say the consultants, but adult to adult. If the old arrangement sounded like binding nuptial vows, the new one suggests a series of casual, thrilling—if often temporary—encounters. For others, the arrangement is troubling. Attractive, mobile, young technical experts and professionals may fare well, at least for a while. But down the road, will those folks be cast aside for someone younger, more attractive, more current? Or will wisdom, not technical expertise, be what keeps people employed 20 years hence? No one knows. Says Kevin Sullivan, senior vice president at Apple Computer: "Experience or knowledge? It's a dilemma."

Source: Excerpted from Brian O'Reilly, "The New Deal," *Fortune*, June 13, 1994, pp. 44–45.

What is most certain in this environment is the need for new business strategies that develop, use, and empower teams that facilitate innovation and the pursuit of quality. Even as loyalty to the organization decreases, loyalty to team members who are part of creative problem-solving teams more than offsets the decrease. As Texas Instruments's chief executive, Jerry Junkins, has stated, "No matter what your business, these teams are the wave of the future."[31] More will be said about motivational team-building strategies in Chapters 13 and 14.

SUMMARY

The primary purpose of this chapter has been to develop an understanding of the "why" of human behavior in order to help managers create a climate of positive motivation. We examined some of the prominent theories of motivation, such as Maslow's hierarchy of needs, McClelland's achievement theory, Herzberg's motivation-maintenance theory, expectancy theory, reinforcement theory, and equity theory. Moreover, we have looked at the role managers play in satisfying the human needs of their subordinates at work. We hope that as you have read this chapter, you have seen the interrelations between the theories and effective management.

The three primary purposes of motivation were discussed, along with the need of positive motivation. We showed how human behavior affects motivation and developed a model to show that motivation is goal directed.

Let us build a few bridges in this summary by using Maslow's hierarchy of needs as the basic building block. For more workers, lower-level needs are relatively well satisfied but can be reactivated if threatened. The big challenge is to create an environment to motivate people through higher-level needs—esteem, achievement, recognition, competence, self-actualization, and advancement.

According to McClelland's achievement theory, there is a high positive correlation between the need for achievement and effective performance.

Herzberg's theory supports Maslow's concept of a hierarchy of needs: The motivators relate to the highest levels (esteem and self-actualization), and the maintenance factors relate to the lower-level needs, primarily the security needs.

According to expectancy theory, employees assess in advance what their behavior may accomplish and consider possible outcomes. Thus, the actions of the supervisor and the organization significantly influence the behavior chosen by subordinates. Workers not only expect fair treatment from superiors, equitable wages, and decent conditions of employment, but also want to work in an environment in which there is a knowledge base, an atmosphere of approval, and consistent discipline. People are negatively motivated when these expectations are not met. Usually, these negative feelings are reflected in inefficiency and a high turnover rate.

Reinforcement theory—based on the law of effect—assumes that workers' desire for rewards from positive feedback leads to improved performance. It was shown that the best-run U.S. companies use this form of positive motivational tactics to improve performance. However, if workers perceive rewards to be inequitably distributed, in the form of either underpayment or overpayment, performance may be adversely affected.

In some cases, money can be a powerful motivator; in other instances, it can even be a demotivator or serve as a negative motivation. We noted that a knowledge of motivation theory is helpful in providing managers with the insight to create a climate for positive motivation. It can also provide managers with the ability to manipulate people unethically. Character is very important in dealing with people.

Finally, we noted that worker diversity, the shift to a service-based economy, and increasing globalization are creating tremendous challenges in motivating today's workforce.

KEY TERMS

motivation, 359
content (need) theories, 363
process theories, 363
hierarchy of needs, 364
motivators (motivating factors), 371

maintenance (hygiene) factors, 371
expectancy theory, 374
reinforcement theory, 377
equity theory, 378

11.1 What Do You Want from Your Job?

learning exercise

Rank the listed employment factors in their order of importance to you at three points in your career. In the first column, assume that you are about to graduate and are looking for your first full-time job. In the second column, assume that you have been gainfully employed for 5 to 10 years and that you are currently employed by a reputable firm at the prevailing salary for the type of job and industry. In the third column, try to assume that 25 to 30 years from now you have found your niche in life and have been working for a reputable employer for several years. (Rank your first choice as 1, second as 2, and so forth, through 10.)

Employment Factor	As You Seek Your First Full-Time Job	Your Ranking 5–10 Years Later	Your Ranking 25–30 Years Later
Employee benefits			
Fair adjustment of grievances			
Good job instruction and training			
Effective job supervision by your supervisor			
Promotion possibilities			
Recognition (praise, rewards, and so on)			
Job safety			
Job security (no threat of being dismissed or laid off)			
Good salary			
Good working condition (nice office surroundings, good hours, and so on)			

Questions

1. What does your ranking tell you about your motivation now?

2. Is there any change in the second and third periods?

3. What are the changes, and why do you think they occurred?

11.2 Giving Praise

learning exercise

Objectives

1. To provide participants with an understanding of the characteristics of effective praise

2. To provide participants with an understanding of the benefits to be gained from praising employees

3. To provide participants with feedback regarding the type of praise they and others give

4. To provide participants with feedback regarding the type of praise they and others like to receive

General Description

One of the most common, effective, and inexpensive approaches to motivation is giving praise. Yet few managers understand the characteristics of effective praise; nor are they aware of the different forms praise can take. This exercise explores a number of different aspects of the use of praise.

Materials Needed

Two sheets of paper and one pen or pencil per participant.

Instructions

1. All participants should think of two people—subordinates, co-workers, friends—whom they have praised within the last two months (or believe are praiseworthy).

2. Each participant should then write down what he or she said to each of the two people praised. If a participant has not actually praised anyone within the last two months or cannot remember what was said in praise, he or she should write down the praise that would be appropriate for each of the two people. A separate sheet of paper should be used for the praise statement directed at each of the two people. Participants should not use the real names of the persons praised. Also, the participant's name should not appear anywhere on either of the two pages.

3. Participants should now divide themselves into groups of five or six. Each group should then combine their praise statements and trade them with another group. Each group will now have praise statements written by members of another group.

4. One member of each group should read the praise statements aloud, one at a time. Each statement should then be discussed by the group. The discussion should focus on these questions: (a) How would you feel if the praise statement had been made about you? (b) How effective do you feel the praise statement would be in motivating the employee or in improving the employee's job satisfaction? (c) Why is the praise statement effective or ineffective? (d) How could the praise statement be improved?

5. After all groups have discussed each of the praise statements, a representative of each group should present to all the participants the general conclusions reached within the group regarding (a) the general effectiveness of the praise statements discussed and (b) the characteristics of effective praise statements.

Source: R. Bruce McAfee and Paul G. Champagne, *Organizational Behavior—A Manager's View* (St. Paul, Minn.: West Publishing, 1987), pp. 177–178.

*L*eadership *in* **Action**

Leadership is of the spirit, compounded of personality and vision; its practice is an art . . . that combination of persuasion, compulsion, and example— that makes other people do what you want them to do.

—SIR WILLIAM SLIM

LEARNING OBJECTIVES

After studying the material in this chapter, you should be able to:

▶ **Define** what leadership is.

▶ **Explain** some of the traitist ideas about leadership.

▶ **Explain** what the behavioral approach to leadership is and discuss some of the more popular theories.

▶ **Describe** the contingency-situational approach.

▶ **Present** a logical argument in favor of an ideal leadership style and the contingency-situational approach to leadership.

▶ **Present** some insights into diagnosing the proper leadership style to use in various situations.

▶ **Compare** and contrast transformational leadership with transactional leadership.

Kenny Clark—An Effective Supervisor

The most effective supervisor one consultant has met was encountered in an organization development and change effort. His name was Kenny Clark, and he was maintenance supervisor in a chemical plant of an international corporation.* The consultant was called in because the plant was suffering from the results of the ineffective, autocratic leadership of a former plant manager. Such leadership at the top had adversely affected all levels, resulting in low morale and losses from plant operations.

In gathering data about the plant through interviews, questionnaires, and observations, the consultant discovered that one maintenance crew was completely at odds with other departments in the plant. Unlike the rest of the plant, this crew—under Kenny's supervision—had very high morale and productivity.

In the interview with Kenny, the consultant discovered that Kenny was a young man in his early thirties who had a two-year associate's degree from a community college. The consultant was impressed with his positive attitude, especially in light of the overall low plant morale and productivity. Kenny said the plant was one of the finest places he had ever worked, and the maintenance people had more know-how than any other group with whom he had been associated. Kenny's perception of his team was that they did twice as much work as other crews, that everyone worked together, and that participative management did work with his people.

Kenny's boss reported Kenny was wrong about his team doing twice as much work as other crews; actually, they did *more* than twice as much. He also maintained that Kenny was the best supervisor he had seen in 22 years in the industry.

*A real company that would not permit the use of its name.

Through leadership training, Kenny became an effective manager.

One thing the consultant was curious about was why pressure and criticism from the old, autocratic manager seemed not to have had any effect on Kenny's crew. The crew gave the consultant the answer. They explained that Kenny had the ability to act as an intermediary and buffer between upper management and the crew. He would get higher management's primary objectives and points across without upsetting his people. As one crew member described it:

The maintenance supervisors will come back from a "donkey barbecue" session with higher management where they are raising hell about shoddy work, taking too long at coffee breaks, etc. Other supervisors are shook up for a week and give their men hell. But Kenny is cool, calm, and collected. He will call us together and report that nine items were discussed at the meeting, including the shoddy work, but that doesn't apply to our crew. Then he will cover the two or four items that are relevant to our getting the job done.

Unfortunately, Kenny did have a real concern at the time of the consultant's interview. He was being transferred from the highest-producing crew to the lowest-producing one. In fact, the latter was known as "the Hell's Angels crew." The crew members were considered to be a renegade group who were constantly fighting with production people as well as with one another. The previous supervisor had been terminated because he could not cope with them. In the course of this chapter, we will return to Kenny and what happened with the renegade crew.[1]

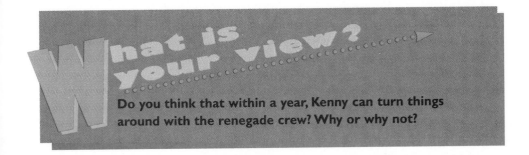

Do you think that within a year, Kenny can turn things around with the renegade crew? Why or why not?

This case illustrates that effective leadership is found in many levels of our society and not simply with the more glamorous top-level positions. We agree with John W. Gardner that effective leadership is dispersed throughout our society, be it held by the president of the United States, a school principal, or a shop foreman.[2]

On the other hand, there is an unfortunate amount of ineffective leadership in our society. Although no single model of leadership exists that everyone agrees with, this chapter should help you identify the need for leadership and how to nurture and use it.

Need for Effective Leadership

There is currently a need for effective leaders at the top levels of our organizations, from the U.S. Congress to our profit-oriented and not-for-profit organizations. In fact, H. Ross Perot, the hard-driving founder of EDS (later sold to GM), strongly believes that "our country cries out for leadership at the business level and the political level. Lack of leadership is the biggest problem we have in making this nation competitive."[3]

> To a large extent, the Boy Scouts of America is contributing to the development of effective leadership in the United States. For example, about 80 percent of the members of Congress (including Gerald Ford, who later became president) and 60 percent of U.S. astronauts have participated in scouting. And Ben Love, chief Scout executive, is still trying to represent that type of leadership model to today's young men.[4]

John P. Kotter of Harvard University maintains that the arena of international economic competition is the major force behind our need for more competent leaders in the business world. He compares wartime, when there is a much greater need for effective leaders in the military and government, to the business world today. "During war, an army still needs competent administration and management up and down the management hierarchy, but it cannot function without lots of good leadership at virtually all levels. No one has yet found how to administer or manage people into battle."[5]

In the business world also, we need leaders at all levels if we are to adapt successfully to the new environmental realities discussed in Chapters 3 and 4.

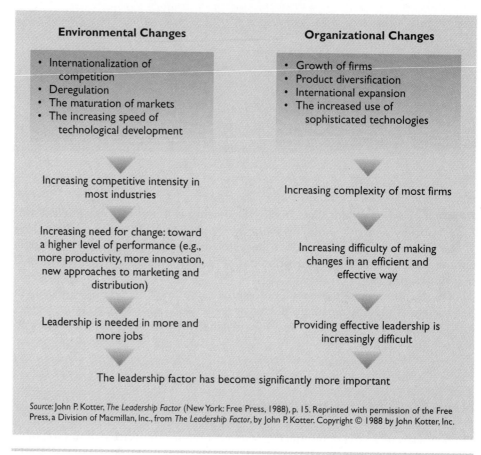

Environmental Changes

- Internationalization of competition
- Deregulation
- The maturation of markets
- The increasing speed of technological development

▼

Increasing competitive intensity in most industries

▼

Increasing need for change: toward a higher level of performance (e.g., more productivity, more innovation, new approaches to marketing and distribution)

▼

Leadership is needed in more and more jobs

Organizational Changes

- Growth of firms
- Product diversification
- International expansion
- The increased use of sophisticated technologies

▼

Increasing complexity of most firms

▼

Increasing difficulty of making changes in an efficient and effective way

▼

Providing effective leadership is increasingly difficult

▼

The leadership factor has become significantly more important

Source: John P. Kotter, *The Leadership Factor* (New York: Free Press, 1988), p. 15. Reprinted with permission of the Free Press, a Division of Macmillan, Inc., from *The Leadership Factor*, by John P. Kotter. Copyright © 1988 by John Kotter, Inc.

FIGURE 12.1
Some environmental changes and their effect on leadership.

Figure 12.1 summarizes some other environmental changes in the business world and their implications for organizational leadership.

Leadership and Ethics

Leaders, because they are in influential positions, have the power to influence ethical issues and decisions affecting many people. Fortunately, we are provided with ethical standards and guidelines by our culture, religion, and values. Many of these guidelines have been enacted into laws to ensure that ethical standards are adhered to by the citizenry.

Sometimes it takes laws a long time to have an effect. For instance, two of the most powerful and influential leaders in the first half of the 1980s were Ivan F. Boesky and Michael F. Milken. The top graduate schools of business in the country sought them out to speak to their MBA students. They were role models for many of these students, and the most desired career field upon graduation was the financial world of Wall Street and investment banking. Milken was considered the most powerful financier since J. P. Morgan and had led Drexel Burnham Lambert, through innovative junk-bond financing, to become Wall Street's most profitable firm.

Now, though, both men are criminals. Boesky pleaded guilty to charges of insider trading in December 1987 and received a prison sentence of two years and a substantial fine. He was also barred from Wall Street for life. Actually, he may have gotten off relatively easily "because he promised to put in prison stripes an even bigger crook: Mike Milken."[6]

Despite such highly publicized cases of greed and unethical behavior, most managers and professionals are ethical in their behavior and practices.

A consultant for the U.S. Army Corps of Engineers has found that its managers and professionals go to extra lengths to avoid even the appearance of unethical acts. For example, the consultant recently invited one of the key top managers from the Corps's largest district to be his guest for lunch and a round of golf at a country club. The manager accepted, but only on the condition that he pay for his own meal and greens fees. He explained that the Corps is careful to see that its employees do not accept gifts or gratuities from firms with which they have business relations. In this way, they avoid a possible source of prejudice in the awarding of contracts on the basis of quality and competitive price. Managers in leadership positions have a special responsibility to set a good example for their subordinates in the areas of ethics and social responsibility.

Leadership Versus Management

People often equate *leadership* with *management*. Reporters, for example, comment on the U.S. president's "exercise of leadership" or "lack of leadership." Sometimes they are actually referring to his efforts to lead the American people in a given direction. More often, though, they are talking about his performance of management functions when he does such things as propose new programs (planning), rearrange agencies (organizing), attempt to inspire confidence during a difficult period (leading), or remove a department head when things go wrong (control).

One explanation for such a broad interpretation of leadership may be that we sometimes use the term *leader* when referring to a manager. Although the two are similar, there are some significant differences.

Leadership is based on a person's ability to influence others to work toward achieving personal and organizational goals. But *management* involves much more. While leadership is part of it, it also includes performing the other functions—planning, organizing, and controlling.

Leadership, then, is an important part of management, but it is not the same thing. Keep in mind, though, as you study this text, that *effective managers must be effective leaders*, as shown in MAP 12.1.

Like management, *leadership* has been defined in many different ways by many different people. Nevertheless, the central theme running through most of the definitions is that **leadership** is a process of influencing individual and group activities toward goal setting and goal achievement. As a leader, you work to ensure balance among the goals of the organization, your own goals, and those of the group. In the final analysis, the successful leader is one who succeeds in getting others to follow.

leadership A process of influencing individual and group activities toward goal setting and goal achievement.

MANAGEMENT APPLICATION AND PRACTICE   12.1

The Godmother of Quebec's Businesswomen

Jeannine Guillevin Wood has been called the godmother of Quebec's businesswomen. Although she shrugs off the designation, the 65-year-old CEO of Montreal's Guillevin International Inc. has become a business legend in the province and beyond. In 25 years, she transformed a small family appliance wholesaler in the city's east end into a multimillion-dollar electrical products distribution empire spanning Canada and stretching into the United States.

"It is true that I was one of the first to show that women could do certain things around here, and for that I am glad," she says. "But the battle is not yet completely won, for there are still a few people who will not accept [women in business]. Those kinds of people I find it best to ignore."

Few colleagues or competitors have managed to ignore Guillevin Wood. The company of which she is CEO and principal shareholder is Canada's third largest distributor of electrical products and a major vendor of automation, security, and safety equipment. It employs 1,100 people in 105 offices, distributing 82,000 products to 33,000 customers. Annual sales in the company year ending January 31, 1990, exceeded $422 million (Canadian) and showed profits of $5.9 million.

Guillevin Wood also sits on the boards of several major Canadian concerns. In October 1990, in the face of a recession, her company expanded in the Maritimes—part of a commitment to Canada-wide growth and community service. That same year, she became the first woman appointed to the policy committee of the blue-ribbon Business Council on National Issues. "You might say that I have won some recognition," she concedes.

Guillevin Wood's life might have taken a far different course. Until 1965, she led an obscure but comfortable existence as a Montreal housewife and mother, content to spend the summers golfing and the winters in Florida. But her first husband, François Guillevin, died suddenly, leaving her with a 15-year-old daughter to care for, as well as control of the family business. (She is now married to businessman Keith Wood.) At the time, F. X. Guillevin & Son Ltd. was an electrical wholesaler with 35 employees and annual sales of $1.5 million, mostly from the distribution of household appliances. Guillevin Wood decided to take the reins into her own hands rather than sell the business. "I had no other choice," she recalls. "It was a

good old family firm with a lot of good employees who had given their lives to the company. How could I let them down?"

It was a brave decision, considering that she had no business experience of any kind. Over the next 20 year, however, she acquired 11 other companies and forged working partnerships with firms in France and the United States to fashion what is now Guillevin International. She also gained wider recognition so that by 1976 she had twice been named "Man of the Month" by Montreal business organizations. Other accolades followed.

Jeannine Guillevin Wood

"There really is no secret to my success," she says. "It was just the result of plain old discipline and a lot of hard work." It is advice that she offers by example to others, male and female—the kind of advice expected from a godmother.

Source: Adapted from "MacLean's Honor Roll: Advising by Example," *MacLean's*, December 31, 1990, pp. 22–23.

Classifying Leaders

A leader has to work effectively with many people, including superiors, peers, subordinates, and outside groups. But the qualities of leadership are seen especially in a manager's relationship with subordinates.

There are many ways to classify leaders or leadership styles. The two most important, however, are (1) by the approach used and (2) by the orientation toward getting the job done.

Approach Used   One common way of studying leadership is in terms of the basic approaches used by leaders: autocratic, democratic, and laissez-faire.

Autocratic leaders—often called **authoritarian leaders**—make most decisions themselves instead of allowing their followers to participate in making them. These leaders are usually thought of as "pushers," somewhat like the image of military drill instructors.

Democratic or **participative leaders** involve their followers heavily in the decision process. They use group involvement in setting basic objectives, establishing strategies, and determining job assignments.

Laissez-faire leaders—also called **free-rein leaders**—are "loose" and permissive and let followers do what they want. You might think of this approach as similar to teachers who handle classes loosely, with few homework assignments, class sessions that seem to drift from one issue to another as they arise, and little direction or discipline.

Orientation Toward Job   Another way to categorize leaders is to examine their attitudes toward getting the job done. Some leaders emphasize the task, others emphasize followers or subordinates, and, as you will find out later in this chapter, some emphasize a combination of both, as shown in Figure 12.2.

Task-oriented or **production-oriented leaders** focus on getting the job done. They emphasize planning, scheduling, and processing the work, and they exercise close control of quality. Another term used in describing this approach is *initiating structure* through telling people what to do and how and when to do it.

People-oriented or **employee-centered leaders** focus on the welfare and feelings of followers, have confidence in themselves, and have a strong need to develop

autocratic (authoritarian) leaders Leaders who make most of the decisions themselves instead of allowing their followers to participate in them.

democratic (participative) leaders Leaders who focus on the welfare and feelings of followers, have confidence in themselves, and have a strong need to develop and empower their team members.

laissez-faire (free-rein) leaders Leaders who are "loose" and permissive and let followers do what they want.

task-oriented (production-oriented) leaders Leaders who focus on getting the job done.

people-oriented (employee-centered) leaders Leaders who focus on the welfare and feelings of followers, have confidence in themselves, and have a strong need to be accepted by their team members.

FIGURE 12.2
Differing leadership orientations.

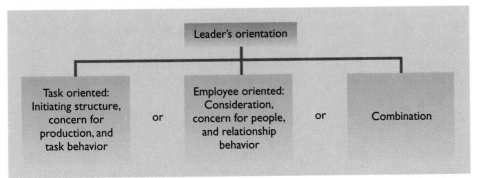

and empower their team members. Other common terms used to describe people-oriented leaders are *relationship centered* and *considerate*.

Some Popular Leadership Theories

Leadership research and theories can be classified as *traitist, behavioral,* or *contingency-situational*. We present them to you chronologically as they have evolved over the years.

Traitist Theories

traitist theories
Theories of leadership that claim leaders possess certain traits or characteristics that cause them to rise above their followers.

According to **traitist theories,** leaders possess certain traits or characteristics that cause them to rise above their followers. Lists of such traits can be very long and tend to include height, energy, looks, knowledge and intelligence, imagination, self-confidence, integrity, fluency of speech, emotional and mental balance and control, sociability and friendliness, drive, enthusiasm, and courage.

Research on Traits   Although most of the research on leadership traits occurred from 1904 to 1947, studies have been conducted as recently as the late 1980s.

The early research on leadership attempted to (1) compare the traits of people who became leaders with those who were followers and (2) identify characteristics and traits possessed by effective leaders. Studies comparing the traits of leaders and nonleaders often found that leaders tended to be more intelligent, somewhat taller, more outgoing, and more self-confident than others and to have a greater need for power. But specific combinations of traits have not been found that would distinguish the leader or potential leader from followers. The underlying assumption of the trait researchers seems to have been that *leaders are born, not made.* But research has *not* shown that certain traits *can* distinguish effective from ineffective leaders. However, respected research is still being done in this area.

One of the earliest trait researchers was Ralph Stogdill, who found several traits to be related to effective leadership. These included social and interpersonal skills, technical skills, administrative skills, and leadership effectiveness.[7]

Another researcher, Edwin Ghiselli, found that certain characteristics do seem to be important to effective leadership.[8] The most important of these are

1. *Supervisory ability,* or performing the basic functions of management, especially leading and controlling the work of others
2. *Need for occupational achievement,* including seeking responsibility and desiring success
3. *Intelligence,* including judgment, reasoning, and reactive thinking
4. *Decisiveness,* or the ability to make decisions and solve problems capably and competently
5. *Self-assurance,* or viewing oneself as capable of coping with problems
6. *Initiative,* or the ability to act independently, develop courses of action not readily apparent to other people, and find new or innovative ways of doing things

The research currently being done in this area does not assume that leaders are born, not made, but looks at traits in a different light. For example, some researchers take the position that, if the characteristics of successful leaders can be identified, then these characteristics can be developed in others who aspire to leadership. In a study involving over 2,600 top-level managers at Santa Clara University and several corporate locations, the superior leaders were most often found to be honest, competent, forward-looking, inspiring, and intelligent.[9]

> Robert Crandall, chairman of AMR Corporation, the parent company of American Airlines, is such a leader. In 1990, he was selected as *USA Today*/FNN CEO of the Year. A competitive impulse and the use of technology have made him "a lethal adversary."
>
> In a nation where short-term thinking is the norm, the tough-talking, fast-driving CEO stands out. In the face of a recession, an annual operating loss, and an industry slump, "Crandall is charging ahead . . . managing for the long term." He's been successful "because he developed a strategic vision and put his entire energy into achieving it," according to *USA Today* and FNN (Financial News Network).[10]

Robert Crandall, CEO of AMR Corporation, exhibits the traits of a superior leader.

Limitations of the Traitist Approach Despite the promise of current research, there are some limitations to the traitist approach. For example we know that people such as Alexander the Great, Napoléon, Joan of Arc, Abraham Lincoln, Florence Nightingale, Geronimo, Mahatma Gandhi, Mao Ze-dong, Adolf Hitler, Winston Churchill, Vince Lombardi, and Martin Luther King, Jr., were different from others. Yet there appear to be no particular leadership traits common to all of them. Moreover, there are many cases in which a leader is successful in one situation but may not be in another.

> The classic example of this tendency was Winston Churchill. As prime minister of Great Britain during World War II, he maintained British morale with brilliant speeches and stubborn courage. Yet in the spring of 1945, as the war was ending and the German forces seemed less menacing, he was defeated for reelection by a relatively unknown politician.

Although the traitist approach did not yield significant findings as to what attributes are the hallmark of a leader, we might observe of those just listed that they all had vision, communicated well, were highly motivated, and motivated their followers.

Behavioral Theories

After the publication of the late Douglas McGregor's classic book *The Human Side of Enterprise* in 1960, attention shifted to behavioral theories. McGregor was a teacher, researcher, and consultant whose work was considered to be "on the cutting edge" of managing people. He influenced all the **behavioral theories,** which emphasize focusing on human relationships, along with output and performance.

McGregor's important work was followed by contributions of other leading behaviorists such as Rensis Likert and Robert Blake and Jane Mouton. Behavioral theories and concepts remain popular and influential today. More recently, William Ouchi's *Theory Z,* which focuses on Japanese-style management, has received considerable attention. A final subject to be examined in this section is the role of effective followers, important in all the behavioral theories.

behavioral theories Theories of leadership that emphasize favorable treatment of employees rather than their output or performance.

McGregor's Theory X and Theory Y   The leadership strategy of effectively using participative management proposed in Douglas McGregor's classic book has had a tremendous impact on managers.[11] The most publicized concept is McGregor's thesis that leadership strategies are influenced by a leader's *assumptions about human nature.* As a result of his experience as a consultant, McGregor summarized two contrasting sets of assumptions made by managers in industry.

Theory X The theory that workers dislike work and must be coerced, controlled, and directed in order to achieve company objectives.

The Assumptions of Theory X.   According to the first set of assumptions, **Theory X,** managers believe that

1. The average human being has an inherent dislike of work and will avoid it if possible
2. Because of this human characteristic, most people must be coerced, controlled, directed, or threatened with punishment to get them to put forth adequate effort to achieve organizational objectives
3. The average human being prefers to be directed, wishes to avoid responsibility, has relatively little ambition, and wants security above all else

Theory Y The theory that workers accept work as natural, seek responsibility, and will exercise self-direction and self-control to achieve company objectives.

The Assumptions of Theory Y.   Managers who accept **Theory Y** assumptions believe that

1. The expenditure of physical and mental effort in work is as natural as play or rest, and the average human being, under proper conditions, learns not only to accept but to seek responsibility
2. People will exercise self-direction and self-control to achieve objectives to which they are committed
3. The capacity to exercise a relatively high level of imagination, ingenuity, and creativity in the solution of organizational problems is widely, not narrowly, distributed in the population, and the intellectual potentialities of the average human being are only partially utilized under the conditions of modern industrial life

You can readily see that a leader holding Theory X assumptions would prefer an autocratic style, whereas one holding Theory Y assumptions would prefer a more participative style.

Now let us see how things turned out with Kenny.

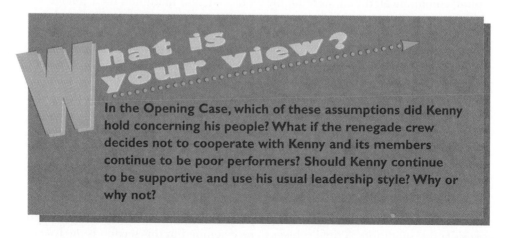

What is your view?

In the Opening Case, which of these assumptions did Kenny hold concerning his people? What if the renegade crew decides not to cooperate with Kenny and its members continue to be poor performers? Should Kenny continue to be supportive and use his usual leadership style? Why or why not?

After Kenny was assigned to the new crew, he had to make a decision about the leadership strategies he would use in dealing with them. His initial diagnosis was that the crew had the ability to do the work but lacked the willingness because of a poor attitude.

In a meeting with members of the "Hell's Angels" crew, the consultant learned that the first day on the job, Kenny called a meeting, shut the door, and conducted a "bull session" that lasted over two hours. Among other things, he told them about his philosophy and the way he liked to operate. He especially stressed that he was going to be fair and treat everyone equally. The crew members were allowed to gripe and complain as long as they talked about matters in the plant, while Kenny played a listening role without arguing with them. In the course of the session, Kenny expressed his expectations of the crew. They in turn told him they would do it his way for two weeks to see if he "practiced what he preached."

As you may have surmised by now, Kenny's leadership made the difference. Before the year was out, his new crew was the most productive in the plant.

Likert's Leadership Findings   Some very effective research into the behavioral approach to leadership has been carried out over a number of years by the Institute for Social Research at the University of Michigan. Rensis Likert and his associates there have studied leadership in several different work settings to see whether valid principles or concepts of leadership could be discovered.

Effect of Supervision Style on Results.   Likert and his team of researchers were strongly convinced that leadership was a causal variable that over time affected, among other things, productivity, profits, turnover, and absenteeism. This conviction seemed to be confirmed by their finding that supervisors who practiced close supervision and were more job centered had lower morale and productivity among their subordinates than supervisors who practiced general supervision and were more employee centered.[12]

Essentially, the leadership style of *close supervision* generally reflects Theory X assumptions about people. Close supervisors do not trust people. They believe in detailed instructions and "keeping an eye on things," often doing the same type of work as the workers they are supervising.

Achievement-oriented employees find it frustrating and demoralizing to work under close supervision, especially for prolonged periods. Consequently, departments in which close supervision is practiced tend to have high turnover of personnel.

Close supervision is not very effective when the work requires any type of initiative or creativity in subordinates. It might work well, however, with new employees or those with low IQs or in the short run in a department where costs have been excessive or where an emergency job must be accomplished.

General supervision, on the other hand, reflects Theory Y assumptions. Likert found that, when asked to give the most important feature of their jobs, leaders practicing general supervision stressed human relations and the development of subordinates. Therefore, these supervisors were called employee centered. This does not mean that these leaders ignored the production or task requirements of their departments. Instead, the leaders emphasized working with and through people in such a way that effective results would naturally follow.

From published research and our own experience, we see four main characteristics of managers using general supervision. They (1) supervise by results (that is, they delegate authority to do the job and periodically check or receive reports on results), (2) emphasize training and development of subordinates through the process of delegation of authority and supervision by results, (3) spend half or more of their time planning and organizing the work of the department and coordinating with other departments and supervisors, and (4) are more accessible to talk over departmental or personal problems of subordinates.

Likert's Four Management Systems. Likert's greatest contribution to behavioral theory was to identify four management systems operating in the actual organizations he studied. These four systems can be arranged along a continuum as shown in Figure 12.3. These management systems may be briefly described as follows:

System 1 (Exploitative-Authoritative). Top management primarily uses an autocratic style, makes all the decisions, and relies on coercion as the primary motivating force.

System 2 (Benevolent-Authoritative). Higher management makes most of the decisions, although some minor implementation decisions may be made at lower levels. A condescending attitude is usually displayed in communicating with subordinates, which results in a subservient attitude toward superiors.

System 3 (Consultative). Although higher management still reserves the tasks of direction and control, ideas are at least solicited from lower levels. As a result, up-and-down communications are superior to those in Systems 1 and 2. Although there is very little cooperative teamwork, certain delegated specific decisions are made at lower levels.

System 4 One of four management systems operating in organizations; one under which higher management views its role as that of making sure that the best decisions are made through a decentralized, participative-group structure.

System 4 (Participative Groups). Under **System 4,** higher management views its role as ensuring the best decisions are made through a decentralized participative-group structure. These groups overlap and are coordinated by multiple memberships (linking pins). There is a high degree of trust, which allows both superiors and subordinates to exercise greater control over the work situation.

A key component of System 4 is the use by managers of group decision making and supervision in the management of the work group. It should be noted that System 4 is similar to the type of management found in many Japanese firms.

FIGURE 12.3
Likert's four-system continuum.

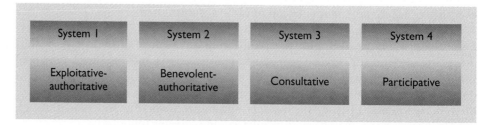

Perhaps the biggest distinction is that in System 4, each individual manager is still held accountable for his or her decisions and executions even though decision making is a group process.

Likert and his team strongly implied that the closer an organization is to System 4, the more effective it will be in achieving its ends. A number of studies have since been published documenting successful shifts from Systems 1 and 2 to Systems 3 and 4, with accompanying improvements in performance and satisfaction.[13] (More details on Likert's management systems will be provided in Chapter 13.)

Blake and Mouton's Managerial Grid®   The *Managerial Grid®* developed by Robert Blake and Jane Mouton focuses on task (production) and employee (people) orientations of managers, as well as combinations of concerns between the two extremes.[14] Figure 12.4 (republished as the **Leadership Grid** Figure in 1991 by Robert Blake and Anne Adams McCanse) shows a grid with concern for production on the horizontal axis and concern for people on the vertical axis and plots five basic leadership styles. The first number refers to a leader's production or task orientation; the second, to people or employee orientation.

> **Leadership Grid®** A leadership model that focuses on task (production) and employee (people) orientations of managers as well as combinations of concerns between the two extremes.

> The *9,1-oriented manager* is described as a stern taskmaster—an autocrat, with some of the characteristics of the close supervisor described in the previous sections. The emphasis is on getting the job done.

> The *1,9-oriented manager* used permissive leadership, with an emphasis on keeping employees happy and satisfied, and tends to avoid the use of pressure in getting work done.

> The *1,1-oriented manager* has been described as an abdicator. This is an extreme of the laissez-faire management style.

> The *5,5-oriented manager* places some emphasis on production but also realizes that people cannot be ignored. Sometimes he or she will use an implicit bargaining approach ("You scratch my back, and I'll scratch yours") to get work accomplished.

> The *9,9-oriented manager* believes that mutual understanding and agreement regarding the organization's goals—and the means of attaining them—are at the core of work direction. He or she has a high concern for both people and production and uses a participative, team approach to getting work accomplished.

Unlike the Michigan researchers, who found that employee-centered supervisors were more productive than production-centered supervisors, Blake and Mouton emphasize that a high concern for both employees *and* production is the most effective type of leadership behavior.

Ouchi's Theory   William Ouchi, in his book *Theory Z*, contrasted Japanese and American industry and concluded that some Japanese corporations could serve as models for American firms.[15] Table 12.1 shows the contrast between typical Japanese and American organizations.

> **Theory Z** A theory of leadership that emphasizes long-range planning, consensus decision making, and strong mutual worker-employer loyalty.

Ouchi felt that Japanese industrial success was a result of better management, an approach he called **Theory Z,** which emphasizes long-range planning, consensus decision making, and strong mutual worker-employer loyalty. The key to increased

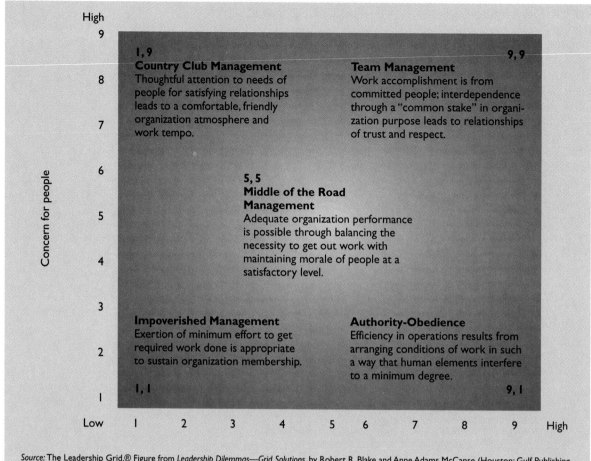

FIGURE 12.4
The Leadership Grid® Figure.

productivity is to get employees involved by using such techniques as self-managing work teams (discussed in Chapter 14), developing interpersonal skills, and broadening career path opportunities and development.

This led to identification of a major difference between Japanese and American companies—the organization structure. According to one report, "The typical U.S. company has 12 layers of management, while the average Japanese [car] maker has seven."[16] Moreover, the Japanese minimize staff positions and emphasize line positions, where the profits are made. As author William Newman has noted, "The Japanese will train their smartest engineers to identify problems, then put them on the shop floor. In the U.S. they'd be sitting at a desk reviewing things."[17]

Some American companies, he discovered, had characteristics similar to those of the model Japanese companies. These organizations, which included some of the best managed in the world—IBM, Procter & Gamble, Hewlett-Packard, and Eastman Kodak—Ouchi called Theory Z companies.

TABLE 12.1	Contrast Between Japanese and American Organizations	

Japanese Organizations	American Organizations
Lifetime employment	Short-term employment
Slow evaluation and promotion	Rapid evaluation and promotion
Nonspecialized career paths	Specialized career paths
Implicit control techniques	Explicit control techniques
Collective responsibility	Individual responsibility
Concern for the whole organization	Concern for parts of the organization

Source: Adapted from William G. Ouchi, *Theory Z* (Reading, Mass.: Addison-Wesley, 1981), p. 58. William Ouchi, *Theory Z,* © 1981 by Addison-Wesley Publishing Company. Reprinted with permission of the publisher.

Ouchi and others note that all Japanese management techniques can be used in American settings. The forecast for the future, however, is that more American firms will become Theory Z companies.

Since the Ouchi book was published, many American firms have significantly improved their leadership and management practices. Nowhere is this more evident than with the Big Three American automobile corporations. A combination of increased sales, reduced levels of management, and more effective use of teams, especially product development teams that reduce the time to get new products to showrooms, has greatly improved both quality and profits. For example, in the second quarter of 1994, GM, Ford, and Chrysler all posted profit records of $1.9 billion, $1.8 billion, and $1.8 billion, respectively; these were the most profitable quarters ever by U.S. automakers, and the third and fourth most profitable quarters by any U.S. firm.[18] As MAP 12.2 highlights, the auto firms still believe they can do better, particularly in regard to reduced cost and improved quality.

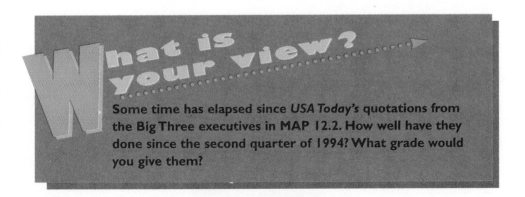

Some time has elapsed since *USA Today's* quotations from the Big Three executives in MAP 12.2. How well have they done since the second quarter of 1994? What grade would you give them?

Followership   All the behavioral theories emphasize more effective and improved management of employees. Today, there is increased emphasis on the importance of followers and recognition of McGregor's notion that talents are widely distributed among employees—not confined to managers and professionals. Effective

MANAGEMENT APPLICATION AND PRACTICE   12.2

Big Three Shift to Success and Won't Rest on Laurels

Big Three auto leaders are pumped with pride over their record second-quarter profits. But they're not losing sight of the competition and the need to keep cutting costs. **Chrysler CEO Robert Eaton, Ford Vice Chairman Allan Gilmour** *and* **G. Richard Wagoner, president of General Motors' North American Operations,** *talked about the challenges their companies face. They spoke with USA TODAY'S* **Micheline Maynard** *and* **Blair S. Walker.**

ON THEIR COMEBACK:

Wagoner: (Sales) came back this year a little faster than some of us had expected. We're all more competitive in our cost structure. Each of us has important products coming in at the same time, and we're all trying to bring new products in while focusing better on the customer.

Gilmour: We're a business that goes with the economy, only (our success is even more) exaggerated. For GM and Ford, European business is picking up. We're all working hard and have been (able) to get more efficient.

Eaton: Clearly, the competitiveness of the domestic industry has made a 180-degree shift from what it was not too many years ago. We were looked at as being behind both the Japanese and the Europeans. Frankly, now we are the benchmark in many areas.

Allan Gilmour (Ford): "We've got to [improve] our efficiency in every way we can."

ON WHEN THEY CAN RELAX:

Eaton: Clearly, it was the best quarter ever in Chrysler's case, and that's true for the others as well. We're proud of our accomplishment. (But) we're not satisfied. Once you become satisfied you start to lose competitively, and go away in this market. This is as competitive an industry worldwide as you can imagine.

Wagoner: North America is extremely competitive. . . . starting (to improve sales) in a down market is a

challenge. There're a lot of things (in the second-quarter results) that say: 'Hey, great news, GM people. but you're nowhere near where you could be and where you need to go to be competitive.'

Gilmour: It's very easy to be mesmerized by these big numbers because these are big companies. (But) the return on sales isn't yet where it needs to be. We all have further work to do. I'm much less excited about the records than I am about the fact that we're seeing a good solid recovery.

Robert Eaton (Chrysler): Proud of earnings gain, but "we're not satisfied."

ON SALES MOMENTUM:

Wagoner: When your financial results show you're in a turnaround, it makes customers feel a little better. And you're viewed as much more able to address customer needs.

Gilmour: When momentum comes, profits go up. Sales pick up (because buyers want cars and trucks from successful companies). People don't want to buy orphans (cars made by a company that exits the business).

ON AREAS FOR PROGRESS:

Wagoner: Most of the stuff we do, we look at and realize we can do better. We are not the benchmark for the industry (on cost cutting and efficiency). We have some significant cost-reduction targets. Wall Street's read is right: We hope we can run faster.

G. Richard Wagoner (GM): "Most of the stuff we do we . . . realize we can do better."

Eaton: Our goal is continuous improvement in everything we do, and that includes earnings.

Gilmour: We've got a heck of a lot of new products coming this fall (such as Mercury

Mystique and Ford Contour midsize cars and a new Lincoln Continental). The first thing to do is get those launches. We've got to (improve) our efficiency in every way that we possibly can. Some people say efficiency is a code word for greed, but we think it's a code word for value. No one needs to pay for anyone else's sloppiness. . . . We have a big, big focus on teams and (corporate) organization and things like that. A lot of that is very important to do: modernizing our processes, (using) computers, (finding) new ways of organizing people.

ON THE SALES OUTLOOK:

Gilmour: We're a considerable ways away from the peak. We had six or seven years of recovery in the

1980s, after a good solid mess at the beginning (of the decade). When the last downturn began in 1989, it lasted a good long time. You'd expect that with this recovery. There are several good years ahead of us.

Wagoner: Consumer confidence in absolute terms is good compared with where it was a couple of months ago. But we have to be more vigilant if it doesn't run through '95 or '96. We'd rather see a gradual upturn (sales increase) of 4% a year vs. say, 8% all at once. It's important for us. We need a couple of good years.

Source: *USA Today*, Friday, July 29, 1994, pp. 1, 2B.

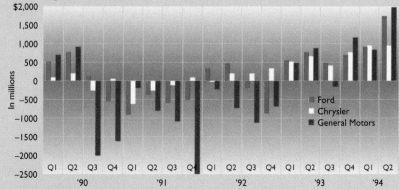

Big Three shift to success

Improving quality and cutting costs, have helped the Big Three—GM, Ford and Chrysler —soar to record profitability. **Executives talk, 2B.**

The automakers have slashed employment

800 700 600 500

717,000

589,000

In thousands

'88 '89 '90 '91 '92 '93 '94

...but quality has improved

180 160 140 120 100

Problems per 100 cars in the first three months

159

113

'88 '90 '91 '92 '93

Earnings have soared

$2,000
1,500
1,000
500
0
−500
−1000
−1500
−2000
−2500

In millions

Q1 Q2 Q3 Q4 Q1 Q2 Q3 Q4 Q1 Q2 Q3 Q4 Q1 Q2 Q3 Q4 Q1 Q2

'90 '91 '92 '93 '94

■ Ford
□ Chrysler
■ General Motors

Note: 1992 Ford earnings, 1st-quarter '92 GM earnings, and 1st-quarter '93 earnings do not include one-time charges.

Source: *USA Today*, July 29, 1994, pp.1, 2B

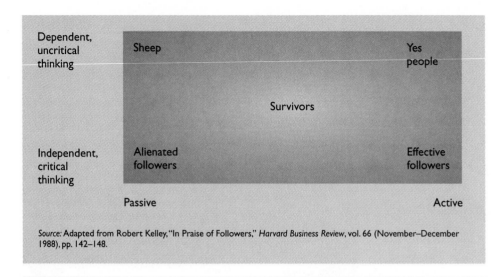

FIGURE 12.5
Types of followers.

followers are "well balanced and responsible adults who can succeed without strong leadership," according to Robert Kelley. The less effective types of followers identified by Kelley, as shown in Figure 12.5, include the following:[19]

Sheep are passive and uncritical thinkers, lacking in initiative and sense of responsibility; they perform the tasks assigned them and no more.

Yes people are active but uncritical thinkers. These are livelier people, but just as unenterprising as sheep. They depend on their superior for inspiration. Bosses lacking in self-confidence like such followers.

Survivors are more independent thinkers and somewhat active. These people are adept at surviving change within the organization.

Alienated followers are independent thinkers who are passive. At some time, something turned them off. They are often cynical, but rarely do they openly oppose a leader's efforts.

Effective followers, by contrast, are independent thinkers who carry out their assignments with energy and assertiveness. These people are self-confident and can succeed without strong leadership. Behaviorists believe that if more managers used such concepts as Theory Y, System 4, 9,9 leadership, and Theory Z, there would be more effective followers and fewer sheep, yes people, survivors, and alienated followers.

Is There an Ideal Leadership Style?

For some time there has been a debate about whether there is an ideal, or normative, leadership style. This debate usually centers on the idea that an ideal style does exist: It is a style that actively *involves* employees in goal setting through the use of participative management techniques and focuses on people *and* task.

Support for an Ideal Leadership Style

Researchers in leadership continue to give considerable support to the idea that there is an ideal leadership style—one that incorporates a participative management approach. Early research in motivation theory also supported the participative management approach as the ideal. The concept has both intellectual and moral appeal, especially in developed countries, where lower-level needs are relatively well satisfied. Many management practitioners feel that this concept makes sense, and in numerous cases both performance and attitudes improved when participative management was introduced.

A work supporting an ideal leadership style comes from Japan. Jyuji Misumi evaluated 34 studies covering a 35-year period beginning in 1949.[20] Misumi argues that there are four leader types: (1) the performance oriented (P), (2) the group maintenance oriented (M), (3) the performance and maintenance oriented (PM), and (4) neither performance nor maintenance oriented (pm). He concludes that performance maintenance (PM) is superior to the other types and results in high levels of both performance and satisfaction. The PM style appears to be quite similar to Blake and Mouton's 9,9 team style and Likert's System 4, where managers focus on both production *and* interpersonal relationships.

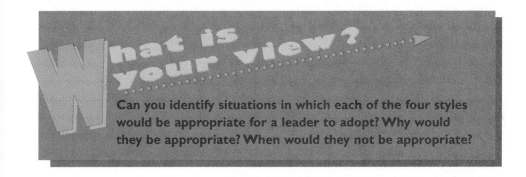

What is your view?

Can you identify situations in which each of the four styles would be appropriate for a leader to adopt? Why would they be appropriate? When would they not be appropriate?

Arguments Against an Ideal Leadership Style

Several classic research studies have challenged the viewpoint that there is one ideal leadership style. Essentially, they say that under various conditions a directive approach may actually get better results and that a participative approach may not work effectively in all situations.

One such study challenged the assumption that leaders who are high in both task and interpersonal behavior will have more satisfied and productive subordinates than those who are not.[21] Another study, judging the leadership effectiveness of 100 managers by three criteria—need fulfillment, salary level, and career progress—concluded there was a lack of empirical support for Blake's 9,9 leadership style.[22] In this study, the more desirable style seemed to be 1,9, or a leader's behavior of low initiating structure and high consideration (low task and high people orientation).

Finally, leadership experience reveals that in some situations an autocratic approach might be best, in others a participative approach; in some a task-oriented approach, in others a people-oriented approach. This conclusion emphasizes that leadership is complex and that the most appropriate style depends on several interrelated variables.

Contingency-Situational Theories

Like the traitist theories, the behavioral theories are inadequate to explain what constitutes effective leadership in all situations. Indeed, most researchers today conclude that no one leadership style is right for every manager under all circumstances. Instead, **contingency-situational theories** prescribe that the style to be used is contingent upon such factors as the situation, the people, the task, the organization, and other environmental variables.

The most popular contingency theories are (1) Tannenbaum and Schmidt's leadership continuum and (2) Hersey and Blanchard's life-cycle theory. Some authors also include the Vroom-Yetton approach to decision making, discussed in Chapter 6, as a leadership contingency model.

Tannenbaum and Schmidt's Leadership Continuum

In a 1958 issue of *Harvard Business Review*, there appeared an article entitled "How to Choose a Leadership Pattern," by Robert Tannenbaum and Warren Schmidt. The article was so popular with practicing managers that it was reproduced in 1973 as a "classic," along with a retrospective commentary by the authors.[23] The original article had been so well received because it sanctioned a range of behavior instead of offering a choice between only two styles of leadership—democratic and authoritarian. It helped managers analyze their own behavior within a context of other alternatives, without labeling any style right or wrong.

Leadership Continuum   Tannenbaum and Schmidt's concept is presented as a **leadership continuum,** as shown in Figure 12.6. The continuum is based on Mary Parker Follett's **law of the situation,** which states that there are several alternate paths managers can follow in working with people.[24] Therefore, in making leadership decisions, managers must consider forces in themselves, their subordinates, and the situation, which are interrelated and interacting:

Forces in the manager include his or her (1) value system, (2) confidence in subordinates, (3) own leadership inclinations, and (4) feelings of security or insecurity.

Forces in subordinates include their (1) need for independence, (2) need for increased responsibility, (3) problem-solving capability, and (4) expectations with respect to sharing in decision making.

Forces in the situation include (1) the type of organization, (2) the group's effectiveness, (3) the pressure of time, and (4) the nature of the problem itself.

The key point is that the successful manager is the one who has a high batting average in assessing the appropriate behavior for a given situation, as shown in Tips 12.1.

The criteria for a situation in which the more democratic approach is possible are that (1) the leader must have a high tolerance for ambiguity, confidence in subordinates, and a supportive higher-level management, and (2) the employees must have the necessary job knowledge and skills, a high need for independence, and a desire to achieve.

Role of Subordinates   An important warning, however, is that a leader must communicate clearly to subordinates just what degree of involvement they will have in a given situation. Will the workers *make* the decision? Does the supervisor only want to *consider* subordinates' inputs before making the final decision? One mistake leaders

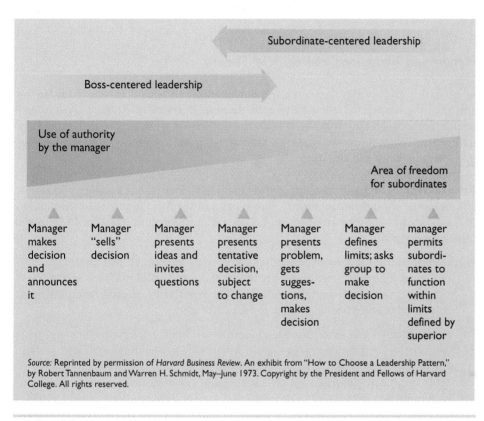

Subordinate-centered leadership

Boss-centered leadership

Use of authority by the manager

Area of freedom for subordinates

| Manager makes decision and announces it | Manager "sells" decision | Manager presents ideas and invites questions | Manager presents tentative decision, subject to change | Manager presents problem, gets suggestions, makes decision | Manager defines limits; asks group to make decision | manager permits subordinates to function within limits defined by superior |

FIGURE 12.6
Continuum of manager-nonmanager behavior.

TipS 12.1

Which Leadership Style to Use

Says Ann Wardlow, principal of Emerson Elementary School: You have to know your people. I use a different leadership style with my experienced teachers, whom I know well and who are very capable. I seldom have to emphasize lesson plans, adherence to school policies, and so on. But I keep a close eye on my new teachers, especially a couple who seem very shaky. One in particular seems a bit headstrong in his dress and behavior, as if he's trying too hard to be one of the kids. Another is constantly in my office, afraid to make decisions on her own. But there's no doubt that you must know your people—their capabilities, experience, and knowledge, their role, attitudes, and relationships with peers and their students—to be able to handle each effectively. A subtle suggestion from me will get the message to some; with others I must be perfectly blunt and direct. The trick is in being skilled enough to know which approach works with whom. To use the same approach with every person would be disastrous.

make is to "fake" a high degree of involvement, already knowing what the decision will be. In other words, the manager thinks, "I know their thinking on this will be identical to mine, so I'll let them feel that I've involved them in my decision." Beware! *You* do not like to feel manipulated, and the leader who plays such a human relations "game" may eventually be hurt or surprised by it.

Hersey and Blanchard's Life-Cycle Theory

A leadership theory that has attracted considerable attention is what Paul Hersey and Kenneth Blanchard call the **life-cycle theory.**[25] It draws heavily on previous leadership research. Hersey and Blanchard take a situational approach, with one major difference: They emphasize leaders' using an adaptive style depending on the diagnosis they make of the situation.

life-cycle theory A theory that the leader's style should reflect the maturity level of employees and that draws heavily on previous leadership research.

Basic Concept   The basic concept of the life-cycle theory is that a leader's strategies and behavior should be situational, based primarily on the maturity or immaturity of followers and the nature of the task. The following definitions should help you understand the theory.

> *Maturity* is the capacity of individuals or groups to set high but attainable goals and their willingness and ability to take responsibility. These maturity variables, resulting from education and/or experience, should be considered only in relation to a specific task to be performed.

> *Task Behavior* is the extent to which leaders are likely to organize and define the roles of their followers, to explain what activities each is to do and when, where, and how tasks are to be accomplished. It relies on establishing well-defined patterns of organization, channels of communication, and ways of accomplishing jobs.

> *Relationship behavior* deals with the leader's personal relationships with individuals or members of his or her group. It involves the amount of support provided by the leader and the extent to which the leader engages in interpersonal communication and facilitating behavior.

Figure 12.7 shows the relationship between the maturity of followers and the leadership style based on the task and relationship behavior of leaders. The style of the leader should change as the maturity of the followers increases. To use the chart, first determine the maturity level of the members of a group (mature or immature). Then trace a line upward until it intersects the curved line. That intersection determines which of the four basic leadership styles is most effective for that situation. The Q number represents a given quadrant of leadership style.

The Theory in Practice   Hersey and Blanchard used the example of parents' relationships with their children to illustrate their theory. Negative consequences will probably result if parents tend to use only one leadership style during their children's development years. For example, children may either run away or engage in many rebellious, antisocial behaviors if parents tend to use only a very directive leadership style (high task and low relationship). The point at which children are likely to rebel is probably in the early teen years. On the other hand, if parents use primarily a permissive style, the result is frequently children who warrant the label of

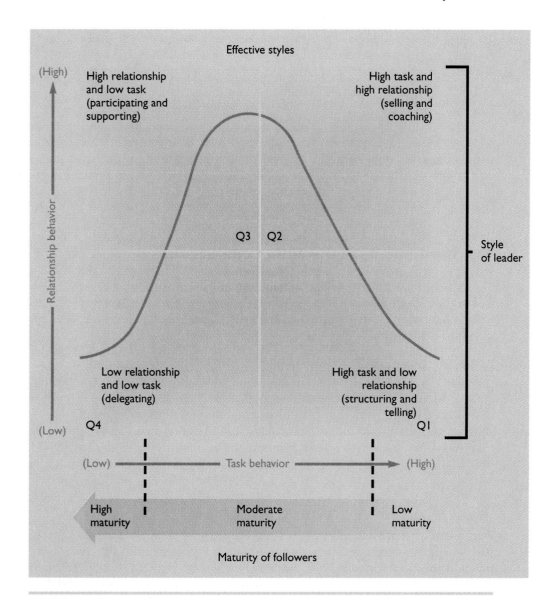

FIGURE 12.7
Situational leadership theory.

"spoiled brats," with little regard for rules, regulations, or the rights of others. The key is to use more directive behavior in the early periods and, as the child (worker) matures, to provide less direction and control, as shown in the following example.

"My relationship with my boss has changed a lot, I guess, in the four years I've been here," said John Dixon, a lab technician. "She was constantly checking my work when I first started, giving me detailed instructions, making sure I understood what was expected of me [Q1 in Figure 12.7]. Then, as I began to learn the ropes, she opened up a bit and seemed to be more personal, more interested in me and my feelings [Q2] as well as the work. In a year or so, after I had proved myself as her best technician, she pretty much let me handle the work side of things—I knew as much about them as she did—and most of our discussions were on the social side or about what a good job I was doing [Q3]. Now that I've been here four years and have proved what I can do, I only see her once or twice a week [Q4]. She spends more of her time with the new people."

A key point to remember in either a family or a work environment is that, in regard to a specific task, leaders may have to modify their strategies when circumstances change. Our conclusion is that, of the various leadership theories, the contingency-situational approach probably best explains what is required for effective managerial leadership.

Transformational and Transactional Leadership

Transformational leadership has become the most influential theory and way of looking at leadership that has emerged in more recent years. It is closely related to what some writers call charismatic leadership and developmental leadership, discussed in Chapter 14.

John MacGregor Burns[26] and Bernard Bass[27] were the first to identify and explore the differences between transactional and transformational leadership. Both authors make the case that transformational leadership is a paradigm shift to a more visionary and empowering leadership style, particularly needed in a world of rapid and turbulent change. As Burns states, "the result of transforming leadership is a relationship of mutual stimulation and elevation that converts followers into leaders and may convert leaders into moral agents."[28]

Transformational Leadership

Bass and others have taken Burns's general framework and applied the concepts to the field of management. Their research has resulted in identifying a number of past and current transformational leaders. A recent study found three factors that were an integral part of being a **transformational leader**—charismatic leadership, individualized consideration, and intellectual stimulation.

transformational leader A leader who provides charismatic leadership, individualized consideration, and intellectual stimulation.

The most important factor of transformational leadership is *charismatic leadership*. To receive a high score on this factor, a leader should need to instill pride, respect, and esprit de corps and have a gift of focusing on what is really important as well as a true sense of mission. The second factor, *individualized consideration*, indicates that the leader uses delegated assignments to provide learning and development and gives personal attention to individuals. The third factor, *intellectual stimulation*, indicates that the leader has vision and presents ideas that require rethinking of past methods of operation and allows for development of new ways of thinking.[29]

Some leaders who have scored exceptionally high on the charismatic leadership factor are Lee Iacocca, R. David Thomas (founder of Wendy's), George Patton, John F. Kennedy, Dr. Martin Luther King, Jr., Ronald Reagan, Sam Walton (founder of Wal-Mart), and General Norman Schwarzkopf. While charisma is important for effective leadership, it may be exercised to meet objectives that do not benefit society—Hitler and Saddam Hussein are cases in point.

TipS 12.2

Treating People as Individuals

There was a time when people were [treated as] "factors of production," managed little differently from machines or capital. No more. The best people will not tolerate it. And if that way of managing ever generated productivity, it has the reverse effect today. While capital and machines are or can be managed toward sameness, people are individuals. They must be managed that way. When companies encourage individual expression, it is difficult for them not to renew. The only true source of renewal in a company is the individual.

Source: Robert H. Waterman, Jr., "The Renewal Factor," *Business Week*, September 14, 1987, p. 100.

Research today reveals that transformational leaders are not limited to only world-class leaders. For example, Kenny, in the Opening Case, demonstrates many of the characteristics of the transformational leader. A business leader whom almost all experts identify as a transformational leader is Jack Welch, who was first introduced in the Opening Case in Chapter 8. Quite interesting is that James Harmon, a GE Human Resource executive, observed early in Welch's career that he demonstrated transformational leadership qualities.

Transactional Leadership

Of course, not everyone can be a transformational leader, and there are many leaders who fall into the category of **transactional leaders.** These leaders identify desired performance standards, recognize what types of rewards employees want from their work, and take actions that make receiving these rewards contingent upon achieving performance standards.[30] In essence this exemplifies an exchange process, a quid pro quo or "I'll do this if you'll do that." The transactional leader operates within the existing culture and employs traditional management strategies in getting the job done.

Two researchers, Karl Kuhnert and Phillip Lewis, have identified two levels of transactional leadership.[31] The first level follows the transactional approach just described and tries to integrate employee personal goals with the goals of the organization. At its best, it is similar to the management by objectives approach described in Chapter 7. But difficulties may arise if leaders do not have effective participation and communication skills in carrying out the MBO process or if rewards (pay increases, promotions) are not under the leader's direct control.

A second level of transactional leadership that is less common and of a higher order "involves promises or commitments that are rooted in 'exchangeable' values such as respect and trust. . . . Thus, lower-order transactions depend upon the leader's control of resources (e.g., pay increases, special benefits) that are desired by the followers. . . . If such rewards are not under the leader's direct control, the leader's bargaining power is diminished. Higher-order transactional leadership, on the other hand, relies on the exchange of non-concrete rewards to maintain followers' performance. In this relationship the leaders directly control such exchanges since they rely upon nontangible rewards and values."[32] The second level represents a step toward transformational leadership.

transactional leaders Leaders who identify desired performance standards, recognize what types of rewards employees want from their work and take actions that make receiving these rewards contingent upon achieving performance standards.

MANAGEMENT APPLICATION AND PRACTICE 12.3

Early Career Manifestations of Transformational Leadership

Jim Harmon states that when Jack Welch was a GE plant manager, he demonstrated many of the qualities and philosophies that he now employs and espouses as chairman and CEO of GE. Back then, he absolutely detested the unnecessary baggage that comes with turf protection and bureaucracy. Although he had to live with a certain amount of bureaucracy because the company insisted on it, he was able to finesse it. He strongly believed in surrounding himself with solid technical personnel who were not "yes people." He also believed in empowering all levels so that workers at the shop level became involved and excited.

Another change he made was doing away with many artificial distinctions between the categories of salaried and hourly employees and made all the plant workers nonexempt salaried. Early on, he would call operators in and chat with them about issues, problems, solutions, and opportunities. He had great difficulty understanding why some managers of his day could not step through those boundaries. He hated to go to corporate headquarters because of the homage and imperialism, but he played the game; today, he has changed the game, and GE's "Workout" strategy ensures people step through these boundaries.

Source: Interview and discussion with Jim Harmon, September 1993.

Comparison of Transactional and Transformational Leadership

One who believes that some people have the ability to grow and develop through levels of leadership and become transformational leaders is George McAleer, former Air Force pilot and now on the faculty of the National Defense University's Industrial College of the Armed Forces. McAleer agrees with Bass's thesis that transactional leadership can result in lower-order improvements, but if one wants higher-order improvements transformational leadership is needed.[33] This is the challenge that faces select military officers who were chosen to spend a year at a senior service college such as the Industrial College in Washington, D.C. This year is critical in one's military career: Out of this select group, approximately one in five will become a general or admiral in the next five to ten years.

In McAleer's words, "What made them successful up to this point in their career may not necessarily be the best avenue for them to proceed over the next several years. That's the formidable task my colleagues and I have at the Industrial College. Part of the challenge is encompassed in a course entitled 'Strategic Decision Making.'"[34] The challenge is to convince these officers that the leadership style that will serve them best in the future as strategic decision makers is transformational.

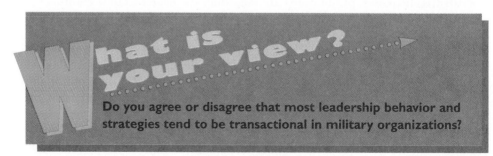

What is your view?

Do you agree or disagree that most leadership behavior and strategies tend to be transactional in military organizations?

TABLE 12.2   CONTRASTING LEADERSHIP APPROACHES

	Transactional	Transformational
Characteristics	Exchange process	Relations orientation
	Evolutionary ideas	Revolutionary ideas
	Within existing structure	Emerges in crisis
	Reactive	Proactive
Motivation	Contingent reward (extrinsic)	Inspiration; recognition (intrinsic)
Power	Traditional	Charismatic
Focus	Outcomes	Vision
Leader	Specifies task	Consultant, coach, teacher
	Clarifies roles	Emphasis on empowering the individual
	Recognizes needs	Gives autonomy; good listener; informal; accessible; model of integrity
	Manages by exception	
Subordinates	Seek security; needs fulfilled	Transcend self-interests for the organization
	Separate organization from individual	Do more than they are expected to do
Outcomes	Expected performance	Quantum leaps in performance

"Leadership: Good, Better, Best." (Bernard Bass)

Source: George McAleer's presentation at APT Type and Leadership Symposium, Crystal City, Virginia, March 5–7, 1993.

One way to start the change process is to contrast the two leadership styles, as in Table 12.2.

Men and Women as Leaders

Historically, literature has highlighted primarily men as leaders and described their leadership roles and behaviors. During most of our history, men have had the leadership spotlight because of their roles in war, hunting, business, and government and as providers. In patriarchal societies, most women played the traditional role of homemaker. In a number of countries of the world, patriarchies still exist, with men the primary leaders in families, business, and government. In the United States, however, this situation has changed dramatically in the past few decades, and women are now finding themselves in leadership positions in business, government, and professional fields as never before.

Recognizing this changed situation, Judy Rosener has conducted research and written about the workforce in America and the way women lead. She makes a case that women today, moving into higher management, are not adopting the style and habits that have proved successful for men, but are instead drawing on the skills and attitudes they developed from their unique experience as women. They are straying from the command-and-control style associated with men and are using what Rosener calls an "interactive style of leadership."[35]

She came to this conclusion after she had conducted a survey of men and women leaders sponsored by the International Women's Forum. Contrary to other studies, hers found that the men and women respondents earned comparable amounts of money and that as many men as women experience work-family conflict. The major difference was that the men described their leadership style in transactional terminology, whereas the women described theirs in transformational terminology. Intrigued by this discrepancy, she interviewed some of the women respondents who described themselves as transformational. In her words, "These discussions gave me a better picture of how these women view themselves as leaders and a greater understanding of the important ways in which their leadership style differs from the traditional command-and-control style. I call their leadership style interactive leadership because these women actively work to make their interactions with subordinates positive for everyone involved. More specifically, the women encourage participation, share power and information, enhance other people's self-worth, and get others excited about their work. All these things reflect their belief that allowing employees to contribute and to feel powerful and important is a win-win situation—good for the employees and the organization."[36]

As might be expected, Rosener's article, which appeared in the *Harvard Business Review*, generated quite a debate. In a subsequent issue, readers and the author faced off over this issue. For example, Cynthia Epstein wrote in and challenged Rosener's methodology. Epstein made the case that the category is "people, not men and women." In Epstein's words:

"Do women bring a different managerial style to the workplace? This is a loaded question because most people are oriented toward finding differences between men and women and tend to downplay the similarities they show. Judy Rosener, in "Ways Women Lead" (November–December 1990), falls into the same trap, under the guise of reporting on her study of manager styles, because her mode of investigation is impaired to begin with. Instead of observing men and women at work to ascertain whether they indeed act differently, she asked them to describe their styles.

"Much current research shows that men and women tend to stereotype their own behavior according to cultural views of gender-appropriate behaviors, as much as they stereotype the behavior of other groups. Thus it was not surprising for Rosener to "find" that men tended to "command and control" and women leaned toward "transformational" patterns, using interpersonal skills.

"An example from my own research on women attorneys was the lawyer who described her style as caring but who was characterized as a barracuda by a male associate."[37]

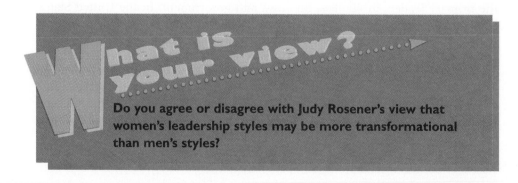

What is your view?

Do you agree or disagree with Judy Rosener's view that women's leadership styles may be more transformational than men's styles?

SUMMARY

Leadership is a process of influencing individual and group activities toward goal setting and goal attainment. The successful leader is able to get others to follow in achieving organizational goals. It has also been shown that leadership is complex and that there are various factors affecting the leadership style used in different countries, organizations, and situations.

The case for an ideal leadership style was presented, along with the case for the contingency-situational approach to leadership. We examined the relationships between ethics and leadership.

Findings supporting the traitist theory of leadership were presented. Then the research and theories of the behavioral approach were given. Included were ideas by McGregor, Likert, Blake and Mouton, and William Ouchi. The general conclusion of these was that participative, employee-centered leadership is the ideal.

The contingency-situational leadership concepts of Tannenbaum and Schmidt and Hersey and Blanchard were also presented. The general conclusion was that leaders must be prepared to adapt their leadership styles according to forces in the follower, the situation, and the leader. We also examined some concepts that leaders can apply to inspire self-confidence and develop people.

We believe that leadership is situational. That is, the style to be used is contingent on many factors, including the manager, the subordinates, and the situation. It is important, however, for you to be keenly aware that there are forces in most organizations that create many situations for which the most effective leadership style is participative.

There is currently a great need for leaders for today's organizations—especially for transformational leaders, who have charisma, show individual consideration, and provide intellectual stimulation.

KEY TERMS

leadership, 393
autocratic (authoritarian) leaders, 395
democratic (participative) leaders, 395
laissez-faire (free-rein) leaders, 395
task-oriented (production-oriented)
 leaders, 395
people-oriented (employee-centered)
 leaders, 395
traitist theories, 396
behavioral theories, 397
Theory X, 398

Theory Y, 398
System 4, 400
Leadership Grid®, 401
Theory Z, 401
contingency-situational theories, 408
leadership continuum, 408
law of the situation, 408
life-cycle theory, 410
transformational leader, 412
transactional leaders, 413

DISCUSSION QUESTIONS

1. Do you believe there is an ideal leadership style? Explain.

2. Should a supervisor use one leadership style with certain workers, another with other workers, and perhaps a third with others? Defend your answer.

3. Can you correlate McGregor's Theory X and Theory Y with task-oriented and people-oriented leadership styles?

4. Which of the various leadership theories discussed in this chapter do you think is the most applicable in the real world? Support your position.

5. Discuss Tannenbaum and Schmidt's leadership continuum and contrast it with Hersey and Blanchard's life-cycle theory. What is the primary difference in the conclusions reached in the two theories?

6. How valid is the "law of the situation"?

7. Are there really any transformational leaders? Defend your answer.

8. (a) Can good leaders be poor managers? (b) Can good managers be poor leaders? Explain your answers.

9. Do you agree or disagree with Judy Rosener's thesis that a higher percentage of women in leadership positions are transformational compared to men in leadership positions? Support your position.

PRACTICING MANAGEMENT

12.1

case

Which Leadership Style?

Ron Paul received his B.S. degree in accounting from a major university in the Midwest and began his career at the Chicago office of Jones & Jones (J&J), a large accounting firm, in 1971. Nine years later, he became a partner in the firm, one of the youngest ever. The firm's executive committee spotted Paul's leadership potential and aggressive style and, in 1983, called on him to open a new office in a suburb of New York. The work was predominantly doing audits that required considerable judgment and self-control on the part of subordinates. Paul was quite task oriented, yet he used a democratic leadership style. He insisted that the entire office be on a first-name basis and encouraged subordinates to participate in decision making.

Long-range goals and objectives were known by everyone, but the methods of achieving the goals were very unstructured.

The office grew rapidly, and the professional staff increased to over 30 by 1988. Paul was considered to be a highly successful leader and manager.

Paul was then transferred to Dallas, Texas, to try to salvage an office that had been losing money and whose employees seemed to lack both ability and motivation.

Paul took over as managing partner in Dallas in early 1989. He started out with the same aggressive managing style that had worked so well in New York. He immediately replaced nearly the entire professional staff of 25 people. Short- and long-range client development plans were made, and the staff was expanded quite rapidly to ensure that a sufficient number of employees were available to accommodate the expected growth. Soon, there were about 40 professional staff members.

But the aggressive style that had worked in New York did not work well at all in Dallas. The office lost two of its best clients within one year. Paul soon realized that the office was badly overstaffed and decided to fire 12 staff members, whom he had hired only one year earlier, to minimize losses.

He was convinced that the setback was temporary and continued with his strategy. The staff was increased by six professionals over the next few months to again accommodate the expected increased workload. The expected new business did not materialize, so the staff was again trimmed, by 13 professionals, on "Black Tuesday" in the summer of 1991.

Following these two layoffs, the remaining staff members were insecure and began to question Paul's leadership ability. The firm's executive committee sensed the problem and transferred Paul to a New Jersey office, where his leadership style has operated quite effectively.

Questions

1. What were the sources of Ron Paul's power as a leader?

2. To what extent does this case illustrate the contingency approach to leadership?

3. Why did Paul's strategy work in New York but not in Dallas? Explain.

12.1

Using Effective Leaders as Role Models

Think of two of the most effective leaders you have had direct contact with and who have had an influence in your life. These leaders can be anyone—a parent, a teacher, a coach, a boss, a student leader, a religious leader, or a relative or friend.

List at least six characteristics and/or beliefs that made these people such outstanding leaders. Next, on a scale of 1 (poor) to 5 (excellent), rank how well you measure up against these characteristics and beliefs.

Do you think you could develop more of these characteristics (score better) if you made a concerted effort? What does this imply about the traitist theory of leadership?

Selecting a Leadership Strategy

learning exercise

This exercise is based on the Hersey-Blanchard life-cycle model. For each of the following situations, select the best leadership alternative.

1. The interdepartmental task force you manage has been working hard to complete its divisionwide report. One of your task force members has been late for the past five meetings. He has offered no excuses or apologies. Furthermore, he is way behind in completing the cost figures for his department. It is imperative that he present these figures to the task force within the next three days. Should you

   a. Tell him exactly what you expect and closely supervise his work on this report?

   b. Discuss with him why he has been late, and support his efforts to complete the task?

   c. Emphasize when the cost figures are due and support his efforts?

   d. Assume he will be prepared to present the cost figures to the task force?

2. In the past, you have had a great deal of trouble with one of the people you supervise. She has been lackadaisical, and only your constant prodding has brought about task completion. Recently, however, you have noticed a change. Her performance has improved, and you have had to remind her less and less about meeting deadlines. She has even initiated several suggestions for improving her performance. Should you

   a. Continue to direct and closely supervise her efforts?

   b. Continue to supervise her work, but listen to her suggestions and incorporate those that seem reasonable?

   c. Incorporate her suggestions and support her ideas?

   d. Let her take responsibility for her own work?

3. Because of budget restrictions imposed on your department, it is necessary to consolidate. You have asked a highly experienced member of your department to take charge of the consolidation. This person has worked in all areas of your department. In the past, she has usually been eager to help. While you feel she has the ability to carry out this assignment, she seems indifferent to the importance of the task. Should you

   a. Take charge of the consolidation but make sure you hear her suggestions?

   b. Assign the project to her and let her determine how to accomplish it?

   c. Discuss the situation with her, encouraging her to accept the assignment in view of her skills and experience?

   d. Take charge of the consolidation and indicate to her precisely what to do, supervising her work closely?

4. Your staff have asked you to consider a change in their work schedules. In the past, you have encouraged and supported their suggestions. In this case, your staff are well aware of the need for change and are ready to suggest and try an alternative schedule. Members are very competent and work well together as a group. Should you

   a. Allow staff involvement in developing the new schedule and support the suggestions of group members?

   b. Design and implement the new schedule yourself, but incorporate staff recommendations?

   c. Allow the staff to formulate and implement the new schedule on their own?

   d. Design the new schedule yourself and closely direct its implementation?

Source: Adapted from W. Alan Randolph, *Understanding and Managing Organizational Behavior* (Homewood, Ill.: Richard D. Irwin, 1985), pp. 256–257.

I became personally convinced that in order to enlist the support of our entire organization in quality improvement, we had to radically change our entire corporate culture.

—DAVID T. KEARNS,
CHAIRMAN,
XEROX CORPORATION

Managing Change, Organization Development, Conflict, and Stress

LEARNING OBJECTIVES

After studying the material in this chapter, you should be able to:

● **Appreciate** the impact of change and development on individuals and organizations.

● **Describe** some ways to cope with and manage the changes that inevitably occur in organizations.

● **Define** organization development, name its objectives, and show how the process works.

● **Discuss** how to manage conflict.

● **Discuss** ways of dealing with stress.

The Ritz-Carlton Hotel Corporation

This opening case could easily have been placed in our leadership chapter because it involves transformational leadership. It could also have been a good choice to introduce Chapter 14 because it encompasses team development, empowerment practices, and total quality We have chosen this chapter because the case is a classic "textbook" example of the effective management of change and organizational development.

In 1850, Cesar Ritz was born in Neiderwald, Switzerland. "Blessed with virtues of ambition, courage and taste, Ritz strived for excellence in everything he did, and when he entered the hotel industry, his ideals were not to be compromised."

After working as a waiter at Voisin, then the most fashionable restaurant in Paris, Ritz teamed with the renowned French chef Auguste Escoffier, with whom he had worked in several of Europe's famous hotels. While both were employed at the Carlton Hotel in London, Cesar Ritz went to Paris to find a place for a hotel of his own. After selecting the perfect location for his hotel, he contacted Marnier La Postolle, an old friend and the originator of the liqueur Grand Marnier, who gladly loaned him the money to open his hotel.

June 1898 marked the opening of the Ritz of Paris of the Place Vendome, with, of course, Escoffier as *chef de cuisine*. The hotel, conceived by Cesar Ritz according to his own standards of perfection, initiated the European deluxe hotel industry. Ritz's idea was to create not a "grand hotel" but a new and original one, a home that would equal the comforts, security, and service that discriminating patrons would provide for themselves—a nonhotel.

Cesar Ritz insisted on certain criteria that would be the foundation for the Paris Ritz and all future hotels bearing the Ritz name: a central location, preferably overlooking a public park or square; comfortable and attractive rooms; food and beverage services second to none; and a wine cellar that would appeal to the finest connoisseurs. Combining all of these elements, Ritz still considered the most crucial aspect of his "perfect" hotel to be service. In order to provide the finest service and quality, the number of employees was to exceed the number of guests.

Horst A. Schulze, president and chief operating officer of the Ritz-Carlton Hotel Company.

Both Ritz and Escoffier had an interest in the Carlton Hotel in London. They combined their efforts and established the Ritz-Carlton Company to give rights to the Ritz-Carlton name internationally. Under the supervision of Cesar Ritz, hotels developed all over the world, including New York City, bearing the Ritz-Carlton name, but few were able to survive the rigid standards established by Cesar Ritz.

The last sentence highlights the problem. Despite the Ritz-Carlton tradition, a number of the properties bearing the name failed to maintain the consistency and standards of excellence of the original founders.

This changed in 1983, when the current Ritz-Carlton Hotel Company acquired the rights to the name and bought the Ritz-Carlton in Boston. The hotel chain today owns outright only a few of the properties, but the company's 11,500 employees manage all 30 of the Ritz-Carlton properties located around the world. Under the ownership of William B. Johnson, an Atlanta investor, and the transformational leadership of Horst A. Schulze, president and chief operating officer, the company's 30 properties have met or exceeded the standards of excellence of the original founders. Evidence of this achievement is reflected in the following:

1. In 1992, the Ritz-Carlton was selected best hotel chain in the United States by the Zagat U.S. Travel Service.

2. In 1992, Horst Schulze was chosen Corporate Hotelier of the World by *Hotels Magazine*.

3. In 1992, Ritz-Carlton became the first hotel company to win a Malcolm Baldridge National Quality Award (established by Congress in 1987 to promote quality management).

4. In 1994, the company was rated by *Consumer Reports* as the number one luxury hotel chain in the world.

At present, most Ritz-Carlton hotels are located within the United States; however, 10 or 12 new developments will be located outside the United States.

After a consulting trip to Honolulu in June 1994, one of the authors took a week's vacation and stayed at the Ritz-Carlton Kapalua, on the island of Maui. We had never stayed in a Ritz-Carlton and were curious to see if it lived up to its reputation. Afterwards we rated our stay a 10+ on a 10-point scale. Here are just a few reasons why:

▶ A basket of fruit was in our room upon arrival.

▶ A minor problem was presented to a staff member who solved it without fanfare. Later we found out that any staff member to whom a guest presents a problem is empowered to solve that problem.

▶ On two occasions when we asked for directions regarding a location on the hotel's 32 acres, we were not simply given directions; we were escorted there.

▶ The food was consistently excellent in all three of the hotel's restaurants.

Horst Schulze is given the credit for catalyzing the chain's reputation for quality and service. In regard to the awards received, Schulze has stated, "We are not resting on the momentary glory or satisfaction of these awards. We have embarked, and have worked diligently the last three years, on total quality management (TQM). We know that through TQM we will continuously improve our product and services. It is our intention to not only serve you with genuine care and comfort, but to fulfill all your needs in our hotels and give you complete service excellence all of the time.

"Today every employee, from housekeeper to server to manager, is committed to the ultimate dream and vision through TQM: 100% guest satisfaction."

Although the hotel's corporate managers have used consultants such as Joseph M. Juran and Steven Covey in their search for excellence, they have created their own version of total quality management. According to Sue Musselman, assistant to the vice-president of quality, it was pursuit of the Malcolm Baldridge Award that gave the organization the quantum leap in improving processes and services. Just a few of the tailored features of the Ritz-Carlton's focus on quality, service, and guest satisfaction are as follows:

1. President Schulze participates in employee orientation programs at each new hotel.

2. In the two-day orientation program for new employees, Rebecca Powell, the training manager, emphasizes that "you serve but you are not servants"; rather, "you are ladies and gentlemen serving ladies and gentlemen."

3. In addition to the orientation program, 100 more hours of training are provided to employees.

4. When processes are improved or reengineered in one hotel, the information and concepts are shared with all hotels. (We will discuss this process, called *benchmarking*, in the next chapter.)

5. Every worker is empowered to spend up to $2,000 to fix any problem a guest encounters. Patrick Mene, director of quality, has reported that employees do not abuse this privilege. "When you treat people responsibly, they act responsibly."

Are employees achieving President Schulze's goal of 100 percent guest satisfaction? In the eyes of one customer, they are. "They not only treat us like a king when we hold our top-level meetings in their hotels, but we just never get any complaints," said Wayne Stetson, the staff vice-president of the convention and meetings division of the National Association of Home Builders in Washington, D.C.

The Ritz-Carlton credo—found in MAP 13.1 and carried by each employee—explains in more depth the chain's success. This is a hotel that has created a culture where the employees practice their credo.[1]

-MANAGEMENT APPLICATION AND PRACTICE 13.1

The Ritz-Carlton Credo

THREE STEPS OF SERVICE

1
A warm and sincere greeting. Use the guest name, if and when possible.

2
Anticipation and compliance with guest needs.

3
Fond farewell. Give them a warm good-bye and use their names, if and when possible.

" We Are Ladies and Gentlemen Serving Ladies and Gentlemen "

THE RITZ-CARLTON

CREDO
The Ritz-Carlton Hotel is a place where the genuine care and comfort of our guests is our highest mission.

We pledge to provide the finest personal service and facilities for our guests who will always enjoy a warm, relaxed yet refined ambience.

The Ritz-Carlton experience enlivens the senses, instills well-being, and fulfills even the unexpressed wishes and needs of our guests.

THE RITZ-CARLTON BASICS

1. The Credo will be known, owned and energized by all employees.

2. Our motto is: "We are Ladies and Gentlemen serving Ladies and Gentlemen". Practice teamwork and "lateral service" to create a positive work environment.

3. The three steps of service shall be practiced by all employees.

4. All employees will successfully complete Training Certification to ensure they understand how to perform to The Ritz-Carlton standards in their position.

5. Each employee will understand their work area and Hotel goals as established in each strategic plan.

6. All employees will know the needs of their internal and external customers (guests and employees) so that we may deliver the products and services they expect. Use guest preference pads to record specific needs.

7. Each employee will continuously identify defects (Mr. BIV) throughout the Hotel.

8. Any employee who receives a customer complaint "owns" the complaint.

9. Instant guest pacification will be ensured by all. React quickly to correct the problem immediately. Follow-up with a telephone call within twenty minutes to verify the problem has been resolved to the customer's satisfaction. Do everything you possibly can to never lose a guest.

10. Guest incident action forms are used to record and communicate every incident of guest dissatisfaction. Every employee is empowered to resolve the problem and to prevent a repeat occurrence.

11. Uncompromising levels of cleanliness are the responsibility of every employee.

12. "Smile – We are on stage." Always maintain positive eye contact. Use the proper vocabulary with our guests. (Use words like – "Good Morning," "Certainly," "I'll be happy to" and "My pleasure").

13. Be an ambassador of your Hotel in and outside of the work place. Always talk positively. No negative comments.

14. Escort guests rather than pointing out directions to another area of the Hotel.

15. Be knowledgeable of Hotel information (hours of operation, etc.) to answer guest inquiries. Always recommend the Hotel's retail and food and beverage outlets prior to outside facilities.

16. Use proper telephone etiquette. Answer within three rings and with a "smile." When necessary, ask the caller, "May I place you on hold." Do not screen calls. Eliminate call transfers when possible.

17. Uniforms are to be immaculate. Wear proper and safe footwear (clean and polished), and your correct name tag. Take pride and care in your personal appearance (adhering to all grooming standards).

18. Ensure all employees know their roles during emergency situations and are aware of fire and life safety response processes.

19. Notify your supervisor immediately of hazards, injuries, equipment or assistance that you need. Practice energy conservation and proper maintenance and repair of Hotel property and equipment.

20. Protecting the assets of a Ritz-Carlton Hotel is the responsibility of every employee.

I t was shown in Chapter 2 that organizations can have life cycles similar to those of products and civilizations. They can go through a period of growth and ascendancy and then a period of stagnation and decline. The process of decline can be reversed, however, by a process of renewal, propelling a new cycle of growth and ascendancy.

The Opening Case presents an example of organization development and renewal in a company and its ascendancy to new standards of excellence. Organization development is a major factor in any organizational change effort. We next examine organizational change and how to effectively manage this change.

Managing Organizational Change

You have heard the adage that nothing is certain but death and taxes. But a third certainty could be added—*change*. In management, change is expected as a part of everyday life. Change takes many forms, including new methods of doing the work, new products or services, new organization structures, and new personnel policies or employee benefits. Change is now occurring at an explosive rate, and it may accelerate into the late 1990s to the point of becoming impossible to predict.

Forces Causing Change

As discussed in previous chapters, numerous factors affect an organization, and most are continuously changing. Forces leading to or causing change originate both outside and within the organization, as shown in Figure 13.1

You might compare this situation to yourself as a human organism. You respond to external stimuli, such as the temperature outside, whether it is raining or sunny, the work schedule for the day, and situations that arise during the day. You also respond, however, to internal stimuli, such as your need for food, whether you

FIGURE 13.1
External and internal change forces.

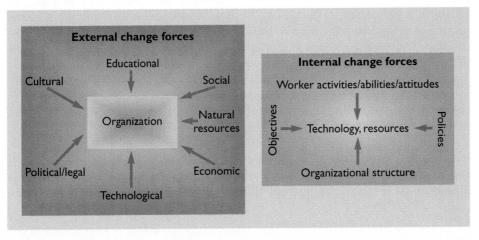

feel alert and well rested, whether you have a cold or fever, or your mood. Substitute an organization for yourself, and we have a very similar situation.

External Change Forces   Although it is difficult to generalize, it seems that *external change forces* have a greater impact on organizational change than internal stimuli, since management has little control over them and they are so numerous. Yet as shown in Chapter 3, an organization depends on and must interact with its external environment if it is to survive; its resources are obtained from outside, as are the clients and customers for its products and services. Therefore, anything that interferes with or modifies that environment can affect the organization's operations and cause pressure for change.

An enormous variety of external forces, from technological discoveries to changing lifestyles, can pressure an organization to change its goals, structure, and methods of operation.

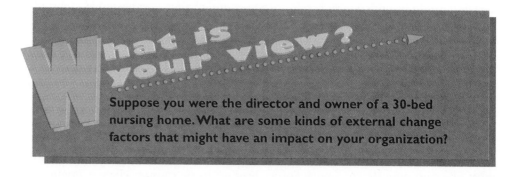

Suppose you were the director and owner of a 30-bed nursing home. What are some kinds of external change factors that might have an impact on your organization?

Some experts believe that one of the basic changes needed in today's organizations is a change away from some of the fundamental values that are widely held in American society, including (1) a short-term rather than a long-term perspective, (2) a focus on the ends rather than the means, and (3) an emphasis on the individual over the community.[2] Taken together, these three values form the *ethic of personal advantage.*

Internal Change Forces   Pressures for change may also come from within organizations. These *internal change forces* may result from new organization objectives and cultures, as we saw in the case of the Ritz-Carlton Hotel Company. Or they may be caused by new managerial policies, technologies, or employee attitudes. For example, top management's decision to shift its goal from short-run profit to long-term growth will affect the goals of many departments and may even lead to reorganization. The introduction of automated equipment and robots to perform work that was previously done by people will cause changes in work layout and routine, incentive programs, and personnel policies and procedures. Worker attitudes concerning child care, health and fitness, or flexible working hours, for example, may lead to many changes in management policies and practices.

External and internal forces for change, however, are not found in isolation, but are often interrelated. This linkage frequently results from changes in values and attitudes that affect people in the system. Some of these people enter the organization and cause it to change from within. For example, many of the changes now occurring in organizations are the result of the activist attitudes of the 1960s and early 1970s concerning pollution, equal employment opportunity, product safety, and equal rights for women.

Results of Ignoring Change

Institutions in our society, including business and government organizations, help preserve many things of worth from the past. These include values and social, cultural, and technological innovations. This role of institutions is important in connecting the past, present, and future and allowing the continuation of a high standard of living. On the other hand, to protect themselves against further change, institutions harden their resistance by formalizing rituals, customs, and traditions. This resistance sometimes leads to inability to cope with a new environment and paves the way for stagnation, decline, and failure. Thus, unless an organization plans for and copes effectively with the challenge of change, the results can be disastrous. The same reasoning applies to managers and employees, who face change at an even more accelerated pace.

Ways of Dealing with Change

There are two major ways of dealing with organizational change. The first is a *reactive process*, whereby management adapts in a piecemeal, one-step-at-a-time manner in dealing with problems or issues as they arise. The second is a *proactive process*, which involves deliberate actions to modify the status quo.

The Reactive Process of Change In using the **reactive process of change,** management tries to keep the organization on a steady course by solving problems as they come up. For example, if you are a department store manager and complaints about salesclerks suddenly increase, you might set up a short training program to correct the problem. If one of your major suppliers goes bankrupt, you quickly search for another source of supply. If new government regulations require you to have better fire protection, you buy more and better extinguishers. In each of these cases, you initiate change in *reaction* to something that has already happened.

> **reactive process of change** Management tries to keep the organization on a steady course by solving problems as they come up.

This approach involves little planning and is usually not viewed by managers as "threatening," since it is aimed at solving a current, visible problem. Over a period of time, however, a series of small, incremental problems can add up to a significant change in an organization, and "quick fixes" may be inconsistent with one another—sometimes the end result is not desirable.

The Proactive (Planned) Process of Change On the other hand, with the **proactive** or **planned process of change,** management tries to change things by setting a new course rather than correcting the current one. Also, planned change seeks to *anticipate* changes in the external and internal environments and find integrated ways to cope with those predicted new conditions. Because of the rapidity and complexity of changes in today's world, we feel that managers must understand and practice planned organizational change.

> **proactive (planned) process of change** Management tries to change things by setting a new course rather than by correcting the current one.

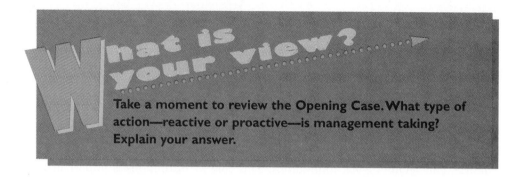

Take a moment to review the Opening Case. What type of action—reactive or proactive—is management taking? Explain your answer.

Planned Change

organizational effectiveness The result of activities that improve the organization's structure, technology, and people.

If management wants to plan for change, then it must decide what needs to be changed in the organization. In general, management seeks to change things that prevent greater organizational effectiveness. **Organizational effectiveness** results from activities that improve the organization's structure, technology, and people so that the firm achieves its objectives.

The choice of the particular technique used to achieve organizational change depends on the nature of the problem that is causing the organization to be less than ideally effective. Management must determine which alternative is most likely to produce the desired outcome. The diagnosis of the problem includes specifying the outcome that management desires from the change. In general, the desired outcome is improved employee behavior or activities that will result in improved performance. This can be achieved by changing the organization's structure, technology, and/or people.

This classification of organizational elements in no way implies a distinct division among them. According to the systems concept, a change in one element is likely to affect other elements. In general, the more change is required, the more likely it is that management will change all three elements.

As you can see from Figure 13.2, management must decide (1) the desired outcomes and (2) the type of change programs to use to (3) change the specific organizational element—including those activities needed to get the work done effectively.

Changing the organization's *structure* involves modifying and rearranging the internal relationships, including such variables as authority-responsibility relationships (recall the discussion of downsizing in Chapter 8), communications systems, work flows, and size and composition of work groups.

Changing the organization's *technology* may require altering or modifying such factors as its tools, equipment, and machinery; research direction and techniques; engineering processes; and production system, including layout, methods, and procedures. Changing technology may result from or contribute to changing tasks to be performed, as well as products and other inputs. For example, mechanization changes the very nature of the work employees do.

Changing the organization's *people* may include changing recruiting and selection policies and procedures, training and development activities, reward systems, and/or managerial leadership and communication.

Managers and employees are likely to support change if it is directed at the *real* cause of the problem, is *an effective solution*, and does not affect them adversely.

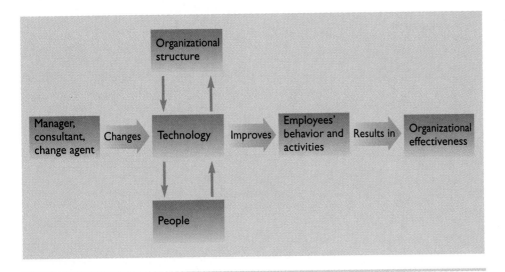

FIGURE 13.2
Organizational effectiveness results from changing structure, technology, and
people.

A neutral response—a "wait and see" attitude—is probably the most frequent
response of employees to change. However, many employees may initially show
resistance. Most managers consider resistance bad. But is it? What if the employees
see problems in the changed policies that the manager has not anticipated? How
will the change affect the organization's "social system"? When there is resistance,
managers should reexamine the proposed change to see whether they can find a
solution acceptable to all. And that change must be brought about through people.

The Process of Managing Change

Managing change requires using some systematic process that can be broken down
into steps or subprocesses. Many models can be used for this process, but one of the
most logical and popular ones emphasizes the role of the change agent. A **change
agent,** who can be either a manager from within the organization (such as Donald
Beall, Rockwell's CEO) or an outside consultant, takes a leadership role in initiating and introducing the change process. As you study this change process, notice
that it involves two basic ideas necessary for organizational effectiveness. First,
power is redistributed within the organizational structure. Second, if the structure
is changed in addition to power redistribution, both changes result from a planned
change process.

The proposed change process, as you can see from Figure 13.3, goes through
six phases. It shows the stimuli on the power structure and the responses.

1. *Pressure and arousal.* The process begins when top management feels a need
or pressure for a change or an opportunity presents itself for improving the
future position of the organization. This is usually caused by some significant
problem(s), such as a sharp decline in sales or profits, serious labor unrest,
and/or high labor turnover, and arouses management to take some action.

change agent The
individual, either a
manager from within
the organization or an
outside consultant,
who takes a leadership
role in initiating and
introducing the
change process.

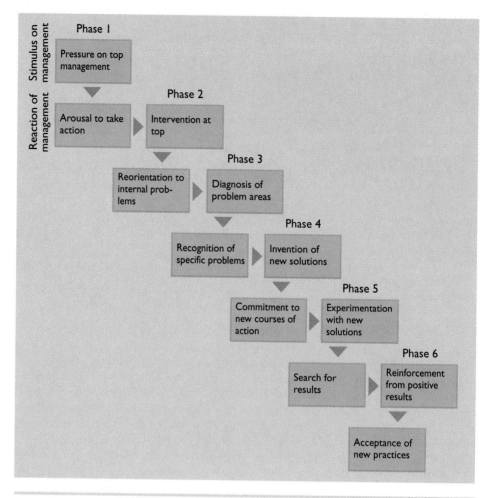

FIGURE 13.3
Model of the change process.

2. *Intervention and reorientation.* A change agent is assigned the task of defining the problem and beginning the process of getting organization members to focus on it. The agent may be able to intervene and reorient the organization's thinking toward ways of attacking the problem or capitalizing on the opportunities.

3. *Diagnosis and recognition of problem(s).* Information is gathered and analyzed by the change agent and management. The most important problem areas are diagnosed, and those that need it are given attention.

4. *Intervention of and commitment to solutions.* The change agent should stimulate thought and find solutions by creatively developing new and plausible alternatives. If subordinates are encouraged to participate in this process, they will probably be more committed to the course of action finally chosen.

5. *Experimentation and search for results.* The solutions developed in Phase 4 are usually tested in small-scale pilot programs and the results analyzed. One unit, or a certain part of a unit, may try out an idea before it is tried in the organization as a whole.

6. *Reinforcement and acceptance.* If the course of action has been tested and found desirable, it should be accepted more willingly. Improved performance should be a source of reinforcement and thus should lead to a commitment to the change.

Using Organizational Development (OD) to Promote Change

Many institutions attempt to cope with changes by developing innovative ways not only to deal with change but also to promote it. One of these innovative methods is a management concept and approach called *organizational development (OD)*. This approach is not perceived in the same way by all its practitioners and experts, but we feel that the concept shows great promise for helping organizations go through a process of change and revitalization, especially in shifting to a more participative culture. **Organizational development (OD)** may be defined as an organizationwide effort, managed from the top, to increase organizational effectiveness through planned interventions in the organization's processes, using behavioral science knowledge.[3] While the effort should be "managed from the top," this does not necessarily mean by the chief executive officer. Instead, "the top" could be the dean of a college in a university, or in a large corporation, the manager of a branch plant or even the head of a major department. Some OD experts give the impression that OD cannot occur in an organization without the aid of either an outside or an internal consultant. However, a healthy organization can develop itself using regular managers and employees as the primary OD practitioners.

organizational development (OD) An organizationwide effort, managed from the top, to increase organizational effectiveness through planned interventions in the organization's processes, using behavioral science knowledge.

What is your view?
Would you characterize the change in the Opening Case as OD?

The objectives of typical OD efforts include the following:

1. To increase trust and support among organizational members
2. To create an environment in which the authority of an assigned role is increased based on expertise and knowledge (expert power)
3. To increase the level of personal—and group—responsibility in planning and implementation
4. To increase the openness of communication among organization members
5. To find synergistic solutions to problems (*synergy*, as discussed in Chapter 8, is the action of two or more organisms working together to achieve an effect of which each alone is incapable).

A Basic OD Model

As with other aspects of planned organizational change, models make it easier to understand OD. Perhaps the most popular model is the *action-research model*—Figure 13.4—which can be used in several contexts, organizations, or organizational units.

In one way, the *research-diagnosis phase* is similar to a doctor's diagnostic method. Like a doctor learning the patient's medical history and present symptoms, the manager or change agent gathers information from members of the organization. Often this information encompasses organizational strengths, problems, and opportunities or more specific factors. The difference between the doctor's diagnosis and the change agent's is that the change agent often provides feedback to organization members so that they can help in developing plans that are concerned with specific actions to be taken. In other words, organization members help to write their own prescriptions.

The data gathered by the change agent are assembled, synthesized, and summarized, with members of the organization helping to develop action plans (*action-planning phase*) that are then implemented (*implementation phase*). The *evaluation phase* sometimes employs the same methods used in the research-diagnosis phase so that OD becomes an ongoing process. Let us illustrate the action-research model with a class in principles of management taught by a young, inexperienced instructor.

Two weeks into the semester, a college teacher we will call Professor Clark noticed that students were beginning to cut class, and some were even sleeping during lectures. She decided to try the action-research and feedback process in an effort to improve class performance and to create a more effective learning environment.

She asked members of the class to respond, anonymously and in writing, to two questions: What are the strengths of this class? What are the problems that are preventing this class from reaching its potential effectiveness? In summarizing the responses, she was dismayed to find that very few strengths were given and the top-ranked problem was that "the class is dry and boring."

Professor Clark reported the findings to the class and divided them into teams to analyze the problem. The consensus of the teams was that it was "dry and boring" because (1) it was offered at 1:00 P.M., when most of the students had just

FIGURE 13.4
Action-research model of OD.

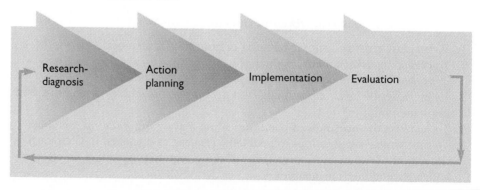

Research-diagnosis   Action planning   Implementation   Evaluation

eaten lunch and were sleepy; (2) the text was highly theoretical, with few examples of practical applications; and (3) the lectures were primarily a rehash of the text, and a course that uses lectures exclusively is a very passive form of learning.

When the groups were asked to make recommendations as to what could be done to make the class more effective, they suggested (1) using more real-world management examples and bringing in executives as guest lecturers; (2) using short cases, critical incidents, and experiential learning exercises to illustrate the text; and (3) requiring students to work occasionally in their groups to develop case reports and presentations.

The text could not be changed, and time did not permit bringing in guest lecturers, but the other suggestions were implemented. At the end of the semester, students evaluated the course as "excellent" and indicated that the change in approach had created an effective, stimulating learning environment.

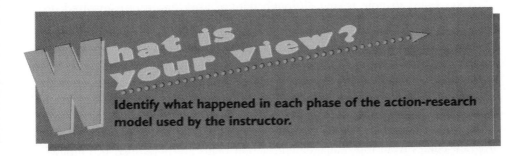

What is your view?

Identify what happened in each phase of the action-research model used by the instructor.

Selected OD Interventions

In Chapter 13 we explore in-depth OD interventions involving total quality management, partnering, and self-managing work teams. In this section we identify three approaches that have been useful in changing an organization's effectiveness. These interventions are (1) Likert's System 4, (2) confrontation meeting, and (3) quality of work life (QWL) programs and quality circles (QC).

Likert's System 4   Recall that we discussed Likert's System 4 (participative group) in Chapter 12. This OD intervention strategy emphasizes democracy and participation in organizations, together with a focus on goal attainment.[4] It is particularly useful in changing an organization's culture from a System 1 or 2 to a System 3 or 4. There is one large paper company that is attempting to shift many of its mills from an environment of benevolent autocracy to System 3 and 4. An outside consulting firm is working with one division at a time, since the transformation takes time.

One General Motors assembly plant successfully used this method to move from System 2 to System 4. It conducted training sessions about System 4 management, held team-building sessions at all organizational levels, and improved both hourly workers' and foremen's jobs. Performance increased dramatically, while grievances and costs decreased.[5]

Confrontation Meeting   The confrontation meeting is particularly useful for organizations that do not have time to spend on a more in-depth OD program. A *confrontation meeting* is usually a one-day session conducted to resolve problems of organization performance by generating and analyzing data about group problems and then formulating action plans to respond to them. It can also be used to discuss problems that arise following the instituting of a change. The meeting generally follows this procedure:

1. A top manager introduces the issues and goals.
2. In small groups, participants gather information about organizational problems.
3. A representative from each group reports on its findings.
4. In natural work groups, participants set priorities for the problems and determine early action steps.
5. A top management team continues to meet to plan follow-up action.
6. The group reconvenes four to six weeks later to report on progress.

A key point to note is that although natural work groups are involved, top management plays a major role in initiating and continuing the process.

Quality of Work Life (QWL) Programs and Quality Circles (QCs)   In response to Japanese competition in the automobile industry, Ford Motor Company and General Motors Corporation have worked with the United Auto Workers union to implement **quality of work life (QWL) programs,**[6] which essentially systematically study factors that affect the work environment, such as working conditions, jobs performed, supervision, and company policy. Although commitment to a QWL program comes from top management, action plans are developed by employee and first-level supervisory groups. Under QWL programs at companies such as GM and Ford, teams of 3 to 12 workers from different departments focus on diagnosing and recommending solutions to various QWL problems.

In one reported study from two plants, the programs resulted in substantial dollar savings and greatly increased supervisor and employee participation in job-related problem solving.

quality of work life (QWL) programs
Efforts by employee and supervisory groups to study systematically factors that affect the work environment, such as working conditions, jobs performed, supervision, and company policy.

T*i*pS 13.1

How to Implement Effective Quality Circles (QCs)

1. Managers at all levels, especially at the top, should be committed to the concept and give it their unqualified support.

2. Only volunteers should be allowed to participate in the program.

3. Projects undertaken should relate directly—or at least indirectly—to participants' work.

4. Projects should be team efforts, not individual activities.

5. Participants should be trained in effective quality control and problem-solving techniques.

6. Circle leaders should also be trained in group dynamics and leadership of workers as a group.

7. QC groups should be given feedback regarding their recommendations and solutions.

Source: Reproduced from Donald C. Mosley, Leon C. Megginson, and Paul H. Pietri, Jr., *Supervisory Management,* 2nd ed. (Cincinnati: South-Western Publishing, 1989), Chapter 16, with the permission of South-Western Publishing Co. Copyright 1989 by South-Western Publishing Co. All rights reserved.

An integral part of most QWL programs is quality circles. **Quality circles (QCs)** are small groups of workers, along with a supervisor leader, who belong to the same division or unit of the plant. For best results, membership in a QC should be voluntary. The group meets regularly, say once a week or twice a month, to identify problem areas, investigate the causes of the problems, and recommend solutions to management. Tips 13.1 gives some suggestions for the most effective use of quality circles. Problems and opportunities can be brought up by QC members, operating managers, or staff personnel. QC sessions are neither gripe nor bull sessions, and the groups usually receive training in decision-making techniques.

quality circles (QCs)
Small groups of workers and a supervisory leader who belong to the same division or unit of the plant and meet regularly to identify problem areas, investigate the causes of problems, and recommend solutions to management.

Promise and Limitations of OD

OD is not a panacea for all organizational problems. It requires the support of top management and works much better in some environments than in others. For example, it lends itself to organizations that can benefit from a change to a culture that favors a participative problem-solving approach for achieving effective results.

Because participation is the key to effective organizational development, the messages found in Tips 13.2 are especially relevant and useful.

Conflict Management

One problem often encountered in OD programs is excessive conflict between either individuals or departments. Even more significant is the amount of time a manager spends in **conflict management,** dealing with opposition or antagonistic interaction.

conflict management
Dealing with opposition or antagonistic interaction.

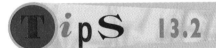

Tips 13.2

Messages Regarding Participation, Individual Development, and Organizational Change

▶ When participation is effective, it produces important beneficial outcomes for individuals and organizations.

▶ Participative competence is required if participative efforts are to result in beneficial outcomes for individuals and organizations.

▶ Many individuals are not prepared adequately to participate in organization development activities.

▶ Currently popular organization development interventions, such as total quality programs, self-directed work teams, and sociotechnical systems interventions, are predicated on effective participation.

▶ Many failures or disappointments in organization development may be traced to ineffective participation.

▶ Individual development and organization development should go hand in hand.

Source: William A. Pasmore and Mary R. Fagans, "Participation, Individual Development, and Organization Change: A Review and Synthesis," *Journal of Management,* vol. 18, no. 2 (June 1992), p. 377.

"Hang on, Griswold! Don't give up the turf!"

Causes of Conflict

Conflicts usually arise in an organization as a result of problems in communication, organizational structure, personal relationships, and change. Let us briefly examine each of these causes.

1. *Communication.* Misunderstandings due to semantics, unfamiliar language, or ambiguous or incomplete information.

2. *Structure.* Power struggles between departments with conflicting objectives or reward systems, competition for scarce resources, or interdependence of two or more groups to achieve their goals.

3. *Personal.* Incompatibility of personal goals or social values of employees with the role behavior required by their jobs. Certain personality characteristics, such as authoritarianism or dogmatism, may also lead to conflict.

4. *Change.* Fears associated with job security or the loss of personal power and prestige causing abnormal behavior. Change can be threatening.

A two-dimensional model that is useful in examining possible responses or approaches to dealing with conflict is found in Figure 13.5.

Although she is usually not given credit, Mary Parker Follet's ideas on how to deal with conflict (discussed in Chapter 2) were the forerunners of the above model. Her preferred style (integration) is comparable to the collaborating style.

The collaborating style is most useful in OD interventions; however, the other four styles are useful in certain situations. Tips 13.3 provides suggestions of when to use each style.

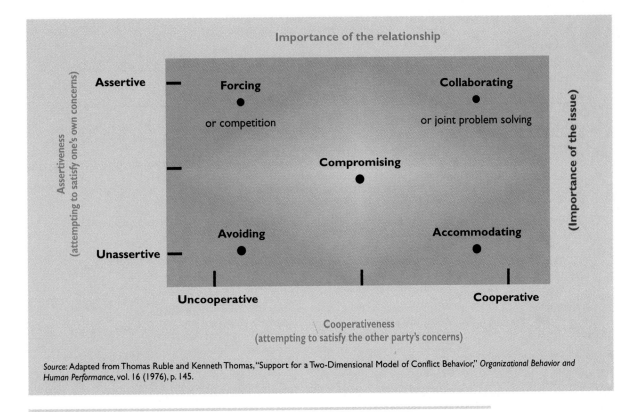

Source: Adapted from Thomas Ruble and Kenneth Thomas, "Support for a Two-Dimensional Model of Conflict Behavior," *Organizational Behavior and Human Performance*, vol. 16 (1976), p. 145.

FIGURE 13.5
Two-dimensional model of conflict behavior.

The names have been changed, but the following true situation that occurred in a bank reveals how conflict can cause major problems in an organization.

> Mark Johnson, president and chief executive of ABC National Bank, was worried about his two chief executive officers, Jim Smith and Jack Jones, who were barely speaking to each other. The two men's antagonistic behavior toward one another was beginning to affect morale and the bank's effectiveness. Personnel throughout the bank were choosing sides, and even some bank customers were aware of the conflict.
>
> Three months earlier, Mark had called Jim and Jack into his office and requested that they settle their differences and work more effectively together. Unfortunately, Mark's request had not been heeded, and more decisive action was called for.

The situation just presented was triggered by a combination of structural and personal factors. Before the conflict erupted, several changes had occurred. The bank had employed a management consulting firm that had recommended a reorganization of the bank that was implemented by the president and the board of directors. Jack Jones, under the old organization, had had 70 percent of the departments and employees reporting to him. Now, Jim Smith, under the new

When to Use the Five Conflict-Handling Orientations

Conflict-Handling Orientation	Appropriate Situations
Competition	1. When quick, decisive action is vital (in emergencies) 2. On important issues where unpopular actions need implementation (in cost cutting, enforcing unpopular rules, dscipline) 3. On issues vital to the organization's welfare when you know you're right 4. Against people who take advantage of noncompetitive behavior
Collaboration	1. To find an integrative solution when both sets of concerns are too important to be compromised 2. When your objective is to learn 3. To merge insights from people with different perspectives 4. To gain commitment by incorporating concerns into a consensus 5. To work through feelings that have interfered with a relationship
Avoidance	1. When an issue is trivial, or more important issues are pressing 2. When you perceive no chance of satisfying your concerns 3. When potential disruption outweighs the benefits of resolution 4. To let people cool down and regain perspective 5. When gathering information supersedes immediate decision 6. When others can resolve the conflict more effectively 7. When issues seem tangential or symptomatic of other issues
Accommodation	1. When you find you are wrong and to allow a better position to be heard, to learn, and to show your reasonableness 2. When issues are more important to others than yourself and to satisfy others and maintain cooperation 3. To build social credits for later issues 4. To minimize loss when you are outmatched and losing 5. When harmony and stability are especially important 6. To allow subordinates to develop by learning from mistakes
Compromise	1. When goals are important, but not worth the effort or potential disruption of more assertive modes 2. When opponents with equal power are committed to mutually exclusive goals 3. To achieve temporary settlements to complex issues 4. To arrive at expedient solutions under time pressure 5. As a backup when collaboration or competition is unsuccessful

Source: K. W. Thomas, "Toward Multidimensional Values in Teaching: The Example of Conflict Behaviors," *Academy of Management Review*, vol. 2, no. 3 (July 1977), p. 487. With permission.

organization, wound up with 70 percent under his jurisdiction, including some key departments that had previously reported to Jack Jones. The personalities of the two men were entirely different in that Jack was much more autocratic and authoritarian in his relationships with others. This fact was a primary reason for the consulting firm's recommendation to shift key departments in the reorganization.

The conflict was aggravated because Mark Johnson was retiring as president in two years, and both executive vice-presidents wanted to succeed him. Under these conditions, both men were competing intensely for the top job, and the resulting power struggle caused dysfunctional consequences in the bank.

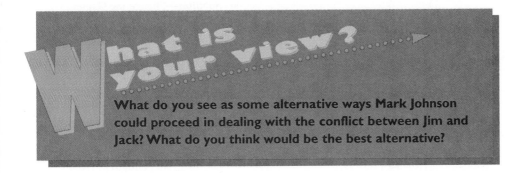

What is your view?

What do you see as some alternative ways Mark Johnson could proceed in dealing with the conflict between Jim and Jack? What do you think would be the best alternative?

Using Principled Negotiation to Resolve Conflict

A real breakthrough in conflict management and resolution is found in the concepts proposed by Roger Fisher and William Ury of the Harvard negotiation project. They emphasize that, whether negotiation involves a peace settlement among nations or a business contract, people often engage in *positional bargaining*. This common form of negotiation involves proposing and then giving up a sequence of positions. The idea is to give up things that are not very important. Hence, proposals are "padded" initially. For this form of negotiation to succeed, it must meet three criteria of fair negotiation: "It should produce a wise agreement if agreement is possible; it should be efficient; and it should improve or at least not damage the relationship between the parties."[7]

When people bargain over positions, they tend to back themselves into corners defending their positions, which results in a number of either *win-lose* or *lose-lose* outcomes. Moreover, arguing over positions often endangers an ongoing relationship by straining and sometimes shattering it. In a marriage, this results in divorce, and in business, the result can be the breakup of an otherwise successful operation. Many negotiations involve more than two parties, and in these cases, positional bargaining compounds the problem of negotiating an agreement.

In their work with the Harvard negotiation project, Fisher and Ury developed an alternative to positional bargaining that they call *principled negotiation,* or negotiation on the merits. The four basic components of principled negotiation are

1. Separating the people from the problem
2. Focusing on interests, not positions
3. Generating a variety of possibilities before deciding what to do
4. Insisting that the result be based on some objective standard

Consultant facilitators for a number of join ventures and partnerships involving multiple parties have noted that educating the joint venture parties in the concepts of principled negotiation has resulted in a high percentage of win-win resolutions in dispute settlements. Table 13.1 illustrates the difference between positional bargaining and principled negotiation. Notice that in positional bargaining, one can play either "hardball" or "softball."

TABLE 13.1   CONTRAST OF POSITIONAL BARGAINING AND PRINCIPLED NEGOTIATIONS

Problem—Positional Bargaining: Which Game Should You Play?		Solution—Change the Game: Negotiate on the Merits
Soft	**Hard**	**Principled**
Participants are friends	Participants are adversaries	Participants are problem solvers
The goal is agreement	The goal is victory	The goal is a wise outcome reached efficiently and amicably
Make concessions to cultivate the relationship	Demand concessions as a condition of the relationship	Separate the people from the problem
Be soft on the people and the problem	Be hard on the problem and the people	Be soft on the people, hard on the problem
Trust others	Distrust others	Proceed independent of trust
Change your position easily	Dig in to your position	Focus on interests, not positions
Make offers	Make threats	Explore interests
Disclose your bottom line	Mislead as to your bottom line	Avoid having a bottom line
Accept one-sided losses to reach agreement	Demand oe-sided gains as the price of agreement	Invent options for mutual gain
Search for the single answer: the one *they* will accept	Search for the single answer: the one *you* will accept	Develop multiple options to choose from; decide later
Insist on agreement	Insist on your position	Insist on using objective criteria
Try to avoid a contest of will	Try to win a contest of will	Try to reach a result based on standards independent of will
Yield to pressure	Apply pressure	Reason and be open; yield to principle, not pressure

Source: From *Getting to Yes*, by Roger Fisher and William Ury. Copyright © 1981 by Roger Fisher and William Ury. Reprinted by permission of Houghton Mifflin Company.

Stress

Writer-consultant Peter Vail has used the metaphor "permanent white water" to describe the roles of managers operating in today's world of rapid and chaotic change. He goes on to state that "perhaps even the metaphor of permanent white water is not adequate. We are not talking about a wild river; we are talking about an unpredictable wild river."[8] In this world of rapid, chaotic, and unpredictable change, there is more stress than managers have ever before had to face.

stress Any external stimulus that causes wear and tear on one's psychological or physical well-being.

    Stress may be defined as any external stimulus that causes wear and tear on one's psychological or physical well-being. Just as our primitive ancestors in times of danger geared themselves for either fight or flight, many of us, in a world of permanent white water, maintain a constant fight-or-flight readiness. Unless we learn to manage stress in both organizations and individuals, it can have a drastic impact both physically and mentally.

    The costs of stress to organizations are enormous. Without question, a person under severe and/or prolonged stress cannot function as effectively as a person leading a more balanced life. However, we do not want to imply that all stress is negative, since a certain amount of it can have a quite positive effect.

Positive Aspects of Stress

Stress is inescapable. Holidays can be stressful; exercise can be stressful; attending a Broadway play or an athletic event can be stressful. Our point is that life is full of stressors that can stimulate, energize, and add zest. We call the constructive dimensions of stress *enstress*, which can enhance, enrich, and be a powerful motivator.

Some readers may remember their high school days as student leaders or athletes. For a student leader, it was both stressful and a powerful motivator to preside over the first student council meeting. There was also a great deal of tension before a football, basketball, or baseball game, but the experience was also a powerful "upper." In the business world, setting difficult goals rather than easy ones is a stressor, but it is also a powerful incentive. Working with an important problem-solving task force causes stress but also motivates. Moreover, people differ in the amounts of stress they can handle. Test pilots and astronauts thrive in careers that other people would find too stressful. Figure 13.6 provides insight into both positive and negative outcomes of stress.

Job Burnout

Although there are some positive aspect of stress, organizations are primarily concerned with preventing the negative outcomes, such as job burnout. **Burnout** is a stress-related malady with primary roots in the setting where people invest most of their time and energy.[9]

burnout A stress-related malady with primary roots in the setting where people invest most of their time and energy.

FIGURE 13.6
Positive and negative outcomes of stress.

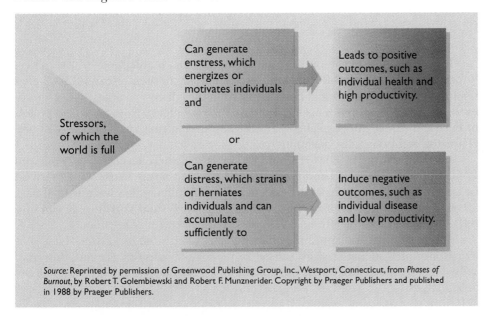

Source: Reprinted by permission of Greenwood Publishing Group, Inc., Westport, Connecticut, from *Phases of Burnout*, by Robert T. Golembiewski and Robert F. Munznerider. Copyright by Praeger Publishers and published in 1988 by Praeger Publishers.

TABLE 13.2   MBI SUBSCALES AND PHASES OF BURNOUT

The adapted Maslach Burnout Inventory, or MBI, consists of 25 items, rated on a scale of 1 (very much *unlike* me) to 7 (very much *like* me). Three subscales are involved:

Depersonalization, high scores on which distinguish individuals who tend to view people as things or objects, and who tend to distance themselves from others; Example: "I worry that this job is hardening me emotionally."

Personal Accomplishment, high scores on which indicate respondents who see themselves as not performing well on a task that they perceive as not being particularly worthwhile; Example: "I have accomplished few worthwhile things on this job."

Emotional Exhaustion, high scores on which come from individuals who see themselves as operating beyond comfortable coping limits, and as approaching "the end of the rope" in psychological and emotional senses. Example: "I feel fatigued when I get up in the morning and have to face another day on the job."

Assignments of Individuals to Burnout Phases

A simple decision rule generates an eight-phase model of burnout. That is, emotional exhaustion is considered most characteristic of advanced phases of burnout, and depersonalization is considered least virulent. Three subscales, each presented in terms of high and low, generate the progressive phases of burnout:

	Progressive Phases of Burnout							
	I	**II**	**III**	**IV**	**V**	**VI**	**VII**	**VIII**
Depersonalization	Low	High	Low	High	Low	High	Low	High
Personal accomplishment	Low	Low	High	High	Low	Low	High	High
Emotional exhaustion	Low	Low	Low	Low	High	High	High	High

Source: Reprinted by permission of Greenwood Publishing Group, Inc., Westport, Connecticut, from *Phases of Burnout*, by Robert T. Golembiewski and Robert F. Munznerider. Copyright by Praeger Publishers and published in 1988 by Praeger Publishers.

The seriousness of the burnout problem has been highlighted by researchers Robert Golembiewski and Robert Munzenrider. Using in their research an adapted version of the *Maslach Burnout Inventory* or *MBI*, they discovered that 40 percent of more than 12,000 respondents in 33 organizations suffered from advanced phases of burnout.[10] Table 13.2 explains the subscales used in research with the MBI and charts the eight phases of burnout.

A person scoring in Phase I would be operating where enstress is at work and would be highly energized and motivated. In Maslow's terms, such a person would be operating or functioning at the esteem and self-fulfillment level of the need hierarchy. To a lesser extent, this applies to Phases II, III, IV, and V. Where we run into difficulty is in Phases VI, VII, and VIII, the advanced stages of burnout.

There are three distinguishing characteristics of burnout candidates. First, they experience predominately stress caused by job-related stressors. Second, they tend to be idealistic and/or self-motivated achievers. Third, they tend to seek unattainable goals.[11]

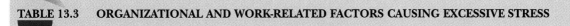

TABLE 13.3 ORGANIZATIONAL AND WORK-RELATED FACTORS CAUSING EXCESSIVE STRESS

A highly centralized organization with decision making concentrated at the top

Many levels and narrow spans of control

Excessive and continuous pressure from higher levels

Conflicting demands on lower levels

Lack of clarity with respect to organizational and work objectives

Widespread autocratic leadership and close supervision

Little or no participation in decision making by supervisors and workers

Inconsistent application of company policies

Favoritism in decisions regarding layoffs, salary increases, promotions, and the like

Poor working conditions

Poor communication

Lack of structure and job descriptions

Widespread permissive leadership

Source: Reproduced from Donald C. Mosley, Leon C. Megginson, and Paul H. Pietri, *Supervisory Management*, 2nd ed. (Cincinnati: South-Western Publishing, 1989), p. 493, with the permission of South-Western Publishing Co. Copyright 1989 by South-Western Publishing Co. All Rights reserved.

Managing Stress and Job Burnout

Table 13.3 lists organizational and work-related factors that can cause excessive stress and burnout. All of these factors are under the influence and control of higher management. Organizational development interventions are particularly well suited for these types of stressors.

OD Interventions Golembiewski and Munzenrider are strong advocates of using OD interventions to cope with stress and job burnout, because interventions can create a balance of enstress and distress for individuals and their employers.[12] The researchers suggest three types of high-stimulus interventions, namely, interpersonally oriented team building, confrontative "stress management workshops," and basic policy or structural change. There are also three types of low-stimulus interventions, including flexible work hours, some kind of job rotation, and mild role negotiation.

Before any intervention is used, however, the starting point is the action-research process, presented earlier in this chapter, to select the appropriate intervention. We have found that using the action-research process and tailored organization development programs, including a segment on stress management, is very effective. An example is given in Case 13.1, "Organizational Development in Action," at the end of this chapter.

Other Strategies to Cope with Stress and Job Burnout There are many strategies to cope with stress and job burnout. Table 13.4 lists over 30 strategies, running the gamut from physical to spiritual. Our stress level is affected to a large extent by how we feel, how we think, and how we act. To illustrate this connection, try the experiment in Learning Exercise 13.1.

TABLE 13.4   WHOLE-PERSON STRESS MANAGEMENT

Physical Strategies	Intellectual/Mental Strategies
Progressive relaxation	Cognitive restructuring
Biofeedback	Systematic desensitization
Autogenic training	Stress inoculation
Visualization	Covert sensitization
Sensory awareness	Thought-stopping
Deep breathing	Reframing
Hot tubs, jacuzzi, sauna	Values clarification
Massage	Paradoxical intention
Yoga	
Exercise	
Diet	

Social Strategies	Emotional Strategies
Interpersonal skills training	Catharsis/emotional discharge
Assertiveness	Covert assertion
Support groups	Self-awareness
Networking	Withdrawal

Spiritual Strategies	Environmental Strategies
Meditation	Time management
Prayer	Problem-solving
Faith/hope	Goal-setting
	Lifestyle assessment
	Decision making
	Conflict resolution

Source: Nancy Loving Tubesing and Donald A. Tubesing, "The Treatment of Choice: Selecting Stress Skills to Suit the Individual and the Situation," in *Job Stress and Burnout*, Ed. Whiton Stewart Paine, p. 161, copyright © 1981 by Sage Publications, Inc. Reprinted by permission by Sage Publications, Inc.

In developing strategies to cope with burnout, the causal variables are how we act and think, the intervening variable is how we feel, and the end result variable is enstress. By taking positive action or developing action plans, we influence not only how we feel but also the resulting outcomes.

Physical exercise is a powerful strategy in dealing with excessive stress. In addition, changing how we think is a powerful way to change how we feel and behave. A good way to start this process is to talk to a trusted friend or counselor. If this person is a skilled listener, just talking can dramatically change the way one is thinking about a particular concern or problem.

An excellent special report of stress reduction strategies is found in an article on how to feel great; synthesis of these strategies appears in MAP 13.2.

MANAGEMENT APPLICATION AND PRACTICE 13.2

Strategies That Make You Feel Great

▶ **Savor the moment.** Happiness, said Benjamin Franklin, "is produced not so much by great pieces of good fortune that seldom happen as by the little advantages that occur each day."

▶ **Take control of your time.** There is nevertheless a place for setting goals and managing time. Compared to those who've learned a sense of helplessness, those with an "internal locus of control" do better in school, cope better with stress, and live with greater well-being.

▶ **Act happy.** Study after study reveals three traits that mark happy people's lives: (1) They like themselves, (2), they are positive thinkers, and (3) they are outgoing. In experiments, people who feign high self-esteem begin feeling better about themselves.

▶ **Seek work and leisure that engage your skills.** Even if we make a lower but livable wage, it pays to seek work that we find interesting and challenging.

▶ **Join the movement movement.** A slew of recent studies reveal that aerobic exercise is an antidote for mild depression.

▶ **Get rest.** Happy people live active, vigorous lives, yet they reserve time for renewing sleep and solitude.

▶ **Give priority to close relationships.** People who can name several close, supportive friends—friends with whom they freely share their ups and downs—live with greater health and happiness.

▶ **Take care of your soul.** Actively religious people are much less likely than others to become delinquent, to abuse drugs and alcohol, to divorce, or to commit suicide. They're even physically healthier.

Source: Adapted from David G. Meyers, "Pursuing Happiness," *Psychology Today*, July–August 1993, vol. 26, pp. 32–35 and 66–67.

In addition to the strategies that make you feel great, Figure 13.7 identifies 101 ways to cope with stress.

SUMMARY

Organizational change is now occurring at an explosive rate. It has accelerated into the business revolution of the 1990s. There are internal and external forces causing change, and they must be considered in any change program. There are two ways of dealing with change—reacting to it or being proactive and planning for it.

The process of managing organizational change includes six phases: (1) pressure and arousal, (2) intervention and reorientation, (3) diagnosis and recognition of problem(s), (4) intervention of and commitment to solutions, (5) experimentation and search for results, and 6) reinforcement and acceptance of new practices.

Organizational development (OD) is an organizationwide effort to increase organizational effectiveness through planned intervention in the organization's processes, using behavioral science knowledge. The action-research model of OD was explained (Figure 13.5) and three popular intervention strategies discussed. In many change programs, there is a need to shift an organization to a more participative, problem-solving orientation. Likert's System 4, confrontation meetings,

Get up 15 minutes earlier • Prepare for the morning the night before • Avoid tight-fitting clothes • Avoid relying on chemical aids • Set appointments ahead • Don't rely on your memory ... write it down • Practice preventative maintenance • Make duplicate keys • Say "no" more often • Set priorities in your life • Avoid negative people • Use time wisely • Simplify mealtimes • Always make copies of important papers • Anticipate your needs • Repair anything that doesn't work properly • Ask for help with the jobs you dislike • Break large tasks into bite-sized portions • Look at problems as challenges • Look at challenges differently • Unclutter your life • Smile • Be prepared for rain • Tickle a baby • Pet a friendly dog/cat • Don't know all the answers • Look for the silver lining • Say something nice to someone • Teach a kid to fly a kite • Walk in the rain • Schedule play time into every day • Take a bubble bath • Be aware of the decisions you make • Believe in you • Stop saying negative things to yourself • Visualize yourself winning • Develop your sense of humor • Stop thinking tomorrow will be a better today • Have goals for yourself • Dance a jig • Say hello to a stranger • Ask a friend for a hug • Look up at the stars • Practice breathing slowly • Learn to whistle a tune • Read a poem • Listen to a symphony • Watch a ballet • Read a story curled up in bed • Do a brand-new thing • Stop a bad habit • Buy yourself a flower • Take stock of your achievements • Find support from others • Ask someone to be your "vent-partner" • Do it today • Work at being cheerful and optimistic • Put safety first • Do everything in moderation • Pay attention to your appearance • Strive for excellence, NOT perfection • Stretch your limits a little each day • Look at a work of art • Hum a jingle • Maintain your weight • Plant a tree • Feed the birds • Practice grace under pressure • Stand up and stretch • Always have a "plan B" • Learn a new doodle • Memorize a joke • Be responsible for your feelings • Learn to meet your own needs • Become a better listener • Know your limitations and let others know them too • Tell someone to have a good day in pig latin • Throw a paper airplane • Exercise every day • Learn the words to a new song • Get to work early • Clean out one closet • Play pat-a-cake with a toddler • Go on a picnic • Take a different route to work • Leave work early (with permission) • Put air freshener in your car • Watch a movie and eat popcorn • Write a note to a faraway friend • Go to a ball game and scream • Cook a meal and eat it by candlelight • Recognize the importance of unconditional love • Remember that stress is an attitude • Keep a journal • Practice a monster smile • Remember you always have options • Have a support network of people, places, and things • Quit trying to "fix" other people • Get enough sleep • Talk less and listen more • Freely praise other people • P.S. Relax, take each day at a time ... you have the rest of your life to live.

Source: Charter Hospital of Mobile.

FIGURE 13.7
101 ways to cope with stress.

and quality of work life (QWL) programs and quality circles (QCs) can be used to achieve that objective.

Managers spend a vast amount of their time dealing with conflict. The four primary sources of conflict are problems in communication, personal relationships, organization structure, and organizational change. There are several conflict management methods: competition, collaboration, avoidance, accommodation, and compromise. Each is listed in Tips 13.3. Principled negotiation has been a real breakthrough in conflict management. The concepts proposed by Fisher and Ury emphasize that in the negotiation process, people often engage in positional bargaining—proposing and then giving up a sequence of positions. The four basic components of principled negotiation are (1) separating the people from the problem; (2) focusing on interests, not positions; (3) generating a variety of possibilities before deciding which to do; and (4) insisting that the result be based on some objective standard.

In today's work environment, stress is inescapable. There are both positive and negative aspects of stress. While managing all kinds of stress is important, organizations are primarily concerned with preventing the negative outcomes, such as job burnout. Several ways of managing stress from both organizational and individual standpoints were discussed.

KEY TERMS

reactive process of change, 427
proactive (planned) process of
 change, 427
organizational effectiveness, 428
change agent, 429
organizational development (OD), 431

quality of work life (QWL)
 programs, 434
quality circles (QCs), 435
conflict management, 435
stress, 440
burnout, 441

DISCUSSION QUESTIONS

1. How could an OD approach be used to convert a highly structured system with an autocratic style of management to a more open system with a participative style of management? Assume that the change is necessary because of low morale and declining profits.

2. Discuss why participative management seems to be effective in an increasing number of situations. Does this trend negate the contingency theory of management?

3. Is change really as pervasive as the authors claim? Explain.

4. (a) What are some of the primary reasons people resist change? (b) What are some of the ways a manager can ensure that change is accepted or at least not resisted?

5. Discuss the limitations and promise of OD as a change strategy to move an organization from one state of development to an improved state.

6. Is all conflict undesirable? Explain.

7. Do you think principled negotiation holds as much promise as the authors suggest? Why or why not?

8. Discuss the positive and negative aspects of stress.

9. (a) Have you experienced burnout (either as a student or as an employee)? (b) How did you cope?

PRACTICING MANAGEMENT

13.1

case

Organizational Development in Action

Several years ago, a consultant was contracted by the vice-president and division manager of a chemical division of a large corporation to help with an unprofitable plant in his division. The problem was due in part to marketplace conditions and in part to the autocratic leadership style of the plant manager.

Morale was so bad at this nonunion plant that employees bypassed the plant's management and contracted the division manager to complain about their treatment at the plant. After an investigation, the division manager concluded that the autocratic leadership style of the plant was a major factor in poor results.

The vice-president had been a follower of Rensis Likert for 20 years, and he appreciated the potential benefits of participative management. He concluded that the solution would be to shift the plant from an autocratic management system in the direction of a consultative (System 3) or participative (System 4) system. Toward achieving this objective, he (1) removed the plan manager and placed him in a staff role elsewhere in the corporation, (2) replaced him with a new plant manager he believed shared his philosophy about participative management, and (3) asked the consultant to meet with him and the new manager to explore how to shift to a participative management system and culture.

Entry and Approach

In the meeting, the decision was made to use an OD action-research approach that would serve as the basis for a tailored management development program. In the action research, a strength/problem profile was developed; several questionnaires were used to develop "before" measurements that could be compared with "after" measurements a year later. The research was carried out through interviews with all managers, supervisors, and engineers. Group meetings with operative personnel were also held to gather data. Management also decided that after training had been given in group dynamics and team building to all managers, task forces would be established to develop action-planning recommendations regarding key problems.

The Outcome

In June 1986, a year after the program was initiated, the plant was producing at its top performance level and making a profit for the first time in its history. Although improved market conditions were a factor, it was concluded that the style of the new plant manager and his effective use of the OD program had played a key role in the turnaround.

At the start of the OD program in May 1985, the Profile of Organizational Characteristics questionnaire revealed that the plant was being operated essentially as a benevolent autocracy (System 2 in Figure 13.8). At the end of the first cycle of the OD program, completed in June 1986, the questionnaire revealed that the management system had shifted from a benevolent autocracy to a consultative management system (System 3). A new cycle of the OD program was initiated to focus on shifting the plant even further, to a participative-group management system (System 4). Figure 13.9 shows the "before" and "after" measurements using the Profile of Organizational Characteristics questionnaire.

In addition, two tailored instruments were used in the May 1986 evaluation phase of the OD program. The instruments and results are shown in Figure 13.9 and 13.10. Again, there was significant improvement in one year's time. It is worth noting that the top two ratings in June 1986 were in processes involving downward communication and the confrontation of problems and opportunities.

Source: This case was first reported in Donald C. Mosley, "System Four Revisited: Some New Insights," *Organizational Development Journal*, vol. 5 (Spring 1987), pp. 19–24.

May 1985		June 1986		
System 1	**System 2**	**System 3**	**System 4**	
Virtually none	Some	Substantial amount	A great deal	1. How much confidence and trust is shown in subordinates?
Not very free	Somewhat free	Quite free	Very free	2. How free do they feel to talk to superiors about job?
Seldom	Sometimes	Often	Very frequently	3. How often are subordinates' ideas sought and used constructively?
1, 2, 3 Occasionally 4	4, Some 3	4, Some 3 and 5	5, 4 based on group-set goals	4. Is predominant use made of (1) fear, (2) threats, (3) punishment, (4) rewards, and (5) involvement?
Mostly at top	Top and middle	Fairly general	At all levels	5. Where is responsibility felt for achieving organization's goals?
Very little	Relatively little	Moderate amount	Great deal	6. How much cooperative teamwork is there?
Downward	Mostly downward	Down & up	Down, up & sideways	7. What is the usual direction of information flow?
With suspicion	Possibly with suspicion	With caution	With a receptive mind	8. How is downward communication accepted?
Usually accurate	Often inaccurate	Often accurate	Almost always accurate	9. How accurate is upward communication?
Not very well	Rather well	Quite well	Very well	10. How well do superiors know problems faced by subordinates?
Mostly at top	Policy at top; some delegate	Broad policy at top; more delegation	Throughout but well integrated	11. At what level are decisions made?
Almost never	Occasionally consulted	Generally consulted	Fully involved	12. Are subordinates involved in decisions related to their work?
Not very much	Relatively little	Some contribution	Substantial contribution	13. What does decision-making process contribute to motivation?
Orders issued	Orders, some comment invited	After discussion, by orders	By group action, except in crisis	14. How are organizational goals established?
Strong resistance	Moderate resistance	Some resistance at times	Little or none	15. How much covert resistance to goals is present?
Very high at top	Quite high at top	Moderate delegation to lower levels	Widely shared	16. How concentrated are review and control functions?
Yes	Usually	Sometimes	No—same goals as formal	17. Is there an informal organization resisting the formal one?
Policing, punishment	Reward punishment	Reward some self-guidance	Self-guidance problem solving	18. What are cost, productivity, and other control data used for?

Source: *Organization Development Journal*, vol. 5 (Spring 1987), p. 23.

FIGURE 13.8
Profiles of organizational characteristics.

FIGURE 13.9
"Before" and "after" scores on communication flow.

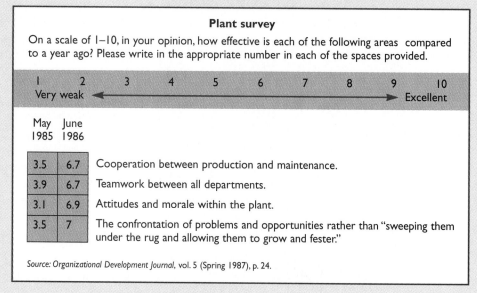

Communication

On a scale of 1–10, in your opinion, how effective is each of the three basic communication flows in your organization compared to a year ago? Please write in the appropriate number in each of the three spaces provided.

1	2	3	4	5	6	7	8	9	10
Very weak									Excellent

May 1985	June 1986	
3.9	7.1	Downward communication—the effective transfer of information, including goals, objectives, policies, changes, performance feedback, and so on, from top management to lower levels of organization.
4.8	6.9	Upward communication—the effective transfer of information such as performance reports, problems, suggestions, feelings, attitudes, gripes, and so on, from lower levels to top management of the organization.
3.7	6.5	Lateral or diagonal communication—the effective transfer of ideas and information between and among departments, including interdepartmental cooperation, indepartmental service relationships, committees, task forces, and so on, comprising members of different departments.

Source: Organizational Development Journal, vol. 5 (Spring 1987), p. 24.

FIGURE 13.10
"Before" and "after" scores in cooperation, teamwork, morale, and confrontation of problems and opportunities.

Plant survey

On a scale of 1–10, in your opinion, how effective is each of the following areas compared to a year ago? Please write in the appropriate number in each of the spaces provided.

1	2	3	4	5	6	7	8	9	10
Very weak									Excellent

May 1985	June 1986	
3.5	6.7	Cooperation between production and maintenance.
3.9	6.7	Teamwork between all departments.
3.1	6.9	Attitudes and morale within the plant.
3.5	7	The confrontation of problems and opportunities rather than "sweeping them under the rug and allowing them to grow and fester."

Source: Organizational Development Journal, vol. 5 (Spring 1987), p. 24.

Questions

1. What is your evaluation of the OD approach used in this situation?

2. Would you have handled the assignment differently? Explain.

3. What does this case illustrate about the potential for the effective use of OD?

Creating an Organizational Culture

Assume you start your own business sometime after graduation. It can be any business of your choice that has a good opportunity for growth. After ten years, the business has become quite successful and now employs 102 people.

1. Identify the business you have chosen.

2. Assume that initially you believed there is a positive correlation between having a strong culture and business success. Identify the specific actions you have consequently taken over a ten-year period to develop a strong organizational culture.

Up in Smoke: Are You Burned-Out?

Directions

Rate each question on a scale of 1 to 5 (1 = never; 2 = rarely; 3 = sometimes; 4 = often; 5 = always).

Do You:	Never	Rarely	Sometimes	Often	Always
Feel less competent or effective than you used to feel in your work?	1	2	3	4	5
Consider yourself unappreciated or "used"?	1	2	3	4	5
Dread going to work?	1	2	3	4	5
Feel overwhelmed in your work?	1	2	3	4	5
Feel your work is pointless or unimportant?	1	2	3	4	5
Watch the clock?	1	2	3	4	5
Avoid conversations with others (co-workers, customers, and supervisors in the work setting; family members in the home)?	1	2	3	4	5
Rigidly apply rules without considering creative solutions?	1	2	3	4	5
Get frustrated by your work?	1	2	3	4	5
Miss work often?	1	2	3	4	5
Feel unchallenged by your work?	1	2	3	4	5
Does York Work:					
Overload you?	1	2	3	4	5
Deny you rest periods—breaks, lunch time, sick leave, or vacation?	1	2	3	4	5
Pay too little?	1	2	3	4	5
Depend on uncertain funding sources?	1	2	3	4	5
Provide inadequate support to accomplish the job (budget, equipment, tools, people, etc.)?	1	2	3	4	5
Lack clear guidelines?	1	2	3	4	5
Entail so many different tasks that you feel fragmented?	1	2	3	4	5
Require you to deal with major or rapid changes?	1	2	3	4	5
Lack access to a social or professional support group?	1	2	3	4	5
Demand coping with a negative job image or angry people?	1	2	3	4	5
Depress you?	1	2	3	4	5

Scoring and Interpretation

Add up your scores for the Up in Smoke test and insert your total:

_____

Scores	Category
94–110	Burnout
76–93	Flame
58–75	Smoke
40–57	Sparks
22–39	No fire

Burnout. If your score is between 94 and 110, you are experiencing a very high level of stress in your work. Without some changes in yourself or your situation, your potential for stress-related illness is high. Consider seeking professional help for stress reduction and burnout prevention. Coping with stress at this level may also require help from others—supervisors, co-workers, and other associates at work, and spouse and other family members at home.

Flame. If you have a score between 76 and 93, you have a high amount of work-related stress and may have begun to burn out. Mark each question that you scored 4 or above, and rank them in order of their effect on you, beginning with the ones that bother you the most. For at least your top three, evaluate what you can do to reduce the stresses involved, and act to improve your attitude or situation. If your body is reflecting the stress, get a medical checkup.

Smoke. Scores between 58 and 75 represent a certain amount of stress in your work and are a sign that you have a fair chance of burning out unless you take corrective measures. For each question that you scored 5 or above, consider ways you can reduce the stresses involved. As soon as possible, take action to improve your attitude or the situation surrounding those things that trouble you most.

Sparks. If your score is between 40 and 57, you have a low amount of work-related stress and are unlikely to burn out. Look over those questions that you scored 3 or above, and think about what you can do to reduce the stresses involved.

No fire. People with scores of 22 through 39 are mellow in their work, with almost no job-related stress. As long as they continue at this level, they are practically burnout-proof.

For many people, both the job and the home represent potential for high stress and burnout. For this reason, having at least one "port in the storm" is important. Ideally, if things are going badly on the job, rest and comfort can be found in the home. Similarly, if home conditions involve pressure, conflict, and frustration, having a satisfying work life helps. The person who faces problems on the job and problems in the home at the same time is fighting a war on two fronts and is a prime candidate for stress overload and burnout.

chapter

14

Team Development and Empowerment Strategies

The effort of two or more individuals working as a unit toward a common goal is greater than the sum of the effort of the individuals working as individuals.

—WILLIAM B. CORNELL

LEARNING OBJECTIVES

After studying the material in this chapter, you should be able to:

▶ **Define** a group and identify the types of groups.

▶ **Identify** the stages of group development.

▶ **Compare** the advantages and limitations of groups.

▶ **Describe** the variables that determine a group's effectiveness.

▶ **Explain** what is involved in implementing successful total quality management and partnering programs.

▶ **Describe** the role of self-managing work teams.

▶ **Explain** how to manage work groups.

Cianbro

Like many other management teachers, the authors have had experience in consulting or conducting research with hundreds of organizations. Cianbro stands out as one of the peak performers from the standpoint of "walking their talk."

Cianbro is a construction company that has been in business 40 years. The corporation is headquartered in Pittsfield, Maine, and has fully operational regional offices in Portland, Maine; Enfield, Connecticut; and Landover, Maryland. Its mission statement, as follows, is succinct, visionary, idealistic, and powerful:

CIANBRO

The Constructors—Building a Better Future

A Team dedicated to safety, dignity, and respect for all; the betterment of its environment and communities —serving clients with quality, innovation, and efficiency.

Cianbro successfully practices the empowerment strategies discussed in this chapter. More so than most organizations, Cianbro has an unusual ability to learn, grow, and develop from experience. By realizing that we live in a changing world, and through problem solving and innovation, Cianbro employees have continually added to their strengths and overcome difficulties.

This point is illustrated by the following story, related to one of the authors by the company's visionary president, Peter Vigue:

Ten years ago, a fatality occurred on a construction project where Cianbro was the prime contractor. For moral reasons, management decided to make safety the number one priority goal for the company. This safety goal was communicated to all employees, and, with the involvement of employees, methods were designed to achieve a "safety first" environment. For example, physicians were hired to design and tailor an exercise program for employees. Every morning, all supervisors now meet with their employees and lead them through a ten-minute exercise routine. A short meeting follows, during which safety issues or any other issues are discussed and dealt with by the work team. As a by-product, the bottom line has improved, and insurance and workers' compensation costs are much lower.

Similarly, action plans, strategies, and policies have been developed for achieving quality, inno-

---

CIANBRO

TO OUR CUSTOMERS:

When the Cianchette brothers combined efforts to form this company, it represented more than just the establishment of a heavy construction enterprise. It marked the birth of an extended family: "the Cianbro Family." Our family today is comprised of enthusiastic people with the drive, determination and pride that we established as the foundation 40 years ago. Our employees have exercised foresight by realizing that the world is constantly changing. Through innovation and progressive problem solving, they've kept Cianbro one step ahead.

A company must be flexible to meet an ever changing business environment and yet maintain its integrity. We are entering our fifth decade in the construction business, and the experience and pride that have resulted have been instrumental in Cianbro's success. We will continue our progress. And we will remain one step ahead, because our experience has provided insight to the future. At Cianbro, we've combined state-of-the-art techniques with our belief that a successful company of the future is one that maintains the quality and integrity of the past.

Peter G. Vigue
Peter G. Vigue
President

The Opening Case represents leadership in action at its finest. Cianbro's founder and its current president have created a climate of ethics and teamwork in conducting their business. The vision and managerial behavior of top management has been the causal variable in the company's emphasis on the customer, quality, and the achievement of outstanding end results. This chapter

vation, and efficiency goals. The customer/client is involved from the beginning in developing with Cianbro a project management plan oriented to providing the best-planned and executed construction operation possible.

VISION STATEMENT

Cianbro Corporation is a full-service *construction company* that will achieve *excellence* in *serving* our *clients* while continuously improving the quality of our *resources*.

CONSTRUCTION **_COMPANY:_** The focus of our efforts will be to provide safe and efficient construction services in the Northeast and Mid-Atlantic regions of the United States. We will pursue construction related activities for growth that will fully utilize our resources and expertise.

EXCELLENCE: Our Company and the activities in which we are involved must be measured by a standard of excellence. The Cianbro team will be recognized for excellence in the safe environment in which we perform our work, the quality of our services, the management of our resources and our community involvement.

CLIENT SERVICE: The needs of our clients are the targets on which we focus our business activities. We will meet these needs with a variety of construction related services in a safe, quality, innovative and efficient manner.

RESOURCES: Our resources will be managed in an environment of continuous improvement that will add value to our Company. Our responsibility to our employees is to create an environment of trust, sharing and caring while providing opportunities that will challenge their talents and energies in a safe and rewarding work place.

The company is a strong supporter of both total quality management and partnering. In fact, it was at a partnering workshop where one of the authors first worked with Cianbro. Many of Cianbro's projects are similar to the L. L. Bean Returns Center, where a total quality management approach in both design and construction is used.

Cianbro has also developed an employee stock ownership trust in which the employees own a large percentage of the corporation, thus sharing the risks and profits of each project. As owners, the employees are highly motivated and the spirit of cooperation and concern for the client/customer is permanent.

A booklet elaborating on the company's background, experience, services, safety record, and philosophy is sent to each customer prior to the start of a project. Two key ingredients are the company's philosophy and way of operating as expressed by its president and vision statement.

Cianbro emphasizes safety first.

---

discusses the importance of empowerment strategies such as total quality management, partnering, and self-managing work teams. Many things are involved in creating a climate for effective teamwork and achieving successful empowerment strategies. The most important ingredient, however, is the support and philosophy of top management. Also, since empowerment strategies rely not only on individual

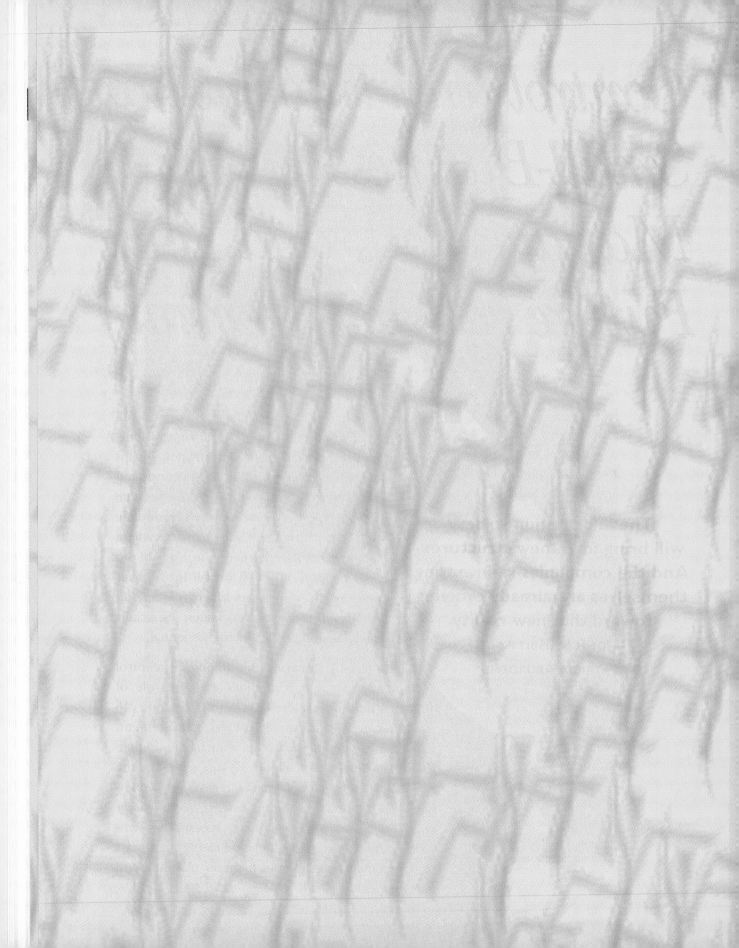

Understanding the Control Function and Managing Information

The right information, at the right time, is nine-tenths of any battle.

—NAPOLÉON

LEARNING OBJECTIVES

After studying the material in this chapter, you should be able to:

- **Explain** what management control is.

- **Identify** and describe the steps in the control process.

- **Explain** the relationship between controlling and the other management functions.

- **Describe** the characteristics of effective control systems.

- **Discuss** the more popular control techniques.

- **Explain** the need for information management and describe the more popular information technologies.

- **Define** a business information system and explain how it operates.

Information Management Fuels Dillard Department Store's Success

Dillard Department Stores, Inc. is a department store chain that is less well known than Wal-Mart but every bit as successful. Over the past ten years, earnings have grown by 25 percent, compounded annually.

Dillard's growth has largely resulted from acquisitions. It bought Macy's midwestern division (ten stores) in 1986 and New Orleans–based D. H. Holmes (18 Gulf Coast stores) in 1990. Aside from acquisitions, Dillard hopes to build from eight to ten new stores each year. William Dillard, chairman and CEO, says the company has committed to open six stores in Mexico and is looking at over a dozen other sites.

A major factor in Dillard's success has been a near-fanatical focus on computer technology. Are Estée Lauder cosmetics selling as fast as anticipated in Santa Fe? How much business is each store doing as of 11:00 A.M. today? Within seconds of the request, Dillard's integrated electronic-mail and electronic data interchange (EDI) information system flashes the numbers on the screen, enabling mangers to digest the information and take appropriate action, including exchanging forms-based information such as purchase orders with suppliers.

Dillard's information system makes it possible to order goods from suppliers and get them onto the sales floor faster than most other retailers. Its Quick Response program orders basic items, such as Gant dress shirts and Christian Dior lingerie, from the vendor each week—electronically—based on the previous week's sales. This system gives Dillard's a tremen-

dous advantage over typical retail stores that require three to five weeks longer to do the same thing. More bad news for the competition: Dillard's goal is to reduce its average turnaround time from 12 days to eight in the near future.

To give you an example of how quickly Dillard's management steps in to exercise control, consider the 1990 D. H. Holmes acquisition. Immediately upon closing the deal, dozens of Dillard's personnel descended on Holmes's 18 stores on a Friday. Over the weekend, each store installed all-new, computer-linked point-of-sale registers and tied them directly into Dillard's mainframe in Little Rock. Merchandise in all stores was tagged with Dillard's bar-coded labels, permitting monitoring of sales information at the register. By Monday morning, the stores were open for business as usual—the Dillard's way!

Obviously, the management of information plays a central role for this efficient and highly profitable firm.[1]

Dillard's Quick Response program allows basic items to be ordered every week without human intervention.

Organizational life is filled with daily examples that reflect the need for managerial information and control. Control difficulties may be reflected in any number of ways—dissatisfied clients, unpaid bills, cost overruns, lack of profitability, unmet schedules, and so forth. Managerial control consists of the things management does to see that plans are carried out as intended. And as you can see from the Opening Case, accurate information plays a central role in helping managers exercise effective control.

There are many names for the control function: It is often called *monitoring*, *evaluating*, *appraising*, or *correcting*. We choose to call it *control* because none of the other terms carries the connotation of setting standards, measuring actual performance, and taking corrective action.

What Control Is

You might think of controlling as being similar to the road markers on a highway. The markers tell you whether or not you are on the right track. If you are not on the right track, you take corrective action to get on it. **Control** can be defined as the process by which management checks to see if what actually happens is consistent with expectations. It is concerned with ways of making things happen as they were planned to happen.

control The process by which management checks to see if what actually happens is consistent with expectations.

For example, in the late 1980s, Nestlé's Beech-Nut subsidiary shocked its parent corporation by admitting to having used additives and substitutes in the apple juice it labeled as "100 percent pure." Top Beech-Nut managers, when made aware of the mislabeling, attempted to conceal the truth from their own superiors. Ultimately, Beech-Nut was required to pay about $25 million in fines and penalties; several top managers were charged with criminal offenses.[2]

Another classic example of lack of control was the ultramodern Denver International Airport. Its opening was delayed several months until early 1995 because a $193 million, high-tech baggage-handling system could not be made to operate properly. Denver officials had to pay over $50 million extra to install a conventional system that would not destroy baggage.[3]

Organizations that do not exercise proper control run tremendous risks. Beech-Nut, Nestlé, and the new Denver International Airport received much adverse publicity as a result of these incidents. Similarly, consider the consequences for Exxon following the *Exxon Valdez* oil spill in 1989. Certainly, these events were not supposed to happen, but a breakdown in the control function allowed them to occur.

We live in a world of controls and control systems. Some common examples of controls with which you might be familiar are listed in Table 15.1.

Total and Partial Control Systems

Some control systems are total systems; that is, they are designed not only to detect the problem but also to correct it. When there is a self–correction feature, the system is often referred to as **cybernetics.** An internal home sprinkler system is a total, or cybernetic, control system because it not only detects a fire but also puts it out. On the other hand, a smoke detector is a *partial system*, since it only *warns* of trouble; another step must then be taken to remedy the situation.

cybernetics A control system that includes not only a detection but also a self-correction feature.

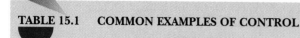

TABLE 15.1   COMMON EXAMPLES OF CONTROL

Nonbusiness	Business
Hotel Automatic sprinkler system	*Toyota Motors* Auto assembly line worker sounds alarm when item on line is found to be defective
Auto Oil pressure gauge on dashboard	
Human body Production of white blood cells to combat infection	*International Paper Company* Metal sensors shut down debarking machine if metal placed there by militant environmentalists in effort to sabotage equipment is detected in logs
Home Electrical circuit breaker system	
Highway Radar system designed to detect speeders	
School Detention hall after school	*Coca-Cola Company* Salespersons report on prices charged by competitors so that Coke may respond in effort to protect market share
	Citicorp Loan officers closely monitor payments by borrowers and amplify collection efforts on overdue accounts
	Al's Supermarket In effort to avoid pileup of old inventory, manager conducts monthly supersales

A good example of a total control system, with all the necessary steps for control, is probably found in your classroom, office, or home in the form of a thermostatically controlled air conditioning or heating system. The standard (or planned temperature) is established when you set the thermostat at, say, 68 degrees. The temperature in the room is monitored constantly by the system. When the temperature falls to 66 degrees, this information activates the burners and the system produces heat. When the room reaches 70 degrees, the thermostat deactivates the burners and the room cools. When the room reaches 66 degrees again, the heater is again activated. The process repeats itself continuously and may be thought of as a total, self-regulating control system.

Managerial control systems operate the same way.

How Controlling Relates to Other Management Functions

Controlling is related to, is affected by, and influences all the other managerial functions—especially planning. In fact, as you will see shortly, the initial step of the control process is actually a planning step—establishing a goal, standard, or performance objective. Thus, you might think of control as answering the question, How are things going?

Controlling Complements Planning Some organizations and managers lay out careful and elaborate plans, but unless they have effective controls available, they find that accomplishing the plans becomes just a matter of luck. You might even think of planning as being "incomplete" unless good controls are also established.

Since control implies comparing actual results with standards, it is sometimes difficult to distinguish between a plan—a standard—and a control. Earlier in this book, we labeled targets, objectives, goals, policies, and procedures as plans; control is needed to ensure that these plans are satisfactorily achieved.

Is the red traffic light at a busy intersection a plan or a control? What about a No Smoking sign in a room containing flammable materials?

Controlling Is Linked to Other Functions   The control function of management is also related closely to the other managerial functions. It helps ensure that planning, organizing, and leading are being performed effectively, as the following example shows.

> The highly computerized Nasdaq stock-trading system, which prides itself on being "the market for the next hundred years," was plagued by computer glitches during the summer of 1994. Trouble with computer software and phone lines twice made it impossible to trade Nasdaq's 4,800 stocks. Then, on August 1, a squirrel chewed through a power line near Nasdaq's main computer center in Turnbull, Connecticut. Nasdaq's computers automatically switched to a backup battery system—called "the Uninterruptible Power Supply"—which failed to engage. Trading was restored after 34 minutes when operations were switched to a backup computer in Rockville, Maryland.[4]

Obviously, the control function itself must be controlled. For example, questions such as the following should be asked: Is the system providing timely information? Are the control reports accurate? Is performance measured at sufficiently frequent intervals? These are aspects of controlling the control function.

Types of Control

There are three basic types of controls. As shown in Figure 15.1, they are (1) feedforward, (2) concurrent, and (3) feedback controls.

Feedforward Control   **Feedforward control** attempts to anticipate problems or deviations from the standard *before* they occur. It is thus an active, aggressive approach to control, allowing corrective action to be taken before a real problem develops.

    Hart Schaffner & Marx uses feedforward control by inspecting bolts of cloth before using them for its expensive tailored men's clothing. And Motorola goes one step further, by stationing its personnel on key suppliers' premises, where control can be exercised even before goods are shipped to Motorola's production plants.

feedforward control
Control that attempts to anticipate problems or deviations from the standard before they occur.

Concurrent Control   **Concurrent control,** also called **steering control** or **screening,** occurs while an activity is taking place. For example, when driving a car, you must adjust your steering continuously, depending on turns in the road, obstacles, and changes in terrain to keep the car safe and move toward your objective.

concurrent (steering) control or **screening**
Control that occurs while an activity is taking place.

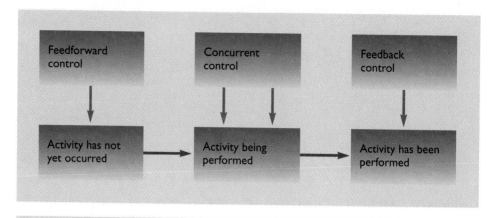

FIGURE 15.1
Three types of controls.

feedback (postaction) control Control or correction that occurs after an activity has taken place.

Feedback Control   **Feedback control,** also known as **postaction control,** is historical. That is, the measured activity has already occurred, and it is impossible to go back and correct performance in order to bring it up to standard. Instead, corrections must occur after the fact. Examples of feedback controls are disciplinary situations, performance appraisal interviews, financial and budgetary results, and final inspections of products.

Perhaps you are thinking, "Since feedback controls occur after the fact, why even bother? Isn't it too late to do anything about the past?" For a partial answer, consider the following situations, which illustrate that feedback control is also future-oriented, and can often prevent the same problem from occurring again.

Suppose that a quality control inspector in a garment factory finds that one sleeve of each shirt in a completed batch is three inches longer than the other. What can be done? Most or all of the material in the shirts will be scrapped. Thus, the inspection occurred too late to salvage the shirts. But detecting the errors at a final control point is still better than having the shirts bought by a customer in that unsatisfactory condition! Likewise, when a local bank falls 20 percent short of its profit objectives for the first quarter, *that is history.* What is important is finding out the reason *why it happened.* The hope of feedback controls lies in finding out why performance was poor and taking the steps necessary to remedy the situation in the future.

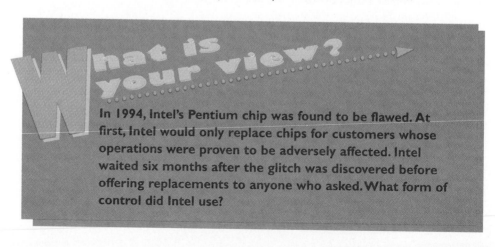

What is your view?

In 1994, Intel's Pentium chip was found to be flawed. At first, Intel would only replace chips for customers whose operations were proven to be adversely affected. Intel waited six months after the glitch was discovered before offering replacements to anyone who asked. What form of control did Intel use?

All three forms of controls—feedforward, concurrent, and feedback—are useful. Feedforward and concurrent controls should be sufficiently timely to allow management to make corrective changes and still achieve objectives. But there are several other factors involved, despite the appeal of these two forms of controls. First, they are costly. Second, many activities do not lend themselves to frequent or continuous monitoring. Third, at some point excessive control becomes counterproductive, as in the case of sales representatives who spend their time filling out control reports for the home office instead of making customer calls. *Management must therefore use the control system that is most appropriate for the given situation.*

Steps in the Control Process

The control process usually consists of at least four steps, as shown in Figure 15.2: (1) establishing standards of performance (planning), (2) measuring actual performance, (3) comparing performance with standards and analyzing variances, and (4) taking corrective action if necessary.

Step 1: Establishing Performance Standards

While establishing performance standards is part of planning, it is the basis for controlling and is usually the first step in the control process. Standards are important for managers need to set clear objectives that channel the entire organization's efforts. For our purposes at this time, we define a **standard** as a unit of measurement that can serve as a reference point for evaluating results. Accordingly, goals, objectives, quotas, and performance targets will all be considered *standards* in this discussion. Some specific standards are sales quotas, equal employment opportunity targets, budgets, job deadlines, market share, and profit margins.

standard A unit of measurement that can serve as a reference point for evaluating results.

FIGURE 15.2
How the control process operates.

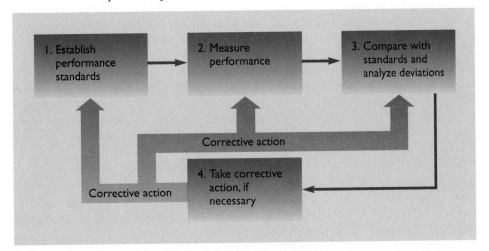

As you see from this list, standards can be expressed in physical, monetary, or time dimensions.

1. *Physical standards* might include quantities of products or services, number of customers or clients, or quality of products or services.
2. *Monetary standards* are expressed in dollars and include labor costs, selling costs, materials costs, sales revenue, gross profits, and the like.
3. *Time standards* might include the speed with which jobs should be done or the deadlines by which they are to be completed.

All of the above are *quantifiable standards*; that is, they can be expressed in terms of numbers (units, dollars, hours, and so forth). This enables managers to communicate their performance expectations to subordinates more clearly and permits the other steps in the control process to be handled more effectively.

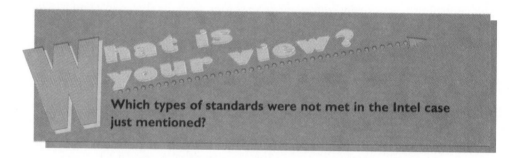

Which types of standards were not met in the Intel case just mentioned?

Nonquantifiable, or *qualitative, standards* also play an important role in the control process. Sometimes managers and subordinates are not as much aware of the nonquantifiable standards, but these are still very important. Although difficult to express quantitatively, such standards as hiring "qualified" personnel, promoting the "most proficient" person, having a cooperative attitude, and wearing appropriate dress on the job, can be critical.

Step 2: Measuring Performance

Setting standards is futile unless there is some way to measure actual performance. While standards establish what will be measured and what level of performance is satisfactory, other important questions must also be answered. For example, *how often* should performance be measured—hourly, daily, weekly, yearly? *What form* will the measurement take—a phone call, a visual inspection, a written report? *Who* will be involved—an operating employee, a supervisor, a middle-level manager, or the top officer of the company?

J. Willard Marriott, Sr., founder and senior executive officer for over 50 years of the hotel and food chain empire that bears his name, was obsessed with customer satisfaction (the performance standard). He felt so strongly about this that he made a practice of reading every complaint card sent in by his customers. In fact, it is said he read the original, raw, unedited cards, rather than typewritten summaries of them. One senior Marriott officer summed up the impact of Marriott's control: "You had 100 or so property managers working 26 hours a day, eight days a week to make sure the boss had a very, very light reading load."[5]

Other considerations in measuring performance are ensuring that the measurement is easy to do, relatively inexpensive, and easy to explain to employees and others. Among the many ways of measuring performance are (1) observation; (2) reports, both oral and written; (3) use of automatic devices; and (4) inspections, tests, or samples. At many large and small companies, internal auditors make use of these methods.

Some examples of using observation are a supervisor overseeing the activities of subordinates, and a basketball coach studying the players during a game. Some automatic measuring devices are a car's speedometer and odometer and the counters that indicate the number of units a machine produces. Examples of inspections, tests, and samples include, respectively, traffic police, final examinations, and spot-checking of units being produced.

Step 3: Comparing Performance with Standards and Analyzing Deviations

A critical control step is comparing actual performance with planned performance; facts about performance, standing alone, are relatively worthless, as the following example illustrates.

Assume that a business reported these figures last month.

Total sales	$250,175
Number of finished products produced	1,100
Number of customer calls	1,112
Number of new customers	87
Number of new salespersons hired	3
Average shipping time to customer	5 days
Employee turnover	18%
Number of lost-time accidents	7

Does this list contain any significant information about the company's progress? Can you tell if the company is doing well?

In order to judge the business's performance, you must be able to compare the results cited with other pertinent data. What was the company's sales goal? How many customer calls are considered "good"? How many new customers was the company attempting to gain? How many new salespersons had the company wanted to hire? What "norm" is there for the average shipping time? Only when you compare *actual* performance to established performance *standards* are you in a position to exercise control.

Deviations in performance must be analyzed to determine why the standard is not being met when performance falls short. Chapter 6 showed how important it is in decision making to identify the real causes of performance problems, rather than just the symptoms.

Step 4: Taking Corrective Action If Needed

If corrective action is needed, it must be taken in whatever form is most appropriate. The standard of performance may be modified or steps may be taken to improve performance—or both may be done concurrently. The corrective action

MANAGEMENT APPLICATION AND PRACTICE 15.1

Spelling for Success

At *Success* magazine, Editor-in-Chief Scott DeGarmo got tired of making the same complaints to the same people about errors. So in 1990, he instituted a new control system that hits editors in their wallets. In the course of his job, DeGarmo checks all copy handed in by his senior editors. If he finds any grammatical or typographical errors, the person responsible pays. Each misspelling costs $25, as does a misplaced hyphen. Getting someone's name wrong really hurts—a whopping $500 fine.

Admittedly, this is a pretty drastic approach, but DeGarmo said he felt it was not unreasonable to hold people responsible for their mistakes, and spelling correctly—and correcting others' spelling—is an editor's job. "When my people see a typo anyplace," said DeGarmo, "I want them to step on it like a roach."

DeGarmo had tried other tactics, "but all the so-called positive reinforcement hadn't worked." He decided that clearer performance standards were needed. "It's not enough to ask people to do their best. You've got to tell them what you want; in my case, it was perfection."

Scott DeGarmo, editor-in-chief of *Success* magazine, devised an interesting control system to reach his goal of 100 percent accuracy in the publication.

Sources: Adapted from Associated Press wire service report, January 1991, and Roger Ailes et al., "*Success* Magazine's 7th Annual Renegades: Break the Rules and Win," *Success*, February 1994, pp. 36–44.

may be to alter either the planning or the control system. If corrections are needed, you can either change the original standard, which may have been too low or too high and/or alter the measurement system itself.

A practical example of the control process in action appears in MAP 15.1.

How Management by Exception (MBE) Aids Control

management by exception (MBE) or exception principle A form of control that focuses on recognizing and addressing only exceptional, significant performance problems.

One technique that can help managers determine whether corrective action is needed is **management by exception (MBE),** or the **exception principle.** MBE is the practice of recognizing and addressing only exceptional, significant performance deviations.

MBE enables higher-level managers to direct their attention to the most critical control areas and permits employees or lower levels of management to handle routine variations. As shown in Figure 15.3, performance is measured against the standard set in order to determine whether a deviation from the standard exists. If a deviation is found that is not exceptional, no action is taken; if the deviation is considered exceptional, it is analyzed and evaluated to determine what type of corrective action should be taken. MBE can be practiced by managers in all functional areas. Even first-line managers can use this principle to help with their daily supervision.

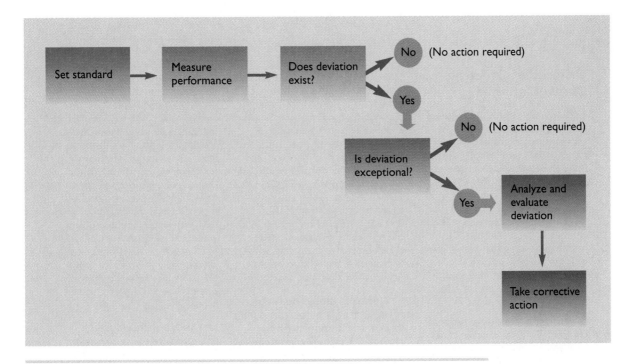

FIGURE 15.3
How management by exception (MBE) operates.

A final warning should be added: Managers who practice MBE must temper the process with various methods of remaining visible to and communicating with their personnel, for it is important for employees to receive recognition for making things go right.

Characteristics of Effective Control Systems

To be effective, a control system must meet at least the following five criteria. The system should be (1) focused on appropriate activities, (2) timely, (3) cost-effective, (4) accurate, and (5) acceptable to those involved with it. The more nearly these criteria are met, the more likely it is that effective control will result. See Tips 15.1 for further suggestions.

Some Effective Control Techniques

There are many qualitative and quantitative control techniques. The most popular qualitative methods are observation and regular spot inspections. But the most important methods are the **quantitative control methods.** These methods include budgets and budgetary control, audits, ratio analyses, break-even analyses, and time-performance charts and techniques, such as Program Evaluation and Review Technique (PERT).

quantitative control methods Techniques that use specific data and measurable criteria to evaluate the quantity and quality of output.

Tips 15.1

Criteria for Effective Control Systems

1. **Controls should be focused on appropriate activities.** As control systems influence where job energies are directed, managers must ensure that appropriate activities are "controlled." For example, a sales manager may cut prices drastically to reach the sales quota for the division; unless he or she is also working under a profit standard, reaching the sales standard, in itself, is not necessarily desirable. Managers must therefore make sure to control the proper balance of activities in the system.

2. **Controls should be timely.** For controls to be effective, they must identify deviations in time to allow management to take corrective action. For example, in late 1993, a computer system at Whirlpool Corp. flashed a warning signal: After "just a few washloads," the machines were springing bad leaks. Whirlpool engineers found the cause to be a faulty hose clamp. Production was immediately halted, and the computer system identified each of the few hundred purchasers of the machine so that mechanics could be sent out to replace the defective part.

3. **Controls should be cost-effective.** Control systems are not inexpensive, and so their costs should be controlled. Thus, management must constantly raise the question of the *cost versus the benefits of the control system.* For example, should a company inspect each item it produces? At first glance,

this seems desirable, but sometimes it is impractical and uneconomical. Surely, this procedure will differ for a manufacturer of parachutes compared to a manufacturer of notebook paper or pistons for an automobile engine. Mass manufacturing processes often use **statistical quality control (SQC) techniques** by which control is based on inspecting random samples instead of every item. With the high costs of sophisticated control systems, equipment, and personnel, it is easy to control an organization right into bankruptcy!

4. **Controls should be accurate.** Care must be taken to ensure that control measurements are accurate. Measurements are often imprecise, and may be based on inaccurate data. For example, on August 10, 1994, Alan Greenspan, Federal Reserve chairman, told Congress that "economic reports issued by the government on everything from inflation to employment often aren't very accurate and shouldn't be seen as precise measures of the economy's health."

Also, honest—but careless—errors can be made in reporting data. For instance, when 1,500 Charleston County, South Carolina, civil servants opened their W-2 form envelopes in early 1994, the forms said they were dead—the deceased box was marked with an X. When the computer making out the W-2s completed the entry for a worker who had died, it kept going for all the line employees. The forms were regenerated at a cost of $600.

Finally, sloppy management control can result in errors. A case in point was Equitable Assurance Society, which was badly burned by inaccurate controls during the 1980s. It rapidly diversified from basic life insurance into new products such as real estate, financial brokerage, and mortgage operations. Costs escalated, payrolls expanded, but profits did not keep up. One reason for the problem was that Equitable's control system had for several years overstated substantially—12 percent versus 4.5 percent—the profitability of one of the company's major new products.

5. **Controls should be accepted by those involved.** People tend to resent controls, especially those they consider unnecessary or excessive. Sometimes too the standards set by management may be perceived as unreasonable or unfair, and employees show their resentment by finding ways to beat the system. If controls are to be accepted, it is important that people clearly understand the purpose of the control system and feel they have an important stake in it.

Source: For more details, see "Equitable's Troubles Show Mounting Risks Facing Life Insurers," *Wall Street Journal*, November 30, 1990, pp. A1, A6; John H. Verity, "The Gold Mine of Data in Customer Service," *Business Week*, March 21, 1994, p. 113; "Greenspan: Statistics Are No Crystal Ball," *USA Today*, August 11, 1994, p. 4B; and "The Grimmest Tax News of All," *Business Week*, March 14, 1994, p. 8.

---

statistical quality control (SQC) techniques Control based on inspection of random samples rather than every item (see Tips 15.1).

Using Budgets and Budgetary Control

The budget is the most widely used control device in both business and government. In fact, it is used so extensively that for many people, the word *budget* means *control.* While *preparing* of the budget is an integral part of the planning function, *administration* of the budget is an integral part of the control function. The budget itself is the end point of the planning process, that is, the statement of plans. To avoid the negative reactions often associated with the concept of control, some managers refer to their budgetary controls as *profit plans.*

"*Oh, it's great here, all right, but I sort of feel uncomfortable in a place with no budget at all.*"

Nature of Budgets and Budgetary Control   **Budgets** express plans, objectives, and programs of the organization in numerical terms. Thus, they are statements of planned revenues and expenditures—by category and period of time—of money, time, personnel, space, buildings, or equipment. Obviously, planning is an integral part of any budget.

Budgets are control devices in that they are designed to guide the actions of management by providing feedback when actual performance is unfavorable relative to budgeted performance. They become the standard by which actual performance is measured.

The amount needed for each item is projected and budgeted, the amounts actually expended are recorded, and the amounts over or under budget are computed. The results indicate areas that are "over" or "under" and should be corrected by (1) increasing the budgeted amount, (2) reducing expenses, or (3) using a combination of these two procedures.

budgets Statements of planned revenue and expenditures—by category and period of time—of money, time, personnel, space, buildings, or equipment.

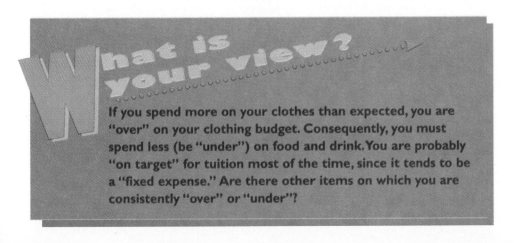

What is your view?

If you spend more on your clothes than expected, you are "over" on your clothing budget. Consequently, you must spend less (be "under") on food and drink. You are probably "on target" for tuition most of the time, since it tends to be a "fixed expense." Are there other items on which you are consistently "over" or "under"?

PRACTICING MANAGER

DONALD TRUMP

Donald Trump—of "the Donald" and the best-selling *Art of the Deal* fame—saw his bubble burst in 1990. Trump, who lived lavishly, as evidenced by his 10-acre, 110-room vacation mansion, his $29 million yacht, and his jet-black helicopter, had been humbled by debt, having to scramble for extensions on interest payments and extended terms on loans. While few people predicted bankruptcy, there was no question that Trump's image as a wheeling-and-dealing risk taker who turned every project into gold had been severely tarnished.

What happened to the man who owned such imposing properties as Trump Towers, the Trump Shuttle, New York's Grand Hyatt and Plaza hotels, and three Atlantic City gaming casinos—Trump Plaza, Trump Castle, and the lavish Taj Mahal? What happened was similar to what happened to Circle K, Drexel Burnham Lambert, Robert Campeau's Canadian and U.S. retailing empire, Harcourt Brace Jovanovich, and other highly leveraged companies: horrible debt management and liquidity ratios. The cash flow was not enough to cover interest payments—and that always spells trouble. Trump recognized this when he admitted, "Gradually I've come to realize . . . that restoring a great asset is not enough when you're paying off a large acquisition debt."

In the 1980s, Trump could do little wrong. His properties became hot items, the Trump name alone was almost enough to assure success, and bankers were quick to lend or to help underwrite junk bond offerings at higher than normal rates—without adequate study or standards. In the late 1980s, however, the real estate market turned sour, and several of Trump's business shortcomings were exposed. The airline had never done well, gaming in Atlantic City had flattened out, and a large tract on Manhattan's West Side remained undeveloped since Trump had shelled out $125 million for it in 1985.

Add to all of this Trump's high-profile pending divorce of his wife Ivana, his alleged affair with model Marla Maples, the death of two of his top casino managers in a helicopter accident, intensified rumors about contractors not being paid, bankers who would not budge in denying Trump's requests for refinancing, and *Fortune*'s report that his personal worth had plummeted in 1990 from $1.7 billion to $500 million because of debt and dropping real estate values, and you have a pretty bleak picture. As one of Trump's banker friends remarked, "You live by the glitz, you die by the glitz."

While things improved—somewhat, for Trump, as he divorced Ivana and married Marla—he was still having budgetary problems in 1995. The Trump Plaza, Taj Mahal, and Trump Castle lost money in 1994, and his personally guaranteed debt was $115 million, which he couldn't refinance without his banker's consent. He was also offering to see $150 million of Trump Plaza stock to the public.

Source: "Trump: The Fall," *Newsweek,* June 18, 1990, pp. 38–45; Mark Memmott, "Business Failures Rise; More Likely," *USA Today,* November 2, 1990, p. 1B; Gary Belis, "Trump Two," *Fortune,* September 24, 1990, p. 216; Donald Trump, *Trump: Surviving at the Top* (New York: Random House, 1990); and "Tempted to Bet on Trump? Think Twice," *Fortune,* May 1, 1995, pp. 132, 134.

budgetary control A system of using the target figures established in a budget to control managerial activities by comparing actual performance with planned performance.

Budgetary control is a system of using the target figures established in a budget to control managerial activities by comparing actual performance with planned performance. Thus, planning the budget is really setting standards, the first step in control, and administering the budget encompasses the rest of the steps. As shown in the profile of Donald Trump, budgetary control is quite difficult in today's world of high finance.

Budgetary control is a simple and direct application of the essentials of the control process: Budget figures are set, and records of actual receipts and expenditures are made. Next, each budget item is compared with the actual performance, and variances can be noted. The manager then has the information needed to take corrective action, such as (1) to increase receipts, (2) to reduce expenditures, or (3) to revise the budget. This process enables managers to check continually and to locate problems early, before they become so large they threaten the very existence of the organization.

Types of Budgets   Most organizations have a budget for each of their major activities. The **operating budget** is the major comprehensive budget for the entire organization, including overall revenues, costs, and financial performance. **Capital budgets** are for purchasing equipment and facilities. **Production budgets** are for producing the organization's basic products and services. **Sales budgets** outline expected sales volume. **Personnel budgets** are for securing and developing human resources. Table 15.2 provides further explanation of these and other types of budgets.

These budgets are discussed as if they were separate and distinct units, but actually they are part of a total comprehensive system. For example, the *sales budget* tends to be the focus of the system, since it reflects the major function of most commercial and industrial organizations. The *production budget*, in turn, is based on the sales budget. The overall *operating budget* of the organization is triggered by the *sales* and *production budgets*.

operating budget
Major comprehensive budget for the organization, including overall revenues, costs, and financial performance.

capital budgets
Budgets for purchasing equipment and facilities.

production budgets
Budgets for producing the organization's basic products or services.

sales budgets Budgets that outline expected sales volume.

personnel budgets
Budgets for securing and developing human resources.

Using Audits for Control

Another effective control method is the use of **audits,** which are efforts to examine activities or records to verify their accuracy or effectiveness. Audits can be performed externally or internally. External audits provide an independent

audits Efforts to examine activities or records to verify their accuracy or effectiveness.

TABLE 15.2   TYPES AND PURPOSES OF BUDGETS

Type of Budget	Brief Description of Purpose
Operating budget	Expresses the organization's anticipated revenues, costs, and financial performance
Sales budget	Provides an estimate of the amount and source of expected revenues
Production budget	Expresses physical requirements of expected production, including labor, materials, and overhead requirements for the budget period
Personnel budget	Provides the details for securing and developing human resources
Expense budget	Provides details for allocation of various expenses, such as selling, general, and administrative
Cash budget	Forecasts the flow of cash receipts and disbursements
Capital budget	Outlines specific expenditures for office, plant, equipment, machinery, inventories, and other capital items
Balance sheet budget	Forecasts the financial status of assets, liabilities, and net worth at the end of the budget period

appraisal of an organization's financial records. They seek to test the reliability and validity of financial records by determining the degree of accuracy and the extent to which financial statements reflect what they purport to represent.

An *internal audit* is an appraisal conducted by an organization's employees in order to verify the accuracy and integrity of the information being used. The internal audit is wider in scope than an external audit and not only considers adherence to organizational standards but also may assess the effectiveness of the control mechanisms used.

It is also possible to apply auditing techniques as a way of determining the overall effectiveness of management. When the technique is used for this purpose, it is referred to as a **management audit.** This type of audit studies the present management personnel of an organization to see how they will affect future operations. It considers programs, policies, organization, operating methods and procedures, financial procedures, personnel practices, and physical facilities and reports on the organization's overall effectiveness.

The management audit highlights major areas needing attention, improves communication by informing all employees of the state of the organization, and acts as a test of the effectiveness of the current management control system. Management audits can be used by any size organization, not just large firms.

In recent years, the auditing process has been broadened to encompass areas other than financial matters, including the environment, safety, affirmative action compliance, and social responsibility.[6] For example, as shown in Chapter 5, *social audits* are now being used to evaluate and report on actions with social implications.

Using Ratio Analysis for Control

Ratio analysis (RA) is a financial control tool that involves selecting two or more components of an organization's financial statement and expressing their relationship as a percentage or ratio. Management can determine its relative performance by comparing its ratios to those of others in the industry and/or by comparing its own present and past performance.

Ratios can be computed for practically any financial measurements, but the most commonly computed ones are liquidity, asset management, debt management, and profitability. These ratios are used as follows:

1. *Liquidity ratios* indicate how well management is prepared to meet its short-term financial obligations, such as payrolls, creditor payments, and interest—that is, whether cash and accounts receivable will cover current debts.

2. *Asset-management ratios* measure how well management uses its assets.

3. *Debt-management (leverage) ratios* indicate management's ability to meet its long-term financial obligations, such as bonds, mortgages, and notes payable. Unfavorable debt-management ratios gained attention in the early 1990s, with a number of organizations so badly overextended that they did not have the liquidity to meet their interest obligations.

4. *Profitability ratios* measure management's overall performance as shown by profits on sales and investments. One such ratio is **return on equity (ROE),** often called **return on investment (ROI),** the net profit owners receive on their investment in a firm. Its major benefit is that it permits a common evaluation of the performance of different organizational units.

---

management audit A means of determining the overall effectiveness of management by considering programs, policies, organization, operating methods and procedures, and so on.

ratio analysis (RA) Financial control tool that involves selecting two or more components of a firm's financial statement and expressing their relationship as a percentage or ratio, permitting comparison of various aspects of performance with that of previous periods or other firms.

return on equity (ROE) or **return on investment (ROI)** The net profit owners receive on their investment in a firm.

Preoccupation with ROE can lead to problems. For example, Du Pont once used a 20 percent ROE as a minimum for approving new product projects. This control technique caused the firm's management to forgo expansion into xerography and instant photography. Yet a disregard for ROE may also be harmful over a period of time.

Using Break-Even Analysis for Control

The objective of most private firms is to make a profit, and even most not-for-profit organizations try to have revenues exceed expenses. Break-even analysis is a useful tool that allows managers to visualize more clearly the revenue-cost relationship. With **break-even analysis,** revenues and costs are charted and analyzed to determine at what volume (of sales or production) one's total costs exactly equal total revenues.

break-even analysis The charting and analysis of revenues and costs to determine at what volume (of sales or production) total costs equal total revenues so that there is neither profit nor loss.

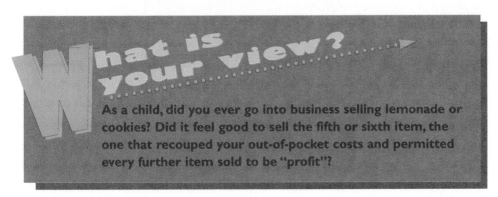

As a child, did you ever go into business selling lemonade or cookies? Did it feel good to sell the fifth or sixth item, the one that recouped your out-of-pocket costs and permitted every further item sold to be "profit"?

How to Compute the Break-Even Point The **break-even point (BEP)** is that point in operations at which total revenue exactly covers both fixed and variable costs. Figure 15.4 illustrates this relationship in a simplified form. Notice the following certain terms. **Total revenue** is the price of each unit of product times the number of units sold. **Fixed costs** are expenses that remain the same regardless of the level of output, such as utilities, depreciation on buildings and other facilities, insurance, property taxes, and salaries of top managers. **Variable costs** are those that vary according to the level of output; variable costs might include materials, parts and supplies, and extra workers' wages.

break-even point (BEP) The point in operations at which total revenue exactly covers total costs, both fixed and variable.

total revenue The price of each item times the number of units sold.

fixed costs Costs that remain the same regardless of the level of output.

There are several ways of computing the BEP. Mathematically, it can be computed by dividing fixed costs by the difference between the price of each unit sold and the variable cost per unit. Therefore, the formula is:

variable costs Costs that vary according to the level of output.

$$\text{Break-even point (in units)} = \frac{\text{Total Fixed Costs}}{\text{(Sales price per unit)} - \text{(Variable cost per unit)}}$$

How to Use Break-Even Analysis Managers can use break-even analysis to study the relationships among costs, sales volume, and profits. Thus, output must be shifted to the right of the chart in Figure 15.4 if more profit is desired. Break-even analysis also provides a rough estimate of profit or loss at various sales volumes. Also, it can be used both as an aid to decision making and as a control device.

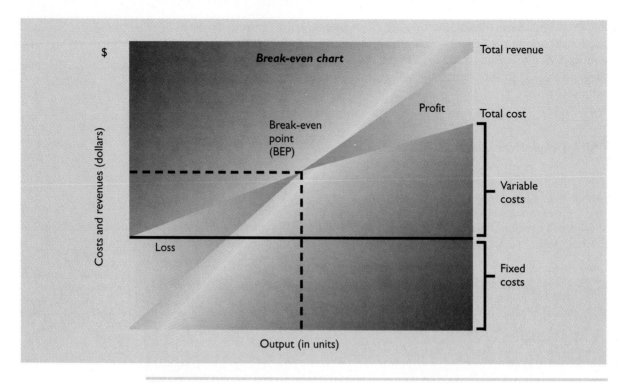

FIGURE 15.4
How the break-even point (BEP) shows cost and revenue relationships.

As an aid to decision making, break-even analysis can (1) identify the sales volume needed to prevent a loss, (2) identify the minimum production and sales volume needed to meet established objectives, (3) provide data to help management decide whether to add or drop a product line, and (4) help management decide whether to raise or lower prices.

An example of this use of break-even analysis occurred recently near a major Southern University. The owner of a small restaurant was having financial problems. When a Service Corps of Retired Executives (SCORE) volunteer asked what was the most popular item, the owner said, "My $5.00 Steak Special." The volunteer put a raw steak on a scale and asked its cost. The cost was $4.00, not counting the other items that were served with it. The owner was told he was losing around $1.65 on each special. He continued the special, though, as an attraction to students.

As a control device, break-even analysis provides one more objective measurement by which to evaluate the organization's performance (as shown in MAP 15.2) and furnishes a basis for possible corrective action. One primary reason for a high BEP is high investment in fixed assets. Management can approximate this break-even point before investing in a new building or machine. Another cause of loss is inadequate control of expenses, as you saw in Tips 15.1. Break-even analysis can help management detect increases in variable costs before they get out of control.

In a classic case of break-even analysis, when Lee Iacocca became chairman of Chrylser Corp. in 1979, he found that the company had to sell 2.3 million cars and trucks to break even (the BEP). By 1982, under the company's stringent cost-saving measures and with selling off inefficient operations, the "new" Chrysler's break-even point had been reduced to 1.1 million units.[7]

MANAGEMENT APPLICATION AND PRACTICE 15.2

Break-Even Point Reflects Ford of Europe's Rising Success

In the early 1980s, Ford of Europe did not perform very well. But then Robert Lutz took over its leadership and things began to change as the company broke away from previous policies and began manufacturing cars that would be competitive in the European market.

The major strategy Lutz undertook was called the "After Japan" (AJ) strategy. The first priority facing Ford of Europe was to gain back the market share the Japanese had gobbled up, and so Ford began designing and manufacturing cars that were specifically equipped to demonstrate to buyers that Ford cars were offering more value for their money.

To make such a statement, Ford had to be competitive with the Japanese in manufacturing efficiency. Lutz, through studying the Japanese automakers, began to reshape operations by copying Japanese techniques. Many changes were made, and seemed to be implemented with few disruptions. The benefits of these changes were noticeable.

Body defects decreased from 835 per 100 cars to 650. The average rate of growth of manufacturing productivity went from 4.8 to 6 percent. The break-even point was reduced from 80 percent of capacity prior to the AJ program to 60 percent of capacity after the program was put into operation.

But then the company became complacent, and costly inventories built up while auto sales in Europe slumped. Also, few new models were introduced. William Fike, a new president, restructured the company, introduced new models, and signed a computer operations outsourcing deal with Computer Sciences Corp (CSC). CSC will develop new control applications geared at improving the efficiency of Ford operations throughout Europe.

Sources: Parviz Asheghian and Bahman Ebrahimi, *International Business* (New York: Harper & Row, 1990), pp. 606–607; Richard A. Melcher, "Ford of Europe: Slimmer, but Maybe Not Luckier," *Business Week*, January 18, 1993, pp. 44–46; and Mark Halper, "Ford Drives Exclusive Outsourcing Deal," *Computerworld*, February 21, 1994, p. 59.

Limitations on the Use of Break-Even Analysis The very simplicity of break-even analysis is one of its limitations. For example, break-even analysis assumes that fixed and variable costs can be separated and classified and that fixed costs, variable costs, and selling price per unit will remain the same during the projected break-even period. Yet all these assumptions are questionable. For one thing, it is often difficult to determine whether a cost is fixed or variable. For example, expenses associated with machinery are normally considered a fixed expense. However, if machinery is operating at capacity and production is to be increased, your expense will no longer be fixed, as you must buy or rent additional machinery to increase production. Also, variable costs per unit may change greatly over a break-even period because of increased prices for raw materials, increased utility rates, and the like.

Despite these difficulties, this type of analysis is valuable to management. Even service types of organizations can find break-even analysis useful, as shown in the previous restaurant example.

Using Time-Performance Charts and Techniques for Control

Scheduling is the term used for planning the timing and sequencing of an organization's operational activities. There are many scheduling techniques available, ranging from appointment books, reservation forms for the use of space and equipment, and rough, longhand memos to mathematical programming of complex and sophisticated activities, such as designing and building a nuclear submarine or building and operating a space shuttle.

scheduling Planning the timing and sequencing of the use of physical and human resources in an organization's operations activities.

Managers need better scheduling and control techniques as the expected use of equipment, space, or human resources approaches maximum capacity. Also, when one operation cannot start until a previous operation or sequence of operations is completed, scheduling and controlling are more important—and more difficult.

Fortunately, several useful analytical techniques have been developed to aid in these planning and controlling processes by permitting managers to see how the various segments of operations interrelate and to evaluate the overall progress being made. The best known of these techniques are the Gantt chart and the Program Evaluation and Review Technique (PERT).

Time Performance: The Gantt Chart

Gantt chart Tool for analyzing performance that shows work planned and work accomplished in relation to each other and to time.

The most popular of the older techniques for analyzing time and performance is the Gantt chart, which was developed by Henry L. Gantt in the early 1900s (see Chapter 2). The **Gantt chart** shows work planned and work accomplished in relation to each other and in relation to time. This relatively simple chart is still a valuable and widely used control technique, especially in firms with many unrelated projects. It is also the foundation on which the more sophisticated types of time-related charts and control techniques, such as network analysis using PERT, are based.

Managing Projects with Program Evaluation and Review Technique

Managing projects is typically more complicated than managing ongoing processes such as assembly lines. Ongoing processes tend to be more predictable; over time, management has gained experience and know-how in responding to problems as they arise. A project, on the other hand, tends to be more complicated for several reasons, including the following:

1. Each project is typically a unique undertaking, something that has not been encountered by management before.
2. A project is often complex in nature, requiring many interrelated activities and participants both internal and external to the organization.
3. Project duration may be weeks, months, or even longer, and over this period many changes may occur that are difficult to predict and may affect project costs, technology, and resources.
4. The nature of projects requires that activities are sequential and dependent on earlier ones. Some activities may be frozen until others are completed.
5. Delays in project completion may be very expensive, amounting to thousands of dollars daily. Late completions may result in lost opportunities and ill feelings.

Program Evaluation and Review Technique (PERT) A technique that aids in scheduling sophisticated, one-time technical projects.

Why PERT Is Important to Management   The **Program Evaluation and Review Technique (PERT)** was developed in the 1950s by the U.S. Navy Bureau of Ordnance for use in developing the Polaris Fleet Ballistic Missile. It is credited with saving two years on that massive project, which involved over 3,000 contractors.[8] PERT aids in scheduling and controlling projects by (1) focusing management's attention on key program steps, (2) pointing to potential problem areas, (3) evaluating progress, and (4) giving management a reporting device. In doing these

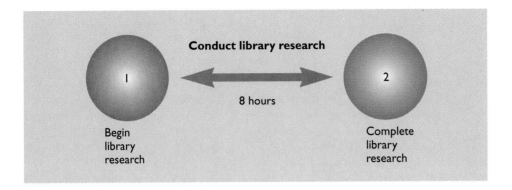

FIGURE 15.5
A simple PERT network.

things, PERT involves using a **PERT network,** which expresses the relationships of events and activities and their timing under conditions of uncertainty. Thus, as shown in Figure 15.5, time is the central control element.

Fundamentals of PERT Timing and sequencing are the primary focuses of the PERT network, or flow plan. The network consists of a series of related events and activities. An event is a significant, specified performance milestone (physical or mental) in the project plan. It is accomplished at a particular instant of time that represents the beginning or end of an activity. It does not consume time or resources. An event is usually represented by a circle or node, as shown in Figure 15.5. An example of an event is your turning in a completed term paper for this course.

An *activity* is a time-consuming element of the program. It represents the work needed to complete a particular event. It is usually represented by an arrow, as shown in Figure 15.5. Your library research for the term paper is one activity, your writing a rough draft is another, and your completing the final draft on your computer is a third.

Steps in Constructing a PERT Network The basic steps in PERT are the same regardless of the type of project, and include at least the following:

1. Identify and define the component activities that must be performed.
2. Define the order in which those activities in the network will be performed.
3. Analyze the estimated time required to complete the individual activities and the entire project.
4. Find the **critical path,** which is the longest path—in terms of time—from the beginning event to the ending event.
5. Improve on the initial plan through modifications.
6. Control the project.

All events and activities must be sequenced in the network under a strict set of logical rules. For example, one rule may be that no event can be considered finished until all preceding events have been completed. This permits the critical path to be determined. Numerous computer programs are available to perform the mechanics of computing the critical path. Figure 15.6 shows a simple project represented by a PERT network.

PERT network A line chart that expresses the relationships of events and activities and their timing under conditions of uncertainty.

critical path The longest path, in terms of time, from the beginning event to the ending event in a PERT network.

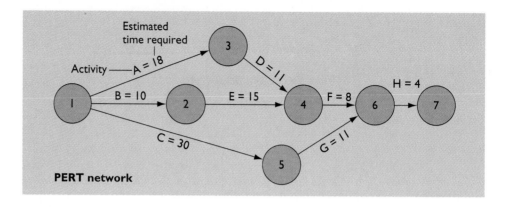

FIGURE 15.6
Project represented by a PERT network.

Many more details about PERT are best left to more advanced courses, such as management science and production and operations management.

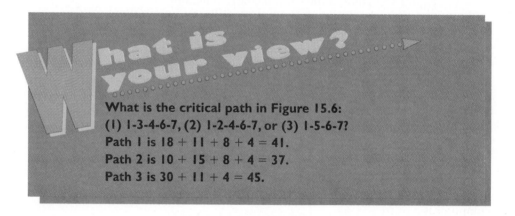

What is the critical path in Figure 15.6:
(1) 1-3-4-6-7, (2) 1-2-4-6-7, or (3) 1-5-6-7?
Path 1 is 18 + 11 + 8 + 4 = 41.
Path 2 is 10 + 15 + 8 + 4 = 37.
Path 3 is 30 + 11 + 4 = 45.

The Role of Information Management

While information has always been a major part of every manager's job, its volume is now rapidly escalating.[9] As today's environments continue to become much more complex and dynamic, managers must obtain, organize, and use huge amounts of information to make decisions. Businesses are recognizing that a high-speed information infrastructure can play a big part in speeding up the pace of operations, while cutting costs. Progressive managers see the potential for doing this every time they can move a transaction from paper to an electronic form, which is the basic concept of the proposed "information highway."[10]

The Information Explosion

The Association for Information and Image Management has estimated that the United States alone generates over 250 million original documents each day. The number rises to over 3.2 billion when copies and computer printouts are included.[11]

In other words, computer technology is carrying us into an era when the number of people involved in the production and distribution of knowledge and information will be vastly more numerous than the production and distribution of things.[12] The futurist John Naisbitt explained this trend best when he said that "although we continue to think we live in an industrial society, we have in fact changed to an economy based on the creation and distribution of information."[13]

One result of this development is the redistribution of power within organizations. For example, power has tended to shift from a few information holders—such as financial officers—to many other managerial and nonmanagerial employees. With practically unlimited sources of information in their own PC, these employees do not have to rely upon others for facts and figures needed to make decisions.

While we have known for years that communications media and computers were rapidly merging into an information revolution, few realized how completely human ingenuity and competitive pressures would turn it into an information revolution. But as computers routinely "talk" to one another via compact discs, phone lines, satellites, and a "million miles of fiber-optic cables networking the nation,"[14] the sharp boundaries between telephones, television, cable, and computers are blurring and will soon become indistinct.

While the first Industrial Revolution (see Chapter 2) was based on breaking up work into its component parts in order to permit mass production, this new revolution is based on unification. Thanks in part to computer networks and multimedia fusions, organizations are becoming more integrated. Enterprises are becoming so closely allied with customers and suppliers that boundaries between them seem to be dissolving. As this unification is global, rather than just national or local, it can result in business units around the world appearing to be "just down the hall." This trend is radically changing our concepts of location, distance, and time.

> Tiris—a unit of Texas Instruments—is managed out of Bedford, England; its line of low-frequency transponders are designed in Freising, Germany; and the units are produced in Kuala Lumpur, Malaysia, from where they are shipped to customers around the world.[15]

As shown in the Opening Case, the effective management of information can give managers and an entire organization a tremendous competitive advantage.

Role of Data, Information, and Systems

In order to understand fully the concept of information management, you need to view the relationships among several key components: data, systems, and information. *Data* are the raw materials from which information is derived. A *system*, as defined in Chapter 2, is an organized whole made up of inputs, processes, and outputs. *Information* is the result of manipulating or analyzing data and presenting it in a format that aids decision making.

> An example will help illustrate these distinctions. Suppose that a Dillard's store (see Opening Case) in St. Louis, as part of a special promotion, sells 23 Liz Claiborne blouses of a certain style over the weekend. This piece of *data*—23 blouses sold—is

just that: a piece of data. In itself, the number *23* is not particularly relevant to management. In order for it to become *information*, a Dillard's manager must also be given another piece of data—the projected sales of the blouses during the promotion. The manager can then know *how far over or under the sales projection* 23 blouses is.

Before data can be meaningfully converted to information, a *system* must be established to make the conversion. Three basic components are involved in converting data into information:

1. *Data input*—the raw data that are entered into the system.
2. *System processing*—system hardware (the physical equipment of the system, including computer, display screens, printers, and the like), software (computer programs), and computer personnel, all of which interact.
3. *Information output*—the reports, charts, graphs, or displays generated by the interaction of data input and system processing. The information outputs used by a large hospital are shown in Figure 15.7.

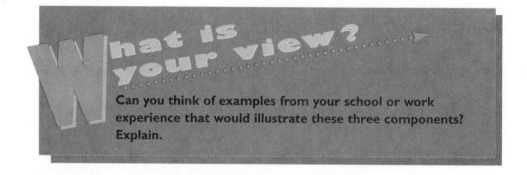

What is your view?

Can you think of examples from your school or work experience that would illustrate these three components? Explain.

Computer Technology's Role in Managing Information

Information management has been aided greatly by advances in computer technology, with its highly efficient processing capabilities. The computer has been a great benefit to management decision making, especially in exercising the control function. While information systems existed before computers, the process was tortoise-slow, costly, and the results far from timely. Today, however, computers have become a necessity for both large and small organizations. The three main types of computers with which you should be familiar are mainframe computers, minicomputers, and microcomputers.

Mainframe computers are full-scale, powerful computers capable of handling huge amounts of data and costing millions of dollars—making them feasible only for the largest organizations, such as the Social Security Administration and General Motors. **Minicomputers** are smaller, have less memory, and cost much less than mainframes. They are used by many organizations as stand-alone computers or as part of a network that could be connected to personal computers.

Microcomputers are the smallest of the computers and can be used as personal computers (PCs) or business computers. First introduced by Apple in 1978, the microcomputer has contributed greatly to the present computer revolution in business.

mainframe computers Full-scale computers capable of handling huge amounts of data and costing millions of dollars, making them feasible only for the largest corporations.

minicomputers Smaller computers with less memory than mainframes.

microcomputers The smallest computers, which are relatively inexpensive and have contributed greatly to the computer revolution.

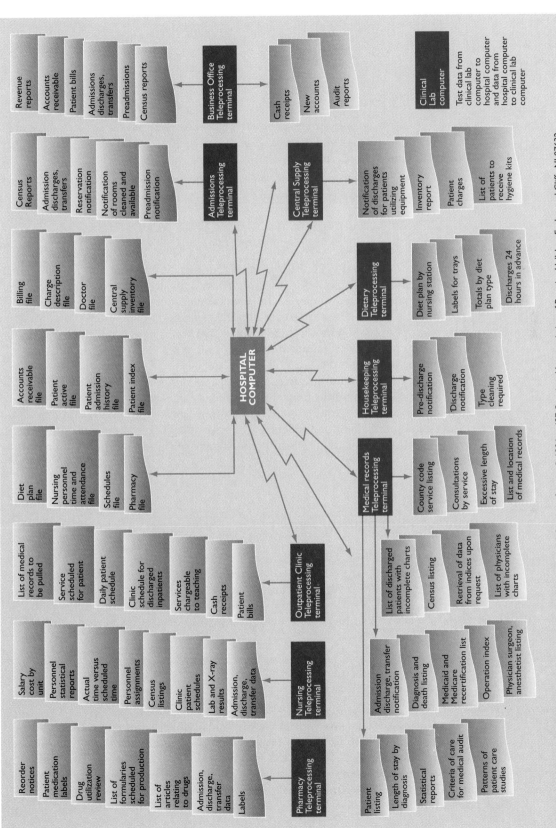

FIGURE 15.7

The information outputs of the Medical University of South Carolina hospital information system. The common database is held in the hospital computer.

Source: Barton Hodge, Robert Fleck, Jr., and C. Brian Honess, *Management Information Systems* © 1984, p. 487. Reprinted by permission of Prentice Hall, Inc., Englewood Cliffs, NJ 07632.

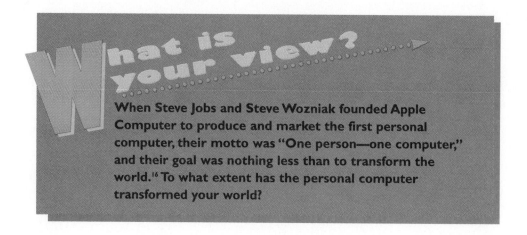

What is your view? ....▷

When Steve Jobs and Steve Wozniak founded Apple Computer to produce and market the first personal computer, their motto was "One person—one computer," and their goal was nothing less than to transform the world.[16] To what extent has the personal computer transformed your world?

The ease with which a PC can be linked to a mainframe or minicomputer means that many managers and others can use it to access the organization's central information pool or database. In some organizations, every employee has a microcomputer or *workstation*. The ease of purchasing microcomputers, along with their low-cost peripheral hardware and software packages, has also facilitated their use, especially in smaller organizations. Microsoft chief Bill Gates says this has resulted in our being in "a PC era."[17]

In Chapter 10, "Communicating for Results," you saw how computer technology has influenced communications through the use of electronic mail. Computer technology has also been applied to design (computer-assisted design) and manufacturing (computer-aided manufacturing) processes. There can be no question about it—the computer has greatly influenced the operations and processes of all organizations.

Business Information Systems

business information systems (BISs) The planned processes by which data are received, computed, stored, and converted into information to suit some business purposes.

Business information systems (BISs) are planned processes by which data are received, computed, stored, and converted into information for a business purpose. The types of BISs are (1) transaction processing systems, (2) management information systems, (3) decision support systems, and (4) executive information systems. The levels of management that make use of these four types of systems are shown in Figure 15.8.

Transaction Processing Systems

transaction processing system The most fundamental business information system, designed to assist the organization in carrying out routine business activities, such as billing or order placement.

A **transaction processing system** is the most fundamental information processing system, designed to help the organization carry out a variety of routine business activities. Common types of transactions might include placing orders, billing customers, and depositing checks, all highly structured processes. As shown in Figure 15.8, transaction processing systems occur at the operations level of an organization.

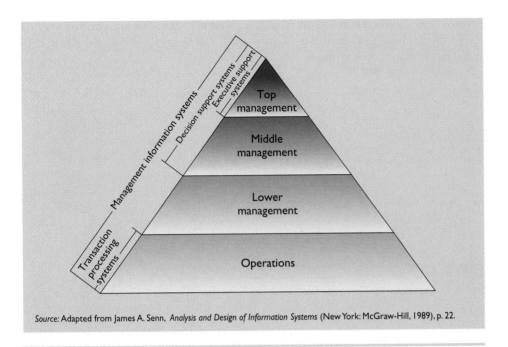

Source: Adapted from James A. Senn, *Analysis and Design of Information Systems* (New York: McGraw-Hill, 1989), p. 22.

FIGURE 15.8
Relationship of information systems to organizational level.

Management Information Systems

A **management information system (MIS)** is geared to assisting managerial decision making in well-structured, recurring situations. In structured situations, managers know what factors are needed in making the decision and what the key variables are. Common MIS systems exist for controlling inventory levels, evaluating sales and financial performance, and a wide variety of other performance aspects. Here are just a few examples of such activities:

▶ Sales status by product, territory, salesperson, and customer, with deviations and projections

▶ Production status by product, department, and plant, including orders behind schedule and reasons for the deviations

▶ Inventory position, both in terms of units or dollars and in terms of comparison with budgeted figures

▶ Personnel skills inventory for all employees, by demographic characteristics

▶ Deviations in expenses such as capital expenditures and labor and materials costs, compiled by budget center

▶ Automatic compilation of all financial ratios, with indicators comparing this information to industry norms and trends

Because the decision process is well understood, the information needed to aid control can be developed and generated on a regular basis in a predesigned

management information system (MIS) A business information system designed to provide managers with information to make decisions regarding well-structured, recurring situations.

format, like that shown in Figure 15.9. Note that management information systems affect all levels of management (Figure 15.8); their greatest use, however, is by middle-management personnel.

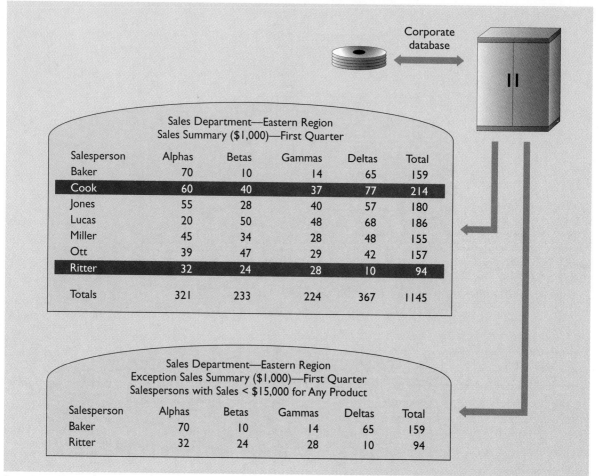

Corporate database

Sales Department—Eastern Region
Sales Summary ($1,000)—First Quarter

Salesperson	Alphas	Betas	Gammas	Deltas	Total
Baker	70	10	14	65	159
Cook	60	40	37	77	214
Jones	55	28	40	57	180
Lucas	20	50	48	68	186
Miller	45	34	28	48	155
Ott	39	47	29	42	157
Ritter	32	24	28	10	94
Totals	321	233	224	367	1145

Sales Department—Eastern Region
Exception Sales Summary ($1,000)—First Quarter
Salespersons with Sales < $15,000 for Any Product

Salesperson	Alphas	Betas	Gammas	Deltas	Total
Baker	70	10	14	65	159
Ritter	32	24	28	10	94

Source: Adapted from Larry Long, *Management Information Systems,* © 1989, p. 22. Reprinted by permission of Prentice Hall, Englewood Cliffs, NJ 07632.

FIGURE 15.9

An operational-level sales summary and exception report. These sales reports were prepared in response to an operational-level manager's request to the computer to "display a list of all eastern region sales representatives who had sales of less than $15,000 for any product this quarter." The report highlights the subpar performances of Baker and Ritter.

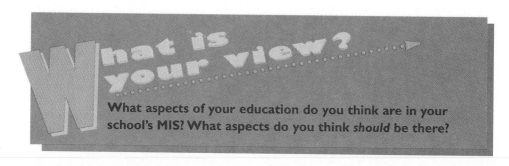

What is your view?

What aspects of your education do you think are in your school's MIS? What aspects do you think *should* be there?

MANAGEMENT APPLICATION AND PRACTICE 15.3

Implementing EIS at ICI

A survey of 700 senior managers in the United Kingdom showed that 55 percent of them desired more effective use of an EIS. In 1985, ICI, a large chemical firm, was one of the first U.K. companies to implement an EIS. By 1990, there were over 100 EIS users at the company, including seven of its board members.

ICI's system quickly and easily converts numbers such as sales, costs, profits, and market share into charts and graphs to permit easy comparison with other figures. The biggest obstacle to the system's implementation was upper managers' fear of technology. For this reason, an important criterion for the system's acceptance was simplicity, so that executives were able to move into hands-on applications after only a half-hour of training.

Source: Lesley Meall, "EIS: Sharpening the Executives' Competitive Edge," *Accounting*, vol. 106 (September 1990), pp. 125–128.

Decision Support Systems

A **decision support system (DSS)** uses computers to facilitate the managerial decision-making process for semistructured situations. Consequently, such systems apply to a broad arena of decisions that, unlike MIS-oriented decisions, have not been faced before or are faced at irregular intervals. A DSS is designed not to replace managerial judgment but to support it and make the decision process more efficient.

> **decision support systems (DSSs)** The business information systems that use computers to facilitate the managerial decision-making process in semistructured situations.

Executive Information Systems

An **executive information system (EIS),** sometimes referred to as an *executive support system*, meets top managers' need for easy access to important information presented in a simple, clearly understandable form. The availability and ease of use of microcomputers permit all sorts of data to be generated by top executives themselves in a variety of formats for communicating information visually, including tables, bar charts, graphs, and on-screen projections. Emphasis is placed on ready accessibility, rather than large quantities of data, and because of its simple format, EIS ideally requires little training time for its executive users. MAP 15.3 illustrates how a major British company implemented an EIS.

> **executive information system (EIS)** A new form of business information system, a subset of DSS, that meets top management's need for easy access to important information presented in a simple, clearly understandable form.

Organizing the Information Activity

Information systems departments vary widely among organizations, so it is not possible to describe any universal practice regarding types of positions and reporting relationships. In some smaller organizations, a single person wears all the information hats. In larger organizations, however, and in those highly dependent on accurate, timely information, information services divisions may employ hundreds or even thousands of people. For example, Merrill Lynch's information services division has over 15,000 employees and operates on a budget in excess of $1 billion. The yearly salary of the chief information officer is over $1 million.[18]

Because of the prominence of information management today, the chief information officer (CIO) typically reports to top management, usually the president or CEO. The CIO at Sears, for instance, carries the rank of senior vice-president and reports directly to the chairman and CEO.[19] Figure 15.10 shows how a small information services division could be organized in a medium-size or small organization.

Emerging Trends in Managing Information

A number of trends are emerging in the information management field. Some of these are as follows:[20]

1. *BIS users are becoming more knowledgeable.* Annually, a dramatic increase in the number of employees knowledgeable about BIS is taking place in almost all organizations. Not only have high school—and especially college—graduates been exposed to BIS; special courses are being offered both within organizations and by local universities, software companies, and equipment manufacturers.

2. *Users may call upon increasing computer power.* End users can access and control more computing power than ever before.

FIGURE 15.10
Organizational chart for small information services division.

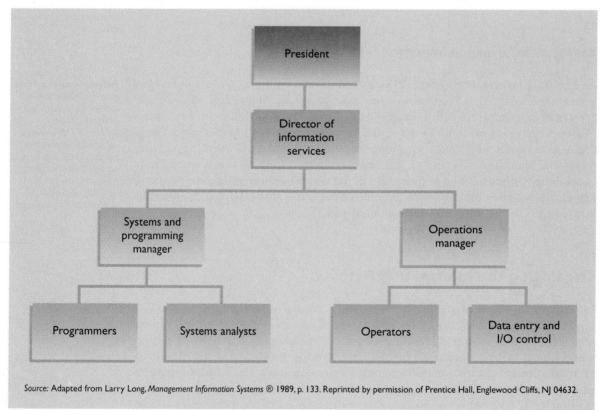

Source: Adapted from Larry Long, *Management Information Systems* ® 1989, p. 133. Reprinted by permission of Prentice Hall, Englewood Cliffs, NJ 04632.

3. *Acceptance of information system (IS) technology is continuously increasing.* While around 10 percent of the general population now considers itself computer literate,[21] this figure is increasing steadily, decreasing the organizational resistance to computer technology. This is especially true at upper-management levels.

4. *The BIS focus is shifting to the end user.* Technical IS personnel have become—and will continue to become—more customer oriented, that is, more concerned about the end users they serve. Software manufacturers are focusing more on "user-friendliness," emphasizing simplicity and formats that PC users themselves find practical. Information quality is continually increasing as a result of the end user's greater willingness to become involved in information-system-related activities.

5. *The BIS is influencing the quality of management decision making at an increasing rate.* There is focus today on the managerial decision-making potential of information systems, with applications such as MIS and DSS.

6. *The BIS is seen as a major productivity tool.* Business information systems will continue to be a major way for organizations to improve their productivity and quality. For example, information systems are capable of boosting efficiency by identifying problem areas in a more timely manner, by reducing duplication of effort, and by permitting more efficient operations, as in production, processes, and quality control. As the move toward certifications of quality programs by professional organizations expands, IS will play a pivotal role in helping companies achieve quality. For example, at the Ritz-Carlton, IS acts as a "manager" in the quality process.[22]

7. *The BIS trend is toward integration.* The technology of BIS—including hardware, software, and database products—is geared toward linkages and interfaces. This not only eliminates costly duplication of equipment but also permits more efficient use of available data and generation of more accurate, timely data.

SUMMARY

Control, which is the process of ensuring that organizational and managerial objectives are achieved, is closely related to each of the other management functions, especially planning. The basic types of control are feedforward, concurrent, and feedback.

The steps in the control process are (1) establishing performance standards, (2) measuring actual performance, (3) comparing performance with standards and analyzing deviations, and (4) taking corrective action if needed.

Management by exception (MBE) is a control technique that helps managers focus attention on exceptional deviations from standards, allowing subordinates to control routine variations.

To be effective, control systems must (1) focus on appropriate activities (2) be timely, (3) be cost-effective, (4) provide accurate information, and (5) be accepted by those involved with or affected by the control system.

Control principles operate in various ways in actual practice. Quantitative control techniques tend to use specific data and measurable criteria to evaluate and correct quantity and quality of output. The more popularly used quantitative techniques include budgets and budgetary control, audits, ratio analysis, break-even analysis, and time-performance charts and techniques, including the Gantt chart and the Program Evaluation and Review Technique (PERT).

Budgets are particularly widely used as both a planning and a control device. The primary benefit of budgetary control is that it allows comparable goals expressed in uniform financial terms to be provided for all organizational units. Also, since the budget serves as a standard of performance, deviations from this standard are readily measurable and provide the basis for corrective action.

Audits, ratio analysis, break-even analysis, and time-performance techniques are all used widely and for different purposes. While auditing is used to verify financial records and assess the overall effectiveness of management, break-even analysis can be used as a planning, decision-making, and control device.

Information management has grown tremendously in organizations during recent years. Data are the raw materials from which information is derived; a processing system manipulates and analyzes data, presenting them in the form of information that aids managerial decision making.

A business information system (BIS) is a planned process by which data are received, compiled, stored, and converted into information to serve some business purpose. Business information systems include transaction processing systems, management information systems, decision support systems, and executive information systems.

Management information systems (MISs) are geared toward helping managers make decisions in well-structured situations, especially in the area of control. The information needed to aid control can be generated in a predesigned format and can be presented on a regular basis.

Decision support systems (DSSs) deal with relatively unstructured situations. A subset of DSS is the executive information system (EIS), which aids management by presenting information that can be easily accessed in a simple, clearly understood format. A number of important trends are emerging in the BIS field, including (1) more knowledgeable users, (2) increasing computer power, (3) greater acceptance of information technology, and (4) a focus on end users of information systems.

KEY TERMS

control, 493

cybernetics, 493

feedforward control, 495

concurrent (steering) control or screening, 495

feedback (postaction) control, 496

standard, 497

management by exception (MBE) or exception principle, 500

quantitative control methods, 501

statistical quality control (SQC) techniques, 502

budgets, 503

budgetary control, 504

operating budget, 505

capital budgets, 505

production budgets, 505

sales budgets, 505

personnel budgets, 505

audits, 505

management audit, 506

ratio analysis (RA), 506

return on equity (ROE) or return on investment (ROI), 506

break-even analysis, 507

break-even point (BEP), 507

total revenue, 507
fixed costs, 507
variable costs, 507
scheduling, 509
Gantt chart, 510
Program Evaluation and Review
 Technique (PERT), 510
PERT network, 511
critical path, 511

mainframe computers, 514
minicomputers, 514
microcomputers, 514
business information systems (BISs), 516
transaction processing system, 516
management information system,
 (MIS), 517
decision support systems (DSSs), 519
executive information system (EIS), 519

DISCUSSION QUESTIONS

1. How is control related to the other functions of management?

2. Discuss the distinction between (a) feedforward, (b) concurrent, and (c) feedback controls. Why is this distinction important—if it is?

3. What steps are involved in the control process? Discuss each.

4. Name and explain the five characteristics of effective control systems.

5. The text states that a budget is both a planning and a control technique. How can this be?

6. What is break-even analysis, and how can it be used for control?

7. What is a business information system (BIS), and how can it help management?

8. In what ways is control of government or nonprofit organizations different from control of profit-seeking firms?

9. You have probably found a slip packaged with a new garment that says something like "Inspected by No. 17." Can you think of at least two ways in which this is a control device?

10. Is information management really as important as the authors claim? Defend your answer.

11. Does a small business, such as a nursery (eight employees) or a dress shop (five employees) need a business information system? Why or why not?

12. In what ways has the PC created an information revolution in organizations? Explain.

13. An entrepreneur who runs a chain of sporting goods stores in a large metropolitan area says, "The best control I have for each of my stores is their net profit picture at the end of each month. That's the overriding reason we're in business, and the only real information I need to know is whether my store managers are doing their jobs." What is your reaction to this statement?

14. Assume you are a student planning to attend college away from home. You will live in a campus dormitory, will purchase a seven-day meal ticket, and will drive your four-year-old, fully paid-for automobile as a means of transportation. Identify the fixed and variable costs you are likely to incur during the first semester of school. Is it helpful to differentiate these? Why or why not?

PRACTICING MANAGEMENT

15.1

case

The Hubble Space Telescope Fiasco

The $1.5 billion Hubble Space Telescope was designed in 1978 to be launched from a space shuttle in the mid-1980s. It was to provide spectacular views of the universe, which would help unlock the secret of how life began. But something went awfully awry!

The prime contractor, Perkin-Elmer Corporation (now a part of General Motors and known as Hughes Danbury Optical Systems Corporation), gave a subcontractor—Composite Optics Inc., of San Diego, California—blueprints with *reversed drawings* for the telescope's tower assembly guidance system. Composite Optics then had to be paid to rebuild the component to the correct specifications.

The telescope was completed around 1986, but the space shuttle program was in disarray because of the *Challenger* disaster. After spending $10 million to store the telescope, NASA placed it in orbit in April 1990—seven years behind schedule and more than $900 million over budget.

No sooner had the telescope been released from the shuttle's manipulator arm than it was beset by glitches. One of its panels got stuck while unfurling. This was corrected by the shuttle crew. Then one of its antennas got caught in an improperly installed cable, blocking the antenna's movement. Then two gyroscopes lost their balance, causing the telescope to point to the wrong place in the sky. This was corrected by rewriting the software. Next, the 25,000-pound instrument developed a vibration, which was corrected with another software patch.

Then came the crowning blow. When engineers could not fine-tune the focus between the telescope's primary and secondary mirrors, they found a fundamental flaw that may have been built in when the mirrors were manufactured. NASA engineers suspected that one of the two mirrors was ground to slightly wrong specifications. A deputy manager of the project said of the grinding, "It was done very carefully and precisely, but it was done wrong!" NASA officials said they had not tested the telescope on the ground, because it would have cost too much.

Unfortunately, this flaw could not be corrected except by installing a new set of properly ground mirrors—which could be done only by a NASA maintenance team. Because of the already crowded shuttle schedule, however, such a mission was not possible until late 1993. Then, astronauts from the shuttle *Endeavor* spent around 30 hours working in space to successfully correct the problem.

Sources: "Hubble Unbound," *Discover*, July 1990, p. 8; Lewis Grizzard, "Hubble in Big Trouble," *Eastern Shore Courier* (Fairhope, Alabama), July 14, 1990, p. 4A; Paul Gillin, "Hubble Trouble," *Computerworld*, December 13, 1993, p. 32; and Barry A. Stein and Rosabeth Moss Kanter, "Why Good People Do Bad Things: A Retrospective on the Hubble Fiasco," *Academy of Management Executive*, vol. 7 (November 1993), pp. 58–62.

Because of improperly ground mirrors, the Hubble Space Telescope could not function properly until astronauts installed corrective lenses—in 1993.

Questions

1. Throughout the text, we have emphasized the difference between *efficiency* and *effectiveness*. To what extent does this distinction apply to the statement by the deputy manager of the project about the grinding of the mirrors that "It was done very carefully and precisely, but it was done wrong!"?

2. Using the steps in the control process discussed in this chapter, explain what went wrong with this project. In other words, at what step(s) in the process did problems develop?

3. If you had been made responsible for correcting the problem, how would you have done it? For example, what control procedure would you have installed?

4. Of the characteristics of effective control systems, which one(s) was inadequate in this case?

15.1 **Controlling Bank Loans**

learning exercise

Assume the morning issue of your favorite newspaper carried a headline that read, "Local Bank Sustains Loan Loss of $30 Million." The article stated that a 51-year-old vice-president had the authority to grant loans of up to $3 million without anyone's approval. This officer had made a series of questionable loans to some of the bank's new borrowers that had resulted in the $30 million loss. As each of the loans had been for less than $3 million, he had not sought anyone's approval.

In defending the bank's policy, a senior bank officer stated in the article, "If you have a bank the size of this one and you don't give people independent lending judgment, the bank will come to a screeching halt."

In general, this bank is a well-managed and successful organization. In this situation, however, the bank lacked effective controls.

Question

1. Assume you were called in as a consultant to install a control system to prevent this type loss in the future. What kind of control system(s) would you install? Why?

Guts, brains, and determination—key ingredients of the American entrepreneurial spirit—have sustained the nation through good times and bad, and launched it on an economic journey unlike any ever witnessed in history.

—JOHN SLOAN, JR.,
PRESIDENT AND CEO,
NATIONAL FEDERATION
OF INDEPENDENT
BUSINESS

Entrepreneurship and Small-Business Management

LEARNING OBJECTIVES

After studying the material in this chapter, you should be able to:

▸ **Discuss** the rewards and challenges of being an entrepreneur.

▸ **Describe** how to become an entrepreneur.

▸ **Discuss** some of the unique problems of managing human resources in a small business.

▸ **Debate** the relationships between government assistance to, and regulation of, small businesses.

▸ **Explain** the growing trend toward family-owned businesses.

▸ **Discuss** the need for tax and estate planning.

Bill Bowerman and Philip Knight of Nike, Inc.

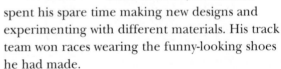

Nike, Inc., designs, manufactures, and markets a wide variety of athletic footwear, apparel, and related items for competitive and recreational uses. At the same time, it tries to maintain its premier position in the industry through quality production, innovative products, and aggressive marketing. Through visionary ideas and strong leadership from its cofounders, Bill Bowerman and Philip Knight, Nike has become the forerunner of its industry—setting a standard by which other athletic shoes are measured. But Nike was not always as respected as it is today.

Nike had very modest beginnings. As track coach at the University of Oregon in the mid-1950s, Bill Bowerman believed he knew what caused most of the shinsplints and other leg ailments his runners suffered—poorly designed athletic shoes. During this time, there was little variety to choose from as far as track shoes were concerned. Other than those for tennis shoes, the only athletic shoe suppliers were two large foreign firms that Bowerman did not think satisfied the need.

Realizing that a new athletic shoe was needed with a heel wedge to offer better support and a lighter sole to provide more stability and traction, Bowerman designed a shoe for his track team. After being turned down by a leading sporting goods company and many other firms, he decided to make the shoe himself. With the help of a friend from a local shoe repair shop, Bowerman cut out white kid leather for the uppers, reinforced them with nylon, set removable spikes in the soles, glued everything together with a strong adhesive, and made his first pair of shoes—which happened to weigh about half as much as regular track shoes. He then let some of his track team members try them on. Philip Knight, one of the runners, approved the shoes by saying, "That feels good!" From then on, Bowerman

Philip Knight, cofounder of Nike, Inc.

spent his spare time making new designs and experimenting with different materials. His track team won races wearing the funny-looking shoes he had made.

In 1962, while Bowerman was busy coaching and creating new designs, Philip Knight was completing a research paper for a graduate course at Stanford. The paper asserted that

Most people seek a sense of meaning, identity, creativity, independence, and achievement in their work and in their lives. One of the best ways to achieve this goal is to become the owner of your own business. Starting and managing a small business, however, is a complex, challenging, rewarding, and sometimes frustrating occupation, as shown in the Opening Case. Success as an entrepreneur requires knowledge, desire, and hard work—plus a little bit of luck.

Germany's domination of the U.S. athletic shoe industry could be ended with low-priced, high-tech, well-merchandised imports from Japan. After receiving his MBA in 1962, Knight went to Japan and convinced Onitsuka Tiger company of the great marketing opportunities in the United States for new shoes. When asked during the meeting whom he represented, Knight made up a company called Blue Ribbon Sports.

Upon returning to the United States, Knight contacted Bowerman and informed him that if they each came up with $500, they would have exclusive United States distribution rights. Thus the partnership began.

In early 1963, Blue Ribbon Sports received its first shipment of shoes from Japan. And with college athletes selling the shoes part-time out of their car trunks, the company earned $8,000 in revenues by 1964—a little over a year after it started. In 1971, with Philip Knight as president, Blue Ribbon Sports changed its name to Nike, Inc., after the Greek goddess of victory. As president of Nike, Knight's responsibilities included handling all the financial operations and other daily business of the company, while Bowerman's job was to offer new design ideas.

Bowerman continued to help the company with his breakthrough ideas. One morning, while sitting at the breakfast table, he noticed his wife making waffles and inspiration struck. After breakfast, he borrowed the waffle iron and proceeded to pour synthetic rubber into it, making a revolutionary shoe. Nike patented the waffle outsole, which offered better traction, in a lighter-weight, more durable shoe and began selling it in 1974. It quickly became the best-selling training shoe in the country, and Nike's revenues reached $4.8 million by the end of that year.

After its common stock offering to the public in 1980, Nike continued to have record increases in revenues. The company has managed to gain and keep the top spot in the U.S. market, being surpassed by Reebok only once, in 1986. Today, Nike focuses on penetrating foreign markets to increase earnings growth. With Knight and Bowerman behind the efforts, Nike is sure to make an impact.

At Nike, the old saying "If it ain't broke, don't fix it" has been revised to "If it ain't broke, then break it and make it better." This sums up the entrepreneurial philosophy that has made Nike a leader in its industry. Problems may arise and things may not go as planned, but Bowerman and Knight somehow manage to find a way to "just do it."

At age 56, Philip Knight is still as successful as ever as chairman of the board and CEO. Bill Bowerman, age 83, has taken a more relaxed position in the company with advancing age but is still deputy chairman of the board of directors and senior vice-president.[1]

Prepared by Donna Counselman, University of Mobile.

This chapter explores the role of entrepreneurs and small-business owners and their growing prominence in today's economy. It also discusses the reasons for and against owning such firms and stresses up-to-date thinking in planning, starting, organizing, and operating a small business. It explains how to achieve optimum benefits from the limited resources available to small firms and how to plan for growth and succession.

Rewards and Challenges of Being an Entrepreneur

Being an entrepreneur can be rewarding in many ways. First, managing a firm you yourself have created brings a certain satisfaction that does not come from directing a business others have built. Second, a small business can win its owner a position of prestige in the community; the owner can become active in the community, which in turn may help the business. Third, business ownership can provide the opportunity to make a great deal of money and can offer certain tax advantages.

Entrepreneurs also must face many challenges, such as inadequate management. During the early life of a small business, some owners tend to rely on one-person management. These owners tend to guard their positions jealously and may not select qualified employees. As you will see later, there are also problems of inadequate working capital, government regulations and paperwork, and growth. Still, if you have a strong need for independence and for being your own boss and are a risk taker, you may want to investigate a career in small business and become an entrepreneur.

Being an Entrepreneur Can Satisfy the "American Dream"

This is a challenging and rewarding time to be studying entrepreneurship and small-business management. Owning and operating your own business are one of the best ways to fulfill the "American Dream." More than four out of ten Americans believe this is one of the best paths to riches in the United States.[2] Every year, around three-quarters of a million people in the United States turn this dream of owning a business into a reality, and many of these dreams become true success stories—look at Wal-Mart, McDonald's, Dell Computer Corporation, Apple, and Hewlett-Packard.

Reasons for the increased interest in entrepreneurship and small business include:

1. The number of small businesses is growing rapidly.
2. Small firms generate most new employment.
3. The number of courses in small business is increasing at colleges and universities.
4. Small businesses are attractive to people of all ages.

The Number of Small Businesses Is Growing Rapidly   The development of small businesses in the United States since World War II is truly an amazing story. As an economic power, U.S. small businesses rank third in the world, behind only the U.S. economy as a whole and the Japanese economy.[3] The U.S. Small Business Administration (SBA) estimates that there are 20 million small companies in the United States, and that number is growing rapidly.

More important than the total number of small companies, though, is the fact that the number of such firms is growing by about 750,000 to 1 million every year, and only one out of nine of them fail. Corporate downsizing has tremendously increased the interest in entrepreneurship. Many former corporate executives have turned to creating their own business as a viable alternative to unemployment or forced inactivity.

These trends are apparently here to stay. So the future of small firms, as a group, is bright, even if some individual businesses do fail.

Small Firms Generate Most New Employment According to R. Wendell Moore, an SBA official, firms with fewer than 500 employees, representing slightly over half of all private employment, produce the most jobs. From 1988 to 1990, in fact, small businesses created 3,107,000 net new jobs, while companies with over 500 employees lost 501,000 jobs.[4] From 1988 through 1991, small companies *"added all net new jobs in the United States."* [5] As Figure 16.1 shows, 80 percent of employees work for companies with fewer than 500 employees.

The Number of Courses in Small Business Is Increasing at Colleges and Universities Another indication of the growing favor of entrepreneurship is its acceptance as part of the mission of many colleges and universities, where entrepreneurship and small-business management are now an academically respected discipline.[6]

FIGURE 16.1
Percentage distribution of business establishments and employees by size of employer.

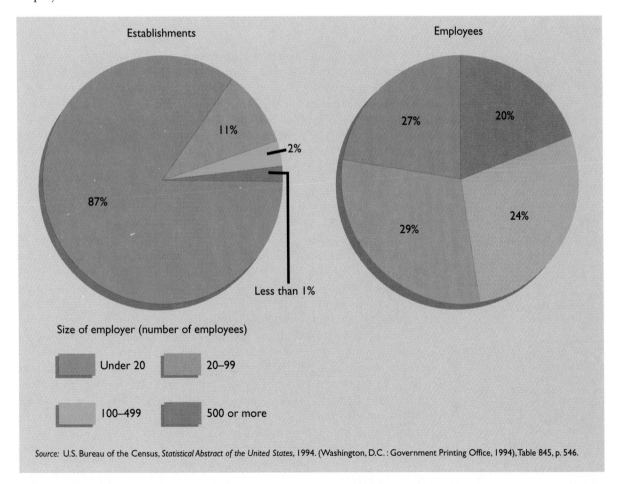

Source: U.S. Bureau of the Census, *Statistical Abstract of the United States*, 1994. (Washington, D.C.: Government Printing Office, 1994), Table 845, p. 546.

Community colleges, especially, are now offering courses for small-business owners. According to a representative of the American Association of Community and Junior Colleges, this activity is "one of the fastest-growing areas in the community college field."[7]

> A long-running survey by the Higher Education Research Institute at the University of California at Los Angeles show that America's students are attracted to the entrepreneurial life. For example, 42 percent of college freshmen in 1991 said succeeding in their own business was "essential" or "very important" to them.[8] Also, many student organizations are being formed on college campuses to encourage entrepreneurship. For example, the Association of Collegiate Entrepreneurs (ACE), founded in 1983 at Wichita State University, now has hundreds of chapters throughout the world.[9] ACE found in one study that a third of all new companies are started by people under 30, many of whom have made their fortunes in computers or high-tech industries. Other such student organizations include the University Entrepreneurial Association (UEA) and Students in Free Enterprise (SIFE).

Small Businesses Are Attractive to People of All Ages   Entrepreneurship knows no age limits. From the very young to the very old, people are starting new businesses at a rapid rate. Particularly heartening is the large number of teenagers and other young people who are now starting small businesses.

> Howard Stubbs is proud of being called "Mr. Hot Dog" in the South Bronx, an area of burned-out buildings, rubble-strewn streets, and open drug deals. Stubbs, a 15-year-old student, borrowed $800 from relatives and friends to buy an umbrella-topped hot dog cart. He buys hot dogs—with all the trimmings— for 33 cents and sells them for $1, while 20-cent sodas sell for 75 cents. Working at his stand on weekends, school holidays, and during summer vacations, he was grossing $10,000 per year after two years. He also cuts his friends' hair—for $5.[10]

What Is a Small Business, an Entrepreneurial Venture, and Intrapreneurship?

small business Any independently owned and operated business that is not dominant in its field and does not engage in new or innovative practices.

mom-and-pop operation Another term for a small business.

entrepreneurial venture A venture in which the principal objectives of the owner are profitability and growth.

small-business owner One who establishes a business primarily to further personal goals, including making a profit.

At this point, we need to distinguish among a small business, an entrepreneurial venture, and intrapreneurship. A **small business**—often called a **mom-and-pop operation**—is any business that is independently owned and operated, is not dominant in its field, and does not engage in many new or innovative practices. It may never grow large, and the owners may not want it to, as they tend to prefer a more relaxed and less aggressive approach to running the business. In other words, they manage the business in a normal way, expecting normal sales, profits, and growth.

On the other hand, an **entrepreneurial venture** is one in which the principal objectives of the entrepreneur are profitability and growth. The business, therefore, is characterized by innovative strategic practices and/or products. The entrepreneurs and their financial backers are usually seeking rapid growth, immediate—and high—profits, and a quick sellout with—possibly—large capital gains.

It is not easy to distinguish between a small-business owner and an entrepreneur, for the distinction hinges on the person's intentions. In general, a **small-business owner** establishes a business for the principal purpose of furthering personal goals, which *may* include making a profit. Thus, the owner may perceive the business as being an extension of his or her personality, which is interwoven with family needs and desires.

On the other hand, an **entrepreneur**—who is an innovative risk taker—starts and manages a business for many reasons, including achievement, profit, and growth. Such a person is characterized principally by innovative behavior and will employ strategic management practices in the business.

With the explosion of innovations in small, service types of organizations, one of the most pressing problems facing executives of large organizations is how to develop the new products and services needed to compete in new and rapidly expanding markets. One answer may be the encouragement of **intrapreneurship**— allowing people the freedom to take an entrepreneurial role to develop new products or services in large organizations. This arrangement involves executives encouraging their employees and managers to come up with new products and ideas for business opportunities. The payoff for the executives is enhanced visibility, prestige, and position.

entrepreneur The goals of an entrepreneur—who is an innovative risk taker—include growth, achieved through innovation and strategic management.

intrapreneurship The practice of allowing people the freedom to take an entrepreneurial role in large, bureaucratic organizations.

> IBM used the intrapreneurial approach when developing and introducing the IBM-PC. It assigned a group of its executives and employees to set up an entirely new division—separate and distinct from the existing organization—to develop the new consumer product. This group formed a new organization, established a separate headquarters and plant, and organized research, design, production, and marketing divisions. The reason for this arrangement? The "old" IBM was oriented toward selling its products to commercial, industrial, and not-for-profit buyers. The PC was oriented toward the consumer. The group that developed the PC is a classic example of the matrix type organization, as discussed in Chapter 8.

What Is Small?

What is a small business? The question may seem easy to answer, but it is not. Many firms you patronize—such as independent neighborhood grocery stores, fast-food restaurants, barbershops or beauty salons, dry cleaners, and campus record shops—are examples of small businesses. However, even with 8,500 employees, the SBA once classified American Motors as a small business eligible for a small-business loan. Why? Because American Motors was small compared to its mammoth competitors—Chrysler (which bought it in 1987), General Motors, and Ford. Perhaps the best definition of small business is the one used by Congress in the Small Business Act of 1953, which states that a small business is one that is independently owned and operated and is not dominant in its field of operation.[11]

Some Unique Contributions of Small Businesses

Small businesses make some of the major contributions that set them apart from larger firms. Smaller firms tend to

1. Encourage innovation and flexibility
2. Generate employment
3. Provide employees with comprehensive learning experiences

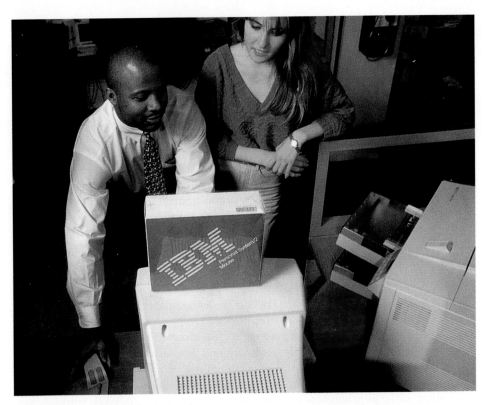

The IBM-PC resulted from the efforts of a small group of employees using the intrapreneurial spirit.

Encourage Innovation and Flexibility   Small companies are often sources of new ideas, materials, processes, and services that large firms are unable or unwilling to provide. Many of today's common products—such as the airplane, auto, air conditioner, instant camera, office copier, heart pacemaker, foam fire extinguisher, sliced and wrapped bread, zipper, safety razor, and computer—emerged from the creativity found in small companies or entrepreneurships. For example, with the outbreak of World War II, there was a need for a machine that could rapidly and precisely calculate artillery trajectories. Dr. John Mauchly and J. Presper Eckert received funding and developed the ENIAC to do that. The team then founded its own company to develop the giant UNIVAC, which was the first business application of computer technology.[12]

Generate Employment   As repeatedly emphasized throughout this chapter, small businesses generate employment by creating job opportunities. A 1992 study by the commissioner and former commissioner of the Bureau of Labor Statistics found that 20 million such jobs were created during the 1980s.[13] Many of these were meaningful, high-paying positions.

Provide Employees with Comprehensive Learning Experiences   Small firms also serve as a training ground for employees who then go on to larger businesses as experienced workers. With their more comprehensive learning experiences, their emphasis on risk taking, and their exposure to innovation and flexibility, these people become valued employees of the larger companies.

> After learning the basics of retailing while working for J. C. Penney in Iowa, Sam Walton and his younger brother, J. L., bought a Ben Franklin Store in Arkansas. They soon owned 15 "Walton's 5 & 10" stores. After failing to interest Ben Franklin executives in the discount store concept, Sam opened his own store, Wal-Mart, in Rogers, Arkansas, in 1962. The rest is history.[14]

Some Problems Facing Small Businesses

Just as small companies make some unique contributions, some special problems affect them more than larger businesses. The major problems that can result in limited profitability and growth or in financial failure are

1. Inadequate financing
2. Limited management knowledge and/or experience
3. Burdensome government regulations and paperwork
4. Inadequate planning for growth

Inadequate Financing Notice in the list above that inadequate financing is one of the primary causes of new business failures. It *cannot be stressed enough that the shortage of capital is the greatest problem facing small-business owners.* Without adequate start-up or operating funds, an owner cannot acquire and maintain facilities, hire and reward capable employees, produce and market a good or service, or do the other things necessary to run a successful business. In fact, two small-business consultants have documented that most start-up businesses fail because of undercapitalization. A later study for the SBA, done by CERA Economics Consultants, Inc., reached the same conclusions.[15]

Limited Management Knowledge and/or Experience Inadequate management, in the forms of limited business knowledge, poor management, insufficient planning, and inexperience, is the second major problem facing small firms. Many owners tend to rely on one-person management and seem reluctant to vary from this managerial pattern. They tend to guard their positions jealously and may not select qualified employees, or may fail to give them enough authority and responsibility to manage adequately.

Most small businesses are started because someone is good at a specific activity or trade, not because of managerial skill.

> This is what happened to Adam Osborne, a publisher of computer books. In 1979, he sold his printing company to McGraw-Hill and used the proceeds to build a portable computer that was used in Afghanistan to file news reports and in the wilds of Kenya to do zoological research. By early 1983, Osborne Computer Corporation was selling 10,000 units per month, for annual revenues of over $100 million. While he had the engineering expertise to design computers, Adam Osborne did not have the management savvy to run a large, expanding company.

Neither did Robert Jaunich II, who was brought in to replace him. Later that year, the company filed for Chapter 11 bankruptcy.[16]

Burdensome Government Regulations and Paperwork   If you want to upset small-business managers, just mention government regulations and paperwork. That is one of their least favorite subjects—and with good reason. At one time, smaller firms were exempt from most federal and state regulations. Now, though, small firms are subject to many of the same regulations as their larger competitors. These regulations are often complex and contradictory, which explains why small-business managers find it so difficult to comply with governmental requirements. While most businesspeople do not purposely evade the issues or disobey the law, they are often just unaware of the regulations and requirements. But, as will be shown later, small businesses often benefit from many of these regulations.

Inadequate Planning for Growth   Historically, the ownership and management of small firms have tended to follow the pattern shown in Figure 16.2. During Stage 1, the owner manages the business and does all the work—possibly with the help of family members. In Stage 2, the owner hires workers to help with the work and routine of management activities as business expands, but she or he still manages the company. In Stage 3, though, professional managers are hired to run the business. At that point, the business takes on the form, characteristics, and many of the problems of a big business.

Growth is a paradox for entrepreneurs. First, if the new owners are incapable, inefficient, or lacking in initiative, their businesses will probably flounder and eventually fail. If the owners are only mediocre, their firms will either fail or remain small. But if the entrepreneurs are efficient and capable and their businesses succeed and grow, they risk losing the very things they seek from their efforts. If the firms become large enough to require outside capital for future success and growth, the owners may lose control, as the following example illustrates.

FIGURE 16.2
Stages in the development of a small business.

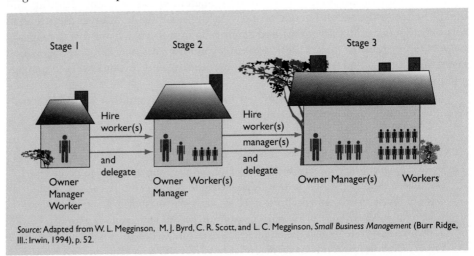

Source: Adapted from W. L. Megginson, M. J. Byrd, C. R. Scott, and L. C. Megginson, *Small Business Management* (Burr Ridge, Ill.: Irwin, 1994), p. 52.

Apple Computer was founded in 1976 by two design geniuses—Steven Jobs, 21, and Steve Wozniak, 19. Jobs sold his Volkswagen microbus and Wozniak sold his Hewlett-Packard scientific calculator to finance the venture out of Jobs's home. From then until 1980, they were able to get by without outside financing. When they sold stock to the public, Jobs was worth $165 million and Wozniak, $88 million. As they could not successfully manage Apple's day-to-day operations, they hired John Scully away from PepsiCo to manage the floundering firm. As the business grew, the men lost control of it. In 1985, after a dispute with Scully, Wozniak sold all of his stock, and Jobs sold all except one share. Wozniak then founded Cloud 9, and Jobs founded NeXT, Inc.[17]

Characteristics of Successful Entrepreneurs

The abilities and personal characteristics of the owner(s) exert a powerful influence on the success of a small business. Also, the methods and procedures adopted in such a firm should be designed not only to offset any personal deficiencies the owner may have but also to build on his or her strengths.

What characterizes successful business owners? One set of such characteristics was suggested by 2,740 readers of *Venture* magazine who responded to the following question: "What types of persons become entrepreneurs, and what psychological factors influence their future in business—and in life?"[18] The results showed that most of these entrepreneurs were firstborn children who had a positive relationship with their fathers. Over 36 percent had held jobs before they were 15 years old, and 23 percent started their first business before they turned 20. Typically, these entrepreneurs were dedicated to their businesses, had a strong sense of enterprise, and were usually hard at work by 7:30 A.M. Ninety-five percent had completed high school, 64 percent had graduated from college, and 30 percent held a postgraduate degree.

A new study of mostly longtime small-business owners by the U.S. Trust Co. generated similar results. Nearly half of them were from poor or lower-middle-class families. On average, they began their careers with a part-time job, such as a paper route at age 10. By 18, they were working full-time, and by 29, they owned their own businesses. While 6 percent dropped out of high school, 23 percent got a high school diploma, another 27 percent had some college, 29 percent finished college, and 17 percent completed professional or graduate school. *Three out of four financed their own college education by working.* On the average, they currently worked 60 hours per week and took only two weeks' vacation each year.[19]

Profile of Small Business Managers

From these and other studies, we can draw the following profile of successful owners of small businesses. In general, they

1. Desire independence
2. Have a strong sense of initiative
3. Expect quick and concrete results

4. Are able to react quickly
5. Enter business as much by chance as by design

Desire Independence   As shown earlier in this chapter, people who start small businesses seek independence and want to be free of outside control. They enjoy the freedom that comes from "doing their own thing" and making their own decisions—for better or for worse.

> Ross Perot left a lucrative job with IBM in 1962 because his suggestion to emphasize software rather than hardware had twice been turned down by IBM's top management. In a search for independence, Perot founded EDS, a data processing firm, which he later sold to GM for several billion dollars.

Have a Strong Sense of Initiative   Owners of small businesses tend to have a strong sense of initiative that gives them a desire to use their ideas, abilities, and aspirations to the greatest degree feasible. They are able to conceive, plan, and carry to a successful conclusion ideas for a good or service.

> Sears was started in 1886 when a batch of watches could not be delivered to the store that had ordered them. Richard W. Sears, a stationmaster and telegraph agent at Redwood, Minnesota, decided to buy the watches and peddle them rather than bothering to return them to the shipper. He was so successful that he left his job and started R. W. Sears Watch Co.[20]

Expect Quick and Concrete Results   Small-business owners expect quick and concrete results from their investment of time and capital. Instead of engaging in the long-range planning that is common in large businesses, they usually seek a quick return on their capital. And they tend to become impatient and discouraged when these results are slow in coming.

> After working as a short-order cook for several years, R. David Thomas accepted a job with a friend in Columbus, Ohio, who owned four Kentucky Fried Chicken restaurants that were on the verge of collapse. Thomas's ingenuity and hard work saved the company and made him a millionaire by the age of 35. He opened his first Wendy's in 1969.[21]

Are Able to React Quickly   Small businesses have an advantage over larger firms in that they can react more quickly to changes taking place in the environment. For example, one characteristic of a small business is its vulnerability to technological and environmental changes. Because the business is small, such changes have a great effect on its operations and profitability. A small-business owner must therefore have the ability to react quickly, as shown by the following example.

> In 1847, 17-year-old Levi Strauss emigrated from Bavaria to America. After peddling clothing and household items from door to door in New York for three years, he sailed by clipper ship to California to peddle tents to gold miners. There was little demand for tents but great demand for durable working clothes. So, the ever

adaptable Strauss had a tailor make the unsold cloth into waist-high overalls, called them Levi's, and was in business.[22]

Enter Business as Much by Chance as by Design An interesting characteristic of many small-business owners is that they get into business as much by chance as by design.

> Frederick Smith wrote a term paper when he was in college that showed the feasibility of rapid delivery of freight by truck and plane. Although the paper received a low grade, Smith founded Federal Express a few years later when he inherited a small fortune.[23]

Need for an Introspective Personal Analysis

Now that you have seen some of the characteristics of successful small-business owners, do you think you have enough of those characteristics to be successful? If so, do Learning Exercise 16.1: Test Your Potential as an Entrepreneur to see if you do. The results will help you make a decision about this important question. No one of these items is more important than any other; rather, you need to determine whether the combination of qualities you have will help you succeed as the owner of your own business.

Growing Opportunities for Entrepreneurs

As indicated earlier, the opportunities for you to become an entrepreneur are practically unlimited. Figure 16.3 gives you a road map of the entrepreneurial process. The process begins when a person has an idea for a new product or service to meet consumer needs. He or she organizes the business; puts up the money for buildings, such as a plant, office, or store; buys the necessary equipment and materials; hires and trains employees; and begins production or operations. The sales resulting from operations bring in revenue, which is used to pay expenses. What is left over is either profit or loss, the reward or penalty for the owner's risk taking.

What the Opportunities Are

While new entrepreneurs may start small, they can eventually become large and profitable.

> Cliffs Notes, Inc., began in 1958, when Clifton Hillegass, age 40, was given rights to course outlines for 16 of Shakespeare's plays. Since he was working as a buyer and seller of college texts at the time, Hillegass hesitated. But then he borrowed $4,000 from the bank and started printing copies of the outlines, while his wife typed some 1,000 letters to college bookstores on a portable typewriter. They have never looked back! Today, Cliffs Notes has an 80 percent market share, and in the late 1980s Hillegass recently turned down a $70 million offer for his company.[24]

Cliff Notes, Inc., chairman Clifton Hillegass.

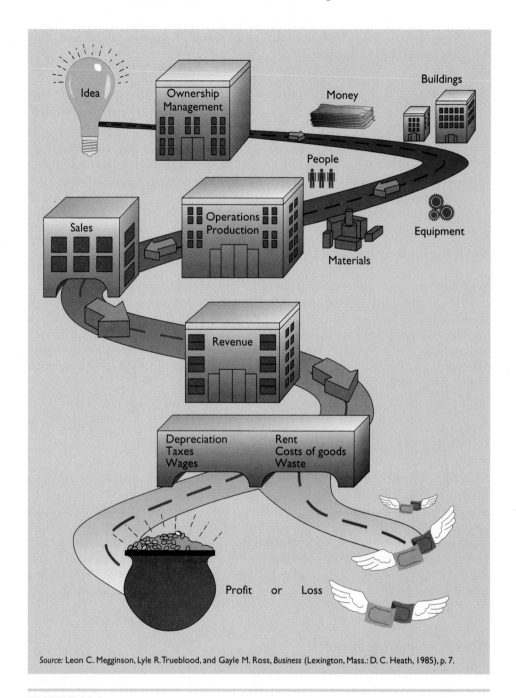

Source: Leon C. Megginson, Lyle R. Trueblood, and Gayle M. Ross, *Business* (Lexington, Mass.: D. C. Heath, 1985), p. 7.

FIGURE 16.3
How a business is formed and operates.

Entrepreneurial opportunities are particularly favorable for women. The number of companies owned by women has grown rapidly, and women are now starting businesses at twice the rate of men. In 1993, women owned over one-third of all small companies.[25] They founded 70 percent of all new firms in 1991,[26] and they are expected to own half the nation's small businesses by the year 2000.[27] Table 16.1 lists the top 25 women-owned businesses, classified by amount of revenue in 1991.

TABLE 16.1   TOP 25 WOMEN-OWNED BUSINESSES, BY REVENUE

Name, title	Company, location	Business	'91 revenue (millions)
Antonia Axson Johnson, chairwoman	Axel Johnson Group, Stockholm, Sweden	Shipping	$829
Gretchen Minyard Williams and Liz Minyard, co-chairwomen	Minyard Food Stores, Coppell, Texas	Grocery stores	$700
Linda Wachner, chairwoman, CEO	Warnaco Group, New York	Lingerie	$548
Donna Steigerwaldt, chairwoman, CEO	Jockey Intl., Kenosha, Wis.	Apparel	$450
Susie Tompkins, creative director	Esprit, San Francisco	Clothing	$450
Norma Paige, chairwoman	Astronautics, Milwaukee	Satellite systems	$415
Jenny Craig, vice chairwoman	Jenny Craig, Del Mar, Calif.	Weight-loss	$412
Helen Copley, chairwoman, CEO	Copley Newspapers, La Jolla, Calif.	Newspapers	$405
Barbara Levy Kipper, chairwoman	Chas. Levy, Chicago	Distributor	$350
Annabelle Fetterman, chairwoman	Lundy Packing, Clinton, N.C.	Pork	$350
Bettye Martin Musham, CEO	Gear Holdings, New York	Furniture design	$280
Linda Johnson Rice, CEO, president	Johnson Publishing, Chicago	Publishing	$252
Dian Graves Owen, chairwoman, co-CEO	Owen Healthcare, Houston	Pharm. supplies	$250
Carole Little, co-founder, co-chair	Carole Little, Los Angeles	Clothing	$205
Linda Jane Lewis-Brent, vice-chair, CEO	Sunshine Jr. Stores, Panama City, Fla.	Convenience stores	$203
Ellen Gordon, president	Tootsie Roll, Chicago	Candy	$200
Donna Karan, CEO	Donna Karan Co., New York	Clothing	$200
Dorothy Owen, chairwoman	Owen Steel, Columbia, S.C.	Steel	$192
Christel DeHann, CEO, president	Resort Condominiums Intl., Indianapolis	Real estate dev.	$180
Adrienne Vittadini, chairwoman	Adrienne Vittadini, New York	Clothing	$160
Lillian Vernon, CEO	Lillian Vernon, Mt. Vernon, N.Y.	Mail order	$160
Helen Jo Whitsell, chairwoman, CEO	Copeland Lumber Yards, Portland	Lumber	$152
Judy Sims, CEO	Software Spectrum, Garland, Texas	Software	$146
Paula Kent Meehan, chairwoman, CEO	Redken Laboratories, Canoga Park,Calif..	Beauty supplies	$140
Lois Rust, president	Rose Acre Farms, Seymour, Ind.	Eggs	$127

Source: *Working Woman* magazine, as reported in Desiree French, "Magazine Names Top Female Entrepreneurs," *USA Today*, April 23, 1992, p. 2B.

Opportunities for Minorities   Entrepreneurship also offers many opportunities for minorities, including African Americans, Hispanics, and Asians.

Opportunities for African Americans.   Small firms hire 10.5 times as many blacks as do larger firms. During the middle to late 1980s, the number of black businesses grew almost three times as rapidly as all U.S. companies.[28] And according to *Black Enterprise* magazine, revenues of the 100 largest black-owned firms grew 50 percent faster than those of the Fortune 500.[29]

The role of black entrepreneurs is fast changing. From opening mom-and-pop businesses, they are now forming companies in electronics, computers, advertising, real estate development, insurance, health care, and automobile dealerships.[30] Also, big companies—such as United Airlines, Pizza Hut, and Kraft Foods—are now helping blacks start small companies.

Among the top black entrepreneurs in the United States are Earvin "Magic" Johnson, co-owner of Pepsi-Cola of Washington, D.C.; John Johnson, owner of *Ebony*, *Jet*, and *EM* magazines; Herman Russell, owner of H. J. Russell & Co.; Earl Graves, owner of *Black Enterprise* magazine and co-owner of Pepsi-Cola of Washington, D.C.; Russell Simmons, owner of Rush Communications and Def Jam Records; Clarence Avant, owner of World African Network; Andre Harrell, owner of Uptown Entertainment; and Oprah Winfrey, owner of Harpo Productions, Inc. (see Case 16.1 at the end of this chapter).[31]

Opportunities for Hispanics.   Hispanics are also forming small firms at a record rate, especially in California, Texas, and Florida. They are particularly active in the food industry, and are now moving into the supermarket arena. The Hispanic food market is the fastest growing in the country, and Hispanic entrepreneurs are trying to cash in on it.

Opportunities for Asians.   Asians have a tradition of self-employment. And the deluge of Asian immigrants into the United States is resulting in a flood of new small businesses. In fact, there are now 57 Asian-owned companies in the United States for every 1,000 Asians.[32]

In addition to their tradition of self-employment, Asian entrepreneurs also receive considerable support from cultural networks when they form a business.

> Dae Song, age 36, could speak no English when he arrived in Baltimore. After learning the dry-cleaning business, he formed his own business. He received $30,000 in loans—and advice and other assistance—from a 30-member Korean support group. He in turn helped other Koreans start businesses.[33]

Husband-and-Wife Businesses   According to the Small Business Administration's Office of Advocacy, the fastest-growing category of new businesses during the 1990s will be jointly managed husband-and-wife-owned businesses. The number of such enterprises nearly doubled during the 1980s, as shown in MAP 16.1, a profile of Lalla Shanna and her husband, Rinaldo S. Brutoco, co-owners of a $16 million-a-year San Francisco gift shop and mail-order firm.[34]

How to Become an Entrepreneur

You have seen the many reasons for starting a small business and some of the available opportunities. Those who do decide to take the important step of starting their own business must do extensive planning in order to increase their chances of success. Now we would like to explain how to actually go into business—if that is what you would like to do.[35] The following steps are usually required:

1. Search for and identify a needed good or service.
2. Study the market for the good or service, using as many sources of information as feasible.
3. Decide whether to start a new business, buy an existing one, or buy a franchise.
4. Make strategic and operational plans and formalize them into a business plan.

Many business owners fail because they see the glamour of some businesses—and the apparent ease with which they are run—and think, "I know I can make a lot of money if I start my own business." While a few do succeed without adequate prepa-

MANAGEMENT APPLICATION AND PRACTICE 16.1

Red Rose Collections, Inc. Hits Inc's Top 500 List

The highly successful, San Francisco–based corporation Red Rose Collections, Inc., was founded in July 1986 as a proprietorship, mail-order company operating out of the garage of its founders, Lalla Shanna and Rinaldo S. Brutoco. From this small beginning, the Brutocos have turned their proprietorship into a corporation that in 1993 earned $16 million in profits. It has been listed on the *Inc.* 500 list, which recognizes the fastest-growing private companies in America, for three years. Red Rose is also recognized as one of the top 100 fastest-growing privately held companies in the San Francisco Bay Area.

The founders of this corporation are one reason why the business has been so successful. Rinaldo S. Brutoco holds the title of chairman of the board, chief executive officer, president, and chief operating officer. He is considered to be the brains of the business aspects, while his wife (and cofounder of Red Rose), Lalla Shanna Brutoco, the creative genius, holds the title of vice-president/merchandising and creative director. She is responsible for merchandise selection and the creative display of the merchandise in each catalog.

Red Rose Collections, Inc., is primarily engaged in the retail sale of products described as "Personal Treasures for Living in a Changing World," offered through its nationally distributed Red Rose Collection mail-order catalog. These products include books, video- and audiotapes, note cards, clothing, jewelry, assorted angel and cherub products, figurines, and personal, home, and garden accessories intended to heighten an individual's sense of personal, spiritual, and environmental awareness and to facilitate self-improvement.

While the Brutocos' company is primarily a mail-order operation, they also own and operate a San Francisco retail store known as the Red Rose Gallerie. This store sells an expanded selection of products

Lalla Shanna and Rinaldo S. Brutoco at their Red Rose Gallerie.

available through its catalog. The retail store also serves as an outlet for overstock and out-of-season items, as well as a testing ground for potential new products before they are published for sale in the catalog.

Source: Prepared by Farrar Brown of the University of Mobile from correspondence and interviews with Rinaldo S. Brutoco.

ration, many others fail. And while proper planning does not ensure success, it improves the chances of succeeding, including finding ways to improve a good or service and to expand its market.

Identifying a Needed Product

Planning starts with searching for a product to sell. The search requires innovative and original thinking—including that of others as well as your own. Hobbies, recreation, and work at home or your place of employment can provide ideas for a new product.

King Camp Gillette was challenged by his boss, the owner of the Baltimore Seal Company, to find a product that "when used once, is thrown away and the customer comes back for more." Until that time, shaving could be done only with a straight razor—a piece of steel that had to be stropped regularly and honed by a professional knife sharpener. While he was trying to shave with a dull razor in 1895, the design for a new razor came into Gillette's mind. He patented the idea and found someone to make the razor with a disposable blade. In 1901, he incorporated a business that later became the Gillette Safety Razor Company.[36]

Studying the Market for the Product

After selecting the good or service and business, look at the market potential for each one. If a market does not exist—or cannot be developed—do not pursue the project any further. On the other hand, there may be a market in a particular location or a segment of the population that needs your good or service.

Small businesses usually select one segment of the population for their customers or choose one niche to serve, since they do not have sufficient resources to cover the whole market. Also, small businesses cannot include as large a variety of goods or services in their efforts as large businesses can. Hence, a small business must find its niche and concentrate its efforts on the customers it can serve effectively.

As shown in Chapter 3, Herman J. Russell founded the Russell Plastering Company when he graduated from Tuskegee Institute in 1957. He soon became known as one of the best plastering subcontractors in the construction industry. Later, he became involved in mostly joint venture construction projects, such as Atlanta's MARTA rapid rail system, the underground people-mover system at Hartsfield International Airport, and the Martin Luther King Community Center.[37]

Deciding Whether to Start a New Business, Buy an Existing One, or Buy a Franchise

After deciding what type of industry you want to enter and doing an economic feasibility study of that industry, you must decide whether (1) to start a new business from scratch, (2) buy an established business, or (3) buy a franchise.

To Start a New Business?   Most successful small-business owners start their own businesses, because they want others to recognize that the success is all theirs. Often, the idea selected is new, and the businesses for sale at the time do not fit the desired mold. Size of company, fresh inventory, personnel, and location can be chosen to fit the new venture.

This idea may be exciting and—when successful—satisfying. But the venture is also challenging, because everything about it is new, it demands new ideas, and it must overcome difficulties. Moreover, because everything is new, a great degree of ingenuity is required.

As shown in Chapter 7, Michael Dell started selling computer parts by mail from his University of Texas dorm room when he was only 19 years old. The results were so gratifying that he dropped out of school, rented a small office, placed an ad in a computer magazine, and created PC's Limited. His new business was so successful that he soon began making an IBM-PC clone using off-the-shelf parts. Now Dell Computer Corporation is a big-time player in the computer industry.[38]

To Buy an Existing Business? Buying an existing business can mean different things to different people. It may mean acquiring total ownership of an entire business, or it may mean acquiring only a firm's assets, its name, or certain parts of it. Keep this point in mind as you consider whether to buy a business someone else has built. Also remember that many entrepreneurs find taking over an existing business not always to be a "piece of cake." Many entrepreneurs, however, have found this way of entering business quite rewarding.

You may remember the 1979 TV commercial where Victor Kiam, president of Remington Products, Inc., holds up an electric shaver and says, "I was a dedicated blade shaver until my wife bought me this Remington Microscreen Shaver. I was so impressed with it, I bought the company." Afterward, sales increased manyfold, market share more than doubled, and profits skyrocketed.[39]

A word of caution is needed here. Past success or failure is not sufficient foundation for a decision of whether or not to buy a given business. Instead, you must make a thorough analysis of its present condition and an appraisal of what the business might do in the future.

Entrepreneur Victor Kiam is submerged by Remington electric shavers while company profits soar.

To Buy a Franchise? According to Colonel Harlan Sanders, founder of Kentucky Fried Chicken, "Buying a franchise is probably the quickest and most successful way of becoming an entrepreneur."[40] Whether that conclusion is true or false, franchising is expanding rapidly and appears to be very successful. Yet the decision to buy a franchise is a serious one, as many have failed, and some franchisees have suffered severe losses. For example, Minnie Pearl Chicken failed because the franchisor lacked adequate capital to service 1,840 franchisees, and Wild Bill Hamburgers was a "franchising fraud that fleeced millions of dollars from more than 100 investors."[41]

Franchising is a marketing system permitting one party—the franchisee—to conduct business as an individual owner while abiding by the terms and conditions set by the second party—the franchisor. One reason franchising is so popular—it accounts for over a third of all retail sales—is its low failure rate. The SBA estimates that only about 5 percent of franchises fail in the first year.[42]

A second reason for the popularity of franchises is the opportunity they give women and African Americans. In 1990, blacks owned 457 McDonald's, 158 Copeland's (Church's and Popeye's), 162 Kentucky Fried Chicken, and 150 Burger King franchises.[43]

One final reason for buying a franchise is that the franchisor uses proven and successful methods of operation and business images to aid the franchisee. A franchise, however, is not a guarantee of success as the costs may outweigh the benefits. Also, it may not fit the owner's desires or direction, or it may not give the franchisee enough independence. Further, overpriced, poorly run, uninteresting, and "white elephant" franchises are potentially disastrous.

Even under the best of conditions, franchisors tend to hold an advantage. Usually, this relates to operating standards, supply and material purchase agreements, and agreements relating to the repurchase of the franchise. Also, there are

franchising A marketing system whereby an individual owner conducts business according to the terms and conditions set by the franchisor.

Franchising offers opportunities to women and minorities.

constraints as to the size of the territory and the specific location. Moreover, you often have no choice about the layout and decor. For example, when Ray Kroc set up McDonald's as a franchise, he controlled the trade name (McDonald's), symbol (golden arches), and operating systems. In turn, he permitted franchisees to use these under controlled conditions—for a fee. Kroc also controlled all aspects of quality that characterized the successful operations of the original drive-in.[44]

Preparing and Presenting a Business Plan

As indicated earlier, a new business results from the prospective owner having both a good idea for producing and selling a product and the ability to carry out the idea. This truth was confirmed in a survey of the 665 fastest-growing private companies in which 88 percent "succeeded by taking an ordinary idea and pulling it off exceptionally well."[45] Other things—such as buildings and machines, personnel, materials and supplies, and finances—are also needed. The needs are identified through strategic, operational, and financial planning. All that planning needs to be formalized into a **business plan,** which is a tool for attracting the other components of the business formation package—the people and the money. A well-developed and well-presented business plan can provide potential entrepreneurs with a much greater chance of success, and reduce their chances of failing.

business plan A plan setting forth the firm's objectives, steps for achieving them, and financial requirements.

Financing the Business

Experience has repeatedly shown that sufficient capital is essential not only for starting small businesses but also for their continued operation. In fact, as we've stated, one of the main reasons for the high failure rate of small businesses is inadequate or improper financing. All too often, insufficient attention has been paid to planning for financial needs, leaving the new business open to sudden but predictable financial crises. Even firms that are financially sound can be destroyed by cash flow problems, for one of the difficulties most commonly experienced by rapidly growing firms is that they are unable to finance the investment needed to support sales growth.

Estimating Financial Needs

The degree of uncertainty surrounding a small firm's long-term financial needs primarily depends on whether the business is already operating or is just starting up. If a business has an operating history, its future needs can be estimated with relative accuracy, even with substantial growth. Even for an existing business, however, an in-depth analysis of its *continuing* financial requirements can be valuable by showing whether the current method of financing the business is unsound or unnecessarily risky.

Finding Sources of Financing

As a general rule, small businesses' long-lived assets, such as buildings and other facilities, should be financed with long-term sources of funds. On the other hand, short-lived assets, such as inventory or accounts receivable, should be financed with short-term loans.

The two primary sources for financing a business are equity financing and debt financing. **Equity financing** involves using owners' funds as a source of funding. **Debt financing** is funding that is provided by lenders who provide funds at a rate of interest that must be repaid by the company.

Equity Financing While **equity** is the owner's share of the firm's assets, the nature of this claim depends on the legal form of ownership. For proprietorships and partnerships, the claim on the assets of the firm is that they are part of the owner's personal assets. Equity financing in a corporation is evidenced by shares of either common or preferred stock.

Debt Financing With debt financing, principal and interest payments are legally enforceable claims against the business. Therefore, they entail substantial risk for the firm (or for the entrepreneur, if the debt is guaranteed by personal wealth).

Despite the risk involved, however, small firms use debt financing for several reasons. First, interest payments on this form of financing are tax-deductible expenses. Second, an entrepreneur may be able to raise more total capital with debt funding than from equity sources alone. Also, debt financing does not dilute the entrepreneur's ownership in the firm. Finally, since debt payments are fixed costs, any remaining profits belong solely to the owners.

Debt securities are usually bonds or loans. In general, publicly issued debt (such as bonds or commercial paper) is more commonly used by large firms, whereas small companies rely more on private loans from financial institutions such as commercial banks, insurance companies, or finance companies.

equity financing
Funds for financing the business that are contributed by the owners.

debt financing
Funding provided by lenders who are paid interest on the use of the financing provided.

equity An owner's share of the assets of a business.

Small Business Administration (SBA) Assistance   One of the primary purposes of the SBA is to help small firms, including those having trouble securing funds from conventional sources, find financing—especially at reasonable rates. The SBA helps these small firms in several ways, including offering guarantees on loans made by private lenders and offering direct specialized financing. Its most popular program—its 7(a) loan program—guarantees loans for up to $500,000. The SBA can also provide some venture capital through Small Business Investment Companies (SBICs).

As the SBA's future is now being debated in Congress, its future activities are in doubt. However, some form of assistance will remain.

Planning for Human Resource Needs

You cannot wait until you need a new employee to plan your human resource needs. Like larger competitors, small businesses must (1) determine personnel needs and (2) develop sources from which to recruit personnel. Small businesses may find it difficult to obtain adequate qualified personnel, since many face labor shortages because of the declining workforce. For example, the average age of the U.S. workforce increased from 26 in 1966 to 34 in 1990, and is expected to increase to over 36 by the year 2000.[46] Because small businesses employ two-thirds of these entry-level workers, they are the first to feel a labor shortage.

To meet this declining supply of potential employees, many small businesses are changing the way they operate. They are spending more on technology, using new methods to attract more applicants, making their workplaces more attractive, and using employee benefits and other incentives to retain valued employees. Small companies are also stepping up automation and even subcontracting out part of their work to reduce the number of employees needed.

While human resource management is important to small firms, job descriptions should be flexible in very small firms in order to give the owner more freedom in assigning work to available employees, whether or not the work fits their job description. These owners cannot afford the luxury of having formal job descriptions.

When seeking a new employee, do not ask for more than is needed to do the job properly. Instead, ask yourself, "Is a college education really needed, or can a high school graduate do the job?" Or again, "Are three years' experience required, or can an inexperienced person be easily trained to do the work?" If an inexperienced person can be trained, is there someone to do the training? Increasing education and experience levels raises the starting pay expected, and you may actually be better off training someone to do things your own way.

Part-time and temporary workers provide scheduling flexibility for small firms, as well as reducing hiring and benefit expenses. Temporary employees include not only students seeking summer jobs, but also out-of-work and retired people.

leased labor
Employees obtained from an outside firm that specializes in performing a particular service.

Leased labor is an important source of part-time employees. These workers may work full-time for the leasing firm and only part-time for the small employer. This is an especially useful source of employees for clerical, maintenance, janitorial, and food service tasks.

Leasing saves labor costs for a business, because the employees' health insurance and other benefits are paid by the agency that supplies the needed labor. Also, leasing allows an owner to cut back on staff when business is slack. The "leased labor" group is fast becoming a permanent part of the American workforce.[47]

Business-Government Relations

Throughout this chapter, we have discussed the operations of a small business within the framework of government assistance and regulation. Now we need to go into a little more detail about this environment. We will look at how the government assists small firms, as well as show how governments control their activities.

Seeking Government Help for Small Companies

Many examples of assistance to small companies have been given throughout this chapter. For instance, you've read that the SBA provides many types of direct and guaranteed loans for small firms. The SBA also offers publications (such as its series of Management Aids), local workshops, Small Business Development Centers, and Small Business Institutes, and it offers information on domestic and overseas marketing.

In addition, the SBA sponsors the **Service Corps of Retired Executives (SCORE)**, whose 750 chapters and satellites nationwide provide 13,000 volunteer members specializing in helping people develop their business ideas. SCORE can match one or more of these counselors to a specific business. It can also call on its extensive roster of public relations experts, bankers, lawyers, industrial relations

SCORE (Service Corps of Retired Executives) A group of retired—but active—managers from all walks of life who help people develop their own business ideas.

A member of the Service Corps of Retired Executives works with some clients.

technicians, and the like, to answer the important and detailed questions one might have about setting up a business. Volunteers will then work with the owner after he or she has started the business. Some clients consult with SCORE counselors for several years.

Another way the SBA helps is by encouraging small-business owners to try to perform more effectively. It does this by making state and national awards for the "Small Business Persons of the Year."

Handling Government Regulations and Paperwork

If you want to see a small-business owner become incensed, mention government regulations and paperwork, which are a growing problem for small companies. The regulations are numerous, complex, costly, and often confusing or contradictory, as the following example illustrates.

> According to Ron Smith, Colorado director of the National Federation of Independent Business, his state has a regulation saying hospitals will be fined if they do not present their annual budgets to the Colorado Hospital—which had been abolished four years previously.[48]

It is frequently difficult to understand and comply with governmental requirements. While most businesspeople are willing to obey the law, compliance is often complex, arduous, time-consuming, and expensive. For example, Murray Weidenbaum, a Washington University professor, found that 150,000 small firms will have to spend more than $10,000 each *just* for pollution permits under the 1990 Clean Air Act.[49]

Entrepreneurs, as well as corporate executives, are now becoming more active in trying to change these requirements through political action and lobbying. They are also retaining lawyers on a permanent basis.

The Role of Family-Owned Businesses

Many small-business owners do not adequately provide for the future. Instead of providing for their business to continue, owners put off selecting a successor until it is too late. Many executives of family businesses, fighting against possible retirement, believe that finding a successor can be done quickly. But the odds are against them, for fewer than one-third of U.S. family businesses pass successfully from the first to the second generation, and only 15 percent make it to the third generation.[50]

Over 80 percent of all U.S. businesses—large, medium, and small—are family owned, and they account for 50 percent of our gross national product, as well as half of our workforce.[51] Yet as indicated, only about one in seven of them makes it to the third generation, often because of unwillingness or inability to deal with the challenges that are unique to family-run enterprises.[52] Most small-business owners do not like to talk about the question of succession. Perhaps this reflects a denial of their own mortality, the same instinct that causes people to be reluctant about making a will. However, to be realistic in ensuring the continuation of your business or in providing an ongoing concern for family members to operate, you must look at this question analytically.

Coping with Family-Owned Business Problems

While family-owned businesses provide a living and personal satisfaction for many people, they must be managed just like any other small firm if they are to succeed. Family businesses are the backbone of America, but they can also be a source of unresolved family tensions and conflicts, which can create obstacles to achieving even the most basic business goals. When close relatives work together, emotions often interfere with business decisions. Also, unique problems, such as the departure of the founder-owner, develop in family-owned firms. When more than one family member is involved, emotions and differing value systems can cause conflicts between members.[53]

We usually think of family businesses as being started, owned, and operated by the parents, with children helping out and later taking over. While this has been the normal pattern, two contrary trends are developing. First, many young people are going into business for themselves—and tapping their parents for funds to finance their ventures. In return, the children often give one or both parents an executive position in the company, including a seat on the company's board. Also, many retirees want to work part-time for the children's businesses, without assuming a lot of responsibility.

Another trend—as shown earlier—is the large number of spouses doing business together. We used to think of married couples running a small neighborhood store, toiling long hours for a modest living. Now, though, a new breed of husband-and-wife entrepreneurs has emerged. They typically run a service enterprise out of their home and use computers, modems, faxes, and telecommunications as the tools of their trade.

Preparing for Management Succession

Any business must be ready for changes in its top management. It is not enough to wait to select a person to step into the top job when it becomes vacant. That key job requires much training and experience, because the decisions the person makes can vitally affect the family, as well as the company and its future. Thus, every transfer of ownership and power is an invitation to disaster. In order to prevent that from happening, the owner should do two things: *Plan early and carefully, and groom a successor.*

When preparing someone for management succession, many small-business owners have some grave concerns about passing the business on to their children. In a survey by Nancy Bowman-Upton of Baylor University, it was found that the main concern of entrepreneurs was treating all children fairly. Of those surveyed, 31 percent gave this as their main concern. Another 22 percent were concerned about the reaction of nonfamily employees. And 20 percent cited family communication, conflict, and estate taxes as concerns.[54]

Another trend in small firms is having two or more children succeed the parent in running the business. For example, a study by John Ward, a professor at Loyola University's Graduate School of Business, found that 55 percent of owners of family-owned firms say they want to include two or more children in future ownership or management of the family business.[55]

Tax and Estate Planning

In projecting the future of a family-owned business, planning is needed to minimize income and estate taxes. A business and its assets may appreciate in value much more rapidly and extensively than the owners are aware, and inheritance taxes can be devastating. Therefore, estate plans should be reviewed frequently, along with possible estate tax liability and the provisions for paying such taxes.

Tax Planning

In planning the firm's future activities, one should consider the influence taxes will have on profits and the business's capital structure. Since tax laws and regulations change frequently, the small-business owner should stay current on these matters. He or she should probably have an annual planning conference with an accounting professional well versed in business tax matters.

Estate Planning

estate planning
Preparation for transferring the equity of an owner when death occurs.

Estate planning prepares for transferring the equity of an owner after death. The major concern usually is perpetuation of a small or family business. Tax rates on estates are now such that the assets bequeathed to beneficiaries may be needed to pay taxes, resulting in removal of equity from a business. By planning for the transition, this problem can be minimized.

From the entrepreneur's standpoint, estate planning can (1) reduce the need for beneficiaries to withdraw funds, (2) help maintain beneficiaries' interest in keeping funds in the firm, and (3) provide for a smooth transition. Estate planning for the above objectives can be in the form of (1) gifts to children, (2) family partnerships, (3) stock sales to family members, and (4) living trusts. Appropriate steps should be taken to ensure compliance with Internal Revenue Service (IRS) regulations, especially regarding valuation of the business.

buy/sell agreement
A contract explaining how stockholders can buy out each other's interest.

Certain actions are possible to ensure that the IRS is bound by a predetermined agreement. One can use a predetermined shareholder **buy/sell agreement,** whereby the corporation agrees to buy back the stock from any of the shareholders—or sell it to someone else for the stockholder. Such an agreement becomes binding on the IRS. In addition, a properly prepared buy/sell agreement ensures a market for the stock and protects minority stockholders.

A number of references may be used to aid in estate and tax planning, but we recommend using the services of a lawyer, accountant, and/or professional tax planner.

S U M M A R Y

Owning your own business can bring about personal satisfaction, prestige in the community, and the opportunity to make a great deal of money, making it rewarding and one of the best ways to fulfill the "American Dream." Some reasons for the increased interest in small businesses are that the number of small businesses is growing rapidly, small firms generate most new employment, there is an increase in the number of courses in small businesses at colleges and universities, and small businesses are attractive to people of all ages.

For a firm to be considered a small business, it should be independently owned and operated and it should not be dominant in its field. A small business tends to encourage innovation and flexibility, generate employment, provide employees with comprehensive learning experiences, and develop risk takers. Several problems seem to affect small businesses more than larger ones; the primary problems are inadequate financing, inadequate management knowledge and/or experience, burdensome government regulations and paperwork, and uncontrolled growth.

Successful owners of small businesses tend to desire independence, have a strong sense of initiative, expect quick and concrete results, are able to react quickly, and enter business as much by chance as by design.

An entrepreneurial venture differs from a small business in that it is characterized by innovative strategic practices and/or products. The principal objectives of an entrepreneurial venture are profitability and rapid growth, whereas small businesses expect normal sales, profits, and growth. Entrepreneurs are characterized by their willingness to make sacrifices, decisiveness, self-confidence, ability to recognize and capitalize on opportunities, and confidence in the venture. Many large companies are now using the intrapreneurial concept to stimulate creativity and encourage competitiveness among their staff.

The opportunities for entrepreneurs are continually growing. These are particularly favorable times for women—especially when you consider that the rate of business start-ups by women is twice that of men. There are also opportunities for minorities, including blacks, Hispanics, and Asians. Husband-and-wife-owned businesses also seem to be able to make use of opportunities, since they are considered the fastest-growing category of new businesses in the 1990s.

When organizing a new business, entrepreneurs usually search for and identify a needed product; study the market for the product; decide whether to start a new business, buy an existing one, or buy a franchise; and make strategic and operational plans, which are formalized into a business plan. If you are going to start a small business, obtaining sufficient capital is very important. Equity and debt financing are two ways a person can raise funds for the needed capital investment and for maintaining the working capital.

Small-business owners must keep their human resource needs in mind. Part-time and temporary workers can provide scheduling flexibility for small firms. Students seeking summer jobs and out-of-work people are examples of temporary employees. Leased labor is a growing source of part-time employers.

The government can have a great effect on the success of a small business. To help small businesses, the government provides direct and guaranteed loans, sponsors the Service Corps of Retired Executives (SCORE)—which helps people develop business ideas—and makes state and national awards through the Small Business Administration. On the other hand, one problem that faces small businesses is government regulations and paperwork.

Family-owned businesses have a hard time maintaining their success from the first to the second to the third generations. Unresolved family tensions and conflicts also seem to be problems family-owned businesses have to deal with. Not only do small-business owners have to plan for someone to succeed them, but also they must consider tax and estate planning.

K E Y   T E R M S

small business, 532
mom-and-pop operation, 532
entrepreneurial venture, 532
small-business owner, 532
entrepreneur, 533
intrapreneurship, 533
franchising, 545
business plan, 546

equity financing, 547
debt financing, 547
equity, 547
leased labor, 548
SCORE (Service Corps of Retired Executives), 549
estate planning, 552
buy/sell agreement, 552

D I S C U S S I O N   Q U E S T I O N S

1. Do you agree that this is an interesting time to be studying entrepreneurship and small business? Why or why not?

2. Discuss some of the reasons for the increased interest in entrepreneurship and small business.

3. Distinguish between a small business and an entrepreneurial venture. If you were to start your own business, which would you wish it to be? Why?

4. What are some of the unique contributions small businesses make? Give examples of each from your own experience owning or working in a small business or from small businesses that you patronize.

5. Discuss the ways in which the government can assist a small business and the ways in which it might pose a threat.

6. What are the characteristics of successful entrepreneurs? Which do you think are the most important? Why?

7. What are some of the problems facing small businesses? Again, give examples from your experience.

8. What are some of the opportunities for women in small business? List and discuss some of these.

9. What are some of the opportunities for minorities in small business? List and discuss some of these.

10. Describe each step that should be taken when starting a new business.

11. Discuss some of the unique problems of managing human resources in a small business.

PRACTICING MANAGEMENT

16.1 case

Oprah Winfrey—A Woman for All Seasons

Oprah Winfrey—actress, talk-show host, and businesswoman—epitomizes the opportunities for America's women entrepreneurs. From welfare child to multimillionaire, Ms. Winfrey—resourceful, assertive, always self-assured, and yet unpretentious—has climbed the socioeconomic ladder by turning apparent failure into opportunities and then capitalizing on them.

Winfrey's wealth, power, and glamour of today are a far cry from her beginnings. She was born on a farm in Kosciusko, Mississippi, on January 29, 1954. Orpah (Ruth's sister-in-law in the Bible) was the name her parents had intended for her, but due to a midwife's mistake, the name Oprah was recorded on the birth certificate. Soon after, her parents separated and Winfrey was left in the care of her maternal grandmother on an isolated farm.

With no playmates, Oprah entertained herself by "playacting" with objects such as corncob dolls, chickens, and cows. Her grandmother, a harsh disciplinarian, taught Oprah to read by age 2½, and as a result of speaking at a rural church, her oratory talents began to emerge.

At age 6, Winfrey was sent to live with her mother and two half-brothers in a Milwaukee ghetto. While in Milwaukee, Winfrey, known as "the Little Speaker," was often invited to recite poetry at social gatherings, and her speaking skills continued to develop. At age 12, during a visit to her father in Nashville, she was paid $500 for a speech she gave to a church. It was then that she prophetically announced what she wanted to do for a living: "get paid to talk."

Her mother, working as a maid and drawing available welfare to make ends meet, left Oprah with little or no parental supervision and eventually sent her to live with her father in Nashville. There Oprah found the stability and discipline she so desperately needed. "My father saved my life," Winfrey reminisces. Her father—like her grandmother—a strict disciplinarian, obsessed with properly educating his daughter, forced her to memorize 20 new vocabulary words a week and turn in a weekly book report. His guidance and her hard work soon paid off, as she began to excel in school and other areas.

At age 16, Winfrey won a full scholarship to Tennessee State University. A year later, she was crowned Miss Fire Prevention by the managers of a local radio station, who were so impressed by Winfrey that they hired her to read their newscast for the final months of her high school career. As a freshman at Tennessee State, Winfrey was named Miss Black Nashville and Miss Tennessee and was a contestant in the Miss Black America Pageant.

Winfrey's second year in college was even more overwhelming than her first. After twice turning down a job offer from the local CBS television station, she accepted a position at WTVF-TV, becoming Nashville's first black woman evening news anchor. She held this job for the rest of her college career.

After graduating from college in 1976, she accepted a position as coanchor and reporter for WJZ-TV, an ABC affiliate in Baltimore, Maryland, and the all-too-sensitive Winfrey began running into problems with the cold realities of journalism. She had "to fight back the tears" when reporting stories that were "too sad." In fact, she was told that if she refused to interview a woman whose family had been killed in a fire, she would be terminated. Winfrey conducted the interview, but minutes later apologized during the live news program.

Oprah Winfrey's success is a true rags-to-riches story.

In 1977, marking a major move in her career, Winfrey, at age 22, joined Richard Sher as cohost of *Baltimore Is Talking*, a morning talk show. Upon completing her first program, Winfrey ebulliently exclaimed, "This is what I was born to do. This is like breathing!"

For the next seven years, Winfrey learned the tricks of the talk-show trade as she and Sher confronted nearly every topic imaginable. Eventually, the general manager of an ABC affiliate in Chicago "discovered" Winfrey after viewing an audition tape sent to him by Debra

DiMaio, producer of *Baltimore Is Talking*. Swanson was so impressed with Winfrey's talent and ratings that he hired her and DiMaio to take over his station's lifeless *A.M. Chicago* in January 1984. After one month, *A.M. Chicago*'s ratings equaled those of *Donahue*, and in three months, pushed ahead. After less than two years, the show was expanded and renamed *The Oprah Winfrey Show*.

The show has been characterized as an hour-long group therapy session in which the host attempts to simplify the problems of a far too complex world. Rather than offering a detached, sterile scenario, Winfrey capitalizes on one of her strongest traits—empathy—holding hands with guests and audience members and crying when she hears testimonials of pain or loss. On one show, Winfrey stated that if there's one thread running through this show, it's that "you are not alone." Winfrey's sentiment was made clear in a now legendary show on incest when she burst into tears as she disclosed to guests, the audience, and millions of viewers that she too had been a victim of incest. She has been quoted as saying, "It was not a horrible thing in my life. There was a lesson in it. It teaches you not to let people abuse you." This made her credibility and ratings skyrocket, helping her earn the Daytime Emmy Award—three for the show and one for the star and host.

Expanding her career into movies, Winfrey received Oscar, Golden Globe, and Academy Award nominations for her performance as Sofia in the highly successful movie *The Color Purple*.

In 1986, King World put *The Oprah Winfrey Show* into syndication in over 130 cities. When the show aired nationwide, it won its time slot by pulling in 31 percent of the viewing audience. With a guaranteed 25 percent of gross earnings, Winfrey quickly became the highest-paid performer in show business.

With her vast fortune, Winfrey turned her attention to business. Using some of the $25 million she earned in 1988, Winfrey's newly formed production company, Harpo Production, Inc. ("Oprah" spelled backwards), of which she is the sole owner, obtained ownership and control of *The Oprah Winfrey Show* and procured a guarantee from ABC that the network would continue to carry the show for the next five years. She spent a reported $10 million on an 88,000-square-foot studio in Chicago for producing motion pictures, television movies, and her talk show. The purchase was supposed to be "the studio in between the coasts, the final piece of the puzzle" enabling Winfrey to do "whatever it is she wants to do economically, and under her own control." The complex represented a carefully orchestrated expansion strategy for her.

In 1994, King World decided to continue distribution of *The Oprah Winfrey Show* through the 1999–2000 television season, and made Oprah a major shareholder. At that time, Oprah began concentrating on topics that can help people improve their lives.

Winfrey gives generously to charities. For example, she has given $750,000 to fund ten scholarships at her alma mater, and organized a benefit sale of her dresses, which raised $150,000 for community-outreach programs. She says, "My mission is to use this position, power, and money to create opportunities for other people." To help improve her own life, Winfrey hired her own personal chef, Rosie Daley, whose cookbook—with the endorsement of Winfrey—is selling "like hotcakes." And to fulfill a personal goal, Winfrey ran a 26.2-mile race by the age of 40 with a time of 4 hours, 29 minutes, and 20 seconds.

If Winfrey's television and motion picture successes are a barometer of her business endeavors, she will surely capitalize on the obvious opportunities and create new ones where others thought none existed.

Sources: "Oprah Winfrey," *Current Biography Yearbook 1987*, pp. 610–614; Barbara Harrison, "The Importance of Being Oprah," *New York Times* Biographical Service, June 1989, pp. 558–564; Richard Zoglin, "Lady with a Calling," *Time*, August 8, 1988, pp. 62–64; Lawrence Ingrassia, "A Select Few Poised to Lead Business into the '90s," *Wall Street Journal*, Centennial Edition 1989, p. A5; Matt Roush, "Her Empire Grows with ABC Series," *USA Today*, May 11, 1990, p. 1D; "Cutting Out the Middlemen," *Forbes*, October 1, 1990, p. 166; Peter Newcomb and Lisa Gubernick, "The Top 40," *Forbes*, September 27, 1993, p. 97; Steven Zausner, "All the Money," *Forbes*, October 18, 1993, p. 22; "King World in Agreement to Continue Oprah Show," *Wall Street Journal*, March 18, 1994, p. 3; Paul Noglows, "Oprah: The Year of Living Dangerously," *Working Woman*, May 1994, pp. 52–55; Eben Shapiro, "Publishing: Oprah Makes Huge Bestseller of a Cookbook," *Wall Street Journal*, May 4, 1994, p. 1; Tracey Wong Biggs, "Oprah Takes a Dream and Runs with It," *USA Today*, October 24, 1994, p. 1; and Gretchen Reynolds, "A Year to Remember: Oprah Grows Up," *TV Guide*, January 7, 1995, p. 14.

Questions

1. What entrepreneurial characteristics does Winfrey have?

2. What has made her so successful?

3. Would you like to work for Winfrey? Why or why not?

4. Do you think Winfrey's "carefully orchestrated expansion strategy" will work? Why or why not?

16.1

learning exercise

Test Your Potential as an Entrepreneur

Do you have what it takes to be a success in your own business? Below is a list of 20 personality traits. Consider each carefully—and then score yourslf by placing a check under the appropriate number with 0 being the lowest and 7 being the highest. Tally your score and find out what kind of entrepreneur you would make, using the key below.

	0	1	2	3	4	5	6	7
I have the ability to communicate.	—	—	—	—	—	—	—	—
I have the ability to motivate others.	—	—	—	—	—	—	—	—
I have the ability to organize.	—	—	—	—	—	—	—	—
I can accept responsibility.	—	—	—	—	—	—	—	—
I can easily adapt to change.	—	—	—	—	—	—	—	—
I have decision-making capability.	—	—	—	—	—	—	—	—
I have drive and energy.	—	—	—	—	—	—	—	—
I am in good health.	—	—	—	—	—	—	—	—
I have good human relations skills.	—	—	—	—	—	—	—	—
I have initiative.	—	—	—	—	—	—	—	—
I am interested in people.	—	—	—	—	—	—	—	—
I have good judgment.	—	—	—	—	—	—	—	—
I am open-minded and receptive to new ideas.	—	—	—	—	—	—	—	—
I have planning ability.	—	—	—	—	—	—	—	—
I am persistent.	—	—	—	—	—	—	—	—
I am resourceful.	—	—	—	—	—	—	—	—
I am self-confident.	—	—	—	—	—	—	—	—
I am self-starter.	—	—	—	—	—	—	—	—
I am a good listener.	—	—	—	—	—	—	—	—
I am willing to be a risk taker.	—	—	—	—	—	—	—	—

Key:

110–140 Very strong   **85–109** Strong   **55–84** Fair   **54 or below** Weak

Prepared by Sherron Boone and Lisa Aplin of the University of Mobile.

Source: William L. Megginson, M. Jane Byrd, Charles R. Scott, and Leon C. Megginson, *Small Business Management* (Burr Ridge, Ill.: Irwin, 1994), p. 31.

Questions

1. How can this survey be of help to you?

2. After taking the survey, do you feel you are well prepared for running your own business?

3. What characteristic do you need to improve on?

Your Future *in* Management

*Hitch your
wagon to
a star.*

—RALPH WALDO
EMERSON

*There is
nothing like
a dream to
create the
future.*

—VICTOR HUGO

LEARNING OBJECTIVES

After studying the material in this chapter, you should be able to:

▶ **Discuss** the outlook for jobs in the management field.

▶ **Describe** the characteristics of successful managers.

▶ **Explain** how companies identify managerial talent in nonmanagerial employees.

▶ **Describe** the four career stages through which individuals progress.

▶ **Relate** some problems encountered by individuals in their first management positions.

▶ **Explain** how organizations help individuals in their career development.

Fast Career Tracks Are Changing

It's the 1990s, and perhaps for the better, the fast promotion track in American firms is slowing down. Promotions in U.S. organizations have traditionally come quickly, much more quickly than in, say, Japan. And those quick promotions have meant that fast-trackers focused on the short run: Many have made their numbers look good with quick-fix budget manipulations, at the expense of a variety of other factors, such as subordinate morale and peer-group relations. But the tide may be turning, as many are sitting in jobs longer than ever before.

The cause? For one, the use of flatter organizations, with fewer rungs on the managerial ladder, permits fewer promotions. For another, U.S. organizations that once moved their best and brightest on the fast track for a new job every 12 to 18 months are asking if this is the best way for personnel and employers to read whether they have succeeded or failed in a job. Consider the case of David Hogberg.

Hogberg, age 37, was working his way up the corporate ladder at Quaker Oats at the rate of about one promotion annually through 1981. But things slowed down when he became manufacturing manager for Kibbles 'n Bits® dog food, and his superior decided to keep him there for three years. "It seemed like an eternity," he said of the position, in which he had 70 people reporting to him. Hogberg wondered if such an extended stint would turn out to be a career setback over the long term. But in fact, it was not. "I got to see the effects of changes I made and [to] work through their implications. It helped me learn to approach every job as a long-term opportunity, to stand back and ask

David Hogberg with other Quaker Oats employees.

what changes we need to make in this whole picture, even if it has been done that way for the last 15 years."

Today, with fewer promotions available, lateral transfers are much more in vogue again, seemingly for the better. Quaker's Hogberg is again an example.

After his three-year stint as manufacturing manger, Hogberg opted to go into production development rather than seek out a plant superintendent's position. Then, three years later, he left a senior product development post to move into marketing as assistant brand manager for Cap'n Crunch® cereal. Currently, as manager of marketing for all of Quakers' "semi-moist" pet foods, such as Gains Burger, he feels that his earlier lateral moves gave him the edge over other candidates: "If I had become a director of product development, it would have been a dead end for me from a career standpoint. My lateral moves have been deliberate, and they worked."

Those fast-trackers with an eye on the top spot—CEO—will have to wait longer and be more patient than in earlier decades. Moreover, they can be expected to spend some time in human resources, public relations, and other staff positions. International experience will also be an ever increasing plus. But staying close to profit-and-loss personalities—branch managers, division managers, and plant managers—remains critically important. As Neil Yeager, author of *Career Map: What You Want, Getting It and Keeping It*, says, "For getting to the top, the bottom line is still the bottom line."[1]

Career planning and development are important to both the organization and its present—and potential—employees. Therefore, in this chapter we discuss several topics relevant to preparing for managerial careers.

Although you may not aspire to become a manager, after studying this chapter you will better understand many career-related issues that affect all people in organizations.

Management Career Opportunities

A career in management has much to offer. Generally, managerial pay and benefits are good, and managerial jobs offer status and prestige and are interesting and nonroutine. Managerial positions entail using judgment and exercising responsibility and offer the social satisfaction of working closely with others. Moreover, effective managers will continue to be in demand through the late 1990s, as you will find in reading this chapter.

We should, however, point out some negatives in a management career. If you dislike the pressure of responsibility and like to work independently rather than with others, a management career is probably not for you. Also, as a manager you will tend to put in longer hours (usually without overtime pay) and have to make several career moves within management ranks as you progress up the ladder as reflected in David Hogberg's career. Both of these conditions require family-life adjustments.

The pros and cons of a management career presented here are broad generalizations; specific management positions vary greatly within firms and industries, ranging from first-line supervisor to chief executive officer. As you will see, the greatest opportunities for future management careers will be in white-collar positions in service-performing industries.

Growth of White-Collar Positions

White-collar and blue-collar are general job classifications used by the U.S. Department of Labor. **White-collar work** includes that done by technical and professional personnel, managers and administrators, salespeople, and clerical workers. **Blue-collar work** includes that performed by craft workers, such as mechanics, carpenters, electricians, and pipe fitters; operative workers, such as machine tenders and assemblers; and laborers.

Until the end of World War II, blue-collar workers in the United States outnumbered white-collar workers. Since that time, however, the number of white-collar jobs has increased. As shown in Figure 17.1, by the year 2000 close to 55 percent of all employees will have white-collar jobs, only about 30 percent will have blue-collar jobs, and the remaining 15 percent will consist of farm and service personnel, such as beauticians, store clerks, and domestics.

Growth of Service Industries

Much of the growth in the number of white-collar jobs is explained by the growth of service-related industries. These industries have accounted for some of the fastest employment growth over the past few decades, a growth that is expected to

white-collar work Work done by technical and professional personnel, managers and administrators, salespeople, and clerical workers.

blue-collar work Work performed by craft workers, such as mechanics, carpenters, electricians, and pipe fitters; operative workers, such as machine tenders and assemblers; and laborers.

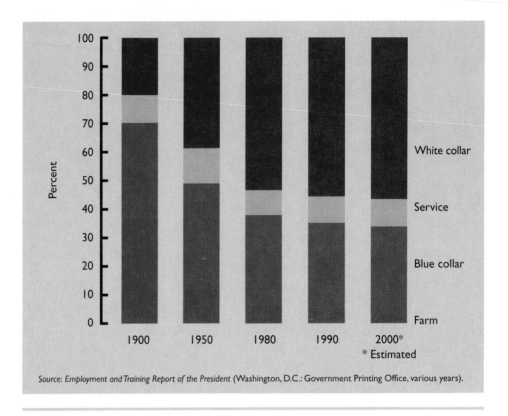

FIGURE 17.1
White-collar positions are increasing, whereas blue-collar and farm jobs are declining.

continue through 2000, and beyond. Service industries include organizations involved in health care; wholesale and retail trade; education; banking; food service; hotels; federal, state, and local government; and numerous others. By the year 2005, around 80 percent of all employees will be working for service-performing industries.

Growth of Managerial, Professional, and Technical Occupations

As shown in Figure 17.2, the Labor Department estimates that the four fastest-growing occupational groups through 2005 will be the (1) professional, (2) service, (3) technical and related support, and (4) executive, administrative, and managerial groups.[2]

Managers held about 15.3 million U.S. jobs in 1993 and despite the "downsizing" trend of many large firms, the job outlook for managers is expected to improve faster than average through 2005 as organizations become more numerous and complex.[3] The bulk of the new positions forecast for managers, officials, and proprietors will involve managing the increasing number of new personnel in the technical and professional fields and in the trade and service industries, which employ a higher percentage of managers.

Small- and medium-size companies offer considerable opportunities for managers. Robert B. Reich, secretary of labor in the Clinton administration, noted

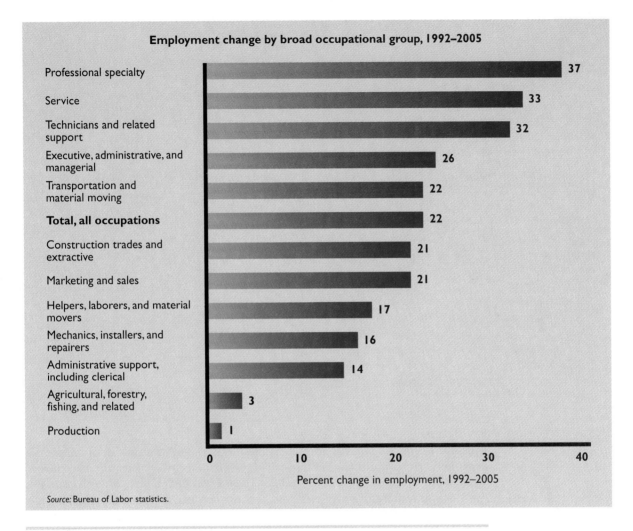

Employment change by broad occupational group, 1992–2005

Professional specialty	37
Service	33
Technicians and related support	32
Executive, administrative, and managerial	26
Transportation and material moving	22
Total, all occupations	22
Construction trades and extractive	21
Marketing and sales	21
Helpers, laborers, and material movers	17
Mechanics, installers, and repairers	16
Administrative support, including clerical	14
Agricultural, forestry, fishing, and related	3
Production	1

Percent change in employment, 1992–2005

Source: Bureau of Labor statistics.

FIGURE 17.2
Employment change by broad occupational group, 1992–2005.

that "in recent years, the Fortune 500 have failed to generate a single new job." Instead, small- to middle-size growing firms, especially those in the service industry, have provided the bulk of new jobs created in the past decade and will continue to do so in the foreseeable future.

The outlook, then, for strong career opportunities is exceptionally bright. But since the levels of education and training required of professionals and technicians will increase, there will be an increasing need for managers with more education and sophistication.

Managerial Opportunities for Women and Minorities

One of the most significant trends in career development during the last decade was the improving position of women and minorities, especially in higher-level jobs.

MANAGEMENT APPLICATION AND PRACTICE   17.1

Most Admired Women Managers in the United States

Working Woman chose a nationally known panel of management experts—male and female—to select the ten most admired women managers in America. The panel was asked to look at all fields, public as well as private. It was found that the most admired female managers communicate with employees, surround themselves with talented people, and are willing to take risks. The list, alphabetically, is as follows:

	Title and Organization	
Gwendolyn Calvert Baker	President and CEO, U.S. Committee for UNICEF	Government
Jill Barad	President and COO, Mattel	Toys
Jane HIrsch	Chair and CEO, Copley Pharmaceutical	Generic drug
Judy Lewent	CFO, Merck	Primary drug
Ruth Owades	Founder and president, Calyx & Corolla	Catalogs
Alicia Phillip	Executive director, Metro Atlanta Community Foundation	Social services
Claudia Rent	President, Mississippi University for Women	Higher education
Mary Singer	President and CEO, First of America Bank–Northeast	Financial
Ella Williams	President and CEO, Aegir Systems	Engineering
Faith Wohl	Director, Human Resource Initiative, Du Pont	Chemical

Source: Clint Willis, "The 10 Most Admired Women Managers in America," *Working Woman*, December 1993, pp. 44–56.

Opportunities for Women   There were 20 million women in the workforce in 1958; now there are around 67 million, which is 46 percent of the total workforce.[4] Women are expected to account for 60 percent of the increase in new jobs through the 1990s. It is therefore expected that by the year 2005, 63 percent of working-age women will be in the workforce, and they will hold 48 percent of all jobs[5] and about half of all MBA degrees, including those from the top schools, such as Harvard, Stanford, and Northwestern. A number of women manage large, well-known U.S. businesses, including Katharine Graham (*Washington Post*), Estée Lauder (Estée Lauder), Donna Wolf Steigerwaldt (Jockey International), and Linda Wachner (Warnaco) (see MAP 17.1; also Table 16.1 on women-owned businesses). Moreover, women have made gains in a number of industries dominated by males, including the automobile industry.

> Susan Insley, Honda of America's senior vice-president, manages Honda's $670 million Ohio engine plant, which is said to be among the most advanced automobile factories. Ditto for Linda Miller of Ford's Dearborn, Michigan, engine plant.[6]

But despite improvement in recent years at lower- and middle-management levels, less than 5 percent of senior management is made up of females, and only 3 percent of overseas managerial assignments are made to women.[7]

Despite the progress being made, though, women's earnings still trail those of men. According to U.S. Bureau of Labor statistics figures, women earned only 57 percent as much as men in 1974, 68 percent as much in 1984, and 77 percent as

TABLE 17.1 HIGHEST-PAID WOMEN MANAGERS

1. **Turi Josefsen**
Executive vice-president, U.S. Surgical Corp. . . . . $26.70 million

2. **Rena Rowan**
Executive vice-president, design, Jones Apparel Group . . . . $6.72 million

3. **Marion Sandler**
Chair and CEO, Golden West Financial Corp. . . . . $6.44 million

4. **Sandra Kurtzigt**
Chair, ASK Group . . . . $3.60 million

5. **Jill Barad**
Presdient and COO, Mattel . . . . $3.46 million

6. **Linda Wachner**
Chair, president, and CEO, Warnaco Group . . . . $3.16 million

7. **Sherry Lansing**
Chair, Paramount Motion Picture Group . . . . $3 million[*]

8. **Jane Shaw**
President and COO, Alza . . . . $2.31 million

9. **Lucie Sallianey**
Chair, Fox Broadcasting Company . . . . $1.50 million[*]

10. **C. F. St. Mark**
President, logistics systems and business services, Pitney Bowes . . . . $1.18 million

11. **Ellen Gordon**
President and COO, Tootsie Roll Industries . . . . $1.09 million

12. **Brenda Lynn**
Executive vice-president, loan production, Plaza Home Mortgage Corp. . . . . $1.03 million

13. **Kay Koplovitz**
President and CEO, USA Network . . . . $1 million[*]

14. **Babette Helmbuch**
President and COO, FirstFed Financial Corp. $989,161

15. **Patricia DeRosa**
Executive vice-president, Gap Division, The Gap $868,191

16. **Nina McLemore**[†]
Senior vice-president, corporate development, Liz Claiborne $839,472

17. **Carol Bartz**
Chair, president, and CEO, Autodesk $821,042

18. **Laurel Cutler**
Executive vice-president and worldwide director of marketing planning,
Foote, Cone & Belding Communications $779,576

19. **Sally Frame Kasaks**
Chair and CEO, Ann Taylor $753,077

20. **Carol Bernick**
Executive vice-president and assistant secretary, Alberto-Culver $693,494

Note: All figures include salary, bonuses, exercised stock options, and other compensation. Excluded are women in private companies and on Wall Street.

[*] Denotes an estimate. These figures do not appear on proxy statements, as the companies are part of larger corporations.

[†] Left company in 1993.

Source: *Working Woman*, January 1994, p. 29.

much in 1993.[8] Also, a 1990 *Fortune* survey of the 4,000 most highly compensated executives and directors showed that only 19 were women. Moreover, the larger proportion of management jobs held by women are in areas such as education, public administration, and health care—not necessarily the highest-paying fields. The 20 U.S. women with the highest compensation in 1993 are listed in Table 17.1.

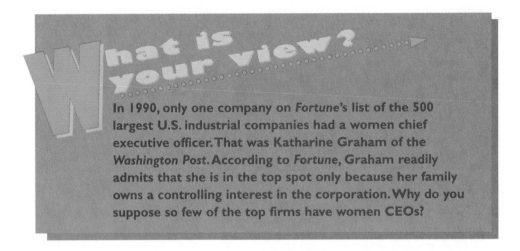

What is your view?

In 1990, only one company on *Fortune*'s list of the 500 largest U.S. industrial companies had a women chief executive officer. That was Katharine Graham of the *Washington Post*. According to *Fortune*, Graham readily admits that she is in the top spot only because her family owns a controlling interest in the corporation. Why do you suppose so few of the top firms have women CEOs?

Opportunities for Minorities   There has been progress, especially in recent years, in the proportion of African Americans, particularly males, in more desirable and higher-paying jobs. Although African Americans have been poorly represented in managerial positions compared to whites, they have recently scored some major high-profile gains in corporate America.

Clifton Wharton became the first African American to chair a Fortune 1000 company when in 1987 he was selected to head up the Teachers Insurance and Annuity Association College Retirement Equity Fund. Upon Wharton's retirement in 1994, Tom Jones, also African American, was selected to replace him as head of the $187 billion fund. Other African Americans in key top management positions include Kenneth Chenault, 43, president of American Express's Travel Related Services Company in the United States; Richard Parsons, president of Time Warner; Anna Fudge, president of General Food Company's Maxwell House; and

Time Warner chief executive Gerald Levin, left, welcomes Richard Parsons as the company's new president. Parsons, a native of the Jamaica Queens section of New York City, salvaged Dime Bancorp from near bankruptcy in 1988 when he joined it as president. As he leaves it in 1994, it is prospering, preparing for a merger with Anchor Savings that will create the United States' fourth largest thrift.

MANAGEMENT APPLICATION AND PRACTICE 17.2

Hispanic Employment at the Top-Scoring Companies

A recent survey of employees of Fortune 1000 firms by *Hispanic Business Inc.* asked Hispanic employees to respond to questions that measured company performance in areas such as diversity gains, benefits, promotions, and value placed on Hispanic employees. The ten most highly rated companies (ranked by highest percentage of Officials and Managers) and their statistics regarding Hispanic employment are shown at right.

Source: Rick Mendosa, "The Best Places to Work," *Hispanic Business*, February 1994, p. 28.

Company	Overall Workforce	Professionals	Officials & Managers
1. Levi Strauss	42.78%	13.06%	23.41%
2. PacBell*	17.00	11.00	13.00
3. Great Western	15.00	8.24	10.72
4. Xerox	6.70	4.40	4.30
5. Allstate	5.44	5.53	4.05
6. Hewlett-Packard	5.90	3.40	3.50
7. AT&T	4.13	2.24	2.94
8. BellSouth	3.12	2.84	2.59
9. Merck	3.12	2.52	2.26
10. IBM	3.32	2.47	2.17

*PacBell is the main operating subsidiary of Pacific Telesis Group.

Source: EEO-1 Report or company summary of the document. Based on most recent year available for each company, 1991–1993.

© Hispanic Business Inc. Reprinting or copying all or part of this information requires written permission.

45-year-old Rich Barton, president of Xerox's U.S. Customer Operations, its largest division with over 29,000 employees. African American–owned businesses have also made considerable progress. In 1973, when *Black Enterprise* released its list of the largest black-owned businesses, earnings from all 100 firms totaled $473 million. By 1993, gross sales of the top 100 firms on the list reached $10.28 billion.[9]

Hispanic workers will probably become the largest group of minority workers in the near future. Because of their relatively lower levels of education and lack of facility in the use of English, however, Spanish-speaking workers are concentrated in occupations with high unemployment and low incomes. MAP 17.2 provides insights into the relative workplace percentages of Hispanics in major companies.

The rapidly growing number of Asians is also making an impact on U.S. management. People from Japan, Vietnam, South Korea, Taiwan, Hong Kong, Malaysia, and Indonesia are joining the ranks of many U.S. and Asian-based corporations in this country.

Career Stages

It is common to view careers in terms of a series of stages through which individuals pass during their lives. These stages are shown in Figure 17.3, with performance level on the vertical axis and age on the horizontal axis. While the specific ages at which a given individual begins one stage and completes another may vary, the four stages reflect distinct periods through which working individuals progress. As shown, the stages are establishment, advancement, maintenance, and withdrawal.

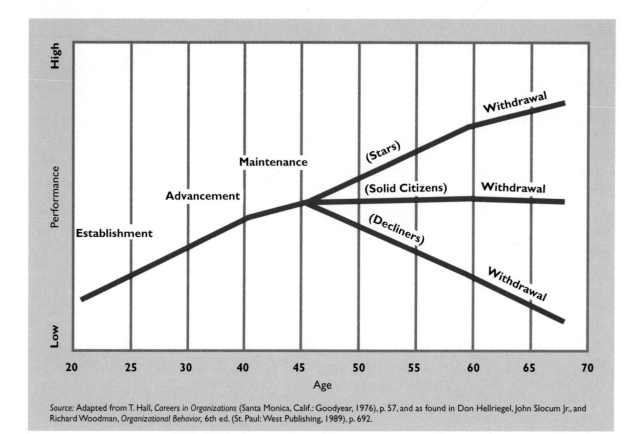

Source: Adapted from T. Hall, *Careers in Organizations* (Santa Monica, Calif.: Goodyear, 1976), p. 57, and as found in Don Hellriegel, John Slocum Jr., and Richard Woodman, *Organizational Behavior*, 6th ed. (St. Paul: West Publishing, 1989), p. 692.

FIGURE 17.3
Working-life career stages.

Establishment (20–25)

The first career stage is establishment (age 20–25). During establishment, a person is a newcomer to the organization and is greatly dependent on others. It is essential that an individual performs well and relates well with his or her superiors. Getting adjusted to the organization's culture and "learning the ropes" is very important, and a mentor can help. A *mentor* is a successful, older, more experienced person who advises, helps open doors, and provides emotional support to and development for a younger employee. The process of becoming a functioning organizational member takes time. Empathizing with other newcomers can help alleviate stress. Much of an employee's work during the establishment stage involves fairly routine tasks. A very important need at this stage is for feedback about performance.

Advancement (25–40)

The advancement career stage often involves new sets of experiences, such as special assignments, promotions, offers from other organizations, and opportunities to become visible to top management. People in this stage typically receive less close supervision and have more latitude in handling their work. A key decision facing someone in this stage is whether to remain specialized (such as in sales or production) or to move into related or even unrelated areas, as David Hogberg of Quaker Oats did in this chapter's Opening Case. Peer relationships become more critical at this stage, as the person is rubbing shoulders with some peers who are destined for success. At the middle to upper age limits of this stage, an individual may become more "tied" to his or her organization through various "perks," such as a company car, profit sharing, a plush office, and fringe benefits like stock options.

College grads will change jobs an average of four times in their careers; many of these changes occur at the advancement stage. As one enters the upper age limits, promotions may be more lateral than upward, as fewer positions are available at higher levels. A source of stress may be the need to balance work and personal life, as the advancement stage may require longer hours, more travel, and relocation as a requisite of promotions.

Maintenance (40–60)

A number of personal changes are associated with the maintenance career stage. Hair turns gray; bodies lose their tone; stamina may decrease. By the early forties, a career that hasn't panned out may lead to a midlife crisis, which can result in radical behavior changes, such as being unable to cope with personal problems, switching jobs or careers, becoming a middle-aged dropout, or getting a divorce.

Three different paths are taken in the maintenance stage by stars, solid citizens, and decliners. **Stars** are individuals who continue to advance, receiving promotions and new job assignments with greater responsibility, and higher status. Frequently stars are assigned roles dealing with important outsiders, such as customers, suppliers, or the government. **Solid citizens** are reliable, steady performers who make up the large bulk of personnel in middle management but have little opportunity for upward promotion. They may lack the interpersonal and competitive skills, may not desire promotion, or they may prove too valuable where they are to compete for the few choice assignments at higher levels. They have reached a *career plateau* where there is little likelihood of advancement to higher-level positions. They face the prospect of doing the same job for an extended period. Many develop off-the-job interests and become involved in community and family activities. **Decliners** are individuals who have little chance for promotion and often are placed in staff positions of decreased responsibility. In many cases, they have failed to keep pace with new knowledge and have become marginal performers.

stars Individuals who continue to advance in their careers, often filling roles dealing with important outsiders.

solid citizens Reliable, steady performers who have reached a career plateau, with little opportunity for upward promotion.

decliners Employees who have little chance for promotion and are often placed in positions of decreased responsibility.

Withdrawal (60–)

This period occurs for most people at around 60 years of age. Many will spend considerable time and energy on mentoring relationships with younger employees. Others may play the role of maverick or entrepreneur, based on their past reputations. In many cases, they devote time to relationships outside the organization, representing their business in community or professional affairs.

MANAGEMENT APPLICATION AND PRACTICE   17.3

Profile of Top Corporate CEOs

A study of 50 corporate CEOs provides some insight into what it takes to reach the top. The CEOs studied headed companies selected from *Forbes*'s listing of 500 major American companies. Among them were such distinguished former American leaders as Lee Iacocca of Chrysler, Robert Smith of General Motors, and Armand Hammer of Occidental Petroleum. Here is what the study found.

PLACE OF BIRTH

Over half (59 percent) of the CEOs were born near metropolitan areas, and 76 percent were born in the mideastern and midwestern industrial states. New York had the greatest representation. Only 6 percent were from outside the United States.

AGE

Ages ranged from 46 to 90 (Armand Hammer), with an average of 59 years.

EDUCATION LEVEL AND SCHOOL

The top CEOs are well educated. Almost all (94 percent) had at least a bachelor's degree. In addition, 26 percent had master's degrees, 8 percent held law degrees, and 4 percent had earned doctorates. Over 46 percent held undergraduate business degrees, while 36 percent specialized in engineering. A large percentage of CEOs with undergraduate engineering degrees had gone on to earn an MBA; over 50 percent of the graduate degrees earned were MBA degrees. Surprisingly, only 36 percent had attended the highly prestigious private Ivy League universities; most had graduated from state universities. Over 40 schools were represented, indicating that graduation from a so-called elite school such as Harvard or Yale is not a prerequisite for the top corporate positions in the land.

CAREER PATTERN

Surprisingly, over half (58 percent) of the CEOs had never worked for another company, working their way to the top in a single firm. Another 38 percent had entered their present firm in midcareer. It would therefore seem that major U.S. companies tend to promote internal candidates to the CEO position.

PROFESSIONAL BACKGROUND

The primary areas of professional involvement were financial, 26 percent; technical, 18 percent; administration, 12 percent; operations, 10 percent; and marketing, 8 percent. While 54 percent headed companies compatible with their own backgrounds, 46 percent had backgrounds unrelated to their firm's product/service mission. Thus the CEOs demonstrated substantial versatility.

OTHER

Seventy-four percent of the CEOs came from middle- or lower-middle-class backgrounds. Seventy-eight percent had performed military service. Over 75 percent played a major role in philanthropic and public service organizations or important national associations. Mean total annual compensation, including salary, bonuses, stock gains, and other forms of compensation, was a whopping $2,544,367.

Source: G. R. Bassiry and R. Hrair Dekmejian, "The American Corporate Elite, A Profile," *Business Horizons*, vol. 33 (May–June 1990), pp. 59–63.

Characteristics of Successful Managers

Perhaps you have started asking yourself, "Do I have the personal characteristics to become a successful manager?" We cannot determine here whether you have the necessary qualities, but we can at least show what qualities research has found to exist in successful managers.

MAP 17.3 above outlines the backgrounds of 50 CEOs of America's largest corporations. Generally, these executives display high educational attainment, have worked their way to the top within their present organizations, and have a variety of backgrounds.

There is no list of the qualities necessary to be a successful manager on which all experts would agree. Remember also that managerial positions vary from the presidents of large companies to supervisors directing the work of only one other employee. However, research does show that some characteristics are generally considered "plus factors" when people are evaluated for managerial positions. These include (1) intelligence; (2) education, including high rank or class standing and leadership in extracurricular activities; (3) broad interests and capabilities; and (4) certain favorable personal characteristics consistent with the requirements of managerial jobs.[10]

Intelligence

You need not be a genius to be an effective manager. Research does show, however, that on intelligence tests, people in management positions usually score above average for our society as a whole.[11] Moreover, managers at higher levels score higher than lower-level managers. You need not interpret these findings, however, as meaning that managers should necessarily be more intelligent than every person they supervise. It is not at all unusual for some or even *all* (in the case of a research group, for example) individuals to have higher intelligence levels than their immediate supervisors. It does mean that you must have a certain minimum level of intellect that will permit you to learn and develop your managerial abilities. So intelligence is a reflection more of your ability to learn than of what you know.

Education

Managers also tend to be more highly educated than nonmanagers. When different variables are compared with measures of success in management, the extent of education has been found to be an important predictor of success. Generally, studies also tend to show that a good class rank, leadership experience in extracurricular activities, and being a graduate of an above-average college substantially increase promotability. However, a comprehensive study by AT&T of 422 college graduates who were placed in the company's general management training program found no correlation between grade point average and subsequent advancement over a period of years.[12] The message here is that grades are critical in landing the first managerial job, but on-the-job performance determines future promotability.

We must point out, moreover, that *age, motivation, initiative, self-study, and good performance help to overcome a lack of formal education.* This is especially true of entrepreneurs.

> Do you remember the profile of Michael Dell, founder of Dell Computer (Chapter 1)? Dell was a college dropout, as were William Gates, founder of Microsoft, and Steven Jobs, cofounder of Apple Computer.

Do not think, however, that you can make your fortune by dropping out of college to start your own business. As you can see from Figure 17.4, the odds are against

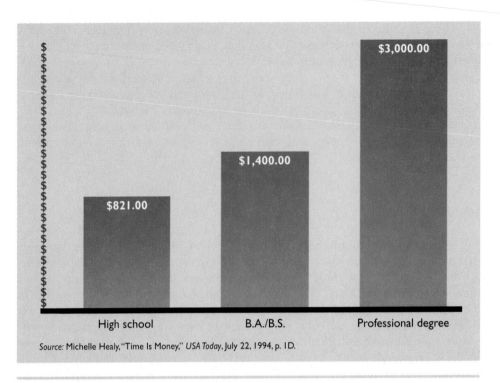

Source: Michelle Healy, "Time Is Money," *USA Today*, July 22, 1994, p. 1D.

FIGURE 17.4
Lifetime employment earnings, ages 25–64, by educational attainment.

you. A college graduate is expected to earn over $600,000 more in a lifetime than someone who has earned a high school diploma; nearly 22 percent of adults age 25 or over now have a college degree.[13]

Broad Interests

From teaching in supervisory and executive development programs, we have concluded that upper-level managers seem to have significantly broader interests than nonexecutives. These interests may range from hobbies to community or church activities. Broader and more intense interests are indicated by top executives who score higher on computational, literary, and persuasive tests than others do. This would seem to indicate that they are capable of comprehending and dealing with a wider range of problems.

Favorable Personal Characteristics

A number of personal characteristics, some clearly behavioral, characterize what firms look for in effective managers. Many of these are related to the human, conceptual, and administrative skills required for managerial jobs, as was pointed

TABLE 17.2 DIMENSIONS FREQUENTLY USED TO SELECT MANAGERS

Dimension	Definition
Oral communication	Effective expression in individual or group situations (includes gestures and nonverbal communications)
Planning and organizing	Establishing a course of action for self and/or others to accomplish a specific goal; planning proper assignments of personnel and appropriate allocation of resources
Delegation	Using subordinates effectively; allocating decision making and other responsibilities to the appropriate subordinates
Control	Establishing procedures to monitor and/or regulate processes, tasks, or activities of subordinates and job activities and responsibilities; taking action to monitor the results of delegated assignments or projects
Decisiveness	Readiness to make decisions, render judgments, take action, or commit oneself
Initiative	Active attempts to influence events to achieve goals; self-starting rather than passive acceptance; taking actions to achieve goals beyond those called for; originating action
Tolerance for stress	Stability of performance under pressure and/or opposition
Adaptability	Maintaining effectiveness in varying environments, with various tasks, responsibilites, or people
Tenacity	Staying with a position or plan of action until the desired objective is achieved or is no longer attainable

Source: Excerpted from George C. Thornton III and William C. Byham, *Assessment Centers and Managerial Performance* (Orlando, Fla.: Academic Press, 1982), Appendix A, pp. 138–140.

out in Chapter 1. As shown in Table 17.2, these include oral communication, planning and organizing, delegation, control, decisiveness, initiative, tolerance for stress, adaptability, and tenacity. Note also that some of these behaviors clearly focus on the important managerial functions of planning, organizing, leading, and controlling.

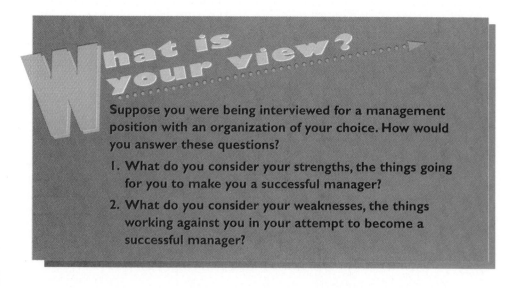

What is your view?

Suppose you were being interviewed for a management position with an organization of your choice. How would you answer these questions?

1. What do you consider your strengths, the things going for you to make you a successful manager?

2. What do you consider your weaknesses, the things working against you in your attempt to become a successful manager?

Initial Management Position

Most first management jobs are in supervisory positions. These managers supervise the doers in organizations—that is, the nonmanagerial assembly line workers, salespeople, tellers, clerks, and office personnel. The classified section of almost any newspaper lists several positions advertised as "manager trainee" spots. These may be positions with a bank, a fast-food chain, a retail company, or some such.

Obtaining Your First Management Position

Although firms often do try to fill initial managerial positions through internal promotion, many operative-level employees in the firm do not have the educational requirements (often a college degree) needed for management positions. Also, operative employees are frequently not capable of becoming good managers because they lack many of the qualities shown in Table 17.2.

The supervisory position is quite a challenging task for recent college graduates, who will probably be younger and have less experience than the employees they supervise. Moreover, there are problems in leading and motivating operative-level personnel, many of whom see limited opportunities for promotion, challenge, or fulfillment in their jobs. In many cases too, first-line supervisors are given limited authority—they must get the job done through influence and persuasion rather than through the authority to reward, promote, or discipline.

Many organizations now have formal management training programs that prepare individuals for their first managerial positions. If you are accepted for a manager trainee position with an energy company such as Exxon, you may begin your career pumping gas in a service station or working on an offshore oil rig. With Wal-Mart, J. C. Penney, or other retail firms, you might rotate through several pre-management positions, taking warehouse inventory, handling customer complaints, or working as a sales person in one of the stores. Many programs provide a rigorous blend of classroom training and on-the-job assignments.

Moreover, many firms interview on college campuses, seeking management trainees from a variety of fields. Since many of you will be—or perhaps now are—involved in interviewing, TIPS 17.1 presents insights regarding some common ethical issues arising from the interview process.

Career Problems You Might Face

What are the most important problems young managers face in their first jobs? Some of them are lack of progress, lack of challenge, insensitivity to organizational culture, difficulties with the first supervisor, and failure to reconcile loyalty dilemmas.

Lack of Progress   New managers, especially recent college or junior college graduates, come from an environment in which they have made steady, sequential progress over several cycles. For example, you will soon earn a grade in this course and the others you are taking, and you will move closer to a degree. After you have passed a certain number of courses, you move from freshman to sophomore or sophomore to junior and then to senior standing. Then you graduate, and so on.

Tips 17.1

Dealing with Career-Related Ethical Issues: Recruiting

As part of the recruiting process, students often face some difficult ethical issues. These include the following situations:

1. Should you accept an organization's invitation for an expense-paid visit even if you know you probably would not accept employment there? If there is a possibility, however slight, that you might be interested in considering a potential job offer, give yourself the benefit of the doubt. But if you are absolutely certain you would never consider working for that employer, it would be unfair to the organization to waste its time and money.

2. You have already accepted a job offer from Company A, and Company B makes you a better offer. Do you take it? An honorable person considers a job acceptance binding, an agreement that can be broken only by mutual consent. Discuss the situation tactfully with Company A. Its options are to (1) say, "A deal's a deal," and try to hold on to you; (2) release you from the agreement; or (3) match or better Company B's offer. The time factor is important here, in that Company A may already have told other candidates, in good faith, that the position was filled.

3. You have received several job offers at different starting salaries. Is it unethical to play the companies off against one another to increase their offers? There is

nothing wrong with letting companies know what you are being offered or that an offer is below others you have received. But you must be careful not to appear manipulative. Letting a company know you plan not to accept an offer because it is lower than that of competitors is certainly acceptable. If the company really wants you, it may appreciate knowing the competitive situation and make a higher offer.

4. Should you expect the company to pay for your visit to their site, and is it OK to travel first class? What about the costs of airport parking, tips, or meals at a fine restaurant? First, who pays for the trip should be clarified when the invitation is extended. If more than just a short distance is involved, the company normally offers to pay for reasonable expenses. But unnecessary expenses, such as first-class travel, meals at the city's finest restaurant, or a night of entertainment, would hardly be considered reasonable. On the other hand, what a company considers standard accommodation may seem luxurious to a penurious student, and so you may have to play it by ear and try to feel out the company recruiter for suggestions as to travel plans, hotel accommodations, and the like.

Source: Adapted from David J. Cherrington, "Ethical Issues in Recruiting," *The Management of Human Resources* (Boston: Allyn & Bacon, 1991), pp. 197–198.

But in your first job, you may feel a distinct lack of perceptible progress, with fewer events changing your basic status. Compared to a school environment, with its rapid progress and feedback of results, the new work environment will probably have a much slower timetable, and it will take a while for you to feel a sense of progress and increased status.

Lack of Challenge   Entry-level jobs often do not require a person to have a college education. College graduates must compete for roughly 20 percent of jobs that do require some college. Indeed, at the establishment career stage, many college graduates experience frustration in their initial job assignments because they are placed in dull jobs that do not entail much responsibility. In reality, though, many employers consider young people's expectations too lofty and unrealistic. Therefore, you will probably have to endure a period during which you have to earn the right to greater authority and responsibility.

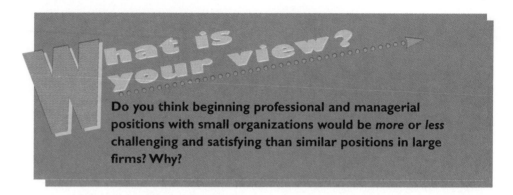

What is your view?

Do you think beginning professional and managerial positions with small organizations would be *more* or *less* challenging and satisfying than similar positions in large firms? Why?

Insensitivity to Organizational Culture   Employees in most organizations face established codes of behavior and interrelationships. New personnel may be idealistic or choose to ignore these codes. Sometimes they are just too naive or unseasoned to be able to recognize them. These failures can lead to reprimand, discipline, or a poor record.

Power coalitions, although they do not show up on the organization chart, are still important ways of accomplishing goals. New employees must learn the organization's behavioral norms, dress codes, and modes of thinking. To fail to understand these realities or to ignore them may lead to misunderstandings, friction, and disillusionment on the part of the new employee.

Difficulties with the First Supervisor   Another initial career problem that confronts new managers is a supervisor who does not support them. Essentially, you will expect your supervisor to give you a feeling of progress by providing feedback about your performance, working with you as you improve your job skills and learn new job concepts, and so on. Also, you will expect the supervisor to relay your ability, potential, and promise to higher-level managers. Supervisors are often less than happy about communicating a subordinate's ability and potential to higher management because of (1) their own job insecurity (the supervisor may see an outstanding subordinate as a threat to the security of his or her own position) or (2) the desire to retain an outstanding employee whose performance would help ensure the success of the departments and the organization.

Ambitious, competent personnel depend heavily on their supervisors to report their talents. Supervisors who jealously safeguard their personnel by keeping them "under wraps" may impede, stall, or even derail many promising careers. If this happens, or if your boss is corrupt or incompetent, you ought to consider changing jobs within or outside the organization.

Loyalty Dilemmas   It requires a delicate balancing act to maintain loyalty to your boss, to your organization, and to yourself.

Managers expect and strongly value their subordinates' general obedience. This may cause problems if you are asked to make decisions or to take actions with which you do not agree. However, unless you are asked to do something illegal or immoral, there are times when you are obliged to follow your boss's directives even if you think there is a better way to do something. Excessive obedience, on the other hand, can create a "yes-person" atmosphere that may not be in the employee's or organization's best long-run interests.

Honest effort is a legitimate managerial request, but to demand success at any price may encourage unethical, immoral, and illegal behavior by subordinates in an

effort to reach goals that may be unrealistic. This dilemma results from the philosophy that "the end justifies the means," which may lead to giving bribes or "cooking the books" in order to fulfill the success-at-any-cost mandate.

A popular management axiom advises telling your bosses what they need to
know so that they will not be caught by surprise. Your bosses will expect you to keep
them informed, even though reports might reflect negatively on your—or their—
performance. It is important to recognize what your bosses *need to know* and not just
what you think they *want to hear*. It is difficult, though, to admit one's mistakes freely
or to convey unpleasant facts to a supervisor, even though that supervisor should
be kept informed of important matters. Loyalty, then, is reflected in communication practices.

> In ancient times, there was an Oriental king who hated to hear bad news.
> Whenever a courier reported bad news or an unfortunate event to him, the courier
> was beheaded. Soon, the king heard no bad news at all.
>
> As CEO of Reliance Electric and later of Acme-Cleveland Corporation, Charles
> Ames stressed the importance of the loyalty dilemma. Upon taking up the reins as
> CEO of Uniroyal Goodrich Tire Company in 1988, he made the following
> promise to its employees:
>
> "We will never act unfairly or lack integrity. Admittedly, this sounds like believ-
> ing in God, the flag, and motherhood, but I am talking about how we *act*, not just
> about talk. In a large corporation, it isn't easy to follow this concept. Effective
> communication is difficult, and the chances of different interpretations of poli-
> cies and situations are great. So we need to work hard to do what's right."
>
> He stressed that he wanted actions and decisions based on logic, facts, and fair
> play, not shaded opinions or distorted facts used to justify actions or decisions.
> "Nor do we want any facts or opinions covered up that might make a situation
> look different from what it really is."[14]

How Organizations Help in Career Planning and Development

Individuals and organizations have recently become more interested and active in
career planning and development. This is a change, for organizations traditionally have
done little along these lines—especially in planning for managerial personnel.

It has long been accepted that professional and managerial careers are highly
desirable because people in those positions are more satisfied with job-related and
personal aspects of their lives. It was assumed that these people had greater
advancement opportunity and more job security. However, corporate downsizing
and elimination of middle-manager and many professional positions means that
midlife career changes among managers and professionals are becoming much
more common.

Role of Career Planning and Development

Career planning involves helping employees choose their goals and identify the
means of attaining those desired objectives. **Career development** is providing the
means of attaining objectives and encouraging employees to use those means.

career planning
Helping employees to
choose their goals and
identify the means of
attaining them.

career development
Providing the means
to help employees
attain objectives and
encouraging them to
use those means.

career path The
sequence of jobs that
can be expected to
lead to career goals
and the ways of pre-
paring for and moving
into those jobs.

An important aspect of career planning and development is providing a **career path,** the sequence of jobs that can be expected to lead to career goals and the ways of preparing for and moving into those jobs. A renowned study shows that it takes an average of 23 years for a person to climb the ladder to the chief executive's position.[15]

Today, *career planning* and *career development* are popular in larger organizations, where it is much more likely than a decade earlier that formal career planning systems exist. If it is in an organization's best interest for its employees to visualize clearly a path or track along which their careers will progress, it is also in a firm's best interest to attempt a reasonable linkage of an employee's talents and interests with the organization's needs.

You, for example, have certain skills and potential skills that you take with you to work. Ideally, a match of your skills and interests with those required by the job should be made. A mismatch costs an organization in at least two ways:

1. You may be ignored and unchallenged, thereby limiting your performance of tasks.
2. Your talent for accomplishing a higher-level task effectively is not being developed fully.

For these and other reasons, organizations are now becoming more concerned about career planning and development. Today's organizations are better equipped than those in the past to recognize talent within their ranks.

Dual Aspects of Career Planning

There is much confusion over just what career planning in organizations is. Career planning must be an integral part of overall organizational planning if it is to succeed. Career planning cannot succeed without *organizational career planning;* nor can it be as effective without *individual career planning.*

Organizational career planning (OCP) focuses on the needs of the organization; *individual career planning (ICP)* focuses on the needs of the individual. As shown in Figure 17.5, an important phase of OCP is making sure that the organization's career planning will match the known and projected needs for personnel and talents in the future. Thus, determining and planning the career moves of individuals that will help them develop and prepare for advancement and greater responsibility in the organization are an example of OCP.

On the other hand, ICP focuses on individuals and their particular needs. Figure 17.5 shows how these types of career planning actually operate in an organization.

Consider the case of Bill Andrews, a talented young geologist with a large, nationally known petroleum company. Bill had a graduate degree in geology and was identified as a comer whom the company felt would be able to take on greater responsibility at higher organizational levels. But when approached about this possibility, Bill felt great uncertainty. He enjoyed the technical work in geology and felt unsure about leaving his specialty. His company practiced ICP, and Bill was given tests and diagnostic measures by the human resources department, as well as in-depth counseling with the company psychologist. The results helped Bill clarify his identity, his interests, and his aspirations. Six months later, Bill accepted a trans-

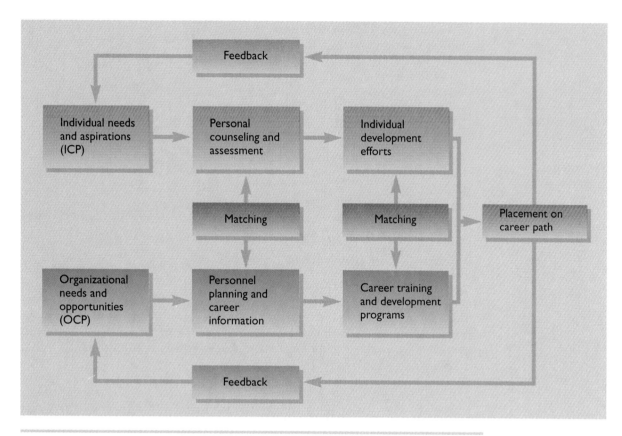

FIGURE 17.5
An example of career planning.

fer to another division of the company, taking on managerial responsibilities. Five
years later, he was one of the most successful project mangers the company had.

Employers more often practice OCP than ICP. Those who embark on an ICP
program usually employ professional specialists to assist individuals in examining
themselves and their career goals. But suppose that the outcome of ICP is that individuals realize the present organization is not the place for them—that their career
needs are not likely to be met and that another organization is more likely to allow
them to reach their goals. It is probably in the organization's best interest to help
individuals reach such a conclusion.

ICP is still relatively new in U.S. organizations, but as they practice more social
responsibility, ICP will be more frequently used and be seen as a logical complement of OCP.

A relatively new concept is the "mommy track," which refers to a career path for
"career and family" women who want to combine serious pursuit of a career with
active participation in rearing their children. What these women need most is the
flexibility to dovetail family and job responsibilities. They are willing to sacrifice
some career progress temporarily in exchange for freedom from weekend work,
shorter workweeks, and flexibility of work scheduling. IBM, Mobil, and Du Pont

are among the growing number of firms that have adopted programs addressing this need.[16]

Organizational Career Development Activities

Most employers are now making more formal efforts to help employees with their career development. The more popular career development activities offered by organizations are listed in Table 17.3. While no firm offers all these programs, larger companies, such as GE, Exxon, and Citicorp, will offer quite a few.

Special Role of Mentoring

In many fields, less experienced workers learn from senior, or more experienced, personnel. For example, in medicine and law, internships help new practitioners to acquire skills and knowledge by working with licensed doctors and attorneys. In the world of organizations, a similar process, though not usually so formalized, is operating quite effectively. Earlier in our discussion of the four career stages, you learned that mentoring was an important process, especially for individuals in the establishment career stage.

Mentors may support their protégés in any number of ways, including

1. Suggesting useful strategies for career development
2. Bringing the protégé's attributes to the attention of upper management

TABLE 17.3   CAREER DEVELOPMENT ACTIVITIES USED BY COMPANIES

- Mentoring
- Tuition aid programs
- Career counseling with performance appraisal
- Manpower planning and forecasting activities
- Intraorganizational job posting
- Job rotation for career development
- Career counseling by specialized staff counselors
- Individual self-analysis and planning workshops
- Lateral transfers in mid-career
- Life and career planning workshops
- Workshops on disengagement or preretirement
- Training supervisors in career counseling sessions
- Time during work hours for career development
- Dual career ladders for technical personnel
- Dual career ladders for professional personnel
- Job enrichment for managers and professionals
- Leaves of absence for professional growth
- Burnout and stress coping problems

3. Providing opportunities for the protégé to demonstrate competence
4. Nominating the protégé for advancement and promotion
5. Protecting protégés in political or organizational skirmishes

Mentors are typically older, senior managers who tend to enjoy strong power and organizational status. Often not the protégé's direct supervisor, the mentor may link with a protégé as a result of favorable impressions of a younger employee's performance or because they click interpersonally.

In most organizations, mentoring is done on an informal rather than a formal basis. However, as more is learned about the positive roles that a mentor system is capable of achieving—for both newer employees and senior executives whose own career advancements may be waning—it could become a more widely used formal career program in organizations.

Ortho Pharmaceutical Corporation, a unit of Johnson & Johnson Company, assigns mentors to the college graduates it hires. The program is touted at campus job interviews.

At Pacific Bell, a unit of Pacific Telesis Group, the firm's 75 summer management interns, hired after their junior year in college, get mentors who later help decide whether the interns will be offered permanent jobs. The system is credited with drawing better-quality new hires.

AT&T Bell Laboratories gives new employees "technical mentors" to help them learn their jobs. It also assigns advisers to women and minority hires.[17]

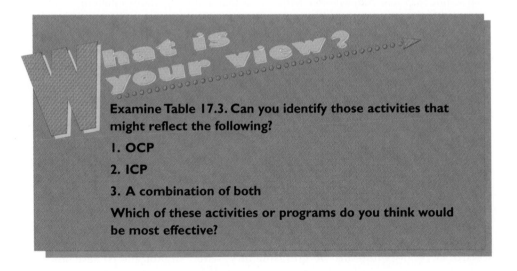

What is your view?

Examine Table 17.3. Can you identify those activities that might reflect the following?

1. OCP

2. ICP

3. A combination of both

Which of these activities or programs do you think would be most effective?

Management and the Future

Now that we have examined the practice of management today, we feel an appropriate final section for this book is one that draws some conclusions about the management process as it will exist in organizations of the future. There is no question that significant trends will have a distinct impact on you and your organizational career.

Continuing Management Trends

Throughout this text, we have discussed new and innovative practices now being seen in organizations in the United States and Canada. These emerging trends point to some broader patterns we think will continue to shape management in the future.

That's Jake

'Next up, we need to decide which is best for the deficit: Buying a Toyota made in Tennessee, or a Dodge made in Tokyo.'

Reprinted by permission.
Tribune Media Services.

Increased Global Interdependence   We have talked a lot about the impact that international business is having on the practice of management. With U.S.-based firms operating overseas and foreign firms opening plants in this country, the distinction between domestic and foreign business increasingly blurs. In fact, many of you may end up working for foreign-owned firms in the United States or abroad (MAP 17.4 illustrates some difficulties encountered in such a career move). The continuing trend toward freer, more open foreign markets in Asia and Europe encourages entrance by foreign firms into these markets and significantly affects strategy, organization structure, leadership, communication processes, and means of control. Since foreign markets are expected to expand more rapidly in the future than home U.S. markets, U.S.-based firms are expected to continue to seek a greater share of international business.

Because of the impact of such rapid change and the increased vulnerability of organizations to external pressures, management will continue to become much more externally focused in the future, as discussed in Chapter 3. There will be increased attention to political, economic, social, and cultural factors and their potential impact on organizations.

New Leadership and Management Styles   A primary management challenge in the future will be managing a workforce that, in general, will be more diverse ethnically and culturally, will have more years of formal schooling, include more professional and technical personnel, be more mobile, and be more inclined to challenge preexisting structures of authority. Employees will continue to demand significant work and more participation in decision making.

We believe that *contingency management* is the appropriate style for today and the future, with emphasis on results. We feel strongly, however, that *more and more situations will require participative management and developmental leadership*, where managers are sensitive to the needs of employees and help to integrate employee objectives with the organization's objectives. We feel equally strongly that there will be fewer situations in which authoritarian management practices and strategies will be effective.

Tendency Toward Leaner, Decentralized Organizations   John Naisbitt, in his best-selling *Megatrends*, predicted a continued power flow toward the individual rather than toward large organizations or government.[18] While organizations have always seemed to value the notion that "bigger is better," there is evidence that the trend toward "appropriate size," which often means smaller, more manageable units, is catching on. This has been reflected in the smaller proportion of managers in place after organizations downsized by eliminating layers of management levels. Also, many organizations, including Johnson & Johnson and Hewlett-Packard, constantly monitor their divisions, product groups, and other organizational units in order to prevent them from becoming too unwieldy. New units, each with their own relative autonomy, are spun off from larger divisions to eliminate complexity and bulk.

Broader Measures of Management Performance   Alvin Toffler, the futurist, in his book *The Third Wave*, forecasts a world in which the performance of managers will be

MANAGEMENT APPLICATION AND PRACTICE 17.4

What to Expect if You Work for a Japanese Firm

It is estimated that 600,000 Americans may get their pay from Japanese companies by the year 2000, as U.S. firms continue to be acquired by the Japanese and the Japanese engage in start-up firms in the United States. Despite all the good things you hear, though, watch out! Working for a Japanese firm may not be all it is cracked up to be, as many Americans are finding out.

In general, the Japanese have been successful in managing U.S. personnel at the operative level, such as factory or clerical personnel. Where they have had trouble is with the hard-driving, upwardly mobile professionals—especially women. The egalitarian culture of equal status, recognition, and reward that goes over so well on the factory floor often frustrates managers and professionals who value individualism and thrive on personal recognition. While factory-level employees generally like the increased participation occurring at the plant level, the managers above them have not shared in it because, all too often, Tokyo calls the shots at their U.S. plants.

American managers complain of so-called shadow managers, Japanese executives who give Americans the titles but reserve the real power for themselves. The facts seem to back this up: Only 31 percent of senior managers of Japanese firms are American, which is quite the reverse of Japan, where foreign subsidiaries fill 80 percent of their senior jobs with Japanese.

Consider the case of William Stewart, age 30, an American who worked for computer giant NEC in both New York and Tokyo. Stewart left the company because of frustration with NEC's lack of a fast track—characteristic of Japanese firms, where promotion is slow and individual recognition discouraged. The key to success in a Japanese firm, he feels, is understanding the "system," which he describes as the process of collecting information and making decisions. For Stewart, it meant 16 hours a day, six days a week, including heavy-duty golfing and after-hours socializing. But it was not the long hours or hard work that prompted him to leave NEC; he just was not interested in having to wait so long in his NEC career to make big-time moves up the career ladder.

Thinking about working for a Japanese firm? Here are some important things to consider:

1. It would be a serious mistake to think of all Japanese firms as being run in the same way or having the same culture. Study them before you decide. Sony is as different from NEC as Apple is from IBM.

2. If you aspire to be a rapid high-flier, look carefully before you leap into a Japanese firm. Do not expect to be a shining star with an individual style. As strong group players, the Japanese promote team play and consensus while downplaying status and reward differentials.

3. Do not anticipate a lot of reinforcement for good work. For one thing, the Japanese *expect* good work; for another, they focus on future *improved* performance rather than letting you rest on your laurels. Japanese managers complain that American workers need too much coddling.

4. Be ready to deal with ambiguity on the job and in the system. Expect to spend lots of energy just figuring out what is going on. This is the process with which Stewart had so much trouble. The differences between Japanese and American firms are likely to be greater than differences among American firms. In short, do your homework before opting for a Japanese company.

Source: Susan Moffat, "Should You Work for the Japanese?" *Fortune*, December 3, 1990, pp. 107–120.

---

evaluated against many criteria—some newly developed—rather than simply by productivity, sales, and profits.[19] The areas measured will also include ethical, environmental, and informational measures, all of which will be interrelated and interdependent.

Changes in Performing the Management Functions

Many of the trends we have discussed will affect the ways managers perform the management functions. Some of the ways these functions will be different in the future are as follows.

▶ *Planning* will profit from better techniques for adjusting to a more technological environment, the use of more sophisticated decision models, greater reliance on the computer, and the need for more precise planning premises and contingency planning. Crises may occur more often as the planning perspective broadens to encompass international arenas.

▶ *Organizing* will be affected by greater reliance on task forces and project management, newer uses of staff and service personnel, greater use of decentralization, reduced levels of hierarchy, and broader span of management as control systems are perfected. International expansion will require greater complexity in organizational design, with appropriate mixes of more centralized, coordinated activity at top management levels in some circumstances and strong decentralization in others, depending on variables in the foreign setting.

▶ *Staffing* will involve more intensive use of personnel planning and career management (especially providing more precise career paths); reduced working time and more leisure time; and greater use of scientific, technical, and professional personnel.

▶ *Leading* will require greater use of motivational tactics designed for creativity, achievement, prestige, and self-expression; more emphasis on personal dignity and worth, security, recognition, and participation; and improved communication, especially upward.

▶ *Controlling* will be influenced by more efficient systems for instantaneous and simultaneous control, greater reliance on computers, and an emphasis on all types of controls, not just financial.

SUMMARY

This chapter has focused on several key aspects of planning a management career. One of these was the extent of management career opportunities. Over the next decade, much growth will occur in white-collar clerical, technical, and professional positions, which will require an expansion in the number of managers needed to supervise the positions.

Generally, individuals pass through four distinct career stages: establishment, advancement, maintenance, and withdrawal.

While there is no generally accepted list of qualities necessary to be a successful manager, several characteristics considered a plus are intelligence, education, broad interests, and certain key behavioral skills including planning, delegating, and communicating.

First-line managers supervise hourly or operative-level employees and constitute the largest group of managers. Some firms look for outsiders to fill these positions, but many companies actively seek to identify operative-level personnel who possess the necessary skills to be effective in a management position.

Newly appointed managers face many problems in their first management jobs. These include (1) feeling of lack of progress, (2) lack of challenge, (3) insensitivity to organizational politics, (4) failure to reconcile loyalty dilemmas, and (5) problems with their own supervisors.

Two main parts of career planning are organizational career planning and individual career planning. OCP focuses on the needs of the organization in attempting to make sure the organization's future needs for workers and various talents are met. ICP focuses on the individual employee in helping him or her map out career objectives and interests. Ideally, OCP and ICP merge so that individuals follow career patterns that are in their own interests and simultaneously meet their organization's labor and career development needs. A career path is the sequence of jobs employees can follow to reach their career objectives. Mentors also play important roles in furthering career movement of younger personnel.

Regarding management practices in the future, a number of trends are evolving. Among these are (1) greater application of participative management styles and use of situational or contingency approaches; (2) emphasis on decentralization and optimum, rather than maximum, size of organizational units; (3) measures of management performance that include social, ethical, and environmental concerns as well as profitability; (4) increased management attention to external environmental variables when making decisions; and (5) changes that will have an impact on the performance of the management functions of planning, organizing, staffing, leading, and controlling.

K E Y   T E R M S

white-collar work, 561
blue-collar work, 561
stars, 569
solid citizens, 569

decliners, 569
career planning, 577
career development, 577
career path, 578

D I S C U S S I O N   Q U E S T I O N S

1. Which type of work do you think offers greater advantages as a career—blue-collar work or white-collar work? Why?

2. Can you think of individuals who have not followed the four-stage career model shown in Figure 17.3? In what ways have their careers differed from the "average"?

3. What is meant by the "loyalty dilemma" managers face in an organization? Have you ever been placed in a loyalty dilemma? What did you do, and why?

4. Search the want ads of your local newspaper and see how many manager positions are advertised. What kinds of skills, if any, are indicated as being desirable? How are the required qualifications described?

5. What is the difference between organizational career planning and individual career planning? Give some examples of each.

6. Describe some of the emerging trends that will affect the future of management.

7. Describe some of the changes occurring in performing the management functions.

17.1

case

Meg Holloran: Early Career Dilemma

Meg Holloran graduated with honors from State University with a major in business. Upon graduation, she accepted a management trainee position with Regents Banking Corporation, a large regional bank holding company in the Midwest. Meg had several offers but selected Regents primarily because of its growth and the fact that the bank's 20-month training program would provide a variety of experiences and a chance to learn the big picture. Along with six other trainees (Meg was the only woman), Meg rotated in 4- to 6-month intervals among positions in branch banking, investments, commercial loans, marketing, and operations. She and the other trainees made good progress and were all impressed that the supervisors to whom they had been assigned seemed genuinely interested in their learning the ropes. Having completed the training period, trainees were asked their choices for initial assignment. Meg selected commercial lending. She enjoyed analysis, was excellent with numbers, and as someone with ambition, realized the instrumental role of commercial lending in the bank's success. As was true with many large banks, commercial lending was the biggest revenue producer for the bank—its "star." The bank's CEO, chairman of the board, and top holding company officers had all been commercial loan people. For Regents, commercial lending was the fast route to the "top."

Meg felt a little dejected when she learned that her first permanent assignment was in branch banking. Several other trainees, she learned, had been given their first preferences, two of whom were placed in commercial lending.

In her next 18 months, Meg was given two separate branch assignments. The first one, which lasted about 8 months, found Meg assigned to a branch near State University. Here she helped individuals open new accounts, put together paperwork for customer loans, managed the safety box system, and, on busy days, operated as a teller. Within 10 months she was reassigned to one of the bank's larger branches as assistant to the branch manager. In this capacity, she performed various jobs assigned by the manager, including interviewing, interpreting budgetary and other performance reports, and interfacing with other personnel on the manager's behalf. She preferred this type of work to that on her first branch job, but she wondered when the move to commercial would come.

Of help to Meg during these early banking career stages was Byron Golson, age 56, a senior vice-president of bank administration (data processing, accounting, human resources, and marketing). Golson was an old friend of the family, and Meg had talked with him on several occasions about her progress in the bank. He had always been helpful, but especially so when she had spent 5 months as a trainee assigned to the marketing department, which reported to him. Last week, some 8 months into her second branch job, Meg learned that she was being transferred to another smaller branch, where she would be assistant branch manager, a line management position. In this capacity, she would directly supervise the teller group, as well as fill in and run the bank in the manager's absence. While she was pleased with the opportunities in the new position, she decided it was time to visit Mr. Golson again for a career-related discussion. After some casual conversation, the meeting went like this:

Meg: Mr. Golson, I've just learned that I'm being moved again, to a new job as branch assistant at Springvale. I'm pleased that I'm being noticed but concerned that they're thinking of me only in terms of branch administration. I'd told them that commercial was my first choice, as I'd mentioned to you. That's the side of banking I'm truly interested in. I'd like your advice. You're familiar with this bank, its ins and outs—what should I do?

Golson: Just be patient, Meg. You should be pleased that you're being given more responsibility.

Meg: I am; don't get me wrong. But commercial is what I really want, and I don't feel any closer than I did two years ago.

Golson: The last thing you want to do in this bank, Meg, is make waves—I couldn't think of anything a female, a young ambitious one such as you, could do to hurt her career here more. Branch administration is where most of our higher-level females are. Meg, look around—like many other businesses, banking is male dominated at the top. You've looked at our annual report . . . check the names. In our holding company, there is only 1 female among 42 senior executive vice-presidents, and that's in a small community bank owned by her father when we bought it. We're trying to change, though—you were among the first female trainees this holding company hired, and Al Bishop (senior vice-president of commercial lending) is flat out an old-line male chauvinist—he'll probably tell you that himself, if you talk with him, and I recommend that you do. He'll be the one who decides if you're brought into his department. But let me give you some honest advice . . . if you want to get ahead around here and especially if you want to ever get into the commercial end, you need to do some things.

Meg: Like what?

Golson: Wearing more makeup would help for starters, and your hairstyle needs some shaping up; those glasses should go, or at least be more stylish. People in this bank have impressions about how a female, especially a female who wants to make it to the top, should look and act. Patrick Lindsay, one of your trainee peers, because he's a male, can probably get by with his fingernails bitten to the nubs, his wrinkled, unpressed clothes, and a directness that often offends his uppers. But you probably couldn't get by. As a female, you're watched more carefully. It's a credit to you that you were one of the first female trainees hired by the bank, and you seem to have impressed people.

Meg: Well, I wanted you to be honest with me and you certainly have been. I guess I was naïve to believe that I was not being looked at differently because I was a female. Hearing this is a surprise.

Golson: Meg, don't get me wrong, it's perhaps more subtle than I'm painting. But you *are* a female, and it *does* make a difference. What you do stands out, fairly or unfairly. But if you play your cards right, I think you can use your femininity to advantage.

The conversation with Golson lasted another five minutes or so, as he talked about how banking and Regents had changed over the past ten years. As Meg left his office, she had mixed emotions—hurt by what she had heard but angered over her own naïveté. Moreover, had she been rejected by Bishop because she was a female? As she did recall, almost all the professional jobs in the commercial lending department were held by males. Is that why she didn't get her first job preference after completing training? She should have known better. "So, I'll have to be more feminine . . . well, I'll be damned."

Questions

1. Should Meg entertain Golson's advice regarding her femininity?

2. What might Meg have done before accepting the position with Regents to learn of any prejudices toward females in the company's management and professional ranks?

3. Assume that you were Meg, preparing for your meeting with Bishop. Develop a plan outlining what you would say during the meeting.

17.1 Career Insight[*]

learning exercise **Part I**

Assume that a large party is being held and the guests are grouped in six rooms according to their personality traits and skills, as listed:

Room A   People who enjoy learning, analyzing, investigating, evaluating, and/or problem solving

Room B   People who enjoy unstructured situations, are imaginative and creative, and have an artistic, innovative, or creative flair

Room C   People who possess good verbal skills and enjoy working with others to inform, help, train, develop, or cure them

Room D   People who enjoy influencing others by persuading or leading, or managing a process

Room E   People who enjoy working with data, have clerical or numerical ability, pay attention to detail, and follow through on instructions

Room F   People who have athletic or mechanical ability and prefer to work with objects, machines, tools, plants, or animals, often outdoors.

Instructions: Fill in the blanks below; then continue to Part II.

1. The people I would most enjoy spending the evening with are in Room _____.

2. The people I would next most enjoy spending the evening with are in Room _____.

3. The people I would least enjoy spending the evening with are in Room _____.

Part II

An important aspect of career management is identifying the types of work you feel best about and enjoy doing. This exercise is designed to give you some idea regarding a match-up of your interests and skills and possible occupational choices.

According to Richard Bolles, one of the top experts in career planning, an important first step in career planning is deciding what type of job offers a fit with your personality and skills. Thus, you are apt to be attracted to people with similar personality traits and skills, and this probably would influence your choice of rooms at the party. The six basic personality types as found in the rooms at the party (given in parentheses) are described in the table on page 589. As each of these lends itself to potential management careers, this exercise should interest you.

[*] This exercise was developed from ideas from several sources, including Richard Bolles, "Career Success Requires We Know More . . . About Ourselves," *Training and Development Journal*, vol. 36 (January 1982), p. 15; John L. Holland, *Making Vocational Choices: A Theory of Careers* (Englewood Cliffs, N.J.: Prentice Hall, 1973), p. 20; and Phillip L. Hunsaker and Curtis W. Cook, *Organizational Behavior* (Reading, Mass.: Addison-Wesley, 1986), p. 86.

Questions

1. To what extent did your choice of rooms match your perceived personality description and occupational environment?

Personality type	Description	Occupational environment
Intellectual (A)	Prefers tasks involving cognitive processes, such as thinking and understanding; tends to avoid work activities that require close interpersonal contact; tends to be more introverted than extroverted	Biology, math, chemistry, physics, and medicine
Artistic (B)	Involves self-expression, expression of emotions, and individual activities; tends to disdain high structure	Art, journalism, music, and photography
Social (C)	Exhibits skill in interpersonal relations; prefers work activities that help other people; tends to avoid high-stress and intelluctual problem-solving work activities	Social work, counseling, teaching, nursing, clerical, and psychology
Enterprising (D)	Desires power and status; likes work activities that involve using verbal skills to influence others and to attain power and status	Law, sales, politics, and management
Conventional (E)	Prefers structure, rules, and regulated work activities; is attentive to details(s); subordinates personal need for power and status to others in the organization	Accounting, clerical, data processing, and credit
Realistic (F)	Likes work requiring physical strength, coordination; tends to avoid interpersonal and verbal types of work; prefers concrete rather than abstract tasks	Engineering, architecture, mechanics, forestry, and agriculture

2. Break into groups of four or five students and compare your room choices. To what extent are they similar? Different?

3. Do you feel that this exercise can provide possible *managerial* career insight? If so, how?

Credits

Unless otherwise acknowledged, all photographs are the property of Scott, Foresman and Company. Page abbreviations are as follows: (T)top, (C)center, (B)bottom, (L)left, (R)right.

Page 2: Philip & Karen Smith/Tony Stone Images; page 7: James Schnepf/Gamma-Liaison; page 14: AP/Wide World; page 30: Tiherry Buccon-Gibon/Gamma-Liaison; page 40: SuperStock, Inc.; page 42: J.P. Lafont/Sygma; page 45: Copyright Yale University Art Gallery, Mabel Brady Garvan Collection; page 49: Frederick W. Taylor Collection; page 51: Boyer-Viollet/Roger-Viollet; page 53L: Historical Pictures/Stock Montage, Inc.; page 53R: Historical Pictures/Stock Montage, Inc.; page 57: Courtesy A. T. & T., Bell Laboratories; page 58: Courtesy Ronald G. Greenwood; page 61: Courtesy Peter F. Brucker; page 64: Bettmann; page 69: Courtesy of IBM; page 74: James Wilson/Woodfin Camp & Associates; page 82: Courtesy Cray Research; page 83: B. Swersey/Gamma-Liaison; page 94: Courtesy H.J. Russell & Co; page 97: Nina Berman/SIPA-Press; page 107: Milt & Joan Mann/Cameramann International, Ltd.; page 109: Peter Charlesworth/JB Pictures Ltd.; page 112: Greg Girard/Contact Press Images; page 117: Edward Basililan; page 122: Lincoln Potter/Gamma-Liaison; page 127: Herman Schwarz; page 140: Courtesy Chick-Fil-A; page 144: Chris Usher; page 147: Courtesy International Paper; page 148: Bettmann; page 151: Jeffrey D. Smith/Woodfin Camp & Associates; page 152: Courtesy George Fraser; page 153: Lowe/Network Stock Photos; page 157: Jeff Greenberg/Photo Edit; page 163: Drawing by Fradon; ©The New Yorker Magazine, Inc.; page 170: Courtesy Gerber; page 172: B. Busco/The Image Bank; page 176: Courtesy Peavey Electronics; page 178: Stephen Marks/The Image Bank; page 191: Courtesy Linda Dean Fucci; page 196T: Fred Mertz; page 196B: Joe Kennedy; page 211: Courtesy Weyerhauser; page 214: Courtesy Hartmarx; page 217: Courtesy Johnson & Johnson; page 218: ©1991 Diane Allen; page 244: Courtesy General Electric Corp; page 250: John Giordono/SABA; page 270: Douglas Kirkland/SABA; page 286: Courtesy Roxanne J. Decyk; page 288: Courtesy Delta Air Lines, Inc.; page 293: D. Wells/The Image Works; page 297: Phi Kappa Phi Journal/Sidney Harris; page 309: Frank Wing/The Image Bank; page 324: Comstock Inc.; page 330: Blair Seitz/Photo Researchers; page 340: Courtesy PFS-TV, Duluth, Georgia; page 347: Courtesy Wendy's; page 359: Courtesy Metropolitan Life Ins. Co.; page 361: Courtesy Quad/Graphics; page 365: Anthony Suau/Gamma-Liaison; page 368: Courtesy Patricia G. Lynch; page 375: Bob Daemmrich/The Image Works; page 394: Brian Willer/*MacLean's Magazine;* page 397: Courtesy American Airlines; page 404L: UPI/Bettmann; page 404TR: AP/Wide World; page 404BR: AP/Wide World; page 422: Courtesy The RITZ-CARLTON Hotel Company; page 424: Reprinted with express permission of Ritz-Carlton Hotel Company; page 436: Copyright 1987, *USA Today,* used with permission; page 454: Courtesy Cianbro Corporation; page 455: The Maine Image from Cianbro; page 482: Courtesy International Paper Company; page 488: Bill Varie/The Image Bank; page 492: Courtesy of IBM; page 500: Robin Thomas; page 503: Drawing by Reilly, ©1976 The New Yorker Magazine, Inc.; page 504: Steve Allen, The Gamma Liaison Network; page 524: NASA; page 528: Philippe Brylak/Gamma-Liaison; page 534: Courtesy of IBM; page 539: David Carter; page 543: Courtesy Red Rose Collection, Inc.; page 545: Boris Spooner/Gamma-Liaison; page 546: Michael Newman/Photo Edit; page 549: Michael Newman/Photo Edit; page 555: Jeffrey Markowitz/Sygma; page 560: Paul Elledge; page 566: AP/Wide World; page 582: Reprinted by permission: Tribune Media Services.

Notes

Chapter 1

1. Peter C. Reid, "How Harley Beat Back the Japanese," *Fortune*, September 25, 1989, pp. 155–164, and Susan Caminiti, "The Payoff from a Good Reputation," *Fortune*, February 10, 1992, pp. 73–77.
2. "Occupational Employment Projections," *Monthly Labor Review* (Washington, D.C.: Government Printing Office, 1991), pp. 17–19.
3. U.S. Bureau of the Census, *Statistical Abstract of the United States* (Washington, D.C.: Government Printing Office, 1993) p. 539.
4. See W. Edwards Deming, *Out of the Crisis* (Cambridge, Mass.: MIT Center for Advanced Engineering Study, 1986).
5. Bruce Nussbaum, "Needed: Human Capital," *Business Week*, September 19, 1988, p. 102.
6. David R. Rosenbaum, "All Roads Lead to Washington and Politics in S&L Calamity," *Arizona Republic*, June 10, 1990, pp. F3–F5, and Kenneth Labich, "The New Crisis in Business Ethics," *Fortune*, April 20, 1992, p. 168.
7. Cited in Fred Luthans, *Organizational Behavior*, 6th ed. (New York: McGraw-Hill, 1992), p. 192.
8. Sarah Smith, "Quality of Management," *Fortune*, January 29, 1990, p. 46, and "Life of a Salesman," *Time*, June 15, 1992, pp. 53–59.
9. John W. Gardner, *On Leadership* (New York: Free Press, 1990), p. 4.
10. John F. Mee, "Management Philosophy for Professional Executives," *Business Horizons*, vol. 1 (1956), pp. 5–11.
11. Myron D. Pottler, "Is Management Really Generic?" *Academy of Management Review*, vol. 6 (January 1981), pp. 1–12.
12. Henry Mintzberg, The Nature of Managerial Work (New York: Harper & Row, 1973); see also, "The Manager's Job," *Harvard Business Review*, vol. 53 (July–August 1975), pp. 49–61.
13. See Fred Luthans, Richard Hodgetts, and S. A. Rosenkrantz, *Real Managers* (Cambridge, Mass.: MIT Press, 1988).
14. Donald Hellriegel, John W. Slocum, and Richard W. Woodman, *Organizational Behavior* (New York: West Publishing, 1992), p. 9.
15. P. J. Guglielmino, "Developing the Top-Level Executive for the 1980s and Beyond," *Training and Development Journal*, vol. 13, no. 33 (April 1979), pp. 12–14; see also, Allen T. Kraut, Patricia R. Pedigo, Douglas O. McKenna, and Marvin D. Dunnette, "The Role of the Manager: What's Really Important in Different Management Jobs?" *Academy of Management Executive*, vol. 3, no. 4 (1989), pp. 286–293.
16. Alan Deutschman, "Odd Man Out," *Fortune*, July 26, 1993, p. 48.
17. Morgan W. McCall, Jr., and Michael M. Lombardo, "What Makes a Top Executive?" *Psychology Today*, February 1983, p. 28.

Chapter 2

1. Lawrence M. Miller, *American Spirit—Visions of a New Corporate Culture* (New York: Warner Books, 1985).
2. Exodus 18.
3. Niccoló Machiavelli, *Discourses on Living*, trans. Alan H. Gilbert, reprinted in *Machiavelli: The Chief Works and Others* (Durham, N.C.: Duke University Press, 1956), vol. 1, p. 203.
4. Daniel Wren, *The Evolution of Management Thought*, 3rd ed. (New York: John Wiley & Sons, 1987), pp. 22–25.
5. For further details, see W. Bowden, M. Karpovich, and A. P. Usher, *An Economic History of Europe Since 1750* (New York: American Book, 1937), p. 600.
6. Christine Ammer and Dean S. Ammer, *Dictionary of Business and Economies* (New York: Free Press, 1977), p. 102.
7. "Unfinished Homework," *Wall Street Journal*, January 6, 1993, p. A1.
8. Adam Smith, *An Inquiry into the Nature and Cause of the Wealth of Nations* (New York: Modern Library, 1937; originally published in 1776).
9. Charles Babbage, *On the Economy of Machinery and Manufacturers* (Philadelphia: Corey Lea, 1832).
10. L. Urwick, ed., *The Golden Book of Management* (London: Newman Neame, 1956). Most of the material in this section is taken from pp. 72–79 of this source and from Frederick W. Taylor, *The Principles of Scientific Management* (New York: Harper & Row, 1947).
11. Taylor, *The Principles of Scientific Management*, p. 47.
12. Henri Fayol, *General and Industrial Management*, trans. Constance Storrs (New York: Pitman, 1949; originally published in French in 1916.)
13. E. F. L. Brech, *Management: Its Nature and Significance* (New York: Pitman, 1948), p. 209.
14. Lillian M. Gilbreth, *The Psychology of Management* (New York: Sturgis and Walton, 1914; reissued by Macmillan, 1921).
15. See Leon C. Megginson, Geralyn M. Franklin, and M. Jane Byrd, *Human Resource Management* (Houston, Tex.: Dame Publications, 1995), Chapter 14, for more details.
16. Max Weber, *The Theory of Social and Economic Organization* (New York: Oxford University Press, 1947).
17. F. E. Fiedler, et al., "An Exploratory Study of Group Creativity in Laboratory Tasks," *Acta Psychologica*, vol. 18 (1961), pp. 100–119.
18. Hugo Munsterberg, *Psychology and Industrial Efficiency* (Boston: Houghton Mifflin, 1913).
19. Oliver Sheldon, *The Philosophy of Management* (New York: Pitman, 1939; originally published in 1923), p. 2.
20. F. J. Roethlisberger and W. J. Dickson, *Management and the Worker* (Cambridge, Mass.: Harvard University Press, 1939), p. 1.
21. Henry C. Metcalf and Lyndall Urwick, eds. *Dynamic Administration: The Collected Papers of Mary Parker Follett* (New York: Harper & Row, 1940), pp. 32–37.

22. Chester Barnard, *The Functions of the Executive* (Cambridge, Mass.: Harvard University Press, 1938).
23. Malcolm P. McNair, "Thinking Ahead: What Price Human Relations?" *Harvard Business Review*, vol. 35 (March–April 1957), pp. 15–18.
24. Richard A. Johnson, Fremont E. Kast, and James E. Rosenzweig, *The Theory and Management of Systems* (New York: McGraw-Hill, 1963), p. 4.
25. *Fortune*, September 24, 1990, p. 64.
26. See for example, David Halberstam, *The Reckoning* (New York: Wm. Morrow, 1986), p. 314.
27. W. Edwards Deming, *Quality, Productivity, and Competitive Position* (Cambridge, Mass.: MIT Press, 1982).
28. W. Edwards Deming, *Out of the Crisis* (Cambridge, Mass.: Massachusetts Institute of Technology, Center for Academic Engineering, 1986).

Chapter 3

1. "The Alaskan Oil Spill: Lessons in Crisis Management," *Management Review*, vol. 79 (April 1990), pp. 12–21; "Alaska Ends Oil Breaks After *Valdez* Spill," *Insight*, June 5, 1989, p. 45; and "Nowhere to Run or Hide," *Time*, May 29, 1989, p. 69.
2. "Costlier Fuels for Pan Am," *USA Today*, January 10, 1991, p. 1B.
3. "The Greening of Corporate America," *Business Week*, April 23, 1990, pp. 96–103.
4. Alan Deutschman, "Scramble on the Information Highway," *Fortune*, February 7, 1994, pp. 129–131.
5. N. H. Snyder, "Environmental Volatility, Scanning Intensity and Organizational Performance," *Journal of Contemporary Business*, vol. 19 (September 1981), p. 16.
6. Rosabeth Moss Kanter, *When Giants Learn to Dance* (New York: Simon & Schuster, 1989), p. 119.
7. George Fisher, "Customers Drive a Technology-Driven Company: An Interview with George Fisher," *Harvard Business Review*, vol. 67 (November–December 1989), p. 114.
8. Myron Magnet, "The New Golden Rule of Business," *Fortune*, February 21, 1994, pp. 60–64.
9. See Michael Porter, *Competitive Strategy: Techniques for Analyzing Industries and Competitors* (New York: Free Press, 1980).
10. Sharon Oster, *Modern Competitive Analysis* (New York: Oxford University Press, 1990), p. 203.
11. See Edmund Faltermayer, "Why Health Costs Can Keep Slowing," *Fortune*, January 24, 1994, pp. 76–82; and Sharon Tully, "The Plot to Keep Drug Prices High," *Fortune*, December 27, 1993, pp. 120–124.
12. Eric von Hippel, *The Sources of Innovation* (New York: Oxford University Press, 1988), p. 17.
13. Fred Luthans, Richard M. Hodgetts, and Kenneth R. Thompson, *Social Issues in Business* (New York: Macmillan, 1990), p. 360.
14. "Abortion Issue Hits Retailer," *USA Today*, September 11, 1990, p. 1A.
15. As reported in *USA Today*, April 26, 1989, p. 1A, and *Fortune*, February 26, 1990, p. 124.
16. Daniel Seligman, "The Unions Present a Bill," *Fortune*, December 3, 1990, p. 189.
17. "Mazda-UAW's Michigan Honeymoon Is Over," *Wall Street Journal*, April 17, 1990, p. B1.
18. David Kirkpatrick, "Environmentalism: The New Crusade," *Fortune*, February 12, 1990, pp. 44–55.
19. Anne B. Fisher, "Is Long-Range Planning Worth It?" *Fortune*, April 23, 1990, p. 282.
20. Ibid., p. 284.

21. Kanter, *When Giants Learn to Dance*, p. 162.
22. John A. Pierce II and Richard B. Robinson, *Strategic Management*, 2nd ed. (Homewood, Ill.: Richard D. Irwin, 1985), p. 178.
23. Jeremy Main, "Making Global Alliances Work," *Fortune*, December 17, 1990, p. 124.
24. "Today's Leaders Look to Tomorrow," *Fortune*, March 26, 1990, p. 32.
25. Joanne Martin, *Cultures in Organizations* (New York: Oxford University Press, 1992), p. 3.
26. Don Hellriegel, John W. Slocum, Jr., and Richard Woodman, *Organizational Behavior*, 6th ed. (St. Paul, Minn.: West Publishing, 1992), p. 502.
27. Thomas J. Peters and Robert H. Waterman, *In Search of Excellence* (New York: Harper & Row, 1982), p. 57.
28. John Wagner and John A. Hollenbeck, *Organizational Behavior* (Englewood Cliffs, N.J.: Prentice Hall, 1992), p. 699.
29. Alan Farnham, "Mary Kay's Lessons in Leadership," *Fortune*, September 20, 1993, pp. 68–77.
30. Cindi Brownfield, "Just a Hamburger Cook at Heart," (Florida) *Destin Log*, September 2, 1985, pp. 1A, 8A.
31. Debra Nelson and James C. Quick, *Organizational Behavior* (St. Paul, Minn.: West Publishing, 1994), p. 497.
32. Peter C. Reynolds, "Imposing a Corporate Culture," *Psychology Today*, March 1987, pp. 33–38.

Chapter 4

1. Quoted in *USA Today*, November 12, 1990, p. 15A.
2. William J. Holstein, "The Stateless Corporation," *Business Week*, May 14, 1990, p. 103, and correspondence with Coca-Cola.
3. See Scott Armstrong, "Drucker Tells of a Revolution Half Done," *Christian Science Monitor*, August 26, 1993, p. 12.
4. Joan Warner, "The Wall Fell Down, and the Continent Took Off," *Business Week*, July 16, 1990, p. 112.
5. Brian Donlon, "Producers Go Global to Cut Costs," *USA Today*, December 7, 1990, p. 3D; "Database," *U.S. News & World Report*, March 18, 1991, p. 17; and *USA Today*, April 13, 1992, p. 3D.
6. "The NAFTA Vote: What's at Stake," *USA Today*, November 17, 1993, p. 3D.
7. For a fuller discussion of these movements, see Andrew Nagorski, *The Birth of Freedom: Shaping Lives and Societies in the New Eastern Europe* (New York: Simon & Schuster, 1993) and "Eastern Europe Is One Hot Market," *Fortune*, January 25, 1993, p. 14.
8. "The Growing Power of Asia," *Fortune*, October 7, 1991, p. 118.
9. Ibid., pp. 118–165.
10. "Cracking the China Market," *Wall Street Journal*, December 10, 1993, p. R1.
11. Valerie Reitman, "Enticed by Visions of Enormous Numbers, More Western Marketers Move into China," *Wall Street Journal*, July 12, 1993, pp. B1, B10.
12. Robert Keatley, "A Boom in Asia: AIG Sells Insurance in Shanghai, Testing Service Firms' Role," *Wall Street Journal*, July 21, 1993, pp. A1, A9.
13. Joyce Barnathan, Pete Engardio, Lynne Curry, and Bruce Einhorn, "China: The Emerging Economic Powerhouse of the 21st Century," *Business Week*, May 17, 1993, p. 54.
14. "The Year for America to Go Global," *Business Week*, January 10, 1994, p. 146.
15. John J. Keller, "AT&T to Unveil Management Shakeup Stressing Globalization and Multimedia," *Wall Street Journal*, July 22, 1993, p. A2.

16. For further details, see Ben Wattenberg, *The First Universal Nation: Leading Indicators and Ideas about the Surge of America in the 1990s* (New York: Free Press, 1990).

17. James E. Ellis, "Why Overseas? 'Cause That's Where the Sales Are," *Business Week*, January 10, 1994, pp. 62–63.

18. Warren Cohen, "Exporting Know-How," *U.S. News & World Report*, September 6, 1993, p. 53.

19. Susan E. Kuhn, "Are Foreign Profits Good for Stocks?" *Fortune*, November 16, 1992, p. 27.

20. Molly Read, "An American Success," *Japanese Times*, October 17, 1992, p. 3.

21. U.S. Commerce Department, as reported in "Say No to Protectionism: Get Free Trade's Benefits," *USA Today*, November 16, 1993, p. 14A.

22. Pamela Sherrid, "America's Hottest Export," *U.S. News & World Report*, July 17, 1987, p. 39.

23. Gary Strauss, "Oil-Gobblers Face Their Biggest Test," *USA Today*, January 29, 1991, p. 4A.

24. "Firefighters to Start on Wells in 2 Weeks," *USA Today*, March 14, 1991, p. 4A.

25. Robert E. Norton, "The Myths of Foreign Investments," *U.S. News & World Report*, May 29, 1989, pp. 44–46.

26. Charley Reese, "Nationalism vs. Globalism," *Human Events*, January 11, 1992, p. 11.

27. Rick Haglund, "What Is An 'American' Car?" *Mobile Register*, March 20, 1994, p. 1F.

28. Cindy Skrzcki, "America on the Auction Block," *U.S. News & World Report*, March 30, 1987, pp. 56–68.

29. Peter A. Buxbaum, "Doing Their Level Best," *Distribution*, April 1994, pp. 42–47.

30. As reported in "Today's Tip-Off," *USA Today*, June 20, 1990, p. 1B.

31. "Joint-Stock Society in Front of the Kremlin," *Business in the USSR*, January 1991, p. 44.

32. John Urquhart, "Canadian Shoppers Flock to U.S. Stores to Get Away from High Prices of Home," *Wall Street Journal*, November 23, 1990, p. A2.

33. Robin Bulman, "Exports Made in America," *Mobile Register*, March 20, 1994, p. 1F.

34. John J. Curran, "China's Investment Boom," *Fortune*, March 7, 1994, p. 118.

35. *Wall Street Journal*, February 26, 1991, p. A1.

36. "Scott Paper to Take Write-Offs in Quarter," *Wall Street Journal*, January 11, 1991, p. A2.

37. Karen L. Miller and James B. Treece, "Honda's Nightmare: Maybe You Can't Go Home Again," *Business Week*, December 24, 1990, p. 36.

38. "U.S. Companies Stay on Guard over Terrorism," *Wall Street Journal*, March 5, 1991, pp. B1, B2.

39. Martha T. Moore, "Crossing the Border Is a Breeze," *USA Today*, May 5, 1990, p. 8E.

40. William L. Megginson et. al, *Small Business Management: An Entrepreneur's Guide to Success*, (Burr Ridge, Ill: Irwin 1994), p. 241.

41. John Huey, "America's Hottest Export: Pop Culture," *Fortune*, December 31, 1990, pp. 56–58.

42. Maria Shao, Robert Neff, and Jeffrey Ryser, "For Levi's, a Flattering Fit Overseas," *Business Week*, November 15, 1990, pp. 76–77, and "Exporting Jobs and Ethics," *Fortune*, October 5, 1992, p. 10.

43. Fred Williams, "Trade Climate Good South of the Border," *USA Today*, May 7, 1990, p. 8E.

44. Ret Autry, "Companies to Watch: Crawford & Co.," *Fortune*, February 25, 1991, p. 92.

45. "Beijing Business," *U.S. News & World Report*, October 29, 1990, p. 17.

46. Laxmi Nakarmi, Neil Gross, and Rob Hof, "Samsung: Korea's Great Hope for High Tech," *Business Week*, February 3, 1992, p. 44.

47. Robert Neff and Kimberly Blanton, "You Can't Eat Sushi at the Local 7-Eleven—Yet," *Business Week*, November 12, 1990, p. 59.

48. Laura Landro, "Sony Corp. Plans Firm to Oversee Movie, Music Units," *Wall Street Journal*, January 9, 1991, p. B5; Catherine Arnst, "The Gold Standard of CDs," *Business Week*, May 24, 1993, p. 146; "Sony Corporation," *Wall Street Journal*, March 17, 1994, p. B4; and "Sony Corp.: Music Entertainment Unit Posts Drop in Pretax Earnings," *Wall Street Journal*, May 17, 1994, p. A1.

49. Carol McPhail, "Study Japan Before Doing Business, Expert Says," *Mobile Register*, May 21, 1993, p. 11B.

50. Based on the authors' experience teaching, speaking, consulting, and doing research in over 60 countries.

51. Joann S. Lublin, "Younger Managers Learn Global Skills," *Wall Street Journal*, March 31, 1992, p. B1.

52. "Ready to Travel?" *Business Week*, March 2, 1992, p. 46.

53. Patrick Oster et. al, "The Fast Track Leads Overseas," *Business Week*, November 1, 1993, p. 64.

54. "Managers Balk at Overseas Assignments," *Wall Street Journal*, June 16, 1992, p. A1.

55. "Many Companies Successfully Meet Expatriation Concerns," *Wall Street Journal*, June 16, 1992, p. A1.

Chapter 5

1. "A Helping Hand," *Sports Spectrum*, January 1994, p. 27; Shelley Wolson, "RB Leadership Award: S. Truett Cathy—Never on Sunday," *Restaurant Business*, May 1, 1992, pp. 110–111; Kerri Conan, "Squawk Swap," *Restaurant Business*, June 10, 1992, pp. 105–109; and Rona Gindin, "Market Share Report: Chicken," *Restaurant Business*, October 10, 1992, pp. 165–188.

2. Milton Friedman, *Capitalism and Freedom* (Chicago: University of Chicago Press, 1962), p. 133.

3. Herbert London, "Profitable Businesses Serve Society Best," *Human Events*, March 13, 1993, p. 9.

4. "'Miracle Drug' to Be Given Away," Mobile (Alabama) Register, October 22, 1987, p. 5A, and various other sources.

5. Herbert London, "Profitable Businesses Serve Society Best," *Human Events*, March 13, 1993, p. 9.

6. "Social Consciousness Spreads," *Wall Street Journal*, September 16, 1992, p. 4B.

7. Christiana Del Valle, "The Politically Correct Pension Fund," *Business Week*, March 21, 1994, p. 108.

8. Rae Tyson, "EPA Order to Pump Gas, Auto Prices," *USA Today*, July 23, 1987, p. 1A.

9. K. E. Aupperle, A. B. Carroll, and J. D. Hatfield, "An Empirical Examination of the Relationship Between Corporate Social Responsibility and Profitability," *Academy of Management Journal*, vol. 28 (December 1985), pp. 446–463.

10. John P. Kotter and James L. Heskett, *Corporate Culture and Performance* (New York: Free Press, 1992).

11. Robert Hay and Ed Gray, "Social Responsibilities of Management," *Academy of Management Journal*, vol. 17 (March 1974), p. 142.

12. From letters to the *New York Times*, August 25, 1918, and *New York Herald*, October 1, 1918.

13. *Dodge v. Ford Motor Company*, 204 Mich. 459 (1919).

14. F. X. Sutton et al., *The American Business Creed* (New York: Schocken Books, 1962), pp. 64–65.

15. Upton Sinclair, *The Jungle* (Cambridge, Mass.: R. Bentley, 1972; originally published in 1906).

16. Various sources, including correspondence with Johnson & Johnson.

17. Gary Strauss, "Businesses: Profits, Planet Do Mix," *USA Today*, June 10, 1992, p. lD.

18. "Firms Give Millions for Children, Elderly," *Mobile* (Alabama) *Register*, September 11, 1992, p. 3B.

19. As reported in the Government Street Presbyterian Church (Mobile, Alabama) *Newsletter*, July 23, 1986, p. 1.

20. See Harry Maier, "Volvo Ad Crushed by Hubbard Lemon Award," *USA Today*, December 11, 1990, p. 2B.

21. Faye Rice, "Who Scores Best on the Environment?" *Fortune*, July 26, 1993, p. 116.

22. Tom Shields, "Smelter's Billows Depart Arizona Sky," *USA Today*, January 15, 1987, p. 3A.

23. Elizabeth Lesly and Laura Zinn, "The Right Moves, Baby," *Business Week*, July 5, 1993, pp. 30–31.

24. "School Daze: Companies Help Workers Cope with Educating Kids," *Wall Street Journal*, October 9, 1990, p. Al.

25. Al Maska, "Business' Educated Investment," *Kiwanis*, September 1993, p. 23.

26. Julie Lawlor, "Best Firms for Working Moms," *USA Today*, September 19, 1990, p. 2B.

27. "What's News—," *Wall Street Journal*, February 19, 1987, p. A31.

28. Robert Johnson, "Aetna Sets Out to 'Do Good' for Chicago but Ends Up in Fight with Neighborhood," *Wall Street Journal*, December 6, 1982, p. A25.

29. For further details, see Chris Welles and Michele Galen, "Milken Is Taking the Fall for a 'Decade of Greed,'" *Business Week*, December 10, 1990, p. 30; S. Schwartz, "Why Mike Milken Stands to Qualify for Guinness Book," *Wall Street Journal*, March 31, 1989, p. Al; and "Mixed Feelings About Drexel's Decision," *Wall Street Journal*, December 23, 1988, p. 1.

30. Milton Moskowitz, Michael Katz, and Robert Levering, eds., *Everybody's Business* (New York: Harper & Row, 1980), pp. 688–689.

31. Lisa Perlman, "Gerber Ends Tours Due to Fears of Corporate Spying," *Mobile* (Alabama) *Register*, April 30, 1990, p. 3B.

32. Patrick Moser, "GM, VW Legal Battle Reaches New Heights," *Christian Science Monitor*, August 25, 1993, p. 9; Audry Choi, "Lopez Concedes He Supervised Shredding Data," *Wall Street Journal*, August 26, 1993, p. A2; and Audrey Choi, "GM Unit Confirms It Hired Detectives to Investigate VW," *Wall Street Journal*, May 16, 1994, p. A9.

33. Andy Pasztor, "Litton vs. Honeywell: Patent Suit Barely Stops to Catch Its Breath," *Wall Street Journal*, September 27, 1993, p. B2.

34. Ron Winslow, "X-Ray Owners Said to Order Far More Tests," *Wall Street Journal*, December 6, 1990, pp. Bl, B3.

35. Desda Moss, "Former United Way Chief Charged with Looting Fund," *USA Today*, September 14, 1994, p. 1A.

36. Christiana Del Valle, "The Feds: At Labor, A Sorry State," *Business Week*, August 15, 1994, p. 8.

37. Ann Reilly Dowd, "Environmentalists Are on the Run," *Fortune*, September 19, 1994, pp. 91–104.

38. Kathleen Kerwin, "Can Jack Smith Fix GM?" *Business Week*, November 1,1993, pp. 128–129.

39. John Waggoner and Ellen Newborne, "Wal-Mart Settles on Ad Claims," *USA Today*, March 18, 1994, p. 18.

40. "Crime and Punishment," *Business Week*, June 15, 1987, p. 85.

41. David C. Walters, "Companies Seem Unperturbed by Tide of Internal Fraud, Study Shows," *Christian Science Monitor*, August 20, 1993, p. 9.

42. "Honda Scandal," *USA Today*, March 15, 1994, p. lB.

43. "Doing the 'Right' Thing Has Its Repercussions," *Wall Street Journal*, January 25, 1990, p. Bl.

44. Courtesy of Rotary International.

45. Patricia Haddock and Marilyn Manning, "Ethically Speaking," *Sky*, March 1990, p. 128.

46. Carol Kleiman, "Ethics Officers Join Establishment," *Mobile* (Alabama) *Press Register*, January 2, 1994, p. 8F.

Chapter 6

1. Barry R. Camp, "Mississippi's Newest Captains of Industry—Melia and Hartley Peavey," Mississippi *Journal of Business*, July 1988, pp. 1–4; and discussions and correspondence with Jere Hess, director of public relations and education for Peavey Electronics.

2. Kathleen Cook, "Why Aren't Women in the Top Jobs?" *USA Today*, August 17, 1987, p. 2D.

3. Richard L. Hudson, "Scientific Saga: How 2 IBM Physicists Triggered the Frenzy over Superconductors," *Wall Street Journal*, August 19, 1987, pp. 1, 6.

4. Patrick Santillo, "The Art of Doing Business in Japan," *Overseas Business*, Winter 1990, pp. 40–41. Santillo is principal commercial officer in the U.S. consulate in Osaka, Japan.

5. Herbert A. Simon, *Administrative Behavior*, 2nd ed. (New York: Free Press, 1978). See also Herbert A. Simon, "Making Management Decisions: The Role of Intuition and Emotion," *Academy of Management Executive*, vol. 1 (February 1987), pp. 57–64.

6. Peter E. Drucker, *An Introductory View of Management* (New York: Harper & Row, 1977), p. 398.

7. Stephen Phillips, "Bad Risks Are This Care Insurer's Best Friends," *Business Week*, December 12, 1990, p. 122.

8. Even ESP is being accepted more by researchers and managers as part of decision making and planning, but there are many skeptics. See C. B. Cheatham, "ESP: A Useful Planning Tool," *Managerial Planning*, vol. 25 (November–December 1976), pp. 38–40.

9. Kathy Rebello, "Bold Freeze on Gas Prices Is Paying Off," *USA Today*, August 29, 1990, p. 1B.

10. Personal experience of one of the authors.

11. Mark Memmott, "It Takes Guts for Executives to Make the Tough Decisions," *USA Today*, July 21, 1987, p. 7B.

12. Isabel Briggs Myers, *Gifts Differing* (Palo Alto, Calif.: Consulting Psychologists Press, 1980). We recommended that students take the Myers-Briggs Test Indicator, available from your university's counseling center. It can be helpful in identifying problem-solving type and in considering careers.

13. Donald Mosley, Fabius O'Brien, and Paul Pietri, "Problem Solving Styles Determine Manager's Approach to Making Decisions," *Industrial Management*, vol. 33, no. 5, (September–October 1991), pp. 5–9.

14. "Bush as the Nation's Manager," *USA Today*, February 8, 1991, pp. 1B, 2B.

15. Victor H. Vroom and Arthur H. Jago, *The New Leadership: Managing Participation in Organizations* (Englewood Cliffs, N.J.: PrenticeHall, 1988).

16. Larry E. Pate and Donald C. Heiman, "A Test of the Vroom-Yetton Decision Model in Seven Field Settings," *Personnel Review*, vol. 16 (Spring 1987), p. 22.

17. Larry Hirschorn, *Managing in the New Team Environment* (Reading, Mass.: Addison-Wesley, 1991), pp. 48–49.

18. One of the authors was introduced to this technique by Mr. Rollie Boreman, Jr., chairman, and Dr. Robert L. Qualls, president, during a consulting assignment with their company, Baldor Electric Company. Since that time, it has been successfully used a number of times.

Chapter 7

1. Sears, Roebuck and Co. annual report, 1993.
2. Patricia Seelers, "Coke Sets Off Its Can in Europe," *Fortune*, August 13, 1992, p. 69.
3. Francis Joseph Aguilas, *General Managers in Action*, 2nd ed. (New York: Oxford University Press, 1992), p. 429.
4. James B. Treece, "Here Comes G.M.'s Saturn," *Business Week*, April 9, 1990, p. 56.
5. John A. Pearce and Richard B. Robinson, Jr., *Strategic Management*, 5th ed. (Burr Ridge, Ill.: Irwin, 1994), pp. 4–5.
6. For further details, see Peter F. Drucker, *The Practice of Management* (New York: Harper & Row, 1954), p. 62.
7. Janice McCormick and Nan Stone, "From National Champion to Global Competitor," *Harvard Business Review*, vol. 68 (May–June 1980), pp. 126–136.
8. Fred R. David, *Strategic Management*, 4th ed. (New York: Macmillan, 1993), pp. 225–228.
9. Bill Saporito, "Woolworth to Rule the Malls," *Fortune*, June 5, 1989, pp. 145–156.
10. Pearce and Robinson, *Strategic Management*, p. 275.
11. Arthur A. Thompson and A. J. Strickland III, *Strategic Management*, 7th ed. (Homewood, Ill.: Irwin, 1993) pp. 103–112.
12. Joseph Weber, "From Soup to Nuts and Back to Soup," *Business Week*, November 5, 1990, pp. 114, 116.
13. Rochard Turner, Laura Landro, and Yumicko Ono, "Matsushita Purchase of MCA Could Help Buyer Break Old Mold," *Wall Street Journal*, March 20, 1990, p. C9.
14. "Whitman Wants to Sell Hussman Unit, Focus on Food, Soft Drinks," *Wall Street Journal*, March 20, 1990, p. C9.
15. Gary P. Latham and Edwin A. Locke, "Goal Setting—A Motivational Tool That Works," *Organizational Dynamics*, vol. 8 (Autumn 1979) pp. 69–80, and Anthony J. Mento, Robert P. Steel, and Ronald Karren, "A Meta-Analytic Study of the Effects of Goal Setting on Task Performance: 1966–1989," *Organizational Behavior and Human Decision Process*, vol. 41 (February 1987), p. 69.
16. Lou Holtz, *Do Right*, video produced by Washington Publications, Inc., McLean, Virginia, 1989.
17. For further details, see Drucker, *The Practice of Management*, p. 64.

Chapter 8

1. Stratford P. Sherman, "Inside the Mind of Jack Welch," *Fortune*, March 27, 1989, p. 39; GE 1989 Annual Report; Stephen W. Quickel, "CEO of the Year: General Electric's Jack Welch," *Financial World*, April 3, 1990, p. 62; and GE 1993, Annual Report.
2. Adam Smith, *An Inquiry into the Nature and Causes of the Wealth of Nations* (New York: Modern Library, 1937; originally published in 1776).
3. Henri Fayol, *General and Industrial Management*, trans. Constance Storrs (New York: Pitman Publishing, 1949).

4. Max Weber, *The Theory of Social and Economic Organization* (New York: Oxford University Press, 1947).
5. For further information, see V. A. Graicunas, "Relationship in Organization" (originally published in *Bulletin of the International Management Institute* [Geneva: International Labour Office, 1933]), in *Papers on the Science of Administration*, ed. L. Gulick and L. Urwick (New York: Institute of Public Administration, 1937), pp. 181–187.
6. Robert D. Dewar and Donald P. Simet, "A Level Specific Prediction of Spans of Control Examining the Effects of Size, Technology, and Specialization," *Academy of Management Journal*, vol. 24, (March 1981), pp. 5–24.
7. Carol Hymowitz, "When Firms Slash Middle Management, Those Spared Often Bear a Heavy Load," *Wall Street Journal*, April 12, 1990, p. B6.
8. Kenneth Sheets et al., "Ma Bell Dukes It Out," *U.S. News & World Report*, December 17, 1990, pp. 71–72.
9. Hymowitz, "When Firms Slash Middle Management," p. B6.
10. Ibid., p. B1.
11. Chester Barnard, *The Functions of the Executive* (Cambridge, Mass.: Harvard University Press, 1938).
12. Personal experience of one of the authors.
13. Personal experience of one of the authors.
14. For a good explanation of this concept, see Richard S. Buskirk, *Modern Management and Machiavelli* (New York: New American Library/Mentor Books, 1975).
15. Based in part on J. R. P. French, Jr., and Bertram Raven, "The Bases of Social Power," in *Studies in Social Power*, ed. D. Cartwright (Ann Arbor, Mich.: Institute for Social Research, 1959).
16. Personal experience of one of the authors.
17. Personal experience of one of the authors.
18. Jerald F. Seib, "Military Reform Has Given Field Commanders Decisive Roles and Reduced Interservice Rivalry," *Wall Street Journal*, January 14, 1991, p. A12. For further details, see Douglas Harbrecht et al., "Managing the War," *Business Week*, February 4, 1991, pp. 34–37.
19. James D. Treece, "Will GM Learn from Its Own Role Models?" *Business Week*, April 9, 1990, p. 62, and "Can a New Wheel Get GM Moving?" *U.S. News and World Report*, April 16, 1990, p. 14.
20. David P. Garino, "Some Companies Try Fewer Bosses to Cut Costs, Decentralize Power," *Wall Street Journal*, April 10, 1981, p. 27.
21. "Odds and Ends," *Wall Street Journal*, January 25, 1990, p. 1B.
22. Peter Drucker, "The Coming of the New Organization," *Harvard Business Review*, vol. 76 (January–February 1988), pp. 45–53.
23. Hymowitz, "When Firms Slash Middle Management," p. B1.
24. Thomas Moore, "Goodbye, Corporate Staff," *Fortune*, December 21, 1987, p. 72.
25. Ibid.
26. "At Oxy, No Sacred Cattle," *New York Times*, January 20, 1991, p. 2F.
27. Ronald Henkoff, "Getting Beyond Downsizing," *Fortune*, January 10, 1994, p. 58.
28. Wayne F. Cascia, "Downsizing: What Do We Know? What Have We Learned?" *Academy of Management Executive*, vol. 2, no. 1, (February 1993), p. 95.
29. This section is adapted from Michael Hammer and James Champy, *Reengineering the Corporation* (New York: HarperBusiness, 1993).
30. Ibid., p. 31.

31. Ibid., p. 32.
32. Adapted from Thomas A. Stewart, "Reengineering: The Hot New Managing Tool," *Fortune*, August 23, 1993, pp. 44–48.

Chapter 9

1. Communication with Roxanne J. Decyk; Annie B. Fisher, "When Will Women Get to the Top?" *Fortune*, September 21, 1992, pp. 44–45; "Young McDonald Has a Law Office," *U.S. News & World Report*, February 8, 1993, p. 16; and Lisa A. Mainiero, "Getting Anointed for Advancement: The Case for Executive Women," *Academy of Management Executive*, vol. 8 (Spring 1994), pp. 53–67.
2. Ellen Newborne, "Wal-Mart Wins with Folksy Approach," *USA Today*, December 12, 1990, p. 1B.
3. Communication with editors of the *Dictionary of Occupational Titles*.
4. "Services Are Still Buoying the Economy," Business Week, June 23, 1987, p. 39, and "Where the New Jobs Will Be," *USA Today*, March 20, 1987, p. 1B.
5. "Working Moms," *USA Today*, October 2, 1992, p. 1A.
6. Actually, there have been state and federal laws, executive orders, and regulations affecting discrimination since the 1930s, but they were primarily passive or designed to prevent discrimination, not to require positive, affirmative action.
7. "Ex-Quasar Execs Win a Bias Case," *Business Week*, December 24, 1990, p. 32.
8. For these guidelines, see "Adoption by Four Agencies of *Uniform Guidelines on Employee Selection Procedures*," Federal Register, vol. 43 (August 25, 1978), pp. 38290–38315.
9. For some interesting insights, see John M. Norwood, "But I Can't Work on Saturdays," *Personnel Administrator*, vol. 25 (January 1980), pp. 25–30.
10. As reported in "Sexual Harrassment," *Mobile* (Alabama) *Press Register*, May 5, 1994, p. 4D (italics added).
11. As reported in "More People Work Part Time," *USA Today*, July 15, 1993, p. 1B.
12. Champ Clark, "Classified Ads That Click," *Money*, December 1975.
13. Bill Leonard, "Looking for a Job? Then Turn on Your TV," *HRMagazine*, vol. 38 (April 1993), p. 58.
14. Bill Leonard, "Résumé Databases to Dominate Field," *HRMagazine*, vol. 38 (April 1993), p. 59. See also Julia Lawlor, "Job Seekers Going On-Line: Unemployed Now Can Turn to Databases," *USA Today*, April 5, 1994, p. 4B.
15. Hugh Aaron, "The Obsolete Specialist," *Wall Street Journal*, May 16, 1994, p. A18.
16. As reported in "Job Test Preferences," *USA Today*, May 30, 1989, p. 1B.
17. Ibid.
18. Julia Lawlor, "Disabilities No Longer a Job Barrier," *USA Today*, June 22, 1993, pp. 1A–1B.
19. Michael A. Verespej, "How Will You Know Whom to Hire? No More Questions About Medical History," *Industry Week*, September 17, 1990, p. 70; Ellen Newborne, "More Top Firms Test Workers for Drugs," *USA Today*, June 21, 1990, p. 1B; "American Workers 'Just Say Yes' to Drug Testing," *Supervision*, vol. 52 (August 1991), pp. 12–13; and Mark Memmott, "Employers Must Weigh Pros, Cons of Drug Tests," *USA Today*, July 1, 1987, p. 4B.
20. Kathleen Zeitz, "Employer Genetic Testing: A Legitimate Screening Device or Another Method of Discrimination?" *Labor Law Journal*, vol. 42 (April 1991), pp. 230–238.
21. Margaret Mead, "Thinking Ahead: Why Is Education Obsolete?" *Harvard Business Review*, vol. 36 (November–December 1958), p.34.
22. Aaron, "The Obsolete Specialist," p. A18.
23. Leon C. Megginson, *Personnel Management: A Human Resources Approach*, 5th ed. (Homewood, Ill: Richard D. Irwin, 1985), pp. 246–248.
24. David M. Hunt and Carol Michael, "Mentoring: A Career Training and Development Tool," *Academy of Management Review*, vol. 8 (July 1983), pp. 475–485.
25. U.S. Department of Labor, as reported in "Apprentices Learn to Earn," *Mobile* (Alabama) *Register*, May 15, 1994, pp. 1F–2F.
26. "More Employees Evaluate the Boss," *Fortune*, July 29, 1991, p. 13.
27. George S. Galbraith, "Salary Adjustment," *Management Review*, vol. 52 (May 1963), p. 17.
28. For more details, see Heidi J. Hartman, *Comparable Worth: New Directions for Research* (Washington, D.C.: National Academy Press, 1985).
29. Reported in Beth Brophy, "Thanks for the Bonus, but Where's My Raise?" *U.S. News & World Report*, July 20, 1987, pp. 43–44.
30. For more details, see "Family Leave Effective August 5," *US News*, March 1993, pp. A1, A17; Stephenie Overman, "Family Leave Interim Regulations Due," *HR News*, April 1993, pp. A1, A4; and "Q & A on the Family and Medical Leave Act," *US News*, April 1993, p. A2.
31. Kathy Jumper, "Industry Nurtures On-Site Day Care," *Mobile* (Alabama) *Press Register*, December 10, 1989, p. B1.
32. Conversation with a representative of the Labor Relations Statistics Department of the U.S. Department of Labor, Atlanta, Georgia.
33. Figures provided by the Occupational Safety and Health Administration.
34. "Machinists Ratify Pact That Saves Jobs at Pratt & Whitney," *AFL-CIO News*, June 28, 1993, p. 2
35. "Union Membership," *Bulletin to Management* (a publication of the Bureau of National Affairs), March 4, 1993, p. 68.
36. "A Rebellion in Labor's Camp," *U.S. News & World Report*, May 22, 1995, p. 18.
37. Bureau of National Affairs, *Unions Today: New Tactics to Tackle Tough Times* (Washington, D.C.: Bureau of National Affairs, 1985), p. 1.

Chapter 10

1. Peter Moore, "Turning the Tide at Whirlpool," *IABC Communication World*, March 1994, pp. 26–29.
2. Keith Davis and John W. Newstrom, *Human Behavior at Work: Organizational Behavior*, 7th ed. (New York: McGraw-Hill, 1985), p. 425.
3. Noel Tichy and Ram Charan, "Speed, Simplicity, Self-Confidence: An Interview with Jack Welch," *Harvard Business Review*, vol. 67 (September–October 1989), p. 113.
4. Leon Megginson, Charles R. Scott, and William L. Megginson, *Successful Small Business Management*, 6th ed. (Homewood, Ill.: Irwin, 1991), p. 304.
5. Robert W. Goddard, "Communicate: The Power of One-on-One," in *Communication for Management and Business*, 5th ed., ed. Normal B. Sigband and Arthur H. Bell (Glenview, Ill.: Scott, Foresman, 1989), p. R43.

6. "Tell Me More," *Wall Street Journal*, August 9, 1985, p. 19.
7. "Serve You Best," *Fortune*, May 31, 1993, p. 88.
8. Goddard, "Communication," p. R43, and Robert Holland, "Face to Face Communication Comes Face to Face," *IABC World*, January–February 1993, p. 17.
9. "Suggestion Box Pays Off," *USA Today*, August 1, 1989, p. 1B.
10. Robert Bell and John M. Burnham, *Managing Productivity and Change* (Cincinnati: South-Western Publishing, 1991), pp. 16–17.
11. Kevin Kelly and Peter Burrows, "Motorola: Training the Millenium," *Business Week*, March 28, 1994, p. 162.
12. Goddard, "Communicate," p. 17.
13. Davis and Newstrom, *Human Behavior at Work*, p. 315.
14. S. J. Modic, "Grapevine Rated Most Believable," *Industry Week*, May 15, 1989, p. 14.
15. See "Spread the Word: Gossip Is Good," *Wall Street Journal*, October 4, 1988, p. B1.
16. Albert Mehrabian, *NonVerbal Communications* (Chicago: Aldine, 1972).
17. For further details, see "Innovation: Lord Nelson and Milstar," *Business Week*, July 24, 1989, p. 38. For an interesting discussion of paralanguage and telephone communications, see Marilyn Pincus, *Mastering Business Etiquette and Protocol* (New York: National Institute of Business Management, 1989), p. 40.
18. "Lou Gerstner's First 30 Days," *Fortune*, May 31, 1993, p. 57.
19. "Kmart Chief Has No Plans to Resign," *New York Times*, June 10, 1994, p. C3.
20. John Scully, *Odyssey: Pepsi to Apple* (New York: Harper & Row, 1987), pp. 128–129.
21. *Wall Street Journal*, February 5, 1985, p. 1.
22. Davis and Newstrom, *Human Behavior at Work*, p. 431.
23. Jill Lawrence, "Consumers Denounce 'Deceptive' Ads," *Mobile Register*, December 11, 1990, p. 1D.
24. J. Ernest Beazley, "In Spite of Mystique, Japanese Plants in U.S. Find Problems Abound," *Wall Street Journal*, June 22, 1988, pp. 13–4.
25. See Keith Denton, "Open Communication," *Business Horizons*, September–October 1993, p. 64, and Tichy and Charan, "Speed, Simplicity, and Self-Confidence," pp. 117–118.
26. Mel E. Schnake, Michael Dumler, Donald Cochran, and Timothy R. Barnett, "Effects of Differences in Superior and Subordinate Perceptions of Superiors' Communication Practices," *Journal of Business Communication*, vol. 27 (Winter 1990), pp. 37–49.

Chapter 11

1. Reprinted by permission of *Harvard Business Review*. An excerpt from "Pygmalion in Management," by J. Sterling Livingston, September–October 1988. Copyright 1988 by the President and Fellows of Harvard College: All rights reserved.
2. "It's Not What You Preach but How You Behave," *Fortune*, March 26, 1990, p. 36.
3. Warren Bennis and Burt Nanus, *Leaders* (New York: Harper & Row, 1985), p. 7.
4. Tom Peters and Nancy Austin, *A Passion for Excellence* (New York: Random House, 1985), p. 204.
5. Ellen Wojahn, "Management by Walking Away," *Inc.*, October 1983, pp. 68–76.
6. Quoted in Alfred Marrow, *Behind the Executive Mask* (New York: American Management Association, 1965), p. 7.

7. See Karen R. Hardie, *Motivation in Business and Management: An Information Sourcebook* (Greensboro, N.C.: Center for Creative Leadership, 1990), for an excellent discussion of recent materials on the topic of motivation as well as coverage of some earlier works regarded as classics on the subject.
8. Abraham H. Maslow, *Motivation and Personality* (New York: Harper & Row, 1954). Maslow's theory was popularized by Douglas McGregor in "The Human Side of Enterprise," *Management Review*, vol. 46 (November 1957), pp. 22–28, 88–92.
9. David C. McClelland, *The Achieving Society* (New York: Van Nostrand, 1961).
10. David C. McClelland and David H. Burnham, "Power Is the Great Motivator," *Harvard Business Review*, vol. 54 (March–April 1976), pp. 100–110.
11. Ibid.
12. Frederick Herzberg, Bernard Mausner, and Barbara Snyderman, *The Motivation to Work* (New York: Wiley, 1959).
13. Frederick Herzberg, "One More Time: How Do You Motivate Employees?" *Harvard Business Review*, vol. 46, (January–February 1968), pp 53–62.
14. Donald Mosley, "What Motivates New Zealanders?" *Management* (New Zealand Institute of Management, October 1969), p. 37.
15. John E. Rigdon, "More Firms Try to Reward Good Service, but Incentives May Backfire in Long Run," *Wall Street Journal*, December 5, 1990, p. B6.
16. D. A. Ondrock, "Defense Mechanisms and the Herzberg Theory: An Alternative Test," *Academy of Management Journal*, Vol. 17 (March 1974), pp. 78–89.
17. As reported in *USA Today*, January 24, 1990, p. 1A.
18. Rigdon, "More Firms Try to Reward Good Service," p. B1.
19. Victor H. Vroom, *Work and Motivation* (New York: Wiley, 1964).
20. B. F. Skinner, *About Behaviorism* (New York: Knopf, 1974), and *Beyond Freedom and Dignity* (New York: Knopf, 1971).
21. See Edward L. Thorndike, *Human Learning* (New York: Century, 1931), for a discussion of how this law operates in education, training, and development.
22. Harriet C. Johnson, "Beauty Bash," *USA Today*, August 1, 1988, p. 2B.
23. R. Bruce McAfee and Paul G. Champagne, *Organizational Behavior—A Manager's View* (St. Paul, Minn.: West Publishing, 1987), p. 171.
24. Stacy Adams and S. Freeman, *Equity Theory Revisited: Comments and Annotated Bibliography* (New York: Academic Press, 1976).
25. Alfie Kahn, "Why Incentive Plans Cannot Work," *Harvard Business Review*, vol. 71, no. 5, (September–October 1993), p. 55.
26. "Labor Letter," *Wall Street Journal*, May 6, 1986, p. 1.
27. "Retailing's Golden Rules," *U.S. News & World Report*, March 12, 1990, p. 19; Ellen Newborne, "Wal-Mart Wins with Folksy Approach," *USA Today*, December 12, 1990, pp. 1B–2B; and *Wal-Mart Annual Report*, 1994.
28. Edward E. Lawler III, *Motivation in Work Organizations* (San Francisco: Jossey-Bass, 1994) p. xvii.
29. "Motivation: Don't Forget the Middle Managers" (briefings from the editors), *Harvard Business Review*, vol. 71, no. 6, (November–December 1993), pp. 12–13.
30. Brian O'Reilly, "The New Deal—What Companies and Employees Owe One Another," *Fortune*, June 13, 1994, p. 50.

31. Susan E. Jackson and Eden B. Alvarez, "Working Through Diversity as a Strategic Imperative," in *Diversity in the Workplace*, ed. S. E. Jackson and Associates (New York: Guilford Press, 1993), p. 17.

Chapter 12

1. Adapted from Donald C. Mosley, Leon C. Megginson, and Paul H. Pietri, Jr., *Supervisory Management: The Art of Working With and Through People*, 2nd ed. (Cincinnati, Ohio: South-Western Publishing, 1989), pp. 218–219, with the permission of South-Western Publishing Co. Copyright 1989 by South-Western Publishing Co. All rights reserved.
2. John W. Gardner, *Self-Renewal: The Individual and the Innovative Society* (New York: Harper & Row, 1964), Chap. 11.
3. John P. Kotter, *The Leadership Factor* (New York: Free Press, 1988), p. 1.
4. David Whitman, "Beyond Thrift and Loyalty," *U.S. News & World Report*, January 14, 1991, pp. 50–52.
5. Kotter, *The Leadership Factor*, p. 9.
6. Michele Galen, Dean Faust, and Eric Schine, "Guilty, Your Honor," *Business Week*, May 7, 1990, p. 33.
7. Ralph M. Stogdill, "Personal Factors Associated with Leadership," *Journal of Applied Psychology*, vol. 32 (January 1948), p. 35071.
8. Edwin Ghiselli, *Explorations in Managerial Talent* (Pacific Palisades, Calif.: Goodyear, 1971).
9. James M. Kouzes and Barry Z. Posner, *The Leadership Challenge* (San Francisco: Jossey-Bass, 1987), p. 16.
10. Doug Carroll and Mindy Fetterman, "Robert Crandall: Piloting American Airlines Through Turbulent Skies," *USA Today*, December 10, 1990, pp. 1B–2B.
11. Douglas McGregor, *The Human Side of Enterprise* (New York: McGraw-Hill, 1960).
12. Rensis Likert, *New Patterns of Management* (McGraw-Hill, 1961), p. 9, and *The Human Organization* (New York: McGraw-Hill, 1967).
13. The best-known of these studies is found in Alfred J. Morrow, David G. Bowers, and Stanley E. Seashore, *Management by Participation* (New York: Harper & Row, 1967).
14. Robert E. Blake and Jane S. Mouton, *Leadership Dilemmas—Grid Solutions* (Houston: Gulf, 1991), p. 29.
15. William Ouchi, *Theory Z* (Reading, Mass.: Addison-Wesley, 1981).
16. "A Better Crop for B-Schools," *Business Week*, September 14, 1981, p. 128.
17. Ibid.
18. *USA Today*, July 18–19, 1994, sec. B1.
19. Robert Kelley, "In Praise of Followers," *Harvard Business Review*, vol. 66 (November–December 1988), p. 142.
20. Robert J. House, "The 'All Things in Moderation' Leader," *Academy of Management Review*, vol. 12 (January 1987), p. 164.
21. J. L. Larsen, J. G. Hunt, and R. N. Osborn, "The Great Hi-Hi Leader Behavior Myth: A Lesson from Occam's Razor," *Academy of Management Journal*, vol. 19 (December 1976), p. 628.
22. Paul C. Nystrom, "Managers and the Hi-Hi Leadership Myth," *Academy of Management Journal*, vol. 21 (June 1978), p. 330.
23. Robert Tannenbaum and Warren H. Schmidt, "How to Choose a Leadership Pattern," *Harvard Business Review*, vol. 51 (May–June 1973), p. 166.

24. Lyndall Urwick, ed., *Freedom and Coordination: Lectures in Business Organization by Mary Parker Follett* (New York: Pitman, 1949).
25. Paul Hersey and Kenneth H. Blanchard, *Management of Organizational Behavior*, 3rd ed. (Englewood Cliffs, N.J.: Prentice Hall, 1977), p. 161.
26. John McGregor Burns, *Leadership* (New York: Harper & Row, 1978), p. 4.
27. Bernard Bass, *Leadership and Performance Beyond Expectations* (New York: Free Press, 1985).
28. John McGregor Burns, *Leadership* (New York: Harper & Row, 1978), p 4.
29. B. M. Bass, B. J. Avolio, and L. Goodheim, "Biography and the Assessment of Transformational Leadership at the World Class Level," *Journal of Management*, vol. 13 (Spring 1987), p. 7.
30. Robert Albanese, *Management* (Cincinnati: South-Western Publishing, 1988), p. 452.
31. Karl W. Kuhnert and Phillip Lewis, "Transactional and Transformational Leadership: A Constructive/Developmental Analysis," *Academy of Management Review*, vol. 12, no. 4 (October 1987), p. 49.
32. Ibid.
33. Bernard M. Bass, "Leadership: Good, Better, Best," *Organizational Dynamics*, vol. 13 (Winter 1985), pp. 26–40.
34. George R. McAleer, "Leadership in the Military Environment," Association for Psychological Type, Special Topic Symposium, Type and Leadership, Crystal City, Virginia, March 5–7, 1993.
35. Judy B. Rosener, "Ways Women Lead," *Harvard Business Review*, vol. 68, no. 1, (January–February 1990), pp. 119–125.
36. Ibid., p.120.
37. "Ways Men and Women Lead," *Harvard Business Review*, vol. 69, no. 1, (January–February 1991), p. 150.

Chapter 13

1. Excerpts from new handout from the Ritz-Carlton, island of Maui. Edwin McDowell, "Ritz-Carlton's Keys to Good Service," *New York Times*, March 31, 1993, pp. C1–C3. *The Portrait*, the Ritz-Carlton Hotel Company; interviews and discussions with Lenny Litz, general manager, and staff of the Ritz-Carlton, Maui; discussion with Sue Musselman, assistant to the vice-president of quality, Ritz-Carlton Hotel Company, Atlanta, Georgia; and Mark Memmott, "The Quality Quest," *USA Today*, June 28, 1993, p. 2B.
2. Terrence R. Mitchell and William G. Scott, "America's Problems and Needed Reforms: Confronting the Ethic of Personal Advantage," *Academy of Management Executive*, vol. 4 (August 1990), pp. 23–35.
3. D. D. Warrick, ed., *Academy of Management OD Newsletter* (Winter 1978).
4. Rensis Likert, *The Human Organization* (New York: McGraw-Hill, 1967), pp. 26–29.
5. Judith R. Gordon, *A Diagnostic Approach to Organizational Behavior* (Boston: Allyn & Bacon, 1983), p. 612.
6. For greater detail, see Donald C. Mosley, Leon C. Megginson, and Paul H. Pietri, Jr., *Supervisory Management*, 2nd ed. (Cincinnati: South-Western, 1989), Chapter 18.
7. Roger Fisher and William Ury, *Getting to Yes* (New York: Penguin, 1983), pp. 3–4.
8. Peter B. Vail, *Managing as a Performing Art* (San Francisco: Jossey-Bass Publishers, 1989), p. 3.

9. Nancy Loving Tubesing and Donald A. Tubesing, "The Treatment of Choice," in *Job Stress and Burnout*, ed. Whiton S. Paine (Beverly Hills: Sage, 1982), p. 156.
10. Robert T. Golembiewski and Robert F. Munsenrider, *Phases of Burnout* (New York: Praeger, 1988), p. 220.
11. Oliver I. Niehouse, "Controlling Burnout: A Leadership Code for Managers," *Business Horizons*, July–August 1984, pp. 81–82.
12. Golembiewski and Munzenrider, *Phases of Burnout*, p. 219.

Chapter 14

1. B. W. Tuckman, "Developmental Sequence in Small Groups," *Psychological Bulletin* (May 1965), pp. 384–399.
2. See, for example, F. Steven Heinen and Eugene Jacobson, "A Model of Task Group Development in Complex Organizations and a Strategy of Implementation," *Academy of Management Review*, vol. 1 (October 1976), pp. 98–111.
3. Don Heilriegel, John W. Slocum, Jr., and Richard Woodman, *Organizational Behavior*, 5th ed. (St. Paul: West Publishing, 1989), p. 210.
4. Rosabeth Moss Kanter, "Becoming PALs: Pooling, Allying, and Linking Across Companies," *Academy of Management Executive*, vol. 3 (August 1989), p. 184.
5. Donald Mosley, Carl Moore, Michelle Slagle, and Daniel Burns, "The Role of the O.D. Consultant in Partnering," *Organization Development Journal*, vol. 8, no. 3 (Fall 1990), pp. 43–49.
6. Ibid.
7. R. Mitchell, "How Ford Hit the Bull's Eye with Taurus," *Business Week*, June 30, 1986, pp. 69–70.
8. R. Bruce McAfee and Paul J. Champage, *Organizational Behavior: A Manager's View* (St. Paul: West Publishing, 1987), p. 250.
9. Don Heilriegel and John W. Slocum, Jr., *Management* (Reading, Mass.: Addison-Wesley, 1986), pp. 539–542.
10. W. Allen Randolph, *Understanding and Managing Organizational Behavior* (Homewood, Ill.: Richard D. Irwin, 1985), p. 399.
11. Jerry B. Harvey, "The Abilene Paradox: The Management of Agreement," *Organizational Dynamics*, vol. 17 (Summer 1988), p. 23.
12. Laurie Baum, "The Job Nobody Wants," *Business Week*, September 8, 1986, p. 60.
13. Marshall Sashkin and Kenneth J. Kiser, *Putting Total Quality Management to Work* (San Francisco: Berrett-Koehler Publishers, 1993), p. 39.
14. John Hillkirk, "On Management," *USA Today*, October 25, 1993, p. 23C.
15. Micheline Maynard, "New Ideas Without New Blood," *USA Today*, April 2, 1993, p. 5B.
16. Fred R. Bleakley, "Many Companies Try Management Fads Only to See Them Flop," *Wall Street Journal*, July 6, 1993, p. A1.
17. Gilbert Fuchsberg, "Quality Programs Show Shoddy Results," *Wall Street Journal*, May 14, 1993, p. A3.
18. *The Tormont Webster's Illustrated Encyclopedic Dictionary* (Montreal: Tormont Publications Inc., 1990), p. 1238.
19. Jeanne Maes and Michelle Slagle, "Partnering: A Strategic Management Tool for Change," *Organization Development Journal*, vol. 2, no. 3 (Fall 1993), p. 61.
20. *Partnering: The Central Artery/Tunnel Manual* (Boston, Mass.: Massachusetts Highway Department, 1993), p. 2.
21. Steve Page, "Partnering on the Central Artery/Tunnel Project: Changing the Way We Do Business," *Design/Construction Quality Institute Forum* (forthcoming).
22. Roger Daniels, "WINS and Partnering Working Together to Improve the Way We Do Business on the CA/T," unpublished paper, December 1993.
23. Richard Lester, "Creative Leadership for Total Quality," *Journal of Leadership Studies*, vol. 1, no. 1 (November 1993), p. 144.
24. Presentation by Edgar Schein at the Albert Einstein Summer Institute, Cape Cod, Massachusetts, August 1992.
25. Eric Sundstrom, Kenneth P. De Meuse, and David Futrell, "Work Teams: Applications and Effectiveness," *American Psychologist*, vol. 45 (February 1990), p. 120.
26. Charles C. Manz and Henry P. Sima, *Super Leadership* (Englewood Cliffs, N.J.: Prentice Hall, 1989), p. 185. The following discussion has been adapted from Chapter 9, "Creating Self-Leadership Systems: Sociotechnical Design and Teams."
27. Carla O'Dell, "Team Play, Team Pay—New Ways of Keeping Score," *Across the Board*, vol. 26 (November 1989), pp. 38–45.
28. David L. Bradford and Allen R. Cohen, *Managing for Excellence* (New York: John Wiley & Sons, 1984), pp. 10–11.
29. Bradford and Cohen, *Managing for Excellence*, pp. 71–98.
30. John Hillkirk, "Kodak Develops New Ways of Managing," *USA Today*, August 8, 1990, p. 4B.
31. This exercise was developed by Synergistic Consulting Group, 6 Schwaemmle Drive, Mobile, Alabama 36608.

Chapter 15

1. Based on several sources, including Susan Caminiti, "A Quiet Superstar Rises in Retailing," *Fortune*, October 23, 1990, pp. 167–174; Nancy K. Austin, "The Service Edge," *Working Woman*, July 1992, pp. 26, 28; Lynda Radosevich, "EDI Spreads Across Different Business Lines," *Computerworld*, October 18, 1993, pp. 69. 73; and "Dillard Stores' Profit in April Quarter Was Flat, Disappointing Some Analysts," *Wall Street Journal*, May 12, 1994, p. B4.
2. "What Led Beech-Nut Down the Road to Disgrace," *Business Week*, February 22, 1988, pp. 124–128.
3. "Denver Airport," *USA Today*, August 12, 1994, p. 3A.
4. See Eric D. Randall, "Computer Woes Gnaw at Nasdaq," *USA Today*, August 2, 1994, p. 2B.
5. Thomas J. Peters, "An Excellent Question," *Inc.*, December 1984, p. 158.
6. Parviz Ashegian and Bahman Ebrahimi, *International Business* (New York: Harper & Row, 1990), pp. 629–630; S. Andrew Ostapski and Camille N. Isaacs, "Corporate Moral Responsibility and the Moral Audit," *Journal of Business Ethics*, vol. 11 (March 1992), pp. 231–239; and Randall Poe, "Can We Talk?" *Across the Board*, vol. 31 (May 1994), pp. 16–23.
7. Lee Iacocca, *Iacocca: An Autobiography* (New York: Bantam Books, 1984), p. 278.
8. William J. Stevenson, *Management Science* (Homewood, Ill.: Richard D. Irwin, 1989), p. 68.
9. For more on this subject, see "Information Officers Move Up in the World," *Wall Street Journal*, January 25, 1990, p. B1, and Gerald M. Hoffman, *The Technology Payoff* (Burr Ridge, Ill: Richard D. Irwin, 1994).
10. "Truck Lanes for the Info Highway," *Business Week*, April 18, 1994, p. 112.

11. "The Technology of the Nineties," *Business Week*, April 2, 1990, Special Advertising Section, p. 102.
12. Mortimer B. Zuckerman, "Editorial: America's Silent Revolution," *U.S. News & World Report*, July 18, 1994, p. 90.
13. John Naisbitt, *Megatrends: Ten New Directions Transforming Our Lives* (New York: Warner Books, 1982).
14. William J. Cook, "The Call to Arms," *U.S. News & World Report*, April 5, 1993, p. 53.
15. Myron Magnet, "Who's Winning the Information Revolution," *Fortune*, November 30, 1992, pp. 110–111.
16. William R. Allman, "Power to the People: Etched in Silicon," *U.S. News & World Report*, June 18, 1990, p. 8.
17. "Gates Gazes Down Info Highway," *USA Today*, July 18, 1994, p. 3B.
18. John G. Burch and Gary Grudniski, *Information Systems*, 5th ed. (New York: John Wiley & Sons, 1989), pp. 4–5.
19. Ibid.
20. Adapted from Larry Long, *Management Information Systems* (Englewood Cliffs, N.J.: Prentice Hall, 1989), pp. 24–26.
21. G. Vaughn Johnson, *Information Systems* (Omaha, Neb.: Mountaintop Publishing, 1990), p. 352.
22. Julia King, "Quality Conscious," *Computerworld*, July 19, 1993, pp. 89–91.

Chapter 16

1. Nike, Inc. 1994 annual report, pp. 42–43; *Timeline* (Beaverton, Oregon: Nike, Inc., 1993); *Higher Than the Top* (Nashville, Tenn.: Dimensions, 1993), pp. 10–14; Donald Katz, *Just Do It: The Nike Spirit in the Corporate World* (New York: Random House, 1994); and "The 400 Richest People in America," *Forbes*, 1994 edition, p. 125.
2. *USA Today*, October 25, 1985, p. 1A.
3. Robert L. Bartley, "On Clinton's Recipe for Growth," *Wall Street Journal*, July 16, 1992, p. A10.
4. R. Wendell Moore, "The Smaller They Are, the Better They Grow," *USA Today*, March 20, 1992, p. A13.
5. Constance J. Pritchard, "Forget the Fortune 500," *Wall Street Journal*, "Managing Your Career," Fall 1992, p. 12.
6. "Building a Better Entrepreneur," *New York Times Magazine*, March 22, 1992, p. 6A.
7. Roger Ricklefs, "Schools Increase Courses to Help Entrepreneurs," *Wall Street Journal*, February 6, 1989, p. B1.
8. As reported in the *Wall Street Journal*, April 6, 1992, p. B2.
9. Katie Gardner, "Student Entrepreneurs: Minding Their Own Businesses," *Washington Post Education Review*, April 9, 1989, pp. 5–7.
10. Bethany Kanel, "South-Bronx Teenager Relishes Being Known as 'Mr. Hot Dog,'" *USA Today*, May 9, 1988, p. 9E, and *ABC Evening News*, November 14, 1989.
11. W. B. Barnes, *First Semi-Annual Report of the Small Business Administration* (Washington, D.C.: Small Business Administration, January 31, 1954), p. 7.
12. Leon C. Megginson, Lyle R. Trueblood, and Gayle M. Ross, *Business* (Lexington, Mass.: D. C. Heath, 1985), pp. 431–433.
13. Frederic Smoler, "The Man Who Would Bring Back the 1980s," *Audacity*, Winter 1993, pp. 14–16.
14. Correspondence with Students in Free Enterprise, Inc., Springfield, Missouri, and Wal-Mart Stores, Inc.
15. David S. Evans, "The Effects of Access to Capital on Entry into Self-Employment," *Small Business Research Summary*, no. 116, November 1991.

16. Megginson, Trueblood, and Ross, *Business*, pp. 432–433.
17. Adapted from William L. Megginson, Mary Jane Byrd, Charles R. Scott, and Leon C. Megginson, *Small Business Management* (Burr Ridge, Ill.: 1994), p. 341.
18. Nancy Madlin, "The Venture Survey: Probing the Entrepreneurial Psych," *Venture*, May 1985, p. 24.
19. Results of U.S. Trust Co. survey, as reported in "Rags to Riches: The Trail Steepens," *U.S. News & World Report*, November 14, 1994, p. 31.
20. Milton Maskowitz, Michael Katz, and Robert Levering, eds., *Everybody's Business: An Almanac* (New York: Harper & Row, 1980), p. 310.
21. Correspondence with Wendy's International Incorporated.
22. Based on material furnished by Levi Strauss & Co.
23. "Supersonic Delivery," *Time*, September 28, 1981, p. 71.
24. *Forbes*, October 20, 1989, p. 208.
25. Wendy Zellner et al., "Women Entrepreneurs: They're Forming Small Businesses at Twice the Rate of Men," *Business Week*, April 18, 1994, p. 107.
26. "A Woman's Work," *Fortune*, August 24, 1992, p. 59.
27. Julia Lawlor, "Women Start Firms Faster Than You Can Say 'Glass Ceiling,'" *USA Today*, May 6, 1991, p. 3E.
28. Kent Gibbons, "Black-Owned Firms Feel Pinch of Law, Economy," *USA Today*, May 6, 1991, p. 3E.
29. "The Top 100," *Black Enterprise*, June 1989, pp. 57ff.
30. Megginson, Byrd, Scott, and Megginson, *Small Business Management*, p. 48.
31. Elizabeth Lesley and Maria Mallory, "Inside the Black Business Network," *Business Week*, November 29, 1993, pp. 70–82.
32. Margaret Usdansky, "Asian Businesses Big Winners in '80s," *USA Today*, August 2, 1991, p. 1A.
33. Megginson, Byrd, Scott, and Megginson, *Small Business Management*, p. 50.
34. Julia Lawlor, "Caution, Communication Are Key," *USA Today*, August 1, 1990, p. 4B.
35. This section relies heavenly on F. J. Roussel and Rose Epplin, *Thinking About Going into Business?* U.S. Small Business Administration Management Aid No. 2.025 (Washington, D.C.: Small Business Administration.)
36. Megginson, Trueblood, and Ross, *Business*, pp. 350–351.
37. Russell Shaw, "Herman J. Russell: Chairman, H. J. Russell & Co.," *Sky*, August 1990, pp. 41–47.
38. Jeremy Main, "A Golden Age for Entrepreneurs," *Fortune*, February 12, 1990, p. 120.
39. Megginson, Byrd, Scott, and Megginson, *Small Business Management*, p. 38.
40. Ibid, p. 116.
41. Constance Mitchell, "Franchisees Shielded from Fraud," *USA Today*, September 13, 1985, p. 5B.
42. Barbara Marsh, "Franchises Frolic but Focus on Deals at Annual Meeting," *Wall Street Journal*, February 2, 1989, p. B2.
43. As reported in *Black Enterprise*, September 1990, p. 57.
44. Correspondence with McDonald's Corporation, Oak Brook, Illinois.
45. "Behind Success: Ordinary Ideas," *USA Today*, May 30, 1989, p. 7B.
46. Leon C. Megginson, Geralyn M. Franklin, and M. Jane Byrd, *Human Resource Management* (Houston, Tex.: Dame Publications, Inc., 1995), p. 43.
47. Timothy D. Schellhart, "Temporary-Help Rebound May Prove Permanent," *Wall Street Journal*, July 28, 1992, p. B4.
48. Brent Bowers, "The Doozies: Seven Scary Tales of Wild Bureaucracy," *Wall Street Journal*, June 19, 1992, p. B2.

49. Jeanne Saddler, "Small Businesses Complain That Jungle of Regulations Jeopardizes Their Futures," *Wall Street Journal*, June 11, 1992, p. B1.

50. Terence Pare, "Passing on the Family Business," *Fortune*, May 7, 1990, pp. 81–82.

51. Wendy C. Handler, "Key Interpersonal Relationships of Next-Generation Family Members in Family Firms," *Journal of Small Business Management*, vol. 29 (July 1991), p. 21.

52. "When Business Is All in the Family," *Mobile* (Alabama) *Press Register*, February 23, 1986, p. 1C.

53. Margaret Crane, "How to Keep Families from Feuding," *Inc. Magazine's Guide to Small Business Success*, 1987, pp. 32–34.

54. John R. Emshwiller, "Handing Down the Business," *Wall Street Journal*, May 19, 1989, p. B1.

55. Buck Brown, "Succession Strategies for Family Firms," *Wall Street Journal*, August 4, 1988, p. 23.

Chapter 17

1. Adapted from David Kirkpatrick, "Is Your Career on Track?" *Fortune*, July 2, 1990, pp. 39–48

2. U.S. Department of Labor, Bureau of Labor Statistics, *Occupational Outlook Handbook* (Washington, D.C.: Government Printing Office, 1994), p. 15.

3. Ibid.

4. *Statistical Abstract of the United States* (Washington, D.C.: Government Printing Office, 1993), p. 393.

5. Ibid.

6. Lindsay Chappel, "Honda Veers from Tradition in Top Ranks," *Automotive News*, January 3, 1994, p. 3.

7. Nancy T. Adler, "Women Managers in a Global Economy," *Training and Development*, April 1994, p. 30.

8. *Statistical Abstract of the United States* (Washington, D.C.: Government Printing Office, 1994), p. 429.

9. Alfred Edmond, "Coming on Strong," *Black Enterprise*, June 1994, p. 75.

10. This list of personal qualities is derived from J. Sterling Livingston, "The Myth of the Well-Educated Manager," *Harvard Business Review*, vol. 49 (January–February 1971), pp. 79–89; Edgar Schein, *Career Dynamics* (Reading, Mass.: Addison-Wesley, 1978), pp. 235–239; and Leon C. Megginson, *Personnel Management: A Human Resources Approach*, 5th ed. (Homewood, Ill.: Richard D. Irwin, 1985), pp. 261–262.

11. E. E. Ghiselli, "The Validity of Management Traits Related to Occupational Level," *Personnel Psychology*, vol. 16 (Summer 1963), pp. 109–113.

12. Ann Howard, "College Experiences and Managerial Performance," *Journal of Applied Psychology*, vol. 71 (August 1986), pp. 530–532. For an earlier study of AT&T managers, see Frederick R. Kappel, "From the World of College to the World of Work," in *Business Purpose and Performance* (New York: Duell, Sloan & Pearch, 1964), p. 186.

13. Michelle Healy, "Time Is Money," *USA Today*, July 22, 1994, p. D1.

14. Charles Ames, "Straight Talk from the New CEO," *Harvard Business Review*, vol. 67 (November–December 1989), pp. 133–134.

15. "Labor Letter," *Wall Street Journal*, December 16, 1980, p. 1.

16. George T. Milkovich and John W. Boudreau, *Human Resource Management*, 6th ed. (Homewood, Ill.: Richard D. Irwin, 1991), p. 391.

17. *Wall Street Journal*, February 23, 1988, p. 1A.

18. John Naisbitt, *Megatrends: Ten New Directions Transforming Our Lives* (New York: Warner Books, 1982).

19. Alvin Toffler, *The Third Wave* (New York: William Morrow, 1980).

Glossary

acceptance theory of authority The theory that subordinates will accept orders only if they understand them and are willing and able to comply with them.; the concept that a manager's authority originates only when it has been accepted by the group or individual over whom it is being exercised.

accountability The fact that employees will be judged by the extent to which they fulfill their responsibilities.

administrative management The process of management concerned with setting goals and then planning, organizing, commanding, coordinating, and controlling activities to attain organizational objectives.

affirmative action program (AAP) Program set up by a business to take direct and positive actions to increase employment opportunities for women, minorities, and other underutilized groups.

apprenticeship training Combining OJT and classroom instruction to learn jobs requiring long periods of study to acquire specific skills.

assessment center A place where applicants spend a period of time taking tests and doing exercises in order to determine whether they have the skills to succeed in a management position.

audits Efforts to examine activities or records to verify their accuracy or effectiveness.

authority The right to do something, or to tell someone else to do it, in order to reach organizational objectives.

autocratic (authoritarian) leaders Leaders who make most of the decisions themselves instead of allowing their followers to participate in them.

behavioral approaches Management approaches emphasizing favorable treatment of employees instead of focusing solely on their output or performance; also known as the *organic* or *humanistic approaches.*

behavioral theories Theories of leadership that emphasize favorable treatment of employees rather than their output or performance.

blue-collar work Work performed by craft workers, such as mechanics, carpenters, electricians, and pipe fitters; operative workers, such as machine tenders and assemblers; and laborers.

brainstorming A group of individuals generating ideas without evaluating the ideas as they are generated.

break-even analysis The charting and analysis of revenues and costs to determine at what volume (of sales or production) total costs equal total revenues so that there is neither profit nor loss.

break-even point (BEP) The point in operations at which total revenue exactly covers total costs, both fixed and variable.

budget A detailed operational plan or forecast, generally expressed in monetary terms, of the results expected from an officially recognized program of operations.

budgetary control A system of using the target figures established in a budget to control managerial activities by comparing actual performance with planned performance.

budgetary control The careful planning and control of all the activities of the organization in financial terms.

budgets Statements of planned revenue and expenditures—by category and period of time—of money, time, personnel, space, buildings, or equipment.

bureaucracy A highly specialized form of organizational structure designed to provide order and guidance, often characterized as highly restrictive and impersonal; an organization with strict rules and regulations, well-defined authority and responsibility, and lifelong employment based on merit and seniority.

burnout A stress-related malady with primary roots in the setting where people invest most of their time and energy.

business information systems (BISs) The planned processes by which data are received, computed, stored, and converted into information to suit some business purposes.

business plan A plan setting forth the firm's objectives, steps for achieving them, and financial requirements.

buy/sell agreement A contract explaining how stockholders can buy out each other's interest.

capital budgets   Budgets for purchasing equipment and facilities.

career path   The sequence of jobs that can be expected to lead to career goals and the ways of preparing for and moving into those jobs.

career development   Providing the means to help employees attain objectives and encouraging them to use those means.

career planning   Helping employees to choose their goals and identify the means of attaining them.

centralization   Concentration of power and authority near the top, or at the head, of an organization.

chain of command   The authority-responsibility relationships that link superiors and subordinates throughout the entire organization.

change agent   The individual, either a manager from within the organization or an outside consultant, who takes a leadership role in initiating and introducing the change process.

classical approaches   Management approaches that sought efficient operations and regarded workers as just another factor of production, along with land and equipment.

closed system   System that tends to move toward a static equilibrium.

code of ethics   A formal statement that serves as a guide to action regarding problems involving ethical questions.

coercive power   Power arising from perceived expectations that punishment will follow noncompliance with a leader's orders.

collusion   A secret agreement or cooperation between two or more people or organizations to help or harm another one.

communication   The process of transferring meaning from one person to another in the form of ideas or information.

comparable worth   Paying equal salaries to women for performing jobs that are different from but as demanding and valuable as those performed by men.

compensation   Providing employees with a financial payment as a reward for work performed and as a motivator for future performance.

complex/dynamic environment   An organization environment composed of numerous, complex, rapidly changing factors.

complex/stable environment   An organization environment composed of many important and dissimilar factors that do not frequently or drastically change.

concentration   The strategy followed by a firm that operates with a single line of business.

conceptual skills   Mental ability needed to acquire, analyze, and interpret information received from various sources and to make complex decisions.

concurrent (steering) control or **screening**   Control that occurs while an activity is taking place.

conflict management   Dealing with opposition or antagonistic interaction.

conservation   Practicing the most effective use of resources, considering society's present and future needs.

consumerism   The organized efforts of independent, government, and business groups to protect consumers from poorly designed and produced products.

content (need) theories   Theories of motivation that are concerned with the question of what causes behavior.

contingency approach   Management approach advocating the combined use of various other approaches, based on the assumption that different conditions and situations require the application of different management techniques.

contingency-situational theories   Leadership theories prescribing that the style to be used is contingent on such factors as the situation, the people, the tasks, the organization, and other environmental variables.

control-of-information power   Power derived from the possession of knowledge that can be communicated or withheld at will.

control   The process by which management checks to see if what actually happens is consistent with expectations.

controlling   The management function of devising ways and means of ensuring that planned performance is actually achieved.

coproducer arrangement   A relationship between organization and supplier that depends on high interaction and close proximity, and results in fewer suppliers and longer customer-supplier relationships.

corporate downsizing   A popular technique for eliminating layers of hierarchy and reducing the number of operating personnel in general and managers in particular.

cost leadership strategy   A strategy to gain competitive advantage by producing goods and services more cheaply than the competition.

Crawford Slip Technique   A problem-solving technique in which ideas are sorted by task forces that then make recommendations.

creativity   Use of knowledge, evaluation, innovation, imagination, and inspiration to convert something into something else.

credos or **company creeds**   Outlines of the organization's beliefs or general guidelines that it will use in pursuing its mission.

critical path   The longest path, in terms of time, from the beginning event to the ending event in a PERT network.

culture   The knowledge, beliefs, art, morals, laws, customs, and other capacities and habits acquired by a person as a member of a society.

cybernetics   A control system that includes not only a detection but also a self-correction feature.

debt financing   Funding provided by lenders who are paid interest on the use of the financing provided.

decentralization   Dispersion of power and decision making to successively lower levels of the organization.

decision tree   Graphic tool for evaluating alternatives in decision making.

decision support systems (DSSs)   The business information systems that use computers to facilitate the managerial decision-making process in semistructured situations.

decliners   Employees who have little chance for promotion and are often placed in positions of decreased responsibility.

delegation   The process by which managers distribute and entrust activities and related authority to other people in the organization.

democratic (participative) leaders   Leaders who focus on the welfare and feelings of followers, have confidence in themselves, and have a strong need to develop and empower their team members.

demographic forces   Characteristics of the population—size, density, age, sex, and other related features—that contribute to shaping the general environment.

departmentalization   The organization process of determining how activities are to be grouped.

development   The broad scope of improvement and growth of abilities, attitudes, and personality traits.

developmental leadership   An approach that helps groups to evolve effectively and to achieve highly supportive, open, creative, committed, high-performing membership.

differentiation strategy   Targets some unique product attribute that consumers see as advantageous over the attributes of competing products.

disabled person   Anyone with a physical or mental disability that substantially restricts major normal activities such as physical movement learning, walking, seeing, speaking, or hearing.

diversification   The strategy of entering a business or businesses different from the present one(s).

divestment or **liquidation strategies**   Involve a decision to sever a business entity that has lost its appeal.

division of labor   The principle that dividing a job into components and assigning them to members of a group gets more accomplished than would be possible if each person tried to do the whole job alone.

downsizing   Increasing efficiency by reducing corporate staff.

downward communication   Communication that follows the organization's normal chain of command from top to bottom.

eclectic approach   Management approach that draws on the best available information from all approaches and disciplines.

economic factors   Factors in the economy that affect organizations, including the gross national product, interest rates, inflation, and so on.

effectiveness   The managerial ability to set and achieve proper objectives.

efficiency   A manager's ability to get things done, achieving higher outputs relative to inputs.

electronic mail   Transmission of information to other users by means of a computer.

employee referrals   Recommendations by current employees of friends or relatives who have the qualifications to fill specific jobs.

employee benefits   A present or future benefit to supplement the cash payment or wages or salaries a person is entitled to because of being an employee.

entrepreneur   The goals of an entrepreneur—who is an innovative risk taker—include growth, achieved through innovation and strategic management.

entrepreneurial venture   A venture in which the principal objectives of the owner are profitability and growth.

environmental change   The frequency and extent of changes in an organization's environment.

environmental complexity   The number of key factors in an organization's environment and their similarity.

environmental forecasting   The examination of future social, international, and technological changes.

environmental protection   Maintaining a healthy balance between elements of the ecology and the environment.

equal employment opportunity (EEO) laws   Rulings that prohibit employment decisions based on race, color, religion, sex, national origin, age, or disability.

Equal Employment Opportunity Commission (EEOC) and Office of Federal Contract Compliance Programs (OFCCP)   Agencies with primary responsibility for enforcing EEO laws.

equal employment opportunity (EEO) laws   Laws and rulings that prohibit employment decisions based on race, color, religion, sex, national origin, age, disability, or being a Vietnam veteran.

equity   An owner's share of the assets of a business.

equity financing   Funds for financing the business that are contributed by the owners.

equity theory   Predicts that people will compare (1) the *inputs* they bring to the job in the form of education, experience, training, and effort with (2) the *outcomes* (rewards) they receive as compared to those of other employees in comparable jobs.

estate planning   Preparation for transferring the equity of an owner when death occurs.

ethical advisers   Longtime employees of a firm whom younger employees can consult when they face ethical dilemmas.

ethics   The standards used to judge the rightness or wrongness of a person's relations to others in terms of truth and justice.

ethnocentrism   The tendency to believe and act on the belief that one's own cultural value system is superior to others.

executive development program   Generalized programs in which managers participate using case analysis, simulation, and other learning methods.

executive information system (EIS)   A new form of business information system, a subset of DSS, that meets top management's need for easy access to important information presented in a simple, clearly understandable form.

expectancy theory   A theory of motivation stating that individuals are predicted to be high performers when they see (1) a high probability that their efforts will lead to high performance, (2) a high probability that high performance will lead to favorable outcomes, and (3) that these outcomes will be, on balance, attractive to them.

expert power   Power derived from a leader's expertise or knowledge in an area in which that leader wants to influence others.

expropriation   Seizure of foreign-owned assets by a government.

factory system   Productive system based on the use of machines and equipment to achieve output.

feedback   The responses the receiver gives by further communicating with the original sender.

feedback (postaction) control   Control or correction that occurs after an activity has taken place.

feedforward control   Control that attempts to anticipate problems or deviations from the standard before they occur.

fixed costs   Costs that remain the same regardless of the level of output.

flexibility   The ability to use free association to generate or classify ideas in categories.

fluency   The ability to let ideas flow out of your head like water over a waterfall.

focus strategy   Seeks to zero in on the needs of a particular market segment.

formal communication channels   The prescribed means by which messages flow inside an organization.

formal groups   A group prescribed and/or established by the organization.

formal theory of authority   The concept that a manager's authority is conferred; it exists because someone was granted it.

franchising   A marketing system whereby an individual owner conducts business according to the terms and conditions set by the franchisor.

functional authority   The right of staff specialists to command line units in matters regarding the functional activity in which the staff specializes.

functional departmentalization   A form of departmentalization that groups together common functions or similar activities to form an organizational unit.

functional managers   Managers responsible for activities of any one primary or support function.

Gantt chart   Tool for analyzing performance that shows work planned and work accomplished in relation to each other and to time.

general environment   The external environment composed of broad factors (legal/political, international, technological, economic, social, and so on) that affect all organizations.

general managers   Managers who oversee a total operating unit or division, including all the functional activities of the unit.

global corporations   Corporations that operate worldwide, with little regard for national boundaries.

globalization   The opening of markets to competitors throughout the world.

grapevine   The best-known type of informal communication within an organization, the grapevine involves transmission of information by word of mouth without regard for organizational levels.

group   Two or more people who communicate and work together regularly in pursuit of one or more common objectives.

group cohesiveness   The mutual liking and team feeling in a group.

groupthink   The tendency of highly cohesive groups to lose their critical evaluative abilities and, out of a desire for unanimity, often overlook realistic, meaningful alternatives.

Hawthorne effect   The feeling of importance and value, which served as an incentive toward increased production, experienced by workers who were chosen as subjects for a scientific study.

heroes   Role models who make attaining success and accomplishment possible.

heroic managers   Those managers who have a great need for control or influence and want to run things.

hierarchy of needs   Psychologist Abraham Maslow's concept that human needs may be arranged in a hierarchy of importance progressing from a lower to a higher order, and that a satisfied need no longer serves as a primary motivator of behavior.

horizontal integration   Somewhat like concentration, but it normally involves acquiring another firm whose products or services are similar.

human relations skills   Ability required to understand other people and interact effectively with them.

human resource management (HRM)   Planning personnel needs; recruiting, selecting, training, and developing capable employees; placing them in productive work environments; and rewarding their performance.

human relations movement   Management approach emphasizing motivation of employees to achieve a balance of objectives that yield greater human satisfaction and attain organizational goals.

human resource planning   The activities needed to provide for the proper types and numbers of employees to reach organizational objectives.

incentive wage   Wages directly related to the amount an employee produces or sells above a predetermined standard amount.

Industrial Revolution   The period of change that began during the eighteenth century when machine and factory production replaced hand production.

informal communication   Communication flows that travel along channels other than those formally designed by the organization.

informal group   A group that evolves out of the formal organization but is not formed by management or shown in the organization's structure.

integration or **collaboration**   A method of constructive conflict resolution whereby the people involved look for ways to resolve their differences so that everyone gets what he or she wants.

intermediate-range plans   Plans covering a time span of one to three years.

internal environment   The subenvironment composed of factors (its organization structure, personnel, policies, and so on) over which the organization has a large degree of control.

international factors   Economic, political, or social events throughout the world that have a strong impact on domestic organizations.

intrapreneurship   The practice of allowing people the freedom to take an entrepreneurial role in large, bureaucratic organizations.

ISO 9000   A framework for product quality assurance among countries doing business within the community of European nations.

jargon   Technical vocabulary used by various specialists.

job analysis   The process of gathering information and determining the elements of each job, by observation and study, and presenting the results in written form.

job descriptions   Outlines of the skills, responsibilities, knowledge, authority, environment, and interrelationships involved in each job.

job specifications   Written statements about each job and the qualifications required of a person to perform the job successfully.

joint venture   A partnership formed for a specific undertaking, usually sharing the foreign costs of operation, risks, and management with a host government or firm.

laboratory training   A program in which a person learns through interacting with others in a workshop environment to be more sensitive to other people and more aware of his or her own feelings.

laissez-faire, laissez-passer   Theory stating that if entrepreneurs were left alone to pursue their own self-interests, they would be guided by an "invisible hand" that would cause them to act in "the interest of the whole society."

laissez-faire (free-rein) leaders   Leaders who are "loose" and permissive and let followers do what they want.

lateral (horizontal) communication   Communication that is coordinative in nature and involves peers within the same work group and departments on the same organizational level.

law of the situation   The concept that there are several alternate paths managers can follow in working with people, and therefore, in making leadership decisions, managers must consider forces in themselves, their subordinates, and the situation.

leadership continuum   A range of behavior associated with leadership styles from democratic to authoritarian (autocratic).

Leadership Grid®   A leadership model that focuses on task (production) and employee (people) orien-